# THE MAKING
# OF
# THEATRE HISTORY

**PAUL KURITZ**

PRENTICE HALL, Englewood Cliffs, New Jersey 07632

*Library of Congress Cataloging-in-Publication Data*

Kuritz, Paul.
    The making of theatre history.

    Bibliography: p. 442
    Includes index.
    1. Drama—History and criticism.   2. Theater—
History.   I. Title.
PN1655.K87   1988   792′.09        87-11529
ISBN 0-13-547861-8

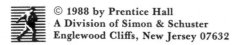

Editorial/production supervision and interior design: Serena Hoffman
Cover design: Ben Santora
Photo research: Anita Duncan
Photo supervision: Lorinda Morris-Nantz
Cover art: Courtesy of the New York Historical Society, New York City
Manufacturing buyer: Ed O'Dougherty

Printed in the United States of America

10  9  8  7  6  5  4  3  2  1

**ISBN 0-13-547861-8 01**

PRENTICE-HALL INTERNATIONAL (UK) LIMITED, *London*
PRENTICE-HALL OF AUSTRALIA PTY. LIMITED, *Sydney*
PRENTICE-HALL CANADA INC., *Toronto*
PRENTICE-HALL HISPANOAMERICANA, S.A., *Mexico*
PRENTICE-HALL OF INDIA PRIVATE LIMITED, *New Delhi*
PRENTICE-HALL OF JAPAN, INC., *Tokyo*
SIMON & SCHUSTER ASIA PTE. LTD., *Singapore*
EDITORA PRENTICE-HALL DO BRASIL, LTDA., *Rio de Janeiro*

For
Oscar G. Brockett,
my teacher and friend

*"The true teacher defends his pupils against his own personal influence. He inspires self-trust. He guides their eyes from himself to the spirit that quickens him. He will have no disciples."*
Bronson Alcott, *Orphic Sayings*

# CONTENTS

# 3
# THE CLASSICAL ASIAN THEATRE   64

# 4
# THE MEDIEVAL THEATRE    119

# 5
# THE RENAISSANCE THEATRE   153

# 6
# THE SOCIAL THEATRE  202

# 7
# THE ROMANTIC THEATRE  252

# 8

# THE REALISTIC THEATRE   305

# 9
# THE MODERN THEATRE   352

# PREFACE

F. P. Dunne, a journalist at the turn of the century, created a Chicago saloonkeeper named Mr. Dooley, and Mr. Dooley once remarked that "If any man comes along with a histry iv Greece or Rome that'll show me th' people fightn', gettin' dhrunk, makin' love, gettin' married, owin' the grocery man, an' bein' without hard coal, I'll believe they was a Greece or Rome, but not before." This book is for the Mr. Dooleys of the world. This story of the theatre tries to give a feeling for the people.

Important theatre has never been just theatre for theatre's sake, but always for the people's sake. The dramatic theatre has been a meeting place for all the forces, ideas, and problems of the world. The men and women of the theatre had their personal flaws, excessive passions, mundane worries, mental anxieties, and physical ills. The theatre has always had its visionaries and charlatans—and sex, and drugs, and rocking music. My story of the theatre stops every now and then to notice the common and uncommon things passing by the theatre's door.

I have given considerable attention to the world in which the men and women of the theatre lived. We hear a lot today about the lack of knowledge of our cultural heritage. In the past a history of an art could discuss just that art, with the assurance that the readers brought with them a knowledge of the world. That is not the case today. This story is written to underline the fact that the theatre always has something to do with its social environment, even when it tries not to. What happens on the stage always influences what goes on off stage, and what happens off the stage always affects what goes on on the stage. Else why have theatre?

Constantin Stanislavski (1863–1938), the Russian actor and director, wanted actors to leave their personal lives and problems at the stage door. Richard Wagner (1813–1883), the German poet and composer, tried to lift the audience out of everyday reality. But as Norwegian playwright Henrik Ibsen's hero Peer Gynt learned, we can never escape ourselves, even if we cannot exactly say who we are. The theatre is always of its day and time. This story includes both time and theatre.

*The Making of Theatre History* surveys world theatre for the reader with a general interest in the theatre. This survey reflects the modern disposition to consider a dramatic text as but one component of a theatrical event. As the reader will discover, actors, directors, and designers throughout history have generated enthusiasm for the theatre in the absence of significant literary texts. Great texts are a historical rarity; great theatre occurs more often.

This book is *a* story of the theatre, not *the* story of the theatre. Whatever enthusiasm the story generates should lead you to read more specific books written by the many fine scholars whose careful research proved so invaluable to me in writing this book. Their works will fill in the gaps and details in my story. Selectivity is a fact of composition, particularly in introductory texts. As ancient story-tellers chanted the same epic saga with different emphases, so different authors narrate different histories of the theatre.

This story uses a representative sampling of theatre from the day of the legendary first actor, Thespis, to the present. It details what time has suggested were important events, people, and ideas in the history of the dramatic theatre. My story is what I believe to be an accurate and interesting account of the social history of the theatre. When reading this history—or any other—always keep in mind the following exchange between the fox and the oriole in an old Indian tale:

"But I want to know the truth."
"What for?"
"Because I want to know the way it *really* happened."
"It happened the way they tell it."
"But they tell it differently."
"Then it is because it happened differently."[1]

[1] Jaime DeAngelo, *Indian Tales* (New York: Hill and Wang, 1953), p. 85.

The story begins with a search for the topic. Chapter 1, "What Is Theatre?" lays out the scope of the story and explores the relationship between the dramatic theatre and society. The story continues in chronological fashion. Each chapter discusses a major period or movement in general, and then investigates it in the particular countries that produced important contributions. It reviews the cultural context, players, texts, playing space, and audience of each country.

Many people have contributed to this work. Countless scholars and historians whose research fueled my narrative are the real heroes of the story; the bibliography notes but a few of them. My parents, teachers, students, and friends are in this story, although you cannot see or hear them directly. My dear wife, Deborah, has lived the life of Penelope while I wrote this book. Stand up and take a bow, dear. My sons, Ethan and Nathaniel, have insisted on testing my narrative skills and patience throughout the effort. My thanks to them, too. Bates College and Prentice Hall have given me the time and assistance to tell this story, and I am grateful to them.

I also wish to thank the following reviewers who saw rough drafts of the manuscript and offered helpful suggestions: Attilio Favorini, University of Pittsburgh; Rosemary Shevlin Weiss, Baruch College; Loren K. Ruff, Western Kentucky University; Briant Hamor Lee, Bowling Green State University; James W. Barushok, Northeastern Illinois University; Albert Bermel, Lehman College and Graduate Center, CUNY, and Eugene K. Bristow, Indiana University, emeritus.

I once took a course called The Rapid Reading of Shakespeare. It entailed reading one play a day for thirty-eight days. The professor told us the goal was not to understand any one play well, but to perceive the movement of structure, characters, and ideas throughout Shakespeare's career. This is what my story hopes to accomplish. In this age of ever-growing specialization, our own small lives need the larger context that a survey can provide. With an idea of our past, we can begin to envision the world of tomorrow.

Paul Kuritz

# 1

# WHAT IS THEATRE?

*Like hungry guests, a sitting audience looks:*
*Plays are like suppers; poets are the cooks.*
*The founder's you: the table is this place:*
*The carver's we: the prologue is the grace.*
*Each act a course, each scene, a different dish.*

George Farquhar,
Prologue to *The Inconstant**

What is theatre? A response should come easily. We all know, or think we know, the answer—that is, until we are pressed to define "the theatre" in such a way as to separate it from everything that is not theatre. Then metaphorical answers arise, like the one by English playwright George Farquhar (1678–1707) that opens this chapter.

Theatre seems "like" something else. To English critic Samuel Johnson (1709–1784) the theatre was like "an echo of the public's voice"; to French playwright Jean Giraudoux (1882–1944) it was like "a trial"; to Swedish playwright August Strindberg (1849–1912) it was like "a lay preacher"; for English actor-playwright William Shakespeare (1564–1616) the stage was like "a mirror" held up to nature. German philosopher Arthur Schopenhauer (1788–1860) liked this metaphor so much

that he exclaimed that "not going to the theatre is like making one's toilet without a mirror."

Today artists and scholars have gone so far as to discard the "like" altogether. A supper, a trial, a public echo, a morning shave, and a lay sermon may all be considered forms of theatre. American composer John Cage (1912– ) insists that "theatre takes place all the time wherever one is; an art simply facilitates persuading one this is the case."[1] And American critic Bernard Beckerman defines theatre as occurring whenever "one or more human beings, isolated in time and/or space, present themselves to another or others. . . . Theater is a potpourri. It can contain anything that man offers to others in his person."[2]

The history of such a theatre would include most human activity from the beginning of time. Games and matches of all kinds, lectures and talks, personal appearances, nightclub acts, the circus, dance, concerts, sporting

* Charles Stonehill, ed., *The Complete Works of George Farquhar*, Vol. I (New York: Gordian Press, 1967), p. 223.

events, every presentation of oneself to another isolated in time and/or space would need coverage. Is this, then, the scope of our inquiry?

***The Beginning of Civilization*** Ten thousand years ago the most common "theatrical" activity in the few civilizations on earth was religious ritual. Civilization began with the development of food production between 8500 and 7000 B.C. Community elders, thought to be in communication with the forces of nature, performed actions to mediate between the natural world of humans and the supernatural world of wind, earth, fire, and water. According to the priest's or shaman's timetable, humans cultivated plants and domesticated animals. Hunters and gatherers settled on irrigated land in the Middle East's Tigris-Euphrates River valley. In 3500 years complex social organizations developed.

The village tribe replaced the roaming band as the fundamental social unit. In *The Edge of History* historian William Irwin Thompson describes the structure of the primary human group of tribal society as comprising four roles: headman, hunter, shaman, and clown. The headman filled the leadership role because of his apparent administrative and organizational skills. The hunter played a prominent role in hunting expeditions because of his great physical strength and speed. The shaman knew

the traditional rituals and magical dances so he communed with the spirit world. The clown made everyone laugh by mocking the other three. For Thompson these roles seemed to perform as a set of complementary opposites; his diagram illustrates this opposition.

The clown's favorite target was the headman; mocking him got the biggest laughs. The shaman helped the hunter provide food for the group by gaining the cooperation of the appropriate spirits. Together, the shaman and the clown constituted the ideational, reflective, thinking sphere of tribal life. Indeed, in some instances both roles were played by one person. But when the duties were divided the shaman conceived religiously and seriously whereas the clown conceived secularly and playfully. Contrariwise, taken together, the headman and the hunter constituted the practical, operational aspect of tribal life. The headman, in fact, planned the hunter's activities. In some cases, just as the shaman could play the clown, the headman could be identical with the hunter. But in all cases, everyone took part in the hunt. The exploits of the hunter or warrior provided the material for stories of model behavior. For example, Sumerian culture left twenty myths, nine epics, and one hundred hymns full of nature and animal imagery. In time the stories themselves took on powers; just the recounting of the legends en-

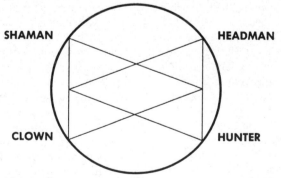

Left Side: Ideational                    Right Side: Operational

*Four basic tribal roles accomplished ideational and operational functions.* (William Irwin Thompson, *At the Edge of History*, p. 108. Copyright © 1971 by William Irwin Thompson. Reprinted by permission of Harper & Row, Publishers, Inc.)

sured the continuation of heroic action and community well-being. Historians have looked to these myths and the rituals surrounding them as a source for a theatre distinct from religious ritual.

***Myth and Theatre***   Some have suggested that the peculiar distinguishing features of the special kind of theatre that interests us reveal themselves when myth and ritual are viewed as the progenitors of theatre. So our question becomes "What is myth?"

Two scholars provide explanatory definitions. Mircea Eliade notes:

> Myth narrates a sacred history; it relates an event that took place in primordial Time, the fabled time of the "beginnings." In other words, myth tells how, through deeds of Supernatural Beings, a reality came into existence. . . . Myth, then, is always an account of a "creation"; it tells how something was produced, began to *be*. . . . In

*A Cayuga man with mask. The dancing shaman-clown may have been the progenitor of the institution of the dramatic theatre.*   (Museum of the American Indian, Heye Foundation)

short, myths describe the various and sometimes dramatic breakthroughs of the sacred (or the "supernatural") into the World.[3]

And, according to anthropologist Bronislaw Malinowski:

> Myth is not simply a piece of attractive fiction which is kept alive by the literary interest in the story. It is a statement of primeval reality which lives in the institutions and pursuits of a community. It justifies by precedent the existing order and it supplies a retrospective pattern of moral values, of sociological discrimination and burdens, and magic of belief.[4]

Myths, then, are sacred histories that narrate the origin of the world and explain why humankind is like it is. "By reciting the myths one reconstitutes that fabulous time and hence in some sort becomes 'contemporary' with the events described, one is in the presence of the gods and heroes."[5]

Myths would seem to involve a subform of theatre featuring a religious history of the beginnings of the world *that is true*. The mythological narrative is not a metaphor, nor is it fictive; myth exists as a true, accurate, and factual record of early history. Myth presents the event itself with the heroes themselves—not reconstructions, fabrications, copies, imitations, or likenesses. The events of a myth always exist in the immediate present and in the immediate presence of the community. Neither time nor place affect the "aliveness" or relevancy of the myth.

In addition, the theatre of myth can have a utilitarian or practical purpose or goal. Mythologist Joseph Campbell identifies four functions that a myth can seek to fulfill:

1. *Metaphysical.*   To reconcile our consciousness with the preconditions of our own existence.
2. *Cosmological.*   To formulate and render an image of the universe in keeping with the science of the time.
3. *Sociological.*   To validate and maintain some specific social order based on a moral code beyond criticism or human emendation.

4. *Psychological.*   To shape individuals to the aims and ideals of their various social groups.

Eliade describes the functional basis of myth in another way:

> "Living" a myth, then, implies a genuinely "religious" experience, since it differs from ordinary experience of everyday life. The "religiousness" of this experience is due to the fact that one reenacts fabulous, exalting, significant events, one again witnesses the creative deeds of the Supernaturals; one ceases to exist in the everyday world and enters a transfigured, aural world impregnated with the Supernatural's presence. What is involved is not a commemoration of mythical events, but a reiteration of them.[6]

This theatre of myth exists (or existed) under the name of *ritual*. Now our question shifts to "What is ritual?"

**Ritual and Theatre**   Ritual is the means through which people "live," to use Eliade's word, a myth. Human beings are not thought to be *true* human beings unless they perform the actions of the gods, heroes, or mythical ancestors. In ritual people seem to find the idea of "imitation," a notion not essential to every kind of theatre, but apparently necessary for the theatre of ritual.

Mythology can exist with or without ritual; ritual has even been found in some cultures without an extensive mythology. Facts do not permit any generalization about whether ritual precedes or follows myth. The variety of individual cultures produces a variety of individual results. Enough evidence does exist to show that myths and rituals tend to be very closely interwoven. Both satisfy a group's needs. Anthropologist Clyde Kluckhohn found that myth and ritual possess common psychological bases. Ritual symbolically presents a community's needs, whereas myth supplies the rationalization for those needs. Together myth and ritual portray the symbolic and often dramatic resolution of the conflicts typical of a particular culture.

A ritual holds as its model some action performed by a supernatural being far in the distant past. The ritual works when it repeats exactly those actions. This repetition imitates the earlier action while also "re-presenting" those deeds. Eliade explains:

> The time of the event that the ritual commemorates or re-enacts is made *present*, "re-presented" so to speak, however far back it may have been in ordinary reckoning. Christ's passion, death and resurrection are not simply *remembered* during the services of Holy Week; they really happen *then* before the eyes of the faithful.[7]

So rituals are not, as we had thought, mere copies or *imitations* of an action; rituals are the *real* actions actually occurring again, here and now. As historian Jane Harrison writes, rituals are "*methektic* rather than *mimetic*, the expression, the utterance, of a common nature participated in, rather than the imitation of alien characteristics."[8]

As a communal event, ritual neglects to distinguish between audience and performer. Everyone involved assumes both roles. In *From Ritual to Theatre*, anthropologist Victor Turner points out that participants share the same set of beliefs and accept the same behavior as normal. Performer and audience both actively affirm certain eternally true and communally believed realities.

**Characteristics of Ritual**   Ritual has been found to be a category of theatre with distinct characteristics. As a subspecies of theatre, ritual exhibits the following characteristics:

1. Ritual bases its action on a sacred, supernatural history, considered to have literal rather than metaphorical or allegorical validity. Myth is history, not fiction.
2. Ritual serves an end outside of itself. Ritual fulfills the common needs of the community.
3. Ritual proceeds through a process by which historical, supernatural figures actually return to the here and now. The figures are *real* and not make-believe or pretended imitations.
4. Rituals do not distinguish between spectator and

performer. Everyone participates in or "lives" the action.

5. Rituals provide the participants with a genuine "religious" experience, distinct from other experiences of everyday life.
6. Rituals affirm the current belief or attitude existing in the group.

Temple rituals kept the Sumerian gods happy with food, amusement, and praise. Ancient Sumerian civilization worshipped a celestial government of gods, each personified with human characteristics. Each god was a personification of a force in nature. Anu, the chief god, and the other gods communicated with humans through signs and omens in nature. Festivals satisfied the gods. For example, the Month of the Eating of Barley and the Month of the Eating of Gazelles sought to influence the gods through sympathetic magic. To make rain for the crops Sumerian priests, in an elaborate ritual, poured water onto a vase of corn or dates. Magical actions lie near the center of theatrical arts.

*Magic and Theatre* The word "superstition" comes from the Latin "superstitionem: a standing still over or near a thing, an amazement, a wonder, a dread." The theatre occasions amazement, wonder, and dread not only in its audiences but also in its performers. Unless certain actions are taken or avoided, unless certain words are intoned or kept mum, the future will bring disaster to the players. The players themselves have the power, the magical power, to cause their future to be bright or bitter. They are told: Never say the last line of the play at rehearsal, never open an umbrella on stage, never wear a green costume. Forbid actual money, jewels, food, mirrors, flowers, or Bibles on stage with you. Unpack your make-up box only after the reviews are in. Wish anything but "Good luck." And never, never have anything to do with a production of *Macbeth*: Do not even utter the name!

Tallulah Bankhead carried a rabbit's foot. The Barrymores exchanged but never ate red apples. On opening nights Sir Henry Irving

A Dogon "Black Monkey" ceremonial mask from the Ivory Coast in Africa was assembled from natural objects and worn in funeral dances to provide the spirit with access to the wearer. (Musée de l'Homme, Paris)

walked rather than rode to the theatre. The Lunts never crossed anyone on a staircase. Ed Wynn wore the same old pair of shoes. And Jack Lemmon whispers "magic time" just before beginning.

When faced with the prospect or even the possibility of losing one's deepest desire, of suffering humiliation and defeat, the impotent will try something, anything. Magic is one of those things. Magical actions grow out of the realization that logical action and scientific thought have limits, that in certain situations the human mind and skill fall flat. People refuse to accept this. Instead, they concoct actions that bring about their desired ends "magically." Magic is the back-up equipment in a person's bag of survival tools. Especially designed to master accidents and to ensnare luck, magical knowledge eliminates both chance and unforeseen circumstances.

*Magic and Ritual* Rituals can be seen as magical acts. By reenacting a myth, by repeating what a god did, one can become god-like. To know the origin of something—in the myth's case, the origin of the universe—is to possess magical power over it. To know the universe is to control the universe. Religious ritual and magic enjoy a close relationship. Psychologist Carl Jung noted that

> the idea, absurd to us, that a ritual can magically affect the sun is, upon closer examination, no less irrational but far more familiar to us than might at first be assumed. Our Christian religion—like every other, incidentally—is permeated by the idea that special acts or a special kind of action can influence god—for example, through certain rites or by prayer, or by a morality pleasing to the Divinity.[9]

But magic can also enjoy an identity apart from religion. Kenneth Burke claims that magic is based on the line "Let there be" and there is; religion is based on the line "Please do such and such" and there is faith and hope. Magic acts by decree, religion by petition. Magic distinguishes itself from religion by having a practical or utilitarian value; magic works only as a means to a particular end. Religion, on the other hand, has less of a functional purpose; religion creates values and supports valuable action.

Magic, then, like ritual, serves a utilitarian function. And, like ritual, magic seems based on the "sympathetic principle": Do what you want done. Never mention *Macbeth* so that people will forget about ever producing the play. Keep real objects off the stage to guard the "reality" of the stage illusion. Wear garments worn in successful performances so that the new play will succeed like the old play. The repetition of a part of a past event—exchanging an apple—can bring about the repetition of the whole past event: brilliant performances and rave reviews. Magic imitates by repeating a partial action of a successful past event so that the whole benefit may be reenacted. As Malinowski states, the magical act consists of "the production of a specific virtue or force and of the launching, direction or impelling of this force to the desired object. The production of the magical force takes place by spell, manual and bodily gesticulation, and the proper condition of the officiating magician."[10]

*Magic and Early Civilization* The world was a magical place. All things shared a common consciousness. People walked and wondered in a horizontally allied universe. Nothing had dominion. Eskimos knew the "Magic Words" after Nalungiaq:

> In the very earliest time,
> when both people and animals lived on earth,
> a person could become an animal if he wanted to
> and an animal could become a human being.
> Sometimes they were people
> and sometimes animals
> and there was no difference.
> All spoke the same language.
> That was the time when words were like magic.
> The human mind had mysterious powers.
> A word spoken by chance
> might have strange consequences.
> It would suddenly come alive,
> and what people wanted to happen could happen—
> all you had to do was say it.
> Nobody can explain this:
> That's the way it was.[11]

In early societies the officiating magician was the *shaman*, the holy doctor of the community. The shaman would put himself into a trance in order to allow a healing power to move through him to the others more effectively. By performing ritual gesticulations and by giving outer form—sounds and movements—to the inner images he experienced as he communed with the "spirit world," the shaman could produce the desired "virtue or force" and launch it into his needy audience.

Some have found the prototype of the theatre in the magical actions of the shaman. The "virtue or force" of the theatrical event would be the powers inherent in the enacted play. The "desired object" would be the audience's response. The "spell" would be the dialogue of the play and the "gesticulation," the actors' movements. The particular "proper condition" of the shaman would find analogy in the actors' "belief" in what they were doing.

But the magic of the shaman is tied to both a belief in the "truth" of what is happening and a clear-cut utilitarian function. The tribal shaman's performance retains all of the fea-

tures of ritual without identifying for us the qualities of a new kind of theatrical event. The theatre can be ritual, the theatre can be magic, but the theatre that interests us is "like" ritual and magic, not identical to them.

*Magic and Movement* The particular manner of gesticulation that found its impetus in early religious theatre may have provided the avenue through which a new kind of theatre was reached. Lewis Spence writes of this manner of movement, better known as the *dance*, and of its relationship to the other features of early religious theatre. The dance is:

a living frieze of ritual action from which the myth emanates in the choral song which frequently accompanied the sacred dance. Yet all three—ritual, dance, and myth—are really one; they were originally indivisible parts of a single thought-process, and only in course of time did they come to possess a separate existence of their own as magical acts, fictions, dances, by which time they had lost something of their first significance as the composite parts of a coordinate process.[12]

*The Hopi Indian Kachina Dance reenacts the visitation of the mythical ancestors to the earth. The dancers become the actual spirits.* (Mennonite Library and Archives, H. R. Voth Collection)

Dance-as-theatre lived as an original, composite part of a coordinate yet single thought process. The dance may lead us to the theatre.

*Dance and Theatre*   Before we examine the dance, a brief review can clarify what, in particular, we are seeking from it. Ritual has been found as a subform of theatre with certain distinguishing features. Magic has been discovered to be associated both with some religious rituals and with some secular, yet superstitious, activities. At this point important questions can be asked: What happens to ritual when one or more of its characteristic features no longer apply? What happens to magic when it is performed for amusement rather than for any utilitarian end? What happens when ritual serves no end other than itself? What happens when the participants believe neither in the actual truth of the myths nor in the actual return of the heroes and gods in performance? What happens when the spectators perceive a distinction between themselves and the performers? What happens when the "religious experience" begins to lose its distinctness from other experiences of everyday life? Johan Huizinga states the matter clearly:

> Living myth knows no distinction between play and seriousness. Only when myth has become mythology, that is, literature, borne along as traditional lore by a culture which has in the meantime more or less outgrown the primitive imagination, only then will the contrast between play and seriousness apply to myth—and to its detriment. There is a curious intermediate phase, which the Greeks knew, when the myth is still sacred, and consequently ought to be serious, but is well understood to speak the language of the past.[13]

When ritual speaks of the past rather than of the present then a new era begins. This "curious intermediate phase" marks the withering away of one or more essential features of ritual as a new species of theatre emerges. This new kind of theatre possesses affinities with both children's play and with religious ritual. Examining the development of dance can clarify that relationship.

*Sacred Dance*   Eliade maintains that all dances were originally sacred. Early dance was modeled on the movements of some superhuman in the far distant past. The physical actions and gestures of the shaman-magician performing the group's rituals constituted the first dance. Movements imitating the group's "totemic" or emblematic animal could have been reproduced to magically conjure up its presence, so that the group might have food, protection, or some of the animal's desirable qualities. Regardless of the object of imitation, "every dance was created *in illo tempore*, in the mythical period, by an ancestor, a totemic animal, a god, or a hero."[14]

One of the earliest forms of ritual dance was the Egyptian Dance of Lamentation. Male and female performers, imitating the sorrows of Isis and Nephthys, the sisters of the slain Osiris, may have performed in connection with certain religious processions or with the proclamation of the new King-God. Like all ritual dance, the Dance of Lamentation had the mysterious, almost magical powers perceived in all dance.

*Profane Dance and the Clown*   To exist only for our perception without utilitarian end the dance must move slightly away from its functional origin. When movement lost its mystery, early people still enjoyed rhythmic motion as a form of naturally delightful repetition. Amusement and delight figured significantly in the dance's early history, and the playing, dancing clown created a new kind of theatrical event. The clowns' presentations of themselves, isolated in time and/or space, before another or others, played a special role for the group. The theatre of the clown, filling a need not met by the theatre of the shaman, concerned itself with impropriety. Through the shaman the group expressed its commonality; through the clown each member released an urge to object, rebel, shock, astonish, or embarrass. African clowns, for instance, delighted by pouring cow urine on their heads and pretending to like it. Clowns could do improper actions, say forbidden words, or become taboos themselves. Yet all the while the clowns know, and the audience knows, that they are *not really* doing the actual actions, saying the actual words, or becoming the actual taboos. Reality is the sphere of the shamen; clowns play in the land of pretense. Yet like the shaman, clowns act on the audience's behalf. Through the clowns, unconscious troubles or irritations are located, named, and brought to a head by expression.

The shaman danced the god's ritual, and the clown mocked the shaman's dance. The actions remained the same, but the experience was vastly different. The web of magic surrounding the religious act was broken by the growth of human inquiry and playful intelligence. Marshall McLuhan explains:

> How art became a sort of civilized substitute for magical games and rituals is the story of a detribalization which came with literacy. Art, like game, became a mimetic echo of, and a relief from, the old magic of total involvement. As the audience for the magic games and plays became more individualistic, the role of art and ritual shifted from the cosmic to the humanly psychological, as in the Greek drama.[15]

Like all cast-off rituals, the sacred dance—instrument of sorcery, worship, and prayer—fell to the status of irrational custom or social play. A new sense of security and a freedom from the immediate struggle for existence let people play with the spiritual forms that had developed as tools for survival.

The religious-mystical experience of ritual was gradually replaced by a new experience. From the Hindu temple dancers of India, from the *wu* priests of China, and from the dancers of the mythic epics of Greece, a new type of theatre emerged. This new form of theatre had its basis in the aesthetic experience of art rather than in the mystical experience of ritual, in the individual vision of the clown rather than in the communal vision of the shaman.

***Art and Theatre***   The difference between the aesthetic experience and the mystical-religious experience lies at the center of the difference between ritual and the newly found form of theatre. A mystical-religious experi-

Zuni Indian Kachina dolls represent both the mythical spirits and their incarnational dancers. The dolls familiarize children with the phases of the initiation ritual. (Denver Art Museum)

ence involves, according to Jacques Maritain, "*an experiential knowledge of the deep things of God, or a suffering of divine things*, an experience which leads the soul through a series of states and transformations until within the very depths of itself it feels the touch of divinity and 'experiences the life of God.'" On the other hand, an individual who has an aesthetic experience perceives "things and brings forth a sign, weak though it may be, of the spirituality within them; he is connaturalized, not with God himself, but with the mystery that is scattered in things and which has come down from God, the invisible powers within the universe."[16] To participate in a ritual is to experience God in oneself; to observe a clown's antics is to perceive a mysterious truth about the nature of the universe and human existence. To one person a performance could have the experience of a ritual; to another, the new experience of art.

The experience of art, like the creation of art, always bases itself on individual insight rather than on ritual's collective affirmation. Susanne Langer defines art as "the expression of a human consciousness in a single metaphorical image."[17] (Ritual expresses the divine or supernatural consciousness in a single actual reappearance.) Henri Bergson believes that "art always aims at what is individual."[18] (Ritual aims at what is universal.) Bernard Beckerman calls this new, artistic form of theatre "drama" and distinguishes it as a "presentation of an *imagined* act."[19] (Ritual presents an *actual* act.) Erving Goffman explains drama as "voluntarily supported benign fabrication."[20] (Ritual consists of mandated, purposeful truth.)

**The Nature of Dramatic Art**  Ritual recalled a past event to present actuality. Drama does not recall the past, nor does it merely imitate the present. Drama envisions a new reality. The dramatic theatre discloses a new breadth and depth of life. Instead of celebrating and invoking the divine or supernatural perspective, the art of the theatre conveys human experiences, human destinies, human greatness, and human misery. Compared with everyday life, religious ritual dazzled people. Compared to everyday existence, dramatic theatre lures human beings from the poverty and triviality of humdrum experience to a vision of the infinite potentialities of life previously only vaguely felt. The sensuousness of the dramatic event confirms the validity of the vision. Dramatic art focuses a clear and intense light on the magic of human possibility.

Drama, the form of theatre now under consideration, usually emerges when some of the characteristics of ritual disappear: when play produces actions organized around the imaginative vision of one person, rather than around the tradition of the group. Play serves as the transition between practical, utilitarian ritual and aesthetic drama. Children play with things and materials. Artists play with the forms of things—lines, designs, patterns, rhythms, masses, and structures. Playing with forms creates new visions. Dramatists shape their particular stories so as to achieve a universal importance not unlike that of the group history of ritual. American philosopher Ralph Waldo Emerson seems to speak to the clown/dramatist when he says, "to believe your own thought, to believe that what is true for you in your private heart is true for all men—that is genius. Speak your private latent conviction and it shall be the universal sense; for the inmost in due time becomes the outmost." Every great work of art, every great piece of dramatic theatre, is individually unique yet accepted by everyone as universally true.

The truth of the drama is the truth of the imagination; the truth of ritual is the truth of sacred history. Both exist in the present. Ritual makes divine history a present, living, mystical experience; drama makes dreamed possibilities a present, living, aesthetic experience. The script of the drama resembles the *illud tempus* (the time of origins) of ritual, as David Cole has written in *The Theatrical Event*. But unlike the figures in the *illud tempus*, the figures of drama come to the present from the future rather than from the past. Within every dramatic theatre, past mates with present to plant the seeds of the future. As Ernst Cassirer has written:

> The great tragic and comic writers . . . do not entertain us with detached scenes from the spectacle of life. Taken in themselves these scenes are but figurative shadows. But suddenly we begin to see behind these shadows and to envision a

new reality. Through his characters and actions the comic and the tragic poet reveals his view of human life as a whole, of its greatness and weakness, its sublimity and its absurdity.[21]

Though the spectators at a drama may be separate from the performers, they are not passive. The spectators see the actors upon the stage, isolated in time and space, as emblems of themselves, representatives of all people. To understand the drama, the spectators repeat somewhat the creative process by which the play was made. They enter into the dramatist's personal vision, through the actors, to turn their pain and outrage, their cruelties and atrocities, their ridicules and miseries of everyday life into means of self-liberation. As the actors undergo for them, the spectators achieve a sense of freedom. The actors' actions resonate in the audience. Perhaps then, drama, too, has a utilitarian purpose, although not as clear as that of ritual. Poet-playwright Shelley expressed the dramatic theatre's purpose when he wrote, ''the highest moral purpose aimed at in the highest species of the drama is teaching the human heart, through its sympathies and antipathies, the knowledge of itself.''

*The Characteristics of Dramatic Theatre* We seem to be finding similarities between ritual and drama after searching for so long to identify their peculiar differences. What about ritual drama? And the drama of ritual? The forms of theatre are not as exclusive as we might have thought. But before we investigate a possible cause for this overlap among theatrical forms, let us enumerate the distinguishing features of dramatic theatre. Drama as a form of theatre has the following characteristics:

1. Drama bases its action on imagined experience, achieving universality by means of a particular individual perspective. Drama is poetry, not history.
2. Drama need not serve a practical end outside of itself. Drama tends to minister to the quality of a society's life rather than to the very existence of that society.
3. Drama proceeds through a process by which

imagined figures appear to exist in the here and now. The figures seem to be actual.
4. Drama distinguishes between spectator and performer. The performer acts while the spectators resonate sympathetically with the performer's experience.
5. Drama provides the audience with ''aesthetic'' experiences distinct from both other everyday experiences and ''religious'' experiences.
6. Drama envisions a new reality, a new belief, a new attitude.

*The Specialization of Civilization* If we return to the areas of overlap, once again William Irwin Thompson can help us, if not to fix finally the various forms of theatre, then at least to understand the reasons for their porous boundaries. According to Thompson, when the tribal unit switches from hunting—food gathering—to farming—food producing—a corresponding food surplus can change the community. That change is the further specialization of role. With a food surplus fewer members of the group are needed to produce food. And because not all members are needed for farming, group unity lessens. Urban culture replaces nomadic existence. The shaman becomes the full-time institution of religious specialists; the headman, the institution of the state; the hunter, the military institution; and the clown, the mocker of the other three, the institution of art.

Institutionalization brings greater social distance as social roles become differentiated. Art comments on the state as the state tries to regulate art. Religion tries to guide the military, and the military tries to justify its activities through religion. Within each institution the basic quadrant is duplicated.

Within the institution of art, the publicist functions closely with the state apologist. Within the military the exploits of the warrior soldier are raw material for artistic formulation. The artisan is art's counterpart to the military's foot soldier and religion's scribe. The celebrational artist is closest to the religious mystic and locates the area where ritual, magic, and drama would most likely overlap. The satirist-critic remains closest to the clown's

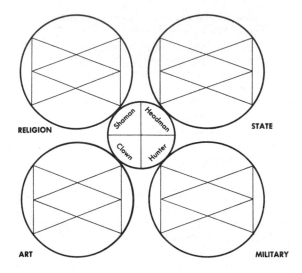

RELIGION · STATE · ART · MILITARY

Shaman · Headman · Clown · Hunter

*When farming communities produced food surpluses, the tribal functions were transformed into the institutions of the state, the military, religion, and art.* (Thompson, *At the Edge of History*, p. 111.)

original function, while the publicist dishes out propaganda and state-created works of art.

Clowns' artistic dances became drama when clowns accompanied their dances with words. But drama is more than the addition of some-thing to dance and the subtraction of some-thing from ritual. Dramatic theatre assimilates various elements to create a new form of the-atre, a new art, greater than the sum of its parts. The way in which the various elements and arts

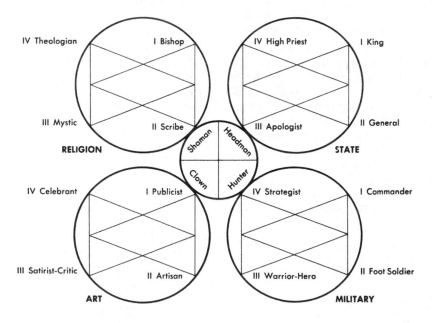

RELIGION
IV Theologian · I Bishop · III Mystic · II Scribe

STATE
IV High Priest · I King · III Apologist · II General

ART
IV Celebrant · I Publicist · III Satirist-Critic · II Artisan

MILITARY
IV Strategist · I Commander · III Warrior-Hero · II Foot Soldier

Shaman · Headman · Clown · Hunter

Left Side: Charismatic-Ideational · Right Side: Routine-Operational

*Within the agricultural community, each institution duplicated the original tribal quadrant.* (Thompson, *At the Edge of History*, p. 112.)

are combined is determined by the individual dramatic artist. Consequently, the individual is more important in drama than in ritual. The history of the dramatic theatre becomes, to a large extent, the biography of individuals with visions of new realities.

### The Rarity of Native Dramatic Theatre

Perhaps ancient civilizations without dramatic theatres did not have room for the dreaming and playing of individuals. Sumerian religious dogma and ritual established a pattern that probably influenced most subsequent civilizations. Later civilizations may have changed the names of gods or epic heroes, substituted other atrocities for those in the Sumerian Lament, and altered the details of the Sumerian New Year's *hieros-gamos* (ritual marriage) between the king and the priestess of the goddess of fertility. But the fact of theatre remained. The Sumerian need to record spoken ideas gave birth to writing and what we call "recorded history."

Later, Egyptian civilization, India's Indus civilization, and Persia's empire-building civilization existed as islands of complex social organization. Using personified natural forces, such civilizations fashioned explanations of the world that formed the basis of myth. Priest specialists tended the myths and developed rituals to influence the forces of nature and the personified gods. Myth and ritual sought to preserve the solidarity and prosperity of the group. But around the fifth century B.C. in India, China, and Greece, an impulse toward individual expression encouraged the appearance of the dramatic theatre within the context of religious celebration.

Most civilizations and cultures never developed their own dramatic theatres. Dramatic theatre is a rarity, spread west from Greece and east from India. But what of cultures without indigenous dramatic theatre? What of native Americans, most native Africans, native Australians, native Europeans? Even native Greeks may have needed the importation of drama from the East. Perhaps the hierarchy of human needs postulated by psychologist Abraham Maslow can help. Perhaps societies need

A harvester vase from Ayia Triada, c. 1500 B.C. Farmers carrying sheaves and winnowing forks celebrate the harvest with song as they dance to the rattle's rhythm. (Herakleion Museum, Greece)

to first satisfy physiological needs—food, drink, sleep, sex—and safety needs—security, protection, and time structure—before they can envision other community needs. Perhaps the satisfaction of these basic needs was better met by group effort and group solidarity than by individual initiative and individual imagination. Perhaps before cultures reached a point at which higher needs could be met, alien cultures imposed alien arts and dramatic theatres. Perhaps; but we can never know.

We do know of the rare moments when collective religious ritual created a fictional theatre event that revealed, in the present, an individual's vision of a new reality. Great dramatic art records those great visions. Clowns, the rebellious dreamers and great visionaries, reordered human existence according to their own imaginations and then presented the results for all to see. Life was reinterpreted and given new meaning. Dramatic theatre explores individuals' dreams about themselves and their societies. This book recounts the story of the dreamers, the dreams, and the people who witnessed them. The history of the dramatic theatre tells nothing less than the tale of people's changing conceptions of themselves and of their universe.

# NOTES

[1] "'45' for a Speaker" by John Cage. © 1954 by John Cage. Reprinted from *Silence* by permission of Wesleyan University Press.

[2] Bernard Beckerman, *Dynamics of Drama* (New York: Drama Books Specialists [Publishers] Inc., 1979), pp. 8, 10.

[3] Mircea Eliade, *Myths, Rites, Symbols: A Mircea Eliade Reader*, Wendell C. Beane and William G. Doty, eds. (New York: Harper & Row, Inc., 1976), pp. 1, 3.

[4] Bronislaw Malinowski, "The Role of Magic and Religion." Reprinted by permission of the publisher from Edwin R.A. Seligman, Editor in Chief, *Encyclopedia of the Social Sciences*, IV, 634–642. Copyright 1931; renewed 1959 by Macmillan Publishing Co., Inc.

[5] Eliade, *Myths, Rites, Symbols*, p. 6.

[6] Eliade, *Myths, Rites, Symbols*, pp. 6–7.

[7] Mircea Eliade, *Patterns of Comparative Religion* (London: Sheed & Ward, 1958), p. 392.

[8] Jane Harrison, *Themis: A Study of the Social Origins of Greek Religion* (New Hyde Park, N.Y.: University Books, 1962), p. 125.

[9] C. G. Jung, *Memories, Dreams, Reflections* (New York: Pantheon Books, A Division of Random House, 1961), p. 253.

[10] Malinowski, "The Role of Magic and Religion," pp. 634–642.

[11] "Magic Words," from *Songs of the Nelsilek Eskimos*, edited by Edward Field, p. 5.

[12] Lewis Spence, *Myth and Ritual in Dance, Game, and Rhyme* (London: Watts and Company, 1947), p. 102.

[13] Johan Huizinga, *Homo Ludens* (Boston: Beacon Press, 1955), pp. 129–130.

[14] Eliade, *Myths, Rites, Symbols*, p. 138.

[15] Marshall McLuhan, *Understanding Media* (New York: McGraw-Hill, 1964), p. 237.

[16] Jacques Maritain, *Distinguish to Unite or the Degrees of Knowledge*, Gerald B. Phelan, trans. (New York: Charles Scribner's Sons, 1959), pp. 247–282. Copyright © 1959 Jacques Maritain.

[17] Susanne Langer, *Problems of Art* (New York: Charles Scribner's Sons, 1957), p. 53. Copyright © 1957 Susanne K. Langer.

[18] Henri Bergson, *Laughter*, Cloudesley Brereton, trans. (New York: Doubleday, 1911), p. 161.

[19] Beckerman, *Dynamics of Drama*, p. 18.

[20] Erving Goffman, *Frame Analysis* (New York: Peregrine Books, 1975), p. 136, © 1974 Erving Goffman. Reprinted by permission of Penguin Books, Ltd.

[21] Ernst Cassirer, *An Essay on Man* (New Haven: Yale University Press, 1944), p. 146.

# 2
# THE CLASSICAL THEATRE

*Man is the measure of all things, of things that are that they are, and of things that are not that they are not.*

Protagoras of Abdera*

## GREECE

"Of all peoples, the Greeks have best dreamed the dream of life." These sentiments by Goethe summarize the place ancient Greece occupies in Western history. The life and arts of classical Greece—especially the theatre, that place of dreams—have inspired people of all ages and countries. Actually, what is considered the "classical" Greek theatre occupied the period between 500 and 400 B.C., when "Greece" consisted of several independent entities.

The three main centers of Greek culture were Ionia, Sparta, and Athens. The Ionians were the first to develop the arts and explore the seas. Their individualistic bent, exemplified by Sappho's (612 B.C.) lyric poetry, contrasted greatly with the more communal and grave nature of their neighbors in Sparta. A

minority of professional soldiers dominated, suppressed, and exploited the Spartan population of serfs. Sparta organized itself into an efficient fighting machine with neither time for, nor interest in, the arts. Athens gathered the best qualities of its neighbors, Ionia and Sparta, to become the dominant cultural center of the fifth century B.C. The individualism of Ionia, represented by the single actor of the Greek theatre, combined with the group solidarity of Sparta, represented by the theatre's chorus, to find artistic expression in an art form unique to Western civilization to that time: the dramatic theatre.

For the first time in the West, Greek dramatic theatre presented, in artistic form, the process and problem of individuation, the relationship between an individual's needs and perspective and those of the community. When we speak of the "Greek theatre," we really mean the "Athenian theatre." And, like all

---

* Paul Edwards, ed., *The Encyclopedia of Philosophy*, Vol. 6 (New York: Macmillan and Free Press, 1967), p. 505.

theatres, the one in Athens existed as a vital ingredient of the whole culture. The single Athenian actor interacted with representatives of society, personified by the chorus.

*Cultural Context* The great period of Athenian civilization flowered after developing for hundreds of years. Had the Greeks known that their world would be studied for thousands of years, they might have kept more and better records. There are few facts about Greek theatre or life upon which scholars can agree. Everything anyone says or reads about Greece and the Greek theatre would be best prefaced with a "probably" or a "could have." With this in mind, we can examine a few of the major cultural phenomena.

H. D. F. Kitto summarized the overriding importance of Athenian society:

> . . .the contribution made to Greek and European culture by this one city is quite astonishing, and, unless our standards of civilization are comfort and contraptions, Athens from (say) 480 to 380 was clearly the most civilized society that has yet existed.[1]

All of Greece aspired to *arete* (excellence). Competition in all areas was the Greek means to this end. In law, ideas and arguments vied for supremacy. In sport, philosophy, dance, and drama, competitors strove for *arete* as offerings to the gods, who were representations of natural powers seen in human terms and forms. And the gods competed for *arete* as well. They vied for control of the moral universe, as the Greeks vied for control of the physical universe. In festive competition, the two worlds came together in an act of joyous celebration. The Greeks were the first Western people to play; play for them existed as an act of both religious and human duty.

While competition led the Greeks toward *arete*, *ananke* (necessity) governed their world. Beyond the gods, the Greek universe rested on an order, a necessity. Though *ananke* was mysterious and often unknowable, reason provided Greeks with a means to glimpse the ultimate order of things and to accomplish remarkable achievements in human inquiry. Reducing facts to a small number of principles, the Greeks created the studies of medicine, natural history, and pure mathematics. The last excited the Greeks as no other field: Because mathematics was based on an order similar to that of the universe, it held the key to *ananke* and regulated the performance of drama.

*Mathematics and the Arts* Mathematics had its first great champion in Pythagoras (581–497 B.C.), who developed the theorem about right-angle triangles. Pythagoras was also the first to think about the mathematically proportional relationship between musical notes. He argued that the order of musical consonance directly paralleled the order of the universe, the music of the spheres. Music held the artistic means of unlocking the mystery of human experience. Consequently, the Greek philosopher Plato (429–347 B.C.) insisted that music hold primacy in the education of the young: Music tuned children's souls to the cosmic symphony. Music (including theatre music) could work magical effects, heal, and inspire, but it could also demean and demoralize. Singing to a musical accompaniment ranked high in Greek esteem; in the Greek theatre music found its premier vocal status.

The Greek artists' concern with the excellence inherent in the human body led sculptors to make rapid progress in the depiction of human anatomy. It also accounts for the Greeks' love of the dance, an invention of the gods. Like everything in Greek society, dance functioned as part of religious celebration. In the Greek theatre dance celebrated the excellence of physicality. Periodically, the Greeks held festivals dedicated to *arete* in which competitors celebrated the gods and humans.

*Politics and the Arts* Pisistratus (605–527 B.C.), the tyrant who presided over the conversion of Athens from a small country town to an international city of cosmopolitan import, achieved this conversion in part by reorganizing the festivals to exploit their peculiar qualities. Pisistratus attempted to emulate in Athens the great international festivals of Olympia and Delphi. His *Panatheneia* featured *rhapsodes* reciting Greek epics. Rhapsodes, who functioned as part poets and part actors, were the forerunners of Greek actors. Pisistratus hoped that the citizens' enjoyment of the rhapsodes' entertainments would help them to gloss over the illegitimacy of his political position.

Each festival, then, was an attempt to bolster the tyrant's political base. But it was also a religious and civic duty displaying to all the world the glories of Athenian abilities. Pisistratus's economic liberalism and artistic patronage both emphasized the supremacy of Athens and furthered the city's connections with foreign states. In this way the festivals resembled leaders' attempts throughout history to enhance their support and power. Dramatic theatre in the West thus arose, in part, to puff a politician's ego.

*Gender, Sexuality, and the Arts*　If we could be transported back to one of the festivals a surprise might await us. Statues and buildings, sporting bright coats of colorful paint, might take us aback. Color decked the theatrical performances as well. The art was different; but human beings' social life differed even more. And because Greeks valued sensual pleasures of all kinds, especially the pleasures of love, love became one of the central themes in Western drama.

Almost no aspect of sexual activity escaped Greek men. But Greek wives did not figure in the sexual satisfaction of their husbands: wives bore legitimate heirs and ran their households. Nonetheless, they were featured characters in the drama.

Physical beauty was openly displayed for admiration. The *phallos*, a representation of the penis that was a religious symbol, decorated every aspect of Greek life, including the theatre. The masculine image, in fact, dominated Greek ideals; the more a woman's body resembled a man's, the more beautiful she was thought. As a result, men stood as the most desirable sex objects. The phallus

reigned. Male Greek dramatic characters rarely yearned for women as much as women yearned for men.

Greeks also allowed homosexuality within regulations designed to safeguard the family unit. Exclusive homosexuality was discouraged; so was homosexual prostitution. The accepted, natural homosexual relationship existed between a middle-aged father and an adolescent 15 to 19 years of age. This relationship may have played an important role in the artist-apprentice life of the Greek theatre. When a young man became old enough to marry the relationship ended. Pederasty—sodomy between men and boys—existed as an integral part of the Greek military and educational systems as well.

Whereas sexual preference was not an issue, gender in Greek society and drama was. Women occupied a very low social position, yet a very prominent position in the drama. Because they usually married when they were between 12 and 15 years of age to men of their fathers' choice, Greek women's sphere of action revolved around their home and families. Even there they lived in quarters separate from their husbands and rarely left except for funerals and festivals. Attending a theatrical event was perhaps a major occasion for some Greek women.

Even while ''woman'' as an abstract quality played an important role in Greek drama, however, women as a part of society functioned as simple, usually ignorant and obedient slaves. Not even as objects of sexual pleasure for their husbands could Greek women find satisfaction; normal males kept either slaves or *hetaerae* (mistresses) for those purposes.

Greek women, then, were unofficial slaves. In addition, one-quarter of Greek society were captive slaves. But unlike slaves of early America, Greek slaves were domestic servants rather than agricultural fodder. Slaves often functioned as messengers in the Greek drama. Slaves could marry, have children, and attend the great religious and civic festivals. At one of these festivals in the sixth century, drama was raised to official status.

*A Dionysian dance.* (British Museum, London)

***Dionysiac Festivals*** The Greeks honored their gods with annual festivals. In Athens, four yearly festivals celebrated Dionysus, the god of the common people's pleasures. The cult of Dionysus was but one of many cults used by the fifth-century rulers for political ends. Pisistratus had brought the cult of Dionysus to Athens to offset the exclusive cults of the nobility. Dionysus, preeminently a nature god, cut across all social and national divisions. By raising the worship of Dionysus to the national level, Pisistratus hoped to transform the agrarian character of the cult as part of a planned urban revolution.

The cult of Dionysus came from the town of Eleutherai. When the citizens of the town voluntarily joined Athens to escape their hated Boeotian neighbors, a wooden figure of Dionysus was brought to Athens to symbolize the town's assimilation. Soon a myth sprang up that Athens did not receive the god with proper honor; as punishment, Dionysus sent a disease to attack the men's genitals. To appease the god and to cure the disease, Athenians had to hold a procession led by a large *phallos* (artificial penis). Every year this procession was reenacted to commemorate the arrival of Dionysus from Eleutherai. The procession eventually preceded the production of plays.

When the Eleutheraians came to Athens they brought with them their traditional myths. One local myth concerned the daughters of Eleuther, the town's namesake. Legend had it that Dionysus had been raised as a girl and occasionally disguised himself as a girl. Eleuther's daughters may have thought their visitor was a woman. The daughters, after beholding a vision of Dionysus clad in a scanty goat skin, supposedly insulted the god and were consequently driven mad in retaliation. To cure his daughters Eleuther was required to institute the worship of Dionysus Melanaigis—Dionysus of the Black Goat Skin. Cross-dressing was thereby associated with Dionysus and the cult of Dionysus; it would, in fact, become the mode of Greek theatrical performance. Around this worship arose the secret cult of Dionysus.

**The Cult of Dionysus and the Emergence of Drama**   The cult of Dionysus, a magical society, preserved some of the structure and functions of the tribal rituals around which the town of Eleutherai had evolved. Membership consisted of women led by a male priest. The central ritual had three parts: first, an orgiastic exodus to the countryside; second, a sacrificial tearing apart and eating of a victim; and third, a joyous return to the city. (The three parts may have served as the structural model for Greek drama.) The ritual reenacted the myth of Dionysus both to promote fertility in the soil and to purge the participants of any irrational impulses. The myth of Pentheus and the daughters of Minyas demonstrate how this cult swept across Greece, especially among the suppressed Greek women. Possessed by Dionysus, Greek women scandalously left their homes and domestic chores to roam the mountains, dancing and swinging sacred branches, called *thyrsi*, and torches. At the pitch of their possessed frenzy, they could grab an animal or a child and tear it to pieces, gorging themselves with its bleeding raw meat. Because Dionysus could appear at any time in animal form, the brutal feast incorporated Dionysus and his power into the members themselves.

The ritual of Dionysus served a cathartic function. Participants purged themselves of individual, irrational impulses. The Greek philosopher Aristotle (384–322 B.C.) would later claim this purgative effect for the drama. The cult grew in popularity by offering freedom through the worship of the god of joy. Worship was open to all, including slaves and women. Worshipping Dionysus, like acting, allowed the celebrants to cease being themselves and to experience freedom. E. R. Dodd explains that Dionysus appealed to people "not only because life in that age was often a thing to escape from, but more specifically because the individual, as the modern world knows him, began to emerge for the first time from

*Dionysus and a comic actor, c. 350 B.C.*   (British Museum, London)

the old solidarity of the family, and found the unfamiliar burden of individual responsibility hard to bear."[2]

The emergence of the individual perspective from the group experience marks one of the conditions for the development of drama from ritual. Through the worship of Dionysus and the establishment of the annual festival called the City Dionysia, the Greeks became the first Western people to complete the transition from the instrumental and functional theatre of ritual to the autonomous, visionary theatre of drama. The City Dionysia housed the fruits of that process.

**The City Dionysia**   Pisistratus succeeded Solon as the ruler of Athens. Solon had, according to Diogenes Laertes, prohibited an actor named Thespis from performing tragedies on the ground that fiction was pernicious. Pisistratus, however, was an advocate of the arts; he used them not only to glorify himself but also to display the greatness and prosperity of Athens. In 532 B.C. Pisistratus enlarged an urban festival, the City Dionysia, even though a thriving Rural Dionysia already existed. The City Dionysia became the most important of the four annual festivals celebrating Dionysus. The others were the Lenaia, the Rural Dionysia, and the Anthesteria.

Perhaps Pisistratus considered this festival to be a public counterpart to the private and secret cult of Dionysus. But in the City Dionysia emphasis fell on the human aspects of Dionysus rather than on the god's mystical powers. At the City Dionysia tragedy took its formal bow to the world and for almost 100 years the City Dionysia was the only festival where drama could be seen. In this way Dionysus, aided and abetted by Pisistratus, brought his illusions, ecstasy, and freedom to the patronage of a new art: the art of the dramatic theatre.

***Thespis and the Drama*** Thespis, the reputed creator of drama, brought the new art to Athens by combining the magic of music, the glory of the dancing human body, and the tales of Greek mythology. Athenaeus wrote that "the old poets—Thespis, Pratinas, Cratinas, Phrynichus—were called 'dancers' because they not only relied upon the dancing chorus for the interpretation of their plays, but, quite apart from their own compositions, they taught dancing to all who wanted instruction."[3] Thespis had taken the rhapsode, the singing-dancing bard, one step further by introducing the actor. Portraying the many character dialogues of the epics had required the rhapsodes to develop some histrionic skill. The actors were bards simply assuming *direct* impersonations by wearing masks, thus making the epics "dramatic." In fact, Aristotle's *Poetics* defines the "dramatic" by contrasting it with the "epic." Putting on a mask seemed the easiest way to cease being oneself. And to cease to be oneself was to engage in the freedom of Dionysus.

Historian Jane Harrison notes a long developmental process that preceded Thespis's performance in Athens. In *Proleomena to the Study of the Greek Religion* Harrison suggests that the religion of Dionysus peculiarly emphasized not only worship but also impersonation of the god. The earlier epics had not featured or involved such gods.

***Festival Organization*** The City Dionysia took place in the month of stags, Elaphebolion—the last half of March and the first half of April. The festival began on the ninth day of the ninth month, the beginning of Athenian spring, when the time was ripe to pay tribute to the empire. The sea was navigable again, so the city filled with visitors, potential audience members. In honor of Dionysus Eleuthereus, the festival celebrated the god's arrival in Athens. From the very beginning tragedy was central to the festivities. Gawdy allegories known as *satyr* plays, choral hymns known as *dithyrambs*, and comedies were added later.

The festival was run by the *archon eponymos*, Athens's chief civil magistrate, who selected the participants and supervised their work. The *archon eponymos* brought together the poet/playwright, the actor, and the city-appointed *choregus*, a wealthy citizen who acted as producer.

Each playwright applied to the *archon* for a *choregus* who would hire a chorus, a choral instructor, a flute player, and mute actors, and who would purchase costumes, masks, set pieces, and properties. The state maintained the theatre building, provided the prizes, and paid the playwright and actors. One month after each festival, the next year's plays would be announced.

A few days before the festival a *Proagon* (a public relations preview) occurred at the Odeum, a small music theatre south of the Acropolis. The day of the *Proagon* coincided with the festival of Asclepius, the god of healing. The coincidence reinforced the drama's connection with the functional nature of ritual. Athens housed the god of healing in a sanctuary above the theatre, and the playwright Sophocles played a large role in introducing this god to Athens. At the *Proagon*, each poet and *choregus* appeared with the actors and chorus in a parade announcing the participants and the title of each play.

Later in the day the city council met with the *choregoi* to begin the selection of judges. Ten lists of judges from among the ten Athenian tribes were deposited in ten urns, one for each tribe. Sealed and deposited under guard in the Acropolis, the urns were protected by a sentence of death to anyone who tampered with them. On the first day of the festival, the urns were placed in the Theatre of Dionysus, the site of the performances, before all whose names were in the urns. The *archon* drew one name from each urn; each of these ten judges took a solemn oath to render an impartial verdict.

The evening before the festival the statue of Dionysus was paraded to the theatre in an elaborate procession. The celebrants wore brilliantly colored garments and golden jewelry. Many sported masks and carried *phalli* on poles. Some may have ridden in chariots while others walked or danced. Performers and *choregoi* paraded along with sacrificial animals and virgins carrying baskets of sacrificial instruments. The procession stopped at the marketplace, where choruses sang and danced before the statues of the twelve gods.

When the procession arrived at the theatre, additional sacrifices were offered, and libations were poured before the statue of Dionysus. In 333 B.C. perhaps as many as 240 bulls were offered. Five choruses of men and five choruses of boys competed in dithyrambic contests. A *dithyramb* was a tumultuous song in honor of Dionysus, led, supposedly, by someone under Dionysus's influence. Before each day's performances, the tribute collected from Athens's allies was paraded before the audience as a display of Athens's power and respect. The honors bestowed on the orphan sons of Athens's war victims were also announced. Lot determined the order of the plays.

**Dramatic Competition**   Each play was preceded by a herald's call or a trumpet blast. The tragic contest featured three playwrights, each with a tetralogy—three serious plays known as a trilogy and a satyr play. When a comic contest was introduced in 486 B.C., three, then five, playwrights competed with one comedy each. At the end of the performances each judge wrote down the winning plays in rank order. The ten ballots were placed in one urn from which the *archon* drew five at random. The names of these five judges were announced while the other ballots were destroyed unexamined. The winning poet and *choregus* were proclaimed by the herald, given a wreath of ivy, perhaps some money, and celebrated with solemn sacrifice and a great banquet featuring the meat from the opening day's sacrifice.

After the five- or six-day festival, the citizens assembled in the theatre to discuss the festival, consider the conduct of the *archon*, vote honors to hard-working officials, and hear complaints of sanctity violations. If the judges' verdict was thought unjust, the case could be tried by a jury selected from the audience. If found guilty, the judges could be imprisoned.

**The Theatre of Dionysus**   The site of the City Dionysia's dramatic contests was the Theatre of Dionysus. As historian Allardyce Nicoll points out, when speaking of the Greek theatre building or, in particular, of the Theatre of Dionysus, we are really speaking of several different things. Greek theatre architecture evolved through different, although by no means consistent, phases, which Nicoll calls (1) Pre-Aeschylean, (2) Classical Athenian, (3) Hellenistic, and (4) Graeco-Roman.[4]

*Pre-Aeschylean* was the performance space used prior to the dramas of the playwright Aeschylus (525–456 B.C.). The theatre consisted of a hillside below the Acropolis, Athens's fortified citadel, and a flat surface at the foot of the hill. The hillside provided a natural rake for an audience of between 14,000 and 17,000 spectators. A flat space called the *orchestra*, the dancing space, may have been either trapezoidal or circular in shape. In the center of the sixty- to seventy-foot level space was the *thymele* (altar). The first spectators probably sat on the hillside in the *theatron* (the seeing place). Later wooden benches were added near the or-

*A model of the temple and orchestra at the Theatre of Dionysus during the Pre-Aeschylean period.*

chestra for dignitaries. A more formal, stone seating arrangement appeared after stone became a feasible building material.

The *Classical Athenian* theatre arrangement has the greatest interest for historians because all existing Greek plays were performed in it. In the Pre-Aeschylean theatre the dancing chorus dominated; in the Classical theatre two or three actors needed a place to change costumes or masks in order to play a variety of roles. To facilitate such changes a temporary dressing room or hut known as a *skene* was constructed at the rear of the orchestra. The movable nature of the *skene* made for great versatility. But

the orchestra, too close to the Temple of Dionysus to construct a suitable *skene*, was moved forward about fifty feet to allow the new stage building to be erected.

Once in place, the *skene* offered playwrights something to incorporate into their plays. Plays began to be set before particular buildings. A stone foundation was provided for the erection of temporary *skene*. Painting some of the building's facade may have suggested the particular place called for in a play. A low platform called a *logeion* possibly linked the orchestra with a *skene* door. The plays of this period seemed to require a door and an upper level, possibly the

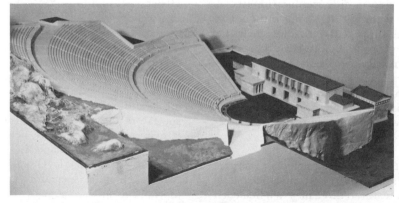

*A model of the Theatre of Dionysus at the end of the classical period.*
(The Cleveland Museum of Art, Cleveland State University Theatre Arts)

*skene* roof, for the appearance of gods. The *skene* was always a separate architectural unit from the *theatron*. Passageways called *paradoi*, formed between the *theatron* and the *skene*, were used for entrances and exits, especially by the chorus. By the end of the fifth century B.C., the *skene* probably had an upper story called the *episkenion*.

*Hellenistic* theatre dates from the time of Alexander the Great (356–323 B.C.) to the first century B.C. As the City Dionysia lost its religious association, plays lost their ritualistic quality. A more realistic or representational mode for both performance and playwrighting emerged. The Greek chorus declined in importance as attention probably shifted to the *logeion* (the stage). The *logeion*, raised to a height of ten to thirteen feet, was supported by a *proskenion*, rows of columns supporting the high platform stage. Between the columns of the *proskenion* painted panels called *pinakes* could show more realistic scenes. The facade of the *skene* contained three huge doors or openings, known as *thyromata*, into which other *pinakes* could be set. As the *logeion* grew larger, playwrights could locate several rooms on the stage.

In time, the influence of the emerging Roman civilization began to change Greek architecture. In *Graeco-Roman* theatres, the orchestra continued to lose importance as the *skene* encroached onto it; in time the *logeion* extended out to approximately one-half of the orchestra's radius. The *logeion* grew deeper until it reached a depth of almost twenty feet.

***Performance Development*** If tragedy began when bardic singers completed the impersonations of the characters in their epic sagas, then the earliest Greek acting was as much physical as vocal:

> . . . whatever most closely links fifth century drama to its earliest manifestations has as much to do with physical expression as with the spoken word, perhaps more.[5]

The actor, the chorus, and the flute player were the performers of the Greek drama. Both the actor and the chorus needed to speak, sing, and dance, accompanied or unaccompanied by the flute player:

> The chorus . . . was never a tedious necessity thrust upon early playwrights unable to think of

*The Theatre of Dionysus from the audience.*

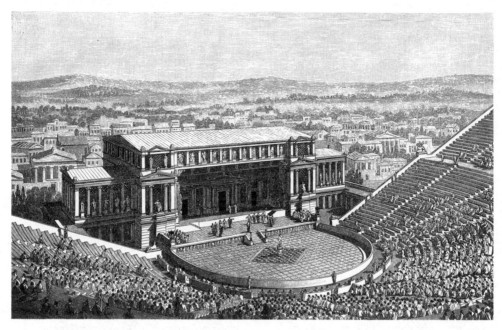

*The Theatre of Dionysus during the Hellenistic period.* (The Bettmann Archives, Inc.)

any other way of writing plays. It was and remained the life and soul of the drama. . . . For all three tragedians a major function of the chorus remained, I believe, to reflect the rhythm of the play in visual terms, even at times when it had no lines assigned to it.[6]

At first only one actor played with a chorus. In 471 B.C., however, actor-playwright Aeschylus introduced a second actor named Cleander. Until the time of the playwright Sophocles (496–406 B.C.) the playwright and the actor were one and the same person. But Sophocles not only declined to act in his plays, he also added a third speaking actor around 468 B.C. After that, the number remained fixed at three. In *The Dramatic Festivals of Athens* A. W. Pickard-Cambridge reports that this limitation occasionally required that one role be divided among two or more actors. Masks helped unify the several performances into one evolving characterization. Mute or nonspeaking roles did not count in the "rule of three" for tragedy. Comedy, on the other hand, could usually

be played by three actors, although occasionally four or five were used. The skills for playing comedy differed so much from those for tragedy that no known individual performed both until 106 B.C.

***The Solo Performer*** Beginning in 449 B.C., as the contribution of the actor to the success of a production became more apparent, a prize was awarded for the best actor. At the same time a new method of casting plays was introduced. Rather than allow playwrights to cast their own plays, the *archons* cast the leading actors of each tetralogy by lot, and then let the playwrights select the other two players. The chorus was drawn from society at large; each member considered it an honor to be trained by either the playwright or a hired specialist.

The Greek chorus performed many functions. First, it served as an intermediary between the reactions of the audience and the action of the play. Second, it maintained the rhythm of the play. Third, it visualized the words with movement, dance, and tableaux.

As interest in individuation and unique human personality increased, the role and importance of the chorus changed and declined.

Actors were judged on the basis of their physical and vocal expressivity. Because the actors played out of doors to a surrounding audience—half of whom were more than 100 feet away, mostly above them—they discovered a unique style perfectly suited to these peculiar circumstances. Simplicity, slowness, referential movement and gesture, and symbolic stage actions probably characterized their playing. Certain types of gestures may have become associated with particular emotions. Grief, for example, may have been communicated by rending garments, tearing hair and beard, slashing at one's cheeks, beating one's head or heart, or bending or bowing the head; sorrow or anguish, by fainting or sinking to the ground; supplication, by kneeling to clasp another's knees or hands or striking the ground with the hands to show distress to the dead. Other gestures were typical as well: smiting the thighs or scratching the ear or cheek in anger, praying with outstretched palms up or down (depending on the location of the particular god), kissing statues or blowing kisses to them,

kissing a friend's face or a suppliant's hand, and solemnly shaking another's hand in greeting.

The actors' performances were sometimes unaccompanied, sometimes spoken but accompanied by music, and sometimes sung. In each case voice chiefly differentiated one character from another. A voice that could "fill" the theatre was judged the best voice. Considering the Greeks' religious view of music, actors used their voices as religious acts. The Greek word for actor, *hypocrite*, also means "answerer"; Greek actors answered the assembled citizenry's questions about the nature of humanity and the relation of individuals to the gods. Greek actors acknowledged the importance of their tasks by preparing for performances with fasting and dieting.

As the age of great playwriting closed, Greek actors rose in public status. No longer beloved amateurs, Greek actors became professionals, earning their livings by touring with great scenes and speeches from famous plays. Eventually a professional guild was formed, The Artists of Dionysus, that gave to star players some rights and privileges unavailable to the general public.

***Music and Dance***   Music, the Greek key to the order of things, and dance, the invention of the gods, constituted the heart of the Greek actor's performance. So important to the drama were they that Athenaeus reports that "Telestes, Aeschylus's dancer, was so artistic that when he danced the *Seven against Thebes* he made the action clear simply by dancing."[7]

Two kinds of music wafted through early Greece: the music of Apollo, the god of music, and the music of Dionysus, the god of revels. Because the theatre was the featured event at the festival of Dionysus, Dionysus's unrestrained music of the reed pipe or flute prevailed over the disciplined and orderly music of Apollo's lyre. The Greek single flute, which resembled an oboe or clarinet, was occasionally joined by Apollo's lyre, percussion instruments, or a trumpet fanfare. The flute player led the chorus into the orchestra and moved through the action of the play accom-

*A Greek actor studying his mask.*

*Greek comic actors, c. 370 B.C.* (The Metropolitan Museum of Art, Rogers Fund, 1913)

panying whoever was speaking, singing, or dancing. Sometimes actors would accompany themselves on lyres. The various Greek musical modes probably resulted in a sound more akin to Eastern than to modern Western music. We cannot be sure, however, because no musical notation existed during the Classical period; the earliest fragments of notation exist from the late Hellenistic age.

Dance probably involved rhythmic movements suited to the type of play: tragic, comic, or satyric. Religious choral dances had been associated with the cults of Apollo and Dionysus. Lucian writes that "you cannot find a single ancient mystery in which there is not dancing."[8] Gestures and physical actions seem to have been keyed to the words spoken or sung. In tragedies, the dance featured the *emmelia*, a stately dance with song or spoken accompaniment. A code of symbolic gestures known as *cheironoma* also worked its way into the performance. In comedies, a *kordax* appeared: "a lascivious, ignoble, obscene dance" with its dis-

tinguishing feature "a lewd rotation of the abdomen and buttocks, often with the feet held close together."[9] In satyr plays, half-human, half-horse characters pranced around in a *sikinnis*, a lively dance that explored all the lewd rhythmic actions those mythological creatures could invent.

***Mask and Costume*** Greek actors wore conventionalized garments based on the dress of everyday life. The *chiton* was a long-sleeved, loose-fitting tunic-like garment; the *chlamys* was a short cloak. An *himation* resembled a long cloak and, together with the *chiton* or *chlamys*, constituted the basic dress. Color and decoration were probably important; stage garments were probably decorated with very colorful symbolic patterns or formal designs. Costumes usually reflected characters' most important traits: status, sex, age, and nationality. Costume accessories and symbolic properties could further clarify the characters' dispositions or identities. Actors wore soft shoes

Thespis was said to have colored his face with a weed known as purslane. Later, he supposedly introduced the use of linen masks. Phyrnichus, the tragic playwright, supposedly introduced the first female mask, and Aeschylus, the first painted mask.

Eventually, each mask, which covered the actor's entire head, included a headdress known as an *onkos*, facial hair, and a characteristic facial expression. Each member of the chorus probably had an identical mask, but a single character in a play could have had several masks, one for each new attitude or emotion. (A good mask actor could, however, make a mask appear to change expression.) In his *Onomasticon* Pollus lists a variety of masks in regular use, for old men, young men, slaves, women, and several specialty masks, to portray River, Justice, Madness, Drunkenness, and the Muses' Horns. Personality masks of famous Athenians were also used; the mask used for Socrates in Aristophanes's *The Clouds* is one example.

***Performance Space*** Greek performers inhabited a theatre space similar to that of the

*A Greek dancer, c. 225–175 B.C.* (The Metropolitan Museum of Art, Bequest of Walter C. Baker, 1971)

or boots, which later may have evolved into thick-soled boots known as *cothurni*. For comedies, *chitons* could be too short, too long, too tight, or too loose. Such comic costumes were probably worn over padded flesh-colored tights to further distort the physiques; when comic characters were stripped "naked," the actors, still clothed in the tights, displayed ludicrously distorted "naked" bodies to the audience. Male characters in comedy (exclusive of the chorus) wore *phalli* that they could manipulate for various bits of comic business.

Masks covered the faces of all but the flute player. For the first performances of tragedy,

*A mask of tragedy, c. 400 B.C.* (Museum of Fine Arts, Boston)

Theatre of Dionysus. However, what was done with that space for scenic investiture is, like just about everything in Greek theatre studies, a subject of debate and conjecture. Did the Greeks maintain a neutral facade for their *skene* and empty orchestra, and rely on the language of the text to supply the details, or did they depend on the words of the text to refer to specific things that were to be visible to the Greek audience? The answer, however unsatisfactory, is probably "Both." Consistency in artistic practice seems to be a fairly new criterion in creating and judging a work of art. The Greek theatre probably used whatever was available to it.

Aristotle credits Sophocles with inventing scene painting, whereas a later Roman writer, Vitruvius, gives the distinction to Aeschylus. The practice probably began in the period when the two careers overlap. *Pinakes* (painted panels) and *periaktoi* (prism-shaped scenic units) were probably used to suggest place or dramatic effect at some point in Greek theatre development. Perhaps *pinakes* were attached to each *periaktoi*, so that pivoting the *periaktoi* would change the setting.

The list of stage machines Pollux provided in his *Onamasticon* suggests that the Greeks may not have had a neutral, conventionalized *mise en scène*, or staging. Scholars are quite willing to accept that the *ekkyklema* (a rolling or revolving platform) was used to reveal tableaux,

and that the *mechane* or *machina* (a hook and pulley system) was used to fly in and out various gods, chariots, or special phenomena; but they have difficulty dealing with some of the other machines Pollux identifies:

> *keraunoskopeion:* a lightning machine
>
> *bronteion:* a thunder machine
>
> *Charon's steps:* a device on which ghosts ascended from hell into the orchestra's center
>
> *hemikuklion:* a device showing a distant view of cities or of people swimming
>
> *anapiesma:* a trapdoor to lift up a river

Consensus suggests that if these machines ever did find their way onto Greek stages, they probably did so in the late Hellenistic or Graeco-Roman periods, when plays portrayed greater realism of situation and character motivation.

Set properties probably helped identify the place of the action. Statues of various gods before temples or palaces, garlands of flowers, altars, watchtowers, chariots and horses, walls, turrets, lighthouses, honorary stone obelisks, tombs, and donkeys could all appear on the Greek stage and become part of the actors' referential actions. Biers, carpets, dummy bodies, litters, and occasional couches could appear in tragedies; all kinds of domestic paraphernalia could abound in comedies.

*A Hellenistic theatre with pinakes.* (Margaret Bieber, *The History of the Greek and Roman Theatre*, p. 111. Courtesy of Princeton University Press.)

*Dramatic Texts*  The Greeks created three forms of drama: tragedy, comedy, and the satyr play. The origin and nature of each of these forms have been topics of considerable speculation among scholars.

Where did tragedy originate? Earlier, we discussed tragedy's association with the rhapsodes. This is one of the most recent speculations. Prior to this hypothesis, evolutionary theories pointed to possible origins in dithyrambs of the cult of Dionysus, mystery rituals, hero cult worship, and the drama of the Death and Rebirth of the Year Spirit.

The word *tragodia*, however, is an Athenian word that was never found elsewhere until Attic drama spread all over Greece. This fact, plus the certainty that the language of tragedy "is an artificial language never spoken by anybody but created or developed for poetic purposes,"[10] has led such scholars as Gerald Else to conclude not a gradual development, but rather a succession of deliberate creative compositions by Thespis and Aeschylus. The theory would support historian Jane Harrison's observation that "tragedy is a rare and special plant, not a universal form of serious literature but a unique creation born at a particular time and place."[11]

The idea of a unique form for Greek tragedy is derived from only thirty-two extant plays by three playwrights—Aeschylus, Sophocles, and Euripides—plus many fragments from other playwrights. This is all that remains from thousands of plays by numerous playwrights.

*Aeschylus*  As a boy Aeschylus (525–456 B.C.) worked in his father's vineyard in Eleusis. In time patriotism and religious fervor led him to other interests. He fought at the Battle of Marathon (490 B.C.), where he saw his brother die; later he fought at Salamis (483 B.C.). Interestingly, the epitaph on his tombstone mentions his career as a soldier but not his life in the theatre, for which he is remembered today.

Aeschylus debuted in the theatre in the City Dionysia of 500 B.C. but failed to win the prize until 485 B.C. Perhaps drawn by the theatre's patriotic and religious atmosphere, Aeschylus wrote drama as he watched his country evolve from a tyranny to a democracy. He wrote more than ninety plays and won the prize twelve times, but only seven of his plays still exist: *The Suppliants* (c. 490 B.C.), the first play in a tetralogy; *The Persians* (472 B.C.), the second play of a tetralogy; *Prometheus Bound* (c. 468 B.C.), the first play of a tetralogy; *Seven against Thebes* (467 B.C.), the third play of a tetralogy; and *The Oresteia* (458 B.C.)—*Agamemnon*, *The Libation Bearers*, and *The Eumenides*—the only extant trilogy. Considered the founder of tragedy, Aeschylus was probably responsible for fixing the form of Greek tragedy by introducing a second actor and by diminishing the importance of the chorus. He was the last playwright to use the tetralogy form, which structurally and thematically relates each play to one another.

The dramas of Aeschylus are distinctive. Group interests supersede those of the individual. Consequently, the chorus plays an important role. In fact, in some plays the chorus holds more than half the lines. Aeschylus's interests are more metaphysical than those of his successors. In his plays action is important, not as it affects individuals but as it affects humanity. Portraying social situations is not as important as examining the nature of good and evil, searching for justice, exploring the relationship of humans to the gods, and determining humanity's fate. Only one of Aeschylus's extant plays, *The Persians*, deals with a contemporary event, the Battle of Salamis.

Majestic and exotic costumes, solemn dances, spectacular effects, and long magnificent descriptive passages characterize Aeschylus's theatre, in which justice ultimately triumphs. Athenaeus states that when defeated for the City Dionysia prize, Aeschylus remarked that his tragedies were dedicated to time and that he knew he would eventually receive his fitting reward. Justice also may have triumphed in Aeschylus's personal life. He was prosecuted for, but acquitted of, revealing some secrets of religious ceremonies in his plays. Accounts suggest that Aeschylus belonged to a secret society and only escaped the fury of his audience by clinging to the *thymele* (stage altar). Other accounts claim that some of the costumes Aeschylus designed were used by the society's high priests.

Late in his life Aeschylus made several trips to Sicily at the invitation of the king. At that time, Aeschylus restaged some of his older plays and wrote new ones in honor of the Sicilian king's new city. He was supposedly killed in Sicily when an eagle mistook his bald head for a stone and dropped a tortoise on it to break the shell. Shortly after his death, the Athenians passed a decree providing a chorus to anyone wishing to revive one of his plays. His son, Euphorion, later won victories by producing four of his father's plays posthumously. Aeschylus's tomb in Gela became a place of pilgrimage; in the fourth century his statue was erected in the Theatre of Dionysus.

**Sophocles**    Born the son of a wealthy munitions maker in Colonus, Sophocles (496–406 B.C.) was known as a handsome and very well-educated young man. He was a good musician and dancer, and won prizes for wrestling and music. In 468 B.C., when he was only 28 years old, Sophocles won his first victory in the theatre. In time, however, even though he had excelled in women's roles, he gave up acting because he had a weak voice. He did continue, though, to stage his plays.

Although Sophocles was notorious for his affairs with young men—the matter became a running joke among theatre people—he married at least twice. His son himself became a tragic playwright.

Like Aeschylus, Sophocles was patriotic and religious. After the battle of Salamis (483 B.C.), the 16-year-old Sophocles danced around the trophy naked and anointed with oil, accompanying himself on a lyre. He served as imperial treasurer in 443 B.C., and was elected twice to a generalship, the highest elective office in Athens. Sophocles later acted as a priest of a healing god and let his home serve as the cult's temporary temple.

Sophocles wrote and produced over 120 plays. He won the City Dionysia with his very first play, defeating Aeschylus. He averaged two plays a year for his entire life and won the City Dionysia prize eighteen times; he never

placed lower than second. But only seven of his plays remain: *Ajax* (c. 445 B.C.), *Antigone* (c. 441 B.C.), *Oedipus the King* (c. 430 B.C.), *The Women of Trachis* (c. 413 B.C.), *Electra* (c. 410 B.C.), *Philoctetes* (409 B.C.), and *Oedipus at Colonus* (401 B.C.). Aristotle credits Sophocles with introducing the third actor and scene painting, and with enlarging the chorus from twelve to fifteen members. By introducing a third actor Sophocles could use more characters and develop more complex plots and situations. A lost book by Sophocles supposedly reviewed the theory and practice of theatre production.

Sophocles was interested in more personal actions and details than Aeschylus. Sophocles abandoned the Aeschylean trilogy to compose separate dramas focused on the human consequences of action. As a result, the chorus in his plays loses some importance as structural emphasis shifts to the individual personality of the central character. Sophocles's drama has more domestic, psychological concerns. For example, his *Electra* is set at the same time as Aeschylus's *Agamemnon*, but Sophocles's characters are interested in the social rather than the metaphysical situation. The character of Electra is most important; her choices and decisions within her familial situation weigh more heavily than any concern with her eternal fate. Sophocles's *Oedipus the King* was considered by Aristotle to be a superior model of tragic construction.

A few months before his death, Sophocles appeared at the City Dionysia for a memorial benefit for the playwright Euripides. At the benefit, his son charged him with senility because he loved the stage so much he had neglected his financial affairs. To defend himself from losing control of his property, Sophocles read from his just-finished *Oedipus at Colonus*. When he sat down he asked, "Is this the work of an idiot?" The case was dismissed. Sophocles's grandson produced *Oedipus at Colonus* after the poet's death.

The cause of Sophocles's death is uncertain. He may have choked on a grape, exhausted himself reading *Antigone* aloud, or collapsed from joy after winning a competition.

*Euripides* Unlike Aeschylus, Sophocles, and Aristophanes, Euripides (480–406 B.C.) opposed the aristocratic nobles who ruled Athens. In fact, Euripides criticized just about everything that had been traditional. By the end of the fifth century, a new philosophy known as "sophism" had found a great proponent in Euripides. His plays illustrate the philosophy's belief in the relativity of history, truth, and even goodness. To make matters worse, unlike Aeschylus and Sophocles, Euripides refused to take part in public affairs. As a result, he was, more than any other figure in ancient Greece, the butt of comic attacks as "the philosopher of the stage."

Born to a merchant on the island of Salamis, Euripides was mocked as the son of a green-grocer, although his family was probably not poor. The attack was more likely aimed at the playwright's close relationship with his mother. As a boy Euripides helped the dancers in the religious festivals, and he may even have carried a torch in one of their processions. His father trained him as a professional athlete but Euripides preferred painting and reading. In time he amassed one of the largest libraries in Greece. Philosophy fascinated him; he studied with the great philosophers of his day. The great Socrates would attend the theatre only if a play by Euripides were in performance.

At the age of 25 Euripides was granted a chorus, and he thus began a career in the theatre that resulted in almost ninety plays. He was constantly assailed by the arch conservative playwright Aristophanes, and his plays frequently lost at the City Dionysia festival to inferior works by playwrights with more orthodox philosophical attitudes. He won only five victories.

Euripides's personal aloofness and austerity contributed to his unpopularity. He wore a long beard, had moles on his face, hated most visitors, lived alone in a cave on an island, avoided society, and refused to cater to his audience's wishes. He wrote plays and staged them, but never acted in them. His contemporaries considered him a misogynist—someone who hates women—although time has cast his work in a more feminist light. In fact, in private life Euripides loved women. According to Athenaeus "when somebody remarked to Sophocles that Euripides was a woman-hater, Sophocles answered 'Yes in his tragedies, for certainly when he is in bed he is a woman-lover.'"[12]

Euripides's reputation as a playwright spread throughout the world. Aristotle called him the most tragic of playwrights. After his death Euripides's plays were, in fact, performed for six hundred years. He influenced all forms of Greek writing and is the most quoted Greek tragedian, perhaps because a great number of his plays remain. Of the nineteen plays, all are tragedies except *The Cyclops*, which is a satyr play: *Alcestis* (438 B.C.), *Medea* (431 B.C.), *Hippolytus* (428 B.C.), *The Children of Hercules* (c. 427 B.C.), *Andromache* (c. 426 B.C.), *Hecuba* (c. 425 B.C.), *Cyclops* (c. 423 B.C.), *Heracles* (c. 423 B.C.), *Suppliants* (c. 421 B.C.), *Ion* (c. 417 B.C.), *Trojan Women* (415 B.C.), *Electra* (c. 413 B.C.), *Iphegenia in Tauris* (c. 412 B.C.), *Helen* (412 B.C.), *Phoenician Women* (c. 409 B.C.), *Orestes* (408 B.C.), *The Bacchae* (c. 405 B.C.), *Iphegenia at Aulis* (c. 405 B.C.), and *Rhesus* (?).

Euripides's plays culminate the development of Greek drama, which began with an interest in the patriarchal community and the question of religion and morality in the emerging state. Euripides's drama concerns the individual and personal emotion and passion. More than Aeschylus or Sophocles, Euripides focused on the complex emotional responses of his characters. His relative realism, interest in aberrant psychology, portrayal of women, and emotive music offended his contemporaries but anticipated the dominant strain of Western dramatic theatre. Technically his plays introduce the extensive use of a prologue and the *deus ex machina* (the appearance of a god to resolve the situation) as a major device for plot resolution.

Euripides recast legendary heroism in his contemporary world of doubt and cynicism. More than his predecessors he modeled his characters on everyday behavior. His Electra is but a simple peasant girl. As mouthpiece for the young people of his generation, Euripides expressed antitraditional attitudes toward customs and beliefs. He even dared to suggest that chance played a more important role in human affairs than fate. Unlike other dramatists Euripides seemed fascinated with female characters; his drama features such great women characters as Medea, Phaedra, Hecuba, Andromache, Hermione, Helen, and Iphegenia. His plays introduce structural techniques that have come to be the hallmarks of "melodrama": sudden reversals, miraculous rescues, startling and resolving discoveries, and contrived endings.

Like Socrates, Euripides was personally unpopular in his town. Too serious and thoughtful, too disgusted with his compatriots, Euripides finally left Athens in 408 B.C. Perhaps because of his friendship with Socrates, perhaps because of the supposed infidelity of his two wives, Euripides felt forced into voluntary exile. He went to the court of Macedonia, where scholars, painters, tragedians, and musicians had gathered.

When Euripides died in Macedonia, perhaps killed by the king's hunting dogs, the king cut off his own hair as a sign of grief. Sophocles publicly mourned his friend's death, and the Athenians sent a delegation to retrieve Euripides's body. The king of Macedonia refused to give over the body; Euripides was buried in Macedonia. He had died, not the most beloved Greek poet—that honor went to Sophocles—but nonetheless the most celebrated.

*Aristophanes*    Aristophanes (c. 448–c. 380 B.C.) probably grew up in the country as a conservative son in an aristocratic land-owning family. In 427 B.C. his first play, which presented a young man's recent experience with the school system of Athens, won second prize. Aristophanes's second play got him into trouble with Cleon, the tyrant who ruled Greece at the time. In retaliation Cleon had Aristophanes prosecuted for falsifying his citizenship. The playwright was acquitted. But in his next play he charged Cleon with slander and lying. Two years later, Aristophanes's third play attacked Cleon with even greater fury; it won first prize at the Lenaea, a Dionysiac festival celebrated in Athens in the

month of Gamelion (January–February). This festival preferred comedy to tragedy. Eventually Aristophanes was awarded a state crown of wild olive for the good advice his plays gave the city.

At first, Aristophanes played in and staged his plays; later he entrusted those tasks to others. Today, only eleven of Aristophanes's almost sixty plays survive: *Acharnians* (425 B.C.), *Knights* (424 B.C.), *Clouds* (423 B.C.), *Wasps* (422 B.C.), *Peace* (421 B.C.), *Birds* (414 B.C.), *Lysistrata* (411 B.C.), *Thesmophoriazusae* (411 B.C.), *Frogs* (405 B.C.), *Ecclesiazusae* (c. 392 B.C.), and *Plutus* (388 B.C.).

Aristophanes was considered an innovator in fourth-century comedy because of his use of colorful language, parody, satire, exaggeration, and vicious attacks on "progressive" education, contemporary philosophy, melodrama, rhetoric, contemporary music, and political corruption. Just the ideas of his plays brought laughter. *Clouds*, for example, ridicules Socrates and his philosophy as having no basis in common sense. *Wasps* presents a man who loves justice so much that he sets up his own home law court. Set at the time of the Peloponnesian War, *Peace* shows a man flying to heaven on the back of a dung-fed beetle to plead for peace amid the protestations of the munitions makers. Disgusted by war, two men in *Birds* plot to establish birds as the superior species. Led by *Lysistrata*, women go on a sex strike until their men stop the war. In *Thesmophoriazusae* women try a Euripides-like playwright on charges of giving away their secrets. In *Frogs*, Dionysus complains of the lack of good playwrights at his festival and travels to hell to bring back Euripides. But Aeschylus convinces him that he was the better writer. The women of the *Ecclesiazusae* seize the government to establish a communal state featuring free love. And *Plutus* offers a debate between Poverty and Wealth about who has helped humanity more.

Plato, who was particularly fond of Aristophanes's plays, included the playwright in his *Symposium*. He also supplied Aristophanes's epitaph when the playwright's son produced Aristophanes's last play after his death. The epitaph read: "The Graces, seeking a shrine that could not fall, discovered the soul of Aristophanes.''

***Characteristics of Greek Drama*** Although Greek tragedies vary greatly in particular structure, they do share some general characteristics: A *prologue* usually precedes the *parodos* (the entrance song) of the chorus. The prologue is expository; it often reveals important aspects of character. The prologue can also initiate the action, as with the arrival of Creon in Sophocles's *Oedipus the King*. The *parodos* supplies additional expository material while setting the proper mood or emotional key. The ensuing action proceeds through a regular alteration of three to six *episodes* (scenes involving interplay among characters or between character and chorus) and *stasima* (choral songs). Sophocles's *Oedipus the King* has four *episodes* between the prologue and the *exodos*, the final scene. The choral *stasima* create a tragic atmosphere and modulate the tone of the play. The *exodos* may feature a messenger speech or a *deus ex machina*. The *exodos* of *Oedipus the King* begins with a messenger's account of the pollution of Oedipus's house and concludes the tragedy.

Comedy was established in Athens in 486 B.C., the time of Pericles (495–429 B.C.), possibly because demagogues wanted a safe means to attack their political opponents. Comedy could have resulted from the combination of a phallic ritual chorus of Dionysus, like the one parodied in Aristophanes's *Acharnians*, and an episodic drama, possibly imported from the Dorian world. All but one of the existing comedies are by Aristophanes; the other, *The Grouch* (316 B.C.), the only example of New Comedy (the next paragraph defines this term), is by Menander. Yet the existing fragments and secondary reports about comedies suggest that Greek comedy retained its original quality. Francis M. Cornford wrote that

> [in] comedy the emphasis [is] on the phallic element and the fertility marriage; and, from that day to this, not only has a marriage been the canonical end of comedy, but this whole form of art, together with other romantic forms which it has influenced, has been marked all through its history by an erotic tone, and its lower manifestations relied openly on the stimulus of sex attraction.[13]

Greek comedy has been divided into three phases—Old, Middle, and New—each with general characteristics. The plays of Aristophanes fall into the category of Old Comedy. Whereas formality and plausibility govern tragedy, informality and fantasy rule Old Comedy. Plots run wildly through the most imaginative situations peopled with the most unlikely characters. Like tragedy, Old Comedy begins with a prologue. The comic prologue, however, posits a ''happy idea'' that is, of course, ridiculous, impractical, or extravagant. In *Acharnians*, for example, a citizen decides to make a separate peace with a warring nation. This scene may be followed by the *parodos* and the *agon* (a verbal contest over the ''happy ideas''). In *Acharnians* the old charcoal burners debate the private citizen. At midpoint the action can become a *parabasis* (a choral passage usually addressed to the audience) concerning some contemporary issue; in *Acharnians* the *parabasis* concerns the Peloponnesian War and political corruption. *Episodes* show the ''happy idea'' in use. A *komos* (the exit) leads to celebration. Episodes show *Acharnians'* private citizen enjoying the joys of his private peace. Old Comedy ridiculed prominent Athenian citizens, mythology, and theology, while applauding sex and excretion.

Middle Comedy is a transitional form, characterized by a decline in the importance of the chorus and an end to the ''obscene'' comic costume. Characters in Middle Comedy resemble contemporary citizens. New Comedy continues the trend of Middle Comedy toward individualization of character and domestication of action. Menander (c. 342–291 B.C.) is the leading playwright of Hellenistic New Comedy.

The satyr play was developed by Pratinas of the Peloponnese as a satellite to tragedy. A satyr play followed each tragic playwright's trilogy, giving the Dionysian spirit a place in Dionysus's festival without diminishing the importance of tragedy. The main character in satyr plays is often Silenus, originally the tutor of Dionysus, but incarnated on stage as the god's most ardent worshipper. Silenus, drunk, can hardly stand, rides an ass, and often falls off. In addition, satyr plays featured a chorus of satyrs, under the leadership of Silenus, performing gross antics and burlesquing the trilogy. Satyr plays appeased citizens who complained that tragedy was alien to the Dionysian spirit. Euripides's *The Cyclops* is the only extant satyr play.

Plays that won the festival dramatic competition could not be staged again. Losers could revise and restage their plays, as Euripides did with his *Hippolytus*, and Aristophanes with *Clouds*. By the fourth century, however, playwrighting had fallen to such a low level that permission was granted to revive old plays, a custom that in time became regular practice.

**Aristotle and Dramatic Criticism** After systematically examining the extant comedies and tragedies of his day, the philosopher Aristotle (384–322 B.C.) proposed some general considerations about the drama that have provided the basis for subsequent speculation. Aristotle wrote about the drama seventy years after Euripides. His treatise, the *Poetics* (c. 335 B.C.), was neither a guide to playwrighting nor an early history of the theatre. It was, however, an attempt to refute the philosophical arguments proposed by Aristotle's teacher, Plato (c. 429–347 B.C.). Consequently, the work provides little information on production practices. Even if Aristotle's statements sound vague to the modern reader, we must remember that the original audience was already familiar with the issues and vocabulary. Nevertheless, Aristotle's *Poetics* contains important statements about the nature and form of Greek tragedy and comedy:

> A tragedy, then, is the imitation of an action that is serious and also, as having magnitude, complete in itself; in language with pleasurable accessories, each kind brought in separately in the parts of the work in a dramatic, not in a narrative form; with incidents arousing pity and fear,

wherewith to accomplish its catharsis of such actions.

> There are six parts consequently of every tragedy, as a whole, that is, of such or such quality, viz. a Fable or Plot, Characters, Diction, Thought, Spectacle and Melody.

> Tragedy is essentially an imitation not of persons but of an action and life, or happiness and misery.

> The first essential, the life and soul so to speak, of Tragedy is the Plot, and the Characters come second.

> Tragedy is an imitation of personages better than the ordinary man.

> There are four distinct species of Tragedy—that being the number of constituents also that have been mentioned: first, the complex Tragedy, which is all Peripety and Discovery; second, the Tragedy of suffering, . . .; third, the Tragedy of character. . . . The fourth constituent is that of Spectacle. . . . The poet's aim, then should be to combine every element of interest, if possible, or else the more important and major part of them.

> As for comedy, it is (as has been observed) an imitation of men worse than the average; worse, however, not as regards any and every sort of fault, but only as regards one particular kind, the Ridiculous, which is a species of the Ugly. The Ridiculous may be defined as a mistake or deformity not productive of pain or harm to others.[14]

Playwrights in subsequent theatre periods looked to Aristotle's *Poetics* for inspiration and justification. Renaissance writers, for example, used their interpretations of the *Poetics* to compose and critique their contemporary dramas.

**The Audience** The approximately 15,000 people who filled the Theatre of Dionysus influenced the writing and performing of the plays. Their vocal responses—stamping feet, cheering, applauding, throwing nuts and raisins, hissing, drinking and relieving themselves, demanding encores, talking to the actors and to the characters, hooting—undoubtedly affected the judges' voting. During comedies actors sometimes threw raisins and nuts back into the audience. Even prisoners were set free to attend the plays, with the knowledge that any crime or assault on a festival day was considered a crime against religion. (A fellow named Ctesicles was put to death for hitting his mortal enemy during a festival procession!) Most importantly, Dionysus himself was thought to be spiritually present in the festive audience.

Because a six-foot actor may appear only three and one-half inches high to spectators in the front rows, and three-quarters of an inch tall to those at the back, the audience may have been inclined to respond most not to the quality of a text, but to the quality of the production. Thus, a miserly *choregus* could doom an otherwise fine script by hiring second-rate singers and using cheap costumes. An audience of men, boys, women,[15] slaves, *hetaerae* (mistresses), and foreigners sitting on a stone theatre slab in March demanded constant stimulation.

Tickets were sold for two *obols* (a day's wage) regardless of location. Pericles founded the theoric fund, which subsidized tickets for the poor. The money collected from selling tickets went to the *architekton* (the theatre owner) for the upkeep of the theatre. Tickets admitted spectators to specified sections of the theatre; perhaps each tribe had its own section, the way fraternities have their own sections at modern college football games. Each section may have been subdivided by sex. The choice, downfront center seats were reserved for the priests, officials, ambassadors, and other distinguished guests.

***Plato and Dramatic Censorship***    Out of the Greek audience came the first critic of the drama, Plato (429–347 B.C.). Plato expressed an antitheatrical attitude that served throughout history as one of the bases for attack on the drama. Plato had no trouble seeing the power

of the drama on people's lives. Indeed, his argument criticized that power. To Plato, if theatre could not affect an audience, it would not exist; but because it can affect an audience, it can do so adversely. In *The Republic* (370 B.C.) Plato wrote:

> When we listen to some hero in Homer or on the tragic stage moaning over his sorrows in a long tirade, or to a chorus beating their breasts as they chant a lament, you know how the best of us enjoy giving ourselves up to follow the performance with eager sympathy. . . . Few I believe are capable of reflecting that to enter into another's feelings must have an effect on our own; the emotions of pity our sympathy has strengthened will not be easy to restrain when we are suffering ourselves. . . . You are doing the same thing if, in listening at a comic performance or in ordinary life to buffooneries which you would be ashamed to indulge in yourself, you thoroughly enjoy them instead of being disgusted with their ribaldry There is in you an impulse to play the clown, which you have held in restraint from a reasonable fear of being set down as a buffoon; but now you have given it rein, and by encouraging its impudence at the theatre you may be unconsciously carried away into playing the comedian in your private life. Similar effects are produced by poetic representation of love and anger and all those desires and feelings of pleasure or pain which accompany our every action. It waters the growth of passions which should be allowed to wither away and sets them up in control, although the goodness and happiness of our lives depend on their being held in subjection.[16]

Plato's views prompted his prize student, Aristotle, to rebut his position by developing the cathartic theory of drama. Dramatic theatre, Aristotle maintained, arouses and then purges the audience of impulses that would be harmful if allowed free rein in society. In this way dramatic theatre functions as the tribal clown; the drama gives vent to an individual's irrational pressures. The actor, as the clown, undergoes in the audience's stead, and the audience acts only vicariously through its empathetic response to the performer.

*Decline* The Peloponnesian War (431–404 B.C.) brought an end to the great period of Athenian theatre. Spartan control of Athens ended the democratic ideal; the death of Socrates (399 B.C.) began the symbolic death of the poetical ideal. Continuous war had exhausted the Greek spirit; specialization and professional "expertism" began to replace good-hearted amateurism questing after theatrical *arete*. Domestic interests seemed safer than national or international concerns.

In the theatre, great tragedy gave way to great comedy. And when great writing faded from the public's view, it was replaced by great acting. Revivals featuring starring actors testified to the lack of playwrights with the vision, know-how, and nurturing community of Aeschylus, Sophocles, Euripides, and Aristophanes. Professionalism invaded the theatre as citizens began to make livings by acting and touring the countryside. Art became more a means of making a living than a gift from the gods to individuals and from individuals to their gods.

But the Greek ideal had caught the fancy of the 20-year-old son of Philip of Macedonia, Alexander the Great (356–323 B.C.). By the time he died at age 33, he had established Greek cities and culture throughout the world. His legacy persisted throughout the history of the theatre.

# ROME

The character Anchises in Book VI of Virgil's epic *Aeneid* charges Rome to "Let others beat out softer lines from the bronze and draw life-like features from the marble—thou, Roman, must think of ruling the people; these are your arts: to impose law in peace, to spare the humble and tame the haughty." After reviewing Rome's contribution to the arts in that civilization's almost 1200-year existence, we could not say that Anchises's injunction had been violated to any substantial degree. Though not as awesome as those of Greece, Rome's achievements provide the basis for the theatre that dominated Western culture. The history of Roman theatre and drama, in fact, establishes prominent characteristics of the Western theatre. We are heirs to Rome far more than to Greece, not only in our theatre, but also in our cultural milieu.

*Cultural Context* Between the dates usually given for its founding (753 B.C.) and its fall (A.D. 476), Roman civilization grew to a Republic, transformed into an Empire, and finally consolidated in the direction of a Christian theocracy. The causes and effects of the dynamic evolutions influenced the development of Western culture and theatre.

*The Republic* Etruscans and Latins inhabited opposite banks of the Tiber River. At the river's ford the two people traded; from that trading center grew the city of Rome. In 509 B.C. the ruling Latins established and controlled a Republican government that excluded from meaningful participation the mass of people known as *plebeians*. The Republic ruled Rome during the fifth century B.C., when Greek society reveled in its Golden Age of theatre.

The plebeians, however, agitated for power. Their threat to throw their weight behind a tyrant produced the Decimviri, Board of Ten, who wrote the Twelve Tables, the basis for Roman law. The plebeians used their rights under the new law to prosper, and many patricians lost their wealth. In time laws were changed to allow patrician children to marry the sons of the newly rich plebeians. Trade created new middle-class citizens, and gradually power shifted in their direction.

The Second Punic War (218–201 B.C.) forced many rural farmers and families into Rome for safety. As Rome grew rapidly, typical urban problems developed. Because the Senate opened its doors to anyone with enough money to get elected, rich men were able to band together in the Senate to guard their interests against the growing population of poor and unemployed plebeians and free citizens. A large workforce caused Rome to abandon its citizen/soldier idea for a professional army of paid soldiers. Ambitious individuals began to court favor with a permanent military organization, rather than with plebeians and free citizens. In a time of great territorial expansion, few senators devoted their time to affairs of state when enormous profits awaited the march of the Roman army. The Senate's interests lay elsewhere: laws were disregarded, and courts were despised. Armed gangs roamed the streets, elections were bought, and few cared. Business was booming; great profits were being made. Naturally, politicians in the luxurious, corrupt, and vice-ridden city passed a cascade of laws against all sorts of luxury, corruption, and vice. The time was one of money lending, interest charging, and land speculation. The nobility and aristocracy were fast replaced by "self-made" successes. A small number of entrepreneurs grew rich as old patrician families grew poor, irritated, and unscrupulous.

In 60 B.C. three men—Caesar, Pompey, and Crassus—agreed to take the government into their own hands. The masses vented their frustrations at free games provided by the government. The self-appointed triumvirate was thus a welcome relief; it could do as it pleased as long as the people were content.

*The Empire* After Caesar successfully marched on Pompey and declared himself Emperor, some citizens feared the consolidation of power in one man. On March 15, 44 B.C., they assassinated Caesar. The resultant power vacuum was eventually filled by Caesar's nephew, Octavian. Octavian was voted the title "Augustus," and the Republic ended. Many reasons have been offered for the Republic's demise: the government's failing to broaden participation in public life, the government's difficulty governing so large a territory, the army's threatening decisive civilian action, the large uneducated population's

playing into the waiting hands of tiny demagogues, and the leaders' looking to the past for answers and seeking a return to the good old days of simplicity, piety, and duty. Edith Hamilton summarizes the causes by noting that "a narrow selfishness kept men blind when their own self-preservation demanded a worldwide outlook."[17]

The Age of Augustus (63 B.C.–A.D. 14) heralded the Golden Age of Roman civilization. Art and literature once again became tools for a leader's self-aggrandizement. When Emperor Tiberius tried to cut the government's expenses by curtailing state support for entertainments, he lost his popularity. A monarchy took root that lasted to the death of Nero (A.D. 68).

From the Emperor Nerva, who ruled from A.D. 96–98, to the stoic Emperor Marcus Aurelius (A.D. 121–180) Rome enjoyed good government and great prosperity. The second century A.D. was especially a time of prosperity. Plutarch wrote of the great lives of the rich people who collected books, built libraries, and hired Greek tutors for their children. India, China, Persia, and Africa were ransacked for booty. As these new territories were conquered, new religious and artistic ideas rode back to Rome on the treasure chests.

The Roman Empire ultimately reached from Britain to Persia, from the Rhone to the Sahara. Although Easterners preferred the Greek culture Alexander had given them in the fourth century B.C., Western people found Latin culture and language superior to their own and, in time, adopted it. The Empire thus contained a diversity of people; it was also characterized by extreme life situations—from absolute despotism to hopeless slavery, from undreamed-of luxury to inhuman squalor, from unbelievable pleasure to unheard-of misery.

The death of Marcus Aurelius led to a rapid succession of emperors and severe internal crises. In the third century, for example, "barbarian" tribes mounted intense attacks seeking new land for their growing populations. Because every communication from Rome to the troubled provinces had to travel cumber-

*The city of Rome during the Empire.*   (New York Public Library Picture Collection)

somely by land, emperors set up subordinate administrative centers throughout the Empire. When Constantine reunited the Empire in A.D. 312, he transferred the capitol permanently to the city of Byzantium, renamed Constantinople, because it commanded the trade routes to the East. In Constantinople the government of the Roman Empire came under Hellenic and Asian influence. The western part of the Empire broke into fragments that took on separate lives of their own. We discuss the final decline of Roman civilization after we examine the society that underwent this extended metamorphosis.

***The Roman Family: The Subject of the Drama***   Reading Roman comedy could give you the exact opposite picture of the values Roman society upheld. A rollicking senator in his nightclothes is a far cry from the discipline, frugality, dignity, and precision that charac-

terized so much of the Roman ideal. These qualities lived in practical people: rulers rather than philosophers, engineers rather than sculptors, soldiers rather than poets. And Roman social structure supported these values.

Roman family life, the subject of Roman drama, had been founded on the basis of the *pater familias* (father's rule), and Roman drama revealed the principle both in operation and in decline. By the second century A.D., the father's absolute rule over wife and children was gone. Once, the father had held the power of life or death, freedom or slavery for his wife and children. But a mother, no longer a possession to purchase, was a human being with whom a man must contract a betrothal and marriage. A woman entered her husband's home of her own free will, usually at the age of 12 or 13, and lived there under her own terms as his equal in every respect. Women engaged freely in birth control and entered freely any profession open to men. Whereas in the time of Cato women could be killed for adultery, new laws made for equal and less severe punishment. Easy divorce was available to men or women. In time a *mater familias* (mother's rule) dominated Roman life. Roman women gave orders to maids; received visitors of both sexes; enjoyed the best education, leisure, and work; and attended religious festivals, games, theatre, and circuses. Adultery headed both sexes' list of social games. Women became actors, clowns, and gladiators; one even became Empress of the empire. Sexual equality was legislated and practiced to an unparalleled degree.

As women emerged from the home to play a role in Roman public life, religion left the hearth to enter the temple. Indigenous Roman religion centered around household gods—tiny, rude figurines to whom farmers offered bits of everyday food. The gods played a unique role in Roman dramas. Unlike the Greek gods, Roman gods had no specific human forms. In the Republic, Romans assimilated the imported Greek mythology and Latinized the gods' names. Educated Romans, however, contented themselves with ethical guidance found in the Greek Hellenistic philosophy. By the end of the Republic, the philosophy preached by Zeno in the fourth century B.C., called Stoicism, had developed a distinctly Roman character.

**Stoicism: Religion in Drama**   Stoicism appealed to the Romans, interestingly, when the extremes of the Empire seemed intolerable. Stoicism held that God (or Zeus, Creative Fire, Ether, the Word, Reason, Soul, Law of Nature, Providence, Destiny, or Order; all were synonymous) dwelt in every person regardless of sex, social status, race, or birth. By recognizing the divinity within, a Stoic could endure pain, sorrow, or death. Striving for virtue— intelligence, bravery, justice, and self-control—and living in accordance with the orderliness of the universe brought one spiritual peace and well-being. Almost alone in Rome, Stoics denounced sexual relations outside marriage, vice and violence in theatrical specta-

cles, and slavery. Earthly existence, rather than the hereafter mentioned by Eastern religious cults, paved the Stoics' path to virtue. Stoicism's faith in astrology, a system of belief in a universe based on the findings of astronomy and cosmology, influenced science, architecture, art, and literature. Stoicism found expression in the only extant Roman tragedies.

But all Romans could not endure everyday life "stoically." During the Empire Eastern mysticism and religious movements wound their way into Roman life. The bleakness and misery of a stoic life made talk of a beautiful afterlife appealing to the mass of Romans. Egyptian ideas of immortality in the cult of Isis, the Jewish expectation of a Messiah, and Mithraism's promised God of Light or Sun of Righteousness found eager adherents among slaves, soldiers, and the distressed. Because the dramatic theatre is, to a great degree, a celebration of the present, this shift toward the future bode ill for the theatre.

In the second century A.D. Mithraism met its most formidable foe: Christianity and its promise of salvation and immortality. And rituals rather than dramas caught the tenor of the times. Both religions had assimilated rites and ceremonials that helped them gain acceptance. Both religions also had similar sacraments: baptism, confirmation, holy feasts of wine and bread. Mithraism's powerful symbolism, candles, music, and pageantry outshone the spartan Christian ceremonies. But Mithraism lacked Christianity's narrative of a Divine Life with which Romans could identify. By the third century A.D. Christianity was one of the Empire's major religions; by that time, about one-tenth of the Roman population was Christian.

Roman expansion brought new religions, but left no time for pure scientific investigation. Engineers rather than scientists dominated that sphere of Roman activity. Amphitheatres, baths, bridges, aqueducts, public works, sewage systems, and roads showed applied science surpassing pure science. Romans had no desire for knowledge for its own sake; knowledge needed a practical use to have value. As a result theatre technology flourished. The development of a true arch made of interlocking wedge-shaped sections and cement encouraged the growth of Roman theatres. Vaulting systems, especially the dome, allowed the Romans to house a large theatre crowd in one space.

***Imported Arts***   Expansion brought different cultures to Rome, each with an art that influenced the development of Roman art. Southern Italy had been settled by Greeks during their Classical period; Aeschylus had written and staged plays for Heiron in the theatre of Syracuse in 460 B.C. In 364 B.C. Etruscan players were imported to Rome to perform dances, musical rites, and ceremonies to stop a plague. Rome celebrated itself: rich citizens financed portraitures, individual portrait busts, and statues. Triumphal arches and frescoes announced the glory of Rome.

The Romans admired poetry that preached; the more preaching, they thought, the better the poetry. Morality and patriotism were favorite themes, and poets served the state by urging citizens to do their duty in these areas. As Horace (65–8 B.C.), the poet and critic, wrote in his *Ars Poetica* (19 B.C.), "the aim of the poet is either to benefit, or to amuse, or to make his words at once please and give lessons of life." But the Romans did not value their own art, especially when they measured it against Greek art. They thought their art had no value independent of its ability to refine the enjoyment of life or to perpetuate the memory of persons or things.

***The First History of the Theatre***   The history of the Roman theatre shows both the assimilative quality of Roman art and the emergence of a distinctly Roman point of view. The Roman historian Livy (59 B.C.–A.D. 17), who wrote the first history of Roman theatre, posited five stages in his somewhat unreliable development of dramatic theatre: (1) dances to flute music; (2) improvised obscene verses and dances to flute music; (3) medleys to flute music with dancing; (4) plotted comedies with singers for the lyrical passages; and (5) the fourth stage with an additional afterpiece. Livy

suggested that Roman theatre evolved from the dance—the premise we postulated in Chapter 1 and the phenomenon we found in the origin of the Greek theatre. In addition, Livy suggested that Roman theatre originally had a function similar to that of primitive religion and superstition. Because no other evidence exists of the first stage of Livy's history, we begin our investigation of Roman theatre with the second.

***Farce***   The link between the theatres of Greece and Rome is the Greek mime player. As historian Allardyce Nicoll points out:

> From the days of ancient Megara to those of Republican Rome there existed a very clear and definite theatrical tradition of a "popular" sort. The literary drama continues its own career, but here is essentially an actors' theatre of antiquity—a thing passed down from generation to generation, changing its name and its medium, but preserving fundamentally the outlines which had been established in dim days before history began. . . .[18]

Greek mime received literary form from the pen of Epicharmus in the fifth century B.C. Travesties of daily Greek life, mythology, and Greek tragedy constituted the repertoire of players known as *phlyakes* (gossips) when they established a beachhead in southern Italy. The *phlyakes* were still servants of Dionysus, and farce was still part of his cult. Players, some masked, others maskless, burlesqued the epic heroes, such as Odysseus and Hercules, with a stable of stock characters: old men, slaves, middle-aged men, gods, thieves, and old women. Scenes from ordinary life, military expeditions, love intrigues, and problems between the sexes provided the fodder for these comic romps.

The *phlyakes*' costumes resembled the old comic costumes; they consisted of plain or striped body stockings stuffed in front and back, phalli, too-short vests, buttons for navels, *chlamys* or *himations* for the men, *chitons* or cloaks for the women, and flat shoes or bare feet. A portable, make-shift platform served as the stage. Curtains or panels at the rear formed a facade that functioned as a door or window.

***The Atellan Farce*** After the third century B.C. no record exists of the *phlyakes*. Apparently the Oscans of southern Italy changed the existing farce into something with a more Latin flavor: the *fabula Atellana*, or Atellan farce, named for the town of Atella. In adapting the southern Italian farce, the Oscans conventionalized four main types of characters and masks: Bucco the braggart, Maccus the greedy blockhead, Dossenus the clever hunchback, and Pappus the stupid old man. Usually only one act long, and often in Greek, the topical and obscene Atellan farces—they probably still used the phallus—resembled human Punch and Judy shows. Their main feature was the *tricae* (tricky bits of stock stage business). They probably also introduced music to the improvisational satires.

In time, as the popularity of the farces grew, Rome welcomed the farce players to the theatrical scene already on hand. Atellan farces met and mingled with indigenous Roman theatricals. The music and dancing that Livy mentioned as imported from Etruria added improvised dialogues to the Roman harvest buffoonery. The farces also combined with the *versus Fescennini* (Fescennine verses) and jesting at the Roman vineyard harvests. Dancing, drinking, and revelry characterized the improvised coarse jokes and personal satires that had grown so immoral that laws sought to keep them in check. Etrurian *isters* (dancing actors) were masked clown-like figures called Phersu: when Latinized, this term became *persona* (mask). These jesting, joking, dancing actors probably came to Rome in 364 B.C. to perform the plague-stopping ceremony Livy described. From then on dancing and flute playing became part of Roman life. Etruscan *mimisti* (dancers) called *histriones* performed to the accompaniment of *tibia* (pipes) and combined with the Fescennine verse singers to create *fabula saturae* (medleys of dance, music, and crude dialogue). When the *fabula Atellana* was rewritten into Latin, it replaced the *fabula satura*

*Dossenus.* (Art Resource, Giraudon)

in popularity. The Romanized Atellana may have been called *fabulae satyricae*.

***Early Written Drama*** After 100 B.C. the Atellan farce had grown so popular that it was

*Pappus.* (Francisco Ficoroni, *Dissertario de larvis scenicis*, Roma, 1754, Plate xxxii. New York Public Library at Lincoln Center)

man with an eye for young women, an easy mark for gulling young men. Each character was recognized by a standard mask and costume.

Although the Atellan farce had a short-lived literary life during the Empire, it remained a popular favorite because of its low-life characters and their coarse, vulgar, and obscene antics. When it took over mime's characteristics Atellan farce became the plebeians' favorite. In addition, farce's characteristic low, four-posted wooden platform with steps leading to it could be set up for easy viewing anywhere, from a public market to a private hall. Nonetheless, no record exists of *fabula Atellana* after the end of the first century A.D.

*Festivals* The Etruscan ruler of Rome, Tarquin, established the Roman festivals,

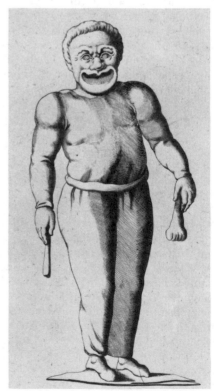

*Bucco.* (Ficoroni, Plate xxxi. New York Public Library at Lincoln Center)

written down. In 89 B.C. C. Novius and L. Pomponius gave the improvised romps a Latin literary form, and farce actually overtook in popularity the literary forms of drama that had been introduced to the Roman festivals. Pomponius is credited with some seventy titles and Novius with forty-four that together suggest the quality of the dramas of rural life: *Maccus the Soldier, Maccus the Innkeeper, Maccus the Maid, The Twin Macci, Bucco the Gladiator, Pappus the Farmer, The Bride of Pappus, Pappus Defeated at the Poll, The Pig, The Woodpile, The Inspector of Morals*, and *The Pimp*. These stock characters referred often to bodily functions. Bucco became a very large-cheeked fool who talked and ate a lot. Dossenus, the mordant wit, sported not only a humped back but also a terrifically exaggerated jaw of large teeth. He usually appeared as a malicious parasite or schoolmaster. Maccus grew more ignorant and developed into a blundering rustic with a taste for stodgy food. Pappus remained a stupid and senile old called *ludi*. Technically the festivals were state religious celebrations honoring various gods. In time the festivals became occasions for entertaining the masses with farces and sensationalism. At first only athletic events, races, and gladiatorial contests occurred at festivals; later other events were added as part of the Roman *fasti* (calendar of festivals). In time *ludi scaenici* (theatrical shows) were featured at the *ludi* as well.

During the First Punic War (264–241 B.C.) Romans saw Greek dramatic performances. Livius Andronicus (284–204 B.C.), arriving in Rome as a prisoner of war, produced the first translation of a Greek tragedy at the *ludi Romani* (the oldest festival), which began in the sixth century B.C. The *ludi Romani*, which honored Jupiter each September 5 to 19, took place in the Circus Maximus, Rome's oldest building for games. By 214 B.C. four days of theatre preceded the festival's races and gladiatorial contests.

Other festivals filled the Roman social season too. In 220 B.C. the *ludi Plebeii* (the people's festival) happened in the Circus Flaminius. Each November 1 to 17 the festival honored Jupiter with at least three days of theatrical entertainments. After 212 B.C. the *ludi Apollinares* honored Apollo between July 6 and 13. The Second Punic War (218–201 B.C.) had increased the Roman demand for drama; the *ludi Apollinares* filled that need with at least two more days of theatre. The *ludi Megalenses* honored Cybele, the *Magna Mater* (Mother Goddess) beginning in 194 B.C., following her arrival from Phrygia. Perhaps as many as six days were allotted for theatrical shows in this April festival. The *ludi Cereales* (April 12 to 19) appeared fully established in 202 B.C. Whether honoring the ancient Ceres or the Greek Demeter, the festival allotted seven days for theatre during the Empire. The *ludi Florales*, begun in 173 B.C. and extending from April 28 into May, had a definite plebeian orientation. The games prided themselves on their violence, coarseness, and lewdness. Drunkenness was the norm. April 28 was also the Feast Day for Roman prostitutes. Consequently, mime, a form of theatre that employed many prostitutes, occupied center stage. The goddess Flora herself was a prostitute whose work financed the festival. Mimes undressed on stage, hares and goats copulated in the circus, and officials threw beans, vetches, and lupines (both types of plants), along with medals imprinted with obscene pictures, into the audience. In 17 B.C. Augustus celebrated the Festival of Saeculum to give credence to the World Renewed as announced by the poet Virgil in his Fourth Ecologue. Theatrical pieces opened the festival and played throughout. The *ludi Funerales* (funeral games) and *ludi Votivi* (games at dedications and triumphal celebrations) increased to almost 100 the annual number of days for theatre.

By 170 B.C. the social season, which lasted from spring to autumn, featured religious festivals with *ludi circenses* (races), *ludi scaenici* (shows), and additional variety acts. Rope dancers, wall climbers, acting bears, choruses of trumpeters and flautists, wind instrumentalists, jugglers, flame throwers, bird flyers, and acrobats competed for the audience with circus races, gladiatorial fights, animal fights, wrestling and boxing matches, and theatre. All events happened simultaneously. By Augustus's time, of the sixty days devoted to public spectacles, forty featured drama.

Although the theatre was the least costly and troublesome and the most frequented, it was also the least appreciated of the events. The popularity of theatre declined, in fact, as spectacle in the circus and amphitheatre grew. By 345 A.D. 175 days were set aside for festivals, but only 100 featured drama. A practice called *instauratio*, however, increased the number of theatrical performances possible. This meant that if any impropriety occurred, such as a dancer's stopping or a flautist's missing a note, the entire festival had to be repeated. *Instauratio* was an almost yearly occurrence; some years it happened three or four times. Because of the odd practice, at least six or seven days were gained for theatre each year.

During the Empire the character of the festivals changed. Mime and pantomime replaced tragedy and comedy in popularity. Because gambling interests could be satisfied more readily in competitive entertainments, racing and gladiatorial fighting increased: the electorate had to be entertained. At the *ludi Florales* slaves bore torches to let the festivals continue into the evenings. The Emperor Nero (A.D. 37–68) gave evening chariot races using pitch-dipped Christians as torches. At one festival in A.D. 88 a circle of lights was lowered into the amphitheatre to turn night into day. The festival theatre in Rome existed as but one part of a complex entertainment and performance network.

### Theatrical Organization and Management

Roman theatre mixed a rising young politico's desire to win popular favor and an impresario's desire for financial profit with the public's desire for an enjoyable day off. Together, the actors, the stage conventions, the Latin text, and a fun-loving audience created a uniquely Roman performance. Each festival was run by a *praetor* or *aedile* (magistrate) who used a government grant to supplement his private finances. The government, decreeing games and theatre, used public funds to help wealthy citizens who either volunteered or were appointed by state officials to run the festivals. The magistrates used these occasions to advance their political ambitions; artistic or social success was not on their mind. Consequently, playwrights sought to avoid offending any family whose son might be next year's *aedile*. The *aedile* contracted with a *dominus gregis* (theatrical impresario) and agreed either to purchase a new play for the company or to allow that company to produce a play from its existing repertoire.

The *gregis* then hired the people he needed, rehearsed the play, presented a preview for the *aedile*, and handled all production arrangements. If he needed more than the resident flautist he hired musicians. By doubling roles a company of five actors could perform almost any scene. Costumes, masks, and properties (the *ornamenta*) were coordinated by the *choragus* (prop master).

The *dominus gregis*, usually a free person, owned a company of slave actors mixed with an occasional free actor. He bought plays with the hope of turning a profit. Once he purchased a play, it became his property instead of the playwright's.

The *dominus gregis* sometimes also acted with his *grex* or *caterua* (company) of actors. The two most famous Roman playwrights featured two of Rome's greatest actor-managers as producers of their plays: Terence (185–159 B.C.) had L. Ambivius Turpio and Plautus (c. 254–184 B.C.) had T. Pubilius Pellio. Turpio, Pellio, Aesopus, and Roscius were Rome's four greatest actor-managers.

Occasionally, the companies competed for prizes that went either to the company as a whole or to individual actors. Companies were notorious both for hiring claques of supporters to fill their theatres and for bribing the magistrates for prizes.

**Players**   The Romans' performance style, which resembled the Greeks', resulted from the actors' extension of voice and movement into music, dance, costume, and mask. Roman acting, however, seems to have required more of a musical or operatic technique than Greek acting. Also, one particular playing convention allowed the actors to exploit the conditions of the Roman playing space: stage left led to the Roman Forum; stage right led to foreign lands and the harbor. In addition, Livius Andronicus (284–204 B.C.) separated the speaking and moving aspects of the actors' work to produce some dramatic effects. For example, one actor performed the actions while another sang the lyrics. Acting was also presentational rather than representational in quality. Actors addressed lines to the audience rather than to fellow actors. The art of acting consisted of conveying the appropriate emotion through the appropriate combination of gestures. Declamation rather than talk characterized the delivery. With such skills actors could both save second-rate scripts and enhance the best writing.

In the first century A.D. Roman rhetorician Quintillian wrote that actors "add so much to the charm even of the greatest poets, that the verse moves us far more when heard than when read, while they succeed in securing a hearing even for the most worthless authors, with the result that they repeatedly win a welcome on the stage that is denied them in the library."[19] Quintillian suggested that Roman actors did not completely abandon reality with their presentational performances: "I have often seen actors, both in tragedy and comedy, leave the theatre still drowned in tears after concluding the performance of some moving role."[20] He reconciled the presentational and representational tendencies in Roman acting when he spoke of "the practice of comic actors, whose delivery is not that of common speech since that would be inartistic, but is on the other hand not far removed from the accents of nature, for, if it were, their mimicry would be a failure."[21]

Quintillian the orator admired the vocal and physical training apparent in Roman acting. In the first century B.C., after, as in Greece, a period of great playwrighting, Roman acting reached its height. But unlike the Greeks, the most famous Roman actors performed both tragedy and comedy. Actors did specialize, however, in certain types of roles: women, gods, youths, parasites. For example, Roscius played masked except when playing his specialty, a parasite, because his own natural squint far surpassed that of the stock parasite squinted mask. Quintillian described how actors used their special gifts to great advantage:

> We have seen the greatest of comic actors, Demetrius and Stratocles, win their success by entirely different merits. But that is the less surprising owing to the fact that the one was at his best in roles of gods, young men, good fathers and slaves, matrons and respectable old women, while the other excelled in the portrayal of sharp-tempered old men, cunning slaves, parasites, pimps and all the more lively characters of comedy. For their natural gifts differed. For Demetrius' voice, like his other qualities, had greater charm, while that of Stratocles was more powerful. But yet more noticeable were the incommunicable peculiarities of their action. Demetrius showed unique gifts in the movements of his hands, in his power to charm his audience by the long-drawn sweetness of his exclamations, the skill with which he would make

his dress seem to puff out with the wind as he walked, and the expressive movements of the right side which he sometimes introduced with effect, in all of which things he was helped by his stature and personal beauty. On the other hand, Stratocles's *forte* lay in his nimbleness and rapidity of movement, in his laugh (which, though not always in keeping with the character he represented, he deliberately employed to awaken answering laughter in his audience), and finally, even in the way in which he sank his neck into his shoulders. If either of these actors had attempted any of his rival's tricks, he would have produced a most unbecoming effect.[22]

***Music and Dramatic Performance*** Although purely Roman music never existed, most Roman plays had musical accompaniment. Music, in fact, filled the Roman theatre, as Greek music transferred to Roman soil quickly took on a new tone in the new society's drama. Plautus, for instance, added music where his Greek models had none; two-thirds of his lines have musical accompaniment. Likewise, one-third of Terence's lines are set to music. And Livius Andronicus was known as the "actor of his songs."

The music played was traditionally associated with each character type. Consequently, before an actor entered, the audience knew what type of character was coming. In addition, music was never separate from the poetry of the drama. It was played before the prologue and between the acts. Even with pantomime, a *scabillum*—made of two boards fastened together and attached to the undersides of each actor's feet—clattered a noisy rhythmic accompaniment to the performance.

The *tibia* (flute), played by the *tibicen* (theatre flautist), accompanied Roman actors. All the musicians sat on stage and moved among the actors. Because two pipes, twenty inches long, were tied to the flautists' mouths, their hands were left free to work the stops.

In the third century the invention of the hydraulic-powered organ quickly raised the wrath of both the playwright Seneca and the orator Quintillian, who thought the instrument's music too "effeminate." But during the Empire organ music filled the theatres and amphitheatres. The actors sang to much of this music; they moved and danced to all of it.

***Theatrical Dance*** Dance in Rome was predominantly religious or ritualistic in nature. But dance played a much less prominent part in Roman society's national and private life than in Greek's. Romans were, as a result, susceptible to the Asian religions' ritualized dances, and they loved the novel religions, musical instruments, and dances brought back from conquered Asian lands.

December 17, the peak of the Roman Saturnalia, became the occasion for great dramatic dancing, exchanging presents, and lighting candles. Pantomime in particular characterized Roman dance drama. In fact, the dance element of the Roman theatre became so popular that it broke away to create a new form of dramatic expression in which Roman actors played an essential role. The actors' use of dance and movement in scripted drama contributed to the growing physicalization of character through dance movement. The audience's appreciation of dance thus owed much to the actors' use of costume and mask.

***Costume and Mask*** Unlike the Greeks, the Romans employed more than three actors to play several roles. Roman masks, which were used to differentiate among the characters, were supposedly introduced by the most famous actor, Roscius, to hide his natural squint. At first masks dominated the Roman stage. The Latin word *persona* (mask) is Etruscan in derivation, which indicates that the Etruscan dancers probably wore masks. Atellan farce players likewise appeared masked. In time, when novel entertainments featuring maskless players grew in popularity, the mask became a rare sight.

Like Greek masks, Roman masks covered the entire head. They were constructed of lightweight linen for easy movement and quick change, often within six lines of dialogue. Hair color denoted character: old people had gray or white hair, or they were bald; young people had black or dark hair; and slaves sported red hair. Tragic masks had more hair and beard than comic masks. The speaker of the prologue wore no mask.

Costumes followed the Greek model, especially in plays based on Greek originals (*fabula palliata*). For these plays the costumes were variants of the Greek *himation*; they were known in Rome as a *pallium* when worn by men, and a *palla* when worn by women. The *pallium* could be freely draped in a variety of ways to denote social rank and attitude. Underneath the *pallium* was a *tunica*, the Greek *chiton* or *chlamys*. Padded body stockings covered low-class characters and slaves. Slaves also wore small scarf-like mantles called *pallii collecti*. Long tunics garbed women and older men; the *chlamys* decked young men, soldiers, travelers, and slaves on errands. Travelers also wore a wide-brimmed hat called a *petasos*.

Colors and accessories completed the costumes' evocative powers and added a measure of symbolism. (To disguise one's identity altogether, one need only put a patch over one or both eyes.) Tragic actors, for example, wore a *soccus* (slipper), a *crepida* (sandal), or went barefooted. All of the properties, accessories, and stage apparati were under the control of the *procurator summi choragi* (a free person from an imperial household who was responsible for acquiring and maintaining the equipment). Generally, *senex* (the old man) could be found in a white or bluish-white *tunica* and yellow *pallium*. A staff and purse rounded out the costume of the white-haired, bearded, toothless, quivering, and feeble miser. *Adulescens* (the young man) wore a rich, bright, and often contrasting colored *pallium* and *chlamys*. If a traveler, he wore the *petasos*; if a soldier, he carried a *machaera* (sword). *Seruus* (the slave) appeared grotesque in a too-short tunic with tight sleeves and no *pallium*. Females wore long flowing garments. Prostitutes were known by their yellow mantles. A cook was identified by a short tunic, spoon, knife, or dish of food; a mourner, by long trailing robes; a pimp, by a variegated costume; a parasite, by a specially wrapped mantle; a slave dealer by a money bag and straight staff; a miser by a curved staff; and a captain by a purple *chlamys*. White indicated cheerfulness; purple, wealth; and red, poverty.

***Social Status of the Actor***   Besides being known as *histriones* and *cantores*, Roman actors were also labeled *infami*. An early edict by the Roman senate clarified the status of acting. Any citizen who became an actor could be punished by death. Unlike Greek actors, who were accorded a measure of dignity, Roman actors were at best considered social inferiors, at worst, things to be used and disgarded. Most actors, in fact, were slaves. Women, too, entered the shunned profession, at first only as mimes; later they may have played other forms of drama as well. Even at the end of the Empire, when some actors had attained respect, admiration, wealth, and even citizenship, the hereditary nature of the profession chained actors to the art from generation to generation. Moreover, actors were forbidden to vote or hold public office. It was also illegal for a citizen to become an actor; soldiers who did so were executed. Acting was still considered an infamous profession entered into only by slaves and free people from non-Roman lands.

The prejudice against acting abated when the nobility became infatuated with pantomimes. In the sixth century A.D. the actress Theodora left her life of prostitution and lewd dancing to marry the Emperor. When the Emperor died the Empress Theodora reigned— and continued to be considered the most powerful actor in history until Ronald Reagan was elected president of the United States. Most of the time, however, actors were thought of as no better than gladiators. Acting, like prostitution, was a necessary evil. The government both attacked and encouraged it.

Like their Greek counterparts, Roman actors formed a *conventicle* (guild). Nominally religious and headquartered in Rome, the worldwide guild associated itself with the goddess Minerva or Athene, goddess of *artes* (skills). Theatre people—actors, writers, and managers—were known as *artifices scaenici* (scenic artists). Included among the *artifices scaenici* were those people responsible for the site and scenery of the theatrical performance.

***Performance Space***   The Roman theatre building, like the Greek, evolved with the development of the drama, but both architecture and drama were slower to develop in Rome than they were in Athens. Because chariot and horse racing, athletic contests, and gladiatorial fights were the first major entertainments, the Roman circus was the first permanent entertainment building. The nomadic Etruscan players who appeared in Rome in 364 B.C. used a temporary stage that became the prototype of the Roman auditorium built over 300 years later.

Both the Atellan and Oscan farces used the *phylukes'* stage; in 240 B.C. the first Roman tragedies and comedies were mounted on this type of stage as well. Temporary stages could be moved for the days of games. Stages were also occasionally erected before temples.

At first the stages were simple; later they were more ornate. The fear of fire within the densely populated city necessitated removing the theatre after each performance. Consequently, both a stage and a seating arrangement were constructed for each performance. A wooden stage no more than five feet high could be reached by stairs from the ground. The audience stood, sat on a hillside, or brought chairs. Later wooden stands were provided.

Roman theatres had carefully planned systems of walls, stairs, corridors, passageways, and doors. Most were built on flat ground rather than on natural slopes, like Greek theatres were. And unlike in Greek theatres, the Roman *scaena* (stage house) was connected with the *cavea* (auditorium) to form one architectural unit. A roofed *parados* (passageway), called a *vomitorium*, led to a semicircular orchestra. A twenty- to forty-foot deep stage (the *pulpitum*) was raised about five feet and had its front edge on the diameter of the orchestra. Besides the three doors in the 100- to 300-foot long *scaenae frons*, at least one door entered the stage from the *versurae* (wings). The stage roof provided excellent acoustics and protection for the expensive *scaenae frons*. Dressing rooms, storage rooms, trap doors, and an extensive cooling system completed the special features of the Roman theatre building.

During the Empire theatres were rebuilt and redecorated to make them richer and more sumptuous. Roman soldiers, settled in conquered lands, wanted popular entertainments. They remodeled Greek theatres and built new ones, making everything bigger, better, more luxurious, more pretentious, and more practical. Roman theatre remains still dot the landscapes of Italy, Germany, Britain, Spain, northern Africa, and Arabia.

**The Theatre at Pompeii** In 179 B.C. unsuccessful attempts were made to build a stone theatre near the temple of Apollo for the *ludi Apollinares*. In 195 B.C. special segregated seating was assigned to senators at the *ludi Romani*. In 154 B.C. the Senate, feeling that people spent too much time at the theatre as it was, stopped an attempt to build a stone auditorium. They did, however, approve plans for a stone auditorium more than a mile outside of Rome. Outside of Rome, in fact, permanent stone theatres were developed with features that would eventually characterize the theatres built in Rome.

In 75 B.C. the first purely Roman theatre, rather than a transformed Greek one, was built in Pompeii. The *cavea* (auditorium) and the orchestra had a semicircular shape instead of the circular form characteristic of Greek theatres. A deep, low stage supported a varied and elaborately decorated *scaenae frons* (rear wall). The painted *scaenae frons* had three doorways in it. Stairs led from the stage to the orchestra where movable seats accommodated members of the city council or guests of honor. The 1500-seat theatre was roofed. The Theatre at Pompeii remains the oldest preserved Roman theatre.

In 55 B.C. the first permanent theatre was built in Rome. The statesman Pompey (106–48 B.C.) built this theatre, which he modeled on a Greek theatre he had visited in Mytilene in 62 B.C., below the temple of Venus Victrix.

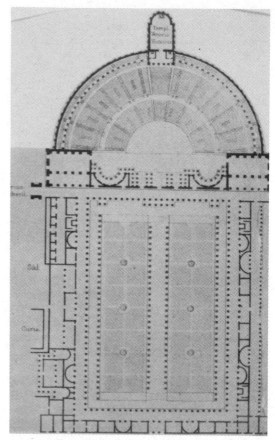

*A plan of the threatre built by Pompey in Rome. (Bieber,* The History of the Greek and Roman Theatre, *p. 181.)*

He disguised the theatre with a temple above the *cavea*. The theatre was dedicated in 52 B.C. with a variety of shows. In 11 B.C. Emperor Augustus completed another theatre, one begun by Caesar, and dedicated it to his nephew Marcellus.

**Vitruvius and Theatre Construction** Late Republican and Augustan theatres were described by the first-century B.C. Roman architect and military engineer, Vitruvius Pollio, in volumes three through nine of his ten-volume *De Architectura* (15 B.C.). Volume five dealt with theater architecture. Vitruvius laid out clear and simple rules for constructing a

*The Theatre at Orange.*

Roman theatre, utilizing contemporary ideas about geometry, astronomy, and astrology. Astrology, an Eastern science practiced by the Chaldeans, determined the influence of each planet on individuals' lives and fortunes according to the precise hours of their births. The seven planets were assigned to each of the twenty-four hours. In Rome, the name of each day of the week was the name of the heavenly body presiding over that day's first hour. Although repeatedly forbidden, astrology continued to influence the astronomy, philosophy, and architecture of the day:

> The Hippodrome was the universe in miniature, its microcosmic image. The arena was the earth, the euripus the sea, the central obelisk the pinnacle of heaven, consecrated to the sun whose course it shared. The Circus was again the circular year, its twelve doors of *carceres* the twelve months or signs. Its limits were marked by the ends of East and West, the rising and the setting; it had three turning points as each zodiacal sign had its three dekans. Each course consisted of seven turns, expressive of the seven days and the

seven stars. The 24 courses of each festival corresponded to the 24 hours of day-night. In turn the imagery of the Circus was imported into the sky.[23]

Vitruvius included an essay entitled "On Astrology" in his work on architecture. In it he wrote:

> I have described the revolutions of the firmament round the earth and the arrangement of the twelve signs and of the constellations to the north and south so as to present them to a clear view. For from that revolution of the firmament and the contrary motion of the sun through the signs and the equinoctial shadows of the gnomons, the diagrams of the analemma are discovered.
>
> For the rest, as to astrology, the effects produced on the human course of life by the twelve signs, the five planets, the sun and moon, we must give way to the calculations of the Chaldean astrologers, because the casting of nativities is special to them so that they can explain the past and the future from astronomical calculation.[24]

Vitruvius's plan for the ideal Roman theatre uses the orchestra to form the center of an astrological circle:

> The plan of the theatre is to be thus arranged: that the centre is to be taken, of the dimensions allotted to the orchestra at the ground level. The circumference is to be drawn; and in it four equilateral triangles are to be described touching the circumference at intervals (just as in the case of the twelve celestial signs, astronomers calculate from the musical division of the constellations). Of these triangles the side of that which is nearest the scene, will determine the front of the scene, in the part where it cuts the curve of the circle. Through the center of the circle a parallel line is drawn which is to divide the platform of the proscenium from the orchestra. Thus the stage will be made wider than that of the Greeks because all the actors play their parts on the stage, whereas the orchestra is allotted to the seats of the senators. The height of the stage is not to be more than five feet, so that those seated in the orchestra can see the gestures of the actors. The blocks of seats in the theatre are so to be divided that the angles of the triangles which run round the curve of the circle indicate the ascents and the steps between the blocks to the first circular passage . . . , the angles which are on the ground floor of the theatre and determine the staircases will be seven in number. The remaining five will indicate the arrangement of the stage. One in the middle should have the palace doors opposite to

it. Those which are to the right and left, will indicate the apartments provided for strangers. The furthest two will regard the direction of the revolving scenes.[25]

This explanation shows the mathematical ratios of the parts of the building: first, the stage depth equals the orchestra's radius; second, the length of the stage building equals two times the diameter of the orchestra; and third, the height of the stage equals one-twelfth the diameter. Roman love of law, organization, and correspondences created a well-planned whole with celestial resonances. Vitruvius created a sacred place for performance.

Because Vitruvius also cared about temporal resonances, much of his writing concerned acoustics. Wood, he proposed, should cover the stage floor and roof for good acoustics. And for the auditorium Vitruvius had another idea:

> In theatres, also, are copper vessels and these are placed in chambers under the rows of seats in accordance with mathematical reckoning . . . . The differences of the sounds which arise are combined into musical symphonies or concords: the circle of seats being divided into fourths and fifths and the octave. Hence, if the delivery of the actor from the stage is adapted to these contrivances, when it reaches them, it be-

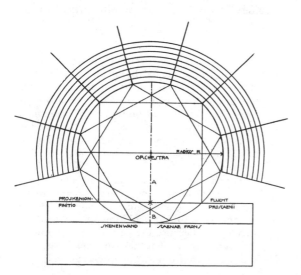

*Plan of the theatre according to Vitruvius.* (Bieber, *The History of the Greek and Roman Theatre*, p. 127.)

comes fuller, and reaches the audience with a richer and sweeter note.[26]

The theatre building housed the scenery for the Roman dramas. The elaborate *scaenae frons* supplied most of the scenic background. Unlike the flat and painted *phylakes'* wall, the *scaenae frons* utilized plastic, three-dimensional ornamentation. Vitruvius called one doorway the *aula regia* (the royal palace door) and two the *aula hospitalia* (the doors to guest chambers). The front wall of the five-foot high *pulpitum*, called the *proscaenium*, equaled the *scaenae frons* in elaborative decoration. Occasionally in a comedy, *pinakes* or *periaktoi* might be found in a doorway to suggest the front of a house. An altar might also have sat on stage before one of the openings for use by characters praying or seeking divine guidance. A front curtain, (the *auleum*) was lowered to reveal the stage and raised to signal the end of the drama. A rear curtain (the *siparium*) may also have revealed certain scenes.

Vitruvius described the basic scenic conventions of the period as follows:

> There are three styles of scenery: one which is called tragic; a second comic; the third, satyric. Now the subjects of these differ severally one from another. The tragic are designed with columns, pediments and statues and other royal surroundings; the comic have the appearance of private buildings and balconies and projections with windows made to imitate reality, after the fashion of ordinary buildings; the satyric settings are painted with trees, caves, mountains and other country features, designed to imitate landscape.[27]

Vitruvius's description suggests an attempt to coordinate scenic decoration with dramatic action.

***Dramatic Texts*** The plays of only three Roman dramatists survive, two comic writers—Plautus (c. 254–184 B.C.) and Terence (185–159 B.C.)—and one tragedian—Seneca (4 B.C.–A.D. 65), a Stoic philosopher, scientist, and imperial tutor. Although thirty-seven plays exist, all in verse, additional fragments

and names survive to suggest a range in Roman drama.

Romans called a play a *fabula*. (Recall from earlier discussion that the *fabula Atellana* was the short impromptu named after the town of Atella in southern Italy.) The term *fabula palliata* covered any Greek New Comedy translated into Latin. The plays of Terence and Plautus fall into this category. A *fabula praetexta* was any serious original play in Latin. A *fabula togata* or *tabernaria* was a Roman comedy based on scenes of contemporary low lifes, whereas a *fabula trabeata* was a *togata* of middle-class life. Additional *fabula* include the *stataria* (the "quiet" play) and the *motoria* (the "bustling" play).

Roman literature, which first appeared in the third century B.C., was modeled after the Greeks'. It may be divided into three parts: Pre-Classical (250–100 B.C.), Classical (100 B.C.–1), and Post-Classical (A.D. 1–150). Unlike Greek drama, none of the extant Roman plays come from the Classical period of the poets Virgil and Ovid and the orator Cicero. The comedies of Plautus and Terence come from the Pre-Classical period and the tragedies of Seneca, from the Post-Classical period.

***Plautus and Terence*** Roman comedy serves as the model for most subsequent Western comedy. The comedies of Plautus (c. 254–184 B.C.) and Terence (c. 185–159 B.C.), the first known black playwright, actually constitute the oldest surviving pieces of Roman literature. Plautus and Terence may even be said to have founded drama as we have come to know it. The scene of their action is always Greece, yet the action is always Roman—walking to the Forum, going to the capitol, worshipping household gods, speaking contemptuously of the Greeks. In addition, not only did Plautus and Terence originate domestic drama, but they also created familiar characters: the hen-pecking but faithful mother and the hen-pecked, randy husband. Plautus also invented situation sex comedy. Lovers in his plays cannot seem to get together without the assistance of a comic slave, the main character and plot mover. The plays of both Plautus and Terence, moreover, show the double standard of sexual mores that dominates Western drama: the exaltation of women for their purity, the placing of women on a special pedestal, the sentimentalization of love, and the use of love intrigue to move the plot action. The slave character appears in these plays as the ancestor of all faithful and unflappable servants. Slaves are, in fact, the chief characters, the only characters with brains, and the only characters capable of fooling everyone else.

Although later editors divided both comic playwrights' plays into five acts of many scenes, the plays were originally performed with continuous action. They also utilized many conventions: asides, soliloquies, chance meetings, failures to see eavesdroppers, discussions of secrets in public, and breaking the dramatic illusion. As in Aristophanes's plays, the comic

A comic slave seeking refuge on an altar.

characters of Plautus and Terence often address the audience; these Roman characters step out of the action to talk about stage machinery, to ask for help, or to explain the length of the play.

Plautus and Terence introduced two basic plot strategies. Plautus used dramatic irony: his audiences know everything, much more than the characters they are watching. Plautus used such comic irony to make the ignorant in his audience feel superior. For example, in *The Haunted House* the audience knows what the father Theopropides does not know—that he is being duped by Tranio the slave. Plautus's technique requires the least amount of audience attention for effect; consequently, Plautus was a favorite among the masses.

Terence, on the other hand, built his plots out of suspense, surprise, plot discoveries, and character reactions to novel situations. The audiences for his plays know as much or as little as the characters. The characters' surprise is the audience's surprise. For example, Terence eliminated the prologue of the Greek original from which his *Mother-in-Law* is derived because the prologue announced the real identity of the child's father before the fact is discovered by a character in the action. In Terence's version the audience discovers the truth along with the character. Terence's plots are more intricate and thus more difficult for a festival audience to follow.

Plautus's plays are mostly populated by average and below average Romans. Slaves, pimps, madams, prostitutes, and parasites help or hinder foundling children as they discover either their true identities or long-lost relatives. For such a middle-class audience Plautus made money the prime motivation for action.

Terence, on the other hand, who deliberately modeled his plays on the Greek New Comedy, wrote for an educated and aristocratic audience. Consequently, fewer below average and average characters appear in his works. His main character is a young Roman gentleman who is well versed in manners and social graces. Great verbal wit replaces the gross physical comedy of Plautus. *The Girl of*

*Andros* (166 B.C.), for example, resembles a Plautine work, but the characters are refined, polite, morally alert, and socially decorous.

**Roman Dramatists** Contemporaries of Plautus and Terence—Titinius, Afranius, and Atta—developed the *fabula togata*, the comedy in native Roman dress. The *togata* arose when the *palliata* was still at the peak of its popularity and existed side by side with it. Although no plays remain, some titles suggest the nature and quality of the action, which was considerably more exotic than the *palliata*: *The Lady Lawyer*, *The Procuress*, *Auntie*, *The Games of the Great Mother*, *What You Will*, *Chums*, *The Auction*, *The Hairdresser*, *Cousins*, *The Divorce*, *Sister-in-Law*, *She Who Gets Slapped*, *Married Man*, *The Omen*, *The Stepson*, *The Spendthrift*, *The Betrayed*, *The Butler*, *Not What He Seems to Be*, *The Suspected Daughter*, and *The Twin that Lived*. Sodomy and female adultery were often the featured subjects. Such literary comedy remained the most popular form of theatre until the Empire.

Although the only existing Roman tragedies are by Seneca, Roman tragedy began as early as Roman comedy. Tragedy started when Livius Andronicus (284–204 B.C.) became the first figure in the history of literature to tackle the problems of literary translation by translating a Greek tragedy into Latin for presentation at a *ludi Romani*. It continued to be performed in Rome for more than 200 years.

In the age of Cicero (106–43 B.C.) eager crowds attended tragedies even though they were more derivative and less original than Roman comedies. One reason for this lack of originality was that Roman tragic writers made no structural changes in their Greek models. Instead they added sentiment and such stylistic modifications as melodramatic effect, inflated rhetoric, plots of horror, eccentric characters, superhuman virtues and vices, and detailed descriptions—everything Romans admired.

Tragic writers were well-known enough to be burlesqued by Plautus. Among the chief tragic writers before Seneca were Andronicus, Naevius (270–201 B.C.), Ennius (239–169 B.C.), Pacuvius (220–130 B.C.), and Accius

(170–86 B.C.). Pacuvius is said to have written the most famous scene in Roman tragedy, in *Ilonia*. In the scene the ghost of the murdered Deiphilus rises to beg burial from his sleeping mother, Ilonia. Supposedly, at one performance the actor Fufius, playing Ilonia, actually fell asleep, and when Deiphilus's voice did not wake him on cue, the entire audience repeated the line in unison, "Mother, I call to thee."

After the death of Accius few, if any, tragedies were written for the stage. Old tragedies continued to be revived and performed to the end of the Republic. Professional theatre people turned their attention to plays that could make larger profits. Tragedies were left to dilettantes writing for their own amusement. To write for stage production was unworthy: actors and the theatre had fallen to too low a repute because of the carryings on of the mimes.

**Seneca** Under the Emperor Augustus and during the first century A.D., the number of plays given private readings for invited audiences increased while the public performance of new drama decreased. The public preferred the mimes. Seneca (4 B.C.–A.D. 65), one of the richest men in Rome, admitted a distaste for commoners and spectacle. Yet Seneca is the only Roman tragedian whose plays survive. So little did Seneca write with the public in mind (or even for the public theatre's conventions) that some scholars have suggested that his ten plays[28] may not even have been staged. Unlike other Roman authors, Seneca, who tried his hand at all the genres, hated Greek models. He substituted instead his own manner, a mixture of his father's rhetorical declamation and his own Stoic philosophy.

Each of Seneca's tragedies concentrates on elemental powers that threaten to disrupt human existence. An omnipresent aura of evil pervades each drama to such an extent that evil itself seems to be the main character. Whereas in his prose Seneca the Stoic tries to combat evil, in his drama Seneca the playwright presents evil as victorious. Evil not only overtakes characters physically and spiritually, but also subsumes the entire environment. In this way Seneca develops the Stoic view of the interrelatedness and correspondence of all parts of the universe.

Senecan drama has distinct characteristics. Elaborate rhetorical speeches dotted with *sententiae* (precise generalities) mix with five acts of violence, magic, death, and obsession. Soliloquies, asides, confidantes, and a single-character chorus constitute some of his dramatic conventions. The first act, a prologue, is given by a character who houses the particular evil upon which the dramatic action will turn. Seneca's Stoic conception of evil differed from the Greeks'. To the Greeks evil was a universal element permeating nature. For Euripides, Medea's reaction to Jason is universal to women of her status in her situation. To Seneca, on the other hand, evil can be either the externalized working of fate or the result of a character's allowing passion to overcome reason. The former, fate, can be negated by reason or endurance. Stoic evil is significant not as part of the natural order of things but in relation to the strength or weakness of a character. Strong characters transcend evil by resistance whereas weak characters succumb to passion and thereby create evil. Reason leads to goodness, passion to evil. Self-control cancels the potential of evil; when reason goes, weakness produces disaster. The single voice of Seneca's chorus presents this Stoic position between each of the five acts. Act II features a discussion between the character of the prologue and another character; one tries to talk the other out of a particular course of action. In Act III choices are made that allow evil to take root in the environment. Act IV brings a messenger to describe the effects of evil on people and place. And, finally, Act V displays the effects of that evil on the main characters.

Through his dramas Seneca shows a world without Stoicism: passion destroys characters. By showing horror, pain, and violence Seneca magnifies the greatness of the Stoic victory over the causes of the debauch. Whether an audience ever saw these dramatizations of Stoic philosophy is a subject of dispute. What is not in dispute is the fact that Seneca's drama suited his audience's voracious appetite for extreme spectacle.

*The Audience*   The Roman audience was truly democratic. All classes attended the theatre, although slaves were forbidden to occupy seats. The good-humored crowd, as easily drawn to sentimentality as to gross brutality and sexuality, enjoyed seeing the wicked or inept punished and the good or excellent rewarded. Yet, unlike the Greeks, the Romans did not strive for *arete*. In fact, they loved mediocrity; the average suited them just fine. The Roman audience desired to see on stage nothing larger than their own small selves. The magistrate who saw a preview could censor any production that threatened to offer more or less. The Roman audience wanted fun and excitement. They shouted to one another, laughed, quarreled, gossiped, and fought for better seats. In his prologues Plautus even speaks of chattering women and crying babies in his audience.

Paid *claques* could sway the audience's sympathies from one production to another. Generally, the audience judged a play by the quality of the staging, the sumptuousness, the acting, and the topicality of some lines. An entertainment could, however, be enjoyed more for who was in the audience than for what was happening on stage. The Roman audience was, moreover, easily distracted. Word of an upcoming gladiatorial contest or a rope dancer could quickly empty a theatre in midperformance. Also, the audience sometimes milled around buying refreshments outside the theatre. Once Augustus sent a message to a knight he saw drinking in the theatre: "When I want a drink I go home." The knight sent back the reply, "Yes but the Emperor is not afraid of losing his seat."

Seating was by rank. The emperor, the *aedile*, and the Vestal Virgins sat in boxes over the left and right orchestra entrances, the *tribunalia*. In 67 B.C. the law reserved the first fourteen rows of orchestra seats for the knights of the equestrian order. Free coin tickets with Roman numerals and Greek letters for the bilingual population designated seats in different sections. The poorest, sitting or standing behind the 40,000 other attendees, shouted freely when they could not hear. So many foreigners and citizens crowded Rome for festival entertainments that the *conquistores* (theatre police) sat or stood on each side of the stage to keep order. Temporary huts for foreigners and visiting citizens crowded the streets around the theatres.

A *praeco* (crier) tried to silence the audience for the start of a performance. A *dissignator* (usher) tried to keep order in the seating. At first, noon pauses let the audience break for lunch. But so desirable were the seats that soon free fruit and food were thrown into the audience so they could guard their seats between entertainments. Figs, dates, nuts, pecans, cakes, cheeses, pastries, and meats rained down on the mob of idle people being fed and entertained to prevent them from overturning the state. The writer Juvenal called the scene *panem et circenses* (bread and circuses). Later, tickets for free prizes were added to the booty dropped into the audience. Fights broke out as the rabble dove for tickets that could give them free furniture, corn, clothing, gold, silver, jewelry, pictures, paintings, animals, ships, houses, and even estates. Chance and hope helped make the theatre a popular event.

To say the audience was vocal would understate their participation. Horace, the Roman poet and literary critic, described their behavior in an epistle entitled ''Audience'':

> Often even the bold poet is frightened and put to rout, when those who are stronger in number, but weaker in worth and rank, unlearned and stupid and ready to fight it out if the knights dispute with them, call in the middle of a play for a bear or for boxers: 'tis in such things the rabble delights. But nowadays all the pleasure even of the knights has passed from the ear to the vain delights of the wandering eye. For four hours or more the curtains are kept down, while troops of horse and files of foot sweep by: anon are dragged in kings, once fortune's favorites, their hands bound behind them; with hurry and scurry come chariots, carriages, wains, and ships; and borne in triumph are spoils of ivory, spoils of Corinthian bronze.[29]

The audience demanded spectacle and novelty; they would be satisfied. Nobles—men and women—occasionally appeared on stage and in the arena. Many emperors tried to excel in acting, dancing, music, chariot driving, and gladiatorship to delight the crowd. Nero even repealed laws forbidding knights and senators from appearing in events. The advent of mime and pantomime brought even wilder audience responses. Lucian of Samosata described a pantomime audience as ''that throng of women and lunatics; [who] clap and yell in unseemly rapture over the vile contortions of an abandoned buffoon.''[30]

***Christian Critics*** Mime and pantomime brought the sharpest attacks from Christians in the audience. One of the loudest and most influential critics was Tertullian (c. A.D. 160–240), who defended Christians against charges of atheism and black magic. Tertullian objected to much that delighted the audience. The very power of the audience's passions, in fact, led to the creation of Tertullian's most hated forms of drama: mime and pantomime. Castrated males acting female roles and dramatic parodies of the Christian sacraments infuriated the early Christians. To Tertullian, too, such spectacles were the carefully chosen instruments of Satan, invented to undermine humanity and to destroy the authority of God. Tertullian planted the seeds of Puritan nonconformity and Bible-based political protests. As the first ''fundamentalist,'' ''born-again'' drama critic, he challenged the theatre with the question, ''Why should it be lawful to hear what we may not speak, . . .why in like manner should it be lawful to see what it is a sin to do?''

***Mime*** *Fabula riciniata* (mime) is first mentioned in Rome in 212 B.C. After 173 B.C. mime dominated the *ludi Florales*. By the time of Julius Caesar (100–44 B.C.) the pen of Decimus Laberius had given mime literary form. In time mime replaced Atellan farce as the afterpiece and intermission fare at the performance of tragedy. Because, unlike pantomists, mime players wore no masks, and be-

*A Roman mime of the first century* A.D. (British Museum, London)

cone-shaped dunce hat, a multicolored, motley patchwork cloak called a *centunculus*, and a *struthem* (phallus). The *archmimus* or *archmima* either dressed lavishly or performed naked. A *stupidus*, an *archmimus*, an old hag character, the *carissa* (artful woman), a parasite, a flatterer, a busybody, a know-it-all, and a glutton all danced grotesquely to flute music, grimaced, mugged, and threw out all sorts of lewd gestures. Even trained dogs joined the action on the mime stage. Women, too, acted in the short, indecent plots featuring low lives engaged in adultery, gibberish, foreign language parodies, stupidity, topical allusions, and puns.

When playing an afterpiece the mimes worked in the orchestra. But after mime surpassed tragedy in popularity, the mimes performed on stage before a *siparium* (rear curtain). They also played in amphitheatres, at the circus, and at nobles' homes with musicians, jugglers, acrobats, and "wonder-mak-

cause mime had an element of indecency, it became the most enduring Roman dramatic form. Although Christian opposition tended to drive the mimes underground after Constantine came to power in A.D. 306, the mimes nonetheless survived into the Medieval period as wandering *jongleurs*.

The strolling mime company of as many as sixty players became a familiar sight throughout the Empire. Led by an *archmimus* or *archmima*, the players usually improvised the action after summarizing the plot for the audience. The subjects and plots were those of the Atellan farce but recast to an urban setting. The *deuteragonist* (secondary mime), the fool who aped the *archmimus*'s actions unsuccessfully, earned the names *stupidus* and *sannio*. The fat-cheeked, bald-headed nit had his ears boxed and rear end whacked at the drop of a hat. He wore a

*A female Roman mime.* (New York Public Library Picture Collection)

ers.'' Catering to the audience's demands, the mimes grew cruder and more obscene. Female players would strip at any request. Indecent songs became popular hits and were heard in the street. Actual sodomy, adultery, and crucifixion culminated the mimes' debased search for applause.

*Pantomime* In time pantomime, mime's child, came to rival its parent. Because Roman pantomime, known as *fabula saltica*, can best be described as interpretive dancing to the music of a singer or chorus, it might be considered more modern dance than drama. The Greeks called pantomime the ''Italian dance'' after its introduction to Rome in 22 B.C. by Pylades and Bathyllus of Cilicia, who added an orchestra and chorus to the solo performance. Unlike mime, pantomime took either a serious or comic tone. The texts were mainly reworked tragedies and mythologies. Also, unlike mime, only one player, the *saltator*, danced all the parts while the chorus sang the lines. Late in the Empire erotic subjects and female dancers entered the repertoire.

The pantomimist wore a new mask for each new character. During a pause or choral interlude the pantomimist changed costume and mask. The basic pantomime garment consisted of a long silk tunic, a cloak, and a beautiful closed-lipped mask. The chorus, orchestra, and stage assistant remained behind the player throughout the performance, in full view of the audience. The dancer-actor used conventionalized steps, positions, and gestures to communicate emotion and attitude. Expressive rhythmical movements of the head and hands, along with natural movements of the body—bends, turns, and leaps—comprised the range of the pantomimist's performance. To accomplish this, the players trained incessantly; they also consumed special diets that avoided rich food. Lucian of Samosata noted that the pantomimist ''must have memory, sensibility, shrewdness, rapidity of conception, tact, and judgement; further, he must be a critic of poetry and song.''[31]

Pantomime was always more popular with the upper classes. But even though it was the favorite art of the Roman Empire, it fell to accusations of immorality and evil influence. Noble men and women owned and used pantomimists for their personal pleasures. In addition, St. Augustine claimed devils brought pantomime to Rome as a plague. Lucian quotes another of pantomime's antagonists who wondered why one should ''sit still and listen to the sound of a flute, and watch the antics of an effeminate creature got up in soft raiment to sing lascivious songs and mimic the passions of prehistoric strumpets, . . .to the accompaniment of twanging string and shrilling pipe and clattering bell?''[32]

*The Amphitheatre* Mime and pantomime were but two of Rome's many theatrical events. The amphitheatre housed many more. By the second and third centuries A.D., for example, tragedy and comedy had been replaced in popularity not only by mime and pantomime, but also by chariot racing and gladiatorial contests decorated with dramatic elements.

Such theatrical events were not new to Rome. Indeed, the games followed the Romans wherever they went. In the third century B.C., for example, the Romans had revived the Etruscan sport of hiring slaves to fight for their lives. But a dramatic element was added: slaves, masked as Charon the ferryman to Hell, dragged dead bodies from the arena with hooks. In 264 B.C., the first gladiatorial combat had taken place in the Forum to celebrate a funeral. In the Republic these spectacles had a political flavor; they were used to buy the masses and keep them happy and quiet. The orgy in the arena provided a form of relaxation, an outlet for the Romans' irrational impulses. Purged, Romans could confidently speak of the value of law and an ordered life. In the Empire the magnificence of the spectacles gauged the popularity of the Emperor. Nonetheless, throughout Roman history, little objection was voiced to the games; they were a matter of course even to the most educated citizens. Only the Stoics and Christians raised objections.

The circus and the amphitheatre were places to see and be seen. Although men and women were segregated by Emperor Augustus in both the theatre and amphitheatre, they could mix in the circus. The games, in fact, offered the only place the mass of people could gather with the emperor and make their wishes known. The spectacles and games were thus Rome's only occasions for public meetings. At the games citizens could petition for particular types of combat, for the appearance of a particular gladiator, for freedom for a brave fighter or an excellent actor, and for amnesty for a heroic criminal. The games and spectacles became political demonstrations of either support or opposition, as the mob cheered or hissed the entrances of political personnel. Among the 200,000 attendees, the senators and the emperor sat nearest the action. Next came the knights and the rest of the throng.

The main events at the circuses were the chariot races. Mock fights, military exercises, and some animal baiting might be included as well. Cellars contained stores, restaurants, and brothels for easy access. But even though the circus riveted the largest crowd's attention, the amphitheatre boasted the most splendid, surprising, bizarre, and monstrous entertainments.

In the amphitheatre's four floors—which rose to 150 feet in height—40,000 to 50,000 spectators watched a *pompa* (ceremonial procession) open the festivities. This parade gave way to a *proelusio* (sham, staged fight). Trumpets announced the real fighting. Nobles, priests, nuns, foreign dignitaries, and the emperor sat in the first row. Only the nuns and the imperial women could sit with their men; other women sat in upper tiers among the ragged proletariat. An awning, representing the starry zodiacal sky, covered the whole audience and cast its colors over the proceedings. Fountains in the arena threw water into the sky to mix with the blood on the ground. Music accompanied the combatants' thrusts and cries. Hesitant warriors were driven on by the whips and hot irons of costumed attendants. Wounded gladiators asked for pity by holding up forefingers. If the audience waved handkerchiefs, they received mercy; if the audience turned thumbs down, they died.

Gladiatorial contests pitted foreigners with native weapons against Romans, individual against individual, and troop of thousands against troop of thousands. Battles raged on land and on artificial sea. A demand for the exotic brought night fighting, animal hunts, battles between women and dwarfs, a day of Negro contests, and a day of combat for each age.

Elaborate scenery and costumes bedecked the Colosseum, which was built in A.D. 80 to replace the stone amphitheatre built in A.D. 29. The characters in the real-life Colosseum dramas were cast from criminals, prisoners, slaves, and, believe it or not, volunteers. Although the Emperor Caligula (A.D. 12–41) forced citizens into the arena, gold rewards actually attracted desperate volunteers. The prospect of glory effectively lured ne'er-do-wells dreaming of their own gladiator schools. A slave either emerged from a combat rich, free, and an international hero, or exited to the mortuary, through a scenic piece known as "Gate of the Goddess of Death," dragged by stage hands costumed as Mercury, god of the netherworld, or as Charon.

Animal baiting was another crowd favorite. Animals could be exhibited and hunted by men and other animals. Criminals, prisoners, and *bestiarii* (hired men) prided themselves on the scars and bites they won in the arena. Panthers, leopards, hyenas, and elephants fought against whole families of hunters and against men trained in nearby arena schools. Domestic deer, rabbits, stags, boars, bears, and bulls roamed elaborate settings in what came to be called *venationes*. More exotic spectacles featured crocodiles, hippopotami, rhinoceri, lynxes, apes, and giraffes. In A.D. 80 Emperor Titus (A.D. 40–81) had 5000 animals hunted in a single day. In A.D. 107 Emperor Trajan (A.D. 52–117) held a four-month festival in which 11,000 animals were slaughtered. Roman scientists squeezed exotic entrails for drugs, sculptors and painters sketched the bloody and warm anatomies, and cooks concocted new recipes.

At other times, however, hunting did not satisfy the crowd. Animals were then paired to fight—a rhino against an elephant, an elephant against a bull—driven on by whips and hot irons. Unarmed men tied to stakes struggled to fight off hungry beasts. Nearby physicians ogled throbbing, newly torn open internal organs.

Shortened pantomimes starred criminals as victims. Several "stars" wore Medea's gifts to Jason's new bride and burst into flame. The robber Laureolus was forced to play the hero of a popular Atellan farce, which climaxed in his crucifixion and tearing apart by animals. Other criminals were costumed as various dramatic characters to suffer public castration. Another criminal, dressed as Orpheus, played music in a beautiful rustic setting housing live birds and animals; then bears entered the stage and tore him to pieces. Other scenes spotlighted sex acts between such mythological characters as Europa and Persiphae and the bull. A costumed Daedalus was eaten by a bear. For improvised *naumachiae* (naval fights), the arena was flooded. Those who fell overboard found hungry fish and marine animals applauding their entrance.

Few found anything wrong with such entertainments. Ovid even suggested that spectacles were wonderful occasions for lovemaking. Cicero believed the sight of criminals fighting for life or death provided the audience with good training for enduring pain and death. After all, the players were public enemies, barbarians, criminals, slaves, and social leeches who had no rights. They were either unimportant or dangerous to society. Even Saint Augustine noticed in his friend Alypius an element of human nature that could enjoy and become fascinated with torture and execution. The undeniability of Augustine's observation makes the fact of Roman spectacle all the more horrible.

***Decline*** In A.D. 568 all spectacles ended in Rome with the arrival of the Lombards, a Germanic tribe considered "barbarian" by the Romans. A series of sporadic incursions by these tribes, which began in the first century B.C., eventually undermined the stability not only of the theatre but also of the unity of the entire Empire. The Germanic tribes—Allemanni, Marcomanni, Burgundians, Franks, and Goths—had turned nomadic to seek protection from the Huns. Meanwhile, the Emperor Diocletian moved the imperial court to Asia Minor to meet a new threat from the Persians. The Emperor was seduced by Eastern mythology and religion; in time he even adopted the costume of an Asian despot. Gradually the Eastern part of the Empire occupied most of the Emperor's attention; it became a separate culture from Rome. The new center was Constantinople, a city of Greek and Eastern character that developed its own art and architecture within a civilization that flourished until 1453.

As important as the physical invasion by the neighboring tribes was the spiritual invasion by neighboring religious ideas. In the second century official polytheism in Rome included the mysteries of Eastern gods. Gods from Iran, Syria, Egypt, and India were "Hellenized" as they traveled through the funnel of Greece to Rome. The new gods suffered, died, and rose from the dead. They were *dei*, unlike the Roman *numina* (household gods).

The passions of the new gods provided meaning and sympathetic solace to Romans confronting chaos and pain in the Empire. As historian Erwin R. Goodenough writes:

> Men lost the reliance of thoughtful Greeks of the Classical Age upon the accumulation of truth by human reason and investigation, and turned instead to ask God to reveal the truth to them. The imparting of this divine revelation was regarded as a divine illumination, or, as they sometimes called it, a new spiritual birth, and it would come as the reward not of the exertion but of the prostration of human effort.[33]

Because Western dramatic theatre showed people struggling with present realities, the influx of revelatory religions decreased the populace's overall appreciation of the theatre's abilities.

***New Religions Rival the Old Theatre*** The most enduring manifestation of the new religious attitude and mythology—the revelation that influenced the entire development of Western theatre and civilization—occurred during the decline of the Roman Empire in Palestine among a tribe known as Jews, who were enjoying the privileged status of limited Roman toleration that alternated with persecution. The idea of a Messiah arose because of the Jews' political persecution and their aspirations for a better future. The Jews believed that, one day, their former kingdom of David would be restored and extended over a wide area by a Messiah. This Messiah would redeem the Jewish people with his strong physical and spiritual powers. The Messiah's wisdom would create the Kingdom of Heaven on earth.

During the time of Augustus, somewhere in Galilee a man named Jesus (Greek for Joshua) was born into a humble family that included half a dozen or more children. In time Jesus regarded himself as having a message for the Jews. He proclaimed that the Kingdom they sought was "at Hand," at most a generation away. Jesus went to Jerusalem to proclaim the coming of a celestial and political transformation for the Jews, but he was arrested by the Roman authorities as a trivial sovereign, the "King of the Jews." Jesus's followers were disappointed by their leader's failure to bring about political change. Historian and Jesus biographer Charles Guignbert suggests that after the disappointment of Jesus's death, his followers found that they maintained their love and devotion to his cause. From the moment of Jesus's resurrection in the hearts and minds of his disciples, his identity transformed. A man so good, so profound, and so gentle, they reasoned, could not possibly have been a man like them. The man Jesus gradually became the mythological "Christ."

*A New Myth for a New Drama* The new mythological empire, born amid the debris of the Roman Empire, dominated the entire development of Western civilization and theatre. Whatever the problematic evidence surrounding the life of Jesus, Christian mythology emerged an equal to the other great mythologies of the world. Western culture and theatre grew from the Christian epic. Although Buddha followed a similar course in the East, the evolution of Christian mythology provides the only Western model of the transformation of an historical person to a mythological divinity and finally to a dramatic hero in the theatre. New dramatic theatre can evolve after the development of new religious mythology and ritual. Thus, the Christian dramatic theatre that flowered in the Medieval period began in the epic mythology and ritual invented in the Roman Empire.

Examining the process of Jesus's elevation to myth can shed light on the origins of other mythic and dramatic heroes. As Christian historian Norman Perrin concludes:

> There is no discernible correlation between the factual element of history and the functional adequacy of a myth, and we have already acknowledged that this is the case for Christian myth. Christian myths, like all myths, function precisely because they are myth, and the only kind of history by which they may be validated is that of the history of an individual or people in the concrete circumstances of life in the world.[34]

The Jewish Messiah became the "Christ" with the Greek translation of the Hebrew *Mashiah*. Greece, the melting pot of all Eastern religions, helped Jesus's life find mythological narrative. Saul of Tarsus, later Paul, was the real founder of Christianity. A man of much wider education than Jesus—he was well-versed in Hellenistic theologies and Stoicism—Paul argued with Peter, one of Jesus's disciples, over Christian membership requirements. Peter maintained that one could receive Christian baptism only after first accepting essential Jewish practices. On the other hand, Paul argued that Jesus had established a new law requiring only baptism, which welcomed non-Jews. Paul's scholarship and rhetoric prevailed, and a zealous, dogmatic missionary program began that plagued much of the world's dramatic theatre.

*The Spread of the New Mythology* Missionaries carried the new interpretation of Jesus's life. In the East, Buddhist missionaries had carried a similar epic. As Norman Perrin explains:

> He who proclaimed the Kingdom of God began himself to be proclaimed as (a) the one who was about to return on the clouds of heaven as Son of Man and agent of God's final judgement and redemption of the world (so apocalyptic Christianity); (b) as the one who died for our sins and was raised for our justification (so Paul); and (c) as "the lamb of God Who takes away the sin of the world" (so the Johannine school). The historical details of the movement from the Jesus who proclaimed the Kingdom of God to the New Testament and its various proclamations of Jesus as the Christ, the Son of God, are forever lost to us.[35]

The new Christ came to redeem not the political and economic oppression of a small tribe in Palestine but the spiritual oppression of all humanity. Christ's kingdom, unlike that of Jesus, was not of this earth. Christ suffered in atonement for others' evil; He redeemed humanity from the inherited sin of Adam.

The early gospels and Paul's letters continued the message of Jesus-as-Christ using Mithraic phrases and imagery. Instead of the Jewish Sabbath, Christians adopted the Mithraic Sun-day with its use of candles, legends of adulation by shepherds, and phrases about "bloodwashing." From the cult of Serapis/Isis/Horus Christians found the identification of Mary with Isis and elevated her to quasidivine rank. The gospels were not written as history but as cathechisms for the indoctrination of newly converted Christians. Historian Joseph Klausner explains:

> The Christian Messiah ceased to be only a man, and passed beyond the limitations of mortality. Man cannot redeem himself from sin, but the Messiah—God, clothed in the form of a man, is the one who by his own freely shed blood has redeemed mankind. And he will come a second time to redeem humanity, since his first appearance, and even his death on the cross, did not suffice to eradicate evil from the world and to convert all men to belief in him.[36]

At first Rome viewed the Christians as a Jewish sect, because Christians worshipped with traditional Jewish rites in the synagogue and Jerusalem's temple. But early Christians also celebrated the *agape*, the love-feast of Jesus's celebration of Passover, a rite that had overtones of Dionysus. Goodenough explains that:

> Christians believed that the Eucharistic bread was "the flesh of our savior Jesus Christ, which suffered from our sins, and with the Father of his goodness raised up again," and that the wine was truly the blood which flowed from Jesus on the cross . . . . So by the secret rite of the Eucharist not a god, but the infinite God himself was not only represented, but by a miracle actually brought immediately present to the wondering hearts of the faithful.[37]

Roman officials worried about the eating of Jesus's body and drinking of Jesus's blood. Christians were put to death on the charge of cannibalism. More died on charges of treason and disloyalty to the emperor. Paul was beheaded; Peter was crucified upside down. All emperors from Nero to Nerva outlawed Christianity, a threat to festivals and theatre honoring others than the "one true God."

Even within the Christian community controversy brewed. Wide variation of belief among the disciples often threatened to break down the unity of the community. Arians held that Jesus was less than God; Sabellians, that Jesus was an aspect of God; Trinitarians, that the Father, the Son, and the Holy Ghost were three distinct persons but one God. Gnostic Christians maintained that the Kingdom of God was within. Jewish Christians sought a political kingdom. Consequently, through dogmatism, spites, rivalries, pedantries, accusations of heresy, riots, excommunications, banishments, and official persecutions, early Christians fought and killed one another to define once and for all how God was related to Himself. And these battles of Christianity played an important—at times a decisive—role in the course of theatre history.

*The Triumph of Christianity* As Christianity made contact with Graeco-Roman civilization it converted the educated. The zeal of the missionaries, the promise of salvation, and the emphasis on love and brotherhood offered Romans an explanation for their suffering and a reason for hope. Even actors and mimes converted.

In A.D. 312 the Emperor Constantine (A.D. 280–337) dreamt he saw Jesus asking him to adopt the Christian banner as his own. As a result, he issued the Edict of Milan to legalize Christianity: Constantine hoped to use Christianity's spiritual strength to buttress his failing Empire. In 325 Constantine convened a council of 300 Christian bishops in Nicaea to settle the relation of God with Himself once for all. The Council set the date for Easter and adopted a common creed upholding the Trinitarian view. In 353 the bishops set December 25 as the date of the Nativity, possibly to absorb the festival celebrating the birth of Mithra on that day of the winter solstice. Jesus had a clear relationship with God, an official birth and resurrection schedule, and an image as the "Sun/Son."

In the fifth century a canon of writings, regarded as having apostolic authority and detailing the passion of Jesus, came to be known as the New Testament. The festive calendar and canon of texts provided the time and source for later dramatic theatres.

In the reign of Theodosius (reigned 379–395) Christianity became the only legal religion in the Empire. But fifteen years after Theodosius died, Rome was ravaged by invading tribes. Many Romans attributed the carnage to the emperor's embrace of Christianity. St. Augustine wrote the *City of God* to counter the fear. He argued that the City of Man—sin—had fallen, but in its place the City of God—virtue—would rise and endure for all eternity.

Justinian (483–565) was the last emperor to attempt to regain the western provinces of the Empire. In 476 Odocer, the Visigoth general, overthrew Romulus Augustus and ended Roman dominance of the west. No emperor reigned in the west until Christmas Day, 800, when Charlemagne declared himself emperor in St. Peter's Church in Rome. At that time the City of God began to arise from the City of Man. The Medieval world of Christian mythology replaced the Roman world of appropriated mythologies. In the East the Christian church became a department of state; in the West the church filled the political power vacuum. As Edward Gibbon (1737–1794) wrote in his monumental history of the decline and fall of the Empire, "The union and discipline of the Christian republic gradually formed an independent and increasing state in the heart of the Roman empire." With the fall of Rome, classical mythology, civilization, and theatre ended. Christian mythology began to create a new civilization and, eventually, a new dramatic theatre.

## NOTES

[1] H. D. F. Kitto, *The Greeks*, rev. ed. (London: Pelican Books, 1957), p. 96. Copyright © H. D. F. Kitto, 1951, 1957. Reprinted by permission of Penguin Books Ltd.

[2] E. R. Dodd, *The Greeks and the Irrational* (Berkeley: University of California Press, 1951), pp. 76–77.

[3] Athenaeus, *The Deinosophists*, Loeb Classical Library, Vol. 1, Charles Burton Gulick, trans. (Cambridge, Mass.: Harvard University Press, 1927), pp. 95–96.

[4] Allardyce Nicoll, *The Development of the Theatre* (London: Harrap, 1966), pp. 268, 272.

[5] J. Michael Walton, *Greek Theatre Practice* (Westport, Ct.: Greenwood Press, 1980), p. 35.

[6] Ibid., p. 53.

[7] Athenaeus, *The Deinosophists*, p. 95.

[8] *The Works of Lucian of Samosata*, Vol. 2, W. H. Fowler, trans. (Oxford, Eng.: The Clarendon Press, 1905), p. 240.

[9] Lillian Lawler, *The Dance in Ancient Greece* (Middleton, Ct.: Wesleyan University Press, 1974), p. 87.

[10] Gerald F. Else, *The Origin and Early Form of Greek Tragedy* (New York: W. W. Norton and Company, 1965), p. 72.

[11] Jane Harrison, *Ancient Art and Ritual* (New York: Henry Holt & Co., 1913), p. 8.

[12] Athenaeus, *The Deinsophists*, p. 259.

[13] Francis M. Cornford, *The Origin of Attic Comedy* (Gloucester, Mass.: P. Smith, 1968).

[14] All quotations are taken from Aristotle, *On the Art of Poetry*, Ingram Bywater, trans. (Oxford, Eng.: Clarendon Press, 1967), pp. 15, 17, 19, 21, 29, 35, 45.

[15] Extant references suggest that women attended tragedies. No references indicate, however, that they attended comedies.

[16] *The Republic of Plato*, Francis M. Cornford, trans. (Oxford, Eng.: Oxford University Press, 1941), pp. 337–339.

[17] Edith Hamilton, *The Roman Way* (New York: W. W. Norton Co., 1970), p. 178.

[18] Allardyce Nicoll, *Masks, Mimes and Miracles* (New York: Cooper Square Publications, 1963), p. 79.

[19] Quintillian, *Institutio Oratoria*, Volume 4, Book 11, H. E. Butler, trans. (New York: G. P. Putnam's Sons, 1922), p. 245.

[20] Quintillian, *Institutio Oratoria*, Volume 2, Book 6, p. 437.

[21] Quintillian, *Institutio Oratoria*, Volume 1, Book 2, p. 277.

[22] Quintillian, *Institutio Oratoria*, Volume 4, Book 11, pp. 345–347.

[23] Jack Lindsay, *Origin of Astrology* (London: Frederick Muller Ltd., 1971).

[24] Vitruvius, *On Architecture*, Volume 2: "On Astrology," Frank Granger, trans. (Cambridge, Mass.: Harvard University Press, 1970), p. 245.

[25] Vitruvius, *On Architecture*, Volume 1, pp. 283–285.

[26] Vitruvius, *On Architecture*, Volume 1, p. 15.

[27] Vitruvius, *On Architecture*, Volume 1, p. 289.

[28] The tenth play, *Octavia*, which is preserved, presents Seneca as a character in the action. Scholars suggest that the work is by another unknown playwright writing after the deaths of both Nero and Seneca.

[29] Horace, "Audience," *Epistle* 2, H. Rushton Fairclough, trans. (Cambridge, Mass.: Harvard University Press, 1970), p. 413.

[30] *The Works of Lucian of Samosata*, p. 240.

[31] Ibid., p. 259.

[32] Ibid., p. 239.

[33] Erwin R. Goodenough, *The Church in the Roman Empire* (New York: Henry Holt and Company, 1931), pp. 23–24.

[34] Norman Perrin, *The New Testament: An Introduction* (New York: Harcourt Brace Jovanovich, Inc., 1974), p. 29.

[35] Ibid., p. 302.

[36] Joseph Klausner, *The Messianic Idea in Israel*, W. F. Stinespring, trans. (New York: Macmillan, 1955), p. 529.

[37] Goodenough, *The Church in the Roman Empire*, pp. 23–24.

# 3

# THE CLASSICAL ASIAN THEATRE

*In the more remote ages of antiquity, the world was unequally divided. The east was in the immemorial possession of arts and luxury; whilst the west was inhabited by rude and warlike barbarians. . . .*

Gibbon, *The Decline and Fall of the Roman Empire*

## OVERVIEW

While the West experienced the slow emergence of a new dramatic theatre, the East enjoyed the flowering of its own classical theatre. Because Eastern classical theatre shares so many features with the classical theatres ending in the West, it seems the next logical stop on our trip through theatre history. Yet despite the similarities, sufficient cultural differences exist between East and West to have created not only two distinct theatrical traditions but also two distinct metaphysical views of the nature of human existence.

Long before Gibbon, people generalized about the differences between Eastern and Western—Oriental and Occidental—civilization. Like all generalizations, these contained as much oversimplification as definition. Yet such definitions seem necessary for Westerners to orient themselves with new phenomena. With this caveat in mind, we can now suggest the major characteristics of the Eastern experience.

The classical Western tradition originated at the time of the Greeks and developed further with Roman civilization. Knowledge was based on observation, comparison of sensations, and experimentation leading to more or less objective conclusions. Westerners observed the changing phenomena of the universe and postulated the principle of progress. Rational people defined reality as a continuum of sensory experiences that were both reliable and worthy of investigation, because underneath the surfaces reside essential forms and ideas of things. Action, work, and accomplishment based on the exercise of the rational mind, within the present material world of existence, allowed Westerners to draw relative conclusions about the nature of their experiences. The conclusions, based on a scientific method of observing particular phenomena, enabled them to exercise some control over nature. Reason enabled Westerners to control the changes within their reality; Westerners stood apart from nature to have dominion over it. In *Zen Buddhism* D. T. Suzuki points out that the Greeks made reason and rationality the means and end of identity.

Easterners, on the other hand, seeking to reconcile the opposites that plagued Westerners, placed intuition at the center. Easterners based knowledge on the intuitive grasp of an inner truth, at the center of one's personality, that does not change or progress. Meditation and contemplation allowed Easterners to form subjective impressions based on dealings with the absolute universal truth within their own natures. The material world is illusory, a mere creation of the senses. Truth resides in religion and philosophy rather than in science. Life is a flux of moments without fixed pattern or static form. Human nature is part of all nature; all nature shares the same inner, eternal truth, and a common spirit permeates the universe. Easterners sought, through renunciation of the illusory material world, to join forces with the inner way of the universe.

*Stasis versus Change* Needless to say, such disparate world views needed disparate dramatic theatres to envision the realities. As Earle Ernst writes in *The Kabuki Theatre*, static societies maintain the performance conventions of their theatres; changing societies alter the dramatic theatre's conventions to more accurately envision new realities. The theatres of Greece and Rome are considered classical because they existed in relatively static societies; the theatre conventions and vocabulary tended to endure for generations. The history of Western theatre, in contrast, details the ever more frequent breakdown and replacement of static societies by an ever-changing milieu. Until the Modern era, the history of Eastern theatre, however, shows the endurance of a static society and theatre that changed only when outside intervention forced new conditions. Western theatre progressed toward new realities envisioned in new dramas. Eastern theatre preserved the eternal truth hidden under the flux of everyday superficiality. Western drama revealed the conflict between humans and gods over the power to change nature. Eastern drama revealed the harmony and unity between the divine and the human. Western theatre showed a struggle between the religious and the human; Western society progressed through these conflicts. Eastern theatre allowed humans to become at one with god so that all differences vanished; Eastern society was forever fixed, despite surface changes. In *Theatre in the East*, Faubian Bowers explains the difference's effect on Eastern performance: Asian performance used frank theatrical conventions within an unchanging repertoire. Audiences came to see *how* a play would be acted rather than to see *what* would happen in a new play. As a result only key scenes demanded attention. In this way Eastern theatre resembled the classical theatres of the West.

*The Natya Sastra* Ironically, the treatises that would serve as the bases for the two divergent theatrical traditions originated within a few decades of one another. The Indian sage Bharata's *Natya Sastra* (c. 200 B.C.–A.D. 200) was to the East what Aristotle's *Poetics* was to the West. A. C. Scott calls the *Natya Sastra* "the seminal philosophy of Asian theatre in general."[1] Greek presence in India at the time of the *Natya Sastra* has even prompted some to suggest that India borrowed Greek ideas. But an examination of the two works shows extreme and fundamental differences. For Aristotle drama imitated an action; for Bharata drama imitated a state of being. Such divergent views of the nature of drama reflect the societies' divergent views of human nature. The Greeks considered their gods to be extranatural; the Indians knew their gods as higher aspects of themselves. Greek life progressed in accordance with an *ananke*; Indian life rested in individuals' own hands. In *The Theatric Universe* Pramod Kale summarizes the fundamental difference by noting that "the *Poetics* is an interpretation of the theatre in terms of large human experience while the *Natya Sastra* is a restructuring of human experience as theatre.''[2]

The Asian theatrical tradition began in India and spread to China and Japan on the backs of Buddhist missionaries. In each new society, Indian theory and practice was modified to assimilate and reflect the peculiar nature of each culture. What began in India with a religious purpose traveled to China and then to Japan, where, in the Modern age, it existed as the only theatre whose tradition had never been broken or seriously altered. The classical theatres of Japan begin with the classical theatre of India.

# INDIA

Archeological excavations revealed dance in India well over 5000 years ago. Dance and drama continued throughout India's Vedic, Epic, and Classical periods. India's ancient Dravidian culture, driven south by an Aryan invasion around 1600 B.C., developed Vedic religion and literature and the Sanskrit language. What is called the Vedic Age lasted approximately 700 years and laid the foundation for subsequent Indian society. Before the Aryan invasion, Dravidian kings amused themselves with minstrels and festivals. They had an alphabet and temples, but they were no match for the nomadic Aryans who quickly dominated India's spiritual and cultural life. India's arts and crafts were left to the native Dravidians. Yet by the time of Buddha (563–483 B.C.) Sanskrit had become an elite language used only at court, in the temples, and by rhapsodes keeping alive the oral literature. The end of Aryan domination was marked by the supplanting of Vedism by Hinduism, but not before the creation of the great religious and philosophical treatises known as the *Vedas* and the *Upanishads*. The *Rig Veda* suggests that dramatic theatre came into being around the eighth century B.C. In addition, Jataka stories depicting Indian life between 600 B.C. and 300 B.C. contain references to theatre.

***The Origin of the Dramatic Theatre*** Dramatic theatre in India, like that in Greece and Rome, seemed to owe part of its origin to religion. In *The Indian Theatre* Chandra Bhan Gupta explains that India's two great narrative epics, the *Ramayana* and the *Mahabharata*, refer to *nata*, *nartaka*, and *nataka*: theatrical arts performed in the cities and palaces during the Epic period. Vedic religion, like the cult of Dionysus, held the seeds of dramatic theatre. As with Dionysus, performers of Vedic rites became people other than themselves. Some villages even forced residents to subsidize public performances of *Stree Preksha* (women's drama) and *Purusha Preksha* (men's drama) in the fourth century B.C. Actors were employed to perform at temples in honor of deities.

The *Natya Sastra* by Bharata, which dates from the third century B.C., tells of theatre arts at festivals and public celebrations, during the Maurya Dynasty, founded by King Chandragupta (reigned c. 321–297 B.C.) after he expelled Alexander's Macedonians from India. The Maurya Dynasty ruled India for 137 years (321–184 B.C.) during which arts and crafts flourished. Kings sent Buddhist missionaries to Ceylon, Syria, Egypt, Greece, Tibet, China, and Japan to spread the new religion. The missionaries used the arts, including drama, to teach Buddhist doctrine. In this way the Indian aesthetic spread across the world.

The Gupta Dynasty (A.D. 320–535) ushered in India's Golden or Classical age in which flourished not only the Buddhism accepted by King Ashoka (reigned c. 274–232 B.C.) but also the dramatic theatre. King Vikramaditya patronized the great playwright Kalidasa (c. A.D. 373–415) and gathered a distinguished circle of poets, philosophers, artists, scientists, and scholars in his new capital city. It was also the age of the classical theatre of the playwrights Bhasa and Sudraka. Scholars developed the Sanskrit literature by writing down the previously oral epics. Buddhist art reached its height with the frescoes at the Ajanta caves. Although civilization was interrupted by Hun invasions, Harsha-Vardhana (A.D. 606–648) recaptured part of India, and his kingdom flourished until the Moslem invasion of 1018.

**The Moslem Influence**   Moslems ruled India. Babur (1483–1530) set up the Mongol Dynasty, which under Akbar (1556–1605) eventually encompassed most of India. Akbar's reforms (which occurred at the time of Shakespeare) created the most powerful empire on earth during the sixteenth century. Under Akbar's leadership Indian music, poetry, and painting enjoyed periods of great development. Unfortunately, the Mongol court did not encourage a new dramatic theatre to replace the atrophied Sanskrit theatre prohibited by the Moslems. Instead, Akbar encouraged metaphysical speculation and religious debate, even though the once vibrant Sanskrit had become merely the language of tedious religionists and academic philosophers. Nevertheless, at a time when Protestants and Catholics warred with one another in Europe, when Catholics held an Inquisition in Spain, and when the Italian philosopher Giordano Bruno (c. 1548–1600) was executed in Italy, Akbar pledged freedom of religion and speech. Unfortunately, the final Mongol, Aurangzeb (1658–1707), a Moslem saint, destroyed all the Hindu art and temples of a thousand years. The empire broke up after his death.

**Religion and Drama**   Religion created the context for all aspects of Indian culture. Because Indians valued the soul more than the body, religious concerns outdistanced political ones, and the Indians became easy marks for imperialistic foreigners. Under alien occupation Indians demonstrated remarkable religious tolerance; rarely was blood spilt by any but Moslem or Christian invaders seeking uniform religious belief. Religion also played an important formative role in the Sanskrit theatre; an entire chapter of the *Natya Sastra* details elaborate pre-performance ceremonies dating perhaps from the ancient Vedic religion.

The term *veda* means knowledge. Sacred Vedic lore comprises some of the oldest bodies of literature in the Indo-European world. The *Rig Veda*, *Sama Veda*, *Yajur Veda*, and *Athara Veda*, for example, date from approximately 6000 B.C. Vedism, the ancestor of Hinduism, worshipped the elements of nature: the sky, the sun, fire, light, wind, water, and reproduction. When personified, the chief forces, which act in the early dramas, became Indra, driver back of darkness; Agni, bringer of fire; and Soma, giver of plants and liquor. Sacrifice and celebration were the centers of the Vedic religion, which knew neither idols nor temples. Near the end of the Vedic period, around the fifth and fourth centuries B.C., the sections of the Vedas resembling parables were collected under the term *Upanishads*: explanations of the relationship between an *atman* (individual's soul) and the *brahman* (universal soul). The *Upanishads* represent the world's oldest philosophical and psychological system of investigation. The belief that *atman* and *brahman* are identical, that the soul within is identical with the soul of the world, resulted in a philosophical position that unites the subjective and the objective, the individual and the world. This metaphysical view permeated Indian society and theatre.

**Hinduism and Dramatic Ritual**   The Vedic age ended as skepticism and free thought arose to lay the basis of a new religion, Hinduism. Hinduism placed the priests at the highest social and spiritual positions; priests guided people toward the proper relationship with *dharma* (the cosmological pattern). The aim of Hinduism was to unify *atman* with *brahman*. A wide diversity of paths could lead to such unification: idols for bathing, dressing, oiling, feeding, decorating, and entertaining; temple festivals and feasts; pilgrimages to the sacred river Ganges; the way of the monk or hermit; and priestly sacraments replete with *devadasis* (sacred courtesan-dancers). The *atman* is reborn until absorbed into *brahman*. The quality of one's actions, called one's *karma*, determined the quality of one's soul's life in the next existence. This means that conduct in life determined one's next reincarnation, and that one's caste or social rank represented one's stage of spiritual development. In this way life itself became the ultimate rite, presided over by the Hindu trinity—Brahma-the-creator, Vishnu-the-preserver, and Shiva-the-destroyer—all aspects of *brahman*.

***The Mythological Basis of Hindu Theatre*** Hinduism manifested itself externally in elaborate spectacle and enormous mythology, internally with hundreds of spiritual paths to liberation, intellectually in an intricate network of philosophical symbols, sociologically in the caste system, and artistically in the Sanskrit dramatic theatre. Indian theatre began with the gods.

Brahma agreed to Indra's petition for the first drama to be a way to celebrate victory over the forces of evil. A reenactment of the deciding battle was Indra's choice of something for all the castes to enjoy; the result was the fifth veda, the *Natya Veda*. From the *Rig Veda* the *Natya Veda* took recitation; from the *Sama Veda*, song and music; from the *Yajur Veda*, mimesis;

and from the *Athara Veda*, sentiment. But when the defeated demons saw the play, they assumed the war had begun again. Although Brahma explained the new art to them, he nonetheless ordered Vishwakarma, the gods' resident architect, to build a sheltering stage house to protect the actors from future attacks by confused spectators. The new theatre was consecrated with the *jaraja* (flagstaff) Brahma had used to defeat the demons in the second battle.

Brahma appointed Bharata the managing director of his theatre and asked him to record the *Natya Veda* so that mortals could also enjoy the new art. The result was the *Natya Sastra*, which, after years of oral transmission, was finally written down in the fourth or fifth century A.D. *Natya* was a term for all theatrical activity: song, dance, and drama. Shiva contributed the *tandava*, a wild violent dance, and Vishnu invented four dramatic styles: verbal,

*Shiva Nataraja, the god of the dance, performs to destroy and then renew the universe.* (Collection William Rockhill Nelson Gallery of Art, Atkins Museum of Fine Arts, Kansas City)

grand, energetic, and graceful. Thus, Brahma created the theatre, Shiva destroyed the chaos of life with ordered dance, and Vishnu preserved the drama. Brahma explained the function of the new art:

> The drama I have devised is a mimicry of actions and conducts of people, which is rich in various emotions and which depicts different situations. This will relate to actions of men, good, bad, and indifferent and will give courage, amusement and happiness as well as counsel to all.
>
> The drama will be instructive to all, through actions and states depicted in it, and through sentiments, arising out of it. . . . There would be no wise maxim, no learning, no art or craft, no device, no action that would not be found in it.[3]

***Hindu Festivals***    During the first 700 years of the Christian era, religious festivities con-

tinued as principal occasions for dramatic theatre. In February or March fertility rituals, erotic games, comic operas, and folk dances marked the Holi festival. Men and women ran through the streets squirting colored water at one another, and theatrical troupes competed for prizes as in the August through October festival of Indra's standard. A tree, shorn of branches, possibly representing the flagstaff used by Brahma to consecrate the first theatre, was paraded to the main square, where it was decorated and adorned to music. Erected in the middle of the town, the *jaraja* (staff), through which the gods' spirits descended to Earth, became the focal point of popular celebrations, dances, poetic songs, juggling, and more ever-popular water squirting. Festivals continued dramatic presentations even after the rise of new religious ideas in India

*A troupe of popular Indian entertainers—male and female acrobats, jugglers, and tightrope walkers.* (Museum für Indische Kunst, Staatliche Museum PreuBischer Kulturbesitz, West Berlin)

***Buddhism and the Theatre***   Hindu festivals, along with Hindu theology and ceremony, grew to displease the Kshatriyas, the second-ranking caste. Great cities, industry, trade, and wealth had created their leisure time for thinking. Consequently, skepticism and immorality increased. At about this time, Gautama Siddhartha (c. 563–c. 483 B.C.), a member of the ruling Brahmin class, rejected both Brahminism's sacrifice and the authority of the Vedas in favor of a personal, self-reliant path toward *moksha* (release). Siddhartha found a way to stop all selfish desires, to do only good, and to eliminate his individuality so that his soul could merge with unconscious infinity. Such enlightenment made Siddhartha the Buddha, free from the cycle of reincarnation. His individual success without Brahmanic aid led him and his disciples to question the authority of the Brahmins and the caste system. When Buddha died, his followers (like the followers of Jesus) split into sects over the question of his divinity. Those who believed him a god came to be known as Mahayana Buddhists; those who denied his divinity, Hinayana Buddhists. Each sect developed its own dogma, literature, and system of rites.

At first Buddhists (like the early Christians) objected to dance and theatre, because they associated them with the Brahmins' demoralization of human nature. When the Emperor Ashoka (reigned c. 274–232 B.C.) adopted Buddhism, conservatives convinced him to ban the theatre altogether. But liberal Buddhists noted that the Buddha himself was supposedly accomplished in dramatic arts. In time Buddhists accepted the theatre for missionary work. (Christians eventually came to the same acceptance of Western theatre.) Asvaghosa, the Buddhist philosopher, tried to sell Buddhism by writing short episodes of allegorical drama. Song, dance, and playlets were featured at Buddhist festivities. But after Ashoka, Buddhism lost influence in India; Indians saw it as more demanding and less fun than Hinduism. As the Brahmins regained power, the Buddhists migrated, carrying with them the Indian tradition of theatre as a tool for propagating the gospel. These missionaries used Prakrit, the popular vernacular, rather than the elitist Sanskrit, to make their message accessible. In India, Buddhism became little more than a branch of Hinduism; Buddha was simply an *avatar* (a human reincarnation) of Vishnu.

***Society in the Drama***   Indian drama reflected the societal structure and attitudes that developed after the Aryan invasion had pushed native Dravidians to the south. A caste system preserved the purity of the Aryan race and prevented Dravidians from gaining political power. The early social structure resembled Thompson's model, which we discussed in Chapter 1. The warriors, Kshatriyas, ruled the society, but their power was challenged by the priests—Brahmins, who, using their exclusive right to education, literature, and law, dominated the other castes.

After the Moslem invasion, the caste system grew rigid and complex. Merchants and free people, the Vaisyas, were above the Shudras, the workers. The outcasts lived in the cellar of Indian society. The Brahmins even devised laws forbidding Shudras access to the Vedas. In addition, professional theatre people were among the social inferiors. Perhaps their low status prompted Bharata both to claim a divine origin for the theatre and to give the drama the status of fifth Veda.

Indian society pursued four goals: *moksha* (release), *karma* (fulfillment of desires), *artha* (wealth winning), and *dharma* (morality). Each caste possessed its own *dharma*. Each person and dramatic character accepted the rightness of things as they were as essential not only to the individual's progressive reincarnation to enlightenment, but also to the harmony of the universe.

As in Greece, women occupied a special place in the Indian universe and drama. The heroines of the epic narrative, the *Ramayana*, became the ideal for Indian women, and Indian drama portrayed the facts of Indian womanhood. In Vedic times women had enjoyed some freedom. They could, like the women of Rome, decide their mates, attend public events, study, and remarry if widowed. But under the growing influence of the Brahmins and the Islamic model, Indian women lost their freedom. Their status became remarkably similar to what it was in classical Greece and Republican Rome. As in Greece and Rome, for example, a lack of romantic love was characteristic. Fathers arranged marriages for their young children. Men had a duty to marry not for love, but to produce a son. Maidenhood, bachelorhood, and prolonged virginity by either sex were considered disgraceful. In marriage, women were expected to provide patient devotion in return for men's solicitous protection. Women addressed their husbands as master, lord, or god, walked behind them in public, prepared their meals, ate only leftovers, and kissed the men's feet at bedtime. To disobey one's husband meant reincarnation as a jackal. In this patriarchal society only men could own property; women were secluded to await self-immolation when their husbands died.

The *devadasi* (temple dancers) served the gods with their singing and dancing, and the Brahmins with their bodies. Some dancers lived in seclusion; others entertained whoever could pay, and gave a percentage of their fee to the clergy. Thus, prostitution was confined to the temple for the glory of the gods. The dancers performed in public ceremonies and at private gatherings. Some learned to read, like the Greek *hetaerae*, so as to charm their clients. If girls, *devadasi* children continued their mothers' work; if boys, they became missionaries.

*A Philosophical Theatre* The *Natya Sastra* summarizes the tradition of sensuous and religious aesthetics with a philosophy of existence *via* sensory pleasure. When ideal and devoted love appears in the drama, it is not a reflection of social reality, but rather a symbol of a soul's devotion to a god. But Indian philosophy was confined neither to the aesthetics of temple dancing nor Sanskrit drama. In fact, Hindu priests were the original Indian philosophers and scientists; their philosophy per-

meated the theatre. Both science and the drama sought the same end. Equilibrium in both art and science meant balancing the flow of *rasa*, the vital juices of Indian medicine, similar to what the West would come to call "humours." The distinctness of Indian philosophy from that of Greece and Rome helps explain the uniqueness of the Indian theatre. Western drama was based on conflict; Eastern drama, on cooperative dance. The West sent heroes into the world to make their destinies according to their free will. The East let heroes flow with the way of the world by withdrawing to inner harmony. Despite (or because of) the differences, Indian philosopher-scientists influenced the development of a remarkable body of literature.

*A Literary Theatre* Classical Indian literature is Sanskrit literature. The word *Sanskrit* means prepared, pure, perfect, or sacred. Sanskrit literature was the written dialect of the scholars and educated priests even after it had passed out of common usage; as such, Sanskrit was India's Latin.

As in the classical world of the West, prose literature was unknown in India until it was introduced by Europeans. As in classical Greece, all Indian writing had poetic content and form designed for oral recitation by rhapsodes. The two great Indian epics, the *Mahabharata* (350 B.C.) and the *Ramayana* (500 B.C.)—the Hindu *Iliad* and *Odyssey*—were written in Sanskrit 1500 years ago, but were sung by professionals for another 1000 years before that. These epics, like the epics of Greece and Rome, provide the subject matter for the dramatic theatre. When written down, the *Mahabharata* (*The Saga of the Bharata Tribes*) grew to seven times the length of the *Iliad* and *Odyssey* combined. Regarded by Indians as the Christian New Testament is by Westerners, the *Mahabharata* contains a philosophical song, *The Bhagavad-Gita* (the song of god). The second epic, the *Ramayana* (*The Tale of Rama*), is the most famous and beloved Indian book. Each epic originally enjoyed musical accompaniment when recited; gradually, and with increasing frequency, as with the *Iliad* and *Odyssey*, dramatic gesture was added to the music. In *The Theatric Universe* Pramod Kale notes that rhapsodists gradually down-played the liturgical aspects of their recitations in favor of the dramatic. Professionals appeared, as in the West, when dramatization crystallized.

Indian arts shared a common aesthetic with Indian narrative epics and dramatic theatre. Paintings, like epics and dramas, did not represent things as much as feelings. The Indian artist's skill did not lie in faithful representation but in evocative suggestion. Line surpassed color in importance, as the soul and spirit surpassed outer form.

*Performance*   Historically the performance of Sanskrit drama stands as the apogee of classical dramatic Indian theatre. The Sanskrit theatre occurred at annual temple fairs, at seasonal festivals in royal manors, at the request of a poet's lordly patron, and before an assembly of scholars or simple villagers. A troupe of Indian players was, as in Rome, but part of a whole entertainment program that included acrobats, wrestlers, tight rope walkers, illusionists, conjurers, hypnotists, magicians, sword swallowers, monkey and mongoose handlers, and snake charmers. But what distinguished the Sanskrit theatre performance from the others was its aesthetic purpose, as explained in the *Natya Sastra*:

> The theatre is a means of recreation and rest for those bowed down by sorrow, engaged in ascetic endeavors or weary after long labor. But it is also a means for teaching people duty, goodness, and achievement in life. It is an instrument for developing their minds.
>
> To those inclined toward righteousness and duty, it teaches righteousness and duty. To those whose minds run on passions, desires and worldly goods, it serves desires and worldly goods. It teaches modesty to the arrogant, self-discipline and control to the violently intemperate, courage to the effeminate, valor to the ignorant and refinement to scholars. To the lordly, it is luxury but to those who sorrow it provides stability. It adds internal wealth to those who already possess

it but to those distracted with envy and worry, the theatre brings peace and composure.[4]

Pramod Kale explains that "on the one hand, theatre is a recreational activity which also instructs and on the other hand, it is a cosmic phenomenon—a quintessence of the universe itself."[5]

Unlike Western drama, Indian drama revealed no search for the meaning of life and death, of human identity and destiny, of individuals' burdens and responsibilities. The performance of Sanskrit drama showed life's answers as clear: "Theatre in ancient India, like the worship of God, was testament of joy. Just as this worship is joyous—so different from the mournful fearful worship of the Judeo-Christians—so is the theatre into its own conception, a song of joy, a celebration of life."[6]

*The Manipulation of Rasa*   The success of an Indian dramatic performance depended upon the troupe's ability to manipulate the audience's *rasa*. A. C. Scott explains *rasa*:

> A state of aesthetic awareness is produced . . . so that the spectator is drawn from the material action of the play into consciousness of an enduring reality. The process takes place both on the stage and in the mind of the individual; it is rather like the western psychiatrist's definition of empathy except that it has a transcendental implication. . . . It is regarded as a highly select occurrence demanding a trained mind both in the performance and in the appreciation of art.[7]

The production of *rasa* began with ceremonies before each play commenced. Each troupe—playwright, master actor, clown, musicians, actor-dancers, crown maker, ornament maker, dyer, painter, and assorted artisans—rehearsed the rites as carefully as the play. Performances occurred both day and night, except during the late evening or the dinner hour. The particular time for an individual play was determined by its subject matter: virtue played before noon, strength and energy in the afternoon, and pathos in the evening.

Work proceeded under the supervision of the *sutradhara* (manager) and the manager's two assistants, the *sthapaka* and the *pariparsvaka*. The first conducted the rehearsals, supervised the construction of the stage settings, and acted as the troupe's agent; the second relayed the manager's orders to the actors, conducted the chorus, and played minor roles. When drum beats announced a play's beginning, the *sutradhara's* assistants unrolled a carpet on the stage and carried in a golden pitcher and Indra's banner on the *jaraja* (staff)—the emblem of Indra, the stage, and the drama. Meanwhile the *sutradhara* scattered white flowers. The orchestra entered next, and the choir, led by the *pariparsvaka*, joined in for a brief concert culminating in the choir's song of welcome. Indra's *jaraja* acted as both a vertical conductor for the descent of the spirits who would possess the actors and as a weapon against any demon who might object to the performance. The *sutradhara* then enacted a sacred rite with the *jaraja* by sprinkling water from the golden pitcher onto the stage and the performers. Prayers to Shiva, the creator and destroyer, focused on the eight-foot bamboo *jaraja* in which Brahma, Shiva, Vishnu, Karitkeya, and three great serpents resided. The first part of the pole was wrapped in white linen, the second in blue, the

third in yellow, the fourth in red, and the fifth in multicolored bunting. The *jaraja* remained on the stage throughout the performance to help the drama achieve poise and equilibrium between the warring aspects of Shiva. The ensuing prologue signaled the beginning of the drama and the entrance of the players.

***Players*** Like Roman actors, Indian actors were *nata* (men) and *nati* (women) of the lowest social order, subject to strict censorship by the Brahmins. Musicians, singers, dancers, indeed all artists, belonged to the lowest caste. Sometimes the king even employed members of theatrical troupes as spies or assassins. Nevertheless, a few respected actors existed: Bharata ranked as a holy sage and the goddess Urvaci was an actress.

All female troupes and all male troupes played throughout India. Women, however, sometimes played "delicate men," and men sometimes played virile female characters. Prologues to Sanskrit plays suggest rivalries among these troupes, who may have had economic difficulties. Some actors actually lived off their wives' prostitution. In fact, law mandated lesser penalties for infidelity with actors' wives than with other wives. In the first century

An all-female Indian theatrical company. (Archaeological Survey of India)

A.D., Patanjali wrote of this problem in his commentary on the *Mahabharata*:

> When an actor's wife appears on the stage, ask her: "Whose are you? Whose are you?" She will always answer: "I am yours."

As in Rome, actresses were usually members of the courtesan guild. Their mothers, who often worked as their impresarios, insisted that they follow strict diets, and that they be allowed precise make-up, stylish clothing, the same education as men, and vocal fan clubs in the audience.

As mentioned previously, the *sutradhara* managed the company. But the term *sutradhara* means the "one who holds the thread of the story," which suggests a link with the Indian rhapsode, the *grantha*. The *sutradhara*, in fact, also acted the leading roles and filled in for missing actors. In addition, the *sutradhara* taught acting to the children of the troupe. The other main player was the *vidushaka* (clown), usually portrayed in the manner of his Greek and Roman counterpart as a bald, dwarfish, fat, gluttonous, teeth-protruding, pink-eyed, trusted friend of the king. The clown, like all players, learned his craft from the *Natya Sastra*.

***The Actor's Technique***   The *Natya Sastra* mandates that an actor present the appropriate state or condition of the character portrayed, use energy to convey the playwright's text, and exhibit appropriate feelings and emotion through the body. The proper relationship between an actor's inner and outer technique leads to an effective performance:

> In your natural form enter the stage circle. Cover your own identity with colors and trinkets. In theatrical performance, after proper consideration of age and dress, he who has the suitable form should resemble the role in nature too. Just as a man's soul, discarding its nature along with its body, enters a different body with its different nature, in the same way, a wise man, exercising his mental facilities, makes others' nature his own, holding "I am he" and along with his dress, speech and body, follows his actions, too.[8]

Dramatic reincarnation followed the four means of the actor's *abhinaya* (craft). The first, *angika* (physical movement), is detailed so minutely that the *Natya Sastra* lists thirty-six different types of glances alone! Finger movements, head shakes, eyebrow maneuvers, cheek inflections, nose tensions, chin angles, neck movements, body postures, walks, and over 500 *mudras* (gestural ideographs) were available to communicate the entire intricate Sanskrit grammar. Kapila Vatsyayan explains:

> Every inch of the human form, every joint of the human skeleton, is given significance, for it is not only the geometrical and physical possibility which is being explored, but its correlation to the meaning, to the attitude or the state the whole will evoke. . . . Character is thus portrayed through a knowledge of types in which particular qualities predominate, and by a systematic use of physical postures, movements, turns and thrusts of the body which correspond to the moods.[9]

Lyrics were repeated two, six, or even twenty times to new accompaniment and increasingly subtle visual interpretation.

This system, the world's most intricate sign language, was rivaled by the second tool in the Indian actor's craft: *vacika* (vocal utterance). Particular pitches and tempos were believed to evoke certain *rasas* (sentiments). The third aspect of the actor's craft, *aharya* (externalization), extended the performance even further, through costume, properties, and make-up. Thus, both realistic and symbolic properties formed peculiar playing conventions. Certain combinations of movements with particular properties could convey darkness, climbing, mourning, crossing a river, swimming, riding, or driving. The convention of touching a stool and bowing before sitting became standard in Sanskrit performance.

These first three aspects of technique constituted the actor's external craft. The fourth aspect, *sattivika* (psychological composition), became the inner and most important aspect of the actor's craft. The Indian actor had to feel

*Codification of single hand gestures for the Sanskrit theatre*   (Bhavnani Enakski, *The Dance of India*)

75

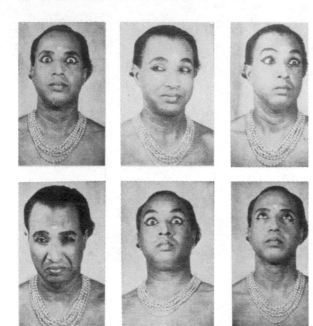

*Facial expressions delineate* bhava *and* rasa *in the classical Indian performance. Top row, left to right: Wonder, Laughter, Fear; bottom row, left to right: Disgust, Anger, Tranquility.* (Bhavnani Enakski, *The Dance of India*, p. 15.)

the character's *bhava* (mood). *Bhava* was an integral part of the theory of *rasa*; *bhava* created the form while *rasa* filled it with emotion.

A Sanskrit actor who mastered all four of these aspects of technique could be considered part of the "inner" school. An actor in the "outer" school knew no rules. The "inner" school was taught by the *sutradhara*. Such a teacher supposedly knew not only the *Natya Sastra* but also all arts and sciences, all customs, and all habits Sanskrit characters might possess. Acting students thus studied oil massage, acrobatics, diet, and eye exercises. A large part of the Sanskrit actor's training involved dance as well.

*Dance*   Indian dance played a central role in the mythological creation of the universe. Shiva, god of the dance, once stood on a demon to subdue it and shook a rattle to calm the demon's anger. The sounds of the rattle created the first rhythm, the rhythm of life. Because Shiva moved to this rhythm, he became the world's first dancer: He danced, and the world took shape. But, as his intensity increased, fire

appeared in one of his hands: Dance was not only the world's creator, but the source of its potential destruction. It originated in an attempt to overcome evil. Aspects of Shiva's dance symbolized the primeval rhythmic energy—an important means to *moksha* (release from the material world).

Shiva symbolized the dance of the universe, the creative rhythm of existence. His statue embodied dance's power over the cosmos. Four arms created the illusion of a body in motion. The front palm of one right hand held a protective pose of security, while another held a drum to sound the rhythm that began the universe. Shiva's left arm reached across his body to create a refuge for the troubled; the other left hand held the fire of destruction and sacrifice. Under Shiva's right foot lay the demon dwarf; the other foot was raised to bless the audience.

Like Greek and Roman theatre, Sanskrit theatre did not distinguish between dancer and actor. Dance filled the stage even while the *sutradhara* narrated. Playwrights designed plots to exploit opportunities for dance. Heroes fell for dancing girls, marriage celebrations ended in dance, warriors prepared for battle with a dance, gods revealed themselves in a dance. As the *Natya Sastra* suggests, "where gods are praised, where the action is graceful, where men and women are indulging in courtship and sweet talk born of desire, in all such graceful and erotic phases, dance composition should be employed."[10]

Dance was built step by step. One hundred and eight single postures could be made of combinations among six postures, thirty-two gaits, and twenty-seven hand gestures. Additional hand, foot, neck, arm, and waist movements could be added. The final combination constituted the *pindibhanda*, the whole body sequence of the dance. And every little movement had to be in harmony with the beat of the music.

*Classical Indian dancer, c. 1800.* (New York Public Library Picture Collection)

***Music*** Indian music, like all Eastern music (and probably like the music of classical Greece and Rome), was difficult for Westerners to appreciate. Chordic harmony, as conceived in the West, was unknown in Indian music; instead, tonal qualities and colors clashed to create grades of consonance and dissonance. Indian music consisted of a melody with a background of occasional undertones; each melody was an improvisation on one of thirty-six traditional modes. The musical line or melodic scheme was known as a *raga*. Each *raga* had five, six, or seven notes to which the musician returned. Each *raga* was named for a mood or personality trait; traditional occult powers, seasons of the year, times of the day, and colors, all had associational *ragas*. Twelve musical notes formed the *ragas*—seven major or natural notes plus five intermediate notes. To this ten microtones were added, to produce twenty-two quarter tones. Rarely, however, did a *raga* use all twelve notes; the very minute and subtle musical score, not separated into bars, consisted of one continuous legato. A complex rhythm and religious-romantic lyrics were added to this score.

Music led from the material, external drama on stage to the spiritual internal peace in the audience. Shiva's drum was so essential to Indian drama that the idiom, "a drama without a drum," came to denote something peculiar. Nine drums, twenty-six flutes, and twelve male and twelve female voices created an aural, emotional continuity on the Indian stage. Bharata wrote that "instruments are the very bed of a performance." Specific instruments played specific types of melodies or rhythms for certain entrances and exits, types of scenes, actions, moods, emotions, attitudes, and production miscues. But whereas later Western music evoked a mental picture or emotional mood for the audience, Indian music focused on its audience's intellectual process. Music that duplicated or imitated the emotion or words of an actor was deemed intrusive.

***Costume and Make-up*** In the Indian theatre, physical decoration was as elaborate and intricate as the music and dance. As in the Greek and Roman theatres, color, closely related to *raga*, carefully regulated the costuming. In addition, region, caste, quality, and station affected the actors' costume colors. Divine women wore white, erotic women, many colors; superhuman mortal women wore yellow, female demons, black. Human men, male gods, and demons wore multicolored garments. Rags and black clothing costumed ascetics. Harem chiefs were known by their red jackets. Kings garbed themselves in many colors; a colorless king was an ill omen. A king in dirty clothing was considered mad or miserable.

Make-up was likewise colorful. The fundamental colors for full body make-up were white, blue-black, red, and yellow. The skin of happy characters and kings was tinted dark orange. Subdivisions of castes were known either by the colors of their skin or by their hairstyle. *Vidusaka* was bald. Boys and servants sported three characteristic tufts, whereas madmen were recognized by ringlets.

**Performance Space** Classical Sanskrit drama played either in the public hall of a temple or in the private hall of a palace. In both instances the intimate, small-roofed hall created a unique playing space that was quite different from those of Greece and Rome. At the time of the *Natya Sastra* each city centered around its temple; consequently, a temporary stage was erected before each city's temple for public performances. Wealthy citizens and rulers hosted private theatricals by erecting a temporary stage in the large dining or music room where harem girls were educated.

According to Bharata's treatise describing the erection of a permanent theatre building as part of a temple or private palace, a theatre had to be built on plain hard soil. After consulting the movement of the stars and offering food in four directions, the builder was to take measurements with a white cotton string. Theatre roofs rising two or three times higher than the structure were to be curved in the shape of a "mountain cave," which was probably a rock-cut architectural style with excellent acoustics. Measurements had to be taken carefully at a specific time on a specific day to ensure quality construction. After the measurements were taken, celebrations, feasts, offerings to the gods, and gifts to the Brahmins commemorated the event.

The ideal theatre building never measured longer than ninety-six feet by forty-eight feet. The theatre hall always faced the temple, even if the theatre was a less desirable forty-eight foot square or equilateral triangular building. The roofed theatre had small windows high in the walls and few doors. Rectangular halls were divided in half, with one forty-eight foot square space for the audience and the other for both stage and backstage areas. The auditorium floor, either flat or tiered, contained risers that were nine inches high and eighteen inches wide. The audience, entering through sexually segregated doors, sat or stood for the performance. Brahmins sat in the front, near the white pillar of the stage, which had gold buried at its base. The Kshatriyas sat near the copper-based red pillar; the Vaisyas, by the silver-based pillar; and the Shudras, by the iron-based pillar. The seating thus reflected the social order, the economy, and the divine order of things. As Pramod Kale writes, "the play hall was a small model of the whole world . . . just as the world was held up by the four castes, the theatre . . . was also looked upon as being held up by four pillars."[11]

The raised earth and clay stage floor was adorned with pictures and reliefs of inlaid gems that led to a golden center. Columns at the four corners of the *ranga* (stage) supported a separate roof. Some historians have suggested that the *ranga* had two levels; others have maintained that the second level was actually a sanctuary to protect the theatre performance from the wrath of demons. The *ranga's* floor was divided into different areas, each associated with a particular deity, because particular deities were said to rule particular areas of the *ranga*; the performance's opening ritual helped pacify them. The sides of the *ranga* functioned as wings. A *yavanika* (painted curtain) hung at the rear to hide the backstage area. Behind the curtain, stagehands produced sound effects. Two

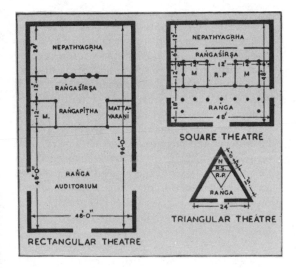

*Floor plans for Sanskrit theatres.* (D. R. Mankad, *Ancient Indian Theatre*, Charotar Publishing House, India)

exits to the backstage framed an orchestra seated at the rear of the stage.

***Scenery*** The Indian stage used little scenery. The makeshift nature of the performance required few scenic items; it exploited instead the Indian love for symbolism, imagery, and costume. Sanskrit texts did not even indicate scenery, though female stagehands may have changed the *yavanika* to suggest various *rasas*—white for an erotic setting, yellow for heroic, a dull color for pathos, multicolored for farce, black for tragedy, and red for violence.

The Indian *ranga* was, like the world, a neutral place where many different locations existed simultaneously. Indian theatre thus aimed for even less illusory imitation than the Greek theatre. By simply circumambulating the *ranga* an actor established a new locale, a technique that predated similar practices in medieval Europe. Consequently, the stage did not attempt to differentiate between the ideal or the real, the symbolic or the natural; all matter was equally illusory, and equally ''real.'' Nor did the Indian stage admit a Western distinction between space and matter. Indian cosmology held that the visible world was composed of an all-pervading substance, ether. Air was simply condensed ether. There was, as a result, no such thing as empty space; all space

contained matter. Thus, there was no need to define spaces on stage.

Properties were likewise symbolic. Players mimed actions rather than use actual objects. Some properties were more real than others; weapons, elephants, toy carts, and mechanical dolls were made from grass or skin-covered bamboo. Real animals appeared when called for. The particular properties, like other production components, were chosen to serve the playwright's text.

***Dramatic Texts*** Like the dramas of all classical theatres, Indian Sanskrit dramas presented imaginative truths rather than historical truths. The Indian playwrights' representations were symbols of larger issues rather than photographs of existing realities. The texts revealed the influence of the *Upanishads*, sacrificial ceremonies, festive processions, ancient dances, and, most importantly, the two great Indian epics. Like the dramas of Greece, the Indian drama also preserved throughout its Classical age the religious tone of the *Mahabharata* and the *Ramayana*.

No evidence of what Western historians would consider a drama existed prior to the reign of Ashoka (c. 274–232 B.C.). When it did arrive, Sanskrit drama, according to Som Benegal, ''exhalted the aesthetic, in contradistinction with the cathartic, quality of drama.''[12] *Rasa* (sentiment) was the primary means employed by the dramatist; only drama, because it was the fifth Veda, could produce *rasa*. A playwright could achieve the eight *rasas*—the erotic or loving, the comic, the pathetic, the furious, the heroic, the terrible or fearful, the odious or loathsome, and the marvelous—by arranging the eight permanent *bhavas* (moods) harmoniously. As the *Natya Sastra* states, ''Theatre is a reenactment of the lives and ways of people, passing through the various phases and enriched by the different *bhavas*.''[13] The different *bhavas* were situations or actions that either produced each *rasa* or that were produced through the evocation of a *rasa*. For example, moonlight, a *bhava*, could produce a feeling of love, a *rasa*, which might then have produced a smile, a *bhava*.

The eight major *bhavas* had thirty-three transitory states, each with a separate determinant and consequence. For example, ''*Chinta* is a painful recollection. Its determinant is the loss or absence of a desired object. Its consequence, tears, sighs, change of complexion.''[14] Transcending all was the ninth *bhava* and the ninth *rasa*, the goal of Indian dramatic theatre: peace of mind and a sense of wholeness after a fleeting glimpse of Enlightenment, the intuitive knowledge of the unity underneath all things.

Sanskrit drama taught not with words but through action. The harmony of the universe was revealed as the characters fulfilled their duties. The diction of the drama created the *rasa*, defined the characters, and structured the action. The plot moved through five songs, each of which had a purpose. Two songs brought characters on and off and revealed their identities. Three were sung by characters on stage: one to change the *rasa*, one to develop the plot, and one to fill in either during a tense scene or a lull in the action.

Sanskrit scholars also employed an extensive system of rules for prosody that included sixty-five metrical patterns and numerous rules of diction and language. Playwrights alternated poetry with prose according to the dig-nity of the topic, characters, and action. Language was vertically proscribed. The hero and leading males spoke Sanskrit, the heroine and leading females spoke a Prakrit dialect, and attendants spoke another dialect. Gods shifted dialect depending on their auditors, but women spoke only prose.

By the end of the Classical era Sanskrit had become a scholar's language with very little popular appeal. Its obscurity to the large public audience encouraged pantomimic action and the introduction of comic characters to explain the action in Prakrit. Eventually, professional companies performed only Prakrit versions of the Sanskrit classics.

***Types of Drama*** Indian dramatic criticism established an elaborate categorization of drama based on subject, hero, and *rasa*. *Natya* (drama) was either realistic or conventional. The first type presented everyday people doing everyday actions without flourish. The second reveled in artificiality, poetic fancy, and lyricism. These two main types of drama had twenty-eight subdivisions. Bharata, however, listed only ten forms of drama in Chapter 18 of the *Natya Sastra*. *Rupaka* (major drama) had seven subspecies, the most familiar of which were the *nataka* and the *prakarana*. *Nataka* showed an exalted mythological figure in a simple plot of five to ten acts and focused on one *rasa* in a mixture of tragedy and comedy. A *prakarana* resembled a *nataka* but usually featured an invented, less distinguished hero. *Sakuntala* is the most famous *nataka*, and *The Little Clay Cart*, the most popular *prakarana*.

***Dramatic Structure*** The structure of Indian drama followed established conventions. Unlike Western plots, which ended in death if a tragedy and in marriage if a comedy, Eastern plots tended to involve separation and reunion. Bharata's *Natya Sastra* described two plot species. One developed a single linear action; another interwove several plot lines through a series of episodes, each marked by the entrance or exit of a character. Both plots sought the resolution of opposites.

*A scene from Kalidasa's* Sakuntala. (National Museum, New Delhi)

Each play opened with the *sutradhara's* invocation to the gods. The prayer may have told of the author and the author's work, the actors and their roles, or something expository about the play. Occasionally another actor joined the *sutradhara* for the prologue, which ended when a character came onto the stage. Bharata insisted that the action of a play develop through five elements—beginning, effort, hope, certainty, and success. Sanskrit drama knew only happy endings; death, calamity, defeat, and the downfall of a king never appeared on stage. The action of the one-to-ten act Sanskrit drama ended when the *sutradhara* exited after giving a *nandi* (benediction) asking a god for prosperity. Minute details of production, written into the text, specified what players needed to do to secure the god's favor. The action followed a poetical rather than a logical organization; consequently, the action slowed to provide for the elongation of a moment. After all, interest did not rest on what would happen next; the stories came from familiar Indian epics. The structure of the drama accentuated how the action was accomplished.

The function of the *sutradhara* emerged from the rhapsodes' dramatic recitation. The *sutradhara*, the "string holder," propelled the story and plot of the play. He laid out each scene, provided background information, spoke characters' thoughts for them, and interpreted the *rasa* of the moment. Although Sanskrit drama could have included any of forty-eight different character types, only a few dominated the action. Indian characterization, in fact, seemed weak by Western standards: Whereas Greek heroes fought their fate to the death, Indian heroes triumphed over all adversity simply because they were at one with the universe, their ally. The heroes and heroines were either noble or quasidivine. Because the playwrights sought the favor of noble patrons, no commoners played hero roles in the action. The heroes were drawn as ideal, self-controlled nobles. The heroines might be the heroes' wives, other men's wives, courtesans, or goddesses. In all cases their identities (like those of Indian women of the time) were defined by their relationships with men.

As in Greece and Rome, the most popular character was the joker/fool/clown. The short, hunchbacked, buck-toothed, deformed, bald, brown-eyed, fat, flat-nosed nit was usually a Brahmin by caste but a buffoon by learning. Other popular characters included a comic villain in gaudy clothes and a polite and eloquent poet-parasite. In general, faithful characters always triumphed through their love, and virtue was always rewarded.

***Playwrights*** From thousands of Sanskrit plays only about two dozen authentic texts survive. The most famous playwrights were Kalidasa (c. fifth century A.D.), Bhasa (c. fourth century A.D.), and Sudraka (c. fourth century A.D.). Other Sanskrit playwrights included Ashvaghosha, Bhavabhuti, Vishakhadatta, and King Harsha.

The name Kalidasa means "servant of Kali," an avatar of Shiva. Only three plays by Kalidasa, the so-called "Shakespeare of India," are known. *Sakuntala*, a seven-act tender romance that was the author's most famous, is typical. Its prologue urges the audience to consider the beauty of nature before watching the story of Sakuntala's siring of Bharata, the father of the warriors in the *Mahabharata*.

Bhasa's most famous play was *The Vision of Vasavadatta*, an almost ideal metaphysical play. Bhasa's thirteen plays range from monologues and one-act plays to six-act dramas.

The third famous playwright, King Sudraka, was a mysterious figure; scholars do not even know if he existed, and, if he did, when. He probably lived between Bhasa and Kalidasa because his only play, *The Little Clay Cart*, seems based on a play by Bhasa. Considered one of the greatest of all comedies, this social play is distinguished by its individualized characters.

*Audience*  The experience of Sanskrit theatre depended as much on the qualities of the spectators as on the abilities of the performers. Unlike the classical theatres of Greece and Rome, the theatre of India catered to an elite audience—called a *kalpavrska* (a tree that answers all wishes)—educated to appreciate the nuances and moods of performance. The prologues of the plays laud spectators for being well read and versed in art and literature. Indian theatre was not democratic; it catered to devoted upper-caste patrons. The aesthetic experience demanded a finely tuned sensibility. The approximately 400 spectators expected to laugh, cry, jump, clap, scream, and fully participate in the theatrical event.

Kings and wealthy Indians filled the theatres for coronations, festivals, marriages, or births. The *sabhapti* (patron of the performance) sat amid his harem on a lion throne.

Lesser nobles sat on the opposite side of the auditorium. Behind the noble spectators sat officers, financiers, educators, poets, astrologers, and physicians. Before the patron sat the Brahmins. In temple performances even *shudras* found a place. Nevertheless, a general rule forbade admission to barbarians, the ignorant, and heretics.

The audience was not interested in how the plot was constructed but in which *rasas* were evoked. Indians knew the goal of their theatre to be the creation of a great *rasa*, a sublime self-realization. The theatrical event itself was a beautiful visual sacrifice; the actors' sacrifices gave the spectators a glimpse of transcendence. To ensure their ability to respond, Indian spectators evolved a series of prohibitions for their stage: A play could neither end unhappily nor display grim realism. Action observed propriety and decorum and avoided painful, disgusting, and debasing scenes. Characters could not undertake long journeys, murder, fight, eat, bathe, kiss, embrace, loosen their garments, or fondle women's breasts. Such actions would interfere with the evocation of *rasa*. Likewise players who bumped into one another, stumbled, dropped accessories, forgot or repeated lines, broke rules of recitation or intonation, sung off key, or missed entrances were judged inferior.

*Decline*  The Sanskrit theatre, the classical theatre of India, declined for many reasons. First, when Prakrit replaced Sanskrit as the popular tongue, Sanskrit became obscure and codified. In addition, Sanskrit drama depended upon the epics for material and adhered closely to rigid conventions and rules of poetic composition. As the clown character became more infrequent, popular taste shifted to Prakrit theatre, leaving the classical dramas to oral readers rather than to actors. Then, the Moslem invasion of India silenced whatever was left of the Sanskrit theatre.

Following the British conquest of India, Indians were educated to ridicule native arts and to aspire to Western models. Educated Indians were sent to England to develop Western artistic skills and tastes. Fortunately, before the

Moslems and British crushed the Indian the-atrical tradition, missionaries who traveled throughout Asia preserved the essential in-gredients of the Sanskrit aesthetic by adapting it to unique cultural contexts. India is, in this way, the source of most Asian theatre. Thus, the profound beauty of the classical Indian aes-thetic survived. In addition, each of the four main modern "classical" theatres, who claim direct descent from India's classical theatre, base their work on the *Natya Sastra*. (They were also viewed by Westerners as dance-based the-atres.) The Kathakali and the Bharata Natyam perform in southern India while the Kathak and Manipuri entertain new generations of In-dian audiences in the north.

# CHINA

Perhaps China's isolation by a large ocean, high mountains, and an extensive desert can account for the distinct nature of its civiliza-tion. China flourished while Greece was still barbaric; Chinese civilization varied from In-dia's as well. In India, priests shaped the so-ciety; in China, politicians did. Indian life fol-lowed the unchanging law of *dharma* toward spiritual fulfillment; Chinese oracles investi-gated the flowing *dao* (the way of life), seeking political stability. Indians' disinterest in action and preference for disengagement from the world created in them an interest in space and the gods of earth, air, and sky. The Chinese veneration for their ancestors developed in them a strong sense of time and thus of his-tory. Indians interested in spiritual fulfillment focused attention on the self and on individ-uals' regulated existence within a group caste structure. Chinese interested in political sta-bility centered attention on the Emperor, per-sonal relationships, and proprieties connect-ing the state with the family. Chinese interests were summarized by the philosopher Confu-cius (551–479 B.C.):

The men of old wanting to clarify and diffuse throughout the empire that light which comes from looking straight into the heart and then act-ing, first set up good government in their own states; wanting good government in their states, they first established order in their own families; wanting order in the home, they first disciplined themselves; desiring self-discipline, they recti-fied their own hearts; and wanting to rectify their hearts, they sought precise verbal definitions of their inarticulate thoughts [the tones given off by the heart]; wishing to attain precise verbal def-initions, they set to extend their knowledge to the utmost. This completion of knowledge is rooted in sorting things into organic categories.

When things had been classified in organic cat-egories, knowledge moved toward fulfillment; given the extreme knowable points, the inarti-culate thoughts were defined with preci-sion. . . . Having attained this precise verbal definition [*aliter*, this sincerity], they then sta-bilized their hearts, they disciplined themselves; having attained self-discipline, they set their own houses in order; having order in their own homes, they brought good government to their own states; and when their states were well-governed, the empire was brought into equilibrium.[15]

These distinctions made Chinese civiliza-tion and theatre more accessible to Western tastes than Indian civilization and theatre. Al-though like the Indians, the Chinese were in-terested in equilibrium, Chinese means were quite different. India was clearly the most metaphysical, theological, and religious of civ-ilizations. China was the most humanistic, nontheological, and philosophical of civiliza-tions. Yet Chinese culture and theatre got their impetus, like all cultures and theatres, from a metaphysical-shamanistic source: the *Yi Jing*, *The Book of Changes*.

***From Ritual to Drama*** The *Yi Jing*, a man-ual of divination, together with Lao-Ze's (604–517 B.C.) *Dao De Jing*, *The Way of Life*, repre-sent the earliest religious sentiments in China. The *dao* is the way, the path of life. Daoists con-sidered intellectual thought superficial, intellectuals dangerous, and wisdom more valuable than knowledge. The way of nature should guide the way of humanity. Human action must seek to conform to, rather than dominate, the natural rhythms of the world. But China produced Confucius, and Indian Buddhism made Chinese culture a curious blend of various outlooks.

Chinese religion, culture, and theatre shifted from dance to song. China's gods were not dancers and neither, for the most part, were its players. Because of Confucius, Chinese religion, culture, and theatre developed in a less mystical and more ethical direction than those of India. Humans in China were more important than gods, so people, not gods, filled the stage. Religion and theatre relied more on history and less on mythology. And even when Indians brought Buddhism to China, the religion accommodated the Chinese point of view. Some scholars consider that Asia is divided culturally between China and India, Buddhism and Hinduism, singing and dancing. The Chinese theatre blended native arts with imported entertainments to create its own style of dramatic performance. But China produced virtually no dance; its classical theatre was called the Beijing opera.

Historians such as E. T. Kirby have argued that Chinese theatre originated in the practices of Daoist shamen, which might have been influenced by Indian practices. China used, for example, Indian motifs in writing, iron, horse-riding warriors, and Indian burial practices. Records of the Zhow Dynasty (1027–256 B.C.) reveal the existence of shamanistic and court dances as well as minstrelsy, juggling, and variety entertainments. Because it is rooted in ancestor worship, Daoism and its *wu* priesthood have always been deeply embedded in Chinese cultural life. Chinese theatre, in fact, seems to have begun in the exorcist rites of the *wu* priests during the early feudal age of the Zhow Dynasty.

Like Hinduism, Daoism denied the value of the world of appearances. In its place Daoism offered immortality through alchemy—that is, better eternal living through science. Male and female *wu* priests, *wu* and *xi*, performed both alchemical ceremonies and rites of ancestor worship. *Wu* ceremonies gradually lost their religious associations, however, and became entertainments at banquets and festivals. The *wu* priests began Chinese entertainment with seances, jesting, miming, rainmaking, soothsaying, and thaumaturgy (miracle making). They also instructed members of a dead person's family to impersonate the deceased as part of a ceremony of commemoration. Arthur Waley explains that beside the *wu* shaman

> there was another functionary, far more regularly connected with Chinese ritual, in whom the Ancestors, the "royal guests" at the sacrificial banquet, habitually took their abode. This was the *shi*, the medium (literally, "corpse") who sitting silent and composed, represented the ancestor to whom the sacrifice was made, or at funerals played the role of the dead man.[16]

Individuals won fame for reenacting important events in a dead person's life. Such scenes were very popular at memorial occasions.

*A Philosophical Theatre*    Before degenerating into alchemical searches for immortality, Daoism provided the Chinese with a sophisticated philosophical and religious outlook that permeated the dramatic theatre. Many Daoist principles guided Chinese society. Chance, change, spontaneity, nonpurposiveness, and reversion to origin serve as keys to understanding the Chinese drama's ideas about the relationship between individuals and society. Early Chinese theatre sought to give free rein to instinct, feelings, imagination, fantasy, and idiosyncrasies. As E. T. Kirby writes, "the origin of Chinese theatre is represented by the mythological figure of Lan Ts'ai ho, one of the Eight Immortals of Taoism and 'the patron saint of itinerant actors.'"[17] With the arrival of Indian Buddhism, Daoism found a mate to produce a distinctive Chinese phenomenon, *Zhan Buddhism* (*Zen* in Japan). But before the arrival of Buddhism, another Chinese philosophy, Confucianism, swept China, and stifled the development of the mystical elements of Daoism.

***Confucianism and the Drama*** Chinese drama, like Chinese religion, was not exclusive; a play could have elements of Daoism, Confucianism, and Buddhism, just as a person could believe aspects of each religion or philosophy. Nonetheless, it was the ideas of Confucius (551–479 B.C.) that provided the framework for Chinese culture and civilization. When proclaimed the state doctrine by Emperor Wu (140–87 B.C.), Confucianism gave homogeneity and unity to Chinese society. Whereas Daoism provided the mythological and ghostly characters for Chinese drama, Confucianism supplied the moral background. Confucianism's veneration of learning made the scholar, rather than the soldier or priest, the Chinese theatre's main character. In fact, Confucianism was known as *ru jia*, the school of the literati.

Filial piety, a main precept in Confucianism, dominates the decisions of many dramatic characters. Confucius taught that goodness and happiness could be attained by maintaining the proper ceremonies and rituals. Adherence to everyday duties could produce the *zhun zi* (perfect person). Chinese drama often shows a *zhun zi* rewarded at the end of a play. In this way Chinese drama served the utilitarian purpose of demonstrating how both adherence to ritual and the fulfillment of duty brought reward.

***Zhan Buddhism and the Drama*** Buddhism reached China in the first century A.D., a time of great prosperity and national confidence. Naturally, Buddhism was not popular. In fact, the Buddhist monk became a figure of great humor on the Chinese stage as a lazy, superstitious ignoramous. But as economic conditions worsened, the life-after-death message of Buddhism in China, like that of Christianity in Rome, began to appeal. At first, Buddhism seemed in conflict with the Confucian desire to make earthly existence as good as possible. Buddhists taught that suffering resulted from desire. To end suffering one must first stop desire. But the Chinese transformed Buddhism much more than Buddhism transformed the Chinese.

Indian Buddhism was too vague for the practical Chinese, who interpreted the new doctrine through the eyes of Confucian ethics. The result was a religion, and an emerging dramatic theatre, that only faintly resembled its Indian ancestor. With the fall of the Han Dynasty (206 B.C.–A.D. 220), Buddhism became more than a court vogue. By 500 Buddhism had swept all classes; by the end of the Dang Dynasty (618–907) the considerably modified religion was instilled in Chinese culture as *Zhan*, the Chinese rendering of the Sanskrit *Dhyana* (meditation). *Zhan* masters in the Dang Dynasty taught a more subjective technique to experience transcendental wisdom using many of the meditative practices of Daoism. Dramatic art became an important way to communicate the experience of *nirvana*, release from the self. The theatre in China expressed the inner life of things and helped facilitate *nirvana*. Theatrical art resembled both Daoism and the Sung Dynasty's (960–1279) Confucian idea of intuitive communion with nature through art. A Chinese painter summarized the artistic technique: "Outwardly, nature has been my teacher, but inwardly I follow the springs of inspiration in my heart."

***Society on Stage*** The dynamics of Chinese religion shaped the society that appeared on stage in historical guise. Each of the three religious-philosophical schools influenced the Chinese social order. Daoism may have provided the divine origin for the Emperor, but Confucianism marshaled the rest of civilization behind him.

The hierarchy of China reflected the Confucian respect for education. The top class consisted of two types of *shi* (scholars): *jin*, officials in the government, and *shen*, nobles attending the royal family. Below were, in descending order, the *nong* (farmers), the *gong* (artisans), and the *shang* (merchants), who, through buying and selling, could both buy into the aristocracy and patronize the dramatic arts. Naturally, the *shang* were the heroes of the dramas. Beneath the other groups were the outcasts—criminals, slaves, prostitutes, and, of course, actors—forbidden to take the imperial exams in Beijing necessary for social mobility. A male of any age could take the public examinations and repeat them if he failed. If he passed, a degree made him a member of the literary class, eligible for appointment to a local government position.

The Confucian ideal rested on the patriarchal extended family. The oldest male was the most venerated. Only sons were educated. Male celibacy was discouraged. Marriages, which were arranged, were based not on romance but on the need to make a family, produce heirs, and continue the devotions to ancestors. Matchmakers arranged marriages; courtesans arranged "celibate" males. Occasionally a family included a concubine under a wife's supervision. Nonetheless, the Chinese family demanded filial piety. The notion that a son's first duty belonged to his parents was tested in countless Chinese dramas. To turn one's back on one's family or to decline a marriage were the greatest sins and the worst crimes against one's ancestors.

Except for professional courtesans educated in singing, music, poetry, and calligraphy, Chinese women occupied a low status. They were, moreover, expected to remain true to their husbands, modest, chaste, and loyal in both life and the drama. On stage, as in life, widows remained chaste, unmarried, and faithful to the dead husbands to whom they still belonged. To enhance their beauty and to ensure that they did not escape, women of an early age bound their feet to reduce eventual foot size. Chinese beauty, in fact, resided more in the feet than in the face. Consequently, a teetering gait, the result of dwarfed feet, signaled refinement and sex appeal.

Because of the severe social restrictions on women, female impersonation became a necessity in the theatre. Female impersonators in the drama imitated the teetering walk using a *tsai jiao*, a foot device that kept the actor on point throughout the performance. Ironically, when women were allowed to act, in the twentieth century, they had to learn the men's technique of portraying women on stage.

*A Literary Theatre* Chinese art and literature contributed to the theatre's cultural milieu. Buddhism and Daoism, rather than Confucianism, dominated artistic development by supplying Hindu motifs, symbols, methods, and forms. Chinese art had no shadows or perspective because art was not an imitation of reality but something made to give pleasure, convey a mood, and suggest an idea through perfect form. The Chinese artist sought a rhythm and an accurate line that suggested or symbolized the soul of a thing. Excellence in technique, rather than innovation in perception or power of feeling, seems Confucianism's contribution to the Chinese aesthetic.

Whereas India had little written history but many artifacts, buildings, and art, China had an enormous written history but few physical remains of its early civilization. Confucianism dominated the list of classical books upon which the imperial examinations were based: the *Yi Jing*, *Book of Changes*; *Shu Jing*, *Book of History*; *Shi Jing*, *Book of Poetry*; *Li Ji*, *Record of Rites*; *Zhun Qui*, *Spring and Fall Annals*; and *Lun Ya*, *Analects*. Chinese writers used a classical, nonvernacular style until the Yuan Dynasty (1279–1368), when unemployed scholars invented the novel to earn livings. The novel became popular with the common people at the time of a great flowering of Chinese drama.

The classical Chinese theatre was called Beijing Opera. As E. T. Kirby writes, "The basic characteristics of the Peking style drama, the national or classical theater that developed in the early years of the nineteenth century, go back in an unbroken continuum for at least one thousand years prior to that time."[18] The performance of Chinese classical theatre was the culmination of a process that began in early dynasties.

*Early Performance* According to Chinese history a ruler in 1818 B.C. abolished traditional temple rites in favor of a Beijing play featuring clowns, dwarfs, and actors. This anecdote underlines both the eclectic nature and the low status of Chinese theatrical performance. The first two kings of the Zhow Dynasty (c. 1027–256 B.C.) contributed their names to two basic kinds of Beijing opera-

*A Yuan theatre performance, c. 1324.* (From a wall painting in a temple in Shansi province; *Pictures of Ancient Chinese Music*, Plate 16.)

drama: *wen* and *wu*. Confucius himself thought that *wen* (culture) was at its best during the Zhow Dynasty. King Wen was thus known for his cultural achievements whereas King Wu achieved fame with military triumphs. In both courts singing actors, jugglers, clowns, acrobats, pole climbers, jesters, dwarfs, and court fools entertained.

In the Han Dynasty (206 B.C.–A.D. 220) trade increased, cities grew, and the arts flourished. Culture was both imported from abroad and developed at home. Military victories were celebrated with dance, music, and song. Professional entertainers, known as *yu* and *bai yu*, enacted stories. Palace singers dramatized stories and performed with masks, song, and dance. During the Han Dynasty Confucianism became official state orthodoxy, the basis for the imperial exams. A popular play at court was *Mr. Huang of the Eastern Ocean*.

The relative peace of the Dang Dynasty (618–907) allowed the arts to develop. Dances with a narrative line were very popular. During this period we also find the first reference to a Beijing opera. The Emperor Minghuang, considered the founder of Chinese theatre, established a Pear Garden Conservatory to train men and women in music. The Pear Garden became synonymous with the acting profession.

In 832 the palace threw out a group of actors for performing a skit satirizing Confucius. A later skit tried to prove that Confucius, Lao-Ze, and Buddha were women. In the eighth and ninth centuries *canjunxi* (adjutant plays) ridiculed a famous government adjutant, Shi Dan, with acting, singing, costume, and make-up. Even women played Shi Dan. Buddhist fables were adapted as *biawen* (mixtures of prose, song, and verse). Court theatricals grew so popular that even a prince played in a short two-character improvised skit featuring a wit and a fool. Buddhism's influence on Chinese literature, art, and dance created a new song and dance form called *daju*, the forerunner of the Chinese classical theatre.

During the Sung Dynasty (960–1279) what was planted in the Dang blossomed. The names of some 280 plays of the period survive. Adjutant plays continued to be popular. But the most important development was the *zaju* (the variety play), which was popular at court and with the public. The *zaju* had three parts: a prelude of low comedy, a one- or two-scene poetic play featuring song and dialogue, and a musical epilogue. During festivals families of professional players performed *zaju* on temporary booth stages open on three sides. Actors were known by nicknames: Orange Peel, Dimples, Silver Fish. A company consisted of a leading male actor and producer-playwright, a director, a comedian, a secondary male actor, an official character, and a musician. Plays were included on variety bills with storytellers, balladeers, puppeteers, medicine men, and fortune tellers.

*Yuan Drama*    Kublai Khan fixed his Mongol capital in Beijing and eliminated the imperial examinations. The Yuan Dynasty (1279–1368), the result of the Mongol invasion, produced the golden age of Chinese literature. Unemployed government scholars turned to creative writing to support their families. The novels and plays they wrote created a popular literature and a popular theatre. Meanwhile, the court drama, like the Sanskrit drama, stagnated into a pale imitation of past models. On the other hand, the dramas of the Yuan were known by every spectator. In all, 700 Yuan titles are recorded, but only 170 texts still exist. The most popular Yuan playwright was Guan Hanqing (1220–1300) who wrote more than fifty plays.

Yuan drama obliquely protested foreign rule and social injustice. Most plays show good characters defeated by evil characters until justice, either legal or poetic, prevails. Characters enter, state their names and backgrounds, and discuss their roles in the play. Character motivation is unimportant because chance serves as the major plot device.

Yuan theatre fell into two schools, northern called *zaju*, and southern, called *chuangi*. *Zaju* drama, centered in Beijing, developed first and was the most prolific. A *zaju* drama consisted of four acts, each with ten or twenty *gu* (songs) sung by a protagonist. Songs, in fact, served as the major structural devices for the well-plotted *zaju*. Each act was built around a set of solos in one distinct musical key and one rhyme scheme; the pipa lute dominated this *zaju* music. One or two wedges, usually a prologue and *xiezi* (interlude) were performed with the four acts.

The most famous *zaju* was Wang Shi-fu's *The Romance of the Western Chamber*, which comprised twenty acts divided into five parts. Other

*A Chinese theatre performance.*    (New York Public Library Picture Collection)

*zaju* included Ji Zhun-siang's *The Orphan of the House of Zhao* and Li Jianfu's *The Story of the Chalk Circle*. As *zaju* became stultified, a new vitality burst forth in *chuangi*, which developed around Hangzhou.

*Chuangi* were not as well structured as *zaju*. They were, in fact, composed without restraint on length; some were thirty or forty scenes long. And unlike *zaju*, *chuangi* used no fixed rhyme scheme; they also utilized a five- rather than a seven-note musical scale. A drum and wooden clapper dominated the *chuangi* orchestra along with a bronze flute and a three-stringed mandolin. Also, whereas *zaju* actors spoke *before* singing, *chuangi* actors sang and then spoke.

Southern dramatists did not produce any work comparable to *The Romance of the Western Chamber*. Kao Ming's *The Lute* was the most popular *chuangi*-style Yuan drama.

**Ming Theatre**   By the time of the Ming Dynasty (1368–1644), the Mongols had been driven out. The new court, wanting to encourage drama at the palace, clamped down on popular entertainments. Actors were frequently arrested for offending the emperor, scholars, and even Confucius. But in the sixteenth century a new blend of theatre arose that used both *zaju* and *chuangi* tunes. The entertainment was called *gunzhu*. Ultimately, the term *zaju* came to refer to short *gunzhu* and *chuangi* to longer ones. Within fifty years *gunzhu* was being performed throughout the country. The magical *gunzhu* plays had thirty-two, forty, forty-eight, or more acts. Each act had its own title so it could be performed as a shortened version of the whole.

Male roles came to be known as *sheng*; female, as *dan*. All roles were balanced, and more than one character could sing in each act. And any character could sing; *gunzhu* featured solos, duets, and choral numbers.

The plays, however, degenerated into displays of poetic skill, and *gunzhu* became an aristocratic, intellectual theatre, out of touch with the average Chinese theatregoer. By the end of the eighteenth century the *gunzhu* audience was a small clique, and *gunzhu* lost it popularity

to one of the many local theatrical genres that developed: *jing-xi*, which became China's classical theatre. Later, in the Manchu or Jing Dynasty (1644–1912), *jing-xi* was called Beijing opera because the theatre was at its finest form in Beijing.

As Yuan and Ming music was replaced by less melodious string music, and as *wu* (military) plays featuring acrobatic skill replaced the lyrical Ming plots, popular audiences returned to the theatres. New troupes combined various styles of music—flute, fiddle, guitar, clapper—into a new form of entertainment featuring *lao sheng* (old men) rather than *dan* (women). Taking plots from popular novels, *jing-xi* playwrights put favorite episodes on stage.

**Revolution and the Drama**   A revolution in 1911–1912 ended the Jing Dynasty. The imperial examinations had been abolished in 1905, and in 1912 China declared itself a Republic. Western-educated Chinese played an important role in turning China away from its past. They wanted an end to the Confucian-based family and society. Students staged the French playwright Alexandre Dumas *fils's* (1824–1895) *Lady of the Camellias* and American Harriet Beecher Stowe's (1811–1896) *Uncle Tom's Cabin*, plays considered clear weapons for literary and social change. During the Communist Cultural Revolution of 1966 to 1967 within the People's Repulic of China, the traditional Beijing opera was completely wiped out. The Communist government attempted to substitute the party for the family as the basic unit of Chinese society. Loyalty to emperor was replaced by loyalty to party leader. Nevertheless, the new government continued to stress the importance of education, and the theatre served educational purposes. A new revolutionary Beijing opera combined Western and Eastern theatre techniques in contemporary, politically relevant plays with clear propagandistic intent.

Throughout its history the theatre in China served as an important way to celebrate special occasions. Performances occurred as part of community festivals, official banquets, family

*A Chinese theatre, c. 1846.*   (New York Public Library Theatre Collection)

celebrations, harvests, and guild feasts. Private homes featured theatrical performances. Restaurants and banquet halls used the theatre as a special treat for a wedding or anniversary party. Actors served wine as guests surveyed menus offering a choice of play as well as of food. The function of the actor in Chinese theatre evolved with the drama.

***Players***   Like all actors of the classical stage, those of China never reached a high station in society. Even before Emperor Minghuang established a drama school to train recruits for his imperial harem, immorality and prostitution were associated with the acting profession. Actresses frequently doubled as prostitutes. So extensive did the doubling become that the Yuan Emperor Jyan Long (1735–1796) banned women from the stage, thereby precipitating the introduction of female impersonation in China. Boys trained to play females were often catamites—that is, they often engaged in sexual relations with men. Boys who ran away from home or were sold to theatrical troupes began training at age 7. Actors remained classed with prostitutes, bar-

bers, and bath attendants. Even descendants were barred from respectable professions until the third generation. Nevertheless, star performers exploited their charisma to set the fashions and styles of the day.

When a professional company organized in the Sung Dynasty, the five to seven members were often members of the same family so that the women players would not cause too great a scandal. Often a company named itself after its leading actress. The leading actor managed the company and hired versatile players to act roles regardless of sex. The manager adapted and devised scripts from a repertoire of well-loved plays and stories. If not performing at noble banquets and weddings, the company was rented to friends. Independent companies were private enterprises; actors invested in their own costumes and properties. After giving two or three performances at one place, the independent troupe moved on. In time, popular troupes could play a whole season in a single city; less favored troupes had to tour. Success allowed the hiring of a business manager to arrange the season, plan individual programs, and hire a company of actors.

*Acting in the Beijing Opera* The Beijing opera's unique style synthesized music, speech, and formalized movement through an elaborate system of commonly recognized acting conventions. Consequently, Chinese playing resembled that of Greece, Rome, and India. Actors had to be acrobats, singers, and dancers who not only observed the strict discipline of each skill but also sought to add their own special charm to their roles. Performance emphasized the rigid conventions of the stage over the text. Each entrance revealed the character's nature with word, song, movement, costume, and make-up.

Etiquette played as important a part on the Chinese stage as it did in everyday life. Each character type, like each person in Confucian society, existed within rigidly proscribed manners. The players were "on stage" only when center stage; elsewhere they could spit, blow their nose, drink tea, and adjust their costume. All entrances came from stage left; all exits went off stage right. Vanquished foes exited before the victors. Throughout their careers actors specialized in playing one type of role. Fathers even taught young sons the intricacies of the hereditary parts.

*Beijing Opera Roles* Beijing opera featured four main roles dating from the early Yuan period: *sheng* the male, *dan* the female, *jing* the painted face, and *chou* the comic. All four character types had rigidly proscribed speech patterns, musical accompaniment, movement, costume, and make-up.

*Sheng* came in seven types and usually entered as unpainted-faced serious males, sometimes bearded. *Sheng* roles included the *wu* (military)—soldiers and warriors—and the *wen* (civilian)—scholars and students. *Wu sheng* were usually frightening and acrobatic. *Xiao sheng* (students) usually sang and danced as lovesick young men. *Lao sheng* were revered patriarchs or government politicians.

The six major *dan* roles were originally played by women, but from the eighteenth century to 1917 only men played them. The *hwa dan* (the "flower") was perhaps the greatest and most compelling type; she was the immoral, voluptuous concubine, the second wife, or the widow. Other *dan* included the virtuous wife or daughter, the comic shrew, the matriarch, and the female soldier. An actor playing a *dan* role sought to portray the symbol of feminine essence rather than reproduce female behavior. The *dan* interpreted feminine behavior. To make the audience see the illusion of a woman behaving on stage, the actor appeared more feminine than women really were and abstracted essential traits to convey the essence of womanhood. Mei Lan Feng (1894–1961) was the most famous *dan* player.

*Jing* stood out from the other roles because of the bizarre patterns painted on their faces to signify the generals, bandits, evil ministers, gods, judges, supernaturals, and demons known for their exaggerated might and swagger. *Jing* entered with one of three dominant characteristics: vigor, power, or wile.

The final type, the *chou* character, spoke in everyday dialect, joked at will, ad libbed from the text, and represented the most life-like character on the Chinese stage. *Chou* mimed and performed wondrous acrobatics as servant, jailer, sentinel, mother-in-law, matchmaker, soldier, merchant, woodcutter, waiter, priest, or general—each one stupid, foolish, and bawdy. The *chou* tried to get laughs to relieve the disgust and emotion building up in the audience.

*Music and Dance* Whereas Indian players were primarily dancers, Chinese players were primarily singers. If Sanskrit theatre resembled modern dance, then Beijing opera resembled Western musical comedy in the demands placed on the performers. Music, closely synchronizing every movement, word, and gesture, timed every action to aural symbols and expressions of character emotion. All movement was dance-like, rhythmical, mimetic, and symbolic.

Music played an important role in Chinese culture and theatre. Lao-Ze believed only music could promote absolute compliance with the unchangeable cosmic and social order necessary to subdue individual passion. Confucius thought that music improved a person's self-control; if a child did poorly in school Confucius advised letting the child dance and sing. Zhu Xi wrote that "correct music keeps the spirits in their fetters."

In the theatre, music created the emotional atmosphere, timed the physical movements, and accompanied some songs. Music was composed to accompany performance but new music was not composed for each play. Standard melodies were used over and over, attaining rich symbolic resonance in the process. From the time of *gunzhu*, nine styles of tunes interpreted the emotions. Disappointment was C major, a languid mood was $B^b$ major, freshness of spirit was $A^b$ major, recklessness was $E^b$ major, sorrow was $G^b$ major, robustness and calamity were $E^b$ Dorian, loneliness was $A^b$ Dorian, humor was $B^b$ Dorian, and sophistication was F Dorian.

Chinese music, which achieved harmony only when the musicians tuned their instruments, divided the octave into twelve semitones, but composers preferred to write music in a pentatonic scale similar to the Western F-G-A-C-D. Each note had a name: "Emperor," "Prime Minister," "Subject People," "State Affairs," and "Picture of the Universe."

The theatre orchestra, sitting on stage left, consisted of gongs, cymbals, drum, wooden clapper, lute-like instruments called *pipa*, and two stringed violin-like instruments. The instruments were divided into the *wen* section (strings and flute) and the *wu* section (percussion). Flute and strings were used for songs; percussion, for entrances and exits. All music was played from memory. The drummer led the eight musicians. Standard styles of music accompanied each kind of play, character, mood, situation, entrance, climax, exit, and interlude. All actors had their own string players.

Singing ability was an actor's most important asset. Chinese audiences appreciated correct pronunciation and strict adherence to rhythm. Speech and song were thus carefully timed to the players' movements. Singing was controlled by convention; each role had a proscribed vocal timbre, pitch, and rhythm. All females spoke in falsetto, except for old women who used their natural masculine voices.

The actors' codified gestures included seven basic hand movements, numerous arm movements, fourteen different ways to point at oneself, twelve special leg movements, and many sleeve and beard movements. Each role required a prescribed method of walking, running, and using the sleeve. For example, the basic hand position for a *dan* player was a circle made with the thumb and middle finger, with the fourth finger touching the middle of the third, and the fifth touching the middle of the fourth. Each foot movement conveyed information about desire, feeling, location, or time. Stylized gestures conveyed opening doors, climbing stairs, mounting horses, or entering boats. Chinese players' movements all exploited the elaborate costumes and showed off the facial make-up.

*Costume* Chinese costume, paying no heed to historical accuracy, mixed styles and periods both to create impressive dramatic effects and to specify subtle nuances of character. Symbolic colors and motifs, derived from traditional patterns, followed strict conventions for rank, status, and character personality. Over 300 costume items could describe a character: forty-six different headdresses, forty-seven dresses, five types of shoes, and six types of girdle were but a few. A *sheng* used five primary colors: red, green, yellow, white, and black; a *xiao* used five secondary colors: purple, blue, pink, turquoise, and dark crimson. Red costumed the loyal and high ranking, veiled a bride's head, and covered a corpse's face. Yellow clothed royalty and shielded the sick. Dark crimson bedecked the military and the barbarian; black, the poor, the fierce, and the simple; green the virtuous; and white the aged, the very young, and the mourning.

Motifs likewise denoted traits. A bat or butterfly meant long life and happiness; a phoenix, good luck and prosperity; a crane, longevity; a tiger, power; a plum blossom, wisdom and charm; a peony, spring and beauty; and a dragon, the emperor. A *yin and yang* pattern suggested the origin of life and metaphysical power. Derived perhaps from the Daoist shaman's use of flags when warring against evil demons, generals sported flags on their shoulders. The higher the general's rank, the more flags stuck out from his shoulders. Ghosts were recognized by the straw hanging from their ears. Strips of tinsel cascaded down the front and back of the lascivious *hwa dan*. *Jing* achieved stature with both high, thick-soled boots, like Hellenistic Greek *cothurni*, and shoulder padding. The higher one's rank, the higher the soles of one's boots. *Dan* "flowered" in toe boots whose bottoms resembled petite three-inch-long wooden shoes. The small shoes gave the actor both the requisite *dan* beauty and a characteristic walk. Good officials wore square hats; bad ones, round hats.

The emperor and civil officials wore round-collared robes that buttoned on the right side. Nobles appeared in long, loose, large-collared, knee-length garments that buttoned down the front. Merchants and farmers wore ankle-length kimonos with large collars. Women dressed according to rank, but all wore short garments over skirts. Sleeves, like the generals' flags, seemed to have Daoist origins. The *shui xiu* water sleeves were long, false, white silk sleeves, attached to a tunic's cuffs; they resembled rippling water when extended. The players moved their sleeves in the music's rhythm to give their action symbolic meaning and beauty. Headdresses capped rank, personality, and occasion. The emperor wore an elaborate hat featuring a yellow pompon; civil officials, soft hats that matched their gowns.

*Make-up* Like costume, make-up defined a character in a conventional and symbolic manner. Two hundred and fifty different designs denoted 250 different roles. The *sheng* used little make-up. If a scholar, a red line on the forehead displayed his beauty. If a *lao sheng*, he sported a beard. Only good characters wore mustaches; villains could not grow hair on their upper lips. The *dan* used a white flour base and red or pink triangular eyeshadow and rouge.

The *jing's* essence was his make-up. His bold symbolic patterns may have originated with the magic of the Daoist *wu* priest. The *jing* could be very brave or very evil; if very good, his oily make-up shined; if evil, his face was powdered and lustreless. Make-up did not follow the contours of the *jing's* face; it symbolized his nature. The more white on a *jing's* face, the more wicked he was. Red meant loyalty and black uprightness. If the mixture of lime, chalk, ink, and soot was green or blue, the *jing* was a demon or bully; if purple, an outlaw. A red beard meant fidelity; blue, fierceness; and white, treachery.

The *chou* had white patches around the eyes and on the nose. The amount of white determined the extent of the clown's cunning. Superstition predicted bad luck for an actor who did not let the *chou* make up first. Occasionally a *chou* drew awful black lines on his face to heighten the impact of his appearance on the stage.

*Performance Space* Permanent theatre buildings arrived late in China. Most performances happened in the open air and in private residences. Stages were also found beside Buddhist temples. Mat shed stages, made of bamboo poles, planking, and rush mat awnings, typified the early performance spaces, but they were temporary structures. The earliest stages were temple porches, red carpets in private gardens, and village threshing floors. Due to their wood construction, however, few early stages endured.

Most Sung Dynasty plays were written to be performed on booth stages at fairgrounds or *wazi* (amusement centers). The booth or mat stages, open to the audience on three sides, had low rails around them.

In the eighteenth century permanent theatres were built first in Beijing and then in Shanghai. Many urban theatres were called tea houses because they adjoined popular restaurants. Tables faced one another and the stage in rectangular buildings that had second-story galleries for wealthy patrons. When women were admitted, they were segregated to the back of the gallery. Theatre connoisseurs reserved benches close to the sides of the stage. Groups of fifty or more theatres clustered in a *wa* (amusement center).

The traditional Chinese stage, like those of Greece, Rome, and India, was bare. Rear doors on each side of the stage provided entrances and exits. The seventeen- to twenty-foot square stage was an open raised platform, three to four feet high, and covered by an ornate roof supported by round black lacquered columns. A two-foot high wooden railing fenced three sides of the carpeted stage. A curved apron extended well into the auditorium. The *zhougun*, a ten-foot high bar between the two downstage pillars, aided the actors' fighting and acrobatics.

*Convention in Staging*   The Chinese proverb "nothing is so vast as a stage" seemed to govern the aesthetics of the playing space. The

A plan of a typical classical Chinese theatre.   (Jack Chen, *The Chinese Theatre*, p. 12. Reprinted by permission.)

| | | |
|---|---|---|
| A Greenroom | D Exit | G Reserved seats |
| B Dressing-rooms | E Orchestra place | H 'Pit' seats |
| C Entrance | F Side seats | |

space prodded the audience's imagination without giving the audience all it wanted. And, more than the text, the actors' need to produce an exciting performance energized the stage space.

The Chinese stage was clearly artificial; no attempt was made to imitate or copy life. In this way it continued the tradition of the other classical theatres. Nonetheless, conventional symbols interpreted action and emotion: Pantomimic knocking at a gate located an exterior; opening an imaginary door changed the location; and climbing imaginary stairs suggested another level. To take a long journey, Chinese actors, like Roman and Indian actors, simply circled the stage. No unity of time or place was attempted.

E. T. Kirby suggests that the stage space owed its nature to the magic of the Daoist *wu* priests:

> The table is similar in form to the offerings table, sometimes called an altar, which is an essential part of all mediumistic ceremonies, and it clearly derives from it. The wall of the temple behind the offerings table is often like that of the theatre, with a doorway to the right and to left. In the theatre, these doorways are called "spirit doors."[19]

Scenic decoration was usually limited to a carpet, a wooden table, and two chairs placed before an elaborate satin embroidered curtain hanging between the two rear doors. A complex set of formal, symbolic gestures and objects filled the space with evocative images that suggested the spirit of an object rather than its physical appearance. A wall painted on blue cloth, for example, represented a fort, a gate, or a mountain pass. An actor carrying two yellow silk flags with wheels painted on them symbolically rode a rickshaw or chariot. A flag with green waves indicated the sea; an embroidered curtain, a bed; black silk streamers, wind or storm; black gauze over the head, a dream; and a whip, a horseback ride.

Stagehands remained on stage to move the table and chairs, distribute properties, and serve tea to the actors. They threw flakes of paper into the air to create a snowstorm, set up one scene while another was still playing, and flashed messages on blackboards to members of the audience. Their waving cloud-painted boards suggested the outdoors.

Properties served the same purpose as scenic pieces. The simple table and ordinary straight-back chairs could be arranged to suggest a throne, a bench, a tower, barriers, or various obstacles. A curtain suspended before two chairs created a bed. Back to back chairs formed a wall, and chairs with backs to the ends of a table suggested a bridge. Chairs also became trees, and tables became hills or clouds. Placing an incense burner on the table made a palace; paper and an official seal, an office; and a curtain hung from a bamboo pole, a general's tent. Pots, basins, cups, fly wisks, brooms, maps, swords, fans, and oars in actors' hands established place and circumstance. An oar wrapped in a garment made a corpse.

***Dramatic Texts*** The product of two or three centuries of cross-fertilization among Chinese theatrical forms, Beijing opera emerged as a universal entertainment in 1790 at the eightieth birthday celebration of Emperor Jian Long. As we discussed previously, Beijing drama owed its literary merit to Yuan and Ming dramas—to the Yuan *zaju* and *chuangi*, which blended to produce the Ming *gunzhu*, which in turn lost popularity to the emerging *jing-xi* or Beijing opera.

The chief difference between *gunzhu* and *jing-xi* was the musical accompaniment and the structure of the plays. Beijing opera featured strings, whereas *gunzhu* had been characterized by flutes. *Gunzhu* was also more literary in its conception. Beijing opera was more theatrical, and more actor centered; its overriding aim was to thrill the audience. (The names of *jing-xi* playwrights were not even listed on the program.) As a result, *gunzhu* texts could satisfy readers; Beijing opera could only please spectators. Unlike *zaju* and *chuangi*, Beijing opera texts were almost incoherent when read. Diction itself mixed dialects from around China; the *chou* usually had a colloquial Beijing dialect. Moreover, because Beijing opera stole plots from legends, history, novels, epics, contemporary newspapers, *zaju*, *chuangi*, and *gunzhu*, almost everyone in the audience already knew the story; they came to see a virtuoso performance.

*A private theatre on the grounds of a mansion in Beijing during the nineteenth century.* (New York Public Library at Lincoln Center)

The text itself was a series of short pieces interspersed with acrobatic displays, an opportunity for improvisation by the actors. Beijing opera was described as a ''musical tragedy with comic interludes.'' Emphasis lay on crisis and climax rather than on exposition and resolution. Plots were of two types: *wen* (civilian) and *wu* (military). In *wu* plays the clash of good and evil climaxed in the defeat of evil. In a *wen* drama characters were usually motivated by revenge: One character wronged another through deceit or abuse, and the second character suffered until a third character entered to resolve the misunderstanding or hurt. Virtue was clear, sorrow great. Good characters possessed all virtues; bad characters possessed all vices. The plays revealed extremes of both ideal and infamous behavior.

*Audience*   Ever since Confucius ordered the execution of an entire company of actors for performing a play not in accord with his moral teaching, the Chinese were a tough audience. Early in their training players thus learned to cater to an audience that retained the teahouse behavior of talking, eating, drinking, and coming and going at will. Performances began early and ended after midnight. Audiences—which represented all professions and all incomes—arrived late to catch only the star performer. (The star performed only after the audience had been warmed up.) All players, in fact, had to earn the right to attention. And when the audience appreciated a performer's work, its thunderous praise was as intense as its disinterested chitchat during the dull parts of the day's entertainment.

The theatre was a social event, and a casual atmosphere surrounded the theatrical experience. At first, performances were free, and only tea had a price. Attendants served the tea, replaced pumpkin seeds at tables, and provided hot towels for the audience to freshen up during the intermissionless performance. Musicians tuned up during scenes of dialogue. Children wandered across the stage and peered into the wings. Stagehands flashed messages to the audience from the stage. Members of the audience checked their programs to see who or what was coming on stage next. The actors rushed to the climax of a play, so that eyes and ears would focus on them.

The dramatic tradition born in India and spread by Indian Buddhist missionaries had taken on quite a new form. The tradition continued to spread across Asia to Japan, making the entire region ''the Indies'' to Western adventurers.

## JAPAN

For over 2000 years the Japanese and the Chinese have lived as neighbors. Yet despite common cultural roots, the people have developed psychologically diverse cultures. Their histories are marked by periods of attraction and repulsion, interdependence and autonomy. The Japanese theatre culminated the journey of the Indian dramatic aesthetic after lengthy transformation during its trek across Asia.

*The Mythological Basis of Drama*
Although the first account of Japanese theatrical activity does not appear until A.D. 712 in the *Records of Ancient Things*, the foundation for Japan's subsequent cultural development was laid in the Yayoi period (c. 303 B.C.–c. A.D. 300). In the Yamamoto period that followed, rulers invented a mythological past in response to Chinese legends that were filtering onto the island. One Japanese legend supplied a mythological origin for the Japanese theatre: Once, the sun goddess, Amaterasu o-mikami, offended by her brothers' playing around, hid herself in a cave to sulk. She sealed the cave with a rock. The world was plunged into darkness. The gods met to coax her out. Finally Amano-uzume-no did a striptease on a sounding board outside the cave. The gods laughed so hard at the dance that Amaterasu peeked out to see what was so funny. As she watched, she calmed down and returned to her place in the

sky. In this way, song and dance rid the world of darkness.

E. T. Kirby considers legend to be the source of Japanese shamanic dance theatre. And in *Japanese Theatre* Thomas Immos describes the legend, like the Japanese noh theatre itself, as a formalization of a basic impulse flourishing in early Japan.

*Religious Ritual and the Drama*   The forms of both the noh theatre and the kabuki theatre, Japan's two great classical dramatic theatres, derived from early court entertainments and religious rituals. In A.D. 782 the Imperial court disbanded its palace entertainers. Many found employment at Buddhist and Shinto temples and shrines, where they incorporated dramatic elements into the religious rites to teach the congregants. Gradually, as the rituals became more secular and theatrical, rivalries developed among temple troupes. Noh dramas emerged from these religious activities. Early noh performances, in fact, raised money to repair shrines and build new temples.

Shinto, "the way of the gods," revered the processes of nature. Similar to early Chinese Daoism, Shinto had neither dogma nor creed, just actions to unite gods, ancestral spirits, and people in one divine way of life. Originally, gods (*kami*) were believed to live in trees. Consequently, groves were sacred places for sacrificial acts, and the Japanese theatre honored the *kami* and their trees. Individuals needed to honor *kami* to protect themselves from *oni* (demons). *Kami* were thus honored by fertility rites, ancestor worship, ritual prayers, and seasonal festivals. Each honor sought to induce the *kami* to make contact with humans.

Early shrines were dwelling places of *kami*, and temples were built on or near the shrines. Dances at the temples reenacted the original manifestations of the gods. Dance and pantomime commemorated the gods' appearances and sought to induce additional revelations.

Rituals, like the theatre that evolved, inspired individuals' awe and gratitude at being alive in the mystery of nature. Shintoism appealed to the senses rather than to the mind. Because the processes of nature could not be evil, the pure of heart followed the ways of nature. Shrines, rituals, and eventually the theatre employed symbols of faith. A mirror represented purity; a sword, courage; and a necklace, charity. The creative power of life was revealed through a love for the pure, the simple, and the natural. Shintoism tended to mystify and simplify everything; rituals, festivals, and the theatre expressed gratitude for life and for community.

*Zen Buddhism and the Noh Theatre*
Tolerant of all religions, Shintoism posed little opposition to Buddhism when it was introduced to Japan by Prince Shotoku Taishi (573–621) in A.D. 552. The Prince, enchanted with the Chinese Buddhist religion, sent priests to study in China and invited Chinese teachers to Japan. (The journey of a priest to China and his return even became a favorite plot of noh drama.) As a result, Shintoism blended with Buddhism to produce *Ryobo-Shinto*, which served the public until the end of the seventeenth century. In 1868, however, an interest in Japanese native history and religion led to the disestablishment of Buddhism, the destruction of temples, and the elevation of Shinto to the position of state religion.

Meanwhile, Buddhism produced a profound change in society. To make its message more palatable, Buddhism retained the essentials of Shinto custom. Buddhism had, in its thousand years, developed philosophically in India and artistically in China. Shintoism gave Japanese Buddhism an appreciation of life and nature. In Japan, Buddhism did not mean disillusionment, as it had in India and China. Indians retreated into themselves and Chinese into their families; but the Japanese embraced the world and all its contradictions, joys, and sorrows.

One Buddhist sect in particular—*Zen*—caught on with the Japanese. *Zen*, the Japanese word for "meditation," was the Japanese pronunciation of the Chinese *zhan*. Through its Chinese counterpart, Zen Buddhism professed a direct experience of nirvana, which thus linked the Japanese to the practices of the Chinese Daoist priests. According to Zen philosophy, the traditional Japanese arts were the most effective way of conveying insight to the uninitiated and transcendental wisdom to the faithful. Landscape painting, gardening, the theatre, wrestling, swordsmanship, and the tea ceremony were prime instruments for instruction. Zen developed a close association with both the Japanese military and artist classes. In the twelfth and thirteenth centuries Zen contributed to a religious revival, especially among the military and artists. In fact, Zen later became the religion of artists. It inspired poets and painters of the fifteenth century to use its language to theorize about and criticize poetry and art.

Just as Chinese Buddhism merged with Daoist rituals, Japanese Buddhism merged with Shinto ceremonies. Zen welcomed Shinto values—simplicity, naturalness, love of beauty, lack of interest in doctrine. Buddhism took ideas and practices from both Shinto and Daoism to create a prayer for long life in a world of suffering.

In time Buddhist plays were danced in markets and temples. Gradually Buddhism infiltrated the early Japanese dance-dramas that had, like the religion, come from China. *Gigaku*, a dance-drama brought from India to China, came to Japan in 612 from Korea. When in India, *gigaku* was a dance to Buddha; in Japan, it was a religious entertainment. *Gigaku* had ten varieties, each accompanied by standard Sanskrit theatre instruments: flute, drum, and cymbal. *Gigaku* performers wore huge masks, which may have inspired the masks in the noh theatre.

*Kagura* ("god music"), the oldest surviving Japanese dance, was the chief feature of worship at Shinto shrine festivals. Performed by priestesses, the dance symbolized the reenactment of Amano-uzume-no's dance before the sun goddess. Until the eighteenth century, *kagura* had been performed at the Imperial court by dancers who were descendants of Amano-uzume-no. Later, *miko* (recruited girls) danced *kagura* at shrines.

In the seventh century *bugaku* arrived from China. Some scholars consider the *bugaku* dancers' angled entrance through the audience to be a source for the *hanamichi* entrance of the kabuki stage. Relying heavily on wind and percussion instruments, masked *bugaku* dancers balanced their movements to suggest the spiritual calm of an Indian Buddhist *mandala*.

The first of Japan's two classical theatres, the noh, derived its characteristics most directly from two native folk dances, the *dengaku* ("field music") and the *sarugaku* ("monkey music"). By the Heinan period (794–1129) the *dengaku* dance had six varieties, each appropriate to a different circumstance. A variety for the common people, for example, incorporated bits of vernacular dialogue, whereas a variety for the nobility used elevated diction. Both entertainments relied on comedy, farce, and country dance. Gradually *dengaku*, professionalized and formalized, became a regular feature at both spring rice-sowing and fall rice-reaping festivities. Crowds assembled to see *dengaku*'s combination of rustic humor, sacred Shinto dance, acrobatics, and juggling. By the mid-fourteenth century, *dengaku* had become an opera alternating dance and recitation.

At the end of the Kamakura period (1184–1335) a miscellaneous form of entertainment called *sarugaku*, perhaps imported from China during the Heinan period, began to be performed. This entertainment absorbed *dengaku*'s characteristics and developed star performers. Featuring occasional nudity, copulation, magic acts, acrobatics, juggling, animal shows, and playlets, *sarugaku* eventually surpassed *dengaku* in popularity. In *dengaku* speaking actors, seated in a row, arose only to dance silently. In *sarugaku*, on the other hand, actors sang and danced simultaneously. In addition, a chorus sang for the actors during strenuous parts of the *sarugaku* dance. By the thirteenth century guilds controlled the *sarugaku* players.

During the fourteenth century a temple prayer-dance known as *ennen-no* found its way into the *dengaku* and *sarugaku*. As a result, new forms of dance-dramas, seeking to prolong the lives of important people, appeared. The new forms, called *dengaku-no* and *sarugaku-no*, were the ancestor of the "no"/"noh" theatre. "Noh," in fact, first referred to *dengaku-no* and *ennen-no* plays stripped of their crudity and humor. But *sarugaku-no* eclipsed the others and became known simply as "no"/"noh" drama. Unlike the other two forms, the noh of the *sarugaku* lineage left a large body of literature. (We discuss the most famous plays, by Zeami, later in this chapter.) But not until 1374, when a noble ruler, Yoshimitsu, recognized the value of the dramatic theatre, did the noh become the first classical theatre of Japan.

*Political Patronage of the Drama*   Japan was settled by a prehistoric race, the Ainu, and immigrants from surrounding areas. Various clans vied for power until a clan in Yamato emerged to dominate an Imperial line. The first emperor (660 B.C.), believing himself to be a descendant of the gods, demanded formal respect from the other clans. In 794 the movement of the Japanese capitol from Nara to Kyoto ushered in a golden age of lavish courts, luxury, and extravagance for the nobility but insolvency and crime for the poor. Each clan maintained a private army of *samurai* to fight for the right to name the next emperor.

In 1192 the emperor surrendered his secular power to the most powerful general, the *shogun*. The shogun, ruling a feudal system of serfdoms, located his government in Kamakura, near Edo. But the Hojo family supplanted the shogun and presided over the flourishing Zen sect of Buddhism. During their reign, the noh theatre lost its rustic qualities and became a sophisticated drama favored by the samurai.

The emperor tried to regain his secular authority but failed. The Ashikaga family ruled from 1392 to 1603, after moving the capitol back to Kyoto. During the Ashikaga rule, northern and southern provinces fought civil wars. For samurai facing death, the noh provided the spiritual solace of Buddhism, a relief from temporal reality, and the reassurance of ultimate salvation. Many noh dramas of the period present the resurrections of dead samurai who ask for prayers for the living.

Great patrons of the arts, the Ashikaga family brought the noh to perfection. Yoshimitsu (1358–1408), the third Ashikaga shogun, renewed formal contacts with China. In 1374 he

fell for a young noh actor named Zeami Motokiyo (1363-1444), the son of Kannami Kiyotsugu (1333-1384), the Thespis or Livius Andronicus of the Japanese theatre. Father and son were invited to live at court as high officials; there, they perfected the noh. Zeami summarized noh's aesthetic goals, standards, and practices in his booklets. He rejected the light and comic elements favored by Kannami. Both father and son, minor Buddhist priests, let Buddhist philosophy permeate their writing and influence dramatic content.

When Kannami died, Zeami continued to refine the noh, seeking quietude, refinement, and understatement. At the court Zeami wrote *Kadensho* (*The Book of Handing on the Flowers*) in 1402 as a manual for his son. But because his son died, and Zeami had no successor, *Kadensho* remained lost until 1908.

Zeami completely controlled the noh until 1427, the end of the Oei era. But Yoshimitsu, Zeami's original patron, abdicated in 1394 to become a Buddhist priest, and Zeami's favor declined during the next reign. His nephew, Motoshiga, replaced him in 1429 as noh master. Zeami was exiled and confined to the island of Sado until the shogun Yoshinori was assassinated in his theatre.

*The Golden Age and a New Drama*   Until accepted by the court in the fourteenth century, noh was a rural, informal entertainment. But by the seventeenth century it appeared solemn and ritualized. Only the *kyogen* ("wild words"), secular, farcical interludes that parodied the noh programs, retained a semblance of human vitality. (We discuss *kyogen* at length later in the chapter.) Noh achieved its final form in the Tokugawa period.

Japan's Golden Age, the Genroku period (1688–1703), spanned the Tokugawa family's reign. Tokugawa politics were based on Confucianism, frugality, and artistic luxury. Confucianism, providing a common political and social ethic, strengthened civil administration. With the Emperor in Kyoto, the shogunate moved to Edo (Tokyo). A new palace flaunted the shogun's prosperity and sophistication; the peacetime samurai needed distraction. Restaurants, brothels, music, and theatre prospered. But anyone other than a noble or samurai who saw a noh performance was punished. The theatre was an aristocratic privilege.

Actors had finally won respectability, but the gain cost them their connection with the common people. In addition, while locked in the palace, the originally full-blooded noh grew artificial and museum-like. The classical theatre, like Japan itself, was isolated for the entire sixteenth and seventeenth centuries. Within the fortress nation, distinct local styles developed; within the noh, various schools emerged. Noh was for the Tokugawa shogun what *kagura* had been for the Emperor: a solemn, stately entertainment. Any mistake in performance could result in immediate exile or death. And the more solemn the noh became, the greater the desire for *kyogen*. In the seventeenth century, when *kyogen* texts were written down, they lost their characteristic improvisational quality.

**Kabuki and the Middle Class** Tokugawa Japan enjoyed a long period of unity and peace, a sense of national identity, and vigorous commerce. All conditions created an economic stability like that in Greece, Rome, India, and China during the periods of their great classical theatres. With the new merchant class rose a new dramatic theatre, beneath the contempt of both nobles and samurai. The new theatre was known as *kabuki*, a common word of the time that meant an unconventional custom or behavior. Because the theatre was like a brothel, and the actors were like prostitutes, and because kabuki arose to replace the theatre forbidden to the common people, it faced opposition and harassment. Its rise followed the rise of the *chonin* (townspeople) who, because of the change from rice to money as the principal means of exchange, achieved greater power than the samurai. Thus, when Japan changed from an agricultural economy to a money economy, it also changed from noh theatre to kabuki theatre. The Genroku era, during Tokugawa Japan, produced *Genroku kabuki*, featuring the art of the dramatist. The kabuki authors usually borrowed scenes from the *bunraku*, the popular doll theatre. All plays were forced to disguise contemporary references in remote settings and historical characters.

Meanwhile, to soften the war-like samurai, the shogun sent them to flamboyant Edo, the home of the new theatre. To the dismay of the government, the samurai became hooked on kabuki. To protect the shogunate's army from kabuki corruption, the theatre areas were licensed. All plays in the "gay quarters" were subjected to strict political censorship.

Kabuki supposedly originated with Oku-

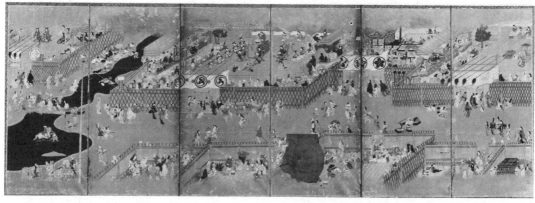

*An Onna kabuki performance in a dry river bed at Kyoto, Japan.* (Museum of Fine Arts, Boston)

ni's kabuki dance at the Grand Shrine of Ozumo in the second half of the sixteenth century. In a dried bed of Kyoto's Kamo River, Okuni, a ceremonial temple dancer, performed an erotic variation on the Buddhist ceremonial dance, *Nembutsu Odori*. Okuni represented characters from noh and *kyogen* plays, and her performances became popular. Okuni's lusty theatre was unlike anything the Japanese had experienced since the *sarugaku*. Playlets from famous stories and historical events filled the program. Kabuki ended with a *so-odori* (general dance) for actors and audience. Okuni died in 1610 but two women assumed her name; kabuki continued as *onna kabuki* (women's kabuki).

The group eventually became known as the pleasure women's kabuki, even though men performed as well. But the entertainment featured women both during and after the performance. Actors' solicitations led to the banishment of women from the stage in 1629. As a result, the young men's kabuki took over and employed catamites (young boys who engage in sexual relations with men) in the female roles. The catamites had lived with and served the samurai, but peace had put them out of work. In time the kabuki featured "humorous" aspects of sodomy. In *The Mirror of Art*, Tominaga Heibei (c. 1652) described the goal of theatre as displaying beautiful boys for customers.

The government tried to stop kabuki. In 1642 all players of women's roles were outlawed, but the ban was eventually rescinded. In 1648 homosexuality was made illegal in an attempt to halt the brawls of samurai fighting over young boys in the theatres. Finally, in 1652, after the death of Iemitsu, the third Tokugawa shogun and a great fan of the kabuki, the young men's kabuki was banned and all actors were ordered to shave their distinguishing forelocks.

But the kabuki returned as the men's kabuki, in which older men assumed falsetto voices and wigs. The men's kabuki was forced to develop impersonation skills rather than simply rely on the exploitation of pretty bodies.

Thus, the art of the *onnagata* (female impersonator) developed.

***The End of Isolationism***  The kabuki capitalized on Japan's growing interest in native religion and ancient history. To increase a sense of nationalism, the shogun had encouraged an interest in Shintoism but neglected to consider the historical position of the emperor, a descendant of the sun god. Gradually, some came to see the emperor not only as the spiritual leader of Japan but also as the rightful political leader.

In 1853 the United States entered Japanese territory, breaking centuries of isolation, to demand trade relations. Then, in 1867, the British demanded to negotiate trading rights with the emperor rather than with the shogun. The shogun resigned, and the 15-year-old emperor became the legitimate ruler of Japan. With the end of the shogunate, government support of the noh ended. The classical theatre of Japan was forced to hide; the noh was considered an arm of the hated shogun. Meanwhile, the kabuki, free from governmental restrictions, flourished.

Mitsuhito ruled Japan under the Meiji regime and oversaw the transformation of Japan from a feudal state to a modern industrial power. The visiting Duke of Edinburgh thought kabuki crude, but in in 1879 United States President U. S. Grant liked it. The emperor and empress enjoyed both noh and kabuki, and in time both theatres were considered to be national treasures worthy of government subsidy and patronage. The noh and the kabuki theatres, in fact, depended on such government support to withstand the barrage of Western entertainment pouring into Japan.

***Society on the Stage***  Throughout their history the noh and kabuki theatres reflected the social behavior of Japan. Japan respected hereditary systems in the Empire, the family, and the theatrical arts. Like the Chinese, the Japanese held *koko* (filial piety) as more important than duty to oneself. Similarly, the Japanese followed their duty to their lord and to their class. *Bushido*, the samurai's code of ethics, was based on Confucian principles. The Japanese court, in fact, loved things Chinese until the end of the sixteenth century. But by then the Confucian social order had been thoroughly made a Japanese reality.

Unlike China, however, where scholars ruled, in Japan the samurai warriors were placed on top of the social order. Just under the emperor and shogun stood the head samurai. The Buddhist revival in the twelfth and thirteenth centuries made Zen priests equal to the samurai.

At the top of Japanese society, then, was the samurai-administrator. Next came the farmer, the artisan, and the merchant. Because they made nothing, merchants were esteemed less than farmers or artisans. Most people were irreligious, sensuous, and spontaneous. The bottom of the social order—courtesans, geishas, and actors—lived off the rest. This stratification lasted 300 years.

At the center of Japanese life was the family. Women, considered inferior, played no part in public affairs. Marriage was, as in China, India, Greece, and Republican Rome, an arranged matter. Female adultery resulted in death; divorce was unknown. Romantic love found expression with a courtesan, a woman of physical charm, artistic talent, and cultivated manners. Rigid class rules of decorum guided all behavior, language, and dress. Cruelty to peasants, workers, and women were commonplace. The samurai sword was the law.

Peace let merchants rise in influence. Untaxed, middle-class merchants prospered with inflation while tax-paying samurai suffered. Rice commodities' futures made merchants millionaires and feudal lords paupers. Osaka became the manufacturing center, Edo the consuming center. The growing middle class, accumulating great power, gave no thought to social revolution. It preferred to release its emotions in theatrical art. At the kabuki theatre middle-class citizens were equal to the samurai, who depended on the kindness of their creditors.

*The Development of an Aesthetic*   Japanese theatrical art and literature were not very sophisticated before they were influenced by the Chinese. Gradually, Japan molded Chinese culture to its own taste. Suggestion was a basic artistic principle. The basic impulse of Japanese art, a love of nature, produced gardens, flower arrangements, and dwarf trees. The Japanese, who admired converting life into beauty, perfected paper folding, calligraphy, tea service, combat, and theatre. To make nature into a dramatic art, the Japanese rearranged and controlled it. As the playwright Chikamatsu wrote:

> When all parts of the art are controlled by restraint, the effect is moving, and thus the stronger and firmer the melody and words are, the sadder will be the impression created.[20]

Like Zen teachings, Japanese dramatic art sought to represent large entities through small details. The theatre artist suggested the whole world with one sharp image. The dramatic poem had to be completed by the reader, the stage setting's few strokes by the viewer, the theatre's sharp lines and bold colors by the audience. Japanese dramatic art contained the spiritual element of sacrifice. The proverb ''Never take up a brush until you are ready to sacrifice not only your fame but even your life for the sake of the forthcoming work'' explained Japanese actors' long waits in their dressing rooms until they were ''ready.'' Japanese artists performed and created in order to give life: ''Know that there is life or death, even in a stroke or dot, and it is your brush that has this mighty power to kill or to give life.''

The structure and order that encompassed Japanese art derived from Chinese philosophy. Through careful control and judgment Japanese theatre artists set the stage for fortuitous and unexpected marvels. Only within a disciplined technique could accident have beauty; chance could not be taught. *Li* (''organic pattern'') was a multidimensional, subtle relationship among a work's parts. Zen art, the noh theatre, framed the universe in microcosm: The relationship among the items in the stage frame had the same relationship as the items in the universe. To the Japanese artist, the process of creating theatrical art was the goal. The point in music and dance was each moment rather than the end of the performance. Meaning existed not after the theatrical event, but within each small moment of the performance.

**Two Distinct Performance Traditions**  As is evident from previous discussions, the classical theatre in Japan consisted of both the noh tradition and the kabuki tradition of performance. Peter Arnott outlines the basic differences between the two theatres:

> *Noh* is austere, *kabuki* flamboyant; *noh* ritual, *kabuki* spectacle; *noh* offers spiritual consolation, *kabuki* physical excitement; *noh* seeks chaste models; *kabuki* delights in the eccentric, the extravagant and the willfully perverse; *noh* is gentle, *kabuki* cruel; *noh* is concerned with the hereafter, *kabuki* bound by the here-and-now.[21]

The texts of the Japanese classical theatre clearly reveal the cultural contexts that shaped the composition of the audiences and performances. Noh texts, structuring the actions of a Zen Buddhist theatre, emphasized allusion and an overriding desire to escape time and place. A noh play sought to prolong the essence of a fleeting moment's mood. The kabuki, too, sought to hold the moment, but the text structured the experience in a way more palpable to a mass audience.

Noh began as popular entertainment but became the possession of an elite audience. Kabuki arose to satisfy the needs of a popular audience deprived of meaningful theatrical experience. The noh audience was wealthy and educated samurai. The kabuki audience was the newly rich merchant class. Noh actors disappeared into their costumes and masks. Kabuki actors were always visible behind the paint and beneath the costumes. Also, noh actors were given samurai status by their audience, the government. Kabuki actors were considered stars by their audience, but social misfits by the government.

We discuss these various differences in detail, beginning with the actors.

**Noh Players and "Flowering"**  The noh players were men and boys who trained from the age of 7. Until the age of 12, student actors danced and recited without criticism or praise. At 12 instruction began in the various roles. Although the greatness of noh actors was not seen until they were 35, after 45 they played less assertive roles. The actors' patron saint, Inari, the former Uzume, had a shrine in every theatre. Since Zeami, noh actors enjoyed high status:

> . . . if the players are too engrossed in practical matters, and think only of money, that will become the ruin of [noh]. Actually a *shite* can get much more income by honesty and thinking only of his art, and the result of aiming at nothing but wealth will be the corruption of [noh].[22]

Twenty-one authentic noh works still exist. The earliest, *Kadensho* by Zeami, explained the artist's role:

> The seed of the flower that blossoms out in all works of art lies in the artist's soul. Just as the transparent crystal produces fire and water, or a colorless cherry tree bears blossoms and fruit, a superb artist creates a moving work of art out of a landscape within his soul. It is such a person that can be called a vessel. Works of art are many and various, some singing of the moon and the breeze on the occasion of a festival, others admiring the blossoms and the birds at an outdoor excursion. The universe is a vessel containing all things—flowers and leaves, the snow and the moon, mountains and seas, trees and grass, the animate and the inanimate—according to the season of the year. Make numerous things the material of your art, let your soul be the vessel of the universe, and set it in the spacious, tranquil way of the void. You will then be able to attain the ultimate of art, the Mysterious Flower.[23]

To "flower," or present the mysteries of the

cosmos, noh actors indicated various visual and auditory symbols with their bodies and voices. Zeami passed along the secret means of accomplishing the feat. Two arts were involved—music and dance—and three forms—*monomane, yugen,* and *hana.*

Zeami defined *monomane* as:

> a thorough personification of a being that one is endeavoring to portray . . . . In actual practice, however, it is essential to draw a line between an object which should be copied as minutely as possible and one the imitation of which should be confined to its general aspects . . . . Here it is the spirit that counts. A mere external *imitation* of an object would make the result "masterless" while by "feeling it with heart and soul to make it one's own," we would have the outcome mastered.[24]

*Monomane* thus suggested imitation of the essence of an individual. The actors so identified with their roles that they no longer felt they were merely imitating an old man, warrior, or woman, for example. They sought, rather, a balance between portraying a particular individual and communicating the universal essence of that person.

*Monomane,* then, was the mastery of the symbolic essence of a role. *Yugen,* symbolized by a white bird with a flower in its beak, was what lay beneath the surface symbol. Originally a poetic term used first by the poet Shunzei (1114–1204), *yugen* became synonymous with elegance and gracefulness rather than with its original meaning of lonesomeness. It captured quietude, elegance, and restrained beauty. *Monomane* "is an attitude in representation, which provides the basis for movements, while *yugen* is an adorning technique to bring them to perfection."[25] Toyoichiro Nogami compares *monomane* to the composition of a painting and *yugen* to its coloring: "No painting is worth our note, if it is not solid in composition, no matter how rich it is in color, or if it fails to command the full attention of the people, if it is poor in color effect, however clever it might be in design."[26]

*Hana,* symbolized by flowers, is the spontaneous adaptation of a particular performance for each particular audience. *Hana,* like "flowering," aroused the interest of an audience. Whereas *monomane* and *yugen* were regular and consistent, *hana* changed. The flower, as Zeami writes, was the perfect symbol for this phenomenon:

> . . . you must understand the reason why they have used the symbol of flowers for *hana.* As every kind of plant and flower blooms at its proper time in the four seasons, people think it is beautiful because they feel it is blooming as something fresh and rare. In the art of No the point at which the audience feels this freshness and rarity will be the interesting part to them. So the "hana" the "interesting part" and the "rarity" are one and the same thing. No flower can remain in bloom forever. It gives pleasure to the eye because its bloom has been so long awaited. In the art of No it is the same, and a *shite* must know first of all that *hana* is a thing which is constantly changing. To change its style, not always keeping to the same one, will make the audience more interested.[27]

An actor bewitched the audience by giving it "the feeling of strangeness":

> By strangeness, therefore is meant merely the change of the occasion to apply a set technique, or the adjustment of emphasis according to the conditions of audience. An actor should be ever attentive to the state of audience. If they are strained and eagerly anticipating, they should be lightly entertained; if their attention is wandering, they should be taken by surprise, baffled of their expectations, and kept in constant suspense, so that they would never be bored, nay, even be excited. They would then be overwhelmed.[28]

*Monomane, yugen,* and *hana* did not tell a story but evoked emotions and moods. Every movement and intonation followed a specific rule. Each episode lingered and sustained a feeling. Symbolic, quintessential actions worked by implication: A simple step became a journey, a lying kimono presented an ill person, a stab at a hat completed a revenge, a downward glance presented tears, a lifted hand produced weeping. Action was slow and deliberate. Each step and gesture, carefully measured, sought economy of movement and complete restraint. Noh actors understated the symbolism of their actions.

A great noh actor did not depend upon innate talent, study, or success; a great actor "knows the nature of things, has broad learning and the qualities of a master, looks after his sons and grandsons, and trains his pupils well."[29] Great actors work not only on their art, but also on themselves:

> To lead a virtuous
> Life, to keep the self upright
> To dissolve the soul
> And to pursue the nature of things—
> These make up the basis of our art.[30]

Off-stage behavior, following rigid guidelines, regulated eating, drinking, quarreling, talking, and laughing. When in the theatre humor was out of place. The Buddhist view of life permeated Zeami's view of comedy: "To be delightful is better than to be funny. To be superb and moving is even better . . . . All the arts repudiate an attempt to amuse."[31]

Following Zeami's injunction, "Let your soul be a mirror which reflects all the laws of the universe," noh actors played two main roles: the *shite* (doer) and the *waki* (assistant). Each role had its own techniques. The *shite* always appeared masked; the *waki*, bare or painted faced. The *waki* questioned the *shite* to provoke the main action. Young boys played the *waki* so as not to overpower the adult *shite*. In the Ashikaga reign, when homosexuality was prevalent, men enjoyed seeing young boys play reserved and graceful *waki* roles. The *shite*, the leading actor, skilled in song and dance, often spoke in the third-person voice about himself or the young *waki*. A third character, the *tsure* (adjunct), assisted the two principal actors by playing subordinate roles. A chorus of ten to twelve men recited the *shite's* lines when he danced. But unlike the Greek chorus, this noh chorus had no identity and did not comment on the action. In a *kyogen* play, a narrator told the play's action.

***Noh Music and Dance*** Noh, like all classical theatres, evolved from dance. Every element of each production highlighted and commented on the dancers, the center of the performance. Noh music achieved form under Zeami's father, Kannami, who introduced the rhythmical intonation of speech sounds to music. This made noh movement's relationship to music more complicated, varied, and expressive.

Drums and flutes, shamanistic instruments used to call the gods, dominated noh music. The flute and the three drums were played by four musicians, who sometimes cried out during a performance. The *ji* (chorus of six to eight singers) recited parts not assigned to others and spoke the voice of the *shite*. The *ji* narrated the opening scene and commented, in a question-and-answer format, on the action. The *ji* took no part in the action other than to chant an accompaniment to the dominant dance.

Noh dance, not miming action but evoking an action's ultimate meaning, followed familiar movement patterns. Each gesture held several symbolic *kata* (forms), of which noh had 300 for dance. But movement never illustrated the words; movement commented on the words. For example, in god plays, which used seven *kata*, characters performed their own type of dance in three to five sequences.

***Noh Costume and Mask*** Noh costumes, which added stature and grandeur to the players, preserved centuries-old official dress. Some noh masks were even considered national treasures. Costumes were brilliantly variegated in color and featured luxurious embroidery and silver and gold brocade. Actors chose their masks and costumes to interpret their roles. They chose costumes, for example, for their silhouettes, and they chose colors and masks for their abilities to lead the audience into another realm. The *shite* wore the brightest colors and most impressive mask; the maskless *waki* wore less vivid colors. The *waki*, if a member of the clergy, often wore black priestly robes. Even more subdued costumes bedecked the musicians and *kyogen* characters. Simple uniforms covered the chorus and stage assistants. The players also wore *tabi* (bifurcated or two-sectioned socks) that were white if formal.

As for Greek, Indian, and Chinese actors, for the Japanese, the noh mask was an object for meditation prior to performance because it was not a mirror of the human face; it was a mirror of reality. Thus, before actors entered the stage they gazed at their masked faces in a mirror until they became reflections of the masks. Young actors were admonished for simply putting their masks on their faces; they had to let their faces be pulled into and cling to the masks.

Noh masks also connected the actors to the gods and nature. Because they embodied the forces that visited the earth at pivotal times of the year, masks were the means through which those forces incarnated themselves. Once on earth, the forces lived in the masks. From the masks, the spirits moved into the masks' wearers. But the masks did not conceal: They revealed these forces in human shape, and they reconciled all human contradictions—male with female, old with young, human with divine, living with dead, past with present. They brought the oneness of the universe to the here-and-now.

*Noh Playing Area*    Originally, noh performances were played on special stands and stages erected in dry river beds. Two ramps led from the dressing area to the temporary stage. Most of the audience sat on three sides of the stage in a 100-foot diameter area; nobles built raised boxes from which to watch the performance. When the aristocracy adopted the noh, playing spaces were erected within palaces, and noh troupes moved indoors. The noh performance area thus became a house and garden within a house and garden. Even the width of gravel separating the stage from the audience was retained.

A separate peaked roof, in the form of a Shinto temple roof, covered the indoor noh stage. The *hashigakari* (a side raised ramp) provided the main entrance and exit to the *butai* (stage). Four fifteen-foot high, square columns supported the roof. Each pillar was named for

a stage function. Actors entered the *hashigakari* and stood before the nearest pillar to announce their names and functions in the play. The actors next moved to the appropriate column: The upstage right pillar, near the *hashigakari*, was the *shite's* pillar. The *shite* stood there when not dancing. Upstage left was the flute player's pillar. Downstage left was the *waki's* pillar; when at the pillar the *waki* purposely upstaged himself to the dominant *shite*. Downstage stood the eye-fixing pillar, used by the *shite* to orient himself during his energetic dance. The orchestra sat at the rear of the stage on a platform for musicians and stage assistants. A low *kirido* ("hurry door") opened left of the platform.

Large jars were placed under the eighteen-foot square stage of seasoned polished wood to increase the resonance of voice, music, and dance, as Vitruvius had suggested to Rome. Seven jars were suspended under the *butai*, two under the platform, and three under the *hashigakari*. Each jar, suspended by copper wires, was set at a 45-degree angle to project the sound into the audience.

The beginning of the drama was signaled, as in the Greek theatre, by off-stage flute music. The musicians entered down the six-foot wide, thirty-three– to fifty-two–foot long raised *hashigakari*. Meanwhile, the eight- to ten-member male chorus entered from the three-foot high *kirido*. At the rear of the stage *koken* (assistants) sat in their black costumes.

The *waki* also came from the dressing room down the *hashigakari*. Three pine saplings served as markers for the actors' progress on the raised ramp. The pines may have represented heaven, earth, and humanity. A pine tree was painted on the rear wall of the *butai*, and a bamboo pattern was painted on the left wall. The painted pines replaced the natural panorama with an artificial one. The pine trees also suggested the legendary old man who, standing beneath a pine to watch a dance, turned out to be a god. The stage pines also allowed a god to descend into the actors, thereby making them the gods' reflections. Consequently, the pines functioned as the Indian *jaraja*—as a conductor between the supernatural world and the human stage.

## NOH STAGE

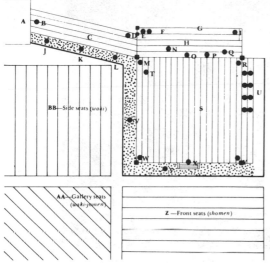

**A** —Green room or mirror room (*kagami-no-ma*)

**B** —Lift curtain (*agemaku*)

**C** —Bridgeway (*hashi gakari*)

**D** —Kyogen position (*kyogen-za*)

**E** —Stage assistant pillar (*koken bashira*)

**F** —Stage assistants position (*koken-za*)

**G** —Pine or mirror board (*kagami-ita*)

**H** —Far up stage area or rear stage (*ato-za*)

**I** —Low sliding door for exits (*kirido-guchi*)

**J** —Third pine (*san-no-matsu*)

**K** —Second pine (*ni-no-matsu*)

**L** —First pine (*ichi-no-matsu*)

**M** —*Shite* pillar (*shite-bashira*)

**N** —Stick drum position (*taiko-za*)

**O** —Large hand drum position (*otsuzumi-za*)

**P** —Small hand drum position (*kotsuzumi-za*)

**Q** —Flute position (*fue-za*)

**R** —Flute pillar (*fue-bashira*)

**S** —Main stage (*butai*)

**T** —Usual position (*jo-za*)

**U** —Chorus position (*jiutai-za*)

**V** —White pebbles (*shirasu*)

**W** —Sight guide pillar (*metsuke-bashira*)

**X** —Stair (*shirasu-hashigo*)

**Y** —*Waki* pillar (*waki-bashira*)

*A plan of a typical noh stage. (On Stage in Japan, p. 14. Reprinted by permission of Shufunotomo Co., Ltd. © 1974.)*

The trees and the stage also represented the legend of Amaterasu o-mikami and Amano uzume-no. After Amaterasu had hid in the cave, the gods brought a flowering sakaki tree, complete with roots. They decorated it with strings of gems cut in moon shapes, and tried to lure the goddess out. They fastened a large mirror in the middle branches of the tree. When Amano danced, her reflection could be seen in the mirror. Because she was possessed, the spirit's reflection was caught in the mirror in the tree. Thus, when Amaterasu peeked out of the cave she saw her own reflection, Amano's reflection, and the spirit's reflection all in the tree's mirror. The noh stage presented the mirror in the tree.

*Contemporary noh stage and auditorium in Tokyo.* (New York Public Library Picture Collection)

***Noh Conventions*** The aesthetics of noh stage decoration foliowed the mythological origin of the theatre. The stage did not represent the actual world of Japan any more than the stage of Greece presented Athens. Instead, the classical stages of the West and the traditional theatres of the East revealed the supernatural world. The spirit world was approached and entered by conventional representation, by hinting at the ideal, by allowing the audience's imagination to be led through visual and auditory suggestions of the ultimate reality. Consequently, little scenery was used. Properties and set pieces remained on stage only for as long as needed. But a fan accompanied almost every role. Opening a fan signaled a dance. Fans could also represent bottles, cups, or weapons. But properties were still not as important as the stage and the masks.

***The Noh Audience*** A noh performance placed great demands on the spectators. Zeami wrote that "the purpose of this art is to pacify and to give pleasure to the minds of the audience and to move them . . . ."[32] To find peace and intellectual satisfaction, the noh audience had to know intricate performance conventions. Like the Sanskrit theatre, the noh needed intelligent spectators for the magic to happen. The audience had to prepare itself so that actions could seem profound and conducive to entry into *nirvana.* Yet, as with the Japanese tea ceremony, a certain amount of boredom was also necessary for the eventual enjoyment of a noh performance. Such an idea seemed strange to Western audiences. But the classical theatre did not end with what an audience saw with its eyes. It drew the audience's imagination into the action so that meaning could arise through joint effort. The classical theatre, seeking to unify actors with characters, sought to unify performance with audience. Zeami advised his audience to forget the theatre and look at noh, to forget noh and look at the actors, and finally to forget the actors and look at the ideas. Only then could the noh theatre be understood. And audiences unable to understand the noh had the kabuki.

***Noh Dramaturgy*** Zeami's *Kadensho* was to

the Japanese what Bharata's *Natya Sastra* was to the Indian and Aristotle's *Poetics* was to Western classical drama. Like Aeschylus's creating Greek tragedy from the rhapsode's narrative, Zeami created noh from the narratives of *dengaku* and *sarugaku*. In *Kadensho*, one of Zeami's twenty-three treatises on drama, Zeami revealed the secrets of effective dramaturgy. A noh script was but a scenario for performance, a libretto for a musical dance-drama shorter than the average modern one-act play. Donald Keene defines a noh script as ''a dramatic poem concerned with remote or supernatural events, performed by a dancer, often masked, who shares with lesser personages and a chorus the singing and declamation of the poetry.''[33]

Each of the five types of noh play had two *ba* (scenes). In the first scene the *shite* entered; in the second scene, the *shite* danced. In every play a chorus sang the actors' lines as they danced. In a god play, the virtues of a god were praised; in a warrior play, the spirits of dead warriors recounted the tragedies of past battles. A play about a woman featured a graceful dance. A mad play showed the tragedy of a woman crazed by loss or injury. Other plays featured devils, demons, ghosts, or festivals.

A noh program consisted of one play from each of five categories performed in a proscribed order. Each play lasted between one and two hours, even though a long text was only ten pages in length.

*Noh Structure*    A noh play traced a journey. The *waki*, a traveler to a shrine or historical spot, met the *shite*, seemingly a local resident who later revealed himself to be someone important. Each play had three sections: the *jo* (the beginning), the *ha* (the middle), and the *kyu* (the end). As in the Greek and Roman dramas, most noh action was reported or seen indirectly in a vision or dream. But the play had no conflict. As the French playwright Paul Claudel (1868–1955) noted, in Western drama something happens; in noh, someone appears.

First, the *waki* entered, introduced himself, and moved to his pillar as the chorus sang a travel song. The *shite*, perhaps disguised, entered and answered the *waki's* questions. The *shite* then danced an interpretive dance symbolizing the recalled event. The *shite* then withdrew as the first part ended.

A comic *kyogen* interlude may have ensued. The drama then resumed with the noh's second scene. The play climaxed as the *shite* reappeared undisguised and danced the finale to resolve the plot. All then exited silently.

The theme of a noh drama usually concerned the afterlife, the sin of murder, the transience of life, the powers of Buddha, or the evil of lust. The plays featured an interplay between the secular and the religious to show the impossibility of separating the two spheres. Buddhist philosophy permeated the texts, which depicted human struggle amid the pain of the material world. Noh plays illustrated Zen doctrines: Zen taught that the phenomenal world was meaningless because it masked the inner truth. Noh action showed a *waki* meeting someone whose true, divine identity was masked by earthly phenomena. In this way noh created a conflict between appearance and reality. What an audience saw was not what it seemed to be: Appearance deceived.

Noh dramas were interwoven with imagery of nature. Each play had an appropriate season for performance and captured the essence of either a season or a time of day. The characters were memories, what remain when life has ended. Thus, when noh plays presented the afterlife, dead figures contemplated their past lives. From the vantage point of death, all was seen as flux and change. As Buddha taught, everything associated with life, even memories, brought pain. To be dead, to be beyond even memory, was to be at peace and rest.

Noh language alternated between verse and prose, singing and chanting. Filled with archaisms, obscure Buddhist references, Chinese derivations, and allusions to lost poems and songs, noh texts seemed almost incomprehensible. The poetry was usually written in alternating lines of seven and five syllables. Each episode of a scene consisted of passages with their own rhythms and linguistic characteristics. Some passages were divided into sections characterized by changes in pitch of recitation or rhythmical drum patterns. Noh diction followed Zen's suspicion of language. Language does not represent rational ideas because words always refer to something other than themselves. Words have no connection with the material world; they always point away from themselves. Consequently, words were used in the noh as echoes of things that once were. Noh employed words to magnify the faint echo, to bring an image back from memory, into physical incarnation upon the stage.

*Kyogen*   The strain of a long noh program was broken by secular interludes called *kyogen*. These short farces, which emphasized situation over character, parodied the noh plays on the program. Usually two *kyogen* accompanied five noh plays. Each *kyogen*, which lasted between ten and twenty-five minutes, featured a *daimyo* (Japanese lord) and his comic servant. Frequently, the servant outfoxed his master but got a beating in the end.

Okura Toraaki (1597–1662), a *kyogen* actor, wrote the following epigram: "The Noh transforms the unreal into the real; the comic interlude, the real into the unreal."[34] Whereas noh made the gods present and the transcendental concrete, *kyogen* made everyone more human than they were—more stupid, more laughable, and, therefore, more unreal.

The *kyogen* possibly derived from a poem by Po chu-i (772–846), which claims that Buddha's power can even transform a fool's mad words into a poem of praise:

> May the worldly writings of my present incarnation, all the wanton talk and fine phrases, be changed into a hymn of praise that shall glorify the doctrines of the Buddha in age on ages to come, and cause the wheel of Law forever to turn.[35]

Comedy also served a religious function. Sorrowful memories gave way to the foolishness of the present. Humans yielded to pain only to triumph against the demons. *Kyogen* provided the reverse side of the story, the human perspective, all the more foolish because of what the audience had just seen. One

hundred and fifty *kyogen* remain, two-thirds of which mock either Japanese lords or Buddhist priests.

*Kabuki Players*   Like all other classical actors, kabuki actors began as outcasts with no civil rights. By law, they wore distinguishing garments, avoided socializing with other classes, and married only into other actors' families. The government also made them live near the theatre. Despised by authorities, adored by the public, kabuki actors actually enjoyed a status similar to modern rock musicians: Like modern movie fans, kabuki patrons followed the actors' private lives. So popular, in fact, were kabuki actors, that one of the first books in which actors talked about acting, the *Yakusha Rongo*, was published late in the nineteenth century. The sentiments expressed in the *Yakusha Rongo* echoed those of Sakata Tojuro (1647–1709) years earlier: "If you wish to be praised, the best way to set about it is to forget the audience and to concentrate upon playing the play as if it was really happening,"[36] and "the actor's art is like a beggar's bag. Regardless of whether you need it at the time or not, you should pick up everything as you come across it and take it with you. . . . There must not be anything about which you are entirely ignorant."[37] Nonetheless, although many actors enjoyed luxurious lives, not until the Meiji Restoration (1867–1912) did they become legal members of society.

Kabuki actors got their name from the noh. Originally the name signified one who officiated at ceremonies or religious celebrations. Each kabuki company followed its manager. He cast the plays, managed the company, played the leading role, and avoided official censure. Ogyu Sorai (1666–1728), an advisor to the shogun, made the kind of objections a manager worked to overcome:

> People are easily influenced by the behavior of actors and prostitutes. Recently there has been a tendency for even high ranking people to use the argot of actors and prostitutes. This habit has become a kind of fashion, and people think that those who do not use such words and phrases are

*A kabuki theatre at the end of the Edo period.*    (New York Public Library Picture Collection)

rustics. I am ashamed that this is so. Such a tendency will result in the collapse of the social order. It is therefore necessary to segregate actors and prostitutes from ordinary society.[38]

Kabuki actors began training at age 5 and reached their prime at 40 years of age. Their craft was characterized by certain styles or patterns of acting known as *kata*. Each family troupe developed unique *kata*, which they handed down from generation to generation. A *kata* known as the *mie* was a static pose; a series of *mie* cumulatively defined a character in time and space. The effect of the *mie* was sculptural: It resembled figures in Buddhist sculpture whose essential quality was balanced tension. The rattle of the wooden clappers that accompanied each *mie* harkened back to the rattle of the serpent that provoked Shiva's original dance. Other *kata* included the swaggering walk, the stylized combat, the impressive entrances and exits, with sound effects, costume, and make-up.

In their dressing rooms, kabuki actors, like noh actors contemplating their faces and figures in a mirror, acquired their external appearances through the inner significance of their visual images. But kabuki actors, not seeking noh's identification with their roles, sought detachment instead. The actors never became their roles any more than painters became their paint or canvas. Audiences, as a result, valued the kabuki actors' technical skill rather than their ability to share the characters' emotional lives. Thus, like the Chinese theatre, the kabuki stressed virtuosity over literary merit. In fact, kabuki players consciously broke whatever illusion or spell the story wove. They might introduce their sons, present a new actor in the company, or answer a question from the audience in midscene or speech.

The basic performance styles and roles in the kabuki repertoire were historically based. The oldest was recognized as an unadorned, slow-motion pantomime, quite unlike the second style. Rough and bravura in action and word, the second style exaggerated every masculine quality. In contrast, another style emphasized femininity. A style derived from the puppet theatre made actors into puppets who performed to narration. The final style resembled abstract dance. Any acting style could appear from scene to scene, from act to act, or among actors in a single scene, depending on the roles the actors played.

Kabuki roles, like those of the noh, used characteristic music, dance, costume, and make-up. Kabuki actors, however, never sang. The noh chorus was replaced by the *joruri* (a solo chanter), who, seated in a niche on stage left, sang both as and about the character. New plays brought new roles and ended the specialization dominant in kabuki role playing.

Roles fell into types, as in the Indian and Chinese theatres. The three basic roles may have stemmed from the 1629 ban on women and the requirement that *onnagata* (female impersonators) register with civilian authorities. The *onnagata* category had three subdivisions: young girl, high-ranking courtesan, and woman from a samurai household. At first, certain families specialized in *onnagata*. Some actors even wore women's clothing off stage, lived as women, and entered public baths through the women's entrance. *The Words of Ayame*, written by an eighteenth-century playwright and catamite, revealed secret instructions for playing a female. Two of the most interesting rules were: "If he does not live his normal life as if he was a woman, it will not be possible for him to be called a skillful *onnagata*,"[39] and "When playing against an actor of little skill, the true artist's aim should be to make his companion's deficiencies appear as qualities."[40]

Two major male role types—good men and villains—were played by the other leading actors. Good men were subdivided into youths, soft, effeminate roles, and silent sufferer roles. Villains could be power-seekers, wicked nobles, or clerics. Comic roles and children's roles filled out the standard types.

**Kabuki Music and Dance** Kabuki music had three categories. The first, ceremonial music, marked the beginning and end of a performance. Ceremonial music featured drums and wooden clappers to add excitement both to scenes of violence and to tableau *mies*. The second, music to accompany special effects, was performed by men hidden in a black box on stage right. The principal instruments were the samisen, drums, and flutes. The third category was on-stage music played in full view of the audience.

The kabuki orchestra created symbolic sound effects for snow, rain, water, waves, wind, and ghostly appearances. The musicians were not fixed on the stage; sometimes up stage left and sometimes right, they always placed themselves in relationship to the dance, the basis of the kabuki.

Influenced by the noh, folk and popular dances, and the bunraku doll theatre, kabuki dance synthesized many diverse elements. Each part of a performance flowed into the next: A cry, beginning with a sound, became a word, faded to a musical phrase, culminated in a *kata*, and ebbed into a comment by the narrator.

Like Japanese haiku poetry, kabuki dance presented literal images, economically and rhythmically. Sometimes the dancers imitated the narration, sometimes other words. Each dance strove toward a *mie*: a series of abstract images of physical pose, elaborate costume, music, and painted face.

Schools of dance taught and licensed students. At first only female roles were danced. In time, as dance became more complex, the *furitsuke-shi* (choreographer) was added to each company. Kabuki valued the choreographer, in fact, much more than the playwright.

**Kabuki Costume and Make-up** Kabuki actors modified historical garments to create a traditional—but quite cumbersome—costume for each role. Court ladies, for example, wore twelve kimonos, and courtesans and supermen walked on stilts. The actors sometimes required stage assistants to help them move and change the fifty-pound costumes on stage. Because kabuki developed when the Japanese government was regulating dress, kabuki costumes followed the government regulations. Commoners, who could wear neither silk, red, purple, nor elaborate patterns, appeared in clothes that were dark gray, blue, or orange with some striping. Actors were forbidden to wear fabrics belonging to the noh; a kabuki actor could even be jailed for wearing too luxurious a costume. Theatre managers swore an oath to uphold these laws of dress.

To suggest changes in emotion, actors changed costume on stage. They were helped by stagehands, who wore black to avoid taking attention away from the major actors. The technique of *bukkaeri* involved a stagehand's pulling a thread that held the garment together at the shoulders; the costume thus fell to the actor's feet, revealing another costume. Another technique, *hiki-nuki*, involved an assistant's pulling several threads and grabbing the costume at the shoulders just as the actor stepped forward to reveal a new costume.

Unlike the noh's *shite*, kabuki actors wore no masks. Instead, boldly patterned make-up characterized roles symbolically. All make-up made the players' faces compromises between the human and the mask. A red line drawn from under the eye to the temples suggested bravery and beauty; indigo or black lines drawn under the eyes indicated wickedness. Red make-up usually denoted justice or strength, and blue denoted evil or the supernatural. Female married characters, like pre-1868 Japanese women, blackened their teeth and shaved their eyebrows.

***Kabuki Playing Area*** Kabuki performance spaces used conventions that combined the noh and nineteenth-century Western illusionism. The kabuki expanded and reoriented the noh stage. The original kabuki stage, modeled on the noh stage, featured a square, roofed platform with four pillars and a runway to backstage. As the runway grew longer it moved from the side to the front of the stage. Called the *hanamichi* (the flower way), this kabuki runway extended from the front of the stage to a dressing room at the rear of the auditorium. Some scholars claim that the *hanamichi* was the original route members of the audience took when giving presents to their favorite actors: They supposedly fastened gifts

to a flowering branch. Other scholars consider the ramp to be an extension of the three steps in front of the *bugaku* and noh stages. In the noh, the steps were used by the shogun to present new costumes to the players. Whatever its origins, the *hanamichi* was used as an extension of the stage, as an area related to the stage, and as an independent stage.

## KABUKI STAGE

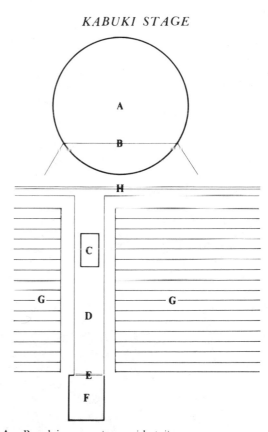

**A** —Revolving stage (*mawari-butai*)
**B** —Panel set (*kakiwari*)
**C** —Trap lift (*kiri-ana* or *suppon*)
**D** —Ramp (*hanamichi*)
**E** —Draw curtain at end of ramp (*hanamichi no age-maku*)
**F** —Room behind curtain (*toriya*)
**G** —Seating area (*kyakuseki*)
**H** —Draw curtain (*joshiki-maku*)

*A plan of a typical kabuki stage.   (On Stage in Japan)*

E. T. Kirby has called transformation the principle of kabuki staging. By the 1660s, transformation of scene and character was evident, and the kabuki stage had added some distinctive features. The *hanamichi* was wider than its noh ancestor, and a curtain revealed on-stage action. Elevator traps, elevator stages, and revolving stages arrived in the eighteenth century. By then, a revolving stage, a double revolving stage, and traps filled the stage area and runway. A rectangular hole in the center of the revolving stage was used to raise and lower scenery. The scenic background consisted of a row of flats nailed together, seams showing. The facade, stopping short of the wings, was clearly two dimensional, and thus underlined the three dimensionality of the actors. Depth was indicated rather than represented on the kabuki stage. In 1827 two concentric revolving stages were featured.

By 1830 the noh roof was abandoned, and the stage stretched the entire width of the auditorium. Other staging conventions developed as well: Stage left was the area for socially important scenes and high ranked characters; stage right was the area for minor scenes and lowly characters. Because characters aspired toward higher social positions all entrances came from stage right. In addition, females walked a pace behind the males. Men moved first with the left arm or leg, women with the right.

***Kabuki Conventions*** Kabuki decoration, like that in all classical stage spaces, emanated from the actors. The stage setting was a decorative background, obviously created to direct attention to and to stand behind the actors on stage. Nevertheless, the kabuki used sophisticated and complex machinery to satisfy the audience's love for gaudy decoration and spectacular revelation.

Platforms defined different spatial areas. Interiors were raised, as in the noh. Three heights defined social standing: One-foot, three-inch ordinary legs supported the platformed homes of ordinary citizens; two-foot, one-inch legs, the homes of samurai, and two-foot, nine-inch legs, palaces and temples. Scenic transformation was the highlight of a performance.

The kabuki floor was emphatically a stage floor. Revolving or revealing platforms, sliding doors, rolling blinds, pulling curtains, revolving stages, opening traps, and rolling wagons established a feeling that the actors rose from and descended back into the floor. The actors played in relationship to the floor rather than in relationship to the space above it. Unlike the Greeks, Eastern designers did not often

*Two* hanamichi *lead to this kabuki stage.* (New York Public Library Picture Collection)

*A revolving kabuki stage.*    (Martha Swope. © 1987)

attempt to have scenery or people fly: They accepted the earth. In other words, Eastern theatre did not show people's aspiring to godhood or positions above their earthly lot. Divinity existed on Earth, on the stage floor, whenever good people met at holy places.

Representation also had a place in kabuki theatre. White mats represented snow; blue mats, water; and gray mats, ground. A closed fan could transform into a whip, a dagger, or a pipe. Open, the fan became a bottle, a headdress, or a lantern. Half-open fans functioned as trays, paper, moons, or flags.

The *hanamichi* itself was divided into ten equal parts, each with a conventional purpose. Seven-tenths of the way to the stage lay the most important acting area where the actors encountered and adapted to their on-stage destinations. The audience witnessed the actors' preparing to meet the on-stage situations.

Actors' personal valets also played conventional roles: taking away the properties, arranging costumes for graceful movement, and serving tea and cushions. In addition, when a

kabuki battle ended, the dead rose to exit the stage.

*Kabuki Audience* Everything about the kabuki served to entertain the audiences, often large crowds who created bloodshed and social uproar. Not only did *haimin* (commoners), *chonin* (townspeople), and *shonin* (merchants), attend the kabuki; the samurai also snuck in. In fact, Tokyo kabuki, notoriously violent and forceful, especially pleased the large number of samurai in the audience. But the new merchant class of the Tokugawa regime constituted the backbone of the eighteenth-century kabuki audience. Consequently, rather than a samurai or a priest, the kabuki hero was a typical audience member: a smart, stylish man-about-town.

The kabuki audience was divided into two sections. In a railed wooden section of boxes on the sides of the auditorium sat the merchants. In the pit before the stage were the poor, uneducated servants and shop assistants. To enter the boxes theatregoers passed through adjoining teahouses. Actors' fan clubs added excitement to the already highly wrought performances. During the opening performances, the clubs gave presents to their actors and questioned them about their personal lives. When the actors appeared on the *hanamichi* the fans eagerly rushed to shake their hands or touch bits of their clothing.

Admission fees reflected supply and demand: The bigger the hit, the higher the price; the longer the run, the lower the price. The producer thus crammed as many people as possible into the theatre. But kabuki also pioneered the art of commercial endorsement. Barkers lured customers with a line of patter and imitations of star actors. The producer hired men who dragged in customers. Souvenir booklets with pictures of the stars were sold. Personality posters endorsed hair decorations, towels, all kinds of products adorned with the names or pictures of star actors brought ready buyers to the teahouses. Customers purchased boxes of rice crackers, cakes, and cosmetics labeled with kabuki actors' names. Occasionally a star performer tossed a used towel into the audience, in the manner of a modern rock star, and created a riot by fans fighting for the blessed object. All was a part of the kabuki experience. As the playwright Kaneko Kichizaemon wrote:

> The actor's duty is to work energetically and industriously regardless of the quality of the play. If he does so, even a play only two-thirds worthwhile will seem satisfactory.[41]

The audience, in a state of constant movement during the five and a half hour program, stopped, like the Beijing opera audience, only for the climax. The kabuki audience came to the theatre to see *mie*, not plays. It appreciated moments rather than sustained durations. It applauded when it wanted—during music, dialogue, or dance—rather than wait for the end of a piece. Shouts at actors' *mie* made the kabuki experience seem like widespread confusion to the uninitiated. A spectator looking for a clearly plotted story would be lost.

**Kabuki Dramaturgy** Full texts replaced improvisations between 1675 and 1750. Before the Genroku period (1688–1703), a practice known as *kuchidate shiki* let actors improvise a plot before each performance. During the Genroku, most of the kabuki's characteristics emerged. As this occurred, the kabuki appropriated the practices and texts of the rival bunraku puppet theatre. As in the Beijing opera, characters were classified by type. Understatement and suggestion were unknown. The kabuki reveled in wild exaggeration.

Kabuki authors wrote for the actors, but kabuki actors did not exist merely to illustrate the authors' words. Early texts do not even assign dialogue by the name of the character; lines are written for individual actors. But narrative line was just one element of kabuki theatre. Masakatsu Gunji notes a major feature: "The chief thing that distinguishes the Kabuki from the drama of the West may be the fact that the play and the acting do not form an integral whole with the play dominant, but more along parallel courses, so that either may take the precedence over the other as the case requires."[42]

Most kabuki plots were a series of melodramatic crises followed by startling climaxes. The plots derived from the noh, *kyogen*, popular songs, folk dances, Japanese current events, and the puppet theatre. They usually featured characters' conflicts between duty to parents and ancestors or duty to the emperor, the law, and their lords. Because the characters usually prevailed, the kabuki was very popular with the audience. Many plots centered around a prostitute living in the gay quarters of the theatre district.

Improvisation often overtook a text spontaneously. The script was a blueprint subject to change at any performance. Texts often contained the phrase "impromptu dialogue follows here." When literary-minded figures came to kabuki companies during the Genroku period, they standardized the texts.

Authors were anonymous individuals until 1680, when Tominaga Heibei was officially listed as the author of a kabuki play. The most famous kabuki playwright, the "Shakespeare of Japan" as some called him, was Chikamatsu Monzaemon (1653–1725). Like Sophocles in Greece, Chikamatsu was the first nonacting playwright of his country. Before writing for the kabuki, he wrote plays for the puppet theatres. In the 1670s he wrote for kabuki troupes after serving in a samurai household and living as a Buddhist priest. Chikamatsu, like other kabuki playwrights, was a member of the theatre company. Only the chief actor could read a finished script. The head playwright read the script to the rest of the company. Many playwrights hired assistants to fill in their plot outlines, in much the same manner as contemporary serial writers. Chikamatsu's stage heroes came from all walks of life and showed the honor of simple people. In fact, Chikamatsu was the first Japanese playwright to put everyday events on stage. His heroes were usually torn between duty and the heart.

Kabuki playwrights followed the aesthetic of *yatsushi*, translating everything into present and familiar terms under the guise of fictional or historical circumstance. Government disapproval of kabuki and the fear of insurrection created this practice: *Yatsushi* made characters both people in society and famous historical figures. Playwrights used these two identities as a source of continuous cross-reference. Perhaps Chikamatsu was referring to *yatsushi* when he said that "art lies in the tenuous space between existence and appearance." Within the confines of *yatsushi*, kabuki playwrights developed two styles. A romantic style of acting and writing flourished around the Kyoto and Osaka areas. The other style, playing in the Edo area, emphasized rough and vigorous action and sentiment. The two styles produced different literary forms. The first were based on the lives of historical figures; the second displayed the domestic tragedies of merchants and hard-luck samurai. The first consisted of a prologue and five or six acts; the second featured only a prologue, a middle scene, and a resolution. A single program lasted twelve hours; it included a history play, a dance, a domestic tragedy, and a one-act comic dance-drama, all thematically related.

*Conclusion*  Japan produced the last of the great Eastern classical theatres. The classical theatres alive in the East shared features with the classical theatres dead in the West. Throughout Western theatrical history, people had looked to Asia and traveled to Asia, seeking the roots of the dramatic experience. With the fall of Rome to Christianity, Western theatre broke with its classical heritage. Since that time, Asian theatre practice was often seen as too mysterious, playful, or profound for some Western tastes. Yet Eastern theatre continued to lure Westerners. The theatre of the East brought people back to the beginning of things. People were confronted with the absurdity, the irrationality, the beauty, the profundity of life. In Eastern theatre people intuited great truths, beyond the grasp of the Western heritage of reason.

# NOTES

[1] A. C. Scott, *The Theatre in Asia* (London: Weidenfield & Nicolson, Ltd., 1972), p. 36.

[2] Pramod Kale, *The Theatric Universe* (Bombay: Popular Prakashan, 1974), pp. 1, 2.

[3] Som Benegal, *A Panorama of Theatre in India* (Bombay: Popular Prakashan, 1968), pp. 11–12.

[4] Kale, *The Theatric Universe*, p. 32.

[5] Ibid., p. 36.

[6] Ibid., p. 49.

[7] Scott, *The Theatre in Asia*, p. 235.

[8] Kale, *The Theatric Universe*, pp. 58–59.

[9] Kapila Vatsyayam, *Classical Indian Dance in Literature and the Arts* (New Delhi: Sangeet Natak Akademi, 1968), p. 14.

[10] Kale, *The Theatric Universe*, p. 143.

[11] Ibid., p. 23.

[12] Bengal, *A Panorama of Theatre in India*, p. 11.

[13] Kale, *The Theatric Universe*, p. 35.

[14] Benegal, *A Panorama of Theatre in India*, p. 13.

[15] Ezra Pound, *Confucius*. Copyright 1947, 1950 by

Ezra Pound. Reprinted by permission of New Directions Publishing Corporation.

[16] Arthur Waley, *The Way and Its Power* (London: George Allen & Unwin, 1942), p. 26.

[17] E. T. Kirby, *Ur-Drama: The Origins of the Theatre* (New York: New York University Press, 1975), p. 70.

[18] Ibid., p. 58.

[19] Ibid., p. 65.

[20] Donald Keene, *No: The Classical Theatre of Japan* (Palo Alto: Kodansha International Ltd., Publishers), p. 95.

[21] Peter Arnott, *The Theatres of Japan* (New York: St. Martin's Press, 1969), p. 132.

[22] Zeami, *Kadensho* (Kyoto: Sumiya-Shinobe Publishing Institute, 1968), p. 67.

[23] Makoto Ueda, *Literary and Art Theories in Japan* (Cleveland: The Press of Western Reserve University, 1967), pp. 68–69.

[24] Toyoichiro Nogami, *Zeami and His Theories on Noh*, Ryozo Matsumoto, trans. (Tokyo: Tsunetaro Hinoki, Hinoki Bookstore, 1955), p. 50.

[25] Ibid., p. 51.

[26] Ibid., pp. 60–61.

[27] Zeami, *Kadensho*, p. 82.

[28] Nogami, *Zeami and His Theories on Noh*, pp. 65–66.

[29] Ueda, *Literary and Art Theories in Japan*, p. 111.

[30] Ibid., p. 111.

[31] Ibid., p. 108.

[32] Zeami, *Kadensho*, p. 64.

[33] Keene, *No*, p. 25.

[34] Ueda, *Literary and Art Theories in Japan*, p. 107.

[35] Arthur Waley, *The Life and Times of Po Chu-I* (London: George Allen and Unwin, 1949), p. 194.

[36] *The Actors' Analects*, Charles J. Dunn and Bunzo Torigoe, eds. and trans. (New York: Columbia University Press, 1969), p. 79.

[37] *Analects*, p. 86.

[38] Earle Enrst, *The Kabuki Theatre* (New York: Oxford University Press, 1956), p. 6.

[39] *Analects*, p. 53.

[40] *Analects*, p. 60.

[41] *Analects*, p. 89.

[42] Masakatsu Gunji, *Kabuki*, John Bester, trans. (Palo Alto: Kodansha International Ltd., 1969), p. 17.

# 4

# THE MEDIEVAL THEATRE

*Love not the world, neither the things that are in the world. If any man love the world, the love of the father is not in him.*

I John 2:15

*The composition of religious imagery should not be left to the imitation of the artists, but formed on principles laid down by the Church and by religious traditions.*

Second Council of Nicea

## OVERVIEW

The overriding, dominant institution of the Medieval period was the Christian church, which altered every aspect of classical society. The church redefined the function of art; it also took over the Roman Empire's political order, Greece's science, and Rome's literature, and transformed them to instruments of its own end. The Medieval age spans the period between the collapse of the Roman Empire (476) and the collapse of the Holy Christian Empire (1517).

***The Holy Roman Empire*** The process of rebuilding Western civilization following the fall of Rome depended upon the Pope's obtaining and exercising the powers of the Roman emperor. In *The Church in the Roman Empire* Edwin R. Goodenough concludes that Romans made Christianity into a great legal system. God ruled as emperor, and the emperor dreamed of universal authority, law, justice, and order. The political theory and ambition of the Roman Empire were transferred to the theological world of the Holy Christian church.

***Creed as Scenario*** At the center of the transformation was Jesus of Nazareth. The process of mythologizing continued as the religion *of* Jesus was displaced by the religion *about* Jesus. The Constantinopolitan Creed adopted at a Council of Nicea embodied the new Christian mythology, served as a test for othodoxy, and eventually inspired artistic theatrical representation:

We believe in one God, the Father all Governing, creator of heaven and earth, of all things visible and invisible;

And in one Lord Jesus Christ, the only begotten Son of God, begotten from the Father before all time, Light from Light, true God from true God, begotten not created, of the same existence as the

Father, through whom all things come into being, Who for us men and for our salvation came down from heaven, and was incarnate by the Holy spirit and the Virgin Mary and became human. He was crucified for us under Pontius Pilate, and suffered and was buried, and rose on the third day, according to the Scriptures, and ascended to heaven, and sits on the right hand of the Father, and will come again with glory to judge the living and dead, His kingdom shall have no end.

And in the Holy Spirit, the Lord and life-giver, Who proceeds from the Father, Who is worshipped and glorified together with the Father and Son, Who spoke through the prophets; and in one, holy, catholic, and apostolic Church. We confess one baptism for the remission of sins. We look forward to the resurrection of the dead and the life of the world to come.

According to Malinowski, as we discussed in Chapter 1, this statement of Christian reality, the creed, embodies a mythology "which lives in the institutions and pursuits of a community. It justifies by precedent the existing order and it supplies a retrospective pattern of moral values, of sociological discrimination and burdens, and magic of belief."[1]

Although the history of the Medieval age and theatre surveys the Christian monarchy's attempt to enforce its view of reality, uniformity of belief was never attained. So vast was the time involved, and so sweeping the changes that occurred, that historians have, as a result, divided the Medieval period into three parts:

*Early:* c. 700–c. 1050
*Middle:* c. 1050–c. 1300
*Late:* c. 1300–c. 1500

During these periods, complexity and diversity in life and theatre increased as the power of the church declined. The Early period's rural economy eased into the Middle period's courtly chivalry, which continued to evolve into an urban, bourgeois, monied culture—the beginning of modern capitalism. Institutions emerged during the 800 years that continued to affect the Modern age: constitutional monarchy, parliaments, trial by jury, anti-Semitism, universities, Christianity, Islam, vernacular languages and literatures, and harmonic music.

*An Educational Theatre* Throughout the development of the Medieval age art and theatre received new commissions. The classical theatre had served an essentially aesthetic function. According to Christianity, on the other hand, everything existed for something other than its own sake. Consequently, art and theatre became instruments of religious education. Whereas classicism focused on the world of the senses, and art served to stimulate those senses, Christianity was "not of this world." Art remained the Christian's enemy until the church came to political power. Once the church was in power, however, the arts and theatre served the Christian state. The medieval religious theatre sought to inculcate the creedal mythology upon which the power of the church rested. The history of medieval religious theatre shows that the church used the arts to keep abreast with changes in the culture—a culture moving from agricultural to urban, feudal to national, and ecclesiatical to secular.

## EARLY PERIOD: C. 700–C. 1050

The church's influence on every aspect of medieval society derived from an early consolidation of power. Church officials moved to fill a perceived power vacuum. From the fourth century on, the Bishop of Rome claimed direct descent from Peter and, forthwith, primary authority in the governance of Rome. Pope Damascus (366–384) asserted the Roman church's authority over all others. Pope Gelasius (492–496) claimed superiority for priests because they alone had to answer to God for the souls of kings. The population's search for answers to the fundamental questions of life and death was steered by the most powerful political empire.

***Enduring Non-Christian Rituals*** By answering the people's questions with baptism and conversion, the church extended its political influence. Nevertheless, as E. K. Chambers points out in *The Medieval Stage*, peasant beliefs and customs remained shaped by pagan mythology in the wake of Christian missionary efforts. Goodenough ascribes this consequence to Christianity's strategy of adopting local beliefs and rituals as little more than variations on the One Truth Faith. Heathen temples were rededicated to Christian saints who just happened to be celebrated with the very rites used to glorify the old gods. Pope Gregory's 601 decree details the church's position:

> Destroy the idols; purify the buildings with holy water; set relics there; and let them become temples of the true God. So the people will have no need to change their places of concourse, and where of old they were want to sacrifice cattle to demons, thither let them continue to resort on the day of the saint to whom the church is dedicated, and slay their beasts no longer as a sacrifice, but for a social meal in honor of Him whom they now worship.

The Roman Pantheon, built to Jupiter Vintex and the Roman gods, was rededicated to the Virgin Mary and the Saints. The Roman festival to Jupiter Vintex became All Saints Day and Halloween. Saint worship replaced pagan polytheism. The Virgin Mary assumed the chair of Ceres, Venus, Minerva, and Diana as the new "Queen of Heaven." The bodies and relics of Christian martyrs miraculously acquired the magical powers previously only available through paganism. And adoration of Christian relics could produce miracles suitable for dramatic representation. The Roman emperor's censors and incense joined pagan candles as integral parts of the developing Christian rituals, mythologies, and doctrines.

***Sin Creates New Rituals*** During the first part of the Medieval era, church leaders formulated a philosophy of life suitable for the City of God planned for western Europe. From birth, every individual was considered a sinner doomed to Hell after death. Christ became human to suffer on behalf of all people. Because of His sacrifice God could forgive people their sins if they asked Him for forgiveness. In addition, the Christian church was God's sole agent on Earth empowered to distribute His forgiveness. Moreover, the ritual of baptism stood as the only way to wash away original sin and gain an appointment with God's representative. The church's Mass was the means to forgive all subsequent sins. Missionaries like St. Patrick of Ireland (c. 389–c. 461), Augustine of Canterbury (d. 604), and Boniface of Germany (c. 680–755) carried this Good News to the barbarians.

Sexuality provided the church with abundant examples of sin. The Romans had continued the Greek reverence for the penis by appropriating the Greek word *phallos* and elevating it over their own *fascinum*. *Phalli* decorated Roman civilization; Christians undecorated Roman civilization because they shared Rome's view that nudity and homosexuality were shameful. The Christian attitude about sex derived from Roman attitudes and early Christian writings.

Saint Paul (c. 5–c. 67) began to formulate the Christian sex code from ambiguous statements made by Jesus in the four Gospels. Because celibacy was considered a holier state than marriage, an underlying misogyny developed in early Christianity. Christians also disapproved of any sexual activity not leading to procreation. And even procreative sex was only tolerated, never enjoyed. Virtue lay on the side of abstinence. Most church leaders, as a result, never married. In fact, the issue of clerical celibacy eventually divided the Christian church into Eastern and Western sects.

***Islam: A Rival Cosmology*** During the Early Medieval period another messenger received different Good News from God: Islam burst upon the medieval scene as the prophet Mohammed (c. 570–632) claimed his place as the true successor to both the Hebrew prophets and the Christian Jesus. Mohammed sought a common basis for all monotheists. Finding Judaism inappropriate for Arabs and Christianity too idolatrous, Mohammed borrowed Jewish, Christian, and Persian teachings to formulate a new major world religion. The minaret call became the Islamic equivalent of the Jewish trumpet and the Christian bells. In 622 (year 1 in the Moslem calendar) Mohammed traveled from Mecca to Medina to claim religious and political leadership. Finding Saturday and Sunday already taken, the Prophet made Friday his holy day. He also turned fellow Arabs from warring with one another to warring with the unbelievers, the infidels.

Unlike the religions of Greece and Rome, but like the Asian religions, Judaism, Christianity, and Islam were religions of a book. The Torah, the Bible, and the Koran all consisted of series of messages believed to be written by God. The Five Pillars of Islam, derived from the most widely read book in history, were: (1) a belief in one God and in Mohammed as His sole prophet; (2) a strong reliance on prayer; (3) a need to fast during the ninth month, known as Ramadan; (4) a deep need to give alms; and (5) a mandatory pilgrimage to Mecca. The notion of a Holy War held an especially prominent place in Islamic doctrine. Like Christianity and early Buddhism, Islam expressed a feverish desire to convert the entire world to its view of truth. But the evangelical zeal of both Christianity and Islam clashed, setting a pattern that continued to the Modern age.

Though Islam used Jewish and Christian sources, Islamic attitudes on sex derived from elsewhere. Mohammed regarded sex as a good aspect of life, and there rested Christianity's problem with Islam. Islam considered sexual intercourse as the greatest of pleasures for both men and women. Sex kept men young. Therefore, to Christendom Mohammed and Islam looked like the incarnations of sensuality, sexuality, and evil. The Koran created humans not from Biblical dust but from semen and drops of congealed blood. Marriage, therefore, stood above celibacy as the premiere relationship; in fact, even polygamy was permitted. And homosexuality and bestiality were more tolerated in Islamic lands.

***The Monasteries***   In 799 the political aspirations of the church solidified as Pope Leo III, unpopular in Rome, fled to Germany for protection. Together the church and the state created stability and order among the citizenry. Stability increased further as orders of monks created rural community centers known as monasteries, which provided sanctuary for both the monks and manuscripts of classical antiquity. In addition, pilgrims, merchants, and minstrels met at the monastery. The self-sufficient organization of the monastery's labor helped raise the Early Medieval age's respect for work; *ora et labora* (pray and work) was the motto. Human existence began to be perceived as endless work in penance or punishment for original sin. When not in the fields or mills, monks copied and illustrated manuscripts for their growing libraries. As the monasteries prospered, monks assumed supervisory and administrative positions and relied on lay brothers and peasants to do manual labor. The monasteries thus became the religious equivalent of medieval manors.

Peasants had as much faith in the monks' protection of their souls as they did in their lords' protection of their bodies. Medieval people concerned themselves with two existences; they knew they had both natural and supernatural lives—the former a consequence of original sin, the latter, of the Grace of God. The monks explained existence to the fallen creatures by relating everything to the truth of the Gospels as enumerated in the Creed. The peasants trusted the monks' preachments because they could not read, and, even if they could, the Bible was reserved for the clergy. Thus, faith became the source of knowledge and, therefore, an important Christian religious principle. Medieval individuals demonstrated their faith in God through their faith in the clergy's explanations. As an added benefit of such faith, they could anticipate salvation. Meanwhile, on earth feudalism reigned.

*Feudalism* Feudalism provided protection and economic security to people deprived of the Roman army and economic system. Gradually, medieval society acquired a rural character following the Roman urban-centered culture, and Rome's money economy gave way to barter on self-sufficient estates. Great landlords ruled independent manors. Lords produced only what could be consumed on the manor; a shortage of money and inadequate transportation prevented the selling of any surplus.

But life in the manor was far-removed from classical court life; no courtiers existed to be impressed by a lord's art or architecture. And by the end of the ninth century, kings began to be elected from an hereditary aristocracy. Kings paid their lords with land for their loyalty; they also waged war, but had no jurisdiction except over their own lands. Competition was unthinkable; lords ruled through God's ordinance.

Personal contractual relationships formed feudalism. One human being was bound to an other. Like baptism, serfdom was an involuntary tie; both were essential for survival. At first estates were worked by peasants bound to the land. Tenant farmers paid a percentage of their harvests to the lords for the right to farm their land and enjoy their security systems. But the development of the heavy plow and the modern horse harness increased the speed of tilling and cut the cost of land transportation. The harness also meant that peasants could live away from their place of labor. In time peasants were producing a surplus to take to market; this surplus raised the peasants' standard of living, and resulted in their having extra money to spend. Artisans and merchants arose to help peasants find ways to spend their money. Democratic capitalism was born. With the rise of cities, medieval society moved into its Middle period, but not without leaving a distinctive art and literature.

*An Antiartistic Bent* Feudalism's anti-individualistic bent resulted in a general, stereotypical art and literature. And because the dramatic theatre usually celebrates the individual perspective, theatrical activity was rare. All was meaningful only in relation to the church: Sacred objects and manuscripts, religious hymns, and printed sermons constituted the early medieval artistic expression. Dance was outlawed along with Gnosticism (the belief in a noncorporeal Jesus), whose Acts of John included a Jesus who said, "Forgiveness is our *choregos*—to sing is my desire, let us dance together. . . . Those who do not dance will not comprehend what shall befall. . . . You who dance, see what I have accomplished." Satan and his minions were, in fact, the only dancers in medieval art.

Early medieval art served the philosophy of the church, which, though based on Judaism, quickly put its ancestor in the enemy camp. Nevertheless, Christians took over the Jewish idea that music was the proper form of worship. In fact, the first Christian music was probably the singing of psalms using the elaborate Jewish chants, which assign a number of notes to one syllable. As the Christian Mass developed into the early locus of artistic expression, antiphonal singing split a congregation into two singing groups. Gradually the clergy took over most of the Mass, and singing occurred only between priest and choir or between two parts of the choir. Music became, as St. Basil had hoped, a means of attracting people to church.

Like Pisistratus in Greece, Asoka in India, and Constantine in Rome, the Carolingian ruler Charlemagne (742–814) used music and the other arts to celebrate his power and patronage. Indeed, scholars and artists enjoyed Charlemagne's patronage. Scholars actually scanned classical texts for confirmation of their Christian beliefs. Moreover, Charlemagne's circle of literati used the word *renovatio*; they were renovating the classical tradition in the body of Christ. Some historians call the appreciation of art *via* the body of Christ the Incarnationalist strain of Christianity: The coming of Christ into the world made the things of the world sanctified. Throughout the Medieval age Christians who enjoyed the arts used this Incarnationalist argument to justify the celebration of life. The eventual production of the Corpus Christi plays (which we discuss later in this chapter) may be seen as a triumph of their position over the objections of Christians bewailing the transitoriness of earthly things.

Charlemagne's patronage also consolidated Latin as the language of the church; clergy learned to read and write. *Aix-la-Chapelle*, Charlemagne's literary academy, creatively assembled classical culture and old bardic songs dealing with legendary heroes. Pagan epics were Christianized to make them worthy of preservation. Charlemagne shifted the center of Western culture from the Mediterranean to Central Europe, where it remained until the Italian Renaissance.

Early medieval art was simplified and stylized. It renounced spatial depth and perspective, and it treated bodily proportions and functions arbitrarily. Art was impersonal and the artist unobtrusive. In addition, building for the glory of God demanded an organization as thorough as Gregory the Great's organization of the chants. To protect themselves against barbarian raids, medieval people constructed fire-proof buildings. The characteristic Romanesque architecture thus featured stone castles and churches. Great wealth poured into building churches, which were shaped as crosses but modeled on Roman courtrooms. Apses in the east allowed priests to face the rising Sun/Son. An immense nave led to each apse. Over time, more and larger windows were added. Priests stood in the church apse under a dome and before a table or altar representing the tomb of Jesus, and the congregants viewed them through the lattice work of the Roman attorneys' bar. The clergy even adapted the clothes of the emperor's civil dress tunic and mantle for their ceremonies. Color and symbol played an important part in ecclesiastical decoration: Red represented the martyr's blood and Christ's agony; white, the Lamb's pure fleece; green, verdant surroundings; violet, Advent and intercession; purple, extreme unction; and black, death and Good Friday. In addition, most churches housed a patron saint in relic form; as lord of each religious manor, the relic was kept under the altar. A bishop or abbot was the

saint's vicar who cured, saved, and destroyed in his church through miracles. During the Early Medieval period artists portrayed the inner emotions and spiritual yearnings of individuals seeking the miraculous.

Gradually, church leaders overcame their objections to representational art, which had been typified by the fifth-century Bishop of Salamis: "Which of the ancient Fathers ever painted an image of Christ and deposited it in a church or private house? Which ancient bishop ever dishonored Christ by painting him on door curtains?" The Nicene Creed served as justification for artistic representation: If Christ was God made flesh, then people could represent flesh, for to deny the flesh was as heretical as the Gnostic position that Christ was only an illusion. So the representation of Christ stood as an affirmation of orthodoxy. By the tenth century the image of an agonized Christ on the cross dominated Western art and religion. Pain and suffering occupied the minds and bodies of Westerners. No wonder the simple acts of secular players met with so much appreciation and so much scorn.

***The Secular Theatre*** The church's frequent attacks on the theatre during the Early Medieval period constitute most of the evidence for the existence of a secular theatre after the collapse of the Roman Empire. Because the church monopolized the written word, only its own Latin dramas were documented. In contrast, the early secular players lacked scribes, so popular performances were ephemeral, occasional, and, of course, scriptless. Scenarios and roles passed orally and adapted to particular places and times.

The mime tradition occasionally popped up too—in written references, for example, to *histriones* and *mimi*. Actually, the classical mime and the Germanic rhapsode seem to have intermingled and influenced one another, until they were almost indistinguishable. What emerged was an extremely versatile *homme de théâtre*—a poet, singer, musician, dancer, dramatist, clown, acrobat, juggler, mime, female impersonator, puppeteer, magician, tight-rope walker, knife thrower, and bear baiter. In short, Early Medieval entertainers were street performers who lived from hand to mouth as they traveled alone or with partners from manor to manor.

Later the term *jongleur* (entertainer), derived from the Latin *iocularis* (laughable) appeared. The *jongleur* could be solemn and dignified when playing surreptitiously at a monastery, or foolish and bird-brained when playing for children of all ages gathered along the side of a road. Often driven from town, these secular players kept the theatre alive in Europe. In *The Medieval Stage* E. K. Chambers identifies them, in fact, as descendants of classical entertainers. Consequently, they were the enemies of the church. Gaiety had little place in the City of God. Happiness and joy represented too much delight in things of the flesh. Smiles and laughter meant that Satan was winning souls. Yet even Charlemagne patronized these players. But the church railed on. The history of the secular theatre is, as a result, written as ecclesiastical attacks.

***Attacks on Actors*** And did the church attack! Almost every church council and synod issued a stern warning to the players and their audiences. Clergy were forbidden to attend performances. Priests were accused of neglecting their duties to attend shows. Performers were accused of using devils' masks in their entertainments, and they could be baptized only after renouncing their profession. No Christian could marry a player for fear of excommunication. And monks were warned against housing strolling players in their monasteries.

Stories of actors who forsook the stage appeared as saints' legends to provide models for other actors. In the third century, during a performance for Emperor Diocletian, an actor named Genesius supposedly left the satire of Christian baptism to receive real Christian baptism. Enraged, Diocletian tortured the actor to force him to sacrifice to the pagan gods. His refusal made him a saint but cost him his head. Actresses could emulate the beautiful, but dissolute Pelagia the Penitent, a great actress from Antioch, who, hearing the powerful

preaching of Bishop St. Nommus of Edessacus, asked to be baptized, gave her wealth to the Bishop, and left the acting profession to wear men's clothing as a hermit on Mt. Olivet. The models of Christian goodness were also encouraged by the lords of the manor, because players took peasants away from their work.

***Festivals*** Wandering players found their best audiences at the fairs and festivals allowed by the church. Winter solstice festivals still incorporated pagan rites and rituals to revive the year spirit with evergreens, dancing, and costume. Likewise, spring fertility pageants sought to revive the Earth with phallic maypole dancing. Sword dances celebrated the triumph of life over winter: When a clown named Bessey disrupted a sword dance and died of an accidental stab wound, a doctor was summoned to raise her from the dead. Sometimes sword dances employed Christian heroes and myths—for example, St. George and the Dragon in England, St. James in Spain, St. Patrick in Ireland, and St. Anthony in Italy. Midsummer nights' fire festivals sought to cleanse the crops to make them grow. Lewd dancing often damaged church property because the church had insisted that existing pagan worship sites be converted to Christian churches. Dancers liked the processional dances and properties of French Christmas *caroles*—called *Springtanz* in Germany. Blackened faces and belled knees characterized the May and Winter Morris Dancers, who sometimes enacted folk characters like Robin Hood and Maid Marion.

Professional players undoubtedly had a hand in these festivities. And even the church contributed. In *The Medieval Stage* E. K. Chambers notes that *ludi* (folk festivals) were permitted and, to some extent, directed by the church. Church personnel tried to make the Teutonic Totenfest, the Celtic Wassail, the Yule celebrations, and the Roman Saturnalia nothing more than local variants of the one true Christmas celebration. In the same way the church tried to mold the Celtic May Day into a more acceptable Easter Festival.

Clearly Early Medieval people had a difficult time renouncing the world, even a medieval world with so little to renounce. The theatre sustained them with simple acts of wonder and joy. The players were religious outlaws performing in violation of ecclesiastical and divine decree. Like guerrilla soldiers, the players employed tactics to outmaneuver their powerful opponent. But when the church began to feature some of the guerrillas' own strategies, the City of God had already begun to give ground to the scraggly individuals from the City of Humanity.

***Christian Ritual***   Scholars are divided on the question of how much influence the persistence of secular minstrels had on Christianity's entrance into the theatre-producing business. In *The Medieval Stage* E. K. Chambers suggests that wise church leaders concluded that popular entertainment might be turned to serve Christian purposes. Before the church used sung dialogues that comprised a minimum of impersonation, a few invented dialogues did exist in the eighth-century poem "Christ" by Bynewulf and in the ninth-century *Book of Cerne*. When dramatic theatre arose in the church, it came through the church's most glorious work of art: the Latin Mass.

The Christian Mass differed from the ritual model we outlined in Chapter 1. Benjamin Hunningher elucidates the points of contrast:

> In Christianity it is not man who in common with other men and by his own force reaches God and participates in Him, but God who bestows his Grace on man, and on man as an individual. In Christ's words, "My Grace is sufficient for Thee," lies the core of the Gospel. All Christians praise and exult in God's Grace, but what has their exaltation to do with the *ecstasis* and *enthousiasmos* of the heathen worshipper, flung out of himself by his wild dance, feeling God, united with God, portraying Him with his own body. The presence of the mask corroborates this identification.
>
> For primitive and ancient religions and the theater that arose from them, in the beginning was the deed, and the deed was with man, and the deed was man. Christianity replaced this with

"In the beginning was the Word, and the Word was with God, and the Word was God."[2]

Christian ritual was based on words rather than on action, the necessary basic material of dramatic theatre. Also, a clear distinction existed at all times between priest and congregation, shaman and audience. The history of Christ was merely remembered in the Mass—not reenacted, as in ritual. Thus, from the beginning, the Mass was more of an aesthetic experience than a religious experience. The priest did not become Christ; the priest imitated the passion of Christ.

The Mass has important implications for the development of a Christian dramatic theatre. If the Mass had more elements of dramatic theatre than of ritual, then the Mass already embodied the function of dramatic theatre: to envision a new reality. The Mass embodied all the new realities medieval individuals ever needed to envision. The Passion of Christ encompassed all that was and all that ever would be. All new realities were revealed through the scriptures and anticipated in the life of Christ. Consequently, an imaginative artist's new visions were not only unnecessary, they were unwanted and heretical. Subsequent attempts to give the Mass more of the powers of ritual, like the introduction of the doctrine of transubstantiation, seem to verify the aesthetic, commemorative nature of the original Mass rather than any ecstatic origin. Ecstasy, masks, and dance were associated with pagan rituals, Satan and his earthly disciples, the infidels, and the Jews.

***Mass and Hours***   Medieval Christians celebrated two varieties of worship: Mass and Hours. The two-part service began with Hours—devotional readings, prayers, a sermon, and songs, each one of which changed with the church's calendar of Jesus's life. The second part of the service—the Mass—remained constant throughout the church year; the sacrament of bread and wine never changed. To vivify the events related in Christ's biography, the church added theatrical elements. For example, on Palm Sunday someone rode an ass to church, and palms were distributed. On Maundy Thursday a member of the clergy washed feet. On Good Friday the altar cross was draped in black and deposited in a symbolic tomb or sepulchre. Properties took on symbolic functions as well: A dove represented Mary, the Mother of Christ, and keys, the Kingdom of Heaven guarded by St. Peter.

Song, the church's premiere artistic expression, likewise evolved theatrically. Antiphonal singing, a musical dialogue between two parts of the choir, suggested the choral exchanges of the early Greek theatre. When the choir answered the cantor in dialogue, the form resembled the early Greek drama of Thespis.

But unlike the Greek dramatic theatre, this medieval theatricality did not yet involve impersonation. In the ninth century, however, liturgical elaboration, featuring awesome architecture, costume, processions, and new melodies, sporadically ushered in the church's initial flirtation with dramatic theatre.

**Tropes** Drama emerged through what was known as a *trope*. Originally a *trope* was a musical term for a short cadence in a syllabic melody. *Trope* gradually began to refer to a text added in the eighth or ninth centuries to a chant in the Mass's Introit, Kyrie, or Gloria. Karl Young defines *tropes* as "deliberate, and perhaps unsanctioned, literary additions to the authorized liturgical text."[3]

The oldest extant *trope* was written for an Easter service at the monastery of St. Gall in Switzerland in approximately 925. After the third reading of scripture, four brethren costumed themselves—one in an *alb* (a white floor-length under tunic with narrow sleeves), three others in *copes* (also ecclesiastical vestments)—and sang the following verses before the sepulchre:

"Quem quaeritis in sepulchro, O Christicolae?"
"Iesum Nazarenum crucifixum, O caelicolae."
"Non est hic, surrexit sicut proedixerat."
"Ite nuniate quia surrexit de supulchro."

All of the congregants then sang the *Te Deum*.

The "Quem Quaeritis" *trope* sought to nourish faith in the fact of Jesus's resurrection. Faith dramatized might triumph over reason. By 1000 the Easter dialogue was found sporadically in Germany, England, France, and northern Spain as well.

**Liturgical Drama** Because liturgical drama was always a local and sporadic occurrence, it did not evolve in an orderly manner. Some complex dramas, in fact, predated some simple *tropes*. *Tropes* must, however, have succeeded in their goal—"to fortify unlearned people in their faith"—because, by the end of the tenth century, liturgical dramas were more frequent. Other episodes of the Easter story, for example, were dramatized: the visit of Peter and John to the sepulchre, the journey to Emmaus, the incredulity of Thomas, the Marys shopping for spices, and the harrowing of Hell. Christmas episodes, like the visitations of the shepherds and Magi, likewise appeared in the Mass. The ranting of King Herod, with its comedy and anti-Semitism, proved a popular favorite. So did *The Prophets Play*, in which Old Testament Hebrew prophets testified against Jews who failed to recognize Christ as the Messiah.

Anti-Semitism was gradually becoming not only a way of delighting audiences, but also a way of unifying Christendom against a common enemy.

Early in the church's history the Jews were identified as Christianity's principal enemy. St. Augustine believed that as long as Jews failed to accept Jesus as the Messiah their history would be one of suffering. Anti-Semitism originated in the early church almost as a way of proving the truth of St. Augustine's prophecy; it arose as a tool for religious and political goals. Throughout the Medieval age anti-Semitic hatred grew such that it gave Western civilization a legacy that boiled to the Modern age. Dramas were statements of Christian faith and belief. And, as most playwrights even today often learn, audiences' actions are more easily manipulated by hatred and fear than by love and trust. In *The History of Anti-Semitism*

Leon Poliakov writes that the drama was the most powerful vehicle the church employed to titillate spectators' violence toward the Jews. The perfidy of the Jews was contrasted with the sanctity of Christ and the Virgin.

***Liturgical Playing Conventions*** Performances originally confined to monasteries occasionally moved, in the Middle Medieval period, to cathedrals and larger audiences. Performances may have occurred only once or twice a year at a given church. The most popular play remained the Marys at the Tomb. Gradually, other subjects appeared in church: the raising of Lazarus, the conversion of Paul, the wise and foolish Virgins, Pentecost, and Daniel and the lions' den. By the middle of the Medieval era, a play called *The Antichrist* had become the most elaborate in staging and rabid anti-Semitism.

Playing conventions resembled those of the Sanskrit theatre. Scenery was at first improvised, and chairs represented different locations. Eventually the altar and sepulchre were incorporated into the action. A star led the three kings down the nave to discover a child behind an altar curtain.

More elaborate structures moved the action into the nave. A single scenic structure, variously called a *mansion*, *sede*, *locus*, or *domus*, inhabited a neutral playing space known as the *platea*, *playne*, or *place*. Because the medieval nave lacked pews, it was spacious enough to let the audience roam with the play's action from scene to scene. A house setting for the raising of Lazarus play or a throne and a wall for a hand to write on in the *Play of Daniel* were typical settings needed for liturgical drama. When more than one setting was needed, all sets remained on stage simultaneously.

At first the plays were little more than living tableaux staged in the church's apse. Symbolic pantomime and male actors moved the dramas toward a more realistic manner of impersonation. But throughout the liturgical drama, iconographical, rather than individual, representations of Biblical characters greeted the audience. Formal, restrained, and decorous speech and gestures matched the mood of Early Medieval art. Conventionalized gestures, often like those of classical and Asian theatres, expressed emotion. When attacking Jews, however, naturalistic and elaborate actions ruled; the playing of Herod, Judas, Pilate, Roman soldiers, and devils left little to the imagination.

The earliest record of a text with stage direction appeared in 965 in the *Regularis Concordia*, a manual written by Ethelwold, Bishop of Winchester, to reform and regulate worship practices in the Benedictine monasteries. Ecclesiastical directions called rubrics in such worship manuals as the *Regularis Concordia* detailed the actions for the playlets' lines.

Contemporary ecclesiastical garb was the basis for Biblical costuming. The most common garments were the *alb* and the *dalmatic*, a long cloak with elaborate designs. The Marys wore *copes*, angels wore *stoles*, and Mary Magdelene dressed as a medieval whore. Female impersonation was aided by the *amice*, a white linen cloth worn around the neck and shoulders and drawn over the head to conceal the sex. Realistic costume details and properties included wings for angels, crowns for kings, censers, Eucharistic wine bottles, candles, silver vessels, Eucharist containers, a crown of thorns, gifts from the Magi, palms, staves, swords, books, and mitres.

***The Comic Impulse*** Liturgical plays occasionally used vernacular words, phrases, and secular melodies, especially for comic characters. And the comic desire to mock and ridicule went beyond the Jewish characters in the liturgical drama. The church itself let the lower clergy vent some hostility toward their superiors on the Feast of the Boy Bishop, December 28, and on the Feast of Fools, the day of circumcision, eight days after Christmas. Ribaldry and disrespect were the order of the day. For one day the community's shamen played the clown's role. They brayed the liturgy, diced on the altar, mocked the bishop's sermons, wore ecclesiastical garments inside out, and sang obscene lyrics to the sacred chants. The feast climaxed with a burlesque procession, during which women emptied chamber pots and threw garbage from windows onto masked priests burning old shoes in censers. Singing was done by a female-impersonating choir. The church reacted to the growing sacrilege and its popularity by abolishing the feasts. But the feasts' supporters did not give up. Some formed clubs and societies known in France as *sociétés joyeuses*.

## MIDDLE PERIOD: 1050-1300

In the Middle Medieval period the church reached its political and intellectual peak, but it started to lose individuals' faith. As national states emerged, popes sought to strengthen their secular control. Secular leaders tried to maintain the people's happiness; but the clergy judged secular governments by their ability to carry out their divine mandate. Consequently, secular kings could hold divine right only after being consecrated by God through the clergy. Nevertheless, courts produced lore to rival the mythology of the church. Infidels captured Jerusalem, and heretical scholars captured young minds in cathedral schools and universities. No wonder the church stressed the end of the world: Events suggested erosion even before the City of God could be completed.

The church seemed bent on preparing humanity for the Last Judgment. Pilgrimages to the Holy Land could gain one favor. Marching in a Crusade against Moslems in Jerusalem, Turks in Byzantium, or Jews at home demonstrated one's love of God. Magnificent cathedrals with stained glass windows proclaimed not only the glory of God but also the eternal power of the church at a time of growing temporal power and patronage for the arts and theatre.

***The Church Reacts to Secularism*** When kings and knights evolved a code of chivalry, the church consecrated the knights as an Army of Christ about to embark on a holy mission, the search for a Grail, the symbol of a lost faith. When knights focused their actions on their ladies, the church countered by elevating the cult of the Virgin, the only lady worthy of men's attention. Worship of the Virgin took over many traits of chivalric love, and miracle plays demonstrated the Virgin's ability to motivate men with the power of her love. Saints plays showed Christian knights working miracles far greater than any deed of any mortal knight. Thomas Aquinas espoused the idea of a treasury of saints, a religious Round Table, ready to do battle whenever priests needed indulgences for sinners in distress. But even with all of the effort, by the twelfth century the Christian faith was no longer universally held.

But Christianity was still universally enforced. It reacted by lashing out with a vicious offensive. In 1095 Pope Urban called for a Crusade to free the Holy Land from Moslems not only for religious reasons but also to appease estateless nobles hungry for land, booty, and tales of derring-do. Knights appreciated the opportunity to enhance their reputations with further adventures. Merchants, hoping to reopen trade routes to the East, rallied behind the church. The Crusades thus exposed feudalism to new ways of thinking, which further weakened the church's hold on Westerners. The church next turned its attack to the infidels at home.

As cities developed, people lived in closer proximity and exchanged ideas. Individuals found reinforcement for their doubts. The church had sought to unify Christendom with a common language, faith, and dogma. But urban religion displayed more emotion than rural Christianity. As a result, personal religious experience became more meaningful as institutional religion diminished in importance. Gradually, the pope came to be seen as a man with human motivations, and local religion came to be valued over universal religion, just as vernacular language began to be valued over Latin. The church organized new orders of monks, the Franciscans and Dominicans, to work for Christian unity. In 1215 the doctrine of transubstantiation was proclaimed as further proof of the validity of the church's doctrine: Christ worked among people as the consecrated Host. The Eucharist recalled individuals to faith and existed to alter the destiny of the human race.

*Anti-Semitism* But heresies continued to arise, and the church sought out their source. The twelfth century marked the peak of medieval anti-Semitism as the church scourged the Jews. The Gospel's hatred of the Jews, the Jews' nonconformity within the Christian culture, and economic rivalry made the very word "Jew" a term synonymous with abuse and deceit. After all, considering the proof available to them, why could Jews not accept Jesus as the Messiah? Jews were simply creatures of Satan, not of God; they were not human. The church considered a Christian who married or cohabited with a Jew guilty of bestiality. Because Jews worked and waited for the Antichrist, their true Messiah, they could not accept the Christian Messiah. But their Messiah would be the son of the Devil and a Jewish whore, because the real Messiah was the Son of God and a Jewish virgin. Jews were tried on trumped-up charges of desecrating the Host, the source of all Christian power, the reincarnated Christ.

The rise of the Christian merchant class and a change in the church's attitude toward business had made Jewish usury no longer either necessary or desirable. Christians, in fact, were now eager to profit from usury. Also, Jewish commentaries accompanying the Moslem translations of Aristotle had created the impression that Jews were in league with the Moslems, which fueled the fires of heresy in the schools. Infidels must be destroyed at home as well as abroad.

*The Inquisition* A small Renaissance in the twelfth century had sown seeds of innovative religious thinking, contention, and disputation. A church thus beset by sects with different interpretations of religion, the world, and politics felt it had no choice but to censor and establish rigid tests of dogma and secular knowledge. In 1215 the Fourth Lateran Council ordered all Jews and heretics to wear a distinguishing form of dress, usually a yellow patch and a horned cap. And in 1233 Pope Gregory IX established an Inquisition under the leadership of the Dominicans. Moreover, Thomas Aquinas (1225–1274), the brilliant church philosopher, declared that "heresy is a sin which merits not only excommunication but also death." Death awaited those found guilty of heresy. Special commissioners known as *inquisitores* investigated and ordered secular rulers to sentence heretics and sorcerers. Tortured suspects produced abundant evidence and numerous confessions. In Spain, Inquisition bonfires of both heretics and heretical books became great social festivals called *Autos Da Fe* (Acts of Faith).

*A New Merchant Class* Stability in medieval society had not only produced a free exchange of ideas but also a free exchange of goods. Money replaced land as the primary means of exchange, wealth, and power. Money even traveled with the serfs to central markets.

The population shifted from rural manor to urban town. Merchants gathered and settled alongside monasteries, near castles, and beside major highways. New towns supported the Crusades' efforts to keep the commercial roads open. The urban life of the new merchant bourgeois class created a secular culture, and competition among merchants stimulated individual initiative, new ideas, and success in business. As a result, originality and individuality appeared as valuable traits to nurture.

With the rise of the money economy, the power of the land-owning lords decreased, and merchants gained political power and independence from kings and lords. Regulations managing the sale of goods both promoted commerce and stifled unwanted competition. Artisans and theatrical players came to the cities for the large potential market. Industries attracted skilled workers seeking to improve their economic status; freedom, in fact, awaited the serf who could remain a year and a day in a town. Meanwhile, successful merchants impressed their friends and associates by patronizing the arts.

***Secular Mythology and Chivalry*** As the lords' economic status declined, kings consolidated their power. These secular authorities demanded a secular mythology and creed to rival those of the church. From these demands came chivalry, a way of life for the kings' knights, a term derived from the French word *cheval* (war horse). Unlike the old feudal knights, chivalric knights claimed their titles not by birthright, but by merit. Knights earned investiture, just as the bourgeoisie earned power. Tournaments that allowed future knights to rise from pages to squires, squires to shield bearers, and shield bearers to knights prospered; they took the form of secular festivals for royal engagements, weddings, births, coronations, military victories, and alliances.

The literature and arts of chivalry embodied a new spiritualization and sensuality among the educated. Indeed, as wealth shifted from rural landlords to urban merchants, so did the arts. The church reemployed its power in a display of monumental architecture; pointed arches, ribbed vaults, buttressed walls, and magnificent stained glass windows characterized the Gothic style of architecture. But the laity assumed more of the artistic creation of both the cathedrals and the dramatic theatre, and the influence of the clergy diminished.

Crusaders returning with memories of Moslem arches and poetry influenced Western architecture and literature as well. Because these crusaders also wanted their exploits sung throughout the land, new epics flattered medieval knights and kings. Poets and rhapsodes sang for and about whoever could pay them. Literature and art were thus secularized by the money economy: Anyone with money could enjoy art and literature. As a result, secular minstrels replaced the church as the source of poetic expression. *Troubadors*, minstrels working in a particular court or circuit of courts, found political patronage and protection. In time, in fact, all minstrels and players enjoyed some security.

Another consequence of secularization is that vernacular literature prospered in the twelfth and thirteenth centuries. Heroic epics became chivalric romances. In *Chanson de Roland* (1100) and *Parzival* (1203), for example, the heroes are Christian knights. In addition, *Aucassin and Nicolette* (1200), *Arthur and the Round Table* (1148) by Geoffrey of Monmouth, and the *Roman de la Rose* (1230), the most famous and influential poem of the age, all combined Christian virtue with the Islamic emphasis on love.

***The New Woman*** During the Middle Medieval period, women began to enjoy a higher status, not only in literature but also in everyday life. Laws let women inherit estates and royal palaces. Poets redefined love as the most important principle of education and the ethical power most attuned to the deepest human experience. Love was associated with the source of all beauty and goodness; women were the incarnation of this love. Women, symbolizing these new definitions, became important symbols in Western literature, art, and drama. A new source of dramatic tension emerged: Will the lovers get together? Biblical heroes were replaced by knights acting out of chivalric love. Men fell in awe of women; loving a woman brought out the best in a man. Man-the-suitor replaced man-the-buyer and subduer of women. Every man dreamed of sacrificing his own identity and desires to a woman, the superior being. The most desirable woman was, naturally, the most unattainable; love for her would produce the most pain. Emotional exhibitionism, longing, and renunciation both proved the depth and truth of love and made wonderful situations for the drama. Chivalric love for a lady worked like a vassal's love for his liege.

Heretofore, the preeminent woman in Christendom had been Eve: the instrument of the devil and the supreme temptress. The church based its canon law permitting wife beating on Eve's sin. To counter the new enthusiasm for chivalric women, the church elevated the Cult of the Virgin, the only woman to whom any man should show such love. Great pilgrimages led to shrines of the Virgin, which appeared throughout Europe. Cathedrals took the Virgin's name; plays demonstrated the power of her loving mercy; feasts commemorated her life. Thus medieval man saw woman as either the saint of chivalric love or the evil manipulator of Eden. And so, when the love of the Virgin proved insufficient to turn the tide of secular love, the church found another incarnation for woman as witch, which would flourish during the late Renaissance.

***Return of the Rhapsodes***  Verse remained the standard medium for poetic expression. Listeners and memorizing rhapsodes alike preferred verse. Troubadors drew characters by changing voice and gesture. Rhetorical considerations rather than literary matters ruled poetic composition. As H. J. Chayto observes in *From Script to Print*, the resulting illiteracy and scaracity of books produced a heightened facility in memorization skills.

Artists, poets, and players flocked to cities not only for wealthy patrons but also for contact with scholars and students in the new universities. The twelfth-century universities, which replaced monastic schools as centers of learning and culture, retained the basic method of learning: memorization. Though its control on curricula was absolute, the church did not monopolize education in these universities. Instead, the universities arose to meet the needs of specialized bourgeois merchants and court administrators. Graduates became church secretaries, lawyers, theologians, and court bureaucrats. Each university had a distinctive quality that the drama captured in its characterizations of various scholars and professors. In addition, students' switching universities after a few years created a familiar medieval character: a wandering scholar with songs and poems of wine, women, and a debauched life.

***The Classics and Scholasticism***  The liberal arts curriculum was taught within an educational philosophy known as "scholasti-cism." Founded by Peter Abelard (1079–1142), a Paris logician, scholasticism sought to reconcile all of the church's proclamations and creeds through the application of classical reason and logic. The clergy still had no rival in their control of medieval thought; they provided the only means of salvation. Professors of liberal arts, however, began to peruse new translations of classical works without regard to theological orthodoxy.

Students read aloud, thereby making the teaching of writing part of their oral training. Beginning at the age of 12 or 14, a university student found dictation the only pedagogical method. Nevertheless, universities were hotbeds of debate and discussion. Abelard, for example, shocked the church with his suggestion that students be allowed to examine Scripture: "The doctors of the Church should be read, not with the necessity to believe, but with liberty to judge." He even went so far as to say that "by doubting we are led to inquire, by inquiry we may perceive the truth."

After Abelard, Thomas Aquinas explained the existence of separate spheres for faith and reason. In this way, he proposed, reason could not subvert faith, nor vice versa. Theology was distinct from philosophy: "For then alone do we know God, when we believe that He is far above all that men can possibly think of God." Students, eager to experience the passions of men like Abelard and Aquinas, considered all propositions, even those raised in the theatre.

On March 7, 1277, however, the Bishop of Paris issued a formal condemnation of 219 such philosophical propositions issuing from the city's university. Included were the ideas that Christianity hindered education, that theology was based on myth, and that philosophy, rather than theology, was the basis of truth. The Inquisition carried on the Bishop's work.

***Variety Entertainment***  Wandering scholars, sometimes called *goliardi*, shared the highways with strolling minstrels and traveling players. As cities grew, and larger audiences increased the players' wealth, entertainers banded together into pairs, threesomes, or troupes to perform on portable wooden scaffolds in manors, guild halls, universities, and marketplaces. A poor reception meant the players were drummed out of town and back onto the highways.

Most plays were never written down. Variety entertainment and farce constituted the players' repertoire. Acrobats, contortionists, tumblers, rope walkers, dancers, jugglers, magicians, puppeteers, animal impressionists, animal tamers, and animal baiters (both male and female) interspersed their acts with lines of patter, jokes, repartee, and insult. A harp, a viola, a drum, and a trumpet occasionally accompanied the narrative, songs, and miming. One or two performers played dialogues, debates, and one-line jokes. Secular playlets, like the Frenchman Adam de la Halle's *The Play of Robin and Marion* (c. 1283), also appeared on occasion. In *The Play of Robin and Marion* a knight falls in love with a shepherdess. After overcoming various obstacles and singing songs, the rightful lovers get together and dance a celebration of their love.

Nobles' sons, hoping to earn eventual knighthood, sometimes tried to work their way up from court entertainers. The would-be knights sang of the ideal chivalric love. Known as *troubadors* or *trouvères*, these aristocratic bal-

ladeers traveled in style, occasionally with their own retinue of *jongleurs* and servants. Sometimes they even traveled to another court, thereby blurring the distinction between entertainers who traveled and those who were in residence with a royal family. Interestingly, whenever the sons of knights or peasants served at a court as entertainers, the whole theatre profession's reputation rose. Evidently, from the very beginning of Western civilization, families preferred to stay home and be entertained; even today, modern technology—phonographs, radios, televisions, and even pianos—resembles in entertainment style the home theatrical company.

The troubador's stock in trade was the *chanson de danse*, a dancing song with a poetic narrative that featured group dancing, singing, and miming. Court troubadors tried to differentiate themselves from common minstrels by writing more complicated meanings into their songs, using more obscure symbolic associations, and composing more distinctive music. But the minstrels quickly copied the troubadors' work. And gradually, courts employed not only rhapsodes but also clowns or fools for entertainment. Some of the clowns became so popular that one actually played be-

*A booth stage at a village fair.*   (The Bettmann Archives, Inc.)

fore a pope, another had a town named after him, and another, William Somers, became the English king's best friend. Some fools and jesters enamoured kings so much that they obtained valets and attendants. A few jealous students even dropped out of the university to try their hands at professional fooling. Kings traded fools or gave clowns as gifts, as children today trade and exchange bubble gum cards. Fool-keeping ultimately became so fashionable that some cardinals and bishops were known to have male or female troupes. Dwarfs, grotesques, mental deficients, and lunatics rounded out the royal home-entertainment troupe.

Fools told stories. Often they acted all the roles themselves, but sometimes they cast their *marottes*, miniatures of their own heads mounted on sticks and used as ventriloquists' dummies, as some of the characters. Fools enjoyed the freedom to interrupt, challenge, and insult the king and his court at any moment. So that everyone would not feel this same freedom, the fools needed distinctive costumes. The chosen garb clearly descended from the clothing of the classical mimes: A hooded cap with asses' ears fell to the shoulders; it sometimes sported bells or a coxcomb (a strip of red cloth notched like the comb of a cock). Underneath the fool's cap a shaved head mocked the monk's devotion to his Lord. A motley jacket of patchwork cloth and tights with a tail jingled with more bells; fools obviously had a difficult time surprising the king with a performance. Props—worked as slapstick devices—might have included the *marotte*, a sack on a stick, or a sack filled with dried peas.

Companies of entertainers might also be found in the hire of town corporations, wearing the town's livery, and receiving salaries to perform at local celebrations and festivities. Town, court, and independent companies thus traveled between performances at their home bases; letters of commendation assured their safety and hospitality.

Players generally found a manor's great hall most suitable for their performances. The lord's raised dais at one end looked out over the playing space. Although banqueteers on the sides of the hall forced players to perform in the round, the kitchen entrance doors and the musicians' gallery enhanced their performance possibilities.

In the fourteenth century, when ordinances against vagabonds and beggars encouraged minstrels to find sponsoring households, fooling became a very popular pastime. A *société joyeuse*, an amateur company of fools, might celebrate the Feast of Fools, New Year's Day, the Twelfth Night, or a royal entry or military victory with a performance. Students and law clerks played farcical plays called *sotties* that flourished through the end of the Medieval era. Usually in verse of no more than 400 lines, *sotties* featured five fools enacting allegorical characters to teach a moral lesson through satire.

Mummings and disguisings were also enjoyed by the bourgeoisie as amateur secular theatricals. Winter processions of costumed and masked townspeople went from house to house for singing, dancing, and a short game of dice with each host. Tournaments and jousts provided mock battles and luxurious pageantry set in a Court of Love under the jurisdiction of a noble lady. Allegorical associations, biblical symbols, and chivalric heraldry created a potpourri of images. Poetic debates on questions of love played a prominent part in the military training exercises with music, script, dance, and song. Such questions as "Can real love exist between married people?" provided early sources for Renaissance operas, ballets, and masques.

***Religious Drama Outside the Church*** In the middle of the Medieval period the church moved some performances outside the church's liturgical services and cathedral walls. In the early thirteenth century, for example, occasional performances of religious plays depicting the miracles of the saints occurred outside the walls of the church. Plays may also have been performed on the steps of a church. By the middle of the thirteenth century the laity were contributing to Christian drama, and staging passed to their hands. Outside the walls of the church, in the marketplaces and guild halls of new cities, the Christian message proclaimed to numerous people the entire Passion of Christ. Nevertheless, liturgical plays remained a part of the Mass until the sixteenth century.

The church drama's growing popularity produced edicts and criticisms from many church officials. Some claimed the humorous elements had passed beyond the church's control; others forbade clergy from participating any further. In 1170 Herrad of Landesberg, Abbess of Hohenburg, denounced the buffoonery in the Christmas plays. Other church leaders urged the banning of all church drama.

Liberal heads prevailed, and outside the church the drama continued the playing conventions of liturgical drama. A mansion or several mansions stood on a neutral platea. Scripts detailed the permissible actions. In the Anglo-Norman *The Play of Adam* (1150), for example, the characters receive the following directions·

> Adam must be well trained when to reply and to be neither too quick nor too slow in his replies. And not only he, but all the personages must be trained to speak composedly, and to fit convenient gesture to the matter of their speech. Nor must they foist in a syllable or a clip one of the verses, but must enounce firmly and repeat what is set down for them in due order.[4]

Directions such as these usually reacted to problems in past productions. *The Play of Adam* shows vernacular passages interspersed with Latin. Contemporary and non-Christian characters, such as Dame Douche, mix with biblical and Christian characters.

In time these religious plays became completely vernacular. Outdoor performances in the vernacular provided a great opportunity to draw large audiences; people could understand what was being said as well as what was being done.

***Saints Plays***   As early as 1170 plays were performed in England that were based on the lives of the church's chivalric knights—the saints. In France, Miracles of Our Lady the Virgin plays served the same purpose as the saint plays. The most famous saint plays were Jean Bodel's *St. Nicholas Play* (c. 1200) and Rutebeuf's *Miracle of Théophile* (c. 1261). Other favorite plays dealt with the miracles of St. Catherine and St. Paul.

Saint and martyr plays varied in length because they were usually associated with a local church's festival. Saint and martyr plays, reveling in great spectacle and realism, featured battle scenes, torture, and bawdy humor. Usually the plot hinged on the local saint's intercession between a local sinner and God. If the sponsor were a guild, the guild's patron saint starred in the show.

Saint plays provided living witness to supernatural events not directly related to Christ's own life. If a miracle could happen once, why not again? All one needed to do was stop the Jews, who were featured characters in the saint plays. Plots of Jewish mutilation of the Eucharistic Host, desecration of images of Jesus and the saints, and ritualistic murder of young Christian children gave Christian audiences visual reinforcement for their beliefs. Jews were given distinctive characteristics on the stage to visually connect them with Satan and the animal kingdom. Horns, tails, goats' beards, and foul body odors were unmistakable. In addition, at the time of the Inquisition, plays justified the church's torture, burnings, and executions. Presented as such absolute paradigms of evil, Jews lost their humanity and receded into the shadows of the occult. Jews, devils, and barnyard, monster-like animals traded traits willy-nilly on the medieval stage. In French plays revealing the miracles of the Host, Jews burn, trample, and stab the Host, yet it remains. Repentent usurers, asking for forgiveness and baptism, are booed, derided, and burned to the delight of the audience. Plays depicting the miracles of the Virgin could not fail to arouse the throng with the Blessed Mother's harangues against the Jews, the murderers of her beloved son.

# LATE PERIOD: c. 1300–c. 1500

The Medieval age concluded as the church's power and authority diminished, the bourgeoisie's power and influence increased, and individuals' minds turned again to the things of this life. The Gothic style of art peaked. Knighthood decayed in long wars. Movable type and plague further erased the Old World.

By the fourteenth century, attendance at church rituals declined, especially among the young who attended only on feast days. Frequently empty churches witnessed the Mass. Popes continued to condemn heretics almost as often as heretics condemned the church. Corruption became a favorite target for church reformers. Priests were accused of shooting dice and of sins of the flesh. Pilgrimages to the Holy Land became excuses for debauchery and adultery. John Wyclif (c. 1320–1384), a professor at Oxford University, and Jan Hus (c. 1369–1415) of Czechoslovakia, leading critics of clerical corruption, anticipated the Protestant Reformers of the early Renaissance.

***The Rise of Humanism***   Classicism, preserved throughout the Medieval age, had lost much of its original meaning by the end of that time. By "comedy," medieval scholars understood a poetic vernacular narrative beginning with horror and ending with joy; by "tragedy," they meant a grandly written work that began quietly and ended in horror.

The Romans and Greeks were predisposed to the ancient civilizations that had flourished there. With the revival of humanistic interests in antiquity came not only the best of the past, however, but also the worst: A vogue for magic, witchcraft, and alchemy lasted well into the Renaissance. Nonetheless, humanists saw individuals' sinfulness as irrelevant to the possibility of creative endeavor. God was, after all, the Creator.

During the Late Medieval era humanist scholars translated and collated manuscripts. In 1469 Cosimo de Medici, a wealthy bourgeois, established a Platonic Academy in Florence where such work was done. Gradually, classical models received attention not only for their form but also for their inspirational content. In 1486, for instance, Vitruvius's *De Architectura* was discovered and published. But Gothic humanists read plays and imagined theatres through eyes trained by liturgical plays, saints plays, and cosmic mystery cycles. As a result, humanist recreations of the classicism of Greece and Rome produced the work of William Shakespeare, Hans Sachs, Pierre Corneille, and Lope de Vega. As writers, artists, and theatre workers followed Italy's lead, the medieval world faded away in the birth of the Renaissance.

***The Feast of Corpus Christi***   To abort the coming of secular humanism, the church moved to bring the message of the Gospel closer to the people. A Feast of Corpus Christi, ordered in 1264 by Pope Urban, lay dormant until 1311. The church hoped to use this festival to revitalize the faith. It would shift emphasis from individual sinfulness to the redemptive power of Christ in the miracle of the Host. The Host enabled individuals to participate fully in the creative act.

The Feast of Corpus Christi occasioned the church's greatest achievement in theatre and drama. Also, the feast sometimes featured the church's greatest creation next to the Mass, the cycle of mystery plays: a detailed history of the universe from the beginning, through the Passion of Christ, to the Final Judgment. The Feast, like the drama, celebrated God's gift of the Holy Sacrament, the redemptive power of Christ continuing to alter human destiny. The message of the Corpus Christi Festival, occurring on the Thursday after Trinity Sunday (sometime between May 23 and June 24), addressed both the new merchant class and the monied artisans. In fact, the festival, celebrating the creative power of the Host, made the merchants and artisans the creators of the festival itself. The marketplace, not the church, was the site of theatrical endeavor.

A Corpus Christi procession in the fifteenth century. (National Szechenyi Library, Budapest)

***The Gothic Arts*** The Gothic arts surrounding the Feast of Corpus Christi bridged the medieval and Renaissance worlds. In *The Social History of Art* Arnold Hauser calls the Gothic style the most fundamental change in the whole history of modern art. Nature became the object of imitation; depth of feeling grew in characters with normal human motivations. Situations were recognizably contemporary. The physical agony of Jesus's crucifixion, the torment of tortured saints, the grief of Mary's mourning, and the sadistic glee of Jewish fiends imitated what people believed they saw around them. Piers Plowman, the hero of the fourteenth-century poem of the same name, demonstrated how a simple peasant, searching for Christian perfection, could become a human manifestation of Christ. Artists reveled in a new-found sensuousness and sensitivity. The laity assumed greater control over the creative vision of their work. The building of cathedrals and the staging of plays became the laity's arts.

Gothic art and theatre struck a balance between the Early Medieval life-forsaking view and the Renaissance life-affirming view. The theatrical view of nature and life as worthy of artistic representation triumphed over the Christian view of nature and earthly life as blocks to individuals' knowledge of God. Gothic art presented spiritual characters in a contemporary framework. Universal truths came through particular instances. In this way, the church hoped to make its old and eternal truths relevant. No longer sinful and unclean, art and theatre celebrated human life. Individual lives with unique qualities and features appeared more frequently on stage and in art; particular details crept into the representations. Natural realities were believed to house and preserve ideal and divine truths. Nature and people were drawn not as opponents, but as sharers of the Holy Spirit.

But in time, the Florentine painter Giotto (c. 1266–c. 1336) managed to create a three-dimensional effect on a flat surface by modeling in light and shade. And Leon Battista Alberti's (1402–1472) treatise on painting and perspective (1435) represented a major event in the history of visual representation. The new relative relationships of objects to the position of the viewers raised dangerous notions of relativity and point of view to an unsurpassed status.

***War and Plague*** Warfare and plague likewise undermined Medieval individuals' faith in absolute justice. The 100 Years' War (1337–1453) between France and England diminished the stature of knights incapable of either winning the war or making a peace. When the war did end, English medieval society lay in ruins, but French nationalism revived. And new methods of warfare dominated. England was forced to look west to the sea for new lands. Death and misery seemed to be knighthood's only products.

The Black Death, a bubonic plague that hit Europe between 1347 and 1350, killed over one-third of the people in western Europe. The rich fled to the country; the poor died trapped in cities. The plague's chaos lowered the world's intellectual level, corrupted manners, unhinged minds, aroused expectations of the Apocalypse, and spread an obscene interest in the Devil that latched onto Jewish and female scapegoats. Surviving serfs demanded freedom with greater vigor; in a reduced labor market a citizen's work doubled in value.

The world turned upside-down and—of all things—danced. Dancing manias such as tarantism (a nervous disease characterized by hysteria and a mania for dancing), St. John's Dance (epilepsy), and St. Vitus's Dance (chorea) swept Europe. Strange seizures kept victims glued to their partners, dancing, until the mass hysteria ended in death or amputation for hundreds or thousands of people. Dancing led a grotesque procession of citizens, drawn from all ranks and professions, to a common grave. *Danse Macabre*, *Danse des Morts*, *Totendanz*, and the *Dance of Death* figured in many Gothic paintings and tales. The bizarre image was contrasted with the procession of Corpus Christi, which led Christians to their common salvation in heaven.

***Movable Type and Printing*** In 1454 printing arrived with the introduction of movable metal type; by 1500 nine million books and pamphlets were available. Typography rode the tide of middle-class wealth, skill, and organization; it presaged future merchanization of handicrafts. Printed words were the West's first mass-produced things; books were the West's first uniform and repeatable commodity.

Print also revolutionized the entertainment professions: The storyteller, the rhapsode, the troubador, and the minstrel all grew less essential; people could read tales that were once enacted for them. For the first time, too, narration became a private matter. Memorization gradually became a lost art.

Typography diminished not only the oral entertainers' importance but also the importance of oral facility to society. From 1450 to the twentieth century, when the whole system of language became suspect, a visual bias slowly replaced the oral orientation. Characterization, for example, no longer a troubador's vocal and physical manipulations, depended on words printed on a page; print replaced the visual and auditory techniques of characterization. Reading became a silent pastime; punctuation began to accommodate the needs of the eye rather than the needs of the mouth and ear. In print medieval individuals saw their vernacular ideas legitimized.

But whereas future audiences would see the world through print—would know linear, sequential, and visual stimuli—medieval audiences could only enjoy plays in performance; copies were unavailable for them to read. And the medieval theatre continued to give words their music. The theatre continued to emit simultaneous, multiple-sourced stimuli.

***Mystery Cycle Plays*** The glory of the Late Medieval period's religious theatre sprang from the Feast of Corpus Christi. Like previous church dramas, those of the Late period sought to make the church more relevant to the common people. As the Passion Play of Lucerne announced, drama existed to Honor God, Edify Man, and Glorify the City. In France, the new plays were known as *mystères*; in England, "mystery cycles"; in Italy, *sacre rappresentazioni*; in Spain, *autos sacramentales*; and in Germany, *Geistliche Spiele*. All were produced by the laity, all were in the vernacular, and most celebrated the Feast of Corpus Christi.

Vernacular cycle plays, which flourished in the fifteenth century, may have resulted from both a continuation of the translation of liturgical plays into the vernacular and initiatives independent of the liturgical dramas. The dramas' didacticism and proselytism could have received impetus from a procession of church personnel and laity following the elevated Host from the town church through the town's streets. The plays of the Feast of Corpus Christi may have been in response to the popular *chansons de geste*, epic tales in the vernacular. In any event, the church produced its own epic, woven from the tales of Jesus, saints, martyrs, and biblical heroes, from the Falls of Lucifer and Adam, to the Day of the Last Judgment.

The drama of the Late Medieval age was part of the church's teaching through sermons, schools, wall paintings, and stained glass. According to V. A. Kolve in *The Play Called Corpus Christi*, the Christian artist helped develop medieval individuals' imaginative capability by creating concrete images of past, future, and invisible things. Such creations were superimposed on a living picture of the present. The creation of a cyclical drama, depicting humans' entire cosmological existence, showed how the Sacrament of Bread and Wine summarized all that went before and justified all that would come. Costume, scenery, and language, contemporary with medieval life, gave vividness and urgency to the church's stories. In addition, by removing Old Testament characters and the career of Jesus from their Jewish contexts, the church further legitimized the growing anti-Semitism of Europe.

***Religious Festivals and Drama*** Most religious plays of the Medieval period were directly related to particular feasts in the church calendar. All church seasons but Lent had dramas associated with them. As we have just discussed, the great medieval cycle plays, or mysteries, occasionally and incidentally developed out of festival processions at the time of the Feast of Corpus Christi. From the thirteenth

*Jean Fouquet's* The Martydom of St. Apollina. (New York Public Library Theatre Collection)

century on, three-dimensional images had been paraded in processions. Guilds were assigned particular images or *tableaux vivants* to produce for the processions. Sometimes parades would stop for brief sequences of action or speeches by the costumed participants. At the end of the procession dramatic plays could be presented, sometimes on specially constructed stages, sometimes on the floats or pageant wagons used in the procession, and sometimes on the ground surrounding the wagons.

By the middle of the fourteenth century, spring and summer outdoor cycle plays celebrating the Feast of Corpus Christi were often seen in Europe. Gradually, other occasions—Easter, Whitsuntide, or the feast day of a particular city's patron saint—boasted a program of mystery plays. But usually the plays were not annual events; intervals of from two to ten years passed between productions. When the plays were performed, they began at sunrise and ended at night. Trade centers such as Coventry, Mons, Lucerne, Valencia, and Florence used the plays to show off their commercial assets, as Athens had in the fifth century B.C. As Arnold Hauser noted in *The Social History of Art* the city is more suitable for the creation of art than the country.

By the fourteenth century, the Feast of Corpus Christi was a principal festival in Europe. Costumed guild members, the bejeweled Host, torches, banners, adorned pictures, detailed effigies, and icons of scriptural significance, such as Noah's Ark and the Tree of Knowledge, made the procession a wonder to behold. As the procession wound through town streets, priests could stop for worship and communion. During the ten to fifteen stops, guild members on pageant wagons or floats may have recited or improvised a few lines of appropriate dialogue or played a few pantomimic actions from their representations of biblical scenes. If dramatic interpolations occurred during the procession they were probably brief, so as not to delay the rest of the marchers. At the end of the procession, parade marchers may have joined the onlookers for plays featuring the scenes from the parade. Churchyards, cemeteries, old Roman amphitheatres, city squares, and town halls may have served as sites for performance.

The feast, the procession, and the drama combined the historical time of Christ with present time in one universal time scheme. In *The Medieval Theatre* Glynne Wickham suggests that the Old Testament was presented as a prologue and prediction of the New Testament, Adam as a prediction of Christ, Eve of Mary, and the Cross of Calvary of the Tree of Knowledge; Noah's Flood prefigured the Last Judgment. Time was, in this way, united and compressed; in Lucerne, the entire history of the universe took but two days to relate. The glory of Christian drama coincided with the peaks of both Yuan theatre and saragaku-no drama in the East.

*Organization of Religious Drama* The Late Medieval period's religious plays marked a new method of organizing the production of church plays. Civic organizations and town officials could act as producers; the church often merely approved the scripts and production techniques while supplying ecclesiastical costumes and properties. In addition, the organization of plays varied according to the amount of money available.

In Europe, religious guilds or confraternities—clubs of the laity and clergy dedicated to charitable work—occasionally presented the plays. The confraternities aided their members in good times and bad, baptisms and executions. The guilds not only staged religious plays but may also have organized parades on feast days, donated windows to churches, and commissioned murals. In France, the most famous confraternity was the *Confrérie de la Passion* (1398). Societies of *jongleurs* occasionally helped out as well. In Italy, the *sacre rappresantazioni* were organized by *compagne*; in Spain, by *confradia*. Germany sometimes found guilds, other times wealthy merchants, to bankroll the productions. In Lucerne, the city council and the Brotherhood of the Crown of Thorns, whose membership consisted of clergy and the city's first families, shared the expense and supervision. In England, the so-called N-town Cycle may have been produced by the Coventry Franciscans.

Elsewhere in England, a joint committee of town councilors and trade guild officials usually supervised the production of plays. The committee could assign individual plays to particular guilds, regulate fidelity to the text, choose playing locations, and levy fines on poor productions. For example, the shipwrights, watermen, or fishermen might stage the play of Noah; goldsmiths, the story of the Three Magi; and bakers, the Feeding of the Five Thousand or the Last Supper. Armorers might feature a beautiful sword in their staging of the expulsion from the Garden. Plasterers and carpenters could collaborate on the Creation, while scriveners worked on the Disputation in the Temple. The whole event resembled a trade fair.

With the rebirth of towns and a money economy, the laity usually won the upper hand in production. And as the Gothic cathedral grew more complex than the Romanesque, the cycle plays outdistanced the liturgical dramas. More people got involved in the productions; consequently, more time was needed to plan, build, and rehearse. Moreover, as the lodge evolved to coordinate the labor pool and money needed to erect a cathedral, the confraternity developed to meet similar demands in staging the epic dramas. Labor began to divide; specialization of skill developed among workers.

Cycles, like cathedrals, required strict regulation in construction. Precise rules regarding work contracts, management hierarchies, and labor restrictions appeared. The medieval stage director organized the workers: Choir boys played women characters, artisans built settings, nobles and rich merchants loaned costumes, and priests copied scripts. Individual artists submerged their egos for the common task. In England, the central corporation of the city could have had the banns (formal announcement) of the play read, keep the official text, and formulate production responsibilities. Individual guilds might have borne the expenses. Some producing organizations might have selected a single stage manager, or director, to oversee the production. Many directors acquired reputations and invitations from towns to repeat their successes.

### A Celebration of Community

Like cathedrals, dramas created a sense of community. In Lucerne a public proclamation from the pulpit announced the unifying occasion. Tryouts were open to all who wished to participate in the drama. In *The Medieval Theatre* Glynne Wickham maintains that no other medieval event could compare in unifying, fulfilling, and democratizing a community.

When plays were performed in a town courtyard, townspeople could watch from their windows or rent their spaces to people seeking a better view. Eager audience members arrived early to claim good seats. Scaffolding provided seats for wealthy and honored guests; the poor stood. Lavatories were erected. Some productions charged an admission fee, others were free. Food and drink were either brought from home or purchased at the performance site. The violence and crudity of some episodes forced some producers to forbid admission to children, the aged, and pregnant women. Once inside, men might be segregated from the women. A barrier, ditch, fence, water, or guards kept the excited audience from the stage. At night, guards patrolled the stage to safeguard the scenery, costumes, and properties.

During the sprawling, transforming, dynamic production, spectators moved about, jostling one another for a better view. A holiday mood stirred crowds of up to 6000, motivated by deep religious inclination, a search for fun, and occasional promises of excommunication or remission of sins. Brawls and quarrels sometimes broke out; prayers were used to restore order. As a prologue, a Mass calmed and quieted the crowd. After the opening Mass or prayer, an anthem or sermon might precede the first scene. When the cycle ended, honored guests, and perhaps the players, enjoyed a banquet.

### The Cycle Texts

The cycle texts related key biblical events to the life of Jesus. Every cycle was composed of many individual plays, each about twenty-five to fifty minutes in length. The Wakefield cycle, for example, had thirty-two plays; the Lincoln, forty-two. During a cycle's history new plays were added, unpopular plays were dropped, and standard works rewritten.

The cycle's episodic structure ignores any cause-to-effect relationship between incidents. By eschewing chronology, the telescopic structure makes distant character's thoughts more contemporary. Anachronisms in the texts, in fact, may have been deliberate attempts to make Christian mythology contemporaneous. The vernacular verse's rhyme and alliteration facilitated both memorization and audibility. Latin was reserved for important proclamations, especially by God. Characterization was minimal. Setting did little more than establish place. Comic scenes juxtaposed reality with ideality, humanity with divinity. Devils, villains, buffoons, and Jews romped across the stages of the universe causing untold misery.

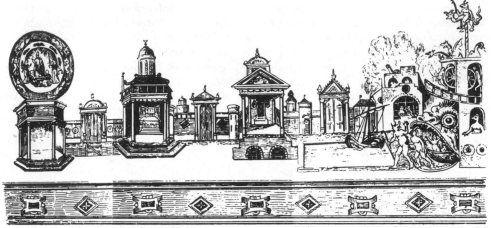

*Arrangement of the mansions for the 1547 Valenciennes Passion Play.* (Drawing by Gerda Becker With after Cohen, *Le Théâtre en France au Moyen Age*.)

Surviving texts date from the end of the Medieval era. Despite their being composed by a succession of authors, remarkable unity and tonal consistency survive in the works along with certain national characteristics. German plays tend to favor grotesque, almost nightmarish scenes; anti-Semitism and crude satirical references likewise proved popular. The extant French plays show a more restricted scope than the English plays. The typical French cycle concluded with the Resurrection. French plays also featured devils, but seem inclined toward rhetoric and intellectual argument. English plays offer simplicity and restraint by contrast.

The names of certain playwrights survive: Jean Bodel, Rutebeuf, Arnoul Greban, Benedikt Debs, Renward Cysat, Hans Baldung, Feo Belcari, Sir Henry Francis, and Miles Blomfield. These individual names underline the growing interest in individual creation. Authors were, according to Glynne Wickham in *The Medieval Theatre*, educated, knowledgeable in church doctrine, familiar with the rhetorical tricks of contemporary preachers, and capable of composing moving verse. Clergy, lawyers, and notaries all wrote plays in service of the church.

One of the most popular dramas comes from the nativity plays in Wakefield. *The Second Shepherd's Play* (1375) is a farce using popular hu-mor and everyday characters: Shepherds freezing in a northern European winter complain of taxation and overwork. One of their lambs is stolen by the poor Mak, who hides the booty in his wife's bed. When confronted by the angry shepherds, Mak's wife pretends the lamb is her baby. Mak is caught and punished just as angels announce the birth of the Savior who will become the Good Shepherd and the Lamb of God.

The Passion of Christ revealed in the cycle plays was almost cinematic in intent. The playwrights sought a moving plot rather than an intensification of any one situation. A multiplicity of particulars and flowing transitions characterized the Gothic drama, conceived, as V. A. Kolve suggests in *A Play Called Corpus Christi*, as a game. Drama was often called a game: Borrowing from the secular tradition that named drama *ludus* in England, *jeu* in France, and *Spiel* in Germany, the Gothic playwrights fancied human history as a match between God and Satan. Latin liturgical dramas had had little relationship with games. But once in the streets, amid a holiday crowd, religious drama acquired gaming or playing qualities. The cosmic game of the cycle was hosted and refereed by the Nuntius, Expositor, Poeta, or *Maître du jeu*, a character who framed each episode with narrative or morals.

Kolve formulates a protocycle to outline the

basic cycle mystery. Episodes dealt, he suggests, with the seven ages of the world first espoused by St. Augustine in the concluding pages of *City of God* (413):

The Fall of Lucifer
The Creation and Fall of Man
Cain and Abel
Noah and the Flood
Abraham and Isaac
   Moses and the Exodus and/or Moses and the
    Laws
   The Prophets
Nativity Plays
   The Baptism
   The Temptation
The Raising of Lazarus
Passion Plays
Resurrection Plays
   The Assumption and Coronation of the Virgin
Doomsday

The plays show God intervening in human history, just as the Host intervenes in secular society by leaving the church during the Feast of Corpus Christi. Eternal time is presented as more important than human time.

Anti-Semitism peaked during the theatrical games. The festival plays show Jews under the tutelage of Satan, working charms and making potions for use against Jesus. The Hebrew language is mocked as gibberish. Accuracy was unnecessary; medieval realism had its own conventions. Jews were heretics, and all heretics were alike. Consequently, some plays show Jews worshipping Mohammed. The character of Judas is drawn as a usurer haggling over Jesus with Caiaphas. Erich Auerbach explains:

> . . . an occurrence on earth signifies not only itself but at the same time another, which it predicts or confirms, without prejudice to the power of its concrete reality here and now. The connection between occurrences is not regarded as primarily a chronological or casual development but as a oneness within the divine plan, of which all occurrences are parts and relations. Their direct earthly connection is of secondary importance, and often their interpretation can altogether dispense with any knowledge of it.[5]

***The Staging of Cycle Plays***   Gothic realism in dramatic construction carried over into the staging of the plays. The cycle plays were, in fact, extremely elaborate. But the precise manner by which the elaborateness took form has been a matter of scholarly dispute. Historians generally agree that most of the mystery cycles of Europe ultimately took place on fixed stages. Most historians also agree that in Spain wagons containing some scenery and actors for the *autos* were part of the Corpus Christi procession, but for performances the wagons were moved to fixed platform stages. England presents a problem. Individual English guilds sometimes built pageant wagons, scenery, costumes, properties, special effects, and even acted in the plays. But some historians argue that the wagons were movable stages upon which the plays were performed along the procession's route. Within this processional staging, each play may have been performed several times a day, each time at a different location and before a different audience. Other historians, interpreting the primary historical evidence differently, argue for fixed staging. These historians suggest that the pageant wagons were merely floats in the Corpus Christi procession similar to those in a modern Thanksgiving Day Parade. The floats may have stopped only for a brief excerpt from a longer play, which, as in Spain, could have been performed after the procession on a fixed platform stage. The floats may have been mansions drawn to a fixed stage platea. In any case, staging practices were probably not universal. Local producers most likely used whatever technique suited their peculiar needs.

Fixed platform stages could be anywhere from 120 feet to 200 feet wide and sixty to eighty feet deep. Cycle stages could be circular, square, or rectangular, depending on the location of the necessary changing and off-stage areas. Flat ground or a raised platform functioned as the platea; one large or several small plateas might exist for a production. The pageant wagon or carriage was probably about twenty feet by ten feet. Historians who favor the processional staging theory for England suggest either a two-storied wagon with off-stage space below, or a scaffold platform stage

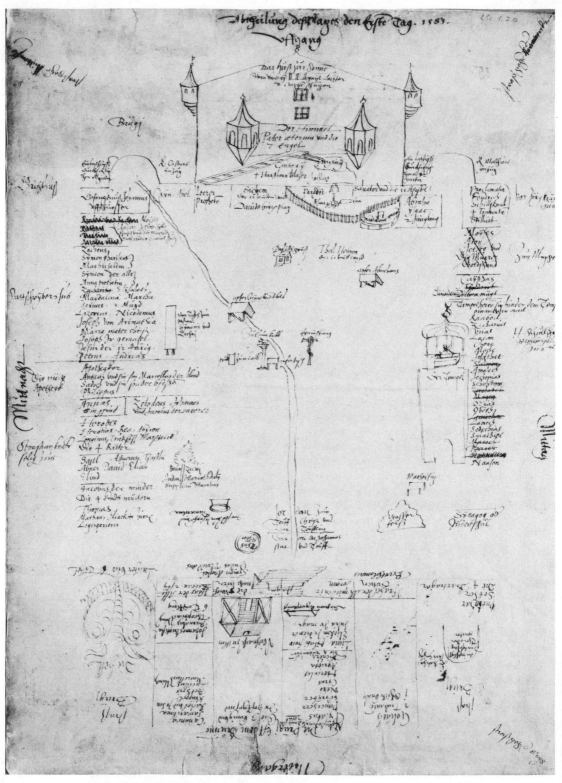

*Renward Cysat's stage plan for the first day of the Lucerne Osterspiel production of 1583.* (Zentralbibliothek, Lucerne)

at each of the stops to which a wagon was drawn for performance. The latter theory would involve a single mansion for each guild's play and a neutral platea at each of the processional stops. If processional staging existed in England, the debated practice was probably inconsistent.

***Scenery for the Cycles*** Medieval pictorial and sculptural art may have served as models for the climactic scenes in the cycle plays. Artists occasionally worked with merchants on scenery, costumes, properties, and special effects. Italian architect Filippo Brunelleschi (c. 1377–1446) designed settings for Italian *sacre rappresentationi* and concocted *ingeni* (secret special effects). For a production of the *Annunciation* Brunelleschi made a "heaven." Italian art historian Giorgio Vasari (1511–1574) describes it:

> . . . Filippo had arranged a half-globe between two rafters of the roof of the church, like a hollow porringer or a barber's basin turned upside down. It was formed of thin laths secured to an iron star which revolved round a great iron ring upon which it was poised . . . children, twelve in all, being arranged, as I have said, on pedestals and clad like angels with gilt wings and caps of gold lace, took one another's hands when the time came, and extending their arms, they appeared to be dancing, especially as the basin was always turning and moving. Inside this and above the heads of the angels were three circles or garlands of lights arranged like some tiny lanterns which could not turn over. These lights looked like stars from the ground.[6]

All action was staged as if part of the present. Medieval people believed the lines of Psalm 90: "For a thousand years in thy sight are but as yesterday." God's history was eternal; past events had to relate to the present. Environment, decoration, and dress visualized the unchanging nature of God's plan for humanity.

As in the Sanskrit theatre, simultaneous settings held the stage. Each *journée* (act) could, in fact, contain anywhere from eight to twenty different locations. Earth was built of many oddly shaped mansions that had curtains for concealment and revelation. Some mansions were elevated; others contained tables, doors, benches, beds, altars, and thrones. At the beginning of each *journée* the Poeta introduced the mansions, which signs helped identify. When scenery changed during intermission, mansions were redecorated or replaced.

On opposite ends of the stage, Heaven and Hell housed the captains of the opposing teams; Earth lay as the gameboard between them. Human characters were the playing pieces. Heaven, which sometimes sat above the Garden of Eden mansion, impressed people with its splendid height and decoration. A golden light shone out of Heaven as its gates opened. Flying equipment let angels with flaming swords or humming harps swoop down to Earth and return home with saved souls. Hell, in contrast, terrified people with a monster's mouth entrance situated below stage level. Resembling a fortress prison, Hell belched forth smoke, noise, screams, fire, and gunpowder explosions. Devils slithered or scampered out to lure, coax, and seize earthlings. Occasionally Hell was built as an infernal condominium containing Limbo, Purgatory, and the Pit.

Other scenery was used as well. A rear curtain, which was half black and half white, facilitated God's creation of day and night. Strips of red fabric fell as Moses crossed the Red Sea. Painted backdrops, representing clouds, hid flying equipment and trickery for special effects called "secrets." These secrets grew in popularity, importance, and complexity during the fifteenth and sixteenth centuries. Imported *maîtres des feintes* (masters of effects) employed machinist skills on pulleys and windlasses; trap doors for miraculous appearances, disappearances, and substitutions; and water for floods, fishing, and walking. Elaborate schemes of torture and execution portrayed the Inquisition. As actors burned at stakes, the odor of burning animal bones and entrails wafted across the noses of audience members familiar with the real odor. Soft animal bladders simulated the sticks Jews used to scourge Jesus. Decapitation and crucifixion were also feigned; weapons contained blood to heighten such effects. Blood concealed in bladders hidden beneath costumes, for example, squirted across the stage. Whips dipped in blood left marks across actors' bare bodies. In France, the severed head of St. Peter bounced three times, leaving a flowing fountain at each spot. A statue of the Virgin had a movable head, arms, and eyes. Herod killed himself with a blade-retracting sword. Live and impersonated lions, tigers, leopards, serpents, boars, dragons, camels, asses, birds, wolves, and snakes recalled the Roman amphitheatre. In 1501, Mons filled Eden with real animals, fish, grass, trees, and bushes. Abraham slaughtered a real lamb. Thunder, flame-blowing dragons, spouting fountains, and sailing ships also appeared on stage. Staffs turned into snakes, wives into pillars of salt, and water to wine, all under the masterly guidance of the *maître des feintes*.

In many cases actors supplied their own costumes. Inside their clothing, they wore pots or leather body suits to protect them from staged beatings and attacks. Costume mostly followed the trend to contemporary realism. Medieval armor bedecked Roman soldiers. Shepherds wore Alpine peasant garb. Pilate was dressed as a medieval lord or city official. Jewish high officials wore the clothes of Christian priests; Jews in general wore the mandated clothing for medieval Jews. Devils exaggerated Jewish stereotypes with features extracted from birds of prey—horns, claws, tails, and scales—and monster-animal heads, the characteristics of infidels. God was modeled on either the emperor or the pope. And church robes fixed with wings clothed gilt-faced angels.

Accessories and properties both symbolized and characterized figures. Archangel Michael was known by his flaming sword, Judas by his red wig and yellow robe, Mary by her white and gold silk tunic, St. Peter by his keys to the Kingdom, and St. Catherine by her wheel. Gloves imported high rank. Wearing white meant one's soul was saved; black, damned. Sword and scales denoted justice; a mirror, prudence; a snake, envy; an owl or spider, Satan; a scorpion, a Jew; a lily or iris, the Virgin; and a clover, the Blessed Trinity.

**Acting for the Cycles** Even with extensive double casting almost 300 actors were needed to produce a play with over 400 roles. Actors of the Late Medieval period were primarily nonclerical. They were mostly local merchants and traders, and occasionally clergy, nobles, and professional players. Consequently, rehearsals worked around business hours. As guilds and confraternities sought to top the previous year's cycle, they may have turned to professional minstrels and *jongleurs*. Companies of fools sometimes supplied comic actors. Most actors were men and boys, though France occasionally let women participate. In 1468, for instance, a glazier's daughter played St. Catherine in Metz. And in 1547, Jeanette Caralieu played the Virgin at Valenciennes. Because the vernacular was spoken, facility in chanted Latin was no longer needed.

A large hall served as the rehearsal space. Because a typical four-day play needed forty-eight rehearsals, the producing organization supplied refreshments to attract the actors to rehearse. For their work guild members and professional players might either be paid a small fee or remitted with indulgences. After a general meeting a script was divided into rehearsal units. Because each play had its own cast, a cycle could show an audience several different Jesuses, Marys, Gods, and Satans. At Lucerne in 1597, for example, Peter Leeman played nine roles, and three actors played Jesus—one as a baby, one at age 12, and one as an adult. Herod was a popular role for actors who enjoyed improvising, but actors were wary of Judas and Jesus: In 1437 an actor playing Jesus almost died during the Crucifixion and a Judas almost expired at his hanging.

Auditions could take place before a guild or committee, although many people played the same role year after year. In Lucerne, actors were allowed two weeks to decline or accept a role. Casting and rehearsals could fall under the hand of a stage manager or director who used the original script, the "register," as his promptbook. Sometimes known as the "pageant masters," the directors, who were occasionally accused of partiality and favoritism, oversaw one or two dress rehearsals at the end of the two-month rehearsal period. One of the most famous directors, Renward Cysat, the City Clerk of Lucerne from 1575 to 1614, directed the city's Passion Play in 1583 and again in 1597, after playing the Virgin in the 1571 production.

Audiences recognized good and bad acting. All actors, working under civic and religious oath, in fact, were subject to a schedule of fines, mostly for tardiness or drunkenness. Actors simply presented the characters' actions without becoming the characters. Music, not histrionics, set and modulated the mood and led the procession and recession. Choruses of angels sang or played trumpet fanfares. Drums and cymbals created thunder. Music did not just heighten tension and create mood; music was Heaven's intervention in human affairs. Instrumental or vocal music bridged scene shifts and transformations. Popular tunes mingled with church hymns in the context of Gothic realism. In Lucerne, where over 100 musicians from all parts of Switzerland crowded the city for its Passion Play, lyrics, using bits of eighteen different languages, mixed sense and nonsense. Rhymes could be taken from children's verse or common magical incantations.

*Decline of Religious Drama*   The peak of medieval religious drama began to bring religion into disrepute. Eventually, religious drama was banned: in France in 1548, in York in 1569, in Chester in 1575, and in Germany in 1597. Heretics and church reformers included the drama in their objections. German Protestant Martin Luther (1483–1546) and his followers disliked plays not for the Anti-Semitism, which they shared, but for the humor and the representation of Jesus. Reformers looked at the stage and saw profanity and superstition. During the years of Wyclif in England (c. 1320–1384), antitheatricalism resurfaced. But the church retaliated: Luther was cartooned on the stage as a fool, and drama thus became a weapon in the growing religious controversy. Moreover, with the growing economic difficulties involved in mounting the enormous pageants, religious drama was doomed. The Counter-Reformation retreated in its use of the stage as a tool for proselytism by checking the scripts carefully. Performances came under closer scrutiny by the church.

*Drama in the Religious Controversy*   As Protestants gained control in some areas of Europe, Catholic drama died out; it was replaced by the Gospels in oratorio form. Nevertheless, in England, John Bale (1495–1563) lashed out at the Catholic church with *The Treachery of the Papist* (1550) and *Kynge Johan* (*King Johan*, c. 1538), a play based on Thomas Kirchmayer's *Pammachius* (1538), which portrays the Pope as the Antichrist. Harold C. Gardiner explains Protestantism's philosophical objections to the drama:

> The subjectivism of Protestantism, which called for an ever-increasing rejection of the mediation of creatures between the soul and God, particularly when these creatures, in representing the saints and holy things, could be misunderstood as incentives to idolatry, would see in the religious stage but another horrible example of how Rome was content with the outward symbol, leaving the reality it represented untouched, uncared for. The individualism which rejected any authoritative interpretation of the Scriptures would scarcely tolerate the traditional meanings of Bible phrase and incident, such as the religious stage propagated.[7]

The warring religious stages did not pass away gradually. Neither did popular favor turn to the newfound classics: on the contrary. The religious plays persisted in holding great attention as rallying points and confirmations of belief in a time of great confusion. Cycle dramas were popular until either new Protestant governments suppressed them as idolatrous, superstitious, or political threats, or growing economic burdens crushed their production. With suppression or economic collapse, the distinction between religious and secular theatre increased.

Banishment and economic hardship turned would-be authors to secular subjects and natural history to replace sacred history and political satire. Common players stepped in to fill the void created by the cessation of the civic-religious festivals. England's Henry VII (reigned 1485–1509) sought to regulate theatrical performances by outlawing any player or minstrel not attached to a household or protected by royal license of the king or his Privy

Council. The time was ripe for secular players to cross to center stage.

***The Rise of Professional Players*** The history of the Late Medieval period's secular theatre follows the rise of professional players. Commercial factors drove wedges between participants in the community religious theatres' productions. The bond between audience and players, the foundation of the religious theatre's power, was lost.

Public theatre became a commodity available for purchase. During the fourteenth century, wealthy merchants and nobles retained permanent companies of professional players. Traveling players cared no more for one town or audience than for any other. When not needed at home, the troupes toured under the names of their patrons—as the Duke of Glouchester's Men or the Duke of York's Men, for example. Richard III (reigned 1483–1485) was the first English monarch to patronize such a troupe of players.

The theatre, no longer a community celebration of a common vision, thus became a commercial attempt to satisfy the aesthetic tastes of a patron. Records show that French troupes, perhaps *sociétés joyeuses*, toured England in 1494 and 1495. Touring companies of five men, one or two of whom were boys, created an audience that in the sixteenth century, eventually supported the erection of permanent theatres. Prosperity in the early sixteenth century let troupes increase their size to six; by century's end, the number had grown to seven or eight.

In 1527 Henry VIII built the House of Revels to stage court entertainments. He also created the Office of Revels under the Master of Revels, a descendant of the *Dominus Festi*, a court official appointed to supervise the Christmas revels. But unlike the *Dominus Festi*, also known as the Lord of Misrule, the Master of Revels was a permanent rather than a yearly appointment. Theatre had become a year-round profession.

***Regulation of the Theatre*** Growing religious tension brought players under greater control. In 1559 an English proclamation forbid the performance of plays unless approved by the Mayor of London, two Justices of the Peace, or the Lord Lieutenant. No religious or political plays were allowed. Noble patrons

*A rural platform stage.* (Centre Culturel de Cambrai)

would be held liable for their players' actions. Later, the Master of Revel's Office assumed a censor's role.

In 1572 an Act for Restraining Vagabonds insisted that all troupes be licensed by a noble or a Justice of the Peace. When renewed in 1597, this Act removed the Justices' power. As a result, many troupes disappeared, and the actor's status was redefined as an agent of a noble household.

***Trouping***   As professional specialization took over, players were differentiated from minstrels. Whereas previously wandering entertainers provided a night's variety entertainment for food and lodging, the new players enjoyed royal patronage and a permanent home. Touring became a luxury rather than a necessity. Resident entertainers held a higher social status than the wandering vagabond entertainers. They could thus afford to become men of letters; some even assumed the elite position of artistic tutor to the lord. Court artists, the forerunners of Renaissance humanists and poets, functioned as chroniclers for the rulers. The street entertainer retained the clown's mantle and functioned as society's satirist.

Thompson's model for a society's distribution of roles (see Chapter 1) also applies to the Late Medieval age. A touring lord's troupe had to walk a fine line between praising and mocking the hand that fed it. On tour the players, experimenting with innovation, changed their performances for the circumstances of a domestic hall, public building, marketplace, university residence hall, street pavement, or raised platform. After bursting into an audience with a cry of "Room," the touring players improvised to suit the moment and addressed the audience to exploit its proximity. Occasionally, word of an innovation or a too-hasty joke got back to the patron, and the players suffered.

Doubling played a major role in the players' acting. By the time of Elizabeth in England (1533–1603), actors averaged three or four roles in a play. Both court and popular audiences enjoyed the phenomenon. Boy actors played both male and female roles, but most companies lacked boy players. Gradually, acting companies developed a hierarchy; leading players did less doubling and minor players did more.

All players needed to sing and dance because song and dance were popular in all forms of drama, and dance and music played an integral part in the emerging secular plays. Even though little documentation exists for theatrical dancing, the practice surely existed. In *From Mankind to Marlowe*, David Bevington notes that the lack of documentation may result from an assumption that such matters did not need to be recorded in the scripts; the players added what was necessary themselves.

One result of the interest in dancing was that the dance manual was invented in the fifteenth century. As the church's influence waned, people sought instruction for dance—an activity long suppressed. Chivalry had elevated dance to social ceremony, so that dance etiquette required training. Players also capitalized on the growing interest in dance. But to rise socially, dancers needed to create their own dances. Such an incentive produced the "Dance Master," an agent of royalty, who toured to teach courts the dances he had created under his lord's generous patronage.

***Humanist Dramas***   Adam de la Halle, who wrote the oldest medieval secular play, *The Play of the Greenwood* (c. 1276), mixed the peasants of Arras (including himself and his father) with supernatural events. After de la Halle wrote *The Play of the Greenwood* and *The Play of Robin and Marion* (c. 1283), secular plays were set on paper more frequently. French farces, for example, prospered between 1450 and 1500. Such verse farces appeared as *Pierre Pathelin* (c. 1470), in which a poor lawyer cons a roll of cloth for his wife before being tricked himself by a wily shepherd. In some farce *sotties* allegorically costumed actors taught moral lessons through satire.

In Germany, too, farces popped up in pre-Lenten Shrovetide folk festivals. The most famous player-author was the German singing master Hans Sachs (1494–1576), who created *Fastnachtspiele*. In *The Wandering Scholar from Par-*

*adise* (1550) Sachs clearly showed the spirit of his Roman predecessors' improvised farces. A simple peasant widow thinks the wandering scholar from Paris is from paradise. The scholar goes along with the widow's confusion and agrees to take her deceased husband's belongings to him. The widow's new husband, however, chases the scholar, but ends up tricked himself.

In England, John Heywood (c. 1497–c. 1580), the first writer of English comedy, brought literary merit to the farce with plays like *Johan, Johan* (1533), *The Four Ps* (1545), and *The Play of the Weather*. In *The Four Ps* a lying contest matches a Palmer, a Pardoner, a Pothecary, and a Pedlar. Jupiter enters *The Play of the Weather* to learn why people are always dissatisfied with the weather. *Johan, Johan* struggles in a love triangle involving his wife and the village priest. Perhaps because of his association with St. Paul's cathedral (he was singing master there), Heywood used Latin dramatic models for instruction in rhetoric and oratory. In 1520, a work by Plautus (254–184 B.C.) was acted in Latin in London when Henry VIII ordered its performance for visiting French hostages. Then the St. Paul schoolboys acted Plautus's *The Menachmi* in 1527. In 1546 Cambridge University ruled that any student who either refused a role in a play or missed a play's performance would be expelled. Heywood branched out from farce in 1559 with his published translation of Seneca's *Troas*.

*Classical Models*  In the fifteenth century the Italian effort to revive interest in Roman drama spread throughout Europe to schools, universities, and courts. Plautus, Terence, and Horace provided solutions to practical problems facing playwrights who wished to write for small companies and unruly audiences. Not since Hroswitha, the German playwrighting Nun of Gandersheim in Saxony—far ahead of her time in the tenth century—had the classics been so studied and copied for the stage. Hroswitha had imitated Terence's dramaturgical technique using Christian heroes as her subjects. She explained why she, and perhaps Christians of the Late Medieval period, found the classics so alluring:

There are many Catholics, and we cannot entirely acquit ourselves of the charge, who, attracted by the polished elegance of the style of pagan writers, prefer their works to the holy scriptures. There are others who, although they are deeply attracted to the sacred writings and have no liking of the works of Terence, and, fascinated by the charm of the manner, risk being corrupted by the wickedness of the matter. Wherefore I, the strong voice of Gandersheim, have not hesitated to imitate in my writings, a poet whose works are so widely read, my object being to glorify, within the limits of my poor talent, the laudable chastity of Christian virgins that in that self-same form of composition which has been used to describe the shameless acts of licentious women.[8]

By the time her plays were discovered in 1501, Europe had begun to learn the ancient lessons Hroswitha prized so highly. And the printing press allowed new literary secular plays to survive and disseminate.

*Morality Plays*  The evolving dramatic structure of the secular plays depended upon a variety of influences. In *From Mankind to Marlowe* David Bevington suggests that the writing was modified by both the small size of the troupes and the public's love for spectacle. The resultant plays sought maximum effect with minimal means. Morality plays were, in fact, the upshot of the suppression of blatantly religious dramas, the small size of the troupes, and the desire for spectacle. Morality plays, beginning in the religious plays of the fourteenth century, derived from the Pater Noster plays performed in England by guilds. They thrived as Europe's dominant form of secular drama between about 1400 and 1550, mostly in England and France.

Morality playwrights continued the medieval method of dramatic construction. Simultaneous scenes gave works a panoramic effect. Comic and serious scenes were juxtaposed to show both moods as integral parts of the human experience. Doubling forced playwrights to introduce new characters while progressively abandoning old ones. Soliloquies commented on the action. Character existed simply as the compression of several qualities.

***Interludes*** In time the features of morality plays blended into what was known as an "interlude" in the early sixteenth century. *Interlude* was a term applied to just about everything entertaining. Generally speaking, an interlude lasted about one hour and consisted of an episode of about 1000 lines. The interlude was the first dinner theatre since the private Roman theatricals; plays might occur between courses or after the meal. They usually concluded with a prayer for the lord and his lands after having provided some entertainment or edification for everyone in the audience. The Prologue to Henry Medwall's *Fulgens and Lucrece* (c. 1497) adequately summarizes the interlude's goals:

This was the substance of the play
that was showed here today,
Albeit that there was
Divers toys mingled in the same
To stir folk to mirth and game
And to do them solace.
The which trifles be impertinent
To the matter principal;
But nevertheless they be expedient
For to satisfy and content
Many a man withal.
For some there be that looks and gapes
Only for such trifles and japes;
And some there be among
That forceth little of such madness
But delighteth them in matters of sadness
Be it never so long!
And every man must have his mind,
Else they will many faults find
And say the play was nought

Interludes were another dramatic "game," adapted to the political or religious tastes of the host. The same satire could just as easily be directed at Luther as at the pope. In 1543, however, censorship made casual improvising more difficult. Nevertheless, certain playing conventions established themselves for the interludes. Overall, the interlude used classical playing conventions: a neutral space before a facade for disappearances, appearances, exits, and entrances.

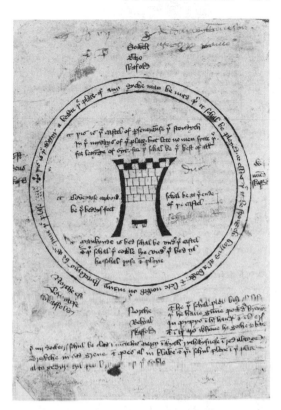

*Manuscript drawing for staging* The Castle of Perseverance, 1400–1425. (Folger Shakespeare Library, Washington, D.C.)

Though a particular space might be reserved for the interlude, the players used the entire available space. Although interludes were frequently performed at schools, colleges, and law students' Inn of Court, the great hall of a noble's residence served as the primary site. Opposite the head table stood a "screen," a wall separating the dining hall from the kitchen, which contained two or three doorways. Sometimes a low platform, placed before the facade created by the screen, gave the actors a raised level. Above the screen might be a musicians' gallery in which players could perform. Because the large crowd seated at tables around three or four sides of the hall might block entrances and exits, interluders played in the round or three-quarters.

Costume distinguished rank and profession. Lovers wore the colors of their lady, men the colors of their confraternity, and servants the livery of their lord. Allegorical characters donned imaginative dress—fame entered as eyes, ears, and tongues; vanity, as feathers; wealth, as gold and silver coins; and flattery and ignorance, as either Protestant or Catholic clerics. In the round, costume was the most important visual aspect. It also identified characters before they spoke. Interluders employed costume both as expressions of character and as satires of the day's fashion. A character's change of clothing, for example, might symbolize a change from vice to virtue, or vice versa.

*Variety Entertainments*   The theatrical impulse broke into all aspects of Late Medieval society. In the Low Countries, Chambers of Rhetoric—arts societies sponsoring competitions—staged independent, civic festivals featuring allegorical dramas as propositions and rebuttals to debate questions. Royal entries and street pageants celebrated coronations, weddings, military victories, and visiting heads of state. Processions and allegorical or didactic plays greeted honored guests and told of their lives and exploits in heroic and mythological terms. Panoramic *tableaux vivants* (living pictures), drawn from the Bible, history, and myth, were narrated in the guest's honor. Humanism delighted in things theatrical, and the theatre once again celebrated humanity.

By 1500 the middle class dominated the economic life of newly centralized nation-states. Vernacular literatures celebrated regional differences. Traders sought faster and less expensive means of turning a profit. With their superior ships and nautical instruments, the Portuguese and Spanish led efforts to locate new sea routes to the riches of the East. Europe hoped to break the monopoly on spices and slaves fueling the Italian Renaissance economy. Europe's eventual success indeed shifted the commercial axis from the Mediterranean to the north.

Throughout Europe the beauty and joy of nature was toasted by art. Church opposition to the things of the Earth counted for less and less. In fact, the church joined in the celebration of life. God no longer appeared to be the omnipotent preserver of all creation; instead, God visited as a small, internal source of individual sustinence.

Italy's economic boom led Europe to a new age. A rising civic spirit replaced warring religious zeal. The laity learned rhetoric, philosophy, and literary criticism from Greek and Roman models. Contemporary individuals replaced historical Christ as the center of interest. The effort to establish the City of God had resulted in doctrinarism, hypocrisy, and intolerance. Medieval society began to grasp not only the forms of classical culture but also its spirit.

As people of the theatre attempted to reinvent the classical spirit, as an interest in simplicity, exactitude of expression, and life dawned in individuals minds, the dramatic theatre envisioned new realities through attempts to refashion old ones. In the theatre of the Renaissance dreams of a humanistic world supplanted plans for a theocentric one.

# NOTES

[1] Bronislaw Malinowski, ''The Role of Magic and Religion,'' in Edwin R. A. Seligman and Alvin Johnson, eds., *Encyclopedia of the Social Sciences*, Vol. 4 (New York: Macmillan, 1967), pp. 634–642.

[2] Benjamin Hunningher, *The Origins of the Theatre* (New York: Hill and Wang, 1961), p. 60.

[3] Karl Young, *The Drama of the Medieval Church* (Oxford: Clarenden Press, 1933), Vol. I, p. 178.

[4] Allardyce Nicoll, *World Drama* (New York: Harcourt Brace and World, 1949), p. 147.

[5] Erich Auerbach, *Mimesis: The Representation of Reality in Western Literature*, p. 555. Willard R. Trask, trans. Copyright 1953 by Princeton University Press; copyright renewed 1981 by Princeton University Press.

[6] Giorgio Vasari, *The Lives of the Painters, Sculptors, and Architects*, Vol. 1, A. B. Hines, trans. (Everyman's Library, 1927), pp. 295–297.

[7] Harold C. Gardiner, *Mysteries End: An Investigation of the Last Days of the Medieval Religious Stage*, Yale Studies in English, Number 103 (New Haven: Yale University Press, 1946), p. 95.

[8] Nicoll, *World Drama*, pp. 141–142.

# 5

# THE RENAISSANCE
# THEATRE

*What a piece of work is a man! How noble in reason! How infinite
in faculty! In form, in moving, how express and admirable! In action
how like an angel! In apprehension how like a god.*

William Shakespeare,
*Hamlet*, Act II, Scene 2

*I do not feel obliged to believe that the same God who has endowed us
with sense, reason, and intellect has intended us to forgo their use.*

Galileo Galilei

## OVERVIEW

In many ways the Modern age began in
1500. Great scientific discoveries and great religious and philosophical revolutions created
instability in the West. Europe responded to
the breakdown of the old medieval order religiously, scientifically, aesthetically, theatrically, and individually. Suddenly the names of
individual people—Luther, Loyola, Galileo,
and Shakespeare—appear as authors of ideas;
the names of characters—Don Quixote, Dr.
Faustus, and Hamlet—grace stage personalities. The dissolution of the old age forced individuals either to choose from an array of op-
tions or to create new ones. Uncertainty
produced a panorama of human experiences
and dramatic expressions.

***The Growth of Humanism*** By building
upon the Gothic interest in individual personality, natural laws, and truth, the Renaissance
broke with the old age in art and literature. The
printing press exploded across Europe both the
new information returning from sea voyages
and the ancient treasures brought to Italy by
scientists and scholars fleeing the fall of Constantinople in 1453. It also spread humanist
ideas, made the movement international, and
changed Europe's mode of experiencing phenomena. Interest shifted from the Latin of
Rome to the Greek of Athens, from a new life
in Christ to a second chance in a New World.
The prospect of life after death gave way to the
hope for a better earthly life modeled on the
vision of an ancient past.

Because of the rediscovery of past civilizations, the Renaissance was the first age to
think of itself as an historical entity. But the
Renaissance was still a religious period even
though religion was secondary in popular consciousness and in the dramatic theatre. The
Renaissance world, still theocentric, was simplified and classicalized. In fact, educated

Catholics spread the humanist ideas throughout Europe.

In Italy, the first to experience a Renaissance and give the movement a name (*Rinascita*), humanists wrote history, orations, letters, poems, and plays. The great humanist, Erasmus of Rotterdam (c. 1466–1536), believed he espoused "the philosophy of Christ," and so was a Christian humanist. Following Erasmus's lead, humanists believed that morality in ethical conduct was the proper concern of the laity as well as of clergy. Humanists stimulated individuality of thought by emphasizing the study of ancient dramatic literatures in education, providing new models for theatre artists, and advocating new standards for dramatic criticism.

In Italy, Renaissance art and theatre evolved through many schools; the Renaissance theatre grew out of the tumult of the late fifteenth and sixteenth centuries. As Arnold Hauser writes, "the Renaissance appears to be the particular form in which the Italian national spirit emanates itself from universal European culture."[1]

***Science and Trade***   The fall of Constantinople in 1453 encouraged the search for an alternative trade route to the riches of the East. Scientific thought focused on the creation of better navigational devices and seafaring ships. Once mastered, the ocean offered new commercial routes. As new lands opened to trade, local cultures either withered or were Westernized because the superior firepower and military organization of Western explorers subjugated those of the native populations. The conquest was fast: In little over 100 years European civilization had spread around the Earth.

Overseas exploration and settlement brought data for scientists to investigate and dramatic artists to conjure. The scientific method—the use of observation and measurement to test theories—led individuals to rely on their senses rather than on inherited authority. Instruments evolved to extend the powers of sensory observation. Scientists contented themselves in exploring one bit at a time;

metaphysical conclusions were left to the theologians battling outside laboratory doors.

The Renaissance began an information explosion. In fact, the breakdown of traditional Asian, African, and American institutions and attitudes that began in the Renaissance continued into the Modern age. Not until the nineteenth century would scholars and scientists again be as respected. Those seeking to expand industry and trade through science and technology explained the world as an empirical reality capable of being ordered and understood by a systematic recording of sensory experiences. The theatre became a place to hear new explanations. As scientists rose in import and respect, the idea grew that there existed literally nothing that humanity might not achieve: Human power seemed beyond limit. The theatre showed people testing their limitations.

The emergence of science depended on the economic needs of new, strong state governments. The printing press, a visual, sequential, uniform, and lineal presentation of thought, experience, and perception, seemed appropriate to Renaissance national ambitions and scientific methods. Mathematics, which allowed quantitative physics to replace qualitative considerations, led Galileo Galilei (1564–1642) to declare that "nature is written in mathematical language." To make nature contribute to state power, rulers patronized science. In turn, the middle class allied itself with governmental machinery. Large-scale industrialists slowly replaced artisans. English and Dutch trading companies sold public shares in their overseas ventures.

Europeans also imported labor to fuel the Renaissance. Christopher Columbus (1451–1506) began transatlantic trade by bringing native American slaves to Spain. By 1502 Negro slaves were imported to the Americas to replace the natives who had died of imported diseases.

But slavery was not new to Europe. Italian joint stock companies had organized a slave trade based in Cyprus, which controlled the entire Mediterranean slave market. The Italian Renaissance depended, in large measure, on the labor and profits made from Tartar, Circassian, Armenian, Georgian, and Bulgarian slavery. Even petty shopkeepers, nuns, and priests could afford slaves. The rediscovery of Greek and Roman civilizations seemed to legitimize the practice. But the fall of Constantinople in 1453 to the Turks sealed off the source of slaves, because their price rose to preclude all but nobles and rich merchants. In time African slaves replaced the Eastern European slaves.

*City-States Patronize the Humanist Arts*
Italian city-states created the model of political organization that spread across Europe and found representation on the stage. Throughout Europe, regional merchant classes vied to surpass the Italian city states. As a result, nationalism and competition spurred artistic activity as a sign of superiority. Playwright Niccolo Machiavelli (1469–1527), the personification of Italian political theory, contributed his name to its practice. Machiavelli's name became associated with the deceitful intriguer frequently found on the Renaissance stage. Machiavelli, like his stage counterpart, separated political practice from Christian ideals. His ideas, neither new nor innovative, nonetheless frightened his contemporaries because of the accuracy with which he described common practice. He first clarified and justified the dual nature of the morality operating in Renaissance society. His book, *The Prince* (1513), contains statements such as "Men are so simple, and yield so much in immediate necessity, that the deceiver will never lack dupes," and "The great majority of mankind are satisfied with appearances, as though they were realities, and are often more influenced by the things that seem than by those that are." *The Prince* gave rise to hypocritical characters on stage and in life who used fraud to gain power.

Within the Renaissance's preoccupation with intrigue and power politics, humanists considered themselves nonpolitical reformers, educators, and moralists. They represented the earliest and most important philosophers of the Renaissance. They read Aristotle's *Poetics* through the eyes of the Latin Horace and championed the Roman Seneca. Indeed, their learning about ancient Greece and Rome sped the rationalization coming to philosophy: People began to reason about doctrine and the physical world. But humanist reasoning tore apart the fusion between Christianity and antiquity that scholastics had worked so long to perfect. Faith and reason were no longer compromised. Consequently, both faith and reason gained passionate advocates. By the end of the Reformation in 1648, reason and faith had gone their separate ways, and no longer did a passionate concern exist for imposing one truth on everyone. Where uniformity of belief did exist, where church and state succeeded in enforcing universal truths, intellectual and artistic stagnation resulted. In contrast, the humanists' success in establishing pluralism led to rapid intellectual and theatrical development; beauty could exist for its own sake and truth could advance unfettered by external authority. Nevertheless, no Renaissance thinker was ready to deny the idea of a divinely ordered universe. An orderly cosmology, in fact, girded Renaissance stage realities.

*The Renaissance Cosmology*   Based on the work of Pythagoras in the sixth century B.C., Renaissance cosmology contained an inherent paradox: the coexistence of unity and multiformity. All things in the Renaissance universe were believed to be interrelated parts of the *anima mundi* (world soul), from which and to which individual souls emerge and return. Such cosmology provided the acceptable patterns of beauty for Renaissance artists. Art and theatre had to reflect and reveal the harmonious patterns that made up the universe; they directed the audience's attention to the present universe, not to past sins or future glory. All things existed in a chain of being that, in art and on the stage, depicted and described the relationship between physical things and conceptual things. For example, between such physical things as stones, plants, and animals, and such conceptual things as angels and God stood people. In this way people were the measure of all things, the chain link capable of experiencing both the physical and conceptual orders of things. Renaissance art and theatre expressed the experience of both orders in the human experience.

The Pythagorean cosmos of the Renaissance juxtaposed science, politics, religion, and theatre with one another. The cosmos, like Renaissance dramatic art, created beauty through a reconciliation of opposites, a whole that defined each part. As a result, Roman and Greek astrology and alchemy were practiced feverishly. In fact, Vitruvius's use of astrology may have influenced directly the Renaissance idea of a theatre. Countless Renaissance dramas use alchemical and astrological metaphors to describe the chain of being as the dance of elements and planets.

The Renaissance artist was a creator imitating God's creation of the cosmos. The parts of an artistic creation were unified as the universe is unified. The theatre, in fact, was considered as a microcosm of the cosmos. The zodiac, often painted above a stage, illustrated the universe as an organism with physical parts and spiritual essences. Kings claimed the sun as their cosmological counterpart; they sat in the center of both their revolving zodiacal kingdoms and their new theatre buildings.

Numbers were considered the ultimate constituents of nature and reality. Creation was, therefore, ordered numerically, and the mathematical orderliness of creation caused theatrical beauty. Numbers and mathematical correspondences even linked works of art, such as plays and theatre buildings, to the cosmos by repeating and echoing significant numerical relationships. The number four, the tetrad, was considered most representative of the cosmos because it was an arrangement of two pairs of opposites made harmonious. Michelangelo laid out the Medici Chapel as a tetrad, an artistic description of the operation of the universe on every level: four elements, four seasons, four humors (the fluids once considered responsible for health and disposition),

each related to one another and to every other conceivable tetrad. Next to the tetrad, the circle was most important because it encompassed the tetrad. Time consisted of recurring circles or cycles of tetrads, seasons, and zodiacal phases.

***An Elite Art*** As always, the majority of Renaissance men and women bought inferior goods and appreciated only average works of dramatic art. An elite intelligentsia patronized most of the important theatrical works of the age. The Renaissance thus marked the development of a gulf between the educated minority and the uneducated majority that would have an important influence on the development of Western art and theatre. For the first time conscious attempts were made to create a unique theatre for an exclusive class from which the majority of people were barred. Humanists wrote in Latin, neither from a great love for the church nor to gain a wider readership; they wished to separate themselves from the popular vernacular. During the Renaissance, humanist scholars replaced church leaders as authority figures, and artists solicited their judgments. An "educated" or "appreciative" audience replaced the popular audience as the primary focus of the patronized artists' attention. In the theatre, court tastes and expectations diverged from popular tastes and expectations to create a dynamic tension for the artists.

Gradually artists separated themselves from craft guilds to gain direct sponsorship from nobles or wealthy patrons. Italy set the model. Italian princes demonstrated the use and appreciation of art and theatre. European rulers looking to Italy saw humanists confer a new status on theatre artists by recognizing the value of dramatic art as a means of propagating their own ideas. Humanists hatched the idea of the "unity of the arts": painting as silent poetry, poetry as spoken painting.

***The Idea of the Courtier*** By acting certain ways, rulers could prove the legitimacy of their high position in the chain of being. Baldassare

Castiglione published *The Book of the Courtier* (1528) to help men and women recognize "perfect" specimens of their sexes. A courtier was versatile rather than specialized in his abilities—a true "Renaissance man." Equally adept in mind and body, courtiers displayed both military finesse and social grace. Experienced in art, poetry, music, and the sciences, able to retain their composure and control under all circumstances, courtiers avoided ostentation and exaggeration. They were unrestrained, nonchalant, effortless, yet always dignified. In fact, Castiglione recommended that to avoid being conspicuous nobles should wear only black.

Castiglione's ideal influenced the stage more than societies plagued by religious and political warfare, disease, and oligarchical governments. Nevertheless, court ladies tried to appear talented, wise, judicious, dexterous, modest, prudent, magnanimous, continent, kind, mannerly, discrete, affable, and knowledgeable on any subject. As the ideal caught on, dramatic heroes avoided affectation more and more. "True art," Castiglione wrote, "is that which does not seem to be art." A beautiful body, grace, humor, integrity, nobility of birth, truthfulness, and sincerity had to appear natural rather than learned.

During the Renaissance, men like Leonardo da Vinci (1452–1519), Michelangelo Buonarroti (1473–1564), Raphael (1483–1520), Titian (c. 1490–1576), Francis Drake (c. 1540–1596), and Lope de Vega (1562–1635) seemed to validate the possibility of accomplishing Castiglione's ideal. By the seventeenth century 100 different printings of *The Book of the Courtier*, including translations into Latin, German, Spanish, English, and French, testified to the popularity of Castiglione's vision. By the eighteenth century Castiglione's model, which equated sexual love with animal lust, had swept Europe and fundamentally altered the drama.

### Revival of Sex and the Occult

The Renaissance found a twist in the relationship between love and sex. The revived interest in the Greeks and Plato caused humanists to support new attitudes on sexuality that were represented on the Renaissance stage. Because the Greeks offered positive justifications for homosexuality, Christian values were quickly challenged. At the same time, the concept of "Platonic love" flourished as a frequent theme in Italian literature. Platonic love was intellectual, nonsexual, and, at times, antisexual love. In *The Book of the Courtier* Castiglione made spiritual love most important; a kiss was merely a way to unite the souls of a man and a woman. On the other hand, Marsilio Ficino (1443–1499), a founder of Florence's Platonic Academy, a center of interest in the revival of classical drama, wrote that homosexuality was best suited for a love between souls. By the sixteenth century, Platonic love had come to suggest homosexuality.

Renaissance society experienced a general reawakening in matters of sexuality as well. Protestant Martin Luther's (1483–1546) belief in "salvation by faith" eliminated the need for celibacy among Christian clergy. Luther tolerated bigamy and concubinage but another Protestant, John Calvin (1509–1564), liked concubinage and bigamy less; Calvin considered sinful all intercourse not leading to procreation. The Council of Trent (1545–1563), Catholicism's rebuttal to Protestantism, reaffirmed virginity as a holier state than marriage. The Council also established an Index of Prohibited Books, which included works discussing sex.

Theatrical art shared the new interest in sexuality. Classical subjects had involved rape and incest and birth; Renaissance drama did, too. As women donned more clothing in society, artistic nudes increased in popularity. Because women were forbidden to sing in Catholic churches, *castrati* (men deliberately castrated to preserve their high voices) filled choir pews and enacted the female roles in Italian operas. Female impersonators also enjoyed great success in the theatre: Nathaniel Field as Ophelia, "Dickie" Robinson as Desdemona, William Ostler as Rosalind, and Robert Gough as Juliet and Cleopatra.

In the sixteenth century an epidemic of syphilis created a fear of venereal disease, which, in turn, gave rise to the invention of the condom. By the end of the seventeenth century traditional religious views on sex were declining as science worked to save the day.

In addition to sex, Neo-Platonism in the fifteenth century also increased the general belief in magic and evil powers. The Jews had been expelled from many countries. In Germany, Jews who did not convert to Christianity faced Martin Luther's demands that their synagogues and homes be destroyed and their prayerbooks seized. Witchcraft became a new scapegoat. In 1486 *Malleus maleficarum*, a handbook for witch hunters, appeared. Witches were blamed for everything: impotence, infertility, and miscarriage. Witch hunting, encouraged by Catholic popes and Protestant reformers alike, peaked around 1600. Witches even became characters in the drama. The hunt did not end until the end of the eighteenth century; the executed numbered at least one quarter of a million and possibly several million.

### Reformation    and    Counter-Reformation

Despite a great desire to curb sexual excesses, the Christian church was rendered virtually impotent by its own internal disorders. Religious disputes relaxed the church's grip on the drama but disrupted the peace of the audience. For over 100 years eruptions of violence based on dogmatic differences plagued Europe. Each controversy halted temporarily society's movement toward secularization, because religion insisted on playing a dominant role in politics. Continuing the spirit of early reformers John Wyclif and Jan Hus, dissatisfaction with church practices climaxed in the actions of Martin Luther, a German monk who created what came to be known as The Reformation.

Fundamental to Luther's objections was the nature and source of religious authority. Luther and his Protestant followers insisted that the Bible and personal experience guide individuals' actions; every individual was considered to have the powers of a priest. Grace was thought to come directly from God rather than indirectly through priests. The role of Protestant clergy was to spread and teach the Bible and await the miracle of God's grace. A person was "justified by faith alone" rather than by Good Deeds, as the anonymous morality play *Everyman* (c. 1500) had claimed.

The ramifications of Luther's interpretation were revolutionary. If every individual were a priest, then there would be no need for special individuals to offer Mass, to ordain other clergy, to hear confessions, to forgive sins, or to anoint the dying. A church institution was obsolete. Consequently, early Protestantism was an anarchical and personal movement advocating a private meeting between a person and his or her God. But such a movement was hard to enforce, and in time a test of Protestant orthodoxy arose. Gradually doctrines and hierarchies equal to those of the Catholic church out-dogmatized the church itself. The weak spot in Protestantism's hope for establishing a unified, reformed church was the individualism implied in a personal interpretation of the Bible. How could a consensus emerge if any interpretation were allowed? It could not. In time a host of sects arose, each with its own divinely inspired interpretation.

The peasants, however, believing the Bible's condemnation of the rich and hoping that its promises to the poor were about to become reality, rallied to Lutheranism. But the ruling Protestant middle class were content to convert key clergy and land-holding princes. Luther sided with the forces of law and order against the masses demanding justice. To Luther the peasants were "murderous rabble" mistaking his call for religious reformation as a call for social revolution.

The Catholic church, meanwhile, set out to reform itself. In 1545 its Council of Trent reaffirmed the belief that good deeds alone could earn one salvation and established seminaries to train priests in the hope of eliminating clerical abuses. From the Council's work came St. Ignatius Loyola (1491–1556), founder of the Society of Jesus (1534). Crucial to the arts, the Council ended the liberal relationship between the church and artists that had existed in the early Renaissance: No longer was choice of subject left to the artist; no longer were nudes allowed; no longer was music allowed to overpower the text. Giovanni Palestrina's musical styles became the absolute liturgical model.

Luther had objected to ''idolatry'' and Calvin to ''Popery''; both men meant pictures, statuary, and dramatic impersonation, which, they claimed, profaned the faith. Music alone became favored by the Reformers. Luther believed that ''next to the Word of God, music deserves the highest praise.'' Music thus became the Protestant weapon; the Jesuits thought Luther's chorales or *lieder* ''destroyed more souls than his writings and speeches.''

Political interests influenced the course of the religious controversy as much as any deep-seated religious conviction. The same printing presses published religious and political broadsides, which were almost interchangeable. Yet after 1648 most religious sects were discredited in the eyes of the peasants. Scientists no longer worried about how discoveries would fit into official thinking because official theology had disappeared. The public had exhausted its concerns for a universal agreement on the truth of anything. Intellectual and religious pluralism thus grew out of the Renaissance's Reformation; each church, state, and profession pursued its own truth, its own way. And the theatre of the time reflected this multiplicity of opinions. Some Protestants even revived old antitheatrical arguments.

**The Theatrical Revolution** Italy housed the first artistic, literary, and theatrical efforts that arose from the renewed interests in classical antiquity. The basic idea of medieval Gothic art was juxtaposition within an expansive and open panorama of multiple points of view; Italian scholars, in contrast, discovered in classical art a hitherto unknown concentration. In drama the discovery gave birth to concentrated scene construction in playwrighting and single-point perspective in painting.

Classical dramatic works were seen to have a different method of obtaining unity. Medieval simultaneity seemed incompatible with the Renaissance desire to create the illusion of

a different reality. Theatre people could no longer justify the existence of actors silently waiting on stage when not part of the scene. Nor could the simultaneous on-stage presence of unused settings satisfy the age's desire for truth. Humanist scholars rejected the artistic conventions of medieval illusionism, and new principles of unity in dramatic art developed.

Theatrical space was unified according to standards of proportion. Dramatic themes were restricted to suit the new concentration of dramatic form; plays were either serious or comic in tone. Plot actions needed rational motivation. Logic was applied to theatrical beauty. The relationship between a play's parts and its whole design became an issue of mathematical proportion. Art and theatre entered a rational, logical phase.

Logic and reason (especially the logic and reason of the ruling elite) dictated a life ruled by formal codes designed to protect society from anarchy and emotional excess. Dramatic art, like society, came to be based on order and discipline. Greek and Roman theatrical art was admired for self-control and the suppression of passion. Renaissance artists, copying the ancient masters, subordinated spontaneity, inspiration, and ecstacy. The emotionalism of the Gothic era disappeared; Christ was portrayed without pain, Mary suppressed her feelings toward the Christ child, and kings on stage contained their passions in regular metered verse. Theatre praised the normal behavior of moderate persons; it condemned and punished the individual behavior of immoderate persons: Both tragic and comic heroes were flawed by immoderation. Economy also characterized artistic technique: A small number of figures inhabited both painting and the stage.

**Neo-Classicism** The new classicism led Renaissance artists to believe that the universal principles that govern the world must govern dramatic art as well. Art must symbolize the order, calm, and social stability to which human existence aspired. Consequently, Renaissance theatre showed the orderliness of society. It demonstrated that happiness and perfection resulted from knowing one's place and obeying the rules. By the sixteenth century, the flux characteristic of the fifteenth century's fascination with the individual personality had given way to an interest in group stability. A play, like a state, needed an orderly arrangement of parts according to rules.

*The Scientific Manipulation of Space* Mathematics and science proved as useful to theatrical art as to the state. Renaissance artists studied nature like scientists. The metaphysical symbolism of Gothic art gave way to theatrical representations drawn from the observable world. Nature thus came to replace the classical masters as appropriate models for dramatic imitation, even though such imitations limited the artists as much as the forms of the classical masters. Artists sought the truths of geometry, perspective, anatomy, and politics. By observing, reasoning, and calculating, Renaissance theatre workers achieved in their work a power and control over nature; they could predict and manipulate the illusion of nature according to the very laws with which God manipulated nature.

The visual arts offered the most startling demonstration of the power of the new aesthetic. Around 1435 Leon Battista Aliberti (1402–1472) explained mathematics in art. Single-point perspective drawing and scene painting framed a consistently organized and unified space. Filippo Brunelleschi (1377–1446) was credited by his contemporaries with the invention of linear perspective. In the theatre, stage settings utilizing single-point perspective placed the vanishing point directly opposite the seat of the noble patron. In this way the dynamics of the theatre experience imitated the experience of everyday life: The closer one sat to the seat of power the better things looked, the more orderly things appeared. Mathematics and theatre served the state. As Rabelais put it, "Physics gave birth to beauty and harmony."

Enclosed space became a Renaissance ideal. Both the picture-frame stage and the printed texts of plays summarized the transformation from the medieval open stage and orally transmitted theatre. Visual stimulation grew in importance. In the theatre, plays, roles, and settings came to exist first on the printed page; playwrights began to describe scene and action in printed stage directions. On the page the visual sense became isolated and elevated in importance. As Shakespeare wrote in *The Rape of Lucrece*, "To see sad sights moves more than hear them told." Seeing was believing. The Renaissance marked the first time playwrights either allowed others to print or personally supervised the printing of their plays.

*Individuality* The artist's individuality and personality mattered as never before. In the fourteenth century artistic biography and autobiography appeared. Attention shifted from the works to the personalities of the artists. Self-portraits grew more frequent as artists grew self-conscious. Some artists even attained "superstar" status. The painter Raphael (1483–1520), for example, lived as a grand seigneur in his own palace. Michelangelo was so highly regarded that he could effect the ultimate Modern pose: the scorn of public recognition. Gradually artists were considered as rare geniuses worthy of veneration; talent did not come through imitation of masters alone, but as the God-given gift of inspiration. Spontaneity was again the ideal. Originality was the competitive tool that, in later ages, would mushroom to an unbelievable extreme.

Artists, however, found themselves torn between their conservative patrons and the liberal antagonists of the state. To work for the former made the artists mouthpieces for the existing order; to support the latter made them outcasts in the role of Thompson's clown-satirist (see Chapter 1). In either case, for the first time, Renaissance artists were considered among the great minds of the age.

*New Themes* Renaissance artists invented new themes to catch the tenor of the times. People became the center and measure of a theatrical work. Even when exploring theological or mythological ideas, the stage rendered a human moment. The practice became clear in Miguel de Cervantes's (1547–1616) portrayal of a medieval chivalric knight caught in the alien world of the Renaissance (*Don Quixote*, 1605). On his steed Rozinante (Once Upon a Time), Don Quixote battles the new technology and windmills, and blames his defeat on necromancy (the art of revealing future events by alleged communication with the dead) and the occult. In the world of the Renaissance, medieval heroes like Parzival (a fool whose search leads to knighthood) or adventures like those of Gawain (King Arthur's favorite knight) were impossible. Instead, new heroes emerged from medieval legend. Like Don Quixote, *Doctor Faustus* (1588), Christopher Marlowe's (1564–1593) Renaissance man risks Hell for a glimpse of the infinite. Doctor Faustus is a humanist scholar who thirsts for infinite knowledge. He wants to understand more and thereby attain greater power over nature. Not content to live on in his work, Faust despairs of his smallness within the omnipotence of the cosmos. He thus strikes a deal with Satan for years of power in the cosmos. But with that power, Faustus moves out of harmony with the cosmos and dies. This Renaissance hero defined Western culture for the twentieth-century German philosopher Oswald Spengler, who called subsequent ages "Faustian." The conflict of Faustus, in fact, became the essential modern conflict: enduring a limited material existence while longing for immaterial infinity—the danger versus the pleasure of acquiring knowledge and power for their own sake.

*Mannerism and the Baroque*    In Italy, artists wrestled with aesthetic problems after the classical influence had waned. As classicism degenerated, slavish imitation of great masters had led to hackneyed formulas. With the ebb of classicism, artists expressed different values and experimented with different structures. The result was mannerism and the baroque styles, which concluded Italy's Renaissance. Mannerism, the style of aristocrats throughout Europe, enjoyed an international scope, the first since the Gothic. The baroque style's emotional and nationalistic flavor appealed more to the masses. The baroque's close connection with the Counter-Reformation led Catholic courts to favor it over mannerism; in fact, it attracted people to the movement's patron, the Catholic church, by reflecting a world in which the individual was dwarfed into insignificance. Only in the one true church could individuals find meaning and self-respect.

Baroque theatre architecture and scene design emphasized spatial grandeur with an agitated rhythm. Sweeping waves, curves, arcs, profuse ornamentation of twisted columns, brilliant colors, and light and shadow connected all the parts. Spatial depth on stage was achieved with oversized foregrounds. Stage compositions, appearing incomplete and disconnected, made the work seem accidental rather than composed. An almost anticlassical attitude prevailed; less consideration was given to the audience in arrangement and composition.

Mannerism, on the other hand, has been considered by some historians to be a cultural phenomenon that affected all of Europe well into the seventeenth century. Preoccupied with consciously cultivating style, mannerism emphasized how one acted and spoke over what one did and said. Playwrights performed verbal acrobatics with metaphors, inversions, antitheses, and unusual rhythms. Blank verse, amplifying and exaggerating feelings, gave the vernacular a status previously reserved for Latin. Mannerism ended the imitation of nature. Instead, dramatic art came to exist and originate spontaneously in the minds of the theatre artists.

Mannerism's form, structure, and unity came from the artists' individual souls rather than from nature or rules. Philosopher Giordano Bruno (c. 1548–1600) wrote that "rules are not the source of poetry, but poetry is the source of rules, and there are as many rules as there are real poems." Consequently, mannerism's symbolic naturalism left a work open to many interpretations. Certain themes, moreover, dominated the mannerist stage: elegance, calculated sensuality, preciosity, refinement, affectation, studied gesture and pose, adoration of the female body, erotic perversion, voyeurism, prostitution, homosexuality, incest, sadism, melancholy, dreams, allegories, occultism, satire, mechanical inventions, landscapes, ruins, and cityscapes.

In the theatre, mannerism blended reality with the shadows of unreality. Comedy could be found in tragedy, tragedy in comedy; tragicomedy was born in mannerism. Characters on stage broke from the fictional world to directly address the real audience. With mannerism stage characters no longer felt a part of a larger cosmos. Stage heroes disengaged from society to observe nature scientifically. From such vantage points these dramatic heroes hoped to change and alter things. Generally, seemingly obsessed heroes acted within open, almost formless, structures. Numerous episodes, excursions, and scenes, almost medieval in conception, created plots that took cinematic jumps in time and place. Colloquial and metered speech existed side by side. Michel de Montaigne (1533–1592), who from his observations of nature developed the art of the essay,

was one of the first writers to try to create such heroes; Shakespeare's Hamlet was one of the first heroes.

Renaissance theatre was diverse. Religious plays ended everywhere but in Spain. Court spectacles, created by the great artists of the day, replaced church spectacles. Learned, humanist dramas were never popular outside the courts. The popular theatre ranged from the Italian *commedia dell'arte* to the English Shakespearean tragedies.

Renaissance ideas and theatre practices changed and altered in transmission. Indeed, no orderly progression or evolution in dramatic ideas or theatrical style can rival in impact the chaotic and incomplete movement of ideas that existed into the Modern age. But, as we discuss next, the Renaissance ideas began in Italy, where scholars fleeing the Turks in Constantinople deposited their treasured collections of ancient treatises.

# ITALY

The Italian Renaissance began around 1350, peaked in 1500, and faded by 1600. (Late Medieval period art coexisted with that of the Italian Renaissance.) But why did the Reniassance begin in Italy? The Crusades had established Italy as the preeminent financial and transportation center of Europe. Italian guilds were the first to enjoy free competition. Italy developed the first banking system. Rural landowners maintained urban residences and personal contacts with city officials. All of these factors contributed to the initial breakdown of medieval feudalism. In addition, the classical dramatic heritage of Rome lay underfoot and around every corner.

By the fourteenth century northern Italy's wealthy merchant class had developed the beginnings of a secular culture. Widespread lay education and money allowed leisured merchant-princes time to patronize theatrical entertainments. Ambition for worldly success and glory replaced the medieval desire for eternal

salvation from the shame of pride. The reminders of ancient Rome dotting the environment led some nobles to seek the old glories to justify their abandonment of medieval ways. Ancient Greek and Roman authors had written for urban societies like theirs; the classical playwrights shared their interest in worldly affairs. In the fifteenth century Italian life was still primarily secular, but in the sixteenth century a new ecclesiastical interest appeared. The Counter-Reformation revitalized the church's interest in art. By the sixteenth century mannerism had introduced artificiality and contrivance to classical form and imitation of nature.

In Florence noble and burgher classes merged into ruling political groups led by dominant families. Family rule over city-states became hereditary: by the Medici in Florence, the Della Rovere in Urbino, the Gonzaga in Mantua, the Este in Ferrara, and the Sforza in Milan. Each separate Italian state, like the ancient Greek city-state forebearers, competed in love for the classics and artistic glory.

Periodically families attempted to expand their city-states. Other times outside invaders capitalized on social unease and political intrigue: France and Spain invaded Italy, and Rome was sacked. Churches and monasteries were plundered, priests murdered, and nuns raped. St. Peter's was made into a stable, and the Vatican into a barracks. Artists, theatre workers, and scholars scattered throughout Europe, taking the ideas of the Renaissance with them.

In this disintegrated environment, the papal state seized political and artistic power. Quickly becoming an important money market, the Vatican patronized the arts extensively. Religious authorities, like their secular counterparts, sought glory in artistic, literary, and theatrical self-images.

**The Medici Family**  The Medici family in Florence of Tuscany created the cultural center of the Renaissance. Florence, the center of the wool industry, banking, and commerce, also supported writers, artists, and scientists. Medici family members organized pageant wagons and scenery or wrote song lyrics for outdoor festivals and carnivals in the fifteenth and sixteenth centuries. Triumphal arches featuring mythological figures paid homage to the noble family. Catherine de Medici (1519–1589), the only child of Lorenzo, wed Henry, the Duke of Orleans (1547–1559), and became the Queen of France when Francis I (1515–1547) died. Catherine's patronage of the arts brought the Renaissance to France.

Under Medici rule, the greatest scholars of the time joined noble literary clubs and tutored the patrons' children. Meanwhile, Florence's Platonic Academy influenced all of Europe. In Rome, for example, Julius Pomponius Laetus (1425–1498) originated the Roman Academy (whose members assumed Latin names) to study the classics. But Pope Paul II suppressed the Academy for its pagan spirit and tortured or imprisoned the members. Later, however, Cardinal Raffaelle Riario revived the Academy to satisfy his interest in the ancient the-

atre. The Academy produced readings of classical plays featuring nobles in the roles; in 1486 it published Vitruvius's *De Architectura*.

**New Literature**  Italian academic authors wrote vernacular works of mixed literary and dramatic quality. By 1464 a printing press operated near Rome, and Aldus Minuccius of Venice published a series of classical authors edited by leading humanist scholars. In time Italian authors' works were set in type. By 1500 the Italian humanists had influenced all of Europe: World libraries collected the products of Italian printing presses. With the work of the humanist authors classical and mythological subjects entered Western literature and theatrical art.

Academies dominated the Italian world by the sixteenth century. Strict, oppressive, and authoritarian like the guilds they replaced, academies published lectures that imitated classical models and Renaissance masters. In time artists reacted against the academic theories.

**New Music**  Italian music did not stir until 1530, after the visual arts had peaked. Earlier a new attitude toward plainsong (early Christian church music) increased interest in individual composition, the literary merit of the lyrics, and the sensuousness of the music. Plainsong, however, was valued more for its beauty than for its doctrinal teaching. A rediscovery of the Greek belief in the innate sympathy between music and words caused composers to attend to the words. Thus, music began to illustrate the words. The stage was set for the arrival of opera.

By 1530 important musical developments had occurred outside the church. The Counter-Reformation had venerated the music of Giovanni Pierluigi de Palestrina (c. 1525–1594) to the point of creative atrophy. Consequently, a new musical form, the madrigal, appeared in northern Italy; as it spread throughout Europe the madrigal became the most important and characteristic Renaissance musical form. At first, because madrigals were closely associated with Italian poetry and the academies that commissioned them, they allowed Renaissance musicians to adopt the Greek prejudice against instrumental music. Madrigals, in fact, illustrated expressively the words of a text by adding dramatic elements to the favorite solo instrument, the lute. Written as cycles, comedies, monologues, and dramatic dialogues with miming, madrigals served as the intermediate step to opera. Elsewhere dramatic authors confined their efforts to recreating the drama of antiquity.

***New Dramatic Texts*** The Italian Renaissance produced no great dramatic literature because efforts were divided among court entertainments, academic recitals, opera, and the popular theatre. In the academies Seneca served as the early model. Albertino Mussato's tragedy of the tyrant of Padua, *Eccerinis* (1315), for example, followed the Senecan formula. *Eccerinis*, the first Renaissance tragedy, mixes Italian history, morality play conventions, and a Senecan chorus of common citizens. The play so impressed his city that Mussato was crowned with laurel, the first such honor bestowed upon a playwright since the first century A.D. During the fourteenth and fifteenth centuries playwrights used Seneca, Ovid, Greek and Roman historians, Italian history, and *sacre rappresentazioni* as sources for dramatic composition.

***Tragic Writing*** In 1498 Aristotle's *Poetics* was published, and playwrights in Italy tried to follow his principles. In the sixteenth century tragedians translated classics to the vernacular for production. In 1502, for example, Aldus printed seven plays of Sophocles; the next year, the plays of Euripides; and in 1518, the plays of Aeschylus. In time the Greeks replaced Seneca as the model. By the end of the century, however, Seneca had resumed his role as primary model of imitation. He was, after all, a Roman.

Gian Giorgio Trissino's (1478–1550) *Sophonisba* (1515), the first important vernacular tragedy, was considered at the time to be greater than Sophocles's *Oedipus the King*. In the play, a general's daughter poisons herself rather than give in to a man she does not love.

With a chorus of fifteen, no act divisions, and blank verse, the play exemplifies Italian authors' temporary shift from Roman to Greek models. *Sophonisba* employs blank verse for a story relayed to a chorus by messengers. First staged at the Teatro Olympico twelve years after the author's death, *Sophonisba* influenced Englishman John Marston's (1576–1634) *Tragedy of Sophonisba* (1606) and Frenchman Jean Mairet's (1604–1686) *Sophonisba* (1634), the first French tragedy written in strict accord with neo-classical rules.

In 1541 Giambattista Giraldi Cinthio (1504–1573) wrote *Orbecche*, the first Italian tragedy to be produced. The play made the author the most popular serious dramatist in Italy. In *Orbecce*, a woman's ghost seeks revenge on the family of her stepdaughter because the woman's affair with her stepson had been revealed by her stepdaughter. The drama ends as the stepdaughter murders her father, and the ghost smiles.

***Comic Writing*** In 1429 the discovery of twelve Plautine comedies thought lost spurred interest in comic writing. As early as 1390, Pier Paolo Vergerio (1370 –1444) had written *Paulus*, a satire on student life. In 1508 Lodovico Ariosto (1474–1533) wrote *La cassaria* (*The Casket*), considered the first modern comedy. In the play, which successfully represents contemporary manners, a clever valet helps two gentlemen free their lovers from a slave dealer. Ariosto continued with *I suppositi* (*The Pretenders,* 1509), *Il negromante* (*The Necromancer*, 1520), *Lena* (*The Bawd*, 1528), and *La scolastica* (*The Academic Comedy*, 1543), taking aim at counterfeiters, astrologers, prostitutes, and students, respectively.

Niccolo Machiavelli turned his attention to the drama with *La mandragola* (*The Mandrake*, c. 1520). This comedy of seduction, unscrupulousness, and cunning shows the steps a young man in love will take to possess an older man's wife. Thinking his young wife is infertile, an old lawyer agrees to try the aphrodisiac the young man (disguised as a doctor) gives him. To save the old man from the aphrodisiac's supposedly fatal effects, the young man agrees to sleep with the old lawyer's wife. Pope Leo X enjoyed a production of the play in 1520.

***The Pastoral***  Vitruvius had enumerated three forms of drama: tragedy, comedy, and pastorals (works portraying rural life). Consequently, the Italians next turned faithfully to writing pastorals. Love and satyrs interested Italian pastoral authors. In 1471 Angelo Poliziano (1454–1494) of Mantua wrote *Orfeo*, the first Renaissance pastoral, for an audience of elitists, nobles, and scholars, the only Italians who found pleasure and satisfaction in the works. The most admired pastoral was *Aminta* (1573) by Torquato Tasso (1544–1595) of Ferrara. *Aminta* shows a shepherd rescuing a woman devoted to the goddess Diana from a lusty satyr. When the woman continues to spurn his love the young shepherd attempts suicide. Of course, the woman changes her mind and the pastoral ends happily. In 1590 Battista Guarini's (1538–1612) *Il pastor fido* (*The Faithful Shepherd*) perfected the pastoral form.

***Intermezzi and Opera***  Italian comedies featured *intermezzi* between the acts. *Intermezzi*, which were extended *tableaux vivants* in song and dance, had evolved from the *mascherata* of both carnival season and court entertainment. They emphasized scenery, costumes, lighting, special effects, music, and dance in allegorical plots. By 1580 the *intermezzi* had become more popular than the plays. Gradually authors related each *intermezzo* to the other, and then to the play itself. At that point *intermezzi* became four-act musical plays interspersed among the five acts of a regular drama. The first of these *intermezzi* dramas, *La Confanaria*, was presented in Florence in 1565.

The evolution of the *intermezzi* helped the development of another interest among Italian authors: opera. When they discovered that the ancient Greeks had chanted and danced their plays, Italian scholars sought to reconstruct the ancient dramatic experience. The result became one of the two most popular dramatic theatres in Italy. Basically, opera originated in the work of one academy, the Camerata of Florence. Interestingly, Galileo Galilei's father

was a member of the academy, which coined two important words: "melodrama," coming from the Greek *melos*, for music, and *opera*, Latin for works. The academy also succeeded in creating *drama tutto per musica* (drama all in music), with poetry following a story, and music following the poetry.

In 1594 the academy, seeking to recreate the relationship between Greek music and drama, presented *Dafne*, a full-length work with text by Ottavio Rinuccini (1562-1621) and Guilio Caccini (c. 1546-1618) and music by Jacopo Peri (1561-1633). All dialogue and choral passages were chanted or related to musical accompaniment. For the marriage of Henry IV (1589-1610) of France to Maria de Medici, Jocopo Corsi (1560-1604) presented Peri's second opera, *Euridice* (1600), with libretto by Rinuccini.

Opera moved first to Mantua, where Claudio Monteverdi (1567-1643) wrote *Orfeo* (1607) and *Arianna* (1608). His greatest opera, *L'Incoronazione di Poppea* (1642), surpassed those of the Florentine originators by combining recitatives with popular music and dance. Opera continued to spread throughout Europe; in time Vienna became the center for opera production. Throughout its development, opera, like Italian drama, caused the artists to reconsider theatrical space.

***Experiments with Stage Space***  In 1486, the year Vitruvius's *De Architectura* was printed in an edition by Alberti, the Roman Academy began experimenting with the production of ancient plays. By the early sixteenth century plays were in production at Italian academies and courts. Students from all over Europe came to study with the Roman Academy's Pomponius Laetus (1424-1498), famous for his attempts to reconstruct Roman staging conventions. Temporary theatres, arranged in court and academic halls, followed Vitruvius's guidelines.

Early auditorium stages adapted medieval staging to Vitruvian principles. Fifteenth-century editions of Terence featured illustrations suggesting the early Italian conception of Vitruvius's Roman theatre. The illustrations in the 1493 edition are subject to dispute among historians, however; the depicted facades with curtained openings for each location may never have existed.

*Serlio* The interpretation of Vitruvius by Sebastiano Serlio (1475–1554) did dominate Renaissance thinking about the use of stage space. Serlio's *De Architecttura* (1545), the first Renaissance work that devoted a section to the theatre, contained illustrations of the Vitruvian tragic, comic, and satyric settings. The treatise circulated throughout Europe and the illustrations often appeared in Renaissance editions of Vitruvius. Serlio assumed that Roman theatres were erected in preexisting halls. In such spaces he described the erection of a Roman *cavea*, semicircular stadium seating

*Tragic, comic, and pastoral settings, as designed by Sebastiano Serlio, 1545.* (Molinari, *Theatre through the Ages,* p. 128, by permission of F. Arborio Mella, Studio dell'illustrazione, Milano.)

around an orchestra area reserved for rulers and guests. His stage was raised to the eye level of the ruler and all scenic perspective focused on the ruler's chair. The stage sloped upward to enhance the illusion of perspective distance. (This phenomenon possibly gave rise to the terms "upstage" and "downstage.")

The oldest surviving Renaissance theatre, the Teatro Olympico (1580), showed several of Serlio's principles in practice. Built by the Olympic Academy of Vicenza and designed by Andrea Palladio (1518–1580), a member of the academy who was an architectural student of Vitruvius, the Teatro Olympico was housed in a preexisting hall. The theatre held thirteen ovoid tiers of seating around a small orchestra, which faced a seventy foot long by eighteen foot deep stage placed before a decorated facade with five openings, one at each side of the stage platform and three in the rear. For the 1585 opening production of Sophocles's *Oedipus Rex*, designer Vincenzo Scamozzi (1552–1616) placed perspective street scenes made of lathe and plaster behind each opening. The vanishing point for each scene lined up with the center of the orchestra. A drop curtain revealed the action of the production.

*Theatre Architecture*  The first permanent theatre was the *Teatro Medici* or Uffizi Theatre designed by Bernardo Buontalenti (c. 1536–1608). Able to hold 3000 to 4000 spectators, this Florence court theatre placed a 66 foot wide

by 180 foot deep stage by 46 foot high facade before a raked auditorium. In 1588 Scamozzi designed his own theatre—*Teatro di Sabionetta*—for the court of Vespasian Gonzaga. The widened proscenium accommodated a single large-perspective vista. A miniature by comparison, Scamozzi's theatre seated only 300 spectators.

The first permanent proscenium arch appeared in 1618, when Parma's prince commissioned Giovan Battista Aleotti to build the *Teatro Farnese* with a 3500-person capacity. Historians have traced the proscenium arch's origin to an enlargement of a single opening in a Terence stage setting, an enlargement of a triumphal arch used in street pageants, and to the picture frame of Italian painters. Whatever its genesis, the arch limited the audience's vision to a single perspective—that of the noble ruler.

Other courts and academies designed garden theatres. Cypress trees were trimmed to Vitruvian dimensions for the production of pastoral plays.

*The Venetian Public Opera House*  The last Italian Renaissance contribution to theatre architecture came in 1637 with the opening of the Venetian public opera house. For the first time opera played outside the courts and academies. To accommodate the cross section of Italian society, the auditorium was divided by class both to allow privacy and to protect the

The stage and auditorium of the Teatro Olympico.  (The Bettmann Archives, Inc.)

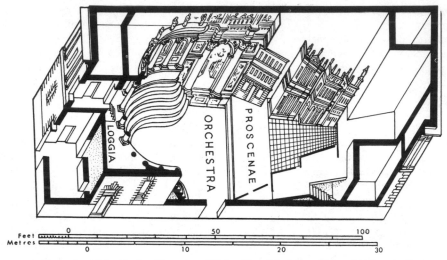

*Floorplan of the Teatro Olympico, 1588.* (Reprinted from Richard Leacroft, *The Development of the English Playhouse*, p. 68. Copyright © 1973 by Richard Leacroft. Used by permission of the publisher, Cornell University Press.)

wealthy spectators. Five balconies, holding over thirty boxes each, surrounded an open floor area called the *parterre* (pit). Low balconies were expensive; high galleries, cheap. The poor occupied the pit. These box, pit, and gallery designations formalized a seating arrangement first utilized for medieval cycle plays and some Asian theatrical events.

***Perspective Scenery*** The proscenium arch framed one of the Italian Renaissance's most important contributions: perspective scenery. Filippo Brunelleschi (1377–1446) has been credited with inventing linear perspective painting and Masaccio (1401–1428) with systematizing the technique. Perspective painting rendered the illusion of distance and three-dimensionality through science. The technique was based on the observation that parallel lines, running into space at right angles to a window frame, seem to converge at a central vanishing point at the viewer's eye level. Brunelleschi, calling the lines "orthogonals," applied the principles of Euclidean geometry to the medieval notion of vision as a pyramid of rays connecting the eye to an object. He deduced a mathematical formula for calculating the reduced size of any image. His friend, Leon Battista Alberti (1402–1472), elaborated and codified the system, which transformed painting from art to science.

Painting, and then the theatre, were reconceived as illusions of objects seen from fixed viewpoints. Perspective laws imposed mathematical and scientific order on the visible world. Dramaturgical laws would impose order on the invisible world. Alberti's treatises on painting (1435), architecture (1452), and sculpture (1464) created an idea of rational beauty according to the ancients' adherence to the "laws" of nature.

The first example of perspective scenery came from Pellegrino da San Daniele for Ariosto's *La cassaria* (*The Casket*, 1508). Individual houses stood before drops painted according to Vitruvius's three descriptions. Serlio had suggested that Vitruvius's three settings could service all plays. Each of Serlio's settings employed the same ground plan: three sets of angled wings stood downstage of one set of flat shutters. The downstage wings featured three-dimensional details, openings, and galleries.

*Scenic Design*   Innovation in design came not from designing for the regular dramas' fixed settings, but from dealing with the popular *intermezzi*. Likewise, scene-changing techniques derived from the popular entre-actes performed either on rolled pageant wagons or on platforms carried on and off the flat apron of the stage or orchestra. Because sixteenth-century audiences enjoyed seeing changes in scenery, designers looked for ways to change scenes more effectively. Theatre became a machine for creating changeable illusions and for controlling the visual experiences of the audience.

The *periaktoi* (prism-shaped scenic devices) described by Vitruvius and Pollux caught the interest of Aristotle de San Gallo (1481–1551). Made from one angled wing and one flat wing, *periaktoi* revolved around a fixed pole to change scenes. But both Serlio's angled wings and San Gallo's *periaktoi* were inefficient. Nicola Sabbattini's (1574–1654) *Pratica di fabricar scene e machine ne'teatri* (*Manual for Constructing Theatrical Scenes and Machines*, 1638) lists three methods for changing the scene: (1) using *periaktoi*; (2) placing angled wings in front of other angled wings; and (3) rolling canvas across angled wings. Changing *periaktoi* or angled wings required that the architectural details on the flats be painted rather than three-dimensional.

Flat wings replaced angled wings when two sides of a building were able to be painted on a single flat. The new technique also eliminated the need for a raked floor, thereby giving actors more playing space. Within fifty years flat wings came to dominate the stage.

The Teatro Farnese first employed flat wings set in grooves; when the front flat was withdrawn the setting changed. At the rear of the stage drops or painted shutters completed the illusion. Later, baroque design conceived all wings as part of one gigantic, grand structure. By 1640 the use of flat wings had spread as far as England.

Meanwhile technicians confronted the problem of synchronizing the changing of flats at each wing position. Working at *Teatro Novissimo* in Venice, Giacomo Torelli (1608–1678) placed slots in the stage floor through which poles were lowered. Below the stage, the poles were attached to wagons called chariots. Above the stage the poles were fastened to flats. As the chariots below rolled on tracks toward the center stage, the on-stage flats above came into view from the wings. To change a scene, flats were removed in the wings, new ones attached to the poles, and the chariots rolled off stage from center. To allow synchronous shifting, an elaborate system of ropes and pulleys attached each wagon to a single winch. The chariot and pole system of scene change remained standard European practice until the late nineteenth century. England and America retained the grooved method.

*Special Effects*   From medieval times special effects fascinated theatre goers. Beams and fulcrums swung suspended platforms into view. Rigging moved both suspended objects and characters upstage and downstage. Wave machines simulated the dynamics of the sea. Hidden ropes moved painted cloth up and down, flat wooden wave cutouts moved up and down and sideways, or long spiral cylinders rotated to illustrate the rising and falling waves. Trapdoors let objects and characters rise and sink, substitutions be made, and smoking fire billow onto the stage. Cannon balls or stones, rolling in rough troughs, created thunder and rain. Wind whistled from the whirling strips of lacquered wood. Music covered the noise of scene changes. A front curtain, at first dropped but later rolled, revealed a play's wonders. Elaborate sky and cloud borders hid rigging and lighting instruments.

Leone di Somi's (1527–1592) *Dialogues on Stage Affairs* (1565) and Sabbattini's treatise addressed particular problems: ''How to Make Dolphins and Other Sea Monsters Appear to Spout Water While Swimming,'' ''How to Produce a Constantly Flowing River,'' ''How to Divide the Sky into Sections,'' ''How to Gradually Cover Part of the Sky with Clouds,'' and ''How to Make a Cloud Descend Perpendicularly with a Person on It.'' Di Somi first suggested that tragedy have less light than comedy and that a stage seemed brighter when the auditorium was dark. Sabbattini added that side lighting pleased audiences more than front lighting.

Joseph Furtenbach (1591–1667), a German who spent ten years in Italy studying theatre technology, experimented with lighting indoor performances. Overhead and wing masking hid lighting instruments which issued a smokey haze through which a performance was viewed. Furtenbach used candles and oil lamps, which smoked and emitted foul odors. He also employed tinsel, mica, and polished brass reflectors to direct the lamplight. To dim or black out, he extinguished the source, lowered a cylinder over the lamp, or rotated the source away from the stage. Containers holding tinted liquids sat before the lamps to color the light.

The Italian scenic ideal was international by the seventeenth century. In Spain, England, and France scenic development occurred neither in the production of classically inspired tragedies and comedies, nor in the popular theatre, but in court entertainments, variously called *intermezzi, entremeses, masques*, and *ballet des cours*. With the Italian scenery traveled the popular Italian players.

*The Commedia dell'Arte*  The courts and academies used amateurs to play in their tragedies and comedies. Meanwhile, Italian professional players delighted all classes with *commedia a soggetto* (plotted plays), *commedia all'improvisio* (improvised plays), and especially with *commedia dell'arte* (skillful plays). These professional players descended from the struggling players who, singularly and in pairs, had eked out livings in the Medieval age. Prosperity in the cities encouraged them to join into troupes, to which Eastern troupes fleeing the Turks added their knowledge of Eastern performance techniques and conventions. By 1600 Italian professional troupes played throughout Europe. The Gelosi troupe, for example, played before Henry IV of France. All troupes shared common features. *Commedia* actor-managers supervised rehearsals, defined the scenarios, read the scenarios to their illiterate companies, discussed the characters and the bits to be employed, fixed the props, and co-ordinated a sharing plan of financial organization (members shared both expenses and profits). The actor-managers then watched their players take over. Traveling from large hall to outdoor fair, each company petitioned a governing body for permission to perform.

The first known important actor-manager was Angelo Beolco (1502–1542), who developed a repertoire of entertainments built around the simple life and common language of a peasant named Ruzzante. Actor-manager Zan Ganassa (c. 1549–c. 1584) toured France and Spain.

The *commedia dell'arte* differed from the *commedia erudita* of the courts and academies. The distinctive features of the *commedia dell'arte*—improvisation within a fixed scenario involving stock characters—possibly evolved from the banding together of specialist entertainers into one troupe. The many diverse performers in one production needed to improvise to bring the work together. Consequently, each company outlined scenarios of action within which stock characters, using stock lines and business, improvised (modern jazz musicians use a similar technique). Players refined, sold, exchanged, and stole scenarios, lines, and stage business. Most scenarios emphasized melodrama and comedy, and plots abounded with love, intrigue, disguising, and duping.

*Commedia* managers considered good actors preferable to good scripts. The *dell'arte* players, in fact, wrote the scenes, created the characters, strung together the speeches, and repeated successful bits of stage by-play. Each company had four lovers, two old men, a *capitano*, and a collection of *zanni* (servants). The lovers, the *inamorata* and *inamorato*, were either fashionable young people of the day or pastoral shepherds and nymphs. Witty, handsome, and well educated, the lovers lived as prototypes of Castiglione's hero and heroine. Fashionably dressed and unmasked to display their natural beauty, the lovers spouted lyrical *chiusetti* (set speeches) on topics like hope, parting, love, and friendship.

The more or less straight lovers inhabited a world of character types. The *capitano*, a braggart to the world but a coward in love and mil-

*Commedia dell'arte characters.*   (Béziers, Musée du Vieux Bitterrois)

itary affairs, sported a wooden sword, cape, long nose, fierce moustache, and a feathered hat. A figure of ridicule, the *capitano* was usually a would-be suitor to the *inamorata*. When Spain invaded Italy the *capitano* acquired a Spanish accent and manner. Stock boasts and threats awaited whomever he met.

Two old men mastered the servant characters of a company. One, Pantalone, the Venetian merchant, spoke maxims with a Venetian dialect. Middle aged or old, Pantalone tried to appear and act young to impress an *inamorata*. But his lust was either too great or nonexistent, his red clothes and Turkish slippers too tight, and his beard too gray and thin. Masked like the *capitano*, Pantalone's brown countenance centered on a long hooked nose. Pantalone, a miser, had an extravagant and deceitful wife if married; if a parent, his children caused him great anxiety. If he had servants, they likely beat him "accidentally." Pantalone's only friend besides the *capitano* was

the other old man, the *dottore*. Only the *dottore* could cure Pantalone's doddering, sneezing, spitting, belching, baldness, and impotence. But the *dottore* was a would-be intellectual. Either a Doctor of Medicine or Laws, the *dottore* had a Bolognese accent that testified to his attendance at the University of Bologna. The *dottore* enjoyed dropping Latin words and phrases to impress his friend. Unfortunately, all were misused: For all his "intellectuality" the *dottore* lacked common sense. Inside his academic cap and gown lived not only glib discourses on philosophy, astronomy, literature, grammar, diplomacy, and medicine, but also a timid victim of parasites, an unfaithful wife, and servants.

The various *zanni* were favorites with the audience, who shared their station in life. Each company had at least one clever servant and one dumb servant. Mostly male, servants helped the lovers and confounded the old masters. A young, crude, and witty female servant, the *fantesca*, waited on the *inamorata*. Whether clever or stupid, Harlequin or Arlecchino was the most popular *zanni*. A shaved head, black hat and mask, and wooden sword or slapstick identified Harlequin, an acrobat and dancer. Harlequin was a patient and faithful valet, always in love and trouble, agile of body, but slow of mind. A crude, lusty, and cynical friend balanced Harlequin's sunny disposition. Called Scapino, Buffetto, or Brighella, the bearded and olive-masked character was probably the great-grandfather of Bluto, the modern-day enemy of Popeye. Without conscience, Brighella lived the life of a Machiavellian hit man. A thief, liar, and drunkard, Brighella liked to scare women with a knife.

Other servants included Pulcinella, a hooknosed, humpbacked poet or valet whose popularity carried him to England as Punch. Pedrolino, the ignorant, licentious, unscrupulous, dull valet became seventeenth-century France's Pierrot. A female servant, the *servetta birichiana* in Italy and the *soubrette* in France, had a blasé unscrupulousness and worldliness; she urged vice on her mistress much in the manner of Emelia in Shakespeare's tragedy *Othello*.

Because *zanni* wore light, thin, pliable leather masks closely fitted to their faces, each character had a distinguishing gesture or bodily pose. But they all specialized in *lazzi*, set pieces of comic business like recognition, reaction, and jealousy. Like the modern Three Stooges, Laurel and Hardy, and the Marx Brothers, *zanni* employed the same *lazzi* time after time. The fly *lazzo*, for example, had a *zanni* catch a fly, tear off its wings, and eat it. When slapped, *zanni* usually had their mouths full of air or water to enlarge the reaction. Dentists invariably used blacksmith or carpenter tools to extract all but the troublesome tooth. Waiters wiped plates and silverware on their dirty pants or aprons before laying them on the table.

Leone di Somi's *Dialogues on Stage Affairs* (1565) explains the acting style used in both the *commedia dell'arte* and written dramas. An actress won high praise if "when she is onstage the audience gets the impression not of a play composed and furnished by an author, but rather of a series of real events taking shape before them."[2] An actor should "observe and imitate the native manner of those persons whom he represents." And "while an actor may think he is talking slowly, the spectator does not get that impression, provided that the words are not separated but given continuous delivery without being so mannered as to raise annoyance." Gestures communicated moods: clutching meant terror; dancing, joy; tearing a handkerchief with one's teeth, grief; pulling back one's cap, despair. Managers checked audibility, volume, pronunciation, rate and tone to make the dialogue resemble "familiar talk, wholly improvised." And always, "when an actor is speaking he ought never to walk about unless he is forced there by great necessity."[3]

The oldest of the 700 extant *commedia dell'arte* scenarios came from the publications of Flaminio Scala (1600–1621). By the seventeenth century Italian *commedia dell'arte* had put Hanswurst in Germany, Pierrot and Columbine in France, and Punch in England. Even regular dramatic writing drew upon *commedia* scenarios and characters. *Lazzi* and songs passed from generation to generation in *zibaldoni* (gag books). By 1650 the *commedia's* influence and popularity had peaked: By that time Europe's audience had been thoroughly educated in Italian popular theatre. Plays of the social theatre, which we discuss in Chapter 6, especially assimilated its scenarios and characters.

***Goldoni and Gozzi*** As late as the eighteenth century the *commedia dell'arte* centered a controversy between two playwrights, Carlo Goldoni (1707–1793) and Carlo Gozzi (1720–1806). Goldoni wanted to change the *commedia* by eliminating the masks, resetting the stories in contemporary society, and using written texts rather than improvisation. Because he reflected the attitudes of the social theatre (see Chapter 6), the resulting plays, such as *Il servitore di due padroni* (*The Servant of Two Masters*, c. 1746) and *La locandiera* (*The Mistress of the Inn*, 1753), were immediately popular. In the lat-

*A commedia dell'arte stage.* (The Art Institute of Chicago)

ter, the mistress, Mirandolina, manipulates the suits of two lovers and a misogynist and ends up married to the servant she loves.

Carlo Gozzi, on the other hand, championed the traditional *commedia*. He wrote plays that retained the masks and fantastic scenarios and that depended upon the improvisation of dialogue and action. Plays such as *Il re cervo* (*King Stag*, 1762), *Re Turandot* (*King Turandot*, 1762), and *Fiaba dell'amore delle tre melarance* (*The Love of Three Oranges*, 1761) were as popular as the up-to-date plays of Goldoni. *The Love of Three Oranges* presents a prince who will die unless he smiles and, later, unless he gets three oranges. The hero of *King Stag* owns a lie-detecting statue to check the sincerity of his would-be brides. But the hero, changed into a deer, nonetheless escapes death only through the intervention of a nearby magician.

***New Dramatic Criticism*** Julius Pomponius Laetus (1425–1498) brought his friends and students to the Roman Academy to stage and watch the first revivals of ancient plays performed outdoors on a wooden stage. Invited guests spread the news of a unique kind of theatre experience. In time courts and princes sought the new dramas for their residence halls. In addition, the rediscovery of Aristotle, Plato, Horace, and Vitruvius renewed discussion of the nature of theatrical art.

Scholars attached their own interpretations to editions of Aristotle and Vitruvius. Giambattista Giraldi Cinthio's (1504–1573) *Intorno al comporre delle comedie e delle tragedie* (*Discourse on Comedy and Tragedy*, 1554), for example, elevated Latin plays over Greek plays. Cinthio, who thought the Greek plays lacked Seneca's beloved maxims (*sententiae*) and majesty, favored Horace's division of drama into five acts, each with a distinctive function. He wanted Act I to present an argument through exposition, Act II to move the action toward a resolution, Act III to introduce obstacles and barriers to the resolution, Act IV to reveal the means for overcoming the obstacles, and Act V to hold the desired end that resolved the argument.

In 1548 Francesco Robortello published the first commentary on Aristotle's *Poetics*. The next year publication of the *Poetics* in Italian opened the discussion to all who could read. As a result, Aristotle's authority rose but drama became a subdivision of poetry rather than a separate art.

*The Neo-Classical Ideal*   Critics ultimately created the "neo-classical ideal." To them great drama revealed a verisimilitude (an appearance of being true or real) based on certain rules and unities. Verisimilitude meant fidelity to truth. Action on stage should appear truthful to reality. Because events seen in life were most appropriate for dramatization on stage, fantasy, the supernatural, soliloquies, and the chorus were off limits. What great person could consider important matters aloud in a multitude of people speaking in unison? Instead, great people confided in their secretaries or confidants.

Verisimilitude required the appearance on stage of only that which could be rendered convincing to an audience. Consequently, battles, acts of violence, and deaths were kept off stage. Lodovico Castelvetro explained that "because of the difficulty of representing actions and making them verisimilar, dramas do not present on the stage the murders and other things that it is difficult to represent with dignity, and it is proper that they should be done offstage and then narrated by a messenger." He also thought that action "cannot last longer than the time allowed by the convenience of the audience, nor represent more things than those which come about in the space of time that the comedies and tragedies themselves require. And as I say, there must always be regard to the ease of the people, for after some hours the

people have to leave the theater because of the human necessities for eating, drinking, sleeping, and other things."

To the critics drama had the moral obligation to praise virtuous action and blame vice as defined by the ruling class. Drama had to teach by revealing the moral pattern of the cosmos, perceptible only to people high in the chain of being. Finally, drama had to deal with eternal truths and qualities rather than with incidental superficialities and quirks of nature. Normal and typical actions had to display decorum, "what fits places, times, and persons." Scientific observation led critics to determine the typical and normal behavior and speech for certain places, times, and people according to class, nationality, sex, age, and disposition. (In the Modern age the classification was carried out by psychologists, sociologists, and anthropologists.)

Neo-classical theorists also had much to say about the peculiar natures of comedy and tragedy. All critics agreed that, even though comedy and tragedy were both classified according to plot, character, thought, diction, and spectacle, the two forms must remain distinct in composition. Comedy was considered a lower form. Tragedy, on the other hand, according to J. C. Scaliger (1494–1558) was "the imitation of the adversity of a distinguished man." Gian Giorgio Trissino believed that tragedy involved true action and characters, whereas comedy involved invented actions and characters. Comedies, which had to employ everyday diction, also had to show middle- or lower-class characters in domestic situations that resolved happily. Tragedies, on the other hand, using poetic diction, had to portray ruling-class characters in historical or mythological situations that resolved unhappily. Comedy taught by ridiculing behavior inappropriate or ludicrous for one's class, nationality, sex, age, or disposition. Tragedy, in contrast, taught by showing the results of poor judgment or error. Aristotle's term "catharsis" came to mean the correction of bad behavioral instincts within the audience by purging pity and fear and inducing good behavioral instincts.

Aristotle's insistence on the unity of action

led neo-classical critics to postulate two related unities: unity of time and unity of place. Unity of action came to mean that events in a plot needed a causal relationship or connection. The unity of time concept arose around 1554 when Cinthio suggested that stage action confine itself to little more than one day's duration. Robortello preferred a limit of twelve hours because some people sleep at night. Segni wanted twenty-four hours because tragic actions are more likely to occur at night. Maggni insisted that the time elapsed on stage equal the actual time passed in the audience, lest anyone find the actions incredible.

From the unity of time came a discussion of place; if stage time and audience time were identical, then place must be the same, too. The first call for a unity of place came around 1570. Lodovico Castelvetro wanted the place of tragedy limited to the space that one person could travel in the actual playing time of a tragedy. Great distances could not be traveled in a short span of time; "It is not possible to have it understood by spectators that many nights and days have passed when it is plainly evident

to them that only a few hours have passed." Thus, because the audience was in one place, the action must be in one place; one could not deny an audience's observation that it had not moved.

In summary, neo-classicism insisted on one plot action occurring in, at most, twenty-four hours, and having one location (or locations possible to visit in the time allowed). This neo-classical ideal, which dominated European drama well into the eighteenth century, had its greatest advocates in the social theatre of seventeenth-century France (see Chapter 6).

***From Italy to the World***    The theory and practice of the Italian Renaissance stage spread north with traveling players and humanists. By 1650 Italy had given Europe a model for a popular theatre replete with plots, characters, and organization. The neo-classical ideal provided a standard for critical judgment. Classically inspired comedies, tragedies, and pastorals, were available for imitation and study; Italian opera and theatre architectural and scenic innovations spread with the rest.

# SPAIN

***Cultural Context***    Between 1470 and 1550 Italy and Spain were very closely connected. Warring entanglements brought humanistic literature, art, and theatre to Spain. Spaniards traveled to Italy to fight or study. Italians taught in Spanish and Portuguese universities and courts. By 1508 Spanish students had studied Latin, Hebrew, and Greek languages and literatures. Readers pored over Greek and Latin translations while political turmoil raged.

***Political Stability***    With the death of Henry IV of Castile in 1474 the reign of his sister, Isabella (reigned 1474–1504), since 1469 the wife of King Ferdinand of Aragon, began. The union of Aragon and Castile brought stability, wealth, and humanist culture to Spain. Together King and Queen revived the medieval Inquisition and expelled both the Moors (Mos-

lems of mixed Berber and Arab descent) and the Jews to unite the Christian nation.

The patriotism generated by the union of Aragon and Castile drew more upon religious ideals than political ones, even though the Inquisition operated as an arm of the state. Catholicism thrived as the national religion. Religious conformity and political loyalty coincided. Whereas in England religion stood as an obstacle to political solidarity, in Spain monarchs used religion to fuse unification. Consequently, Spanish literature and theatre remained religious, and the religiosity of the drama increased with nationalism. The medieval Feast of Corpus Christi revived as a celebration not only of the power of the Host but also of the power of the king. Working with local priests, the Jesuits—priests of the Society of Jesus—formed schools based on classical traditions to prevent losses to Protestantism.

The literature and drama of ancient Greece and Rome entered Spain through these Jesuit schools.

Like that of Italy, Spain's Renaissance depended upon economic prosperity. Spain drew great wealth from the domination of Italy, the sixty-year control of Portugal (1580–1640), and the Spanish-American empire. The New World arose from medieval blueprints. Native American heritage collapsed as Spanish priests replaced native shamen. In a single generation conquistadores baptized the Aztec and Inca lands of Mexico and Peru. Baroque churches modeled on Spanish counterparts dotted the American landscape. Silver and gold mines spewed treasure until disease wiped out the native laborers. Spanish Jesuits and Franciscans built missions resembling medieval manors; like feudal serfs, native Americans tilled the mines and fields.

***The Golden Age*** Spain reigned as a world power from the time of Columbus to the defeat of the Naval Armada by the British in 1588. The nation's distinctive literature, art, and theatre combined Islamic attitudes toward women and honor with Christian faith and doctrine. Vernacular literature had been printed in Spain since 1474 and in Mexico City since 1539. But unlike Italian humanists, those in Spain preferred Bible translation and the narration of mystical religious experiences. Nevertheless, Spain enjoyed a Renaissance, a *Siglio de Oro* (a Golden Age), between 1580 and 1680.

Spanish drama was less historical than that of England and more religious than that of Italy. In 1605 and 1615 Spanish literature reached its peak with the publication of Miguel de Cervantes's (1547–1616) *Don Quixote*, Parts I and II, a novel parodying chivalric novels. Cervantes, a mannerist writer, displayed both an ambivalence toward the struggle of idealism with realism and a new hero, neither all good nor all bad. Don Quixote is both saint and fool.

***Dramatic Texts*** Great drama seemed to arise from a community's sense of purpose, pride in past accomplishments, and a new order envisioned by poet-playwrights. Indeed, stability, confidence, well-being, and economic prosperity let Spanish authors envision new realities. With the unification of Aragon and Castile the Castilian dialect emerged as the language of both literature and the stage.

As early as 1492 Juan del Encina (c. 1469–c. 1529), after studying in Italy, experimented with dramatic writing. Considered the founder of Spanish Renaissance theatre, Encina broke from Christian medievalism to write humanistic plays. Secular influences crept into his simple comic and pastoral dialogues. Then, a sixteen-act dialogue novel, *The Comedy of Calisto and Melibea* (1499) by Fernando de Rojas (c. 1465–1541), though never performed, influenced writers with its characters and situations. Also known as *La Celestina*, this work inspired playwrights to write sequels or borrow plots, scenes, characters, and speeches in the manner of Indian playwrights drawing upon the *Ramayana*.

Playwrights also wrote *auto sacramentales*, religious plays combining elements of secular morality plays with aspects of cycle plays. The power of the Holy Eucharist and the truth of Catholic dogma were ratified in stories mixing humans, supernatural figures, and allegorical entities. Interludes and dances accompanied the religious plays. In 1765 excessive farce and melodrama diminished the religiosity of the *autos* so much that the plays were banned.

The first truly important figure in the history of the Spanish professional theatre was Lope de Rueda (c. 1510–c. 1565), a supervisor of Corpus Christi plays in the capitol who was asked to perform before Philip II in 1551. Rueda was the first Spanish playwright to write for a touring company that depended on a popular audience. Fools and simpletons thus scamper through his farces. Rueda also invented the *paso*, a one-act interlude between the acts of a longer work.

***Lope de Vega*** The style of drama created by Rueda flowered in the hands of Lope Felix de Vega Carpio (1562–1635), the creator of the *commedia's* (drama's) final form. Lope authored 1500 lyric poems and almost 2000 plays, 500 of which survive.

Claiming that he only desired the public's approval, Lope constructed plots driven by love. In addition, contrary to the dictates of the neo-classical ideal, his comedies and tragedies mix elements of one another, a phenomenon he defended in *El arte nuevo de hacer comedias* (*The New Art of Writing Plays*, 1609). Lope wrote *heroicas* (plays with a serious tone) and *capa y espada* (plays involving the mundane business of middle-class intrigue). Always in love or trouble, like a *commedia dell'arte zanni*, Lope suffered during his last years: His favorite son drowned, his daughter was raped, and his beloved mistress went blind and mad. His most enduring plays include *El acero de Madrid* (*The Waters of Madrid*, 1606), the basis for Molière's *Doctor in Spite of Himself*; *Peribanez* (1610); *Fuente ovejuna* (*The Sheep Well*, 1614); *El mejor alcalde el rey* (*The King the Greatest Mayor*, 1620); *El caballero de Olmedo* (*The Knight of Olmedo*, c. 1620), and *El castigo sin venganza* (*Punishment without Revenge*, 1631).

His plays usually feature a conflict between love and honor, great female roles, and an important fool character, the *gracioso*. In *The Sheep Well*, for example, the ruling lord seizes a peasant girl but is driven away by her lover. In retaliation, the lord takes another girl. He then arrests the first girl and her lover when they try to marry. The peasants revolt and overthrow the evil lord in what is considered the first proletarian drama. *The King the Greatest Mayor* also presents a lord abducting a peasant girl. But in this play the girl's new husband appeals to the king for help. To glorify the Spanish monarchy Lope has the king free the girl and execute the evil lord.

***Tirso and Calderon***  Of the 400 plays by Tirso de Molina (c. 1569–1648) eighty survive, most notably the first Don Juan drama, *El burlador de Sevilla* (*The Trickster of Seville*, 1630). Actually named Fray Gabriel Tellez, Tirso, a monk, would have written other plays like *Don Gil de las calzas verdes* (*Don Gil of the Green Trousers*, 1635) and *La brudencia en la mujer* (*Prudence in Women*, 1633) under his assumed name, but his superiors found him out and threatened excommunication. Tirso's plots feature either a "masculine" female character or a woman vying for the attention of a young man.

Yet another major dramatist in Renaissance Spain, Pedro Calderon de la Barca (1600–1681), dominated Philip IV's select group of court playwrights. After attending Jesuit schools and the Universities of Alcala and Salamanca, Calderon wrote over 100 plays before being ordained a priest in 1651.

Whereas Lope had examined love, Calderon explored honor. Works like *La devoción de la cruz* (*Devotion to the Cross*, 1633), *El médico de su honra* (*The Doctor of His Own Honor*, 1635), *La vida es sueño* (*Life Is a Dream*, c. 1636) reveal more didacticism and allegory than Lope's works. In *Life Is a Dream* a Polish king keeps his son locked in a tower, because a prophecy said the son would be evil. To test the prophecy, the king drugs the son and removes him from the castle. The son wakes, shows evidence that the prophecy is true, and finds himself back in the castle. When a revolution frees the son, he wonders if his first freedom was real or a dream. Whatever the truth, he vows to be a good ruler. *El mágico prodigioso* (*The Wonderful Magician*, 1637) presents a Roman Faust character. *El gran teatro del mundo* (*The Great Theatre of the World*, c. 1645), which won the admiration of nineteenth-century playwrights Lessing, Schlegel, and Shelley, shows God as playwright call various actors from his world as theatre. Some complain of the roles they have to play in the Great Playwright's morality play. Grace of God serves as prompter for the drama of life. At the play's end, all actors exit without role, costume, or properties to a great celestial cast party.

Calderon's ability to argue Catholic dogma with great lyricism and imagination made his *autos* the best of the form. After Lope, plays had became mechanical and limited in action, and soliloquies and set speeches took on a cliched character. With Calderon, acting again had to carry the show.

**Professional Players**  By 1550 a combination of religious and secular interests had put primary responsibility for theatrical production with local governments, and city councils asked professional companies to produce their religious dramas. In 1592 a second company broke the city's monopoly on production. In a typical year before 1647, three or four *autos* were produced. After 1647 officials sponsored only two *autos*, although some cities did revive old *autos*. In Madrid all *autos* between 1647 and 1681 were new works by Calderon.

Permanent theatre buildings and a growing number of troupes increased the demand for regulation. In 1603 eight companies held licenses; twelve years later the number was twelve. But companies ignored the regulations; they either organized on a sharing basis (*companias de parte*) or contracted actors for one- or two-year periods. Numbering anywhere from one to twenty, such Spanish troupes contained both men and women. Most troupes toured, but they received a license to perform only if a free performance satisfied a city official. Before 1590 playwrights toured with the companies; after 1590 playwrights merely sold their scripts.

Actors remained officially infamous. But in the Golden Age (between 1580 and 1680) players enjoyed toleration and even an occasional Christian sacrament. In 1587 church leaders objected to the licensing of actresses. No doubt the popularity of the 1575 Italian *commedia dell'arte* troupe's tour contributed to the ease with which women were accepted. The 1596 ban on female performers, in fact, was never enforced. In 1598 a compromise even allowed the wife or daughter of a company member to perform. Transvestism was never a feature of the Spanish Renaissance stage; the *zarabanda*, a licentious and voluptuous dance, caused controversy enough.

Wardrobes were the Renaissance actors' greatest asset. It not only helped them find work, but also became an investment that they could cash in at any time. Actors dressed not according to character or dramatic situation but according to personal success and wealth. Their conventionalized costumes contributed to the stage spectacle. They wore contemporary fashions, adding an alien element only for historical, legendary, fanciful, and old-fashioned characters. These costumes were often the only scenic element filling a performance space.

**Carrios to Corrales**  In a holdover from medieval times, Spanish city councils supervised playing sites and times. Drama gradually moved to the court as the Italian ideal of rulership gained ground in Spain. Meanwhile, Italian scenic practices traveled from the palace to the public theatres. At first scenery rode on *carrios* in the Corpus Christi processions. Bulls with gilded horns pulled pageant wagons carrying city-supplied scenery, costumes, properties, and actors. Such processional staging remained a part of Spain's theatrical scene until the *autos* were banned in 1765.

When not employed by the city council for religious festivals, professional companies used whatever space was available. Professional players performed in courtyards, squares, and the court of Philip III (1596–1621). Because Philip's queen liked the theatre, plays and masques became regular court features. Court entertainments peaked in 1626 when Philip IV (1621–1665) imported Cosmo Lotti from Florence to install Italian scenic technology in Spain. Then, both indoor and outdoor performances enjoyed royal attendance. Seated on gondolas, the royal audience could watch performances on floating barges.

In 1640, Lotti built the Coliseo, a permanent theatre, in the new palace in Madrid, El Buen Retiro. Containing Spain's first proscenium arch and a wing and groove system for changing settings, the Coliseo was the most modern theatre of its time. The royal theatre occasionally opened its doors to the public, donated a percentage of its gate to charities, and featured many characteristics of the permanent public theatres that had been built.

*A reconstruction of the Corral del Principe, Madrid, seventeenth century.* (Museo Municipal, Madrid)

In 1579 and 1583 the first permanent theatre buildings were constructed in Madrid. The *Corral de la Cruz* and the *Corral del Principe* were based on temporary courtyard theatres. A raised platform stood before a permanent two-level facade. The audience sat on three sides of a twenty-six to twenty-eight foot wide by twenty-three to twenty-nine foot deep stage. Three openings in the lower level of the facade allowed entrances and exits, which designated changes of place. The yard or pit before the stage was called the *patio*. Benches, added in the seventeenth century, were known as *lunetas*. The *gradas*, platformed balconies along the sides of the patio, and the *cazuela*, the women's area located at the rear of the *patio* over the *alojeria* (tavern), needed additional benches. Behind and above the *gradas* on the sides of the patio were *aposentos* (boxes) on the first two floors of the houses surrounding the courtyard. Above the *gradas* were spectator *desvanes* (attics), on the tops of the buildings. Two galleries above the *cazuela* housed officials and clergy. Several entrances led to the courtyard. At each entrance two fee takers, one for the confraternities and one for the theatre lessee, split the admission fee. Three-fifths went to the actors and manager, two-fifths to charity.

*Two Audiences* The audience enjoyed a rousing time at the public theatre. Outside the entrances ticket scalpers operated; inside, men and women connived to overcome the sexually segregated seating. *Alguaciles* (armed guards) protected the stage and maintained order in the unruly, noisy mob. Vendors sold both fresh and dried fruits, water, sweets, ale, and rolled wafers called *barquillos*. The *patio* held the most vocal spectators, the *mosqueteros*. Respectable women attended plays only if masked. Police at the door of the *cazuela* stopped women from hurling fruit, orange peels, and cucumbers, or rattling keys at the players below. A shout of "Victor" followed a favorable turn on the stage. The court audience, in contrast, was more subdued. Aristocratic audiences enjoyed the fashionable Italian scenic effects in performances that occurred whenever the king decreed.

Public performances were strictly regulated: none from Lent till after Easter nor during summer months. The curtain fell at 2 P.M. in the fall, and at 4 P.M. in the spring, to ensure the audience a safe return home. But both court and public audiences witnessed the same format: Music began the performance with dancing or a *jacara* (ballad). Next came a *loa* (prologue), another dance, and then a play with *entremeses*. A dance completed the bill.

The Spanish Renaissance ended with the death of Calderon and the positioning of a Frenchman, Philip V (1700–1746), the first Bourbon, on the Spanish throne.

# ENGLAND

With the waning of Spain in 1588, world attention shifted to England. When the Italian Renaissance reached England, however, at the time of Spain's Golden Age, the early Italian Renaissance ideas had blended with mannerist tendencies. During the Elizabethan Age, named for the queen whose reign oversaw the Renaissance, Italian ideas developed politically and artistically in England.

*Political Stability* Political anarchy, which had frustrated Italian and Spanish unification and cultural development, ended in England when the War of the Roses (1455–1485) led to the restoration of the Tudor Dynasty and Henry VII (reigned 1485–1509). The houses of York and Lancaster had struggled for the monarchy. With the defeat of Richard III, the Tudor family established political stability that lasted to the death of Elizabeth in 1603. The war's political heroes and actions became the material of England's Renaissance theatre.

Henry VII encouraged the classical scholarship that had slowed during the wars. English citizens went to Italy to study, and Italians found employment in English noble households. Peasants and the middle class looked for order after the strife. Henry VII's son, Henry VIII (1509–1547), raised as a model Renaissance prince, patronized humanists as long as they agreed with him. Following his father's taste for European entertainment, Henry VIII brought to London the French troupe of players he had enjoyed while in France. Under Henry VIII court theatrical entertainments grew in magnificence; his Master of Revels became a permanent state position.

The defeat of the Spanish Armada in 1588 created a wave of national pride that stimulated the cultural and theatrical Renaissance. Elizabeth I (reigned 1558–1603) had determined to achieve peace for England. Consequently, England ruled France, and Germany remained divided by internal religious wars. Meanwhile, the English theatre flourished.

*Theatre Regulation* Governmental regulation stabilized theatrical development. When Elizabeth took office any gentleman could boast a troupe of players, and illegal companies toured under bogus patronages. In 1559 Elizabeth banned all unlicensed plays, forbid plays with religious or political topics, and made local authorities responsible for all public performances. Thirteen years later only gentlemen of baronial rank or higher could legally sponsor troupes. In addition, public performances required a license from two Justices of the Peace. As a result, the number of English troupes shrank.

Because Puritans, the Crown's major opponents, had won the Lord Mayorship of London and dominated the City Council in 1573, in 1574 Elizabeth passed licensing power to the hands of the Master of Revels. Whereas local Puritan municipalities had forbidden plays on the excuse of plague or riot danger, official licensing encouraged troupes to build permanent theatres. But plays could happen only three weekdays and never during the time of a church service. The domestic calm enjoyed under Elizabeth, however, deteriorated under her successor.

James I (reigned 1603–1625) had been James VI, Stuart King of Scotland. Raised by Calvinists, James believed he was ordained in the chain of being by God and was thus answerable only to God. James did not understand Parliament's role in English government. His lavish expenditure of money added to the Calvinists', "Puritans'," objections to his reign. As a result, the Puritans demanded the removal of church trappings reminiscent of Catholicism. But James refused.

In 1604 James abolished the right of anyone but the royal family to have a troupe of players. From that point on, the theatre and the monarchy were wedded in the eyes of Parliament and Puritans. The premiere company, the Lord Chamberlain's Men, was rechristened the King's Men. New patents specified which building fell under which company's control.

Provincial troupes were outlawed. Theatrical activity centered in London. In fact, Sir Henry Herbert, the Master of Revels, grew wealthy licensing plays. His 100 employees rehearsed players and supplied costumes, scenery, and properties for court performances.

Puritans wanted James to simplify Anglican religious services by eliminating the sign of the cross, rings in marriage, and ecclesiastical garb. Instead, displaying his love for spectacle, James flaunted his wealth and pageantry in court entertainments. The King's strong opposition to the Puritan minority's demands encouraged both extremism and migration to the New World of the Americas.

James's son, Charles I (reigned 1625–1649) tried to bypass Parliament's refusal to finance his schemes: He ruled without Parliament. He refused, for example, to call Parliament to session and raised money through taxation and the sale of titles and monopolies. Open rebellion broke out in 1642. A Parliamentary army led by Oliver Cromwell (1599–1658) defeated the Royalist forces, tried Charles, and beheaded him on charges of treason. The monarchy was destroyed. The theatre, an arm of the Royalist legion, was outlawed. Parliament controlled England, and England's Renaissance ended.

***Economic Prosperity*** Like Spain, England drew its strength from economic ventures in the New World. A colony in Virginia appeared in 1607, and by 1620 the English Massachusetts Bay Colony was outshipping the Dutch of New York. Along the Brazilian, Caribbean, and Atlantic coasts, native Indian slaves worked until imported diseases wiped them out. Entrepreneurs replaced the native slaves with immune and disease-resistant West African slaves.

Elizabeth encouraged merchant capitalism. Overseas trading companies built geographical spheres of influence within monopolies assigned by royal charter. Between 1630 and 1643 over 20,000 men and women sailed to New England, and over 40,000 British arrived in the Southern colonies in America. England traded eastward as well. The British East India Company, for example, held a monopoly on the "East Indies." Merchants wanted both permanent markets for English goods and the products of the New World. Promoters were wealthy and noble; colonists were commoners. Outside of the religiously motivated New Englanders, most colonists preferred to better themselves economically with free land. Convicts and prisoners from the English Civil Wars joined colonists recruited by private companies.

The society imported to the New World reflected the society at home where, as in Italy, rich bourgeois and noble landowners created the ruling class. The crown and middle class ruled as allies. Court life, however, set the fashion. The merchant middle class supported Elizabeth for the order she brought. Trade flourished only in peace time. Old medieval families died out, titled households broke up, and players looked for new patrons. Court life centered in the rapidly growing city of London.

***The Arrival of Humanism*** When humanism arrived in England in the fourteenth century, it prompted the appearance of a secular drama. Law students at Oxford and Cambridge lived in university residence halls known as Inns of Court. Debates and plays allowed these students to develop the skills of courtiers—music, dance, rhetoric. Like the Italian Academies, English Inns of Court—with their Christmas Revels and honors for royal guests, births, and marriages—influenced the revival of classical plays.

The arrival of a printing press in Caxton in 1474 accelerated the English literary Renaissance. (In 1638 a press in Cambridge, Massachusetts, imitated the homeland's output.) After the War of the Roses, the English aristocracy followed the Italian lead: The English court became the center of literary and artistic life. But English nobility did not compose courtly dilettante literature. Instead, the distinguished court favorites were sons of artisans using arts, letters, and the theatre as a means of social mobility. Literature and theatre were in vogue in Elizabethan society. Gentlemen and ladies discussed poetry and dramatic criticism. Many wrote and read sonnets and lyric poetry. Just below the poet in esteem stood the dramatist. The theatre offered security to court poets flattering patrons with literary dedications.

***Dramatic Texts*** In English schools humanist teachers produced Roman dramas and Roman imitations. Performances began at Cambridge around 1520, in 1525 at Eton, in 1527 at St. Paul's, and in 1525 at Oxford. Nicholas Udall (1505–1566), headmaster of Eton, penned the comedy *Ralph Roister Doister* (1534). Cambridge presented "Mr. S's" *Gammer Gurton's Needle*. The plays' common balcony and window scenes show the influence of the street scene in Plautus and Terence. Professional companies, eager for popular novelties, mixed classical features into their medieval repertoires. An interest in Seneca revived with the publication of Nicholas Treveth's commentaries in the early fourteenth century. In 1559 Seneca was first translated into English. *Cambises* (c. 1561) by Thomas Preston (1537–1598) also mixed classical mythology, medieval allegory, and contemporary English life. A comic and serious Senecan spectacle, *Cambises* featured many scenes and locations. It was the most popular play of the day.

In time students and playwrights shifted the attention from classical plays to either plays based on English history or plays adapted from new Italian models. The Italian *novelle* (histories) and vacation stories provided material for Elizabethan tragedy. In addition, despite the neo-classical ideal, violence occurred on the English stage, a fact that helped popularize Elizabethan tragedy. The first English tragedy was written by two students, Thomas Sackville (1536–1608) and Thomas Norton (1532–1584), in 1561. *Gorboduc*, a five-act variation on the Seneca model that went into five printings, was attended by Queen Elizabeth. Then George Gascoigne (c. 1525–1577) translated Lodovico Dolce's play *Giocasta* into *Jocasta* (1566).

The *commedia dell'arte* also contributed references and characters named Pantaloun, Harlakeen, Zani, Arlecchino. The capitano became Sir Topas, Bobadil, and Falstaff. Pantalone appeared as Gremio, Shylock, Polonius, Mammon, Brabantio, and Corvino. Many university students worked in the professional theatre after graduation. Their group came to be known as the "University Wits." One wit, the son of a scrivener, wrote *The Spanish Tragedy* in 1587. Showing clear Senecan influence, this five-act play by Thomas Kyd (c. 1557–c. 1595) used ghosts, chorus, soliloquies, and confidants in a plot of revenge. Elaborate rhetoric echoed through the sixteenth-century Spanish setting.

Like television today, the English public theatre needed new scripts constantly. Unlike the East, the West valued novelty and newness over revivals of old works. Plays dropped out of the English repertoire after the potential audience was exhausted; new plays, which entered the repertoire every two and a half weeks, had a life of about ten performances. In fact, between 1600 and 1642 the practice of consecutive performances of a single play began. At the time Thomas Middleton's *A Game at Chess* (1624) held the record: nine consecutive performances. Each company probably had only one complete copy of each play, the promptbook. The single copy contained all cues, entrances, exits, music, and scene changes. All plays belonged to the troupe and were subject to piracy, printing, and sale without regard to either troupe or playwright. The Master of Revels had authority to appoint another playwright to revise, change, or alter any script for court performance.

***Christopher Marlowe*** Kyd's college roommate, a shoemaker's son named Christopher Marlowe (1564–1593), found work with the Earl of Nottingham's company.

Marlowe, who was the first great English dramatist, translated Ovid's *Amores* (c. 1597). He also perfected blank verse as the standard dramatic diction. A member of London's underworld, Marlowe flaunted his scandalous reputation as an atheist. One day he was murdered in a tavern brawl, perhaps doing espionage work for the government.

Marlowe wrote *Tamburlaine I* and *II* (1587), *Doctor Faustus* (1588), *The Jew of Malta* (1589), and *Edward II* (1592). *Tamburlaine* was the appropriate hero for an age of power, conquest, and looting. But Tamburlaine conquers not only with physical force but also with great wit, poetic diction, and love of beauty. *Doctor Faustus* contains remnants of the old morality play structure. Nevertheless, Marlowe redefined his age's concept of Hell as a human state of affairs rather than a location after death. And, significantly, Marlowe's hero in *Doctor Faustus* is not a royal born prince but rather a poor scholar. With *The Jew of Malta*, a portrait of a Jew revenging the insults suffered at the hands of intolerant Christians, Marlowe ruffled the Puritans. *Edward II* presents homo sexuality in the story of a gay king and the plots of his court and wife to destroy his lovers. The character of Mortimer presents a Machiavellian hero.

***William Shakespeare*** Although William Shakespeare (1564–1616), the premiere wit, never attended a university, his Stratford grammar school education in Latin classics, Christian ethics, and rhetoric was evident in his plays. He became to English drama, in fact, what Lope de Vega became to Spanish drama.

At age 18 Shakespeare married the 24-year-old Ann Hathaway. Two years later Shakespeare fathered twins, one of whom, Hamnet, his only son, died in childhood.

Beginning as an actor, Shakespeare worked his way to great wealth as a shareholder in both an acting company and a theatre building. His first plays— *The Comedy of Errors* (1592) and *Titus Andronicus* (1593)—are clearly based on Roman models. In the 1590s Shakespeare turned to history with *Henry II Part I* (1590), *Henry VI Part I* (1591), *Henry VI Parts II, III* (1591), *Richard III* (1592), *Richard II* (1595), *King John* (1596), *Henry IV Part I* (1596), *Henry IV Part II* (1598), and *Henry V* (1599). When plague closed the theatres between 1592 and 1593 Shakespeare wrote sonnets and poems dedicated to the Earl of Southampton. During the

1590s Shakespeare also wrote *The Taming of the Shrew* (1593), *Two Gentlemen of Verona* (1594), *Loves Labors Lost* (1594), *A Midsummer Night's Dream* (1595), *Romeo and Juliet* (1595), *The Merchant of Venice* (1596), *The Merry Wives of Windsor* (1597), *Julius Caesar* (1599), and *Much Ado about Nothing* (1599).

At the turn of the century Shakespeare produced *As You Like It* (1599), *Twelfth Night* (1601), *Troilus and Cressida* (1602), *All's Well that Ends Well* (1603), *Measure for Measure* (1604), and his great tragedies: *Hamlet* (1601), *Othello* (1604), *King Lear* (1605), *Macbeth* (1606), *Antony and Cleopatra* (1607), *Timon of Athens* (1607), and *Coriolanus* (1608). His last plays were *Pericles* (1608), *Cymbeline* (1609), *A Winter's Tale* (1610), *The Tempest* (1611), and, in collaboration with John Fletcher (1579–1625), *Henry VIII* (1612).

Shakespeare was interested in the relationship between the health of the monarchy and the health of society. In both *Macbeth* and *King Lear*, for example, royal turmoil upsets the entire state. The eventual corruption and disillusionment of England found their way into Shakespeare's plays. With the execution of the Second Earl of Essex (1566–1601) for treason, with his own patron, the Earl of Southampton in jail, and with his father's death, Shakespeare wrote *Hamlet*, a portrait of the tone of the times within the revenge structure of Thomas Kyd's *The Spanish Tragedy*. Shakespeare's hero was a prince and a scholar who spoke to all times and places.

Most of Shakespeare's major tragedies were written under King James. Consequently, his heroes explore the nature of a person's responsibility when living in an evil world. Many of Shakespeare's late plays, showing a mannerist influence, portray decadent chivalry. Like most humanists, Shakespeare tended either to look down on the masses or to celebrate them.

Yet, despite such private political attitudes, Shakespeare pioneered change. His plays suggest both pessimism and hope beneath England's pride and prosperity. Each knight in his plays—Falstaff, Brutus, Hamlet, Timon, and Troilus—is hurt by the discovery of a new reality. Although Shakespeare explored Machiavellian ethics with Richard III, Iago, and Malvolio, his sympathy lay with the failures of public life. Throughout his career, Shakespeare mixed Renaissance, medieval, mannerist, and baroque ideas and techniques.

After 1594 Shakespeare was a shareholder in England's leading troupe, the Lord Chamberlain's Men. Renamed the King's Men in 1603, this troupe featured the principal actor, Richard Burbage (c. 1567–1619), for whom Shakespeare wrote many of his major roles. In 1599 the company erected its own theatre, The Globe. It also performed in the Blackfriars Theatre.

The earliest publication of Shakespeare's collected plays came in 1623 with the First Folio, edited by two of the playwright's fellow players, John Heminges and Henry Condell. The edition contains thirty-six plays including *Henry VIII*, seventeen previously published in pirated quarto form. The 1609 *Pericles* quarto joined the collection in the third edition of the Folio (1664). *Two Noble Kinsmen*, number thirty-eight, is considered a 1613 collaboration with John Fletcher.

**Ben Jonson** Unlike Shakespeare, Ben Jonson (1572–1637), the son of a clergyman and stepson of a bricklayer, edited his own collection of works in 1616. Jonson's first play resulted in his arrest for libel in 1597. But Shakespeare's production of Jonson's *Every Man in His Humor* (1598) provided Jonson with his first success. Later, released from prison after murdering an actor in a duel, Jonson found fame with *Every Man Out of His Humor* (1599); *Cynthia's Revels* (1600); *The Poetaster* (1601), a satire on his fellow playwrights; *Volpone* (1606); *Epicoene* (1609); *The Alchemist* (1610); *Cateline* (1611); and *Bartholomew Fair* (1614). Besides a successful career in the public theatre, Jonson collaborated with Inigo Jones on court masques (we discuss these in more detail in a later section), such as *The Hue and Cry after Cupid* (1608). Recipient of a royal pension, and celebrated as England's first poet laureate (1616), Jonson died rich and famous.

Jonson's plays espoused the psychology of humors. Each character was drawn as psychologically obsessed due to an imbalance among blood, phlegm, and yellow and black bile. The mixture of the four elements in the body, scientists believed, created various temperamental dispositions. With the mechanical psychology, Jonson concocted farcical intrigues among the bourgeoisie. In plays unified according to Jonson's understanding of the classical rules, contemporary characters plot and fail in contemporary settings. *Volpone*, for example, is a black comedy set in the greedy capital of Italian commerce. The main characters, Italian merchant-princes, have the names of birds of prey. *The Alchemist* shows English society seeking a quick fortune with the philosopher's stone, which could turn worthless ore into gold. *Bartholomew Fair* exposes pious hypocrisy with the clergyman Zeal-of-the-Land-Busy.

**Dramatic Technique** Elizabethan dramatists employed a characteristic structure for their plays. After an early point of attack, action followed a chronological order of events. Eschewing the frequent use of recollection, exposition, and messengers, playwrights placed important action on stage in relatively short scenes. Time and place shifted rapidly. The comic mixed with the serious. Characters in serious dramas, facing moral choices and the need for decision, expressed themselves in poetic imagery, soliloquies, and Senecan *sententiae* (pithy axioms).

**Mannerism and Jacobean Drama** Around 1610 playwrights whose work was later called Jacobean adopted such mannerist traits as gratuitous novelty and sensationalism. Mannerist Jacobean plays accepted the moral code of the aristocracy. Tragicomedy, the ultimate mannerist form, came into fashion when two mannerist playwrights, John Fletcher (1579–1625) and Francis Beaumont (1584–1616), collaborated after studying at Cambridge. At the time and during the Restoration (1660), Fletcher's plays were more popular than Shakespeare's. Fletcher actually developed the tragicomic romance's elaborate plot of suspense and surprise at the expense of character examination. Spanish concepts of honor dominate the plays of Beaumont and Fletcher. As mannerists, these playwrights searched for novelties and sensations for the drama. Their *Philaster* (1610), which portrayed a woman who disdained both commoner and noble to find her true love, spurred the popularity of tragicomedy. To get her man the woman disguised herself as a man. Other plays, like *The Maid's Tragedy* (1611) and *A King and No King* (1611), replaced Shakespeare's at the King's Men. Together, Beaumont and Fletcher published a collection of approximately fifty plays.

Adultery, murder, and revenge figured prominently in the plays of John Webster (c. 1575–c. 1634), another collaborator. Only three of Webster's solo creations survive: *The White Devil* (c. 1608), *The Duchess of Malfi* (c. 1614), and *The Devil's Law Case* (1620). In *The White Devil* a beautiful woman finds herself married to the foolish nephew of the Cardinal, but she falls in love with a handsome Renaissance man. She and her lover murder those who learn of their affair but die at the end. Her brothers forbid *The Duchess of Malfi* to remarry because they want her estate for themselves. But she falls in love with a servant and secretly marries. They are discovered, tortured, and killed. The collaboration entitled *Westward Ho* (1607) contains Webster's most famous line: "I saw him now going the way of all flesh."

**Masques**   The court masque, the English version of the Italian *intermezzo* and the Spanish *entremese*, began with the hand of William Cornish in 1512. In the seventeenth century James's pleasure in court performances increased the amount of writing done for court tastes. James I, in fact, revived sumptuous masques, and under his reign the court enjoyed expensive yearly masques. Charles doubled the number.

All court performances except masques were played by professionals. Most dramatists, with the notable exception of Shakespeare, wrote masques. Ben Jonson, for example, wrote many masques for scenic elaboration by Inigo Jones (1573–1652). The

Jonson-Jones collaboration dissolved in 1631, however, in a dispute concerning the prominence of spectacle over language. Described by Jonson as "mirrors of man's life" and by Jones as "pictures with light and motion," masques provided visual symbols for interpretation by the court audience.

The most expensive masque, *The Triumph of Love* (1634) by James Shirley (1596–1666) and Inigo Jones, cost 21,000 pounds when produced by four Inns of Court. A new masquing hall at Whitehall Palace constructed in 1637 let Inigo Jones bring the full glory of Italianate scenery to England. Before Jones, masques scattered medieval mansions around a banqueting hall. In 1605, for his first masque for James I, Jones erected a stage for all of the scenery at one end of the hall. Jonson's *The Masque of Blackness* (1605) used a perspective setting with angled wings revealed by a drop curtain. The following year Jones introduced *periaktoi* with *The Masque of Hymen*, which featured a cloud machine that transported a person from upstage to downstage. In 1608 the first proscenium arch was constructed, for *The Hue and Cry after Cupid*. Then shutters and grooves changed the settings for *The Masque of Oberon* (1610).

Fiscally conservative Puritans winced at the extravagance of the masques. Nevertheless in 1608 Jonson introduced the "antimasque," a counterpoint of the main story featuring humorous or grotesque characters and an ugly setting. Antimasque satyrs, drunkards, gypsies, sailors, beggars, fools, and animals contrasted and heightened the beauty of the goddesses, nymphs, queens, gods, and heroes of the masques.

Dance served as the principal action in the masques' allegorical stories honoring people and occasions. Participating courtiers, seeking to retain their amateur status, refused to learn or speak lines. Thus, the social dances of the period, already known by the reluctant courtiers, became the basis of the formations invented by the dancing masters. All dancers in a masque were of the same sex; double masques used two sexually divided groups. Each dancer was accompanied by a "torchbearer"

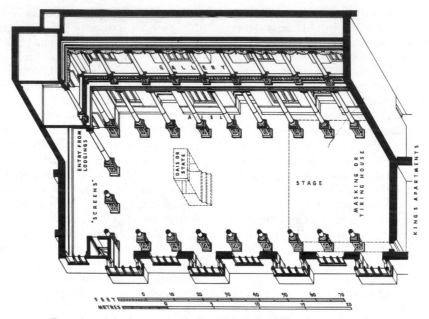

*Floorplan of the banqueting hall at Whitehall, 1606.* (Leacroft, p. 54)

who carried a candelabrum; sometimes these "torchbearers" performed their own dances.

***The Theatre*** In 1574 official licensing encouraged troupes to erect their own theatre buildings. The first permanent theatre in London, opened in 1576 for the Earl of Leicester's Men, was headed by James Burbage (1530–1597), father of the actor Richard Burbage mentioned earlier. Erected in Shoreditch on easily available land outside city jurisdiction, "The Theatre" stood in Holywell near the Bishopsgate on land leased for twenty-one years. The Theatre was in a "liberty," a place once controlled by Catholics, and only subject to the crown. (A flourishing underworld lived in the brothel-filled liberties.) Also in 1576, Richard Farrant opened the first private indoor theatre, the first Blackfriars, named for the liberty in which the remodeled monastery stood. Blackfriars served a private aristocratic audience.

In time other entrepreneurs built theatres: in 1577, the Curtain; 1579, Newington Butts; 1587, the Rose; 1595, the Swan; 1599, the Globe; 1600, the Fortune; 1605, the Red Bull; and 1613, the Hope. The most important theatres were operated by England's leading companies. Burbage ran The Theatre; Burbage and Shakespeare, the Globe; actor Edward Alleyn (1566–1626), the Rose; and Philip Henslowe, the Fortune. When Burbage's lease expired, The Theatre was dismantled, moved across the river to newly leased land, and renamed the Globe. The Globe was constructed from The Theatre's timber, stucco, and thatched roof. From this Herculean effort the Globe drew its emblem of Hercules carrying the Earth on his shoulders. In 1597 Burbage also leased and remodeled Farrant's Blackfriars, but angry neighbors blocked its opening with complaints about noise and traffic. Eleven years later Burbage finally succeeded in establishing an adult company in a private theatre. In 1613 the Globe burned down from a cannon effect during a performance of *Henry VIII*. A new Globe took its place until 1642. In 1617 the first roofed public playhouse, the

*Exterior of the Swan Theatre.* (Courtesy of the Lilly Library, Indiana University, Bloomington, Indiana)

Cockpit (later named the Phoenix) opened. A second roofed public theatre, Salisbury Court, opened its doors in 1629.

Players moved from theatre to theatre. In 1583 the Master of Revels created a troupe for Elizabeth, the Queen's Men, by drawing together the best actors from several troupes. The plague of 1592 further consolidated the troupes. Two companies reigned: the Lord Admiral's Men, managed by Edward Alleyn and financed by Philip Henslowe, and the Lord Chamberlain's Men, a sharing company centered around the Burbage family and leading actors. In 1598 Burbage, Shakespeare, and other actors became householders of the Globe. After 1610 the once common outdoor public performances became little more than summer festivals for companies that had acquired pri-

*Exterior of the Globe Theatre as it appeared in the time of King James I.* (Courtesy of the Lilly Library)

*Exterior of the Globe.* (Courtesy of the Lilly Library)

vate indoor theatres to counter London's troublesome weather.

***Theatre Architecture*** The Elizabethan public theatre drew on many sources for its design. The temporary platforms erected in innyards and gaming arenas, and used for street pageants, tournaments, and cycle plays, made the introduction of the facade-backed raised stage almost inevitable. If available, galleries surrounded the platform's open yard.

Francis Yates argues, however, that the Elizabethan public theatre resulted from a conscious attempt to reconstruct a Roman theatre. Professional players, working at the courts in the company of scholars and university-educated playwrights, may, in fact, have learned of classical theatre models. The geometry of the square and the circle in the theatre groundplan and the zodiacal "heavens"—a roof over the stage—support Yates's theory of Vitruvian influence. The front edge of the platform stage lay on the diameter of a Vitruvian *orchestra*; the facade of the tiring house, the changing room, lay on the base of one triangle; and the other triangles pointed to the entrances both to the stage and to the yard, the *pit*. In addition,

scholars discovered illustrations of Terence stages labeled *Theatrum*, the name of the first English public theatre.

The round basic shape of the public theatres echoed both the Italian reconstructions and the classical models themselves. One of the primary sources of information comes from a copy of a drawing of the Swan theatre by Johannes de Witt, a Dutch visitor. The only surviving copy of the de Witt sketch was made by Arend van Buchell, who added a prose passage that claimed the building could accommodate 3000 spectators, had wooden columns painted to resemble marble and support the heavens, and definitely resembled his idea of a Roman theatre. Van Buchell used a Roman name to label each part, such as *orchestra* and *ingessus*.

Additional support for the classical theory exists. For example, theatres drawn on maps of the period are round or polygonal. And a Ms. Thrale, who lived near the site of the Globe during the eighteenth century, insisted that the remaining foundation showed a round shape within a hexagon. These sources, plus building contracts for the Hope and Fortune theatres and stage directions in the plays themselves, have given shape to both general features of the

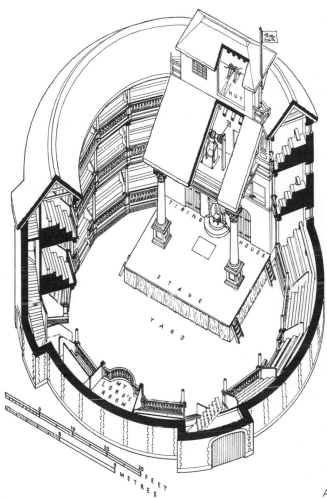

*A floorplan of the Swan, 1595.*   (Leacroft, p. 34)

buildings and particular theories about aspects of individual playhouses.

Elizabethan public theatres probably did have round interiors within round or polygonal wood-framed buildings. In each theatre three roofed galleries surrounded an open, flat pit, possibly raked toward a permanent or temporary platform stage. The raised stage, anywhere from four to six feet high, was located against the facade of a tiring house. The Fortune stage was twenty-seven and a half feet deep and forty-three feet wide within a fifty-five foot square space. A *scaenae frons* (facade), possibly located within the tiered galleries, had at least two large doors and one shallow gallery from which a curtain could be draped or hung. Like the Roman theatre awning, a roof over the stage was sometimes painted underneath to depict the zodiac. The roof was either cantilevered or supported by posts to protect actors and costumes from frequent bad weather.

So much controversy has stirred about particular features of the public playhouses that once-popular reconstructions are rarely attempted anymore. Scholars agree that a ''discovery space'' of some kind was necessary. J. C. Adams suggests that this space was an ''inner below,'' a small curtained proscenium

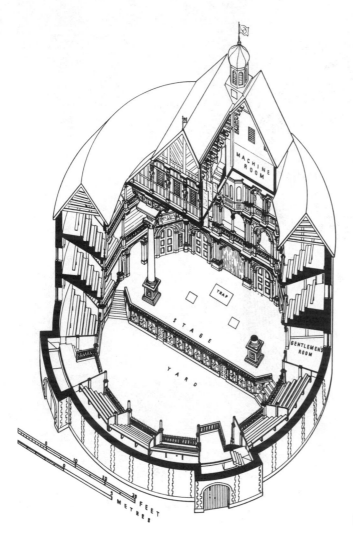

*The second Globe.* (Leacroft, p. 44)

stage located between the facade's doors, used for playing interior scenes and locating set pieces. Adams also proposes that the stage contained an "inner above" as well. C. Walter Hodges claims that a mansion-like structure, a "pavilion," stood between the doors. Such a pavilion would allow better sightlines than an "inner below." It would also be removable; the stage in the Swan drawing, Hodges argues, had the pavilion removed. George Reynolds proposes that a simple raised space, from which stairs could lead to the stage, existed between the doors. Reynolds also suggests the expedient use of medieval mansions on stage for discovery spaces. Francis Yates suggests that a curtain, hanging from a balcony, created a discovery space on the stage below. Yates also speculated that the stage may have had a railing of spikes to keep the pit audience off the stage. Richard Hosley concludes that the space behind the Swan's two double doors served as two discovery spaces. Hosley's space would have been a permanent feature of the architecture, as would Adams's "inner below."

**Private Theatres** As mentioned previously, the first private theatre, the first Blackfriars, was built by Richard Farrant in 1576 for his boys' company to rehearse plays for court performances. The most important private theatre, the second Blackfriars, was erected by James Burbage on a site different from that of the first Blackfriars. When Burbage's lease of The Theatre was about to expire, in 1596, he sought to acquire a private home for his company. Neighbors delayed the idea until 1600, when James's son Richard leased the theatre to a boys' company. In 1608 James I, sensitive to the political nature of the boys' entertainments, ordered the children's company disbanded. Burbage regained control of the theatre and the king authorized the King's Men to play there. Performances began in 1610, after the plague.

The success of Burbage's adult company in a private theatre led others in the same direction. In 1616 Christopher Beeston created a theatre in a Drury Lane cockpit that later, when reconstructed after a fire, was named the Phoe-

nix. In 1629 the Salisbury Court Theatre and the Royal Cockpit appeared. The latter theatre was created by Inigo Jones, working on the orders of Charles I, who wished the King's Men to have a home theatre at his court. With the advent of private theatres, players performed in the public theatres only between May and October.

Private theatres, which grew in importance with the middle class's desire for sensationalism, horror, and spectacle on stage, drew upon previous indoor designs: Medieval manors and town halls, the Netherlands' Chamber of Rhetoric stage (a facade and platform stage used by the literary societies), and banqueting "screen" facades joined Italian reconstructions of classical theatres to produce hybrid playing spaces. The second Blackfriars existed in a forty-six by 101 foot room, thirty-five feet of which was occupied by the tiring house. The remaining sixty-six by forty-six foot space re-

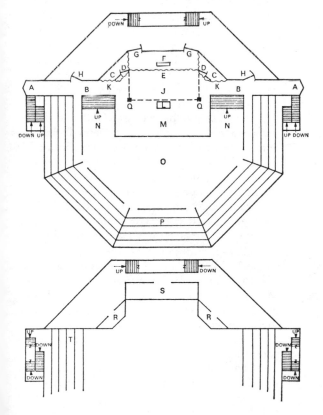

*Floorplan of the Globe, 1599–1613: (A) spectator's entrances; (B) wing access; (C) bay enclosure; (D) enclosure gate; (E) traverse; (F) grave trap; (G) stage door; (H) players' door; (J) area beneath shadow; (K) penthouse; (L) main trap; (M) platform; (N) yard alley; (O) yard; (P) twopenny rooms; (Q) stage post; (R) bay window; (S) twelvepenny rooms; (T) twopenny rooms.* (Gerald Eades Bentley, *The Seventeenth Century Stage*, p. 265. Copyright © 1968 University of Chicago Press.)

mained for stage and audience. Estimates suggest that the stage was eighteen and a half to twenty-five feet deep, twenty-nine to forty-six feet wide, and between three and four feet high. The stage faced an audience seated in one to three galleries. Because fewer spectators fit into these private theatres, higher admission fees were charged. The consequently more respectable audience demanded seats for all.

The Cockpit Court theatre resembled the remodeled Italian halls. Within an octagonal gaming area, three sides were allotted to the stage, and two galleries followed the octagonal lines. The king's box faced the facade's central door. As in the Teatro Olympico of Jones's architectural mentor, a semicircular stage, thirty-six feet wide by sixteen feet deep, extended from a two-storied facade. Five entrances led to the stage.

Jones also converted Whitehall Palace's Great Hall, Tudor Hall, and Banqueting Hall to temporary playing spaces for court masques. Eventually a 120 foot by fifty-seven foot masquing house was built to store elaborate machinery. Jones used wings and shutters to create the perspective illusions. Steps

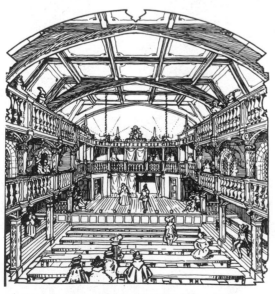

*A reconstruction of the second Blackfriars Theatre.* (New York Public Library Theatre Collection)

led from the stage to the hall's benches around three sides of an open area facing the stage.

*Scenery* Money to build theatres came from speculators. The most famous speculator, Philip Henslowe, kept records that remain the primary source of information on scenic practices. In addition, the accounts of the Master of Revels and textual evidence contribute to a controversy between advocates of "spoken decor" and supporters of "actual decor." Do lines in a play describe location because the details were or were not physically present on stage? The medieval cycle tradition supports the idea that what was described was actually there. But Elizabethan players probably followed a more time-honored theatre tradition: expediency. In other words, players used whatever was easily and inexpensively available.

Nonetheless, whatever scenery existed resembled, at first, medieval rather than Italianate scenery. Properties included chairs, tables, stools, beds, carpets, tapestries, tents, altars, stocks, scaffolds, coffins, bodies, chariots, caves, trees, bushes, flowers, rocks, tombs, steeples, gates of Hell, stars, cages, painted drops of Rome, stables, bedsteads, mountains, houses, and banners. All were probably inconsistently employed. In addition, because the theatres were indoors, lighting was a factor; candles thus appeared on stage and in the wings. Conventions also continued the medieval use of the stage as a *platea* and set pieces as *mansions*. Set pieces may have remained on stage when not in use. Servants changed properties and stored them in either the tiring house or nearby buildings.

After 1603, the demand for spectacle grew as the court's influence on theatrical fare increased. Playwrights and managers sought court protection by adapting to court tastes. Mannerist spectacles, as in the plays of Beaumont and Fletcher and court masques, resulted. And, as troupes gained court favor, their wealth increased. Scenery grew more sumptuous.

Music, always popular with Elizabethan theatre audiences, also grew in importance

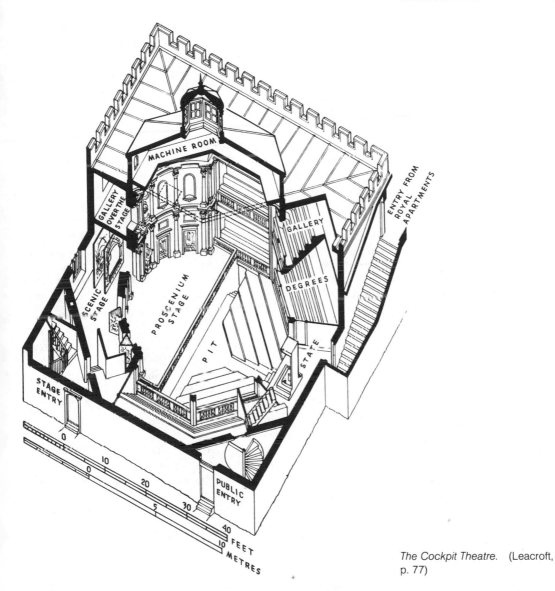

Labels within the illustration: MACHINE ROOM, GALLERY OVER THE STAGE, SCENIC STAGE, PROSCENIUM STAGE, GALLERY, DEGREES, PIT, STATE, ENTRY FROM ROYAL APARTMENTS, STAGE ENTRY, PUBLIC ENTRY

0 10 20 30 40 FEET
0 5 10 METRES

*The Cockpit Theatre.*    (Leacroft, p. 77)

with the court masque. After 1605 illusionistic scenery, dance, and music filled court masques. Incidental songs and "jigs," in fact, appear in many Elizabethan scripts. Trumpets framed entrances and proclamations. Drums beat out battle scene tempos. Background music established moods. Preperformance concerts, popularized by childrens' troupes, were adopted by the adult companies for private theatrical entertainment.

***Companies***    Money seemed to be on everyone's mind in the Renaissance. At first gate receipts offered actors their only source of income. But companies organized by leading actors shared play selection, production responsibilities, and profits after expenses. Expenses included the playwright's fee, salaries for hired people, and the common fund for costumes, properties, and scenic materials. Eventual restrictions on the number of theatre companies meant that individuals in licensed companies could live well.

The construction of permanent theatres provided householders with additional income from occasionally renting the building to amateur groups, fencers, and tumblers. A taphouse increased their revenue with the sale of beer, ale, and wine.

A company of ten to twenty-five men salaried over half of its members on two-year contracts. Boy actors apprenticed to adult actors beginning anywhere from age 6 to 14 and ending at 18 or 21. The master actors trained, fed, and clothed their apprentices. Because the boys usually played young women (but never older women), players boasted that they needed no women, like the whores and courtesans of Europe, to play female roles. English actors based this use of boy actors on classical precedent and English tradition. In fact, jeers and fruit pelted French actresses visiting the English stage in 1632. After apprenticeship some men continued to act; some chose other professions.

Rehearsals were brief, thereby giving performances an improvisational quality like that of the *commedia dell'arte*. A plot (a scenario listing the play's action with entrances, exits, and cues) hung backstage for reference. A system of rules and fines regulated lateness, drunkenness, absence, and robbery. Nonetheless, clown members of the company—like Richard Tarlton (?–1588) and Will Kempe (?–c. 1603)—added to the loose atmosphere of rehearsals and performances. Some actors were given *sides* (scripts containing their lines and cues). Most actors, however, could not read, so they learned their lines from hearing prompters, bookkeepers, or playwrights, reading the scripts once or twice. Memorization abilities were thus high among the players.

Two great companies of twelve to fifteen men dominated the Elizabethan theatre. The Earl of Leicester's Men became the Lord Chamberlain's Men in 1594; then in 1603 it became the King's Men. The company's leading player, Richard Burbage, created Shakespeare's Richard III, Hamlet, Lear, and Othello. The other company, the Lord Admiral's Men, rivaled that of Shakespeare and Burbage. Centered around the acting skills of Edward Alleyn, the literary skills of Christopher Marlowe, and the managerial skills of Philip Henslowe (Alleyn's father-in-law), the company became Prince Henry's Men in 1603 and later Queen Anne's Men. Alleyn, who created Marlowe's heroes and Kyd's Heironimo, became the first great English-speaking actor. He retired from the stage when he saw a real devil during a performance of the title role in *Doctor Faustus*.

In 1603, three, and in 1611, four, adult troupes monopolized London. Royal patronage brought their members yearly salaries and an allowance for room and board to supplement the gate receipts. Patrons sometimes even donated clothing to their companies. In return, the players were required to perform at court for evening plays, masques, and celebrations.

***Acting Style*** The Elizabethan acting style, as all acting styles viewed historically, has been called both formal and realistic. Great acting is always considered "realistic" by its contemporaries; only later, when "new realities" are applauded on the stage, does the old style appear formal by comparison. Elizabethan acting was realistic for its time: References to expansive gestures—strutting and stamping—suggest full-blooded, exciting, and passionate performances displaying elaborate vocal and physical virtuosity. The best actors of the day, like the best actors of any day, fulfilled Hamlet-the-playwright's advice to the visiting players:

Speak the speech, I pray you, as I pronounc'd it to you, trippingly on the tongue, but if you mouth it, as many of our players do, I had as lief the town-crier spoke my lines. Nor do not saw the air too much with your hand, thus, but use all gently, for in the very torrent, tempest, and, as I may say, whirlwind of your passion, you must acquire and beget a temperance that may give it smoothness. O, it offends me to the soul to hear a robustious periwig-pated fellow tear a passion to tatters, to very rags, to split the ears of the groundlings, who for the most part are capable of nothing but inexplicable dumb shows and noise. I would have such a fellow whipt for o'erdoing. Termagant, it out-Herods Herod, pray you avoid it. . . .

Be not too tame neither, but let your own discretion be your tutor. Suit the action to the word, the word to the action, with this special observance, that you o'erstep not the modesty of nature: for any thing so o'erdone is from the purpose of playing, whose end, both at the first and now, was and is, to hold the mirror up to nature: to show virtue her feature, scorn her own image, and the very age and body of the time his form and pressure. Now this overdone, or come tardy off, though it make the unskillful laugh, cannot but make the judicious grieve; the censure of which one must in your allowance o'erweigh a whole theatre of others. O, there be players I have seen play—and heard others [praised], and that highly—not to speak it profanely, that, neither having th' accent of Christians nor the gait of Christian, pagan, nor man, have so strutted and bellow'd that I have thought some of Nature's journeymen had made men, and not made them well, they imitated humanity so abominably. . . .

And let those that play your clowns speak no more than is set down for them, for there be some of them that will themselves laugh to set on some quantity of barren spectators to laugh too, though in the meantime some necessary question of the play be then to be consider'd. That's villainous, and shows a most pitiful ambition in the fool that uses it.[4]

The actors' costumes influenced their playing styles. As in all previous periods, costume in the Renaissance functioned as the most important visual element. Players wore basic contemporary garments for all characters, in all times, in all places. "Ancient" costume denoted old-fashioned characters, and "antique" drapery or greaves (leg armor from the ankle to the knee) on contemporary garments suggested Greece or Rome. Fanciful costumes bedecked ghosts, witches, fairies, gods, and allegorical characters. Robin Hood, Henry V, Tamburlaine, Falstaff, and Richard III became associated with traditional costumes. And racially and nationally stereotyped clothing covered Turks, Indians, Jews, and Spaniards.

*Audience*  Illiteracy forced the Elizabethan audience to develop careful and effective listening skills. The verse dialogue helped as well. Although the audience at the public theatre came from all classes of society, the upper classes attended in numbers greater than their percentage of the population. Working men, stealing away from their jobs, made up most of the audience. The idle, the unemployable, and the underworld constituted the rest of the cross section. Attracted by posters, handbills, processions, theatre flags, and announcements of coming attractions, at least 1500 to 2000 English spectators crowded into a theatre building to see an afternoon performance. London's population was about 160,000 at the time, and any play had the potential patronage of about half that number. By the end of the sixteenth century, wealthy speculators may have purchased seats on the stage; the boxes had been appropriated by prostitutes and criminals.

"Gatherers" took money at the entrances. Vendors sold wine, beer, ale, nuts, apples, cards, tobacco, and playbooks during the intermissionless performances. No one drank water, and tea had not yet become prominent. The strong ale that served as England's primary beverage affected the mood of the audience. Respectable women dared attend only behind masks.

*Attacks on the Theatre*  Attacks on the theatre increased around 1600. The attacks did not come from court humanists. Court performances, in fact, increased from five a year under Elizabeth to twenty-five a year under Charles. But, with the rediscovery of the classics did come Plato's objections to the drama. Antitheatricalism increased, too, as Puritans saw both the building of permanent theatres and the increasing of royal support for what they considered the Devil's work.

Puritans believed the theatre encouraged vice and took men away from their jobs. One year after Burbage opened The Theatre, the Vicar declared that sin caused the plague, and that plays caused sin; therefore, plays caused the plague. Moreover, The Theatre's proximity to whorehouses brought actors into association with other of tools of Satan. Early pamphlets, such as John Northbrooks's "A Treatise against Dicing, Dancing, Plays, and Interludes" (1577) and Stephen Gossen's "The School of Abuse" (1579), prompted defenses by Thomas Lodge, "A Defense of Poetry, Music, and Stage Plays" (1579), and Sir Philip Sidney, "The Defense of Poesy" (1583). Sidney (1554–1586), a poet, critic, soldier, and statesman, actually began English dramatic criticism. His defense, based on the idea of theatre as an effective way to teach morality and virtuous action, constituted the first major English statement of the Italian Neo-Classical ideal. But the Puritans were not impressed. They maintained that the theatre continued the tradition of showiness, flamboyance, and extravagance associated with Roman popery and the church of England's monarch.

Lodge began his defense by quoting Cicero. Gossen, who even quoted the Greek and Roman opponents of the stage, rebutted by attacking female impersonation: Deuteronomy XXII, 5 said, "The woman shall not wear that which pertaineth unto a man, neither shall a man put on a woman's garment; for all that act so do an abomination unto the Lord thy God." Actors were also accused of sodomy and homosexuality. In 1592 Thomas Nashe penned "Pierce Penniless His Supplication to the Devil," invoking the patriotism of the chronicle plays and championing the stout and noble character of English players when compared to the whores who acted on Europe's stages. In 1608 Thomas Heywood recounted a history of esteemed actors and pointed out that neither Christ nor his apostles ever spoke against the theatre. He insisted that plays refine the English language, teach the ignorant, and uphold morality. But then came William Prynne (1600–1669).

In a treatise whose lengthy title barely suggests the torrential venom that Prynne spews at just about everything done outside of work and church, the author complained that the theatre had become more popular than the church. (A similar suggestion made by the Beatles about their music created a modern flurry of Puritan agitation and outrage.) Prynne's treatise was entitled

Histriomastix. The Players Scourge, or, Actors Trageodie, Divided into Two Parts, Wherein it is largely evidenced, by divers Arguments, by the concurring Authorities and Resolutions of sundry texts of Scripture: of the whole Primitive Church, both under the Law and the Gospell; of 55 Synodes and Councels; of 71 Fathers and Christian Writers, before the yeare of our Lord 1200; of above 150 foraigne & domestique Protestant and Popish Authors, since: of 40 Heathen Philosophers, Historians, Poets; of many Heathen, many Christian Nations, Republiques, Emperors, Princes, Magistrates; of sundry Apostolicall, Canonicall, Imperial Constitutions; and of our own English statutes, Magistrates, Universities, Writers, Preachers. That popular Stage-players (the very Pompes of the Divell which we renounce in Baptisme, if we believe the Fathers) are sinfull, heathenish, lewde, ungodly Spectacles, and most pernicious Corruptions; condemned in all ages, as intolerable Mischiefes to Churches, to Republickes, to the manners, mindes, and soules of men. And that the profession of Play-poets, of Stage-players; together with the penning, acting, and frequenting of Stage players, are unlawfull, infamous and misbeseeming Christians. All pretences to the contrary are here likewise fully answered; and the unlawfulness of acting or beholding Academicall Enterludes, briefly discussed; besides sundry other particulars concerning Dancing, Dicing, Health-drinking, etc. of which the Table will inform you.

Youths, Prynne railed, were being led to Satan by watching and acting plays; because of the theatre, the virility of England was endangered. Prynne called the theatre audience "Adulterers, Adulteresses, Whore-masters, Whores, Bawdes, Panders, Ruffians, Roarers, Drunkards, Prodigals, Cheaters, idle, base, prophane and godlesse persons, who hate all grace, all goodnesse, and make a mocke of piety." Classical objections were reworked. The theatre, it was posited, stood for sensory pleasure, for idleness rather than work, for wanton spending rather than thrift. Mostly the theatre stood for the Crown, the symbol of all religious and political abuse.

Defenders of the stage were neither as passionate nor as determined as their critics. Conceding some abuse, admitting an origin in pagan ritual, and agreeing to the arousal of a few instances of antisocial behavior, defenders of the theatre insisted that the instructional value of the theatre outweighed all objections. But the military dictatorship of Oliver Cromwell (1599-1658) represented the victory of Prynne's position in the debate.

***Closing the Theatres*** In 1642 all theatres were closed. No place where Royalist plots could hatch could remain open. Sports, games, and selling were forbidden on Sundays. Maypoles were torn down. Church fast days were enforced. Christmas decorations were outlawed. (As modern Puritans would say, "Christ was put back into Christmas.") Gambling, swearing, dicing, and drinking were fined. Race horses were outlawed. Books containing "scurrilities and gross jests" were censored. Adultery and sodomy became felonies punishable by death. Fornication brought three months in prison.

But the Jews were allowed to return. And in 1656 playwright William Davenant (1606-1668) obtained permission to take money at the door from people anxious to hear "declamations set to music." Davenant's license had insisted that "all women's parts be acted by women." As a result, in 1656, Mrs. Coleman's portrayal of Ianthe in *The Siege of Rhodes*, one of Davenant's operas, made her the first actress in a public "theatre." Meanwhile, some theatres sought to operate illegally and poorly. But some actors, members of the Royalist army fighting for the king, left for Europe. In France actors and Royalists enjoyed the influence of the court. In Germany and the Low Countries English actors spread the Elizabethan version of Renaissance theatre.

The Restoration of Charles II on May 29, 1660, ended the Puritan experiment in England. All sex laws except those against sodomy were repealed, and the players returned. On July 9, playwright Thomas Kiligrew (1612-1683) received from the king the right to establish a company. William Davenant tried to share the monopoly. A debate began that continued into the next age's English theatre, which was being shaped at this time in France.

# FRANCE

From Spain and England European leadership passed to France. But after the glories of Italy, Spain, and England, French culture and theatre seemed disappointing. Nonetheless, after long religious and civil wars—which lasted until 1594—Henry IV (reigned 1589-1610) restored the French monarchy and economic stability. The assassination of Henry IV in 1610, however, reintroduced instability once again.

Italian theatre came to France under the last Valois ruler, Henry III (reigned 1574-1589), who invited the Gelosi troupe of *commedia dell'arte* players to France. Since 1494, in fact, war and marriage had kept France in close connection with Italian culture and theatre. Renaissance developments in France after the wars reflected the late mannerism of Italy. By 1625 a professional theatre had gained a small foothold in Paris. By 1650 Paris had become the political and cultural capital of Europe, ready to export the next major theatrical vision.

***Arrival of the Renaissance*** Francis I (reigned 1515-1547) surrounded himself with strong women. Indeed, the existence of women actresses in France may date from a dance performed by Eleanora for her future husband, Francis I. Francis patronized the arts both to enhance his stature and to appease his queen. He invited Erasmus to join the Italian artists and architects coming to France.

Francis's son, Henry II (reigned 1547–1559), married a 13-year-old distant cousin of the pope, Catherine de Medici, daughter of the Renaissance patron, Lorenzo de Medici. Henry II, however, had little interest in continuing his father's literary and artistic patronage. If he had, the dramatic theatre may have developed sooner. But his wife compensated for her husband. When the royal couple arrived in Lyons in 1548 they saw the Italian players. They also saw Bibiena's *Calandria*, which featured scenery by Mannocio of Florence. Catherine contented herself with the *commedia dell'arte*. During a tournament and masque, Henry was accidentally poked in the eye and died.

Catherine de Medici ruled France for the next three decades of violence and bloodshed. Her attempt at conciliation with the warring Protestants failed. The rebels rioted, demonstrated, invaded churches, and drove out priests. Catholics objected to the laxity of a government that allowed altars to be overturned. Meanwhile, Catherine presided over the development of the *ballet de cour*, the French version of the Italian *intermezzo*. She also supervised the building of the Palace of Louvre, and she patronized The Pleiade, a group of prominent French writers. But, civil war broke out all over France, and theatrical development was stifled again. Little business or theatrical activity was possible amid anarchy.

*Political Stability* Henry of Navarre, wanting to avoid further warfare, converted to Catholicism in 1593. In 1594, he became Henry IV (reigned 1589–1610), saying Paris was "worth a Mass." But, as we discussed earlier, Henry IV was assassinated in 1610 by a religious fanatic. His son, 9-year-old Louis XIII (reigned 1610–1643) entrusted the rule of France to Bishop Armand du Plessis de Richelieu (1585–1642), who became a cardinal in 1624.

Richelieu brought the glory of Italianate theatre to Paris. Because Louis XIII loved plays, by the seventeenth century theatrical interest was high all over France. The Italian

*commedia dell'arte* troupes had established a model for plot and character. Richelieu was succeeded by Cardinal Mazarin (1602–1661), who led France to the dominant position in Europe.

Louis XIV (reigned 1643–1715), who made his divine right to rule absolute and enjoyed the longest reign in French history, spent a great deal of money glorifying himself and France. Middle-class merchants solidified the crown's economic and political base. Old aristocratic families died out or went begging at court. Louis compensated the nobles for their loss of prestige by glorifying them in art and literature. The chivalric ideal revived as the birthright of French gentlemen reading Castiglione's *The Book of the Courtier* (1528), and the French court operated as an elaborate game of chivalry played by the rules of this book.

*The Church Brings Humanism* Protestants disliked the theatre. Where Huguenots, French Protestants, thrived, the theatre and humanism went underground. Because humanism sprang from the study of the classics in Jesuit schools and Catholic universities, humanism was associated with Catholicism. *Sotties* were performed in Jesuit speech classes; translations of Greek and Latin tragedies followed. By 1470 printing presses at the Sorbonne were publishing the works of humanist editors.

Italian Renaissance ideas influenced France more than any other country, but very slowly. Lyons became the first center because an important group of French Renaissance poets settled there due to the city's contact with Italian, Swiss, and German bankers and merchants. In 1550 seven authors joined together under the patronage of Catherine de Medici, as mentioned earlier, to form The Pleiade for "the renewal of poetical themes, the transformation of style, the reconstruction of the language," as their charter promised. Pierre de Ronsard (1524–1585), the greatest French Renaissance poet, wanted to imitate the Greeks by hearing poems sung. By 1570 Henry III had patronized an association of poets and musicians known as the *Académie du Palais*. Unaffected by the academic background, professional players struggled there for survival.

***Professional Players*** In 1402 the *Confrérie de la Passion*, the producer of medieval mystery plays, won a monopoly on theatre in Paris. But in 1548 religious drama was forbidden by decree. The *Confrérie* thus became the controller of all secular drama in Paris. French troupes nonetheless continued to play farces and moralities in the provinces. Meanwhile, English and Spanish troupes toured along with the Italian *commedia dell'arte*. The development of the French theatre between 1580 and 1630 thus occurred in the provinces, rehearsal areas for the main event in Paris.

All troupes wanted to play Paris. Since touring had increased by 1550, troupes competed until 1677 to rent the *Confrérie's Hotel de Bourgogne*, built in 1548. Even if performing in another Paris facility, in fact, a troupe had to pay a fee to the *Confrérie*.

Valleran le Comte (fl. 1590–1613), the most influential actor-manager of the day, arrived in Paris in 1598 with his *Troupe du Roi*, probably self-named after playing for Henry IV. Le Comte's eight- to twelve-member company was organized on a sharing basis. The following year he leased the Hotel du Bourgogne but failed to replace popular farce with the new tragedies of Alexandre Hardy (c. 1572–c. 1632). Farce actually dominated the French stage, and leading actors gained fame for their farcical characters. Each actor had, like a *commedia dell'arte* player, a single character to portray in each farce. Often actors concealed their own identities behind their characters.

By 1607 women were appearing in the companies. Richelieu is credited with making their employment standard.

***The Ballet de Cour*** French conquests of Italy brought Italian dancing masters to the court of Francis I (reigned 1515–1547). Then, the Academy of Saint Cecelia Jean Antoine de Baif created another important vehicle for French players, the *ballet de cour*. Founded in 1570, the Academy proposed the union of words and music in the ancient manner, as suggested by Ronsard. But religious warfare delayed the Academy's efforts.

In 1581 the first modern ballet was created by Baldassarino da Belgriojoso (Balthasar de Beaujoyeux), who adapted neo-classical ideas to French tastes. The *Ballet Comique de la Reine Louise* was an imitation of Tasso's *Aminta* as performed by the Gelosi troupe, but done with book by La Chesnaye, music by Sieur de Beaulieu, and design by Jacques Patin. But the *ballet comique* did not prevail. Instead, when Thoinot Arbeau published his *Orchesography* in 1588, a history of dance classifying each rhythm and offering a simple system of dance notation, France replaced Italy as the center of Western dance theatre. By 1625, the *ballet de cour*, a ballet of entry with separate thematically related sections, dominated court entertainment. French dancing was established; acting had to wait for developments in architecture and playwrighting.

***Classical Models*** Lyons issued the early humanist publications. In 1493, for instance, an illustrated edition of Terence's plays appeared. The illustrations of Terence's stage reveal how French scholars may have staged his plays. In 1506 Erasmus's translation of *Iphegenia in Aulis* appeared; in 1540 classical plays and critical works, including Lazare de Baif's translation of *Electra* and Bouchetel's *Hecuba*, were translated into French. Gradually Italian plays and commentaries on Aristotle were translated into French as well. The Pleiade, formulating rules of grammar and prosody, wrote new French plays based on classical rules. Cardinal Richelieu later established a group of five poets to reform the French stage according to these rules.

In 1552 a college student named Etienne Jodelle (1523–1573) wrote both the first French tragedy, *Cleopatra captive*, and the first French comedy, *Eugène*, for production before Henry II. Following Jodelle, by the end of the sixteenth century, professional playwrights had incorporated neo-classical principles into works for popular audiences. Alexandre Hardy, France's first professional playwright, used a five-act form and poetic diction. His use of ghosts, messengers, and a chorus suggested Senecan influence. But wide-ranging locations, long time intervals between scenes, and on-stage violence drew upon the audience's medieval tastes. Hardy's plays of love and sensationalism encouraged others to write for the stage.

The neo-classical ideal advanced in France when the playwright Jean de la Taille (c. 1540–1607) advocated three unities in a 1572 Preface: "The story or play must be represented in one day, one time, and one place." Slowly, an audience for serious drama developed.

**Theatre Architecture**   French scholars developed their treatment of theatrical space through translations of Vitruvius, Serlio, and Alberti. Vitruvius's treatise had reached France by 1500; Serlio, living at the court of Francis I, published a French edition of his *De Architectura* in 1545. Nevertheless, most court entertainments used medieval-type dispersed decor, though a few attempts were made to use perspective illusions. Henry IV and Catherine sponsored outstanding examples of Italianate scenery. In 1558 Jodelle, as arranger of court entertainments, also tried to create spectacles like those in Italy.

In the *Salle du Petit Bourbon* adjacent to the Louvre, dispersed decor awaited the audience for a *ballet de cour*. The *Salle* measured forty-nine feet by 177 feet and featured two side balconies. The king's chair stood at the rear, opposite the stage.

**Audience**   By the end of the sixteenth century all sections of French society enjoyed the theatre. Ladies attended public theatres but sat masked in the galleries. Posters announced two or three performances each week. Like their Elizabethan counterparts, French audiences had to get home before dark. The macaroons,

bread, and wine sold at the theatre sated them until dinner.

**The Hotel de Bourgogne**   Between 1595 and 1625 Parisian performances occurred at the *Confrérie's Hotel de Bourgogne*, built in 1548, the first new public theatre since the fall of Rome. The theatre, named after a villa that had stood on the site, was the only permanent theatre in the city. Two or three galleries, one of which was divided into boxes, hung from walls around a forty foot by 105 foot space. Above the rear gallery, the *paradis* (an undivided gallery) looked down at the *parterre* (pit). Sixteen hundred spectators viewed the five to six foot raised stage framed by side galleries. A platform, twenty-five feet wide by seventeen to thirty-five feet deep, probably held medieval scenic elements. By 1633 side wings, representing diverse mansion-like locations, stood before a vista-painted backdrop. The Italian architectural side wings and back drop combined with the medieval idea of simultaneous settings to create a unique treatment of stage space.

All other Parisian performances occurred in converted tennis courts. *Jeu de paume* had been a popular game since medieval times. The ninety foot by thirty foot enclosed, roofed tennis courts could seat anywhere from 250 to 1800 spectators. By simply adding a platform stage, actors, illuminated by windows below the roof, could perform to a gallery at the opposite end of the space.

In 1634, Paris's second public playhouse, the *Théâtre du Marais*, was built in a former tennis court. Rebuilt after a 1644 fire, the 114 foot by thirty-nine foot building probably contained a thirty-one foot deep stage within its fifty-three foot high structure. Richelieu permitted an actor-manager, Montdory, to break the *Confrérie's* monopoly. And in the Marais section of Paris a young playwright named Pierre Corneille (1606–1684) began to write plays that would set the tenor of the next theatrical age: France was about to move the West toward a new theatre envisioning a French reality.

# NOTES

[1] Arnold Hauser, *The Social History of Art*, Vol. II (New York: Random House, 1957–1958), p. 9. Copyright © 1951.

[2] Allardyce Nicoll, *The Development of the Theatre* (New York: Harcourt Brace World, Inc., 1966), p. 268.

[3] Nicoll, *The Development of the Theatre*, p. 272.

[4] William Shakespeare, *Hamlet*, the Arden edition, ed. Harold Jenkins (London: Methuen, 1982), pp. 287–290.

# 6

# THE SOCIAL
# THEATRE

*It seems clear to me that God designed us to live in society—just as He
has given the bees the honey; and as our social system could not subsist
without the sense of justice and injustice, He has given us the power to
acquire that sense.*

Voltaire

*The love of justice in most men is simply the fear of suffering injustice.*
La Rochefoucauld, *Maxims*

From the closing of the English theatre and
the end of the Thirty Years' War (1648) to the
rise of Napoleon, the world and its theatre
underwent enormous changes. France held
center stage for that century and a half drama.
Whereas the previous age had achieved direction from Renaissance and Reformation ideas,
the new age, the age of social theatre, moved
according to industrial, scientific, and democratic revolutions. The West's social order
convulsed as well.

The age began with a courtly society and
ended with a bourgeois-centered order. Reason and decorum gave way to emotionalism
and naturalism. Because the age spanned so
great a transition in values, it bred numerous
contradictions. Renaissance neo-classicalism
mingled with early romantic notions, and clas-
sicists embraced new romantic principles.
The court aristocracies succumbed to the
middle class, either peacefully or after
revolution. Court tastes and plays receded
as the public theatres dictated dramatic
sensibilities and standards. Individuals of
the utmost rationality supported anti-rational
movements.

## OVERVIEW

The centripetal axis of the age's theatre was
society. As society's nucleus of power shifted
from monarchy to representative assembly, society's cultural standards, still largely shaped
by Castiglione's *The Book of the Courtier*, transferred from the court to the bourgeoisie. Amid
the shifts, the public devoured, to an unprecedented degree, information, rumor, opinion, epigrams, songs, and theatre. Each sector
of the public found the dramatic theatre a pow-

erful ally, either to protect the old social order or to envision a new, revolutionary one.

The dramatic theatre celebrated this age's contradictory views of society and human nature. The Enlightenment, the Age of Reason, made everything and everybody fair game for freewheeling scrutiny and criticism. Society fell under the same scientific observation as nature, and, as a result, thinkers and dramatic artists envisioned natural humanity, natural religion, and natural rights.

*Reason and Industry*   With the waning of Renaissance and Reformation infatuations, dispassionate professionals found reason and decorum effective conciliators for members of a pluralistic society. Compromise, moderation, balance, and manners replaced the hot arguments of the prior age's metaphysical on-stage and off-stage debates. When reason could not accommodate growing demands for economic justice, however, the enlightened principles collapsed beneath revolutions that ended the social theatre's existence.

Though a majority of people remained farmers, an increased food supply freed many people to work the cities' newly invented textile machinery. Steam engines powered factories, mines, and transportation. The Industrial Revolution began to create less expensive goods, a rise in the general economic level, and a widening gap between rich and poor. In time, women and children worked long hours in urban factories. When faced with urban destitution unemployed women turned to prostitution. Some of the upper and middle classes became aware of growing social unrest and injustice.

But one could only increase one's wealth by increasing the productivity of one's workers and by widening one's markets. From the mid-eighteenth century on, the idea of *laissez faire*, noninterference by the state, popularized industrial investment, began the modern economic structure, and standardized the gap between rich and poor. Governments that interrupted the free market for humanitarian reasons were suspect. The Enlightenment believed rational individuals capable of self-regulation; the drama upheld this notion. In time, the middle class took control not only of the economy but also of the society's theatrical life.

Individuality, sentimentality, and morality thus became hallmarks of middle-class values. Middle-class individuals upheld these values to distinguish themselves from the aristocracy's corrupt neo-classical ideals. Praising the middle-class virtues on the stage implied criticism of the aristocracy. Virtue, in fact, became fashionable and subversive. To be without feeling, like the nobility, meant to be not human.

*Slavery and Feminism*   Colonial slavery continued to fuel the economies. Most Enlightened philosophers protested slavery as contrary to nature and therefore universally wrong. Middle-class sentimentalists considered the suffering of Negro slaves a popular topic for verse and drama; master and slave stood as symbols of vice and virtue.

With the idea of natural rights, women acquired a more public voice. They published pamphlets, for example, on women's rights; they also produced the first public references to birth control. Although official state academies excluded women from membership, female salons of aristocratic women protected and patronized theatre artists and intellectuals. Gradually, both feminism and antifeminism formed as movements in this socially conscious age.

*A New Cosmology*   The age's social ferment originated with the work of Sir Isaac Newton (1642–1727). In *Philosophiae Naturalis Principia Mathematica* (1687), Newton reduced the multiplicity of observable phenomena in the universe to a mathematical order. To explain falling bodies Newton hypothesized gravitation and formulated laws of motion. He also redefined God as a master mathematician, an inventor of a great machine known as the universe. Newton's view found no place for such traditional ideas as divine grace, providence, heaven, or hell. Consequently, no place was found for them on the stage either.

Newton's world picture derived from his observations of the everyday world. His laws predicted events by discovering the order beneath chaos; with enough information, even future events could be predicted. The universe emerged as rational and comprehensible. As a result, an information explosion occurred. Individuals sought knowledge as a way of increasing their power over events and the future. The universe ground on as a great machine susceptible to individuals, observation, analysis, and control.

To reconcile Newtonian science with religion, a natural theology known as Deism arose. If any religious view was implied in the drama, it was Deism. Deism saw no supernatural control over life, no Divine influence over nature, and no celestial revelation in human affairs. Deists advocated doing away with organized churches and priests. All individuals were equal in God's benign sight; all individuals should thus be equal under human law. Religious Deism and political revolution lived as blood brothers.

Newton's laws likewise negated the divine right of kings and the chain of being. God was discovered to be a passive observer of the universe. And because God let the universe operate according to mathematical laws, a new justification for the political and social order was needed. The social contract idea emerged: people living in a state agreed to the form and powers of their government. Divine right gave way to a social contract in the state and on the stage.

### The End of Monarchy

During the age of the social theatre, monarchs tried to substitute personal empires for those of Christianity, only to have their monarchies overthrown by revolution. England's peaceful revolution of 1688 inspired the world; the terror of the 1789 French Revolution shocked the world. English philosopher John Locke (1632–1704) proposed that power to rule came from people, not God; French philosopher Jean-Jacques Rousseau (1712–1778) observed that each individual is born free "but everywhere is in chains." People had a natural right to freedom based on the same natural laws observed by Newton. Reason hoped to work as the tool to win the rights. The new ideas found expression in the dramas of the age.

### A Sense of History

The rediscovery of the historical past in the excavations of Pompeii (1748) and Herculaneum (1737) offered aristocrats an exotic escape from the troubles thrust upon them by Rousseau. Trips to Italy signified intellectuality and aesthetic sensibility. Antiques were collected. Ancient manuscripts were sorted, calendars translated, and history placed in chronological order. Professional journals and books exchanged information. English historian Edward Gibbon (1737–1794) produced his *History of the Decline and Fall of the Roman Empire* (1776–1788). For the first time people began to sense the transitoriness of power and order. And the past and the exotic found representation on stage.

### The Rise of Bourgeois Taste

Aesthetic standards and taste originate in a society's power brokers. During the age of the social theatre power and taste shifted from the court to the bourgeoisie. The transformation happened first in England. Bourgeois sentimentality was an aesthetic and moral reaction to the reserved, emotionless qualities of court art, literature, and drama created in the shadow of *The Book of the Courtier*. The neo-classical rules had been made by the powerful. Rebellion against the court's political order mirrored rebellion against the court's neo-classical aesthetic order. The English playwright Edward Young's (1683–1765) *Conjectures on Original Composition* (1759) led the way.

The age of the social theatre believed in correspondences among scientific law, social justice, and artistic truth. The court's theatrical standards represented both the old cosmology and the old political regime. Reason and rationality, the source of the unities of time and place, became suspect. Instinct, emotion, and genius, as suggested by Young, provided truer champions of the people. German scholar Johann Joachim Winkelmann (1717–1768) encouraged individuals to imitate the spirit of the Greek masters rather than bogus neo-classical forms.

An age that eventually came to value spirit over form necessarily produced great music. Music lived, in fact, as the love of the bourgeoisie. Town concert societies formed. Commissioned music was replaced by music for sale in the marketplace. Opera took on great popularity with the production of *opera seria* (serious opera) and *opera buffa* (comic opera). Women started singing careers; one woman, Barbara Strozzix, even composed an opera in 1659 for performance in Venice.

Literature entered this age under the control of official state institutes for intellectual and literary standards. But new dramatic forms were created to thwart aristocratic officials and delight the bourgeois public. The novel appeared as the age's representative genre. The first English novel was Samuel Richardson's (1689–1761) *Pamela, or Virtue Rewarded. In a Series of Familiar Letters from a Beautiful Young Damsel, To Her Parents. Now first Published In Order to Cultivate the Principles of Virtue and Religion in the Minds of the Youth of Both Sexes* (1740). It was followed by Henry Fielding's (1707–1754) more cynical *Tom Jones* (1749).

**The Novel**   Bourgeois morality invaded the heroic epic to create the novel. In the process virtue came to mean prudence and reputation. A heroine's struggle for personal virtue mirrored her class's struggle. Within the bourgeois heart goodness prevailed; love, considered a danger to the aristocratic social order, moved to the center of the novel's action of virtue-triumphant. Heroes were humanized. The novel told of the inner journey of emotion rather than of the external travels of an epic hero. Characters were analyzed and explained in terms of their feelings. Neo-classical objectivity withdrew as the author and reader, the playwright and the audience, became emotionally involved in the characters. Psychology moved into art, literature, and the theatre.

As in life, the countryside replaced the court as the source of goodness on stage. Untamed nature surpassed the formal garden in beauty. Even urban aristocrats built country homes to get back to nature. But the Enlightenment did not produce a distinctive style in art or scenic design; in 1753 the English artist William Hogarth wrote that "there is at present" a "thirst after variety." The Oriental and the Gothic flickered briefly as fashionable modes.

**Theatre Mirrors the Revolution**   The dramatic theatre caught the tides of social change. The French tragedian Pierre Corneille's hero—prince, general, and noble—was admired for his social position and dispassion. However, at the age's end, the bourgeois hero won admiration for his high moral principles and sensibility. The French comic playwright Molière began the depiction of the honest and witty middle class; the playwright Beaumarchais concluded the development with an observation that the public could never be interested in an aristocratic hero. The neo-classical ideal, perfected in France, fell to the domestic middle-class drama imported from England.

The middle-class drama arose as a conscious alternative to neo-classical Renaissance drama. Class conflict dominated the action of the plays. Middle-class heroes pitted themselves against, or were forced to oppose, a corrupt aristocratic society. In the seventeenth century, the fall of the neo-classical heroes symbolized their class's fate. However, the rising middle class believed it would triumph over social injustices. Problems were seen as existing in the social order rather than within naturally good individuals. Consequently, no great tragedies were produced in the eighteenth century. Opera filled the tragic void, and music embraced the tragic sentiment. Ballad opera provided a melody for the morals.

The breakdown of the old society also corresponded to the breakdown of dramatic forms. Playwrights mixed comedy and tragedy as marriages united poor aristocrats with wealthy bourgeois. In addition, the terror of tragedy and the outrage of comedy were knocked off the stage by the devastating combination of tears and smiles. Further, the excesses of the court theatre ebbed as the bourgeoisie entered the theatre. Morality was rewarded rather than ridiculed. The middle class wanted a wholesome, utilitarian, realistic drama. As a result the dramatic theatre moderated to become not too heroic, not too risqué—something respectable merchants and industrialists and their families could attend.

*Domestic Drama*   In 1731 *The London Merchant* by England's George Lillo (c. 1693–1739) introduced the new genre of drama by building on Jacobean "domestic tragedies." Neither tragic nor comic, the form won the French labels *comédie larmoyante* (tearful comedy) and *tragédie bourgeoise* (bourgeois tragedy). Whereas seventeenth-century theatre mirrored the court's decadent society, the eighteenth-century theatre audience exploited the desire to see itself as good, sentimental, and moderate. Consequently, tragedies and comedies—plays based on human imperfections and flaws—did not convey the appropriate truth of the human condition. Instead, comedies evoked tears, and tragedies avoided inevitable conflicts and calamities. Sentimental comedy and bourgeois drama emerged as the premiere dramatic genres of the day; they remained the most prevalent and popular forms of dramatic theatre in the world, even into the Modern era.

*New Acting Styles*   Acting styles followed these changes in audience sensibilities. All actors strive to imitate nature realistically, within the acting conventions of their age. Throughout the social theatre's history audiences focused their interest on actors' "points," moments by which actors' interpretations and techniques were judged. One favorite point in Shakespeare, for example, centered on Hamlet's first encounter with his father's ghost.

Conventions gradually changed during the age of social theatre. During the neo-classical heyday actors' characteristic restrained grace dictated that they use few gestures. The smallness of the theatres encouraged control and reliance on facial expression. However, as theatres enlarged, acting became more expansive

and exaggerated. An emotional tone of voice gradually overshadowed the rhetorical structure of the language. The "tragic strut" and the exaggerated "start," a reaction to a discovery, became standard.

The great English actor, David Garrick (1717–1779), and his French contemporary, Henri-Louis Lekain (1729–1778), were said to have reformed acting by consciously working against the social theatre's convention of exaggeration. They adopted a "familiar" tone of speech to begin a movement toward naturalism in stage behavior. But the movement never became wholly natural. "Claptrap," tricks to suck applause from an audience at the end of a speech or an exit, continued. Dramatic pauses still heightened effects. At the end of the eighteenth century actors John Phillip Kemble and Sarah Siddons returned acting to grandeur, dignity, and grace with their statuesque poses. Throughout this time, actors continued to play to the audience rather than to one another.

A flurry of acting handbooks were produced in the eighteenth century. Each said that understanding, sensibility, passion, physical beauty, and a sense of humor were essential traits for actors. Acting students were urged to study classical oratory, grammar, the histories of painting and sculpture, dancing, fencing, and etiquette. They needed to use gestures to communicate as gracefully as possible the appropriate passion. Their voices had to avoid monotony and repetition of inflection.

*Passion over Plot*   When English playwright John Dryden (1631–1700) claimed that dramatic art imitated nature, his definition stressed "imitation" and the artificiality of the work. In time, the word "nature" received emphasis. Critics, playwrights, and actors demanded "truth to life" rather than "truth to artistic convention." By the end of the age of social theatre, the prose of everyday life had replaced poetry as the language of the dramatic theatre. Prose was thought more "real," more of "nature." The goal of the playwright shifted from plot construction to arousal of passion and sentiment in the audience. In the process poetry came to be associated with passion rather than, as it had been historically, with plot. This identification of poetry with character passion climaxed in the nineteenth century.

A parallel development occurred in thinking about the work of the actor. In the eighteenth century feelings and emotions became the actor's goal. Actors who actually felt the emotions of a character were viewed as superior. English playwright Aaron Hill (1685–1750) wrote in 1750 that "the performer, who does not himself feel the several emotions he is to express to the audience, will give but a lifeless and insipid representation of them. ..." This idea began a process of rationalization that culminated in the early work of Constantin Stanislavski in the twentieth century.

***The Paradox of the Actor*** The idea that if actors cannot actually feel emotions on stage they cannot play them convincingly replaced the thinking of such older actors as Garrick, Colley Cibber (1671–1757), and Françoise Riccoboni (1707–1772), who thought that actors did not actually take on the identities of their characters. Actors considered actual feeling incompatible with the art's demand for control; real feeling involved a loss of control. How, the traditionalists wondered, could actors effect a series of rapid changes in emotion if they must truly feel each one? Traditionalists maintained that the art of acting was the creation of the illusion of genuine emotion rather than the experience of actual emotion itself.

Great actors, they argued, reproduce the external signs of emotion.

Thus argued Denis Diderot (1713–1784) in his *Le Paradoxe sur le comedien* (*Paradox of the Actor*, 1769), a reply to the growing demand for actual feeling and emotion in acting. Diderot considered actors to be cold and tranquil spectators to their actions on the stage. Aesthetic distance allowed the actors the control necessary to create the illusion of emotional and agitated characters. The English critic Dr. Johnson (1709–1784) joined the debate: "If Garrick really believed himself to be that monster, Richard the Third, he deserved to be hanged every time he performed it." Diderot and his traditionalist followers argued in vain that if actors gave themselves up to their emotions they could not control themselves. (The validity of the traditionalist position was demonstrated by many actors in the next age's romantic theatre.)

The social theatre arose with reason, laws, and rules. In time aristocrats complained of their insignificance in the economic and political lives of their nations. The bourgeoisie demanded more political representation. Championing liberty and the rights and dignity of the individual, the people shook and, in some cases, toppled the monarch. The theatre focused this dynamic agitation by envisioning a new reality.

The Industrial Revolution produced a prosperity that climaxed in political and theatrical revolution. The age of the social theatre, begun in the splendor of French sun kings and the neo-classical ideal, ended with the French Revolution and sentimental domestic drama.

# FRANCE

***The Sun Kings*** All aspects of French life fed and reacted to its monarchy. Despite severe intellectual limitations, Louis XIV (reigned 1643–1715) oversaw a perfect harmony among Catholicism, neo-classicism, and absolute monarchy. The "Sun King" lived as the

Lord's Anointed, the Miracle Child, born of prayers following twenty-two years of a barren marriage. His power secure, Louis boasted "L'état, c'est moi." But even the Sun King sensed his limitations. Louis once asked French critic Boileau, "Who is the greatest writer of the time?'' When Boileau proclaimed Molière, the king replied, "I did not think so, but you know better about these things than I do.''

But France's king did not lack elegance or pleasure. Despite bad teeth and stomach troubles, the king led both the aristocratic society and the bourgeois economy. The bourgeois worked without privilege; the nobles enjoyed privilege without work. Louis, meanwhile, found mistresses, fathered bastards, ate, rode, hunted, played cards, and occasionally danced in the *ballet de cour*. The unconcerned courtier ideal still dominated. But then unsuccessful war shook the people's confidence in the monarchy.

French culture and art peaked under Louis XV (reigned 1715–1774); France enjoyed *le Siècle des Lumières* (the Enlightenment). The king's mistress, Madame de Pompadour, patronized artists, actors, musicians, and encyclopedists while bankrupting France. Meanwhile, the aristocracy and church paid no taxes, and the bourgeoisie picked up the tab for the monarchy's tastes and fun. Louis XVI (reigned 1774–1793) succeeded his grandfather to govern a nation with great private wealth and great public debt. The shy, pious, and humble king became the mark of the very beautiful, very charming, and very cruel Marie Antoinette of Austria. Louis loved her; she despised him. Louis was impotent; Marie demanded very frivolous, extravagant pleasure. Together they became a symbol of monarchical degeneracy, waste, and extravagance.

*Revolution* The monarchy's aristocratic corruption and oppression, coupled with bourgeois demands for equality, caused the Estates General to be summoned in May, 1789, for the first time since 1614. On July 14, citizens went to the Bastille to obtain weapons and disarm the king's old fortress. When fired upon, the people stormed the building and took control. The king yielded. On August 4, liberal nobles and clergy renounced their feudal rights. On August 27, the Declaration of the Rights of Man was issued. The king returned to Paris,

a prisoner; repeated treachery led to his decapitation in 1793.

Meanwhile, France became the symbol of Revolution, and Louis XVI, the rallying point for European monarchs fearing insurrections at home. To the beat of the *Marseillaise*, the French national anthem, a new army fought for the new French constitution on nationalist principles. But in time France faced anarchy; extremists rose to dominate the Revolutionary government. The revolutionist Robespierre (1758–1794), the lawyer Danton (1759–1794), and the journalist Marat (1743–1793) created a Republic. A final revolt in October, 1795, was put down by a general named Napoleon Bonaparte (1769–1821).

*Salon Culture* Throughout the political life and death of the monarchy, French social and economic life struggled on. Nobles spent their days at court glorying in art, literature, and theatre and playing the game of courtier. The rules of the game encouraged a feeling of superiority. Dramatic art displayed the aristocratic virtues of moderation, self-control, objectivity, reserve, and strength; only the bourgeoisie displayed emotion and passion.

Throughout aristocratic France *salons* appeared. Salons afforded men and women the chance to meet for philosophy and flirtation. Behind social masks of ease and natural grace, salons produced great hostesses, great conversation, and artificial levity. Affectation, in fact, dominated the style of elite chivalry and etiquette.

Salons also set the form and content of stage diction. François de La Rochefoucauld (1613–1680) recorded the best of the lot in *Réflexions ou sentences et maximes morales*, a volume of epigrams of pessimism, self-love, and self-delusion. The dramatic theatre of the age gave life to La Rochefoucauld's observations. Amid a Machiavellian atmosphere, salon members enjoyed objectively analyzing one another's feelings and emotions. Some salons, functioning as unofficial academies, created regional artistic styles and literary personalities. Under

Louis XV and Louis XVI salon life replaced court life; neither monarch enjoyed etiquette, society, ceremony, or wit.

**Social Revolution** Though women could occasionally sparkle in a salon, their status remained comparatively low. *Mariages de convenances* between rich old men and poor young women continued, though women could sneak young lovers. Poverty forced the abandonment of almost a quarter of the babies born in 1780 Paris. Nevertheless, the growing demand for rights excluded women. Before the Revolution only an occasional noble woman or banker's daughter could participate in the government.

Sex came under new scrutiny, however, as reason affected every human activity. Royalty actually set the tone. Royal mistresses often became queen. Madame de Pompadour even provided her husband with young girls when she became too old to satisfy him. The name "Sadism" evolved from the Marquis de Sade (1740–1814), who derived sexual satisfaction from giving pain to others. Sexual variation increased in prominence on stage and behind the scenes; homosexuality and heterosexuality prospered. Louis XIV's plan to expel all homosexuals collapsed because his nephew and successor, Phillip, the Duke of Orleans, lived a transvestite and homosexual life. The most notorious transvestite of this time, Chevalier d'Eon de Beaumont, was a good friend of the playwright Pierre Augustin Caron de Beaumarchais (1732–1799). In addition, the court composer Jean Baptiste Lully (1632–1687), who collaborated with Molière on several court entertainments, was a member of the Sacred Fraternity of Glorious Pederasts. Twelve volumes of novels about the Italian womanizer Casanova were popular as well. And the playwright Denis Diderot explored the details of forced celibacy and female sexual variance in his novel, *La Religieuse* (1760).

**The Philosophes** The Age of Reason began with fashionable philosophy among circles of intellectuals (called *philosophes*), but later seized upon Newtonian ideas. François-Marie Arouet de Voltaire (1694–1778), commonly known as Voltaire, dominated the *philosophes* and spread French philosophy as far as Prussia. Voltaire and Jean-Jacques Rousseau (1712–1778) represented two phases in the philosophical mood as aristocratic rule faded into bourgeois control. The son of a watchmaker, Rousseau moved from country to country proclaiming the natural goodness of God, humans, and nature. Evil, to Rousseau, originated in the social environment of private property. Whereas Voltaire favored educating individuals through reason, writing, and reading to create a better social order, Rousseau advocated encouraging instinctive violent action to liberate individuals' frustrated natural sentiments. Each man also had divergent views regarding the dramatic theatre.

The *philosophes* attacked religious superstition and fanaticism by collecting facts from every sphere of knowledge. They held skeptical views of religion, especially of the monarchy's close relationship with the clergy and religious persecution. Voltaire led the group with passionate attacks on doctrine of any kind. Meanwhile, Diderot organized and edited a twenty-year project: producing the first *Encyclopédie* (Encyclopedia). The *Encyclopédie*, however, perceived as an indictment of the existing society, was condemned, seized, and destroyed by agents of both the church and the state.

**Neo-Classical Glory** French neo-classicism arose from balancing conservative Christianity and monarchy with liberal rationalism and humanism. The balance evidenced itself in the drama of the period. The French court was as authoritarian and absolute in matters of theatrical beauty as the church was in matters of revealed truth. Indeed, so powerful were church and state tastes that they combined to mold theatrical art and literature that were consciously international in perspective; there are no French characters, for example, in Racine's tragedies, even though Racine is considered a major French dramatist.

The liberalism of Louis XIII toward artistic creation disappeared with Louis XIV. State art was created in compliance to state rules. In 1648 the *Académie Royale de Peinture et de Sculpture* made art an agent of the government. Painters worked as part of the civil service, and schools codified and regulated artistic representation. Theatrical art raised the prestige of the king, created a new mythology to surround the monarch, and made every aspect of court life splendid. By 1661 every aspect of creative expression was regulated because art academies operated as law courts. Form dominated content.

At the beginning of the neo-classical age personal style, individuality, and initiative were belittled and suppressed. The theatre demanded a universality to match France's international ambitions. Language became formal, characters uniform, and action regulated. Playwrights were made to live by rules rather than by imagination. Theatre demanded discipline, limitation of vision, concentration, and the integration of model principles. Some of the early artistic results had so delicate and sensual a quality that later revolutionaries dubbed them ''rococo'' or florid.

The Enlightenment began to reason away the rules almost as they were written. People of reason argued that art demanded logic, clarity, and simplicity. The playwright Pierre Corneille admitted that ''I believe in the precepts of Aristotle not because they are Aristotle's but because they are in agreement with human reason.'' Molière added, ''The ancients are the ancients, and we are the people of today.''

**The Bourgeois Aesthetic**  Courtly dramatic art died in the eighteenth century because, as economic power moved to the bourgeoisie, so did theatrical influence. Voltaire's and Rousseau's readers were predominantly of the middle class. Merchants wrote, painted, and patronized. And most playwrights came from the middle class, as well.

Sentimentalism in France developed independently from concurrent developments in England. Nevertheless, the French admired, copied, and adapted English models. In 1752, Samuel Richardson's new literary form debuted in translation from his 1740 novel *Pamela*, which contained ideas and used techniques already known to the French through the work of playwright Pierre Carlet de Chamblain de Marivaux (1688–1763). But Richardson was admired more for the ethical than the literary merit of his words. The French dramatic theatre expressed the change in interests and techniques.

This shift in interest from aristocratic court society to middle-class virtue and sentiment arose from a changing audience's demand to see its social origins and class on the stage. Printed texts and academic prefaces announced the change.

**Dramatic Texts**  France had embraced the neo-classical ideal in dramatic composition as a reaction to bloody medievalism. During the seventeenth century well-educated playwrights turned to the public theatres as their English counterparts had done almost a century earlier. Jean de Mairet (1604–1686) wrote for the Montdory troupe at the *Théâtre du Marais*. As we discussed in Chapter 5, his *Sophonisba* (1634) stands as the first French tragedy written by the rules. In 1630 he followed the rules to produce France's first pastoral, *Silvanie*. Later Mairet attacked Corneille's *The Cid* for violating his beloved rules.

**Le Cid Controversy**  French tragedy reached a golden age within the neo-classical ideal. Composition illustrated the belief that reason provided the knowledge of what was right. In 1636 Pierre Corneille's (1606–1684) *Le Cid* employed rationalism but without regard to court or academic tastes. Although the debate that followed established the Italian ideal in France, it also planted the seeds of the ideal's slow demise.

French tragedy depended upon the power of poetic language. Few movements, gestures, or set pieces were allowed to compete with the spare, essential poetic utterances. Shakespeare had used a vocabulary of 24,000 words; Jean Racine (1639–1699) focused on only 2000. The difference did not stop there. The French Alexandrine couplet was longer than the blank verse of Elizabethan iambic pentameter. The French avoided colloquial expressions in writing for the stage; the English sought them out.

Corneille, who was educated in Jesuit schools before beginning a law career, composed the first great French comedy, *Mélite* (c. 1630). Later, in 1634, Corneille was invited by Richelieu to collaborate with other playwrights at the Cardinal's personal theatre. The *Marais's* production of *Le Cid* (c. 1636) helped establish French neo-classicism. Corneille based his success neither on French rules nor on English inspiration. His plays worked because he satisfied two of Aristotle's requirements: (1) the hero is one like us, and (2) the hero suffers from one for whom he has great affection.

In 1660 Corneille contributed to the debate over unity, another Aristotelian requirement:

> The unity of action does not mean that tragedy should show only one action on the stage . . . . There must be only one complete action, which leaves the mind of the spectator serene; but that action can become complete only through several others which are less perfect and which, by serving as preparation, keep the audience in a pleasant suspense.[1]

In *Le Cid* Chimène loves Roderick, but her father insults his father, thereby forcing Roderick to challenge his future father-in-law. Chimène must wish for her fiancé's death. Roderick passes up suicide to lead a small army against the invading Moors. When Roderick returns a hero, Chimène insists a new suitor take up her father's cause and challenge Roderick. But when Chimène discovers that Roderick intends to let himself be killed, she urges him to victory. Roderick wins the duel, and Chimène, following the king's decree, weds the victor. All of the action in *Le Cid* happens in twenty-four hours and in an area surrounding the palace. Critics believed the play destroyed verisimilitude by crowding so much action into such a small area in so short a time. And instead of the requisite tragic ending, the lovers are happy at the play's conclusion.

But the new French Academy (1629), concerned with maintaining correct usage and style, was most concerned with moral questions. Was it proper for Chimène to marry her father's murderer? Should love outweigh duty? *Le Cid* challenged not only the form of neo-classicism but also the spirit of blind obedience to duty at the expense of individual emotion.

Corneille seemed to heed the French Academy's criticism with his next plays. The Roman patriot *Horace* (1640) finds his wife's native Alban homeland at war with Rome and his sister in love with an enemy soldier. Horace's patriotism allows him to kill both his sister and his wife's brothers. *Cinna* (c. 1640) joins a conspiracy against the Emperor Augustus because of his love for Emolie, who seeks to avenge the Emperor's murder of her father. Like *Le Cid*, the play ends happily as the noble Emperor rises above the conspirators to grant clemency to the plotters. And as he dies, the Christian convert *Polyeucte* (1642) sacrifices his pagan wife, Pauline, to the man she loves. Pauline had worked diligently to get Polyeucte pardoned for destroying the pagan idols. Around 1643 Corneille was appointed to the French Academy, but the failure of his *Pertharite* in 1651 caused him to retire for eight years.

Corneille's heroes presented France with characters forced to chose between the claims of society and their personal desires. Corneille, in fact, called upon superheroes to make extraordinary sacrifices for their country. Simple characters struggled in complex historical plots. And despite a capacity for great tenderness and humanity, Corneille's heroes subordinated their feelings and emotions to what reason told them was their duty. Corneille's heroes were always conscious of their motivations, actions, and goals.

Corneille supported the French monarchy and French neo-classicism but only to the point of tyranny. His plays reveal a growing dissatisfaction with the status quo. The early plays resolve when order is restored by a king or ruler; the middle plays present the hero as a rival to the king's authority; the last plays depict a monarchical tyranny that makes heroism impossible.

**Racine**   An orphan educated by Jansenists, Jean Racine (1639–1699) was encouraged by Molière to produce *La thébaïde* (*The Theban*) in 1664. Whereas Corneille drew strong male characters displaying Jesuit free will, Racine sketched impulsive female characters driven unconsciously by original sin toward predestined fates. Beneath civilized social facades, Racine's heroines battled with inescapable primitive passions. Racine, placing complex characters in simple, concentrated plots, revealed the destructiveness of passion. Acute psychological insights and simplicity of expression characterized Racine's technique. Unlike Corneille, Racine placed the conflict within the mind of a single character rather than between two characters. Corneille's heroes could resist temptation; Racine's could not.

Perhaps Racine drew upon his own experiences with his mistresses, Marie Champmeslé and Thérèse du Parc. Racine enticed the latter away from Molière's company to star as his Andromaque. (Unfortunately, her mysterious death, either by poison or abortion, hung a cloud around his career.) In the play *Andromaque* (1667), the heroine is loved by Pyrrhus, the man who killed her husband. Pyrrhus is loved by Hermione, who is loved, in turn, by Orestes. Because only marriage to Pyrrhus can save Andromaque's infant son, she agrees to the marriage but vows to kill herself afterward. However, Hermione convinces Orestes to kill Pyrrhus. She then commits suicide. In *Britannicus* (1669) the Roman Emperor Nero poisons Britannicus to get his fiancée. The fiancée flees, and Nero's trusted councillor is murdered as he tries to capture her. An enraged Nero ends the play wondering what to do next. *Phèdre* (1677) reworks Euripides's *Hippolytus*. But Hippolytus is not chaste. Nevertheless Theseus's new bride, Phèdre, still develops an overwhelming passion for her new stepson. In *Bérénice* (1670) Titus is torn between his duty to Rome and his love for the title character. Titus orders Bérénice from the city but his messenger also falls under her charm.

*Esther* and *Athalie* were written for production in girls' schools. The former relates the story of a Jewish queen who saves her nation from destruction. The characters were considered to be allegorical representatives of King Louis XIV and his mistresses. In the latter Queen Athaliah has nightmares about the crime that brought her to the throne. She accidentally meets the rightful heir living in the temple. A coup ultimately restores the prince to the throne and slays the queen.

*A scene from Racine's* Bérénice *(1678).*
(Bibliotheque Nationale, Paris)

Racine supposedly believed a good play-wright capable of both justifying the most immoral actions and arousing sympathy for the vilest criminal. In his Preface to *Bérénice* (1670) Racine wrote that "the principal rule is to please and to stir; all others are simply means to arrive at that end."

***Molière and His Successors*** Jean-Baptiste Poquelin (1622–1673), known by his stage name Molière, understood the growing bourgeois audience first hand. Molière disappointed his upholsterer father by passing up a law career to run off with the red-haired actress Madeleine Béjart, four years his senior, to found the Illustre Theatre in 1643. As a boy Molière had enjoyed the *commedia dell'arte*, and he had excelled in classical studies with class-mate Cyrano de Bergerac. Nevertheless, two years after the founding of the theatre, Molière, Madeleine, Madeleine's brother, and 2-year-old Armande Béjart (either Molière's daughter or sister-in-law) went bankrupt. They regrouped and toured the provinces for thirteen years before playing Paris in 1659. That year, Molière's *Les précieuses ridicules* (*The Affected Ladies*) was so successful that the king's brother, Phillipe, christened the group the Troupe de Monsieur and gave them the Petit Bourbon, the king's private theatre, for performances. In 1662 the chronically ill Molière married 19-year-old Armande. His rivals charged that Molière, the coiner of the word "moron," was marrying his own daughter. To silence them the couple named their son after the child's godfather, King Louis XIV of France.

The first play after his marriage was *L'ecole des femmes* (*The School for Wives*, 1662). In the play Arnolphe jealously guards his innocent ward, Agnes, while helping his friend, the cynical Chrysalde, woo an overly protected young lady. The lady turns out to be Agnes. Arnolphe vows to marry Agnes himself, but the young man's father arrives to save the day. Conservatives objected to Molière's questioning of the law that gave guardians absolute authority over their wards. To answer his critics Molière wrote a play about their criticism, *La critique de l'école des femmes* (*The Critique of The School for Wives*, 1663).

Molière seemed to enjoy arousing the conservatives. At a time of growing religious pietism, for example, he wrote *Tartuffe* (1664), the tale of a self-righteous, egotistical hypocrite who cons his way into a bourgeois household with claims of religious piety. The title character manipulates the head of the family so thoroughly that, at the end, only the king can rectify the situation. Again the conservatives attacked Molière; after the first performance the play was banned for two years. Molière was, in fact, a vigorous opponent of restraint and convention; he also considered the worst vice to be hypocrisy or posturing. In defense of *Tartuffe*, he wrote "the duty of comedy is to correct men by entertaining them." Later conservatives denounced Molière's recasting of *Don Juan* (1665) as an immoral and atheistic hero whose fake reformation riled the pietists in the audience.

Alceste, *Le misanthrope* (1666), is obsessed and disgusted with his salon-dominated age. Unable to compromise with a world of bribery and flattery, incapable of faking the social insincerity necessary to win Célimène, the woman he loves, Alceste retires from the world to live as a hermit. Harpagon, *L'avare* (*The Miser*, 1668), loves the girl married to his son in a plot borrowed from the Roman playwright, Plautus. Monsieur Jourdain, *Le bourgeois gentilhomme* (*The Would-Be Gentleman*, 1670), is a bourgeois social climber determined to move from his shop to the salon world he admires. *Les femmes savantes* (*The Learned Ladies*, 1672), led by the bourgeois housewife, Philmainte, fawn all over the pretentious, superficial, and conniving pedant, Trissotin, the rage of the salon world.

Throughout his career Molière enjoyed the favor of both popular and court audiences. The playwright ridiculed all but the monarchy, the church, noble privilege, and the idea of social hierarchy. He knew the source of his income. Nevertheless, Molière unmasked social pretensions and championed moderation with stories of heroes whose worst fears come to pass. The king protected Molière from attacks, even by religious zealots.

Marital and health problems caused Molière's death during a performance of the hypochondriac, Argan, in the *Le malade imaginaire* (*The Imaginary Invalid*, 1673), the saga of a man who, though preyed upon by every conceivable medical quack, insists on a doctor for a son-in-law.

After Molière's death comedy continued to satirize contemporary French life. But cynicism crept in. Alain René LeSage (1668–1747) was forced to write for the stage when his uncle squandered his inheritance. LeSage's comedies of manners peaked with *Turcaret* (1709), a depiction of greed and opportunism so fierce that the playwright was offered a bribe to keep it from production. *Gil Blas* (1715–1735), his novel, satirized eighteenth-century France and made LeSage the first French writer without a patron to support himself by writing.

The psychology of love interested Pierre Carlet de Chamblainde Marivaux (1688–1763), who entered the French Academy in 1743. Playwright, novelist, and essayist, Marivaux wrote essays on contemporary life for his periodical, *Le spectateur français (The French Spectator)*. His plays display the concealment and eventual declaration of love by means of badinage so clever as to coin the name *marivaudage*. In *La double inconstance* (*The Double Inconstancy*, 1723), for example, two lovers discover they are not in love when confronted with the real thing. *L'île des esclaves* (*The Isle of Slaves*, 1725) placed aristocrats in the place of their slaves for a three-year period, after which the nobles were cured of prejudice and inhumanity. Servants and masters play *Le jeu de l'amour et du hasard* (*The Game of Love and Chance*, 1730) by exchanging social positions to learn the truth about love and lovers. A poor man woos and wins a rich widow in *Les fousses confidences (False Confidences*, 1737).

**New Dramaturgical Goals** Sentimental comedy, which came to mean the happy resolution of a contemporary family problem, aroused tender emotions for an ordinary character in everyday situations. The valet and soubrette roles of neo-classical drama eventually disappeared. So did humorous roles and comic lines of business. Comedies instead presented series of emotional crises that ended happily and illustrated moral lessons. The re-

*A 1674 production of Molière's* The Imaginary Invalid.   (Bibliotheque Nationale, Paris)

turn to Paris of the *Comédie Italienne* in 1720 provided French comic writers with a new market and hastened the decline of heroic neo-classical tragedy after the death of Racine.

Playwright Antoine Hodar de la Motte (1672–1731) urged a loosening up of the rules of composition to allow more action; he wanted visual excitement to match the linguistic fireworks. Philippe-Néricault Destouches (1680–1754) returned from England with notions of tragedy gleaned from the plays of Joseph Addison (1672–1719). Tragedy moved from heroic and romantic situations toward moralizing sentimental comedy. In time, tragedy disappeared completely, as a new serious genre emerged. The heroism, passion, and romance of tragedy moved to the opera.

*L'opéra*　French opera developed from the work of an Italian, Giovanni Battista Lulli (1632–1687), who felt so at home in Paris that he became Jean Baptiste Lully. Lully teamed with playwright Phillipe Quinault (1636–1688) to produce *Amadis* (1684) and with Molière to produce *Le bourgeois gentilhomme* (*The Bourgeois Gentleman*, 1670). Jean-Phillipe Rameau (1683–1764) adapted French opera to Italian developments.

French serious opera, *tragédie lyrique*, emphasized drama over music. However, most major work occurred in the comic operas, *opéra comique* and *opéra buffa*. In 1761 Carlo Goldoni, the leading reformer of comic opera, settled in Paris. Musical genius Wolfgang Amadeus Mozart (1756–1791) brought the comic opera to the forefront of French culture. But opera too became sentimentalized, as ordinary characters replaced *commedia dell'arte* types. All dramatic theatre moved toward the *drame* or *genre serieux*.

*Le Drame*　The new form of serious drama moved easily between tragedy and comedy, extending neo-classical verisimilitude to the bourgeois. *Le drame*, preferring a safe middle ground to the limits of terror and outrage, never approached the extremes of tragedy or comedy. It sought to teach morality by manipulating the emotions of the audience. Popularized by Denis Diderot's *Le fils naturel* ( *The Natural Son*, 1757), the drama displayed moral truths, preached natural virtue, denounced the crimes of civilized society, aroused pity for the oppressed, and elevated the middle-class merchant to heroic stature.

Whereas the old neo-classical hero could feel guilt, the new bourgeois hero was guilt-free. Society had to bear the guilt, because society, not the good bourgeois, created the problems. Naturally good characters faced a choice, not between love and honor, but between personal will and societal duty. In the new drama, the heroes are controlled by their environment; society shapes their destiny. No longer do the heroes control their own fates.

*Diderot*　The break with neo-classicism progressed with the work of Denis Diderot (1713–1784). Educated by the Jesuits and holding an M.A. from the University of Paris, Diderot urged playwrights to abandon classical heroic passions to write about everyday bourgeois life. In 1758 he wrote, "forget your rules, put technique aside: it is the death of genius." The neo-classical ideal restricted the playwright too much and created a false picture of reality. The playwright should, Diderot argued, take subjects from everyday life, create characters with accurate psychological motivation, and write in vernacular prose rather than in poetic Alexandrines. Diderot wanted to create sentimental comedy in France. *Le drame* was his name for a contemporary play exploring the domestic problems of everyday life; it ends with the reconcilation of a problem after troublesome characters repent for past mistakes.

Diderot tried to practice what he preached with *Le fils naturel* (*The Natural Son*, 1757) and *Le père de famille* (*The Father of the Family*, 1758). The purpose of his drama was "to inspire men with love of virtue and horror of vice." In 1758 Diderot urged, "when you write, you must keep virtue and virtuous people in mind." He observed, "the theatre is the only place where the tears of the virtuous man and the rogue are mingled."

Diderot wrote to improve humanity. His

plays, theories, and criticism sought to make people better. He gathered the great Enlightenment thinkers to write for his *Encyclopédie*, an attempt to record all available knowledge and advance the cause of rationalism. However, in time Diderot saw passion as more important to artistic creation than reason. Imagination stood as the means to stimulate passion. Diderot thus elevated passion over reason, thereby marking the end of one age and the beginning of another. Although the romantic theatre was still a way off, Diderot's work nonetheless evidences a tense compromise between academic rationality and unrestrained emotionalism.

***Beaumarchais***   The spirit of freedom and equality that climaxed the age of social theatre in France found its greatest theatrical voice in Pierre Augustin Caron de Beaumarchais (1732–1799), the son of a watchmaker. Beaumarchais began his career as harpsichord tutor to Louis XV's two old maid daughters. When the American Revolution erupted, Beaumarchais smuggled arms and ammunition to the colonists. He also helped the French and Spanish governments organize funds and ships for the revolutionaries. And he wrote.

*Le barbier de Séville* (*The Barber of Seville*, 1775) and *Le mariage de Figaro* (*The Marriage of Figaro*, 1784) advanced the revolutionary spirit in France with veiled attacks on the aristocracy. In *Le barbier de Séville* Dr. Bartholo jealously guards his young ward Rosine. Count Almaviva connives to win her with the help of the local barber, Figaro, the archetypal common man. *Le mariage de Figaro*, the sequel, shows the married life of the Count and Rosine a few years later. As their love fades, the count plots to get Figaro's fiancé for his mistress. Beaumarchais filled his play with so much hatred for the aristocracy that *Le mariage de Figaro* was suppressed. The eventual performance in 1784 still caused a riot because the barber Figaro represented all French citizens exploited by the ruling class. Figaro's spirit of freedom soared through Beaumarchais's laughing comedies of intrigue. The man of the people, Figaro, spoke

the peoples' thoughts and became the stage voice of the Revolution.

Beaumarchais wanted drama to reflect the peoples' interests of the moment rather than the ancients' universal concerns. He wrote "when my subject seizes me I evoke my characters and I situate them. . . . What they are going to say I've not the least idea: it is what they will do that concerns me." Freedom even for dramatic characters! But for Beaumarchais and for the citizens of France on the eve of Revolution, deeds overshadowed words. A Beaumarchais play, like a Revolution, consisted of a series of exciting scenes.

Beaumarchais also worked for equality by founding, in 1777, the Bureau Dramatique in protest to the exclusion of annual box rentals from the gross receipts upon which playwrights drew their royalty percentages. In 1791 Beaumarchais's work was rewarded. The National Assembly passed the first royalty payment law, securing for authors and their heirs a fee for each performance of a play.

***Theatrical Troupes***   Paris remained the center of theatrical activity. Actors who wanted careers vied to attach themselves to the city's leading troupes. The *Hotel de Bourgogne* troupe descended from Valleran Le Comte (1592–1613) and boasted the acting of Bellerose (c. 1592–1670), the principal actor. The *Théâtre du Marais* followed the actor-manager Montdory (1594–1654). For presenting neo-classical dramas, the *Marais* enjoyed the financial patronage of Cardinal Richelieu. *Mélite*, Corneille's comedy, debuted at the *Marais*, the leading Paris company until 1647 when Floridor (1608–1672) replaced Bellerose at the *Bourgogne*. Corneille then took his plays to the *Bourgogne*, forcing the *Marais* to employ spectacle to compete. The *Marais* finally closed in 1673.

The members of the closed *Marais* joined Molière's company to form the *Troupe du Roi* at the *Hotel de Guenegaud*. In 1679 the Bourgogne troupe merged with them to create the first national theatre, the *Comédie Française*. The *Comédie* monopolized all spoken drama in France, with the exception of the *commedia dell'arte* troupe, the *Comédie Italienne*. (But in 1697 the *Comédie Italienne* was expelled from France after slurring Louis XIV's wife.) Troupes looked for ways to circumvent the *Comédie Française's* monopoly. As a result, new popular forms of dramatic theatre emerged.

For example, the *opéra comique* sang comic dialogue. LeSage wrote for the new troupes by alternating spoken dialogue with verses set to popular tunes. When Louis XIV died, the *Comédie Italienne* returned under the leadership of Luigi Riccoboni (c. 1676–1753), a player of Pantalone. When *commedia dell'arte* declined in popularity, the troupe circumvented the monopoly by playing tragedies and tragicomedies in Italian. In 1723 the *commedia* troupe was named a state theatre; in 1762 it won a monopoly on comic opera. Carlo Goldoni (1707–1793) arrived to write for the troupe.

Actors achieved high status. In 1789 a debate in the National Assembly culminated in extending the rights of citizenship to "Jew, Protestant, and actor." But in 1791 the National Assembly abolished all monopolies, thereby enhancing the opportunities for young French playwrights. As a result, companies disbanded because any play could be performed anywhere. New troupes formed, allied themselves with particular political parties, and espoused their party lines on stage. Consequently, if the message was determined to be unsympathetic to the current ruling faction, actors were arrested and theatres closed. Actress Olympe de Gouges wrote the Declaration of the Rights of Women in 1791, and actress Claire Lacombe organized the Revolutionary Society, a club for working women, in 1793. But the number of politically active actors decreased. In 1795 the National Convention picked the Directory, a board of five, to rule France, and scattered *Comédie Française* actors were finally reunited.

Troupes organized on a sharing plan, assigning shares according to an actor's importance to the troupe. In the *Comédie Française*, *sociétaires* held shares and bound themselves to the company for twenty years. The oldest *sociétaire* functioned as the *doyen* (troupe leader).

*Pensionaires* were salaried actors eligible to become *sociétaires* when positions opened. Whereas the opera company numbered anywhere from 120 to 280, the *Comédie Française* and the *Comédie Italienne* had only between fifty and seventy members each.

Actors retained their lines of business throughout their careers. Kings, lovers, princes, mothers, old men, coquettes, and soubrettes were particular specialty roles. Secondary actors and utility players rounded out the company. In 1786 a Royal Dramatic School opened as an agency of the *Comédie Française* to teach lines of business and the traditional interpretations of the company's repertoire.

**Great Actors** Individual actors dominated the social theatre scene. Molière and the Béjart family stood out during the early years. In 1664, for instance, Armande Béjart replaced Madeleine Béjart, famous as Dorine in *Tartuffe*, as the heroine of Molière's plays. Molière discovered a child actor named Michael Baron (1653–1729) who, before dying while playing Don Diegue in a performance of *Le Cid*, became the principal actor with the *Comédie Française*. Catherine de Brie (c. 1629–1706) continued her soubrette line, playing Agnes in *L'ecole des femmes* (*The School for Wives*) until she was 65 years old. Marie Champmeslé (1642–1698), Racine's mistress, enjoyed the leading roles he wrote for her.

The most popular actress in Paris was Adrienne Lecouvreur (1692–1730). Known for her great beauty and naturalness, she excelled as the heroines of Racine and Corneille, especially Pauline in the latter's *Polyeucte*. Voltaire fumed that though Lecouvreur died in the same year as the English actress Anne Oldfield, the English actress was buried in Westminster Abbey with great ceremony whereas the French tragedienne was refused any kind of Christian burial. Like Molière, she was deposited in an unmarked grave.

Marie-Françoise Dumesnil (1713–1803) excelled in playing passionate roles, blazing her eyes, expanding her gestures, and crying. She was, however, often accused of being

*Adrienne Lecouvreur in Corneille's* Death of Pompey *in 1725.* (Costumes et Annales des Théâtres de Paris, *vol. 4, 1788–1789)*

picious build-up, Lekain drew acclaim as "the French Garrick." Even his small, hushed voice proved no obstacle to fame: Voltaire liked the actor's interest in historically accurate costumes.

The age concluded with the acting of the English-educated François-Joseph Talma (1763–1826), who debuted in 1787 as Voltaire's *Mahomet* at the *Comédie Française*. Talma created an uproar as the king in the Republican drama *Charles IX* (1789) because his radical passion stunned the audience. He refined his performance with accurate costuming and a natural delivery of lines. Talma, foreshadowing the romantic view of acting, claimed acting as "the sphere in which a magnetic personality exercises a power of sympathy which cannot be resisted or defined. That is great acting; but though it is inborn and cannot be taught, it can be brought forth when the actor is master of his craft." Such ideas found sympathetic ears in the political world. In 1799 Talma aided Napoleon in drawing up a new

*Lekain and Mlle. Clairon in Voltaire's* The Orphan of China, *1777.* (From an illustrated edition of Voltaire's plays published in 1883–1885)

drunk on stage. She died in a bed filled with chickens. Dumesnil's chief rival, Claire-Josephe-Hippolyte Leris de la Tude Clairon (1723–1803), was considered by Voltaire, Diderot, and England's David Garrick as the best actress of her age, especially as Phèdre. Clairon liked ensuring both the historical accuracy of her costume and the conversational quality of her lines. She wrote her *Mémoires* in 1799. Her student, François-Rose Vestris (1743–1804) played in her teacher's shadow, but received some attention in Voltaire's *Tancrede*.

Henri-Louis Lekain (1729–1778) entered the theatre after Voltaire had built him a private theatre at Voltaire's home, trained him, and arranged for his debut with the *Comédie Française* in Voltaire's *Brutus*. With such an aus-

*Talma in Voltaire's* Brutus *(1791).*    (From Adolphe Julien, *Histoire du Costume au Théâtre*, 1880)

charter for the *Comédie Française*. Napoleon even featured Talma at state entertainments.

The new sentimental bourgeois drama did not enjoy the favor of the *Comédie Française* and so the name actors of the age never played in them. Simplicity and naturalness were considered threats to their traditional acting style. Actors and critics also commented on the actor's craft. Corneille had hoped printed texts would control actors' interpretations: ''Print-

ing puts our plays in the hands of actors who tour the provinces and whom we can thus inform of what they ought to do, for they would do some very odd things if we did not help them by these notes.'' The ''odd things'' Corneille feared eventually came to characterize great acting in the romantic theatre.

As we discussed earlier in this chapter, in 1769 Diderot's *Le paradoxe sur le comédien (Paradox of the Actor)* suggested that to portray great emotion on stage actors needed to remain coolly in control of themselves. Good actors left the theatre merely tired while spectators exited either happy or sad. Control allowed the actors to repeat their effects from day to day. Actors, Diderot suggested, do not feel the emotions of the characters but merely render ''as scrupulously as possible the external signs'' of emotion. This was the ''paradox of the actor.''

As truth and virtue came to be seen in the free expression of sentiment, greatness in acting had to display the free, rather than the controlled, expression of emotion. The genius actor had an originality of talent based, not on the ability to represent external signs as Diderot had suggested, but on a genuine emotional reservoir of mysterious, secret, undefinable, and irrational feelings.

***Theatre Architecture and Design***    Theatre building and scenic innovation took place at both court and public theatres. In 1641, Richelieu asked le Mercier to build the *Palais Cardinal*, the first French theatre with a proscenium arch. When Richelieu died, the 600-seat theatre was renamed the *Palais Royal*.

The *Salle du Petit-Bourbon* (1577) was the first court theatre in the Bourbon palace. Molière shared this theatre with a *commedia dell'arte* troupe until the building was demolished in 1660. Molière took the theatre's boxes and decorations with him when he left to open his *Psyche* (1671) in the remodeled Palais Royal theatre. At Molière's death in 1673 Lully claimed the theatre for opera. Lully wanted the theatre's chariot and pole system of scene changing which was most suited to stage spectacle (see discussion in Chapter 5). Then, in 1689 the new *Comédie Française* moved into a

*Giacomo Torelli's 1650 setting for* Andromède *by Corneille.* (The Metropolitan Museum of Art, Elisha Whittelsey Fund, 1951)

new theatre, a tennis court in Étoile remodeled by François d'Orbay. In 1782 the *Comédie Française* moved into an ovoid theatre with seats for all spectators.

At the beginning of the eighteenth century, only three Parisian theatres had existed; by 1791, the number had grown to fifty-one. New minor theatres housed the new bourgeois drama rejected by the *Comédie Française*. Musical and pantomime theatres coined the term *melodrame* to describe plays whose dialogue was underscored with music.

Scenery showed the transition from court taste to popular taste. The Italian Cardinal Mazarin, for example, loved opera, the *commedia dell'arte*, and spectacle. He thus commissioned Corneille to write a play to exploit scenery. He also brought the neo-classical visual ideal to France with Torelli's 1645 designs for the opera. When Mazarin died, however, Torelli was ordered to leave the country.

But the Italian influence continued with the Bibiena family. After establishing their reputations in Italy, Fernando (1657–1743), Francesco (1659–1739), Giuseppe (1696–1757), Antonio (1700–1774), and Carlo (1728–

*An* opéra comique *on the Hotel de Bourgogne stage in 1769.* (Bibliotheque Nationale, Paris)

1787) spread their style to Barcelona, Vienna, London, Berlin, and Paris. They developed the *scena per angolo* (angle perspective), which broke design symmetry. They also increased the scale of the settings. The king's single vantage point disappeared on stage, as it would in the nation. Instead, two or more vanishing points appeared at the sides of the stage. No longer could the world be kept within the limits of the king's proscenium arch; no longer would the stage perspective be an extension of the king's auditorium scale. The king and his audience could see only part of the Bibienas' huge buildings. Indeed, the center of the stage often showed only a sharp corner of a building where an horizon once lay. There was thus more happening in the world than what was perceived by the king.

The court viewed two types of neo-classical scenery. For tragedy, the *palais à volonte* presented a single, neutral location. Comedies usually happened in neutral, domestic interiors called *chambres à quatre portes*. But as the neo-classical reality vanished in playwrighting and acting, new stage representations appeared. Diderot and others called for more exact depictions of the environment. Following the rediscovery of Herculaneum and the elevation of sentiment, design frequently emphasized "mood," atmosphere, and the interplay of light with shadow. Moonlight became a favorite lighting effect.

In 1748 Diderot declared that "the perfection of a spectacle consists in the imitation of an action, so exact, that the spectator, deceived without interruption, imagines that he is present at the action itself." Diderot proposed that the space on stage be conceived of as a room with its fourth wall behind the audience. Both actor and character should inhabit a specific room. Such a reconsideration would allow the actor to reveal a character's psychology through realistic action and stage composition.

Diderot was the first person to articulate the power of picturization on stage. He defined the phenomenon as "an arrangement of persons on the stage so natural and true that, rendered faithfully by a painter, would please me on canvas." Diderot demanded stage pictures equal

to paintings in emotional evocation. As a result, pantomimic action increased in importance. Stage settings served to compose the position of the actors.

In time the French recognized that stage pictures were ruined by the presence of spectators on the stage. An on-stage audience left little more than twelve square feet of space for playing. After visiting England for three years, Voltaire advocated increasing stage action, encouraging spectacle, and removing the audience from the stage. Finally in 1759, spectators were banished from the stage. The way was open for spectacle to grow more elaborate.

***Costume*** Neo-classical characters dressed in the *habit à la romaine*, a combination of Roman toga, powdered wig, and plumed head dress. In 1727 Lecouvreur played a tragedy costumed in elaborate contemporary court dress. In time the three-cornered hat replaced the plumed helmet as the appropriate headwear for a classical tragedy. Traditional characters, like Molière's Harpagon and Sganarelle, however, retained their familiar costumes.

Although Beaumarchais went so far as to describe in the stage directions the costumes he wished for his characters, actors generally wore what they liked; the wardrobe was their own. In 1753 Madame Favart wore authentic peasant clothes on stage; in 1761 she appeared in Turkish fashion. Voltaire's *L'orpheline de la Chine* (*Orphan of China*) featured what the French considered Chinese-looking costumes. In 1756 Lekain's bloody hands and disheveled hair upset audiences at *Semiramis*.

By the eighteenth century, utilizing local color and ensuring specificity of time and place became more important in costume. Even Molière began to be staged in contemporary clothes.

***Audience*** During the age of the social theatre, the dominant taste shifted from the aristocrats to the middle class. After 1625, in fact, ladies and gentlemen joined the middle and lower classes at the public theatres. Masked ladies, poets, scholars, politicians, and "would-bes" of all types filled the theatres. The

*Voltaire's Irène at the* Comédie Française *in 1778.* (New York Public Library Theatre Collection)

national theatres, however, were more exclusive. Not until the royal births of 1779 and 1781 were the lower classes allowed into the *Comédie Française*. Also, many bourgeois could not afford the price of admission to a state theatre. Consequently, most of the evolution of bourgeois drama occurred in the minor theatres.

***Dramatic Criticism*** The aristocratic and scholarly audience demanded fidelity to the principles of neo-classicism, and Corneille's *Le Cid* (1636) crystalized French advocacy of the ideal. Paris was in an uproar over Corneille's violation of the neo-classical precepts being formulated in literary salons. Cardinal Richelieu asked his seven-year-old Academy to issue a statement. Jean Mairet and Georges de Scudéry (1601–1667) had already noted that the play strained verisimilitude by doing too much within twenty-four hours and by allowing the heroine to marry her father's murderer less than twenty-four hours after the crime. The verdict of 1638 was written by the Academy's leader, Jean Chapelain, who both praised the play for using the neo-classical structures and blamed the play for stretching the neo-classical

structures. *Le Cid* strained probability by following the demand for unity of time.

As nobles worked to preserve the old regime, critics struggled to save the old forms of drama from the rising bourgeoisie's demand for a more truthful drama. François Hedelin Abbé D'Aubignac (1604–1676) upheld the unities but suggested that the most important principle was suspense. Louis-Sebastien Mercier (1740–1814), voicing the sentiments of many French citizens, attacked the unities along the lines suggested by Diderot. Rousseau joined the assault but attacked all theatre in a diatribe unsurpassed since William Prynne.

Rousseau argued that if theatre taught the love of virtue and the hatred of vice, then the theatre could not exist in a society as corrupt as that of the eighteenth century. In fact, Rousseau blamed the theatre for corrupting society. The theatre taught hypocrisy and exhibitionism as prerequisites for success. Even the ancient plays of Greece and Rome were worthless to Rousseau because contemporary individuals could not put themselves in the place of heroes so alien.

Rousseau thought the arousal of emotion in an audience unhealthy: it made people less sensitive to real-life occasions demanding real emotion. Proposing that actors actually feel the emotions they portray, he condemned acting as an art that corrupts the performers. Plays forced actresses to violate their natural modesty as women. And, by close association with women, the men of an acting company developed feminine traits. Rousseau thought people attended the theatre simply to have their prejudices flattered, their passions aroused, and their vices encouraged. For Rousseau, the Revolution should allow only sporting contests, military tournaments, balls, and patriotic civic pageants to satisfy whatever need people had for spectacle.

The French social theatre ended with the Revolution sought by Rousseau. The change in French society and theatre drew inspiration from events in England.

# ENGLAND

***Monarchy and Society*** The period between 1660 and 1700 is called the English Restoration because the monarchy returned after the Puritans' Commonwealth collapsed. Reacting to conservative morality, English culture reacquired permissiveness and libertinism. The theatre housed the fruits of the reaction. But the Restoration faded into the eighteenth century's Enlightenment. Throughout the period an adventurous spirit permeated English life even as reason tried to dominate.

Charles II (reigned 1660–1685) aped the court life and theatrical patronage of Louis XIV that he saw while in exile in France. But his brother James II (reigned 1685–1688) was, like French monarchs, a Catholic. A stubborn and deliberate man, James II considered himself answerable to God alone, and he relied primarily on spiritual rather than political advisors. The birth of his son revived English fears of a Catholic monarchy.

In 1688 the fearful Whigs controlling Parliament invited James's oldest daughter, Mary, a Protestant, and her husband, William III of Holland, to take the crown from James. England's bloodless Glorious Revolution was complete; England's Parliament had substituted the idea of a social contract for the old theory of divine right kingship.

With George I (reigned 1714–1727), the fun-loving, boorish Prince of Hanover Germany, and his successor, George II, court society almost disappeared. George I could not speak English. Social fashion and dramatic taste fell to his English mistresses presiding over court entertainments. More social than his father, George II (reigned 1727–1760) shifted court interest from the theatre to the opera: German Protestants had always preferred music to theatre. English theatres, taking up the challenge, featured musical pantomimes, musical harlequinades, and the new ballad opera. John Gay's (1685–1732) *The Beggar's Opera* (1728) drew crowds.

***Imported Culture*** English Restoration society began with an injection of French culture and theatre. Charles II, who loved everything French, including the theatre, was actually the first English monarch to visit a public theatre. Charles's love for French culture so influenced English tastes that Samuel Johnson later defined "frenchify" as "to infect with the manner of France, to make a coxcomb." Like France, England had two rival societies: aristocrats, who favored the monarchy, and commoners, who missed Cromwell. The age's middle class developed into a third, and controlling, faction.

Society flaunted frivolity wherever Puritanism had insisted upon solemnity. Sporting events returned. Bullbaiting, bearbaiting, dog and cock fights, foot races, fencing, wrestling, football, bowling, and horse racing provided opportunities for fun and, more important, gambling. Continental sports like ice skating and yachting appeared. Cricket caught on with the gentry. Golf gained a foothold as well, after Scotland entered the Empire.

Sexual variety was evident everywhere. Social clubs discreetly advertised their heterosexual or homosexual interests. Prostitution served both homosexual and heterosexual clients. Masochism found stage representation in such plays as *Venice Preserved* and *The Virtuoso*. Sir John Vanbrugh's (1666–1726) play *The Relapse* contained homosexual allusions to King William's feelings toward some of his courtiers. John Cleland (1709–1789) wrote *Fanny Hill, or Memoirs of a Woman of Pleasure*; pornography became a business. Mary Wollstonecraft (1759–1797), the mother-in-law of Percy Bysshe Shelley (1792–1822), wrote *Mary, A Fiction*, one of the first lesbian novels. Henry Fielding's (1707–1754) novel, *The Female Husband*, likewise focused attention on lesbian love. Fashionable female transvestism let Charlotte Clarke, the daughter of playwright Colley Cibber (1671-1757), act out the role of Lord Foppington in her father's play *The Careless Husband*. Clarke lived as a man with a young widow.

Actresses also entered the English stage. ''Breeches parts'' replaced female impersonation among actors. Between 1660 and 1700 one-quarter of the plays required women to dress as men to show off leg and thigh flesh. Dandyism and foppery came back into style as dress and behavior marked class membership. Tobias Smollet's (1721–1771) Lord Struwell in the novel *Roderick Random* (1748) observed that sodomy was so extensive that it threatened to become a ''more fashionable device than simple fornication.''

As aristocrats tried to get into business, businessmen bought titles, and the theatre became the place to show off one's success. The English capitalist economy eclipsed the French mercantile system. By mid-eighteenth century, the merchant middle class was demanding and buying books and periodicals.

Women also proposed the education of women. Mary Wollstonecraft wrote *A Vindication of the Rights of Woman* (1792), arguing for a social contract for middle-class women. The Anabaptist movement produced nonconforming women who participated in every aspect of English life. Quaker women even preached.

As more people read and traveled, opposition to slavery grew, as it had in France. Playwright Aphra Behn's (1640–1689) 1688 novelette, *Oroonoko*, told the story of the leader of a slave revolt in Surinam. Translated and adapted for the stage, Behn's story quickly became an international hit of the eighteenth century. The Negro hero created the prototype for literature's noble, sexy slave. Behn's novelette also contained the first call for a slave revolt in modern literature. For almost 100 years the stage version by Thomas Southerne played at the Drury Lane theatre. Even the great actor David Garrick (1717–1779) played the rebel leader.

***Bourgeois Aesthetics*** Throughout the West sentimentality stood as the bourgeois value most antithetical to the aristocratic qualities of the courtier. Nonetheless, art, music, and theatre celebrated sentiment as the middle class's influence proliferated. The English garden, a combination of perfect nature and complete artifice, stood as the perfect symbol of the tense times. The garden, rebelling against neo-classicism's insistence on straight lines, regularity, and geometry, declared a faith in picturesque nature.

Composer George Frederick Handel (1685–1759)—born Georg Friederich Händel—followed his Hanoverian patron to England. The son of a barber-surgeon and a graduate of the University of Halle, Handel wrote the opera *Rinaldo* for 1711 London. He also wrote forty-six other operas and thirty-eight oratorios. Because he exploited all aspects of his musical skills and his bourgeois audience's sensibility, and because he let money dictate his artistic choices, Handel won great fame and wealth.

English literature of the age showed the transformation of style from aristocratic to bourgeois. The Restoration began with literature written for patrons and ended with lit-

*Handel's opera* Acis and Galatea *in 1749.*    (Lilly Library)

erature written for the marketplace. John Dryden (1631–1700) worked to give the neo-classical ideal a home in England. Poet, playwright, and critic, Dryden was a Cambridge-educated poet laureate of England whose antipathy toward democracy derived from his allegiance to the monarchy's stabilizing influence on society. But by 1701 the forces of democracy had generated the first daily newspaper in London. Middle-class wealth began to support periodicals and books.

Newspapers and periodicals actually bridged the gap between the scholars and the general bourgeois readers. Gradually, through Richard Steele's (1672–1729) *The Tatler* (1709) and Steele's and Joseph Addison's (1672–1719) *The Spectator* (1711), the new audience grew accustomed to serious literature. Both journalists tried their hands at playwrighting. Cosmopolitanism thus developed as a two-way traffic of magazines, books, and plays began between England and France.

The comparative freedom of the English press encouraged the novel to develop first in England. Samuel Richardson (1689–1761), a printer's apprentice, made the middle class the subject of *Pamela* (1740), the first novel of sentiment. *Pamela* shows an interest in the spiritual life of the main character, little attention to plot, and an emphasis on the analysis of emotions and conscience. Richardson, describing his heroine's flow of passions and feelings, acts as her spiritual counselor. *Pamela* established

the wish-fulfillment theme: a poor working girl marries her boss or master in reward for all her virtuous actions. The novel, and Richardson's *Clarissa* (1747), stimulated numerous parodies and piracies; it also influenced the thinking of France's Rousseau and Germany's Goethe.

***Dramatic Texts*** England repeated France's shift away from neo-classical tragedy and comedy toward bourgeois drama and sentimental comedy. English neo-classical tragedy depended upon Spanish and French models for plots of love and honor. English iambic pentameter fell into heroic couplets to reproduce the French Alexandrine.

Dryden ranked as the foremost serious playwright at the beginning of the age. *The Conquest of Granada* (1670), ten acts of war, related three love stories, but focused on the heroics of Almanzor and his love, Almahide. *All for Love* (1677) condensed Shakespeare's story of Antony and Cleopatra to a neo-classical structure occupying but twenty-four hours and a single location. In his *Essay on Dramatic Poetry* (1666) Dryden raised the issue of the relationship between verse and verisimilitude. Later in the eighteenth century France's Houdar de la Motte attacked the use of verse in tragedy as not verisimilar. But Dryden accepted poetry as a necessary convention of dramatic art. He stressed the imitative, conventional aspects of a play's relationship to reality. As the age continued, however, his position lost ground.

Other neo-classical authors of serious drama included Dr. Samuel Johnson, who wrote *Irene* (1749). Undersecretary of state and journalist Joseph Addison wrote one of England's best neo-classical tragedies, *Cato* (1713). But, a more important dramatic development inaugurated during the Restoration was the practice of adapting Shakespeare to the taste of the times.

***Shakespeare Improved*** Unaltered, Shakespeare was too painful, too outrageous, too worrisome. The Bard needed some enlightened help to accommodate the Restoration's sentimental philosophy: virtuous characters had to triumph. As a result, the reputed illegitimate son of Shakespeare, William Davenant (1606–1668), rewrote *The Tempest* to give Miranda a sister, Dorinda, and Prospero a protégé, Hippolito. Thomas Otway (1652–1685) remodeled *Romeo and Juliet* so that the heroine could awaken before Romeo took poison. Nahum Tate (1652–1715) corrected *King Lear* by eliminating the Fool, marrying Cordelia to Edgar, and sparing the lives of Lear and Glouchester. Thomas D'Urfey (1653–1723) added an attempted rape to *Cymbeline*. The actor-manager Thomas Betterton (c. 1635–1710) renamed *A Midsummer Night's Dream, The Faerie Queen*, and added music by Henry Purcell (c. 1659–1695). Even Corneille's and Molière's works appeared in England only after being "corrected."

***Restoration Comedy of Manners*** Restoration comedy began inasupiciously with the plays of Cambridge-educated Thomas Shadwell (1642–1692). When Shadwell replaced Catholic Dryden as poet laureate a debate began over the merits of comedies written in the style of Ben Jonson. Shadwell thought his play, *The Sullen Lovers* (1668), an adaptation of a Molière play, to be in the spirit of a Jonsonian "humorous" comedy. But Dryden, who even penned a few mannered comedies—such as *Marriage à la Mode* (1672)—preferred Shadwell's "comedy of manners" to the comedy of humors.

A comedy of manners sashayed the fashions and behavior of the jaunty men and women of aristocratic London. Handsome, beautiful, witty, well-dressed, and sexy, the eighteenth-century versions of *commedia dell'arte inamorati* and *inamoratae* wished to impress each other with their wealth, wit, dress, and language. Each play juxtaposes the social appearance of purity and innocence with the personal truth of impropriety and promiscuity; apparent intelligence, with real ignorance; and seeming wealth, with actual poverty. City life is presented as fashionable; country life, as crude. Urban wit always outsmarts rural naivety. City people are civil, country people are naturally rude. City people wrote the plays to celebrate the image they wished to create for their social circles.

Sir George Etherege (c. 1634–1691) attended Cambridge and lived in France as a young man. Such plays as his *The Man of Mode* (1676) represent the full embodiment of the social comedy of manners. Emphasizing the man-about-town, Etherege's comedy introduces Sir Foppling Flutter, the man of mode, recently returned from France and full of the very latest in fashion. Sir Foppling walks into the amorous adventures of Dorimant and Harriet. The lovers marry only when Dorimant agrees to leave his beloved city to be with Harriet in her dull countryside.

William Wycherley (c. 1640–1715) was the son of a steward. After being educated at Oxford, Wycherley lived in France as the protégé of one of Charles II's mistresses. Restoration comedy of manners peaked with his plays. *The Country Wife* (1675) is based on a typical Molière scenario. To conceal his affairs with the city's ladies, Horner pretends he has been castrated. When he meets an innocent country wife in the city for the first time, Horner, proceeding to educate the girl, infuriates her jealous husband, Mr. Pinchwife. *The Plain Dealer* (1676) also shows a Molière influence. Manly, the misanthropic hero, is obsessed with sexual infidelity. His only consolation is the honesty and faith of his friend and mistress. When the two marry behind his back, Manly's insane reaction is checked only when his valet reveals himself to be a woman, Fidelia, madly in love with him.

Aphra Behn (c. 1649–1689), who was raised in the West Indies and who became an English spy in the Netherlands, was the first English woman to support herself writing. Behn's *The Rover* (1677) and *The City Heiress* (1682) were very topical comedies of intrigue.

As sentiment crept into the drama the comedy of manners came to be labeled ''laughing'' comedy. Richard Brinsley Sheridan (1751–1816) revived the fading comedy of manners but with enough fashionable sentiment to satisfy his audience's tastes. For example, in his first play, *The Rivals* (1775), Lydia Languish is made foolish by reading too many sentimental novels. Eventually she comes to her senses and gets her man. Honest Charles Surface is contrasted with his hypocritical brother, Joseph, in *The School for Scandal* (1777). Both brothers seek the hand of the ward of Sir Peter Teazle: one for her love, the other for her money. The brothers' uncle arrives to save Charles and unmask Joseph. *The Critic* (1779)

satirizes the theatrical practices of Sheridan's day.

Sheridan was part owner of the Drury Lane theatre. When the theatre burned in 1809 Sheridan turned to alcohol. He died a pauper.

Oliver Goldsmith (1730–1774) studied medicine, but traveled across Europe playing his flute and begging for money. When he returned to London, he opened a medical office, but no patients came. He could not even get a job as an orderly. He turned instead to the theatre; he wrote a play, *The Good-Natured Man* (1768). *She Stoops to Conquer* (1773), Goldsmith claimed, was based on a mistake he had once made. The comic complications of *She Stoops to Conquer* begin as young Marlowe enters the country estate of Hardcastle thinking it an inn rather than the home of his fiancée. In his work Goldsmith employed humor rather than strictly verbal wit. For him sentimental comedy was sterile.

William Congreve (1670–1729), son of an army officer, wrote comedy that rewarded the witty, duped the dull, punished the sentimental, and prized the objectively detached. In *The*

The School for Scandal *at the Drury Lane Theatre in 1778.*   (New York Public Library Theatre Collection)

*Old Bachelor* (1693) Heartwell falls in love with his friend's former mistress. Complications arise as the character of Maskwell confounds everyone in society by always telling the truth. In the end a trick saves Heartwell from his fate. In *Love for Love* (1695) Valentine is so profligate that he must sign over his inheritance to his unaffected brother Ben, a sailor. To get out of the contract and to win Angelica, Valentine feigns insanity by speaking as Truth. Valentine and Angelica are recast as Mirabell and Millamant in *The Way of the World* (1700). The lovers love freedom as much as they love each other. They eventually marry despite the machinations of Millamant's jealous aunt, Lady Wishfort. When *The Way of the World* met with a cool reception, Congreve retired from the theatre. He became Commissioner of Wines in 1705.

**Sentimental Drama**   Sentiment increased in comedies as more merchants attended the theatres. Richard Steele (1672–1729) catered to the bourgeois sensibility with *The Conscious Lovers* (1722), a play that marks the turn from Restoration bawdy comedy to comedy of sentiment. The purpose of sentimental comedy was neither laughter nor ridicule, but the arousal of "a pleasure too exquisite" for laughter. Emotional appeals returned "bad" characters to their natural states of "goodness." Nasty characters reformed in the last act in such plays by Colley Cibber (1671–1757) as *Love's Last Shift* (1696). Comedy came to mean, as Dr. Johnson defined it, a "dramatick representation of the lighter faults of mankind," and farce, "a dramatick representation written without regularity, and stuffed with wild and licentious conceits."

Verbal wit disappeared in sentimental comedy. Gallant men and women lost their intellects but kept their fashionable clothes. Low-class characters were banished from the plots; most heroes and heroines, as a result, came from middle or upper classes.

Tragedy also fell to sentimentality. The major play of the sentimental movement issued from the pen of George Lillo (1693–1739), an apprentice jeweller. Lillo's *The London Mer-chant, or The History of George Barnwell* (1731) became the best-known play throughout the world. The audience to the first performance had brought with them copies of the old ballad on which the play was based, because they had wanted to mock the play with the song. But by the end of the drama the audience was in tears. The hero, a London apprentice who gets involved with a prostitute and eventually murders his favorite uncle, ultimately repents. Lillo followed this success with *Fatal Curiosity* (1736), an attempt to do for peasants what *The London Merchant* did for apprentices.

New forms of drama appeared as well. John Gay (1685–1732), a silk merchant's apprentice, turned his attention to opera but alternated song and dialogue to create ballad opera, an English opera without recitative. In *The Beggar's Opera* (1728) and the sequel, *Polly*, Gay makes the lives of Macheath, the robber, and his several wives in the crime world a satirical metaphor for London's political scene. His plays encouraged novelist Henry Fielding (1707–1754) to also try his hand at satire. One of Fielding's periodic theatrical attacks on Prime Minister Robert Walpole (1676–1745) occurred at the Haymarket Theatre in *The Historical Register for the Year 1736* (1736). Walpole attended this performance; he even attacked an actor slurring him. The next year Walpole read the play *The Golden Rump* to the House of Commons to show Parliament the kind of attacks and obscenities to which he was subject. In response, Parliament passed the Licensing Act of 1737 to limit such plays. Fielding, however, claimed that Walpole wrote *The Golden Rump* himself to help get the Act passed.

**The Licensing Act of 1737**   The Licensing Act resulted, in part, from Walpole's dislike of the political satires attacking his Prime Ministership. The Act thus forbade any plays "for gain, hire, or reward" not licensed by the Lord Chamberlain. In addition, the Act authorized playing only in theatres within the City of Westminster, which meant that companies could perform legally only at Drury Lane and Covent Garden.

Managers sought to circumvent the Licensing Act by presenting plays not "for gain, hire, or reward." Free plays thus accompanied the purchase of a pint of ale or filled the intermissions between acts of rope dancing and tumbling. Tickets to free plays also bought dishes of chocolate or entrance to an exhibition of painting at which free plays were performed.

Other gimmicks were used as well. Henry Giffaro, for example, opened Goodman's Fields Theatre and charged admission to concerts at which free plays were performed. The great actor David Garrick debuted there as Richard III in 1741. But many theatres also closed. The end of the New Wells Theatre in 1752, in fact, forced William Hallam to send a troupe of players to America for the first time.

In 1752 new legislation required all places of entertainment within twenty miles of London to obtain licenses from local magistrates. The production of "regular drama" was thereby restricted, but Parliament did authorize a few regional theatres as *théâtre royales*. In 1766, however, Samuel Foote (1720–1777) won an exception to the monopoly as compensation for an injury caused by a prank played by the young Duke of York. Foote's license allowed him to produce plays at the Haymarket Theatre during summer months, when the two licensed theatres were closed. In 1777 Foote sold his license to George Coleman. But in 1788 Parliament extended the Act's power to require the licensing of regular drama outside the twenty mile radius.

***Company Rivalry*** Under the Commonwealth, actors sold their wardrobes, and the Globe was torn down. A 1649 Act actually made acting an illegal activity. Yet surreptitious, underground performances continued. And as news of the impending Restoration spread, actors and managers hustled to secure licenses, theatres, and monopolies.

The old Master of Revels, Sir Henry Hebert, ignored the fledgling activities at the Red Bull and Salisbury Court theatres. Meanwhile Charles II issued a monopoly to William Davenant and Thomas Killigrew (1612–1683), who quickly suppressed all other theatrical activity.

Davenant and Killigrew's monopoly lasted until 1843 but not without challenge by George Jolly (1640–1673), the manager of The English Comedians touring Germany. Jolly successfully challenged the monopoly and won a license from the king. But Davenant and Killigrew tricked Jolly out of his license and tried to placate him by naming him their acting teacher.

Killigrew and Davenant eventually split into two companies: Killigrew took the King's Company to Drury Lane and Davenant, the Duke's Company, led by a young actor named Thomas Betterton (c. 1635–1710), to Lincoln's Inn Fields. But actors' dissention and financial troubles broke apart Killigrew's King's Company after Davenant's death in 1682. Killigrew's actors then merged with the Duke's Company operated by Betterton. Christopher Rich, an unscrupulous, unpleasant lawyer with no theatrical experience, won financial control of the company. In 1695 actors led by Betterton broke away from Rich, won a license from William III, and opened Her Majesty's Theatre in Haymarket. In 1707 the Crown reunited the companies under Rich's tyranny. The new company played at Lincoln Fields Theatre until the new Drury Lane reopened in 1710.

In the 1720s managers and actors questioned the legitimacy of Charles II's patents. Because the patents had never been ratified by Parliament, individuals defied them. In 1720 John Potter opened the Haymarket Theatre. And in time four theatres played in London. The Licensing Act of 1737, discussed previously, sought to clarify the situation.

***Theatre Management*** The sharing plan of theatre organization ended after 1690 because actors considered receiving a fixed salary safer than receiving a percentage of the gate. Thomas Betterton tried to revive the practice between 1697 and 1707, but failed. Theatre came to be considered an investment opportunity by bourgeois financial speculators. Individuals with no theatre experience or interest invested in companies by providing mortgage money to company managers. It was thus, in fact, that Christopher Rich assumed control over a company in 1693 (see the preceding section). Rich's son, John, ran the theatre and, using profits from Gay's *The Beggar's Opera*, built the Covent Garden Theatre, which opened in 1732 with a company headed by actor James Quin. In 1767 George Coleman ran Covent Garden; Thomas Harris took control in 1774.

Between 1710 and 1733 Drury Lane operated under the leadership of three actors: Colley Cibber, Robert Wilks, and Thomas Doggett. Actor Barton Booth replaced Doggett in 1713. In 1746 David Garrick and John Lacy managed the Drury Lane building until Garrick retired. In 1776 playwright Richard Brinsley Sheridan took over until 1788, when John Philip Kemble managed the theatre.

Prosperity created large companies—by 1800 any one company might employ eighty actors—and increased emphasis on spectacle. Ticket sales provided the primary source of income. To cover growing expenses either ticket prices were increased or theatres were remodeled to accommodate larger audiences. Promotional gimmicks, like charging half-price after the third act, also increased the gross. All these changes affected the playing style of the actors.

***Actors and Actresses***   Women entered the English stage to satisfy court tastes developed in European theatres, which brandished female players. So the patent given to Thomas Killigrew specified that women must act to

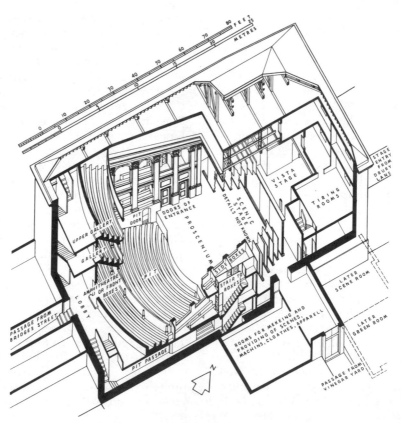

*The Drury Lane Theatre, 1674.*   (Leacroft, p. 95)

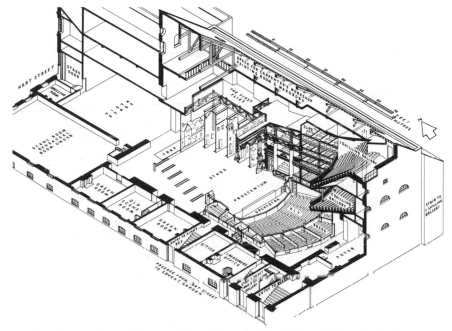

*The Covent Garden Theatre, 1824.*   (Reprinted from Richard Leacroft, *The Development of the English Playhouse*, p. 108. Copyright © 1973 by Richard Leacroft. Used by permission of the publisher, Cornell University Press)

avoid the scandal of female impersonation. But even without this caveat, female impersonation would have been difficult to revive. The dissolution of the companies had broken the training process of young boys. Nonetheless, to lessen the social stigma of appearing on the stage for the first time, actresses took the title "Mrs." even though some single players earned money prostituting themselves. Men continued to act witches and comic old women.

With a decrease in the number of theatres, the number of opportunities for young actors to learn the art of acting also decreased. Consequently, acting schools appeared under the aegis of Davenant and Killigrew, Charles Macklin, and Thomas Sheridan. Acting was taught and practiced along "lines of business"—that is, ranges of character types played regardless of age. Actors owned and guarded their lines of business, and companies cast according to lines of business. Minor actors were hired for a season, leading actors for longer

periods. Benefit performances supplemented a group's or an individual's salary.

Each play was staged by the company's leading actor or actor-manager. If a new play, the first rehearsals could be conducted by the playwright. Fines penalized lateness, memory lapses, and role refusals. A prompter did many of the jobs of the modern-day stage manager, obtained licenses for plays, copied script "sides," collected fines, called rehearsals, cued performances, and made sure the actors entered at the right times from the right places with the right properties.

Actors, playing at the front of the stage, stood full front. The speaking actor always moved to the dominant stage position. Interpretation and pantomimic business were learned along with a role. Acting also developed toward "realism" during this age. Indeed, innovation was rare and sensation-making. Charles Macklin's 1741 noncomic Shylock, for example caused an uproar. Like kabuki actors, eighteenth-century players rushed toward climactic or important moments called "points" to win applause.

The work of several individuals during this period is particularly notable. Thomas Betterton, a squat, clumsy, wild Irishman, was the greatest figure of the Restoration stage. His enormous head and feet, his pocked face, beady eyes, and stooped shoulders never interfered with his success in comedy or tragedy, especially as Hamlet or Sir Toby Belch. Betterton gave the first performance of Congreve's *Love for Love*, adapted Shakespeare to his audience's tastes, and brought to the English stage practices he had studied in France. Nell Gwynn (1650–1687), a whorehouse waitress, decided to become an actress at age 14 after selling oranges at the theatre. She first appeared at age 15 in John Dryden's *Indian Emperor*. Not a good actress, however, she favored roles in men's clothing. She so invigorated the men in the audience that Charles II made her his mistress. Elizabeth Barry (1658–1713), the first great English actress, was fired three times for lack of talent before the Earl of Rochester coached her. She then won fame in 119 different roles. Cruel, vindictive, calculating, and selfish, Barry delighted in treating her lovers badly, especially the playwright Otway. But Barry was nonetheless the first actor to have a monarch demand a benefit performance on her behalf. The mistress of playwright Sir George Etherege, she died from rabies contracted from her lap dog.

Anne Bracegirdle (c. 1663–1748), the beauty of the Restoration stage, used the insignia "Celebrated Virgin" while living as Congreve's mistress. She began acting at age 6 and played opposite Thomas Betterton. Her most famous role was Millamant in her lover's *The Way of the World*. Bracegirdle retired from the stage in the shadow of Anne Oldfield's prominence. Voltaire said Oldfield (1683–1730) was the only English actress whose speech he could follow. Oldfield's performances as Mrs. Sullen in George Farquhar's comedy, *The Beaux Stratagem*, and as the heroine in Nicholas Rowe's drama, *Jane Shore*, created for her a stature unsurpassed for her time. She was the first actress honored with burial in Westminster Abbey.

The man whose plays brought sentiment to the stage won the nickname "Hatchet Face" when his thin body appeared on the stage. The son of a Danish sculptor, Colley Cibber (1671–1757) disobeyed his parents and became an excellent comic actor by age 19. Cibber excelled as fops and as Shakespeare's Justice Shallow. But in tragedy Cibber was usually hissed off the stage. Cibber was a rude, arrogant, snobbish social climber; his autobiography is even entitled *An Apology* (1740). Another man who disobeyed his father to run off to the theatre, Barton Booth (1681–1733), "Booth with the Silver Tongue," succeeded Betterton as England's leading actor. As Joseph Addison's *Cato* Booth displayed the unique ability of being seen and heard at the same time. James Quin (1693–1766) was the last great actor to dominate the

*Macklin as Macbeth.* (Lilly Library)

stage with Thomas Betterton's declamatory style. Best as a warm and intelligent Falstaff, Quin quit the theatre after being hissed off the stage as Richard III.

Other actors had their moments center stage as well. Spranger Barry (1719–1777), a former silversmith, "handsome as a god," exploited his distinguished, noble appearance and beautiful voice as the greatest romantic lover of the Restoration period. His Romeo and Othello were particularly appealing. But gout ended his career. Kitty Clive (1711–1785), delighting audiences in low comedy, parodied Italian opera. And Frances Abbington (1737–1815), who was born in the slums, nonetheless set the standard for stage ladies of quality. Off stage Abbington supplemented her income as a prostitute who recited Shakespeare. Her Beatrice won widespread fame.

### David Garrick

The greatness of David Garrick (1717–1779), the Restoration's supreme actor, was foreshadowed by that of the longest-lived English actor, Charles Macklin (1699–1797). Dark and big-jawed, Macklin developed a naturalistic technique in reaction to the reigning oratorical style. He spoke "plainly and without ornament" as both comic Shylock and Macbeth, dressed for the first time as a Scotsman. Indeed, the rage for authentic costume grew with Garrick.

Considered the greatest English-speaking actor, David Garrick gave time and thought to the process of acting. The son of an army captain and the grandson of a French Protestant, Garrick first acted under the name of Lyddal. On October 19, 1741, when he debuted at the unfashionable Goodman's Fields Theatre as Richard III, Garrick became a spectacular *homme du monde*. "Garrick fever" swept Ireland and England.

The actor, his mistress Peg Woffington, and a company of England's best actors played a wide variety of plays. Speaking "naturally," without flourish, Garrick could display a wide variety of feelings. He also possessed a phenomenal ability to transform himself into a character. But critics noticed a characteristic "hesitating stammer" and a habit of pro-

nouncing the short vowel "i" as "u." Garrick also used pauses to great effect, especially when playing Shylock for sympathy. A vain miser, too sensitive to the press, Garrick wrote verse, plays, and an adaptation of *Romeo and Juliet*. His most famous roles included Lear, Abel Dugger in Jonson's *The Alchemist*, and Benedict. His least successful portrayal was as Othello.

Peg Woffington (1714–1760), England's most beautiful and least vain actress, lived in a *ménage à trois* with Garrick and Macklin. The daughter of a bricklayer, Woffington, lovely in "breeches parts," won reknown for Portia and her versions of William Congreve's heroines. She retired from the stage when her tongue became paralyzed while she was playing Rosalind.

*Theatre Architecture* During the Restoration, the size of England's theatre buildings increased to house the growing bourgeois audience. The stage itself, which combined Elizabethan public theatre architecture with Renaissance court entertainment, was placed equally in front of and behind the proscenium arch. The arch framed a deep stage, which thrust beyond the arch into the auditorium. The thrust apron, representing a holdover of the platform stage, kept the actors close to the audience. Behind the actors stage pictures changed within the proscenium arch. Two doors on each side of the thrust apron led through the proscenium. Window or door frames could be placed over the proscenium doors. In this way, the traditional facade of the public theatre split to form the two sides of the proscenium arch.

During the eighteenth century the thrust apron gradually receded into the proscenium archway. Actors, forced up stage, inhabited the scenery in order to allow new rows of seats to replace the apron thrust. The proscenium doors and windows became spectator boxes. The audience grew larger, and the actors retreated behind the proscenium arch.

Theatres characteristically featured the box, pit, and gallery arrangement of class seating. Two or three galleries, the lowest of which held

*David Garrick as Richard III.* (Lilly Library)

boxes, surrounded benches in the raked pit. During the Restoration, a typical theatre held fewer than 700 spectators. As the age progressed, the auditorium's seating capacity increased to about 3000 spectators, and the size of the apron thrust decreased. A raked stage behind the proscenium arch contained grooves for scenery. In addition, as the audience increased so did the size of the stage house behind the arch. A heightened demand for spectacle increased the need for storage space, dressing rooms, and construction areas.

As early as 1656 William Davenant began to restage plays in his home, Rutland House. Davenant's extravaganza, *The Siege of Rhodes*, designed by student John Webb (1611–1672), son-in-law of Inigo Jones, was presented at Davenant's home and later at the Cockpit. It was the first play to use Italianate scenery in an English public theatre. In 1661 Davenant converted Lisle's Tennis Court into a theatre variously known as the Duke's House, after the king's brother, and Lincoln's Inn Fields Theatre. Lincoln's Inn, the first English public theatre with a proscenium arch behind an apron thrust to use Italianate scenery, opened

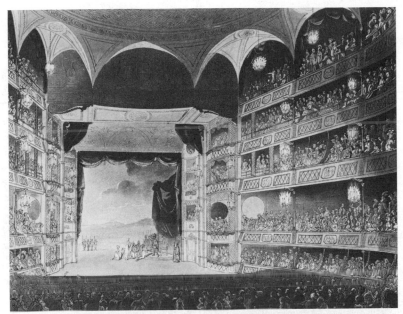

*The interior of the Drury Lane Theatre, 1808.*    (The New York Public Library; Astor, Lenox, and Tilden Foundation)

with a revival of *The Siege of Rhodes*. In 1671 the building reverted to a tennis court when Davenant opened Dorset Garden. Lincoln's Fields reopened in 1685 as a theatre, but closed shortly thereafter. John Rich reopened the building in 1714 but moved his company to Covent Garden nineteen years later.

On May 7, 1663, the Drury Lane theatre, built by Thomas Killigrew, opened as a *théâtre royale* with a play by John Fletcher. The theatre burned in 1672. The new Drury Lane, which measured 58 by 140 feet, was built by Christopher Wren. It offered entertainments only sporadically after 1676. In addition, riot and fire continued to make Drury Lane's history a spotty one. Another theatre by Wren, Dorset Garden Theatre, the Second Duke's House, won fame for opera with William Davenant's musical *Macbeth* (1673) and Shadwell's *Tempest* (1674). Dorset Garden, measuring 57 by 140 feet, operated as the only London theatre from 1672 to 1674. In 1689 the theatre, renamed the Queen's Theatre to honor Mary II, featured variety entertainments.

In 1732 John Rich built his theatre royal on the site of a former convent garden. The theatre, called Covent Garden Theatre, opened with a revival of Congreve's *The Way of the World*. Rebuilt in 1784 and again in 1792, the theatre finally fell to an 1808 fire that also destroyed George Frederick Handel's organ and opera manuscripts.

While John Rich ran his theatre, Henry Fielding's satires drew audiences to the Haymarket Theatre. Built by a carpenter in 1720 to house a visiting French company, the Haymarket remained closed each year until Samuel Foote took control of the theatre for summer seasons.

*Scenery*    Elaborate systems of wings, borders, grooves, shutters, and drops shifted scenery at the signal of a whistle. As always, audiences enjoyed seeing the scenes change. When shifts could not be made aesthetically, *entre-actes* performed before an ''act drop.'' Stock scenery presented the neo-classical essence of a place. So standard were the scenes,

*The interior of the Covent Garden Theatre in 1794.* (Lilly Library)

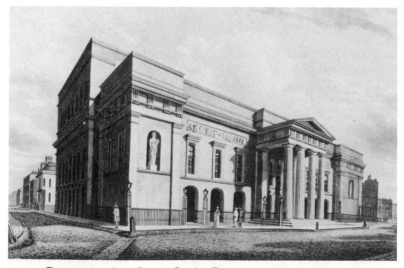

*The exterior of the Covent Garden Theatre in 1809.* (Lilly Library)

The interior of the Little Theatre, Haymarket.    (New York Public Library Theatre Collection)

in fact, that new theatres opened with brand new stocks of settings: temple, tomb, city wall, palace exterior, palace interior, street, chamber, prison, garden, and rural landscape. Ticket prices increased to pay for the new scenery.

In 1765 David Garrick returned from Europe with the idea of specially designed settings for particular plays. To accomplish this feat, however, scene painters were needed. As early as 1749 John Rich had imported Jean Nicholas Servandony (1695–1766) from the Paris opera. But the most important scene painter, Phillipe Jacques De Loutherbourg (1740–1812), worked for ten years at Drury Lane with David Garrick.

De Loutherbourg gave up religious studies to bring new innovation to stage design. He installed border lights along the proscenium for illumination, thereby forcing the actors seeking visibility to remain up stage of the proscenium arch. He also replaced wings with scenic units to break up the perspective. His guiding hand, overseeing all visual elements, brought a new unity to the stage picture.

De Loutherbourg furthered the Restoration's interest in reproducing actuality on stage. He staged travelogues featuring geographical accuracy and romantic picturesqueness. He used light to create illusions of fire, volcanoes, the sun, moonlight, clouds, thunder, gunshots, wind, waves, hail, and rain. He opened the Eidophusikon, a six by eight foot miniature stage and theatre built to perfect his lighting techniques. The invention of the Argand or "patent" lamp in 1785 facilitated these attempts. This lamp had a cylindrical wick and glass chimney, which let operators regulate the blend of oil and oxygen to produce a brighter and more constant illumination. In addition, colored glass chimneys tinted the light.

Costume continued to rest on the whim and wealth of individual actors. But realism began to creep in during the middle of the eighteenth century. Players appeared in contemporary clothing, and expensive garments displayed the ideal dress. Black velvet somehow became associated with tragedy. Shylock appeared in gabardine gown and red hat. David Garrick even used Elizabethan costumes for some productions of Shakespeare.

***The Court Audience Challenged***   The Restoration period began with Charles II's considering the theatre his private property, and ended with virtuous merchants' demanding representation on the stage. Charles II went to the theatre almost every day with his mistresses and courtiers. Baccarat was often played in the court boxes. But as the bourgeoisie increased in power, conservative values appeared more frequently on stage and in the boxes. Audiences enjoyed seeing the novelty of reality and history reproduced on stage.

As the demand for spectacle grew, the audience on stage posed a problem: Peg Woffington, whom we discussed previously, often played Cordelia with an admirer's hand circling her waist. And Mrs. Cibber had to die as Juliet surrounded by sobbing fans. Finally, in 1762, David Garrick banished benches from alongside and behind the proscenium arch.

The demand for virtue began with Jeremy Collier (1656–1726), who objected to the way the theatre flaunted the demise of Puritan control of English life and manners. His *Short View of the Immorality and Profaneness of the English Stage* (1698) was so powerful that John Dryden apologized and William Congreve gave up the theatre. Collier objected to the portrayals of sin-

ners as heroes, the use of obscene language, the ridicule of the clergy, and the profane use of the Bible. He saw sin made appealing.

The Restoration court audience wanted to see itself behaving like the French. To this audience, life was a ribald fashion show moving from salon to salon, and gossip was the chief entertainment. The theatre was the place to see gossip glorified on stage and to hear the latest gossip passed in auditorium galleries. Romantic affairs evolved on both sides of the proscenium arch. Spectators arrived at the theatre to see themselves portrayed on stage as they thought they were—witty, unsentimental, carefree—and to be seen by friends in the audience seated on or near the stage. Plays of four hours length afforded intermissions for social intercourse of all kinds.

As the aristocracy lost economic and political clout to the middle class, however, the theatre, run to profit investors, wooed the new power brokers. Plays moralized to win conservative merchants' approval and attendance. Sentimental comedy replaced licentious Restoration comedy as England's social values shifted. The middle class enjoyed morality, sentiment, and pathos. Crying and sighing replaced laughing and lechery as the chief audience responses. The audience, crying with pity for the heroine, smiled as the sinner converted, the heroine escaped, and virtue triumphed. The theatre refashioned itself to Collier's demands: moral instruction became the theatre's primary aim.

## AMERICA

***A Second Chance***   Although the Spanish and the French brought the first European theatrical productions to the New World, the English brought the culture that eventually dominated North America. Culture was carried by those English individuals looking for a second chance and a better lot. Consequently, they built in America the society unavailable to them at home. Puritans escaping godlessness, Cavaliers hoping to place themselves atop a new social hierarchy, and second-rate actors

dreaming of finally making a living brought their dreams and biases to the New World.

The theatre faced considerable difficulties. The harshness and severity of eking out a basic living left settlers no leisure time to attend the theatre. Life meant work. To stop working for whatever reason jeopardized everyone's lives. Yet even when the struggle abated, the theatre faced its greatest hurdle.

***Theatre Opposition***   Perhaps the greatest

obstacle facing the theatre in America was the attitude brought from England. Puritans and Quakers associated the theatre with monarchical forms of religion and government. Puritans had arisen in England to drive sin out of their country, and "symbolism," associated with both the pope and the theatre, out of their Anglican Church. In addition, the theatre had the reputation of being associated with loose living. The Puritans came from England to escape the licentiousness and obscenity that they saw on stage. America was God's second chance for good people to create a sin-free society: theatre was the enemy.

Theatre also meant sex, and in America sexual prohibitions surpassed those in Europe. Religious groups settled in America to escape fornicators and adulterers. People shook their heads about sexual pleasure even in marriage. In New England sodomy, bestiality, and adultery had death penalties attached to them. Rape was a lesser offense because the Bible did not specifically forbid it. Nevertheless, a short age of women increased prostitution. Casual sex with Indians and imported Negroes kept prostitution from booming, however; laws prohibited marriage to Indians and Negroes but not "fornication" with them.

The New York Dutch burghers' thriftiness, and the Pennsylvania Presbyterians' piety, combined with Puritan and Quaker hostility to present a united opposition to theatre in the northern colonies. Considering actors "inlets of vice," William Penn asked, in *No Cross, No Crown*: "How many plays did Jesus Christ and his apostles recreate themselves at? What poets, romances, comedies, and the like did the saints make use to pass their time withal?" The same number would be allowed in his new community.

Opposition to the theatre united many different religions, all of which were bent on saving souls. Cotton Mather and Jonathan Edwards, colonial heroes and preachers, found God's providence behind everything and fought to preserve the religious life. As Mather wrote in his *Magnalia Christi Americana*:

It is a thing very notorious unto us, that idleness, drunkenness, uncleanness, cheating, lying, profane swearing, and, above all, the profanation of the Lord's day, gains ground upon us. Let all that have any *power* in their hand, unto the utmost of their power endeavor to keep under those enormities.[2]

***Cavalier Culture*** Had transportation and communication been better, Reverend Mather could have found that south of him very little was being done to keep under the "enormities." In fact, southern colonists were encouraging the very things the northerners were trying to stamp out. Southerners viewed entertainment liberally, as a necessary part of life. Still clinging to the Anglican and aristocratic life, southern colonists were willing to pay for horse racing, dress balls, musicals, and theatre. Just as northern colonies imported hostility toward the arts, the southern colonies—Maryland, Virginia, and the Carolinas—imported hospitality.

Nevertheless, both northern and southern colonies evolved hierarchical social structures appropriate to the mannered life of a social theatre. And both societies ended with the rise of democratic and romantic ideals. Historian Loren Baritz points out in *City on a Hill* that whereas northerners came looking for a society distinct from the corrupt one they left in Europe, southerners wanted to recreate the social life that had eluded them.

As the South held onto its rigid social hierarchy of chivalry, dueling, mansions, magnolias, and college honor codes, the North moved to a social system based less on deism than on capitalism. Nevertheless, in both the North and the South manners played an important role. As the neo-classical courtier knew, manners distinguished families of superior wealth, intelligence, and integrity. The daughters of mannered Americans attended finishing schools; the sons attended college. Both sexes seemed superior to their counterparts in Europe. Colonial women, for instance, enjoyed more freedom than their sisters in Europe. Female printers, newspaper publishers, pharmacists, and medical doctors existed in America. Likewise, due to a more pressing need to be "jacks-of-all-trades," American men were more versatile and less specialized than European men.

The colonial societies' prejudices and manners echoed in the arts and sciences. Michael Wigglesworth (1631–1705), the poet whose *The Day of Doom* (1662) became America's first bestseller, was partly responsible for spreading antitheatricalism. One out of every forty-five colonists owned a copy of his rant, which featured these lines:

> Could you find time for vain pastime,
>     for loose licentious mirth?
> For fruitless toyes, and fading joyes
>     that perish at the birth?
> Had you good leisure for carnal Pleasure,
>     in dayes of health and youth?
> And yet no space to seek God's face,
>     and turn to him in truth?
>
> The wicked are brought to the Bar
>     like guilty Malefactors,
> That often times of bloody Crimes
>     and Treasons have been Actors.[3]

And Thomas Jefferson wrote in 1813 that, "we have no distinct class of literati in our country. Every man is engaged in some industrious pursuit, and science is but a secondary occupation, always subordinate to the main business of life."

*Imported Culture*  Neo-classicism's close ties with monarchy ruled out any influence the ideal might have in America. And because neo-classicism never got a foothold in America, a reaction to neo-classical restrictions never occurred. In fact, Americans, like the Germans, looked directly to the Greeks and Romans for their models. Ancient classicism seemed more universal and eternal than the European version of the classics. Thus, Benjamin Franklin was drawn in a toga rather than in a rococo or baroque mode.

Nevertheless, most American students were sent to English universities as much for the status as for the education. Occasionally, American colleges would attempt a "theatrical" or a "dialogue," but the academic attitude toward theatre was best summarized as late as 1824 by Yale President Dwight: "To indulge a taste for playgoing means nothing more or less than the loss of that most valuable treasure the immortal soul." The laws were equally inhospitable. For example, Maryland and Virginia were the only colonies to allow theatrical performances. Portsmouth, New Hampshire's refusal to admit an acting troupe best epitomizes the legal opposition. Plays, it was said, have "a peculiar influence on the minds of young people and greatly endanger their morals by giving them a taste for intriguing, amusement and pleasure."

The American Revolution quenched whatever interest and activity the theatre might have been developing. Theatre was English, and England was the enemy. British soldiers even presented plays in Boston, New York, and Philadelphia. On October 20, 1774, the Continental Congress resolved:

> We will, in our several stations, encourage frugality, economy, and industry, and promote agriculture, arts, and the manufactures of this country, especially that of wool; and will discountenance and discourage every species of extravagance and dissipation, especially all horseracing, and all kinds of gaming, cock-fighting, exhibitions of shews, plays, and other expensive diversions and entertainments.

Aside from taking time, men, and money from the war effort, English plays upheld the social structure Americans were fighting to overturn. The democratic impulse moved Americans against king and Parliament. Stirrings for the natural rights of individuals, a desire for a government based on a social contract among sovereign individuals, a belief in the unalienable right to life, liberty, and the pursuit of happiness, found no mirror in the English plays trouping about the colonies. The Revolution marked the end of the social theatre in America. Democracy brought the beginning of the romantic spirit to American society.

Great theatres emerge in settled communities after generations of political stability have created a clear national identity. But

America was a nation in flux; everyone was on the move. And regional differences in every aspect of social life worked against the development of a clear national identity. Nonetheless, with peace, theatrical activity revived and expanded with the new nation. Thus, the rapid population growth of the 1780s meant a growing audience for theatre. Moreover, as the expanding nation developed a sense of identity, a more peculiarly American theatre emerged. Louisiana, Texas, and Florida brought new possibilities for settlement, theatrical production, and dramatic subjects. As the population moved, seeking its fortune, the theatre followed. The history of the American theatre is, to a great extent, the search for greater profit.

***Second-Rate Companies and Players*** Actors sailed to America looking for an opportunity to act. In 1703 Anthony Aston (1682–1750), claiming his fame as the first professional actor in America, performed in Charleston and New York. In August, 1749, a company of actors led by Walter Murray and Thomas Keane, presenting some plays in a Water Street warehouse in Philadelphia, began the professional theatre in America. Their company presented the standard English fare of the day: *Cato, Richard III, Love for Love, The Beggar's Opera* and, of course, *The London Merchant*. During the next couple of years the company played on Nassau Street in New York and in Williamsburg as the Virginia Company.

William Hallam, the brother of an actor killed by Charles Macklin in a backstage brawl, saw his New Wells Theatre close in 1751. Hallam, the manager of the obscure theatre near Goodman's Fields, featured acting by his brother Lewis (1714–1756) and his sister-in-law, Mrs. Hallam, a relative of Christopher Rich. William decided the troupe had no choice but to go to America under Lewis's leadership. He would retain financial control back home. The brothers would share the profits equally.

The brothers decided that Virginia would be most receptive to the dramatic theatre. The company departed in 1752 with Lewis as principal low comedian, Mr. Rigby as principal tragedian and acting coach, Mr. Singleton as light comedian and juvenile tragedian, Mrs. Hallam as leading actress, and assorted extras. Young Lewis Hallam Jr. (c. 1749–1808) dropped out of Cambridge to travel with his parents. On board for forty-two days the company rehearsed twenty-four plays, which included *The Beaux Stratagem, The Merchant of Venice, Jane Shore, Richard III, Hamlet, Othello, Tamburlaine, The Conscious Lovers*, and *The London Merchant*, the best-known play in the world at the time.

The company landed at Yorktown and immediately set off for Williamsburg. In one summer it converted a warehouse to a box, pit, and gallery theatre. On September 5, 1752, Granville's farcical *Jew of Venice* played to harpsichord accompaniment. For eleven months the Hallams performed twice a week. (They played, for example, Shakespeare, but without mention of the author.) In June, 1753, after having difficulty obtaining a license to perform, the company played New York. It sold tickets to *The Conscious Lovers* at nearby stores and taverns. The group next traveled to Philadelphia to play for two months before sailing to Jamaica, where Lewis Hallam Sr. died.

In Jamaica Mrs. Hallam met, and in 1758 married, David Douglas, a resident of Jamaica since 1751. Douglas and the Hallams consolidated their troupes into a company featuring the acting of 18-year-old Lewis Jr. The new company, called the London Company, went to New York and opened in 1758 with *Jane Shore* and a Fielding play. By playing Romeo to his mother's Juliet, Hallam Jr. became one of America's first starring actors. He later played the title role in Thomas Godfrey's *The Prince of Parthia*. In 1768 the troupe traveled to Philadelphia, Maryland, Williamsburg, and Rhode Island. Along the way the company changed its name to the more acceptable American Company, thereby capitalizing on growing anti-British sentiment. In 1767 America's first home-grown actor, Mr. Greville, dropped out of Princeton to join the American Company. But when the Continental Congress banned theatrical presentations, the company broke up and left for Jamaica and the West Indies.

*The interior of Philadelphia's Chestnut Street Theatre.* (Harvard Theatre Collection)

During the Revolution, the British controlled New York. In deserted theatres British soldiers and female camp followers presented English favorites to amuse the troops. After the war, John Henry, an actor who had joined the American Company in 1766, returned to the mainland. Hallam followed later. Together they created a new company, organized on a salary basis, that monopolized professional theatre from New York to Charleston. In 1778 Hallam, after reopening Philadelphia's Southwark Theatre, offered drama as lectures and moral dialogues. In 1785 the company reopened New York's John Street Theatre.

New companies sprouted up. Thomas Wignall, once with the American Company, started a company in 1791 with Alexander Reinagle, a Philadelphia musician. This new company of English actors opened at Philadelphia's Chestnut Street Theatre. Hallam replaced Wignall with John Hodgkinson. Thomas A. Cooper, a new actor in Wignall's company, overshadowed Hallam as America's favorite actor. Holding the title until the debut of Edwin Forest, Cooper moved to New York in search of better roles. He debuted in New York as Hamlet in 1798. Success eventually led Cooper to the management of the Park Theatre.

By 1800 Philadelphia, New York, Charleston, and Boston stood as America's four centers of theatrical activity. Each company toured a circuit that included at least one of the cities. However, the old American Company confined itself to New York. Distinctive American types began to find their way into the dramas. The Yankees, the Irish, and the comic Negro Sambos, satisfied the nation's need to see itself on stage.

***Second-Rate Plays*** American plays aped their European counterparts. The first extant American play, *Androborus* (1714) by New York Governor Robert Hunter, satirized his political opponents in the manner of English political satire. Thomas Godfrey (1736–1763) penned the first American play to receive a professional production, *The Prince of Parthia* (1767), a curious blend of Shakespeare and Lillo. *The Disappointment* (1766), a comic opera by Thomas Forrest, would have had the honor but the American Company dropped the play in rehearsal.

The Revolution created a flurry of writing, especially of propaganda and satire, for publication but not for performance. After taking a pacifist attitude with his satire, *The Patriots*

The interior of New York's Park Theatre during a performance by Charles Mathews. (Courtesy of the New York Historical Society)

(1776), Colonel Robert Munford (c. 1730–1784) gave America its first Negro character, Ralpho, in *The Candidates* (1798). The stage Negro reinforced the audience's belief and hope that Negroes were docile, innocent, and hard-working children.

Royall Tyler (1757–1826) practiced law in Falmouth, Maine, and Quincy, Massachusetts, after graduating from Harvard and Yale at the same time. When his engagement to John Adams's daughter broke off, in 1787, he moved to New York, where he became fast friends with Thomas Wignall. Struck with the stage, he wrote *The Contrast* (1787) in three weeks. *The Contrast* was the first comedy written by an American for professional production. The play sports Billy Dimple, America's version of Richard Sheridan's Joseph Surface from *The*

*School for Scandal*. In fact, Dimple and his servant, Jessemy, display affectation, hypocrisy, and aristocratic sentiments to contrast with the plain-speaking, democratic sentiments of native-born Colonel Manly and his servant, Jonathan. In the play, American women are caught and torn between the two types of men, and Jonathan accidentally sees a performance of *The School for Scandal*. Later Tyler tried his hand at versions of Molière's *Le Médecin malgré lui* (*The Doctor in Spite of Himself*) and Cervantes's *Don Quixote*.

The title of America's first professional playwright was reserved for William Dunlap (1766–1839). Born in Perth Amboy, New Jersey, Dunlap quickly developed a love for Shakespeare, Pope, and history. In New York during the Revolution, Dunlap attended plays presented by British officers. In 1784 he studied painting in London with Benjamin West, but after seeing London's Shakespearean and contemporary drama, Dunlap succumbed to the lure of the theatre.

Dunlap bought into the management of the old American Company in 1796 and two years later succeeded Hallam Jr. as manager. He supervised the building of the Park Theatre, which opened in 1798, but returned to portrait painting in 1805 when the theatre folded. He came back to the theatre periodically. In 1809 Dunlap managed an engagement of Edgar Allen Poe's parents and in 1812 managed the English actor George Frederick Cooke's American tour. In 1832 Dunlap published the first history of the American theatre.

Dunlap wrote every kind of drama: sentimental, patriotic, ballad, Gothic melodrama, farce, adaptation, translation. After fifty-three plays he discovered that middle-class Americans preferred sentimental dramas. Dunlap's best plays were *André* (1798), a pseudo-Shakespearean tragedy based on an actual event in the American Revolution, and *A Trip to Niagara* (1827), his last play, a spectacle-travelogue through western New York.

By 1800 Dunlap and Tyler ranked as America's foremost contributors to the dramatic theatre. As in other countries, a lack of great plays shifted the burden to great actors. Thus, the nineteenth-century's glorification of individual genius and erratic temperament matched the lack of literary skill.

**Theatre Buildings** The first theatre in America, in New York, was a thirty foot wide by eighty-six foot long building renovated in 1716 under the management of Charles and Mary Stagg. Their Nassau Street Theatre was renovated in 1753 by Lewis Hallam. The new forty foot wide building reopened as New York's New Theatre. The first permanent theatre in America was Philadelphia's Southwark, on South Street above Fourth Street, built in 1766 by David Douglass. The following year Douglass built New York's John Street Theatre, which sat 1000 spectators.

In 1794 Thomas Wignall's new company moved into Philadelphia's new Chestnut Street Theatre, a building that made Philadelphia America's theatre capital. The 2000-seat theatre featured a 400-seat raked pit, thirteen rows of benches, a seventy-one foot deep raked stage, and three tiers of boxes seating 755. Chandeliers lit the Chestnut's auditorium and orchestra pit of thirty musicians. The thirty-six foot wide stage was illuminated by oil lamps. Negroes, isolated in a special gallery, watched the action from afar. George Washington, a lover of the theatre, held a box at the John Street Theatre. When Philadelphia became the capital, Washington reserved boxes at both the Southwark and Chestnut Street Theatres.

The opening of the Park Theatre in 1798 shifted the center of theatrical activity to New York. The Park, the old American Company's replacement for the John Street Theatre, drew architectural inspiration from the Chestnut Street Theatre. In time, permanent theatres

arose in New Orleans, Newport, Charleston, Boston, and Baltimore as well.

**A Disparate Audience** Handbills, luring people to 6 o'clock evening performances on Mondays, Wednesdays, and Fridays, promised all kinds of novelties and enrichment to theatre goers. Sometimes servants arrived at the theatres to save choice seats. Vendors, both inside and outside the theatres, sold their wares before, during, and after the performances. The American audience, however, lacked the refinement and theatrical experience of its European counterpart. No college in America, for example, offered a course in Shakespeare until 1855. Moreover, America was settled by many people who did not miss the theatre, and playgoing meant little more than prize fighting to most Americans. Indeed, theatre audiences generally looked for emotional excitement.

By and large, wealthy, educated members of the audience preferred English plays, English settings, and English style. The poor and uneducated preferred to see themselves in comedies and melodramas featuring raw passion. The growing middle class enjoyed bourgeois sentimental comedy. Plays thus catered to each section of the audience. Because of the great regional differences within the colonies and among the states, and because American audiences displayed these regional interests and tastes, no play enjoyed nationwide popularity. Jealous states housed jealous cities, each preferring its own brand of culture. Audiences, moreover, loved to deflate the pride of players fresh from triumphal engagements in rival cities or states. The United States had no London or Paris or Madrid, where artists and scholars could exchange ideas and excitement. As a result, no national style or subject emerged from the deliberate dissimilarity.

# GERMANY

**Political Disunity** The Thirty Years' War (1618–1648) eliminated the possibility that an intellectual, artistic, or theatrical capital comparable to Paris, London, or Madrid could

arise in Germany. Envious German states, eclipsed by France's importance in the war, admired French thought and dramatic art. Because German princes wanted to appear

French, they assembled the best French minds to teach and outshine rival princes. Just as every Italian prince had sought his own Athens, each German prince tried to build his own Versailles: castle building prospered in Germany.

Every court tried to enhance its authority by patronizing English, Dutch, Italian, and especially French artists and performers. Germany thus followed the courtly, aristocratic neo-classical style of France. French artists and performers were imported, and the Germans imitated French models. Even German theatrical troupes imitated the French. But the Age of Reason, riding into Germany with these artists and scholars, never extended its influence beyond the courts.

Unlike France, England, and Spain, Germany escaped unification under a single strong monarch. Each German prince thought himself a future Louis XIV. The Hohenzollern King Frederick I (reigned 1688–1713) patronized education and science. His son, Frederick II (reigned 1740–1786), who earned the title Frederick the Great by rebelling against his father's militarism, concentrated his energies on German culture and theatre. He reformed the Berlin Academy, made the Bank of Berlin the state bank, and brought French intellectuals, artists, and language to Germany.

### From Neo-Classicism to Sturm und Drang

Religious differences contributed to both the political divisions and the legitimacy of the princes. But as the Enlightenment came to the courts, princes' interests turned from theology to philosophy. The *Aufklarung*, the German Enlightenment, avoided any particular school of philosophical opinion. Nevertheless, Rousseau found more favor in Germany than in France. Philosopher Immanuel Kant (1724–1804), however, opened the door for the development of a unique German school of philosophy by attacking the metaphysical theory of knowledge rooted in the Enlightenment. Kant argued the impossibility of knowing things in themselves. The study of intelligence provided, he posited, the real source of universal truths about the human experience.

German intellectuals eventually rejected rationalism largely because princes had used the philosophy to justify the status quo. The *Sturm und Drang* (Storm and Stress) movement among young German intellectuals, which foreshadowed the Romantic age, eventually proclaimed the world irrational, incomprehensible, mysterious, and without meaning. Germans thought and reacted against French neo-classical rationalism. Elemental human forces, such as instinct, replaced reason as the true driving force of human will and action.

*Sturm und Drang*, a 1776 play by Friedrich M. Klinger (1752–1831), depicted the terrible struggle of a man in a hostile environment. The title named a movement that drew inspiration from Shakespeare and rebelled against eighteenth-century rationalism. *Sturm und Drang* plays opposed more than they advocated, employed a wide variety of forms, expressed a multitude of sentiments, and championed the spectrum of political ideas. Verse alternated with prose in tales of prostitution, seduction, rape, and child murder. All rules were violated, and character was valued over plot.

When faced with the problems of staging their plays, young class-conscious *Sturm und Drang* playwrights began to modify their Rousseau-inspired writings. At heart, the plays blamed the nobility for creating social conditions that left the good bourgeois no choice but to commit atrocities, to violate their natures. Thus, the German stage replaced the German pulpit.

The rise of emotionalism paralleled the shift of power from court to middle class. Peace allowed middle-class merchants to regroup. In addition, the introduction of potato farming after 1750 boosted the German standard of living. The subsequent increase in food supply ushered in both a new prosperity and a population boom.

As power shifted from court to merchant class, German aesthetic demands changed. Native culture and traditions, dismissed by French scholars, revived. But Germans also sought a cosmopolitan and humanistic culture, especially in music, the favorite Protestant art. Despite the political divisions caused by the

Austrian Hapsburg dynasty's domination of the German Confederation, the people shared similar aesthetic aspirations.

*Opera*  Christoph Willibald Gluck (1714–1787), the son of a gamekeeper, toured Copenhagen, Naples, Vienna, and Prague with an opera company. His own opera, *Artaserse* (1741), played in Milan and revealed the neoclassical ideal's movement from spoken drama to the musical stage. As in France and England, opera in Germany seemed the appropriate home for neo-classical heroes, conflicts, and wills. In a preface to his opera *Alceste* (1767), Gluck urged the reform of opera to the guidelines of the Italian Monteverdi. Opera needed, Gluck suggested, to once again emphasize action, psychology of motivation, and emotional expression. Gluck rejected opera's ceremonial formalism and baroque decoration, and he applied to opera the Enlightenment's insistence on the natural reflection of human experience. Gluck introduced common sense, emotion, and meaningful action to opera. He refused to indulge his singers, simplified the musical style, and insisted on suiting credible music to the action. *Orfeo ed Euridice* (*Orpheus and Eurydice*, 1774), *Iphigénie en Aulide* (*Iphigenia at Aulis*, 1762), and his masterpiece *Iphigénie en Tauride* (*Iphigenia at Taurus*, 1778) influenced one of the age's greatest dramatists, Wolfgang Amadeus Mozart (1756–1791).

Mozart grew up as the son of the Austrian court composer. Because Austria dominated the German Confederation, Vienna originated much of Germany's cultural activity. A child prodigy, Mozart reigned as a European celebrity from the age of six. In 1768 he wrote his first operas. In all, he wrote forty-one symphonies and twenty clavier concertos. His five operatic and theatrical masterpieces—*Die Entführung aus dem Serail* (*The Abduction from the Seraglio, 1781*), *Le nozze di Figaro* (*The Marriage of Figaro*, 1786), *Don Giovanni* (1787), *Così fan tutte* (*All Women So Do*, 1790), and *Die Zauberflöte* (*The Magic Flute*, 1791)—dissolve the boundaries between comedy and tragedy and question the relationship between foolishness and heroism.

*Native Arts*  Commercial centers like Hamburg and Zurich first freed themselves from court tastes. Gotthold Ephriam Lessing (1729–1781), the son of a Protestant minister, became not only the chief German exponent of the French Enlightenment but also the conduit through which a German national style emerged.

Lessing's achievements owed much to the pioneering work of Johann Gottfried von Herder (1744–1803), who first declared that great literature would come to Germany only after German replaced French as the language of composition. But French literature dominated the universities. German writers, supporting themselves with other jobs, had to write in French to find a market. A Prussian philosopher and critic, Herder met Immanuel Kant and formulated ideas that eventually coalesced into the *Sturm und Drang*. Herder, for example, defined poetry as a spontaneous, immediate expression that was the natural gift of all individuals—not simply the studied product of reasonable, educated people. Herder, despising the Enlightenment's self-conscious intellectuality, championed the importance of England's Shakespeare over the French neoclassical model.

In time, a literary career became possible outside the court. In the second half of the eighteenth century, in fact, the small middle class began to want to read about itself in German. Middle-class teenagers came to lead the *Sturm und Drang*, and middle-class heroes appeared in literature and art. In the Romantic age the heroes became the disenfranchised bourgeois artists themselves. Romantics saw the artists as heroes, the first articulators of middle-class values through middle-class heroes.

*Second-Hand Dramas*  The German people loved *Hauptaktion* and *Nachspiel*, a long farce and an afterpiece, usually starring Hanswurst, the German descendant of the *commedia dell'arte*'s zanni. The most famous Hanswurst was Joseph Stranitsky (1676–1726). Other clowns, called *Pickelherring* and *Harlequin*, also monopolized the stages. But educated court

Germans wished to replace the farces with dramas modeled on the French neo-classical ideal.

Johann Christoph Gottsched (1700–1766) admired French taste, translated Racine, and wrote such neo-classical imitations as *Dying Cato* (1732). Working to purify the German language, he created a German version of the French neo-classical theatre. However, he found the social, conversational salon life of France unsuited to the philosophical, solitary brooding so popular among thoughtful Germans. In time, German individualism saved German writers and artists from the burden of the French rules advocated by Gottsched.

Gotthold Lessing (1729–1781), also wanting to purify the German language and stage, insisted on means quite different from Gottsched's. In fact, Lessing's theory and practice developed as a reaction to attempts to transplant the French tradition. As a Berlin literary journalist, Lessing published reviews, wrote essays, and penned plays. In 1746 Lessing moved to Leipzig, a cultural center, to work for Neuber's company. His early plays, modeled on French and English dramas, reflect the Neuber interest in reforming the stage. In 1751 Lessing traveled to Berlin to meet Voltaire. Three years later his essays advocated the new sentimental drama.

In 1755 Lessing made a total break with the neo-classical drama by writing *Miss Sara Sampson*, a prose tragedy of domestic life using the Medea myth. The play shows the influence of Lillo's *The London Merchant* (1731) and Diderot's theory of the *drame bourgeois*. Voltaire, however, objected to Lessing's play, the most powerful domestic drama of the century. In 1759 Lessing proclaimed English tragedies superior to the French, and Shakespeare a more suitable model than Racine: Shakespeare was "the voice of nature," unrestrained by human rules. Lessing's Sampson family, English rather than German, gave his play the necessary dignity and seriousness.

Lessing's plays reflected his new aesthetic position. In 1767 Lessing, the dramatist and critic with the new national theatre in Hamburg, hoped to extend his treatise on aesthetics, *Laokoon* (1766), to the theatre. For the new theatre he wrote *Minna von Barnhelm* (1767) and essays later titled *Hamburg Dramaturgy* (1767–1769). In the comedy *Minna von Barnhelm* Tellheim, a poor war veteran, will not marry the wealthy Minna because of his present poverty. When money comes into his life, Minna teases him by pretending poverty as a comic excuse for not accepting his proposal of marriage. Another work *Emilia Galotti* (1772), a drama based on the story of Appius and Virginia, stands as Lessing's most influential play. The play made him, according to the playwrights Goethe and Schiller, the founder of the German theatre. A middle-class girl, Emilia, is killed by her father to prevent her from marrying an Italian prince. Lessing's last major work, *Nathan the Wise* (1779) proclaimed his faith in truth, reason, and intellectual liberty in religious matters. The character Nathan, modeled on the philosopher Moses Mendelssohn, possesses an enlightened religious outlook; he takes from a religion only what makes sense to him and rejects the rest. Nathan acts more morally than the bourgeois who accept the traditional religious creeds without question. The play contains Nathan's famous Parable of the Ring, whose moral is that the only true religion is the religion that helps improve humanity's condition.

***Goethe and Schiller*** While Lessing founded Hamburg realism, Johann Wolfgang von Goethe (1749–1832) and Friedrich Schiller (1759–1805) were developing Weimar classicism. Weimar classicism, like Hamburg realism, evolved as a reaction to French neo-classicism. Both Goethe and Schiller had been members of the *Sturm und Drang* in their youth. However, the playwrights left the bud of Romanticism to create Germany's version of an Enlightenment drama. They came to value the theatrical and social conventions they once attacked. Weimar classicism, born after *Sturm und Drang*, displayed a faith in reason, an admiration for order and discipline, and an inclination toward aristocracy. Weimar classicism was German classicism: it sought the

*Goethe's Weimar Court Theatre.*   (New York Public Library at Lincoln Center)

typical, the universal, the regular, the normal, and the permanent, while directly imitating the Greeks rather than French versions of the Greeks.

Goethe, the son of a lawyer, abandoned his law studies at Leipzig University to follow his loves. A lover of both Greek and Shakespearean drama, the poet, dramatist, and novelist always struggled between the two distinct modes of dramatic representation. *Goetz von Berlichingen* (1773), written for readers rather than for theatregoers, stands as *Sturm und Drang's* greatest play. Modeled on Shakespeare, Goethe's play outdoes the Bard in number of scenes and characters. The next year Goethe's novel *Die Leiden des jungen Werthers* (*The Sorrows of Young Werther*) created a sensation throughout Europe. Young men even committed suicide in sympathy with the hero.

In 1775 Goethe accepted an invitation to Weimar. He lived there for the rest of his life, working to make the city the cultural capital of Europe. In 1786 Goethe visited Italy for two years; he then returned to Weimar, writing in a new style. The new classicism of Goethe had little relationship with the world of Germany. Goethe was interested in ideals and spiritual matters rather than history and domestic af-

fairs. In 1789 he wrote *Torquato Tasso*, a celebration of tradition, restraint, and respect for form. *Faust* appeared in two parts in 1770 and 1831.

While in Weimar, Goethe befriended a young man named Friedrich Schiller. The son of an army officer, Schiller turned from a medical career to attack political tyranny with *Die Räuber* (*The Robbers*, 1781). In *The Robbers*, Karl Moor, the head of a gang of outlaws, fights the corrupt society of his brother Franz. Goethe had predicted a great playwright would appear.

Perhaps Goethe saw Schiller as that great playwright when Schiller settled in Weimar between 1787 and 1792. Schiller had already written *Louise Miller* (1784) and *Don Carlos* (1787). In the latter the tyrannical king of Spain is opposed by his son, Don Carlos, not only for political repression, but also because his father has married his fiancée. Don Carlos's passion is kept in check by his reasonable confidante, the Marquis de Posa.

Disinterested in political tyranny like Goethe, Schiller investigated spiritual tyranny and freedom instead. Though a professor of history, Schiller read Immanuel Kant's aesthetic theory with great enthusiasm. With

The setting for Schiller's The Robbers in 1782 at the Mannheim National Theatre. (Städtisches Reib-Museum, Mannheim, Theatersammlung)

Goethe he edited the journal *Die Horen* in 1794. Weimar classicism advanced with such plays of Schiller's as *Maria Stuart* (1800), *Die Jungfrau von Orleans* (*The Maid of Orleans*, 1801), and *Wilhelm Tell* (1804).

Schiller's *The Wallenstein Trilogy* (1799) chronicled the Thirty Years' War with a Shakespearean scope. *Das Lager* (*The Camp*, 1798) is a portrait of the army of the intellectual Catholic Count Wallenstein. *Die Piccolomini* (1799) reveals the Count's loss of faith in the rightness of the war. As his army suffers defeat, the Count considers a separate peace with the Protestants. But the Emperor loses faith in the Count, and the Count's officers plot to force him to declare a separate peace and a separate state. Meanwhile, the Count's closest aide, General Piccoloni, plots with the Emperor to overthrow Wallenstein. Piccoloni's son, Max, must choose either duty to his father and emperor or his admiration for the Count and his love for Wallenstein's daughter. The final play, *Wallenstein Tod* (*Wallenstein's Death*, 1799), details the mass desertion of the Count and his eventual assassination.

***Bourgeois Drama*** Weimar classicism, un-

concerned with contemporary society, deliberately envisioned ideal reality. The vision was a literary one, derived from the Greeks, and inorganic to German domestic life. Weimar classicism sought to unite Germany aesthetically by appealing to external truths rather than regional differences. But Germans wanted what their counterparts in France and England wanted: a theatre validating middle-class virtues rooted in bourgeois life. In Mannheim the first national theatre in Germany offered a vision far more popular and accessible than the one created by Goethe and Schiller.

August von Kotzebue (1761–1819) and August Wilhelm Iffland (1759–1814) produced what bourgeois audiences wanted and enjoyed. Iffland controlled the Mannheim theatre and, after playing Franz Moor in the premiere of Schiller's *Die Räuber* (1781), wrote the popular play *Die Jäger* (*The Foresters*, 1785). The Weimar lawyer Kotzebue, who gave up his job with the government to write over 200 plays, actually made German drama the most popular in the world at the turn of the century. As chief dramatist at the Weimar court he wrote *Menschenlass und Reue* (*The Stranger, or Misanthropy and Repentence*, 1789). Of his melodramas, thirty-six were translated into English. But Kotzebue, like most of the world theatre audience, disliked the developing Romantic movement. In 1819, a student assassinated Kotzebue for holding reactionary views: passions fueled the coming Romantic age.

***Reforming Actors***    Exiled English comedians performed jigs, comic sketches, and neoclassical tragedy. The Germans preferred *Gammer Gurton's Needle* and plays featuring their own *Pickelherring* to the seriousness of John Dryden. Actors sang, danced, and acted in German. With the English Restoration, German players replaced the English actors who returned home. But not until 1800 were performances permitted throughout the year. Even then, theatres were closed during Lent and Advent and on every Saturday and Sunday. The German instinct for reformation surfaced in the efforts of Caroline Neuber (1697–1760) and Johann Christoph Gottsched (1700–1766).

To escape her father, Caroline Neuber eloped with her husband, Johann. For ten years the Neubers toured with a theatrical troupe. Meanwhile, Gottsched fled Prussia's draft in 1724. The two met and vowed to reform German dramatic fare according to the French neoclassical ideal. Their repertoire offered translations of French plays and new German plays. In Leipzig they worked to raise both literary and performance standards. In 1737 Neuber and Gottsched burned an effigy of Hanswurst and presented Gottsched's versions of Corneille and Racine. But a squabble over costuming *Cato* ended the collaboration. Though their efforts produced many disappointments, Neuber's holding long rehearsals, eliminating improvisation, and introducing a heavy fine system established regular drama in Germany. Even after she and her husband died, in poverty during the Seven Years' War, her methods continued in other managers' work.

Goethe, for example, continued Neuber's work by developing the skills of play direction in his work with his Weimar company. To eliminate regional dialects and the urge to improvise, Goethe established a dictatorial method of directing based on rules and fines.

He taught grace, beauty, and the lyrical speaking of verse. Goethe divided his proscenium stage into a grid and specified the movements he wanted his actors to accomplish. He even beat out the rhythm of a scene as his actors scurried to follow the cadence. During performances Goethe sat in his box and instructed the audience on proper behavior. But as a producer Goethe had to compromise. To attract an audience Goethe added domestic dramas and operas to his bill of Schiller, Terence, Shakespeare, *commedia dell'arte* scenarios, and Calderon.

By the end of this age, the most important German troupe was managed by Frederick Ludwig Schroder (1744–1816). Schroder created ensemble playing through strict discipline. His repertoire included Lessing, Shakespeare, and *Strum und Drang* plays. Schroder's reputation as Germany's greatest actor was rivaled only by that of his mentor, Konrad Ekhof (1720–1778), a postal clerk, who, after becoming an actor, introduced a realistic acting style at the time of Neuber's heroic style. Ekhof was the German Garrick.

***Critics and the People***    In time the German middle class acquired leisure for reading and a taste for the domestic theatre. Commercial connections with England brought German merchants into contact with English middle-class culture. German aristocrats had wanted French culture; the German bourgeois wanted English culture. The English novel brought moralizing and middle-class sentiment to Germany. Domestic drama replaced the heroic drama, the family novel replaced the romance, and middle-class values replaced aristocratic ideals. Theatre audiences cried steadily, often becoming hysterical when bourgeois pathos became unbearable.

Germany's late development of a national literature produced a preoccupation with aesthetic theory. Gotthold Lessing objected to Horace's idea of *ut pictura poesis* (poems are like pictures). Lessing did not believe one could talk about poetry with the vocabulary of painting or painting with the vocabulary of poetry. In 1757 Lessing wrote, ''Each art imitates in

*Friedrich Schroeder as Falstaff in 1780.* (New York Public Library Theatre Collection)

the manner appropriate to it.'' In 1767 he wrote, *''Ut pictura poesis non erit''* (poems are not like pictures). Painting could only reveal the visible moment; poetry could reveal a wider range of things.

Like Goethe, Lessing tried to rescue the classics from French neo-classicism. Lessing, unable to advocate mechanical rules of composition, considered Shakespeare more Aristotelian than Racine. In fact, Lessing reinterpreted Aristotle using Shakespeare as the example. Shakespeare showed how a genius followed organic rather than external rules of composition. German taste had come a long way from Frederick the Great's description of Shakespeare as "farces worthy of the savages of Canada." In time Lessing urged the creation of a bourgeois drama, the only drama capable of fulfilling the dictates of Aristotle. Domestic drama alone could show the actions of ordinary individuals, worthy of pity, while demonstrating moral lessons.

Court audiences enjoyed stock French settings. Permanent theatres contained chariot and pole scenic systems. The success of Lessing's *Minna von Barnhelm* (1767), however, increased the audience's fascination with spectacle and local color. Historical accuracy in scenery and costume crept in with German history. But domestic life required domestic settings.

As the age ended Romanticism elevated the spontaneous expression of feeling inherent in bourgeois drama to new heights. The ability to spontaneously express feeling became the single mark of greatness in art and literature. Bourgeois intellectuals rejected rationalism as aristocratic and French. In its place irrationality stood as the mark of genius. Originality and passion supplanted verisimilitude and decorum. Germany was the last major European culture to receive the Renaissance; consequently, the neo-classical ideal was irrelevant. Germans were ready for something else. That something else was romanticism.

# NOTES

[1] Pierre Corneille, "Of the Three Unities of Action, Time, and Place," in *Critical Theory Since Plato*, ed. Hazard Adams, trans. Donald Schier (New York: Harcourt Brace Jovanovich, 1971), p. 219.

[2] Cotton Mather, *Magnalia Christi Americana* (Hartford: Silas Andrus and Sons, 1855).

[3] Michael Wigglesworth, *The Day of Doom* (New York: American News Co., 1867).

# 7

# THE ROMANTIC THEATRE

*The lofty spirit spurned me coldly,*
*And nature hides from me her face.*
*Torn is the subtle thread of thought,*
*I loathe the knowledge I once sought.*
*In sensuality's abysmal land*
*Let our passions drink their fill!*
                              Goethe's *Faust**

## OVERVIEW

Faust's despair captured the feelings of young men whose revolutionary hopes had been destroyed. The democratic revolution, carried on the back of Napoleon, was crushed by England's Duke of Wellington and buried by the Council of Vienna. An industrial revolution brought thousands of homeless war refugees to overcrowded and polluted cities to live in animal squalor. The aesthetic revolution, promising passion and instinctive action, had been purchased by the bourgeoisie for its sentimental ballad dramas. Intellectuals, theatre artists, and poets rebelled and ran from the smugness and pride of reasonable middle-class merchants, content to increase their profits and

* Johann Wolfgang von Goethe, *Faust*, Walter Kaufman, trans. (New York: Doubleday, 1961), p. 187. Copyright © 1961 by Walter Kaufman. Reprinted by permission of Doubleday & Company, Inc.

mouth hypocritically their faith in democratic principles.

The despairing looked to nature, defined as an unintelligible, mysterious, and meaningless consciousness. But at least nature offered escape and peace. In nature individuals partook of the flow of life-beyond-human-understanding. The darkness of nature provided a refuge and home for those alienated from the present. Wandering through the wildness of nature, individuals pursued goals both inexpressible and unattainable. In nature, they found meaning beyond material and theatrical realization.

Most of these so-called "romantics" preferred to escape the present situation to an ideal past, an exotic culture, or a utopian future. Romantic dramatists attempted to create what they knew could never be made. Romantic theatre people searched for meaning and understanding everywhere but in the failed and befouling present. The overriding, absolute truth was the passion of emotional release, the most ephemeral part of existence. Thus, reality in the romantic theatre lay in the perpetual flux of moods and emotions. Truth lived in the genuineness of emotional irrationality rather than in rational political action. Romantics thus yearned for a world that could never exist. They looked to fairy tales, fantasy, childhood, dreams, madness, drugs, anything to numb the pain of failed revolutions.

***The End of Revolution***   Napoleon and the French fraternity had tried to carry on the Revolution. His defeat signaled the defeat of liberal ideas threatening conservative regimes. The bourgeoisie, tired of revolution and war, yearned for peace, quiet, and prosperity. So did theatrical entrepreneurs. When social problems reached the boiling point, governments either responded slowly, as in England, or suppressed the dissidents, as in Russia.

But the democratic revolution would not stay down. Popular uprisings in 1830, 1848, and 1849 shook Europe. France swung among monarchy, empire, and republic. Count Camillo Cavour (1810–1861) of Sardinia eventually united Italy for nationhood in 1848. Revolts erupted in Poland and Belgium. Otto von Bismarck (1815–1898) united Germany, and Vladimir I. Lenin (1870–1924) upended both the Russian tsar and the bourgeois provisional government.

By 1900 representative bodies expressed some public opinion in most Western nations. But special-interest groups arose to outmaneuver democratic systems and dim the romantics' hope for the democratic ideal. Many theatres offered escape from the day's turmoil. Nevertheless, the democratic revolution continued into the Modern age as nations were born of peoples' desires for representation, justice, and human rights. Romantics looked to native mythology and history to kindle the fires of national pride.

***Industrialism and Imperialism***   Nations prospered with the industrial revolution. As national armies marched around the world in search of raw materials for domestic mills, a cultural imperialism developed that knew no respect for foreigners. Romantics saw both capitalists and industrialists exploit nature and disregard the universal consciousness experienced through nature. Scientists vivisected animals; engineers mined minerals; doctors ripped human corpses in autopsies; good bourgeois husbands demeaned prostitutes, and industrialists tied children to factory machines for twelve-hour shifts. The industrial revolution raped and corrupted nature, the romantics' only home.

Beginning in England, industrialization and imperialism became national policies throughout the West. The industrial revolution increased the food supply, decreased the death rate, and exploded the population; many had to find new places to live. As Americans moved west, Russians moved east; both people destroyed natives in their way. Colonization also expanded trade and created domestic prosperity. European peasants, seeking lives better than those offered in cities' mills, streamed to America, Argentina, Chile, Uruguay, South Africa, Australia, and New Zealand. The theatre followed. For example, Marunal-Naqqash (1817–1865) of Lebanon wrote the first Western-style Arabic play, a comedy based on Molière's *The Miser,* called *al-Bakhīl* (*The Miser*).

New industries and products delighted the bourgeoisie and disgusted the romantics. Capitalism demanded speed. Roads, canals, railroads, and steamships thus increased the speed of goods traveling to foreign markets and raw materials reaching home mills. The Suez Canal opened in 1869; the Panama Canal, in 1914. In 1837 the telegraph increased the speed of placing orders. In 1866 the trans-Atlantic cable connected the supplies and markets of two continents. Mass production standardized both products and the jobs of those producing them.

Romantics reacted by flaunting novelty and individuality in life and in the theatre. As men and women streamed into cities looking for a piece of the prosperity, romantics headed for the country. The overall population shift from rural to urban during the period represented the most significant cultural phenomenon in human history since the change from nomadic hunting and gathering to static farming. The size of the potential theatre audience continued to grow.

Urban celebrations resembling bourgeois masques honored nations' prosperity. In 1851, London hosted "The Great Exhibition of the Works of Industry of All Nations." One hundred thousand exhibits trumpeted the wisdom of industrial capitalism. In 1862 England's International Exhibition even included an exhibit from the Japanese Court. Into the Modern age, world's fairs continued such festivities.

In the nineteenth century imperialism brought Asian philosophy, religion, and art to Europe just as empire had brought Asian philosophy, religion, and art to Rome 1000 years before. The nineteenth century's flirtation with "Orientalism" represented only a part of a deep interest in the East that was building since the Renaissance. European philosophers found solace in Asian philosophy. And the East was represented more frequently on stage.

***Orientalism*** Romantic philosophy rejected the optimism of the Enlightenment. Asian philosophy offered both an appealing resignation to life and a celebration of the life spirit. Asian philosophy reminded romantics of the Greeks and inspired Johann Wolfgang von Goethe (1749–1832) and Friedrich Schiller (1759–1805) to begin the *Sturm und Drang* movement. Asian philosophy seemed to confirm the romantics' view of irrationality as an extension of emotionalism. With Indian philosophy came Asian theatre aesthetics. Indian philosophy put no stock in reason; neither did the disillusioned German philosophers seeking the romantic ideal.

As far as Westerners knew, Asia enjoyed democratic utopias. In 1785 Charles Wilkins had translated the *Bhagavad-Gita*. In 1844 Eugene Burnouf published his *Introduction to Indian Buddhism*. Spense Hardy wrote a manual of Buddhism in 1853, and Barthélemy Sainte-Hilaire wrote a life of Buddha in 1858. Asian culture, in fact, permeated Western thought during the nineteenth century. Philosopher Arthur Schopenhauer (1788–1860) advocated the renunciation of the will to live. Theatre composer Richard Wagner (1813–1883) put Buddhist ideas in his opera *Tristan und Isolde* (1865) and included an episode from the *Ramayana* in his opera *Parsifal*. Indians came West to teach. Artists and writers fell under the spell of Orientalism.

Eastern influence had begun with Voltaire in France. In England, poet Samuel Taylor Coleridge's (1772–1834) *Kubla Khan* (1797) invoked China. Western romantic playwrights, in fact, sought inspiration everywhere but in the contemporary West. The "spirit" of Greek drama was admired more than the form of the Greek writers' works. The English poet Wordsworth wrote that "poetry is the history, or science of the feelings."

The metaphysics of the Age of Reason collapsed for the romantics. Because a world built on reason had no value for them, romantic philosophers looked to nature for value and meaning. The intuitive, unconscious experience of nature revealed the true order of things. An individual artist capable of perceiving nature's order might be able to redeem the rest of suffering society. Philosophers found dramatic art and the study of aesthetics to be the best means of communicating romantic insights. Aesthetic principles were extended to human behavior, morality, and economics.

***A New Vision of Community*** Some romantics attacked society and then hid from it; other romantics worked to redeem society. Most romantics objected to the rules, restraints, traditions, and authorities guiding corrupt and hypocritical bourgeois society. Romantics in the theatre championed individuality. The self was all they could depend on, experience, or express. Romantics dreamed of a community they lacked.

Though cities offered employment and theatrical entertainment, they lacked the country village's sense of community. As a result, urban schools, churches, civic groups, labor unions, and sports teams worked to create the missing sense. Team sports instilled the collective values rewarded at the mills. In 1839 baseball began in America. Spectator sports filled the workers' leisure time with harmless outlets for pent-up anxieties and frustrations. Railroads brought about intercity competition. Sport appropriated much of the theatre's passion and purgation. But artificial comradeship could not erase the social problems festering in the industrial cities.

By uniting the alienated into a single community, utopian socialism promised to resolve individuals' lack of both satisfactory work and rewarding emotional relationships. Henri Saint-Simon (1760–1825), Charles Fourier (1772–1837), and Robert Owen (1772–1858) independently produced pamphlets, books, and journals, and organized lectures and meetings to spread their socialism from England and France to America and Russia. They created a new vocabulary for society that gave old terms new meaning. From their work arose social-action movements and back-to-nature campaigns. But utopian socialism was swallowed by a larger movement: Marxism.

Karl Marx (1818–1883) believed that the working class, the proletariat, would grow so poor that an eventual revolution would establish a utopia. Marx defined capitalism as the difference between the value of labor and the wages labor received. Marx used England to illustrate his ideas about the capitalist system. He found women harnessed to coal cars in mines; 9-year-old children working fifteen hours a day in textile factories; and tuberculosis, occupational diseases, and work-related accidents producing a high mortality rate. The final violent struggle between wage slaves and bosses would, Marx thought, result in the disappearance of the capitalist economy. A dictatorship of the proletariat would abolish all classes; a free and equal society would allow men and women to produce goods and services according to their ability and to consume them according to their need. Marx pictured an economic utopia into whose vision workers could escape. The theatre was notably absent from most of his vision.

In 1917 the forces of democratic revolution struggled against the Russian monarchy, espousing the romantic philosophy of the nineteenth century rather than the Enlightened philosophy of the eighteenth century, which had produced the American and French Revolutions. As a result, the Russian Revolution established the nineteenth century's idea of democracy, just as the French and American Revolutions had established the eighteenth century's image of democracy.

***Poetry over Plot***  Romanticism meant poetry, and poetry meant passion. Joanna Baille's *Plays of the Passions* (1798, 1802, 1812) equated great tragedy with great passion. Plot and character became, in the hands of the romantic poets, secondary to the passion conveyed by poetic diction. Because of the new conception of drama, fewer poetic plays succeeded in the theatre. As a result, audiences grew suspicious of poetry's ability to envision reality accurately.

Prose thus came to dominate the theatre, not because the idea of verse in the theatre was bad, but because romantic versifiers elevated diction over plot, character, and thought. Also, drama suffered because romantic poets sneered at the theatre as the home of bourgeois society. To write for stage production was to cater to the enemy. Instead, romantic poets wrote for readers who could imagine scenes that could (or would) never be staged. To write for an audience in a theatre would violate the romantic poets' station as isolated genius.

***The Genius***  Romantic artists and actors freed themselves from the rules of corrupt society. Because rules interfered with creativity, to break the rules marked artistry. Greatness did not result from following rules; greatness came from the mysterious process of inspiration, which was outside the realm of rationality. Inspiration marked genius. Individuals beyond rationality, whose subjective impressions of the world allowed them to remain in touch with nature's fundamental consciousness, displayed genius. In the solitude of nature, romantic artists expressed their innermost selves, what the Hindus referred to as *atman*.

Nature provided romantic theatre artists with a source of natural genius proportionate to their consistency with the universal flow. By locating their own depths, the artists put themselves in touch with nature's fundamental processes. Romantic artists wanted their creations to imitate the natural, unplanned, unconscious process of nature. They intuited the organic laws of nature. As English writer Thomas Carlyle (1795-1881) wrote, "Genius is ever a secret to itself." English poet Samuel Taylor Coleridge (1772-1834) differentiated the "talent" of playwrights like Francis Beaumont and John Fletcher, competent artisans, from the "genius" of Shakespeare, an artist of imagination and will. Johann Wolfgang von Goethe had said, "I believe that everything which the genius does as genius, eventuates unconsciously."

***Nature and History*** Nature created unconsciously to provide romantic theatre artists with a storehouse of symbols to be read. English poet William Wordsworth (1770-1850) criticized John Dryden for his inability to read nature truthfully. Romantic artists renewed the poetic vocabulary by serving as shamen in touch with the spiritual world. Cultural myths gave the romantic artist-shamen additional symbols and signs to use in the interpretation of nature. The romantics' search through the past for mythological meanings advanced the historiography of the previous age.

The Age of Reason had considered the present as a step toward a future Enlightenment. But romantics without the vision of a utopian future related all values to their particular moment in history. Romantics in the theatre looked for meaning in the past. They postulated an evolution of humans and society. They saw the problems of the day as only a stage in an ongoing process. German philosopher Friedrich Schlegel (1772-1829) described the present as a product of the past.

Romantics found the dark sides of nature and history particularly fascinating. Spanish artist Francisco Jose de Goya (1746-1828) drew phantasmagorical visions. The Mexican playwright Fernando Calderon (1809-1845) set his *El torneo* (*The Tourney*, 1838) in medieval England. The English poet William Blake (1757-1827) sketched mystical encounters. American poet Edgar Allan Poe (1809-1849) explored terror and madness while most Americans closed their eyes to the dark side. Most romantics agreed that art was the appropriate vehicle for making profound insights into the human condition. Indeed, art itself became a refuge from society.

***Transcendental Aesthetics*** Romantic theatrical art transcended the values of the moment. Art embodied the ideal, and it showed reality as pathetic in light of the ideal. Life came to be judged by art. The aesthetic experience came to represent life's most fulfilling moment and to mean the emotional experience of the ideal. The transcendental vision acquired a physical presence in art. In the presence of the magnificent infinity suggested by art, emotion could not be contained. Art aimed for an emotional response. English painter John Constable (1776-1837) called painting "but another word for feeling." Sketches like those by French artist Honoré Daumier (1808-1879) caught the fleeting spirit of the moment. Gardens housed Japanese pagodas as shrines to the transcendental experience of art. French painter Claude Monet (1840-1926) bought Japanese prints, and Ferdinand Victor Eugène Delacroix (1799-1863) collected Japanese porcelain. The East knew how to make art work the romantic magic.

Romantic theatrical art gave life ecstasy, revelation, and a glimpse of the eternal oneness of the universe. In this light, romantics considered art to be a truer, more real experience than life itself. But to glimpse the infinity of existence and to capture that vision in artistic matter eluded numerous romantic artists, who produced a plethora of unfinished works. Many artists gave up altogether; the material reality of art could never embody the truth of spiritual infinity.

Music stands as the romantics' greatest artistic achievement; it approximated the romantic goal most successfully. Because music existed in time rather than in space, it satisfied the quest for infinity. It also probed human emotions most deeply. Music thus invaded the theatre. Philosopher Friedrich Schlegel considered music to be the only universal language. Philosopher Arthur Schopenhauer (1788–1860) revived the Greek investigation of the relationship between mathematics and music. And German playwright Ludwig Tieck (1773–1853) thought music "the last mystery of faith, the fully revealed religion." Dramatic poetry, too, worked to capture music's power. Music and poetry achieved an unsurpassed alliance as the spoken word tried to assume the qualities of music. Tieck even called his plays "prose operas." Western music caught the rhythms of nature as the East introduced expanded percussion sections to Western orchestras.

***Opera***  Music, the most romantic art form, attempted to synthesize the arts in the manner of the ancient Greeks and Indians. As a result, opera emerged as the dominant form of aesthetic romanticism. Romantic opera kept the form of the comic opera, added more expressivity, featured dangerous plots and passionate characters, and displayed the universality of great love amid the powers of untamed nature. Italians, the inventors of opera, dominated the romantic opera world.

Giuseppe Verdi (1813–1901), the son of a tavern keeper, wrote his first opera, *Oberto*, in 1839. He couldn't stop. He wrote *Nabucco* (1842), *Ernani* (1844) from Hugo's play, *Il Trovatore* (1853), *La Traviata* (1853), and *Rigoletto* (1855) from another Hugo play. Verdi claimed

he admired the sixteenth-century composers Palestrina and Rossini more than Beethoven or Mozart. Verdi worked at the Paris Opera between 1855 and 1870. He composed *Don Carlos* (1867) there, but *Un ballo in maschera* (*The Masked Ball*, 1859) played in Rome and *La forza del destino* (*The Force of Destiny*, 1862) played in St. Petersburg. Verdi concluded his career with *Aida* (1887), *Otello* (1887), and *Falstaff* (1893). Gioacchino Rossini (1792–1868) had dominated Italian opera before Verdi with works such as *Il barbiere di Siviglia* (*The Barber of Seville*, 1816), *Otello* (1816), *La Cenerentola* (*Cinderella*, 1817), and *Guillaume Tell* (*William Tell*, 1829). Ludwig van Beethoven (1770–1827), who read Plato, Aristotle, and Shakespeare, had displayed Mozart's genius at the beginning of his career. He wrote only one opera—*Fidelio* (1805)—but finished his career with *The Ninth Symphony* (1824), five string quartets, and the *Missa Solemnis*.

Music carried the romantic vision outside the opera hall. The sonata was replaced by romantic sounding etudes, intermezzi, arabesques, fantasies, rhapsodies, impromptus, improvisations, and variations. Virtuoso playing and conducting appeared as well.

Even satire and burlesque reached new heights with romantic music. In England William Gilbert (1836–1911) and Arthur Sullivan (1842–1900) knocked romanticism itself with their operettas. *Patience* (1881) parodied the aesthetic movement's love of genius. *The Mikado* (1885), a satire on England's rapture with Japan, drew a formal complaint from the Japanese ambassador.

***The Artist as Hero***  Romantic theatre artists modeled their heroes on themselves to an unprecedented degree. Life and dramatic art overlapped; autobiography and fiction spilled onto each other. Wanderer, outcast, rebel, mysterious stranger—each appellation suited both artist and fictional hero. The romantic audience read the stage hero into the artist and the artist into the stage hero.

As a visionary, the artist-hero intuited order

in the universe and apprehended meaning in nature. Communication of that vision would redeem humanity. As a bohemian, the Romantic artist-hero experimented with living arrangements, dress, appearance, alcohol, drugs, and sexual variation. Romanticism used sex to liberate the passions. The artist-hero rebelled against traditional sexual mores. Often romantic theatre workers believed a person's spiritual self could only achieve fulfillment with a sex partner. The act of love would reconcile warring opposites. As a gentleman dandy, the romantic artist-hero also played the master ironist, the man of leisure, in order to reveal the emptiness of bourgeois society. By donning the clothes and behavior of corrupt society, the romantic artist-hero would reveal society's nakedness. English playwright Oscar Wilde (1854–1900) played the romantic dandy with great humor and tragedy.

*The Theatre* Romantic comedy was in short supply. In essence, the romantic vision was one of despair: the ideal could never become real. Even the genius was doomed. Whatever humor the genius had was bitter, ironical, and destructive. English critic William Hazlitt (1798–1830) thought there was nothing to laugh about or ridicule during the Romantic age: "In short, the proper object of ridicule is egotism; and a man cannot be a very great egotist who everyday sees himself represented on the stage. We are deficient in comedy, because we are without characters in real life." [1] An age that revered genius saw no egotism to mock. The object of ridicule had become the source of artistic genius.

Who could mock the romantic genius who had experienced the essential dualities of life, the universal antitheses striving for resolution? Previous ages had found truth in fixed essences. The Romantic age found truth in dualities—for example, the physical against the spiritual. The romantic was torn and broken, alone, isolated, and in search of synthesis and integration. Dramatic art reconciled the dualities of existence, and made individuals whole again, in a glimpse of the ultimate dialectical resolution. The romantic theatrical experience resembled the experience of the Asian theatre. In fact, in 1789 William Jones translated *Sakuntala* by the Indian playwright Kalidasa into Latin for Western intellectuals to read and envy. (Jones thought Latin as alien to Western culture as Sanskrit to Eastern culture.) The romantic theatrical experience sought to redeem individuals in the manner of the Christian religious experience.

Tragedy, the form of drama alien to bourgeois optimism, returned to the stage because the romantic vision was tragic. The romantic hero died in order to return to the oneness of nature. In death, the hero achieved victory over material destiny. An enormous number of romantic tragedies became romantic operas because music made their passionate messages more palatable to the public. But the bourgeoisie would not be denied a taste of the new theatrical vision.

Melodrama, the new bourgeois form, took the surface traits of romantic tragedy but stuck on a last minute happy ending to satisfy bourgeois needs. An orchestra played throughout each play. Composers scored each melodrama and received billing with the playwrights. Music delineated characters at entrances and exits. Certain instruments even became associated with certain melodramatic characters. The counterbass, for example, accompanied the villain; the trumpet, the hero; the flute, the persecuted innocent; and the bassoon, the clown. Melodramas provided songs, dances, pantomimes, and special effects.

Romantic scenery grew out of the "antiquarianism" and "exoticism" of the late social theatre. Landscape painters often doubled as scene painters. In 1808 German critic August Wilhelm Schlegel (1767–1845), the brother of philosopher Friedrich, complained of the disproportion between the actor and the perspective scene. Actors could not touch or use the painted scenery. The romantics countered the objection by accelerating the movement toward three-dimensional realism. They did not, however, produce a new scenic vision; instead, they regularized the design of new settings for each production. Gas lighting darkened auditoriums to enhance the audiences' vision of ideal, remote, or mythic worlds unbroken by nearby distractions.

As audiences demanded more recognizable places and more historical accuracy in decor, realism in scenery and costume increased. The need for directors to coordinate the actors with the music and scenic effects increased as well. Consequently, the Romantic age accelerated the rise of the director to a position of prominence. But the actor retained the dominant position. The actor, not the playwright, was the romantic theatre's principal virtuoso. Great acting, in fact, compensated for the dearth of great plays. A new respect for Shakespeare as a romantic genius brought his characters to the favor of romantic actors; Richard III stood as romantic actors' favorite role.

Key "points," climactic moments in the play, revealed the romantic actors' genius, and touches of real-life nature kept these actors in touch with the source of all inspiration. Some actors even worked to break the rhythm of blank verse to make the language more "natural." Acting featured sudden shifts of intense emotion, volume, and rate as passions seized and possessed romantic actors. Detailed pantomimic action and excruciating death scenes highlighted romantic interpretations.

Romantic actors lived as stars of the human firmament. Stars needed great roles rather than great supporting companies. As a result, resident stock companies declined as stars toured their genius to the masses. The railroad and steamship brought actors to the people and crowds of people to the ever-growing theatres. Stars were forced to extend their engagements to accommodate all the people wanting glimpses of their genius. The long run resulted. And actors were hired for individual shows rather than for seasons.

Romanticism, like sentimental comedy and bourgeois drama, remained a strong force into the Modern era. In 1800 France epitomized the hopes of democratic revolutionaries for political change. England stood as the center of the industrial revolution in economics and society. But Germany housed the revolutionary sentiments in aesthetics. During the nineteenth and twentieth centuries these three revolutions spread out to influence the world.

## GERMANY

The political unification that produced a renaissance in most European nations arrived late in Germany—during the Romantic Age. Count Otto von Bismarck of Prussia used war to forge the German nation. The nationhood frustrated by Reformation bloodshed, Renaissance rivalries, the Thirty Years' War, and the Council of Vienna witnessed the end of Romantic despair.

***Asian Consolation*** Prior to Bismarck's triumph, however, romantic despair grew. Violence, epidemics, loss of life and property, suppression, and exploitation continued. Germany's lack of political freedom led philosopher Friedrich Schlegel and his circle of friends toward the romantic theatrical vision. Schlegel found India's consolation in the life of the spirit appealing. He wrote to playwright Ludwig Tieck that "the real source of all tongues, of all thoughts and utterances of the human mind . . . everything—yes, everything without exception—has its origin in India." In 1800 Schlegel disclosed, "It is to the East that we must look for the supreme Romanticism." Schlegel learned Sanskrit to read Hindu philosophy. He admired India's synthesis of art, science, religion, philosophy, and theatre into one ideal way of living.

Friedrich's brother, critic and poet August Wilhelm Schlegel shared his enthusiasm. August defined romanticism as the opposite of classicism. He admired Shakespeare and, with his wife, Katherine, translated many of Shakespeare's plays into German. In addition, August worked for Madame de Staël, thereby helping to bring, through her writing, the German philosophy to France. The Schlegel brothers also founded the journal *Athenaeum* to disseminate the romantic ideal. Both men continued their Asian studies; the Hindu drama *Sakuntala* reigned as their ideal drama.

*A Philosophical Theatre*    Though indebted to the East, German romanticism found its true springboard in the philosophy of Immanuel Kant (1724–1804). By making aesthetics the basis of a new metaphysics, Kant's theory of knowledge began German idealism. Art, Kant observed, does not depend upon conscious, rational, or intellectual processes. Meaning and sense are not external absolutes, he believed, but rather the products of subjective perceptions and sensations that nature and individual minds share.

Kant thought that religion and theatrical art attain value only as they help intuitive morality find appropriate action. Kant believed that "spirit" was only the mind animated by an aesthetic idea. Playwrights, such as Schiller and Goethe, and philosophers found excitement in Kant's writing.

Georg Wilhelm Friedrich Hegel (1770–1831) lived in Jena with Schiller, Tieck, and the Schlegels. Hegel located truth in the relationship between contrasting opposites. The "dialectical movement" of opposites, the resolution of conflict into a new complex entity, made, he believed, evolution the basic process of life. The dramaturgical mind, Hegel urged, should imitate nature by seeking the unity beneath diversity. Change was the basic principle of nature and therefore of the drama. Individuals had to move, as the Daoists, with the flow of change.

Friedrich Schiller (1759–1805) thought that the flow was driven by two human powers: the *Stofftrieb* (the desire for sensual fulfillment) and the *Formtrieb* (the need for conceptualization). The contrasting principles find resolution in the *Spieltrieb* (the need to play). Play, especially the play of the theatre, soothes individuals' conflicting needs for both change and stasis. Theatrical art, Schiller believed, exists as the ultimate form of human play. The theatre plays to reveal the unity beneath diversity.

Philosopher Arthur Schopenhauer (1788–1860) knew no parents and had no wife, children, or friends. Schopenhauer lived alone with his poodle, Atma, named after the Hindu *atman*. *The World as Will and Idea* (1818), which gathered dust until theatre composer Richard Wagner praised it, begins with an affirmation of Kant: "The world is my idea." Schopenhauer's masterpiece encouraged romantic theatre workers to look within themselves for a glimpse of meaning. Schopenhauer believed that dramatic art gives everyone a glimpse of the truth known by geniuses. Great theatre art suspends the audience's wills, as does Asian theatre, and through a particular play an audience perceives universal truth. Only a genius can accomplish such a feat. Music succeeds in this because music imitates the will itself. Music, like the will, aims directly at the emotions to attain its power. Schopenhauer thought Hinduism and Eastern aesthetic practice would, in time, more profoundly influence the West than Christianity would the East. The modern world testifies to the validity of his insight.

*Nietzsche and Tragedy*    Philosopher Friedrich Nietzsche (1844–1900) looked to Greece, the meeting place of East and West, to formulate his ideas. He had read Schopenhauer and loved Richard Wagner's opera *Tristan und Isolde*. Nietzsche even visited Wagner near Lucerne. In 1872 the 27-year-old University of Basle professor wrote his first book, *The Birth of Tragedy from the Spirit of Music*, and dedicated it to Wagner. Nietzsche rediscovered the prerational exuberance of the Dionysian mystery music that had given birth to Greek tragedy. After the publication of Nietzsche's book, the ancient Greeks could no longer be thought of as the simple, noble, refined, and calm people of Weimar classicism. Instead, the Greeks came to house the struggle between the irrationality, imbalance, and emotion of the Greek god Dionysus and the proportion, balance, and structure of the Greek god Apollo. Nietzsche's

Greek gods personified the romantics' struggle in nineteenth-century Europe.

Tragedy, Nietzsche postulated, grew from the dialectical meeting of Dionysus, the symbol of creative and destructive energy (like the Hindu gods Shiva and Vishnu), with Apollo, the symbol of restraint, meaning, and harmonizing energy (like the Hindu god Brahma). Tragedy synthesized the two energies into an affirmation of life amid a world of suffering. Dionysus gave individuals the intoxicating experience of life in the real world; tremendous terror and blissful ecstasy led people to complete self-forgetfulness. Individuals and nature were reconciled in Dionysus, fused together "as if the veil of maya had been torn aside. He is no longer an artist, he is a work of art."

Apollo, on the other hand, gave individuals the dream experience of the artist's imaginary world. Music keyed the fusion of the Dionysian with the Apollonian experiences. The Dionysian melody of emotional flow met the Apollonian rhythmic beat: "Apollo could not live without Dionysus." Melody was primary, rhythm secondary. Dionysus always precedes Apollo, as reality precedes the dream. Thus Greek tragedy received a romantic history.

According to Nietzsche, the Greek chorus was rooted in the Dionysian experience. In dithyrambic singing, the hero, Dionysus, was not actually present. In dramatic choral singing, however, the hero, Dionysus, was present but in disguise. Dionysus appeared dressed as the Greek mythological heroes, "in the net of the individual will. The god who appears talks and acts so as to resemble an erring, striving, suffering individual. That he appears at all with such epic precision and clarity is the work of the dream-interpreter, Apollo, who through this symbolic appearance interprets to the chorus its Dionysian state."[2] The hero of Greek tragedy—indeed, the hero of all drama for Nietzsche—is Dionysus, suffering from the act of individuation that created his physical manifestation. Only when individuality ends, only when the romantic hero dies, would the suffering end and the spirit of Dionysus escape his physical disguise.

Tragedy shows "the fundamental knowledge of the oneness of everything existent, the conception of individuation as the primal cause of evil, and of art as the joyous hope that the spell of the individuation may be broken in augury of a restored oneness."[3] But Nietzsche thought Greek tragedy committed suicide. Like Gotthold Lessing in the eighteenth century, the Greek playwright Euripides preferred to intellectualize as a critic rather than write as a poet. He thus wrote as an observer of life. Under the influence of the philosopher Socrates, Euripides, said Nietzsche, wrote according to the following principles: "To be beautiful everything must be intelligible," and "Knowledge is virtue." Euripides was not a romantic; he found real tragedy too repugnant, too dangerous, too inexplicable. Nietzsche believed that Euripides retreated to philosophy; Apollo shrank to logic and Dionysus to naturalism. Optimism based on knowledge and virtue replaced the pessimism of individuality. Tragedy became impossible for people like Euripides, who depend on virtue, knowledge, faith, and morality.

Nietzsche lambasted the illusion that the rational mind could "penetrate the deepest abyss of being." He saw science born in tragedy's death: science wishes "to make existence appear comprehensible and thus justified." Nietzsche predicted that science would come to the point "when they see to their horror how logic coils up at these boundaries and finally bites its own tail." His observation predicted not the realistic theatre, but the modern theatre.

***Wagner and Opera*** Music was the key to Nietzsche's idea of the drama. His friend Richard Wagner (1813–1883) sought a continuously developing orchestral music without set numbers. Wagner employed a musical structure based on melody and modulation called *leitmotiv*, a musico-dramatic device for expressing character motivation. Nietzsche liked the tragic insight he found in Wagner's operas. He hoped romantic music could restore tragedy to pre-Euripidean greatness. Romantic tragedy could let the Greek god Apollo redeem individuals with dreams and illusions after the god Dionysus had celebrated the joy of existence within the universal consciousness of infinity. But Nietzsche repudiated Wagner when the composer began to philosophize. *Parsifal* seemed insincere and hypocritical to Nietzsche, and in 1888 he wrote *The Wagner Case* and *Nietzsche contra Wagner*. Two weeks later Nietzsche went mad.

Nevertheless, Wagner dominated German music and theatre during the Romanic era. After living in Paris for three years, Wagner moved to Dresden, where his *Rienzi* (1842), *Der fliegende Holländer* (*The Flying Dutchman*, 1843), and *Tannhäuser* (1845) enjoyed success. He participated in the 1849 revolution and fled to Switzerland, where he developed his theories of music-drama. Wagner proposed a *Gesamtkunstwerk* (a master artwork) synthesizing music, poetry, drama, spectacle, and mythology. Such a synthesis had given classical Greek and Indian music-drama their peculiar genius. But *Das Rheingold* and *Die Walküre*, the first two parts of a proposed tetralogy, *Der Ring des Nibelungen* (*The Ring of the Nibelung*) were refused production and attacked by traditionalists.

In 1864 18-year-old Ludwig of Bavaria became king. Though insane, the young king loved both Wagner's *Lohengrin* (1846) and the composer's ideas for German art. Patronized by Ludwig, Wagner produced *Tristan und Isolde* (1865), *Die Meistersinger von Nürnberg* (*The Mastersinger of Nurnberg*, 1868), and his *The Ring of the Nibelung* (1876). *The Ring* opened his *Festspielhaus*, a theatre built at Bayreuth and financed by worldwide Wagner Societies. *Siegfried* (1871) and *Götterdämmerung* (1874) completed the tetralogy.

Wagner's operas were quasireligious theatrical events expressing the composer's yearning for something in which to believe. Wagner saw himself as a priest, and his *Gesamtkunstwerk* as a ritual for an audience wishing to merge its identity with the Germanic myths. Wagner accomplished what most romantic German playwrights desired.

***Dramatic Texts*** The works of the German romantic playwrights seemed to anticipate the work of Richard Wagner. Indeed, romantic playwrights shared Wagner's goal for his opera *Parsifal*: "to enable everybody to escape, for a while, from the disgusting and disheartening burden of this world of lying and fraud and hypocrisy and legalized murder." Goethe remained the romantics' hero, despite his dislike for the romantics' abandonment of reason and discipline. Old Goethe had turned to the East's Persian poetry for sensuality and mysticism. Meanwhile, Schiller found the ideal of feminine beauty in the Hindu play *Sakuntala* and inserted part of the Hindu playwright Kalidasa's *The Cloud Messenger* in his play *Maria Stuart* (1800).

Ludwig Tieck (1773–1853) heard all about the East from Friedrich Schlegel, but he found Goethe, Shakespeare, and the Spanish writer Cervantes most to his taste. He developed a particular fascination for determining how Shakespeare's plays were staged originally. Visits to England to research and stage Shakespeare's plays led Tieck to abandon the eighteenth century's versions of Shakespeare. Also, Tieck disliked the Englishman John Philip Kemble's acting; he thought it a poor version of French neo-classicism. With his daughter Dorothea, Tieck thus helped translate Shakespeare's plays for a new edition. His interest in Shakespearean staging accounted for Tieck's demand, as Dresden's dramaturg, for simplicity in staging at a time of growing realism in scenic decoration.

Tieck's own plays displayed the romantic love of old fairy and folk tales, such as Bluebeard, and the Puss-in-Boots tale. His play *Zerbina* (1799) introduced the son of Puss-in-Boots in quest of Good Taste. Tieck also tried to write medieval epic dramas. Beneath historical and fantastical details Tieck satirized both eighteenth-century rationalism and bourgeois theatrical tastes.

Heinrich von Kleist (1777–1811) lived unrecognized until after his suicide, when Tieck published his plays posthumously. In Kleist's *Prinz Friedrich von Homburg* (1810), a Romantic hero accepts death as his victory. Although Kleist held many romantic notions, he had little contact with other writers. Kleist's studies with Immanuel Kant and his obsession with the illusory nature of reality infested his plays. Reading Kant, in fact, caused Kleist to drop out of the University of Frankfurt to lead an almost archetypal romantic life. He fought against Napolean in hope of dying. In 1811, he helped a dying woman expire and then committed suicide.

A medical student who had to flee for his life after organizing a secret political group, Georg Büchner (1813–1837), like many romantics, died young. His *Dantóns Tod* (*Danton's Death*, 1835) showed the influence of Shakespeare. But *Leonce und Lena* (1836) seemed more like a play by French playwright Alfred de Musset (1810–1857). Büchner finished medical school, lectured on anatomy and zoology, started to write *Woyzeck* (1896) to reveal the corruption of humanity, and then died of typhus.

Influenced by both Nietzsche's intellectuality and Schopenhauer's theory of music, Richard Wagner wrote the most romantic dramas of the age. Emotion reigned as the most important element in his work. Because diction addressed the rational mind, Wagner chose music to speak directly to the universal soul. Music, moreover, gave his productions a regularity missing in spoken drama. Spoken drama was also inappropriate for Wagner's ideal theatre of myth. He wished to combine the genius of Shakespearean drama with the greatness of Beethoven's music. Wagnerian drama affected the audiences as a drug. French symbolist writer Charles Beaudelaire (1821–1867) actually compared Wagner's overture to *Lohengrin* with opium. Wagner believed an audience could only be affected by a master artwork that was composed, written, and directed by one person.

***Scenic Innovation*** Besides dramatic theory and music, German romantics introduced important scenic innovations. Ludwig Tieck investigated the history of the Elizabethan playhouse and other historical performance conditions. In 1841 Emperor Friedrich Wilhelm invited Tieck to stage Sophocles's tragedy *Antigone*. For the production, composer Felix Mendelssohn (1809–1847) supplied music for the chorus, and Tieck supervised a reconstruction of a Greek stage. In 1843 Tieck produced Shakespeare's *A Midsummer Night's Dream* on a reconstructed Elizabethan stage. Built on the proscenium stage of the Neues Palace, Tieck's Fortune Theatre had two levels, each with three acting areas. German fascination with historical accuracy led Jacob Weiss to publish authoritative histories of costume in 1856 and 1872.

For interior scenes, an occasional box setting appeared. To create the box sets, panels were added between flat wings to form a room. The first complete box set appeared in Berlin in 1826. But scenic innovations were contradictory. Tieck made history by urging simplicity and suggestion at a time of passionate detail in realistic illusion. Richard Wagner made history by demanding greater realism in a reconceived theatrical space.

***The Bayreuth Festspielhaus*** For his Bayreuth *Festspielhaus* Wagner supervised the plans of architect Gottfried Semper. Wagner demanded a classless theatre like the one he imagined in ancient Greece. Wagner's theatre did not have the conventional box, pit, and gallery division. Thirty tiered rows ran without aisle from one side of the auditorium to the other. To improve sight lines, 1745 seats fanned out from the stage. The orchestra pit below the stage floor wafted music out an opening where a pit should have been. The space between the opening to the orchestra and the proscenium arch was known as the "mystic gulf" or "mystic chasm" (see p. 404).

This mystic gulf inhabited the space between the proscenium arch and the front rows of seats. Near the seats, a second, wider proscenium arch framed the stage to make the stage action seem even more remote. Wagner explained that "the scene is removed as it were to the unapproachable world of dreams." The chasm separated the real world of the auditorium from the ideal world of the stage. To underline the division, Wagner darkened the auditorium during performances.

The stage itself was a traditional proscenium arch stage. A raked floor supported a chariot and pole system for shifting wing and drop scenery. Steam vents let fog in to complete the illusion of mythic reality. For his dramatic mythologies, Wagner insisted on the latest technology and the most faithful detail in accurate scenery and costume. Wagner wished to hyp-

notize the audience into hushed, reverential passivity. His vision of ideal reality left nothing to the imagination.

Wagner's success with music drama left the German romantic vision in the hands of musicians; the technological innovations of Bayreuth would serve the realistic theatre of the next age. Meanwhile, the ideas of the German romantics infiltrated England and France through Madame Germaine de Staël's book *On Germany* (1813).

# ENGLAND

The war against Napoleon brought England into contact with German romanticism and exacerbated the ills of the industrial revolution at home. England faced a financial crisis from the war. Theatres folded as attendance plummeted. Theatre goers who could afford to attend wanted nothing more taxing than escapist spectacle. Pressure mounted for social and political reform in a nation beset with almost constant social unrest.

*Reform* The execution of France's Louis XVI had frightened England. But plans for reform were suspended lest they encourage the forces of revolution at home. Napoleon and the spirit of democratic revolution had to be crushed. Laws forbade the organization of workers' unions. The Napoleonic war in Europe increased England's national debt, poverty, unemployment, and radicalism. An urban police force tried to maintain the peace. Even poets like Percy Bysshe Shelley (1792–1822) got caught up in the social turmoil. Gradually Parliament yielded to demands for justice to avert social revolution.

Conflict seemed everywhere. Even in India a struggle broke out between natives unhappy with British annexation and resident Westerners. Indians resented British laws outlawing their customs. Indians, objecting to forced conversions to Christianity, mutinied and recaptured Delhi. The revolution spread. But after a year, armed British forces arrived to restore the peace of subjugation.

In England social conditions were almost as bad. In 1801 only 26 percent of Britain's population lived in cities of 5000 or more. But by 1891 the figure had reached 72 percent. The potential theatre audience was growing. In midcentury almost 80,000 prostitutes worked London. Forty-five percent of English women between 20 and 40 were unmarried. Fifty percent of factory workers were under 14 years of age. Only 27 percent of factory women were married; older, married women were fired and replaced by children. Domestic service was the primary occupation for women.

*The Literary Theatre* Faced with social problems, English literature expressed a faith in the transcendental world spirit. The world spirit, if allowed the chance to inspire, could heal. Individuals needed to open themselves to the world spirit so that genius might flourish. English romantic literature developed, in part, as a reaction to the industrial revolution. In playwright Oliver Goldsmith's *Deserted Village* (1770) and in poet Percy Bysshe Shelley's song of "Despair" (1810), the town, nature, and countryside were contrasted with the city, society, and industry.

William Wordsworth (1770–1850) wanted a poetry of everyday speech. Wordsworth considered nature to be the source of wisdom. With Wordsworth, poet Samuel Taylor Coleridge produced *The Lyrical Ballads* (1798). After Wordsworth and Coleridge traveled to Germany to study German romantic literature and philosophy, Coleridge translated Friedrich Schiller's *Wallenstein* (1799–1800). Coleridge's *Biographia Literaria* (1817) did for dramatic "imagination" what Aristotle's *Poetics* had done for dramatic "action."

Lord Byron (1788–1824) and Shelley developed a more radical romanticism. The son of an aristocrat, Shelley was expelled from Oxford for his pamphlet *The Necessity of Atheism* (1810). He left England to live in Italy. Following his wife's suicide, he married his mistress, Mary Wollstonecraft Shelley.

Philosopher John Stuart Mill had called poetry "soliloquy"; Shelley extended the definition to argue that poetry's function was "to cheer [his own] solitude with sweet sounds." His reader was but an eavesdropper. Shelley combined mysticism and Hellenism with a fascination for science. After his death in a sailing accident, for example, his wife kept his withered heart in an envelope on her desk.

Before his death, Shelley composed two romantic dramas, *The Cenci* (1819) and *Prometheus Unbound* (1820). In the former, Count Francesco Cenci tyrannizes his family and rapes his daughter, Beatrice, but escapes punishment by bribing government officials. But Beatrice, forced to murder her father, is punished by the same judicial system that failed to prosecute her father.

George Gordon Noel Byron, the club-footed son of a libertine, developed aristocratic inclinations. Hints of incest with his sister forced him to leave England for Switzerland. (Many romantics left their native lands.) Byron wanted to reform the English stage. To help the reformation he wrote *Manfred* (1817), a portrait of rebellion against a Christian universe, and *Cain* (1821). Byron made his personality the center of the public's interest; his works were only a part of the unfolding drama of his life. Byron made dissolution and despair fashionable in English romanticism. His works perfected the character of the demonic hero, possessed of death and danger, scornful of sacred Christianity and the middle class. Lucifer was Byron's hero.

The last great character in English romantic literature, Charles Dickens, had one foot in the next age's realism. Indeed, Dickens had a romantic sensibility and a realistic eye. The son of a naval clerk, Charles Dickens (1812–1870) worked in the factories as a child. Many of his novels were serialized in the English press, thereby giving his work dramatic structure and suspense. Several of his works were adapted to the stage as well. Dickens himself claimed he would have preferred being a great actor to a great novelist. He thought the theatre "the most rational of amusements," and he believed that "every writer of fiction, though he may not adapt the dramatic form, writes, in effect, for the stage."

Dickens created a one-man traveling show out of his works: he traveled the world speaking and reading to large and enthusiastic audiences. Even the dour English essayist Thomas Carlyle beamed that "no theatre stage could have had more players than seemed to flit about his face, and all tones were present." Dickens loved great actors, especially France's great actor, Frederick Lemaitre, and England's own stars, William Macready and Henry Irving. In fact, Dickens began an affair with an actress, Ellen Teinan, though many years her senior. Despite poor health he pressed on with his lecture and speaking tours with suicidal passion. His life explained his love for Gounod's romantic opera *Faust*: "I could hardly bear the thing, it affected me so, and sounded in my ears so like a mournful echo of things that lie in my own heart."

Dickens took the misery of London and spun romantic tales. In contrast, Walter Pater (1839–1894), a classics tutor, retreated to the Renaissance. His studies in *The History of the Renaissance* (1873) became a favorite with the romantic dandies and aesthetes of London, who adopted the guise of gentleman in order to send society flying. Playwright Oscar Wilde carried romantic impersonation to the theatre.

***Great Players*** Above all, English romanticism in the theatre produced greatness in acting. From John Philip Kemble to Henry Irving, English actors of the Romantic age demonstrated poet Samuel Taylor Coleridge's belief that imagination was both the means of nature and the means of the artist.

After touring the provinces for seven years, John Philip Kemble (1757–1823) debuted in 1783 London as Hamlet. Kemble wore costumes well but lacked a sense of humor. He founded the so-called ''teapot'' school of acting because his posture resembled a teapot. His weight shifted from foot to foot as his hand gestures mirrored the change of side. Kemble's declamatory style and monotonous, forced vibrato arose from his desire to perform formally and classically. Although critics attacked him for his affected pronunciation, Kemble nevertheless played 172 different roles. He excelled in Shakespeare's *Coriolanus*, but novelist Sir Walter Scott (1771–1832) loved his Macbeth best. Kemble also created the first popular Hamlet since David Garrick; he interpreted the prince as a gentle, philosophical man. As manager of Drury Lane for fifteen years, Kemble appointed William Capon (1757–1827) scene designer of antiquarian settings. Kemble retired in 1817 as the public's attention turned to Edmund Kean.

Kemble's older sister, Sarah Siddons (1755–1831), dominated the English stage for thirty years. She debuted in London in 1775. King George III and all of London were especially infatuated with her beauty and dignity. Portrait painter Sir Joshua Reynolds (1723–1792) even immortalized her as The Tragic Muse. Unlike her brother, Sarah Siddons presented more natural emotions and behavior. Excellent at mime, Mrs. Siddons nonetheless drew criticism for her annoying and monotonous rhythm; some critics dubbed it ''hobbletitrot.'' Her grand style was also unsuited for comedy. Her best role was Lady Macbeth. In addition, the great actor David Garrick hired her to play Lady Anne to his Richard III just before he retired. Sarah Siddons also made costume history by eliminating the hoops and powdered wig from the standard court costume of tragedy. Siddons and Kemble were, paradoxically, known for a dignity that faded when faced with the emotional barrage of George Frederick Cooke and Edmund Kean.

George Frederick Cooke (1756–1812)

*George Frederick Cooke as Richard III.* (Lilly Library, Indiana University, Bloomington, Indiana)

flashed brilliantly when sober, but he was often hissed from the stage for drunkenness. When sober, Cooke was an intellectual scholar and gentleman; when drunk, he was a debauched maniac. He suspected, in fact, that he was insane. Managers did not allow him to debut in London until he was 45 years old. Critics admired his great voice, but found his gestures awkward, even in his great performances of Richard III, Shylock, Iago, and Macbeth. In 1810 Cooke went impulsively to America, where he met American playwright William Dunlap, his eventual biographer. When Cooke died on tour, his body was buried unceremoniously, and his head was used by a stock company for its production of *Hamlet*. Eventually the head found its way to the New York phrenological society. When news of these outrages reached London, Cooke's greatest fan, Edmund Kean, came to New York to give his mentor a proper burial. (Kean did, however, keep one of Cooke's toes as a good luck piece while he was on tour.)

Edmund Kean (c. 1787–1833) epitomized English romantic acting. As a boy Kean wore leg braces. Nonetheless, at age three he was forced to play Cupid in a Drury Lane ballet. Later, pretending to be a deaf orphan, he ran away to sea. Back home he joined Drury Lane and created a sensation as Shylock. He played the part for the first time as a manly, handsome, and witty martyr. Kean's dazzling portrayals of Richard III, Hamlet, and Iago caused Samuel Taylor Coleridge to announce

*Edmund Kean as Richard III.*  (Lilly Library)

that "to see him act is like reading Shakespeare by flashes of lightening." His Sir Giles Overreach in Phillip Massinger's (1583–1640) *A New Way to Pay Old Debts* remained a popular favorite. History also credits Kean with restoring the original fifth act to *King Lear*, even though he abandoned the change after three nights of audience objections. Meanwhile Lord Byron became Kean's good friend. Perhaps Byron agreed with critics who saw Kean as "all violence, all extreme passion," and "possessed with a fury, a demon."

In 1820 Kean traveled to America, and his notoriety spread. But in 1825 a court case involving Kean's adultery with a Mrs. Cox turned the public against him. Kean turned to drink and became preoccupied with death. On tour in America, moreover, Kean refused to play to small audiences. Melancholic and depressed, he ultimately collapsed on stage playing Othello to his son's Iago; he died six weeks later.

With Kean gone the spotlight turned to William Charles Macready (1793–1873). Forced into the theatre to pay his father's debts, Macready debuted at Covent Garden in 1816. His 1819 performance in Richard III elevated him to chief rival of Kean. Macready combined John Philip Kemble's declamation with Edmund Kean's detailed pantomimic action. Critics noted less passion from Macready and so labeled him a snob with a temper. In the 1820s, when Macready toured America and France, audiences witnessed "the Macready pause," his attempt to break blank verse to make his acting seem more "domestic." Although Macready never succeeded with comedy, audiences found the supernatural, mystical quality of his acting very attractive, especially as Lear, Macbeth, and Virginius. He tried to "feel" his roles; he announced "I cannot act Macbeth without being Macbeth."

In 1827 Macready took over the management of Covent Garden and instituted many of the practices begun by Wolfgang von Goethe in Weimar. For example, he blocked the stage action, insisted that players act at rehearsals, worked painstakingly on crowd scenes, and commissioned new, historically accurate set-

*William Macready as Macbeth.* (Lilly Library)

tings. He also, however, lost money. His unsuccessful production of Shakespeare and "gentlemanly melodrama," in fact, forced him to tour. During his last tour of America, Macready quarreled with America's star, Edwin Forrest. Riots broke out before New York City's Astor Place Opera House where Macready was acting, and many died. Macready, the darling of educated theatre goers, retired in 1851. His successors never attained the reverence he and Edmund Kean had enjoyed.

Other actors at this time included Samuel Phelps and Fanny Kemble. Samual Phelps (1804–1878), like Macready, worked as an actor-manager. He especially fostered an intense audience identification with his characters. He consciously avoided emphasizing ''points'' and trained young actors to do likewise. Popular as Bottom in Shakespeare's *A Midsummer Night's Dream*, Phelps also attained fame for restoring original texts to Shakespearean production. At Sadlers Wells, Phelps produced all but four of Shakespeare's plays and proved that poetic drama could still turn a profit. Fanny Kemble (1809–1893), small and dark haired, became a star after her first appearance for her father, Charles, at Covent Garden in

1829. She took her famous rendition of Juliet to America, met a man, married, and retired to a Georgian plantation. After her divorce, she toured America and England giving readings of Shakespeare.

Realism began to characterize English acting with Charles Fechter (1824–1879). Tall, handsome, and French-born, Fechter was the first actor to play the classics with the same natural style used in contemporary plays. Although noted for his uncontrollable temper, Fechter dominated England and the West as the great stage lover. As Armand in the original production of Alexandre Dumas *fils's* (1824–1895) *La dame aux camélias* (*The Woman of the Camellias*, 1852) and as Hamlet in 1861,

*Henry Irving as Shylock.* (Lilly Library)

Fechter transplanted French melodramatic acting to England. His blonde Hamlet with a French accent was the rage.

Romantic acting continued with Henry Irving (1838–1905), who debuted in 1866. Ten years in the provinces preceded Irving's sensational appearance in Leopold Lewis's *The Bells* (1872). Irving's intensity almost overshadowed his ludicrous vocal and physical mannerisms. He depended on clever and original pantomimic action to compensate for a very bad voice. In addition, noble passions were beyond Irving, and his love-making scenes brought laughter. But he so excelled in playing scenes of horror, pride, and sarcasm that Irving received the first knighthood bestowed on an actor. He died after finishing a performance of Alfred Lord Tennyson's (1809–1892) *Becket* with the lines "Into thy hands, O Lord." His lover, Ellen Terry (1847–1928) reigned as England's most popular actress. Audiences loved her utter naturalism on the stage. Terry was especially good as Beatrice in *Much Ado About Nothing* and Portia in *The Merchant of Venice*.

*Actor–Managers*   Actors managed most of the theatres of the period. Moreover, actor-managers became intimately involved in the utilization of their theatres' spaces. Covent Garden, for example, came under John Philip Kemble three years after George Cooke's debut there in 1800. Sarah Siddons debuted at Covent Garden in 1812; four years later William Macready debuted there as well. Kemble retired at Covent Garden in 1817, the year gas lighting was installed. His brother Charles (1775–1854) managed the theatre and dazzled audiences with historically accurate scenery and costumes designed by J. R. Planche (1796–1880). In 1819 a new theatre replaced the Covent Garden destroyed by fire. In 1832 both Charles Kemble's famous *King John* and his daughter Fanny played Covent Garden. William Macready managed the theatre between 1837 and 1839 and oversaw the introduction of limelight there. (For further discussion of limelight, see the next section, *Increasing Spectacle*.) Madame Vestris (1797–1856) and her

husband, Charles Matthews (1803–1878), took control in 1839. They produced their biggest hit, Irishman Dion Boucicault's (1822–1890) *London Assurance*, in 1841. Covent Garden closed the next year, when Vestris left. In 1847 the theatre reopened as the Italian Opera House; thereafter, it entertained opera.

Drury Lane burned down in 1809 but reopened in 1812 with *Hamlet*. Two years later Edmund Kean debuted there as Shylock. William Macready's management of Drury Lane ran up so many deficits that the proprietor refused to renew his lease. Macready thus began a petition drive to break the monopoly of the patent theatres. As a result, on August 22, 1843, Parliament passed the Theatre Regulation Act, freeing all theatres for the production of all kinds of plays.

A new Haymarket theatre, designed by

*The exterior of the Drury Lane Theatre in 1776.*   (Lilly Library)

Nashe, opened with *The Rivals* in 1820. In 1833 audiences lined up to see Julia Glover play Falstaff. Benjamin Webster's management brought gas light and Samuel Phelps's debut to the Haymarket in 1837. The Haymarket stood as London's premiere theatre under Buckstone's management in 1853. America's great star, Edwin Booth, made his London debut at the Haymarket in 1861.

A theatre that opened in 1806 was rechristened Little Drury Lane in 1813 to distinguish it from the patent theatre of the same name. Eventually the building took the name Olympic and housed melodrama. Gas light entered the Olympic four years before Vestris took over its management, in 1830. With J. R. Planche writing burlesques, extravaganzas, and French adaptations, Vestris made the Olympic fashionable. She also introduced the box set to England around 1832; rooms were decorated as contemporary interiors with carpets, fixtures, and three-dimensional details. As mentioned previously, in 1839 Vestris left the Olympic with her new husband, Charles Matthews, to

*The interior of the New Theatre, Haymarket, in 1821.* (Lilly Library)

manage Covent Garden for three years. The Olympic burned down in 1849 but reopened in time for American playwright Anna Cora Mowatt's *Fashion* and Englishman Tom Taylor's *Ticket-of-Leave Man* in 1863. It was demolished in 1889.

The Lyceum was the home of the Drury Lane company in 1809. In 1830 the building burned down, but it reopened four years later as the Royal Lyceum and Opera House. Vestris tried to make a go of the theatre for nine years but went bankrupt trying. Covent Garden used the building later. Another theatre, the Sadlers Wells, had been famous for aquatic drama (plays which required water to fill the pit) before Samuel Phelps made the place the home of Shakespeare in 1843. Charles Kean's management of the Princess (see the next paragraph) came to rival Phelps's staging of Shakespeare at the Sadlers Wells. But Phelps ended his management in 1862.

The Princess opened in 1840 for opera but switched to spoken drama after the Theatre Regulation Act of 1843. Various stars played the Princess: America's Charlotte Cushman and Edwin Forrest in 1845 and William Macready several times. Charles Kean took control in 1850, two years after the Queen had named him Master of Revels. His responsibility as chief provider of court entertainment helped him raise the status of the Princess. Kean introduced curtain raisers to give the gentry time for a leisurely dinner without missing the main event. Besides Shakespeare—with program notes detailing the accuracy of the decor—Kean produced melodramas like Boucicault's *The Corsican Brothers* (1852), Delavigne's *Louis XI* (1855), and Hugo's *Ruy Blas* (1838) starring Charles Fechter. Kean's *Henry VIII* used limelight for the first time.

***Increasing Spectacle*** The population boom and railroads forced the patent theatres to expand their capacities to accommodate the customers. Each patent house eventually seated around 3000 people. Minor theatres operated until they were caught infringing on the patent theatres' rights. Spectacle increased simultaneously because such enlarged houses could no

*Dion Boucicault's* The Corsican Brothers.   (Lilly Library)

longer offer subtle acting. Romantic acting developed, in part, as a response to the large spaces actors were asked to ''fill.'' In addition, in 1858 the new Adelphi theatre replaced house benches with armchairs for the first time.

Scenic designers increased in importance. John Philip Kemble hired William Capon (1757–1827) to fill the Drury Lane's forty-three by thirty-eight foot proscenium opening with detailed spectacle. Capon also worked at Cov-

*Charles Matthews in Dion Boucicault's* Used Up *(1849)*.   (Lilly Library)

ent Garden and advanced historicity in design throughout London. Complex mechanical machines worked increasingly complex effects. Pageantry increased in history plays; processions, coronations, and cavalry marches took on new importance. Museum-quality authenticity became a regular production value with William Macready's productions in the 1830s. Robert Elliston (1774–1831), the manager of Drury Lane for seven years, eventually installed a water system to enhance the realism of his stage effects.

Effects and specially designed settings and costumes increased production costs, hastened the enlargement of the theatres to increase revenue, and necessitated long runs to repay production costs. Featuring a star actor increased a production's chances of recouping its outlay for scenic ghosts, vampires, monsters, thunderbolts, battleships, avalanches, military sieges, seas, earthquakes, fires, castles, and forests.

Mood was manipulated by new developments in lighting, although the number of theatre fires attest to the dangers of such lighting. Limelight, known as the Drummond light because it was invented by Thomas Drummond in 1816, featured a heated column of lime that produced illumination that was filtered and focused through a glass lens. By the 1850s limelight was widely used. In the 1860s the carbon arc spotlight ran a current of electricity between two carbons. The light from the arc was filtered through a lens to produce a spot of light.

Because plays were designed principally to show the historical period, costume developed along the same lines as scenery. John Philip Kemble ensured the historical accuracy of the dress of the principal characters in some of his plays. When Charles Kemble managed Covent Garden he set new standards for historical accuracy in costuming with his 1823 production of Shakespeare's *King John*. In 1834 J. R. Planche wrote a *History of British Costume*.

### Poets Fail on Stage
Romantic poets rediscovered and admired Shakespeare as never before. Unfortunately, the romantics knew more about Shakespeare's poetry than about his dramaturgical and theatrical expertise.

Some notable poets wrote their own literary plays. For example, poet William Wordsworth (1770–1850) wrote *The Borderers*, poet Samuel Taylor Coleridge wrote *Orsino* (1813), *Remorse* (1823), and, with poet Robert Southey (1774–1843), *The Fall of Robespierre* (1794). Poet John Keats (1795–1821) issued *Otho the Great* (1819), Lord Byron penned *Manfred* (1817), *Marino Faliero* (1821), *Sardanapalus* (1821), and *Werner* (1823), a favorite of actor William Macready. Percy Bysshe Shelley wrote the most successful literary play—his 1819 *Cenci*. Subsequent poets fared worse. Alfred Lord Tennyson submitted *Queen Mary* (1876), *Harold* (1876), *The Falcon* (1879), and *Becket* (1879). Robert Browning (1812–1889) wrote *Strafford* (1837), *King Victor and King Charles* (1842), *The Return of the Druses* (1843), and *A Blot in the Scutchen* (1843).

Romantic poets disdained the bourgeois audience, actors, and managers. Aloof from the theatre's unique demands, the poets' failures exaggerated the growing gulf between literature and the theatre—that is, between poetry and stage diction.

### Minor Dramatic Forms Dominate
*Melodrama* dominated the romantic stage. Combining the styles of Germany's playwright August Kotzebue (1761–1819) and France's playwright Guilbert de Pixérécourt (1773–1844) English melodrama flourished as the "outlaw" dramatic genre sneaking around the rights of the legitimate patent houses and playing in "minor" theatres. Melodrama stole from poets—such as Robert Southey, Lord Byron, and Walter Scott—the Arabian Nights, French plays, German plays, anything potentially exotic, lofty, or as thrilling as Lewis's *The Bells* (1871), Rose's *The Prisoner of Zenda* (1896), and Marcel's *The Sign of the Cross* (1895).

Minor playwrights wrote for the minor theatres. Edward Bulwer-Lytton (1803–1873), for example, wrote popular pseudoromantic melodramas like *The Lady of Lyons* (1838), *Richelieu* (1839), and *Money* (1840). James Sheridan Knowles (1784–1862) presented *Virginius* (1820), *William Tell* (1825), and *The Hunchback*

(1832). Douglas William Jerrold (1803–1857) succeeded with *Black-Eyed Susan* (1829).

Real and imagined crimes were great subjects for melodrama; George Dibdin Pitt's *Sweeney Todd, Demon Barber of Fleet Street* (1847) established the model. Irishman Dion Boucicault (1822–1890) brought his local dialect and picturesque scenes to the stage with *London Assurance* (1841), *The Corsican Brothers* (1852), and *The Octaroon* (1859), a melodrama about an American Negro. Another Irishman, Oscar Wilde (1856–1900), brought his romantic passion and devastating wit to the theatre. Such plays of his as *Lady Windemere's Fan* (1892) and *The Importance of Being Earnest* (1895) represent the comparatively few English romantic plays popular in the modern repertoire.

Other outlaw forms followed. *Burlesques*, for example, satirized contemporary pretensions. *Extravaganzas*, originally based on myths or folk tales, in time became indistinguishable from burlesques. *Burletta* escaped the Licensing Act, which, as discussed in Chapter 6, had limited the number of theatres that could legally produce regular drama, with a three-act form and a minimum of five songs.

*A New Audience* Novelist Charles Dickens observed that, "It being a remarkable fact in theatrical history, but one long since established beyond dispute, that it is a hopeless endeavor to attract people to a theatre unless they can be first brought to believe that they will never get into it." Stars and spectacle brought in the audience; romantic poetic dramas and Shakespeare gradually lost popular favor with the bourgeois public.

Eventually patent theatres included melodramas, burlettas, and extravaganzas in order to compete. Evenings' entertainments provided something for everyone, often in six-hour programs. Sometimes as many as three plays, plus variety acts, filled a night at the theatre. Melodrama evaded the monopoly of spoken tragedy while burletta skirted the monopoly of comedy with music. Music touched the bourgeois audience's sentiments, and happy endings let everyone go home smiling.

The Industrial Revolution brought the working class to the theatre in large numbers for the first time. Their overwhelming numbers dictated the tastes to which the managers now catered. The new audience was less discriminating, less literate, and less interested in

*Charles Kean in Kotzebue's* The Stranger *(1849).* (Lilly Library)

activating imaginations worn down by hard labor. The new audience wanted something livelier than the bourgeois sentimental comedies that had satisfied the previous audience of merchants. As a result, English theatres developed fast-moving, colorful, gaudy, and gigantic spectacles of escape. Variety acts became the proletariat's *intermezzi*. *Othello*, for instance, played with elephants, entre-acts of an exotic fantasy play, a version of the *Tale of Puss-in-Boots*, and an episode from Aladdin.

Sophisticated audiences turned up their noses at the melodramas and burlettas, but they had a difficult time explaining why. Mr. Curdle, in Charles Dickens's novel *Nicholas Nickelby*, complains of the "modern" theatre: "As an exquisite embodiment of the poet's visions, and a realization of human intellectuality, gilding with refulgent light our dreamy mo-ments, and laying open a new and magic world before the mental eye, the drama is gone, perfectly gone." Mrs. Curdle agrees: "What man is there, now living, who can present before us all those changing and prismatic colours with which the character of Hamlet is invested?" The sophisticates preferred Bulwer-Lytton. But Mr. Curdle could not even remember what there was about the old "unities" that he missed. He tried to explain to Nicholas that they are "a completeness—a kind of a universal dove-tailedness with regard to place and time—a sort of a general oneness, if I may be allowed to use so strong an expression . . . a unity of feeling, breadth, a light and shade, a warmth of coloring, a tone, a harmony, a glow, an artistical development of original conceptions . . ."[4]

# FRANCE

***Monarchy Restored***  Napoleon wished to preserve and extend throughout Europe the democratic achievements of the French Revolution. But the restored monarchy that replaced him worked to eliminate the achievements. A coalition of European powers defeated Napoleon behind the might of the British navy. Six monarchs and the highest ministers of Europe met in the Congress of Vienna (1815) to celebrate their victory.

Prince Metternich of Austria led the reaction to liberalism. Legitimate rulers were reestablished, and Europe was redrawn according to old dynastic lines. In France the Bourbon Louis was restored to the throne. Meanwhile the middle class looked forward to economic freedom and stability but intellectuals and workers despaired. Louis's death brought Charles X, an ultra conservative Royalist, to the throne in 1824. No attempts were made to ease the growing social problems. Consequent uprisings in 1830, 1848, and 1849 led to the establishment of a democratic Republic. Meanwhile, France sought worldwide colonies in Asia and Africa to fuel its industrial revo-lution. But the Empire ended in defeat by Germany's Otto von Bismarck in 1870.

***Antibourgeois Sentiment***  French romanticism and theatre rode a roller coaster of hope and despair throughout the political turmoil. Salons reopened to celebrate the romantic heroes of the day; the leading *cénacle* (group) orbited around writer Victor Hugo (1802–1885). Generally, the romantic movement had a very antibourgeois bias. Leadership originated among intellectual aristocrats who read Madame de Staël's account of German romanticism. In time, however, leadership did pass to plebians such as Hugo, and French romanticism became bohemian in character.

The French Academy could not dictate theatrical taste after the Revolution. As the Revolution and the Restoration produced unexpected disappointments, intellectuals isolated themselves. In addition, many artists and playwrights fostered a contempt for the middle class, which had undermined the democratic revolution. Rival artistic circles created various versions of French romanticism. Most romantics defined themselves as outside the avaricious, narrow-minded, and powerful bourgeois society.

Romantics also distinguished themselves from corrupt society. French theatrical romantics chose a life in art rather than a life in society. They championed geniuses over the ordinary individuals who supported the monarchy. They wore clothing, facial hair, and head gear to mark their separation from society. Their manners were equally shocking to the bourgeois. Romantics defied every tradition, especially learning and maturity. Youth, they believed, was superior to age; youth had not yet sold out its ideals or imagination for a few dollars.

### Art as Religion

Many French romantics elevated youth and dramatic art to godhead. The artist was their god, and the artist was their hero. Also, God was the artist, and the hero was the artist. Art for art's sake replaced art for the bourgeois' sake.

Victor Hugo wrote a Preface to his play *Cromwell* (1827) that proclaimed a romanticism, not of the monarchy's disillusioned supporters, but of bohemian liberals. Marie-Henri Beyle (1783–1842), better known as Stendhal, set a literary controversy in motion with *Racine and Shakespeare* (1823). Stendhal suggested that playwrights who wished to write for a contemporary audience should imitate Shakespeare rather than Racine. Racine showed, Stendhal said, the classicism of grandparents; Shakespeare was of the present.

"Art for art's sake" was announced by Théophile Gautier (1811–1872) in the Preface to his novel *Mademoiselle de Maupin* (1835). Painters carried on Gautier's cry. But a member of Hugo's circle, Eugène Delacroix (1798–1863), preferred Racine to the romantic vision. Nevertheless, his own romanticism offended the public with rich colors, sensuous effects, exotic subjects, and an interest in the threats and mysteries of the world.

Delacroix was not alone in his interest in the non-European. In 1829 Victor Hugo claimed, "In the age of Louis XIV all the world was Hellenist; now it is Orientalist." The East influenced French theatrical romanticism as second-hand Orientalism spilled in from Germany. In 1823 Casimir Delavigne, and in 1825 Michel Beer, wrote plays based on Indian legends. In 1813 Etienne Joury wrote the tragedy *Tippu Sahib*. Gautier outlined a *Sacontala* ballet in 1858 and a novel, *La partie carrée*, which featured the Indian goddess Kali. In 1835 the *Faust* translator Gerard de Nerval (1808–1855) adapted *The Little Clay Cart* by the Hindu playwright King Sudraka. And music turned eastward when, in 1810, Joury wrote an opera based on an Indian *sari*.

### Vaudeville and Mélodrame

French playwrights took great inspiration from Shakespeare and the German romantics. But the *Comédie Française* continued to play neo-classical dramas to almost empty houses. The *vaudeville* and the *mélodrame* arose to circumvent the monopoly. These two outlaw forms served as transitional genres to romantic tragedy.

The *vaudeville* was a bourgeois corruption of neo-classical comedy. Contemporary characters appeared in an episodic plot broken frequently by song and dance. The *vaudeville* had many features in common with the *mélodrame*, which derived from monologues with musical accompaniment, the domestic dramas of Denis Diderot, and pantomimes of mythological or contemporary events featuring special effects. *Mélodrame* extended the naturalism advocated by Denis Diderot. From 1798 to 1830 *mélodrame* dominated French public taste with popular tomb scenes, heroic escapes, rescues of persecuted innocents, and punishments of traitorous villains. Audiences lined up to see daring feats by heroes trying to rescue persecuted innocents.

During the Revolution the playwright Guilbert de Pixérécourt (1773–1844) had fled France. But he returned to enjoy great success in the Empires and Republics. He subsequently lost a great fortune in a fire and died after a long illness.

Pixérécourt's plays both popularized and standardized the French *mélodrame* of bourgeois theatres. In 1797 his *Victor* made his name synonymous with *mélodrame*. Written as an opera, *Victor* dropped the songs and debuted with simple musical accompaniment to the spoken dialogue. Roger, the bandit hero, derived from Friedrich Schiller's Karl in *The Robbers*. In fact, Pixérécourt read works by Shakespeare, Sir Walter Scott, Wolfgang Goethe, Friedrich Schiller, and August Kotzebue to find scenes and characters for his plays. He adapted popular novels, such as Defoe's *Robinson Crusoe* (1805), and he wrote over fifty historical and picturesque plays such as *The Mines of Poland* (1803), *The Spanish Moors* (1804), *Christophe Colomb* (1815), and *The Scotish Chiefs* (1819).

*Mélodrame* developed distinctive characteristics. It presented the bourgeoisie with a popular version of neo-classical tragedy, stripped of subtlety, poetry, and unhappy endings. A plot of intrigue moved from contrived climax to contrived climax. Plot mechanics propelled simple characters with strong moral virtues or vices. Fierce conflict—not within a single character, but between characters—moved the action. Bloody violence resulted from chance and coincidental discoveries, meetings, and fortuitous properties. Unmotivated reversals led to spectacular *coups de théâtre*. Set in exotic locations and swimming in mysterious moods, *mélodrame* attempted to adhere to the old unities by changing scenes between each of the three acts.

Melodramatic plots built to one *coup de théâtre* after another *coup de théâtre*. Monologues usually conveyed the exposition as expeditiously as possible. The last-minute happy endings followed three acts of violent struggle and conflict that grew not out of any inner struggle or desire, but from stock characters. There were six stock characters: the powerful and insensitive villain, a male; the sensitive yet persecuted hero, male or female; the persecuted innocent, usually a woman; the *niais* (clown), usually an ally of the hero, who spoke slang or a local dialect to provide comedy in tense situations; the villian's accomplice; and the faithful friend. Usually the villain forced the persecuted innocent to suffer, and the hero punished the villain, forced him to repent, or killed him. The clown helped rescue the persecuted innocent or trap the villain. Characters

used disguises, secret passages, tricks, letters, secrets, eavesdropping, pretenses, discoveries, rumors, intrigues, arrests, accusations, and escapes to further their ends. When performed by a hero the device was good; when done by a villain the same action was evil.

The plots and characters used emotional thrills to teach simple moral virtues. Bourgeois sentimentality ruled; inherent goodness triumphed because of the emotional sensitivity of the hero and persecuted innocent. The standards, beliefs, and hopes of the bourgeois majority, as represented by the hero, triumphed over the deviant actions of the individual, represented by the villain. The diction was prose but the dominant quality of *mélodrame* was spectacle.

A melodramatic text was judged, actually, by its potential for spectacular staging. Haunted, exotic, or Gothic forests, gardens, innyards, palaces, ships, prisons, bridges, waterfalls, mines, caverns, and tombs housed such spectacular production numbers as dances, reviews, parades, floods, sieges, duels, battles, eruptions, avalanches, storms, fires, and wrecks. Elaborate and detailed settings rivaled those of the opera. Some scenes played without words as *tableaux mouvants*.

### The Well-Made Play and Romantic Tragedy
*Mélodrame* produced two important offshoots. First, it developed into the *pièce bien faite* (well-made play), under the guidance of Eugène Scribe (1791–1861), Eugène Labiche (1815–1888), and, later, the son of Alexandre Dumas *père*, Alexandre Dumas *fils*. Scribe wrote for ten months of the year, averaging ten plays a month. In his 400 plays, *vaudevilles*, comedies, *mélodrames*, and librettos—favorites of the bourgeoisie—he arranged topical characters and events in carefully constructed plots. Labiche's more than 170 plays made him the nineteenth century's bourgeois Molière. Of his *vaudevilles* and farces, *Le chapeau de paille d'Italie* (*The Italian Straw Hat*, 1851) is best known. French realists later combined the dramaturgy of the well-made *mélodrame* with "realistic" urban subject matter.

Second, *mélodrame* paved the way for the serious romantic tragedy of Alexandre Dumas *père*. Romantics appropriated the dramaturgy of *mélodrame* and put it in a classical five-act form. Without music, romantic drama, emulating Shakespeare, chose an early point of attack. As a result romantic drama features less exposition than *mélodrame*. The neo-classical unhappy ending characterized the romantics' view of life; it was retained. Romantic authors used poetic diction to accomplish both the musical effects of the orchestra and the emotional thrills of the spectacle.

Bourgeois values are not miraculously rewarded in romantic tragedy. Instead, bourgeois values cause the death of the hero, the persecuted innocent, or both. The romantic villain upholds the bourgeois values and becomes the force of evil or death.

Alexandre Dumas *père* (1802–1870) established romantic drama in France with such history plays as *Henri III et sa cour* (*Henry III and his Court*, 1829), influenced by the 1827 appearance in Paris of Charles Kemble's company, and *La Tour de Nesle* (*The Tower of Nesle*, 1832). *Henri III and his Court* assembled standard romantic and melodramatic features: astrology, magic, duels, a magic mirror, Catherine de Medici, silent love, drugs, humor, storms, visions, and secret passages. Although written in prose, the play appeared at the *Comédie Française*.

In 1829 Alfred de Vigny (1797–1863) translated *Othello* for the *Comédie Française*. The romantics of Paris were overcome with the greatness of Shakespeare's vision. The play demonstrated the truths expressed two years earlier in Victor Hugo's rallying cry, the Preface to his play *Cromwell*, which had made Hugo a hero among young French literati.

### Hugo and Hernani

The son of an army officer, the clean-shaven and well-dressed Victor Hugo led a scruffy lot of weirdly attired bohemians. Throughout his life Hugo displayed an insatiable appetite for sex with a wide variety of women. Passion ruled every aspect of his life. Exile appealed to him more than life under Louis Napoleon. Considered the greatest of all French poets, Hugo rose to demigod

status following the 1827 publication of his play *Cromwell* and its provocative Preface. Playwrights studied the Preface. Alexandre Dumas *père* wrote in its light, and Hugo, in turn, led a band of poets and artists to the opening performance of Dumas's play, *Henri III and his Court*.

Hugo had submitted his play, *Marion de Lorme*, for production. He envisioned a new national drama teaching and leading the democratic people of France. *Marion de Lorme*, a romantic tale of a seventeenth-century Parisian courtesan, had won the praise of Honoré de Balzac, Ferdinand Delacroix, Alexandre Dumas *père*, Alfred de Musset, and other members of his circle when Hugo read the play to them. Dumas even carried Hugo on his shoulders until Mrs. Hugo called the group to refreshments. But the censor turned down the play. The fifth act's characterization of Louis XIII seemed to ridicule a royal ancestor. Hugo appealed to the king, but lost. He quickly wrote *Hernani*, a drama about "a soul who lives apart." *Hernani* presents a hero in rebellion, dueling against the authority of a villainous king. The outlaw, Hernani, vies with Don Carlos for the hand of Dona Sol, engaged to her aged guardian. When Carlos becomes king of Spain, Hernani plots against him. However, the king magnanimously restores Hernani to his title, land, and beloved Dona Sol. But the guardian claims Dona Sol as his own. Honor-bound Hernani accepts death as his fate without Dona Sol. Dona Sol joins Hernani in a joint suicide that echoes Shakespeare's *Romeo and Juliet*. When his circle heard Hugo read *Hernani*, they cheered the play and the playwright. Censors approved the play for production at the *Comédie Française*.

Interest spread about the new play in rehearsal. Hugo had published his letter to the king to protest the censorship of *Marion de Lorme*. Passages of *Hernani* somehow found their way into newspapers and journals and even onto the *vaudeville* stage. The discussion of the new play heated to debate and argument. The press printed a flurry of attacks and defenses. Anonymous threats of riot, death, and "small civil war" appeared in the press. Hugo lost many of his oldest friends. Even Mademoiselle Mars, the thirty-year veteran actress of the *Comédie Française*, objected publicly to the "bad taste" of several lines her character, Dona Sol, was required to say.

The play opened on February 25, 1830, an extremely cold winter's evening. Braziers lit the theatre. While a party of supporters planned its activities with Mrs. Hugo, the playwright attended last minute rehearsals. Volunteers came and left the Hugo house all day. Around 3 o'clock in the afternoon a group of eighty or ninety bohemians—singing, screaming obscenities, and chanting—arrived at the *Comédie Française*. The group, including Théophile Gautier and his shoulder-length blonde hair, Gérard de Nerval, Hector Berlioz, Honoré de Balzac, and Stendhal, entered a side door and took over the pit and the upper gallery. For four hours they sang, cheered, ate, drank wine, and relieved themselves in corners of the national theatre of France.

When the bourgeois merchants, lords, and ladies arrived in their carriages and powdered wigs, they entered their theatre to see a drunken, unkempt mob carrying on amid a mess of food and the odor of wine and urine. Aristocrats scolded the mob from their boxes. Those in the pit and gallery shouted back. Even when the play began the audience was as active and vocal as the players on stage. Endless interruptions and yells from both supporters and detractors stopped the action. Yet by the end of the fifth act all were at least quiet.

*Hernani* was a tremendous popular success. The same drama played in the auditorium and on the stage for forty-five nights. Box-office receipts broke all records as audiences stayed an hour after each performance to cheer and argue. The public found what Hugo had promised in his Preface to *Cromwell:* a drama that was not just a mirror of life but a "concentrating mirror, which instead of weakening, concentrates and condenses the coloured rays, which makes of a mere gleam a light, and of a light a flame."

*The opening night uproar at Victor Hugo's* Hernani. (Victor Hugo Museum, Paris)

After *Hernani*, Hugo wrote *Le roi s'amuse* (*The King Takes his Pleasure*, 1832), famous as the basis for the opera *Rigoletto*, and *Ruy Blas* (1838). Throughout his career Hugo tried to provide, as he explains in his Preface to *Ruy Blas*, "melodrama for the crowd, tragedy that analyzes passion for the women, and for the thinkers, comedy that depicts human nature."

Following *Hernani*, Dumas *père's* interests turned toward "cape and sword" *mélodrame*. Plots and characters, similar to those in the Spanish Renaissance drama of Lope de Vega, found melodramatic expression in such plays as *Les trois mousquetaires* (*The Three Musketeers*, 1844) and *Le Comte de Monte Cristo* (*The Count of Monte Cristo*, 1845). Urban problems eventually replaced capes and swords as the realistic theatre arrived.

**Great Players**   England's Edmund Kean, John Philip Kemble, and William Macready thrilled the French romantics with their realistic portrayals of emotion. French actors began to study and imitate the English "points," especially moments of madness or death. Stars shone in France as well as in England, but the French stars were mostly female.

A "sweet thing" on stage but an iron monster off stage, Mademoiselle Mars (1779–1847) won the reputation as the greatest comic actress of the Romantic age. She ran the *Comédie Française* shortly after debuting at age 16 as Agnes in Molière's *L'ecole des femmes* (*The School for Wives*). Mars, the illegitimate child of *Comédie* actor Montel, excelled as women of intelligence and manners, especially as Célimène in Molière's *Le misanthrope* and as Marivaux characters. Although she did not understand the romantics, Mars agreed to play in Dumas *père's Henri III* and Victor Hugo's *Hernani* as Dona Sol. She frequently offered the romantic playwrights help in improving the good taste of their scripts.

Influential lovers such as Napoleon and the Tsar of Russia, smitten by her beauty, helped Mademoiselle George (1787–1867) succeed in the theatre. When she refused to accept the defeat of Napoleon, however, the *Comédie Français* dismissed her. Popular attention returned when George played in Hugo's *Lucrece Borgia* and *Marie Tudor* and in Dumas's *Christine*. The rapid rise of Rachel (1821–1858) to stardom eased George into retirement as an elocution teacher.

Marie-Thomas Dorval (1798–1849), like George, used her connections to advance her career. The mistress of poet Alfred de Vigny, Dorval played in his *Chatterton* and displayed great passion on stage and off. Hugo also cast her in his *Angelo* (1835). Poet Théophile Gautier said she was "nature itself." Dorval worked from spontaneous inspiration, totally immersing herself in her roles. She often acted opposite the great Frédérick Lemaître.

The most famous French romantic actor, Frédérick Lemaître (1800–1876), excelled as characters with passionate temperaments, such as Hamlet and Othello. Dumas *père* wrote *Kean* for this "Talma of the Boulevards," as Lemaître was nicknamed. Novelist Honoré de Balzac (1799–1850) wrote *Vautrin* for him. Hugo, casting him as the hero of *Ruy Blas*, thought Lemaître was actors Lekain and David Garrick rolled into one man, "untameable, robust, pathetic, strong, fascinating as the people." Rachel was Lemaître's female counterpart.

With neither romantic passion nor romantic scripts, Rachel created romantic stardom by reviving neo-classical roles and playing them, not with inappropriate romantic gusto, but with subdued simplicity. Rachel began as a cafe singer. Noticed by influential critics, she was admitted to the *Comédie Française* at age 17 after playing at a minor theatre for two years. She debuted as Camille in Corneille's *Horace*. In 1843 Rachel played her greatest role, Racine's Phèdre. She tried romantic drama but only succeeded once, in Eugène Scribe's *Adrienne Lecouvreur*. Instead Rachel toured the world as Roxanne in Corneille's *Bajazet*, Hermione in Racine's *Andromaque*, and as Phèdre. But off stage she helped create the image of the romantic actor—uncooperative, egotistical, and temperamental. English critic George Henry Lewes compared Rachel to Edmund Kean and dubbed her "the panther of the stage." On her deathbed Rachel advised, "In

*Rachel as Bajazet.* (Lilly Library)

tradition of giving advice. Sarah Bernhardt (1845–1923) abandoned her idea of becoming a nun to rule as queen of the French stage—the one and only, the impetuous, The Divine Sarah. Bernhardt's golden voice and eccentric life created a sensation. She slept in a coffin. She lived in a menagerie of wild animals. She said ''great actors have always been judged by the naturalism they exhibit in their acting,'' but ''all art whatsoever presupposes enlightened selection, and no purpose is served by being brutally natural.''[5] Bernhardt, who debuted in 1862, played Racine's Phèdre, *Hernani's* Dona Sol, and *Ruy Blas's* Queen. She toured London, New York, Russia, and Australia. She played the role of Hamlet and said ''it is not male parts, but male brains that I prefer.''[6]

Bernhardt achieved her greatest success as

*Sarah Bernhardt as Cleopatra.* (Lilly Library)

studying for the stage, take my word for it, declamation and gesture are of little vail. You have to think and weep.'' Spoken like a romantic. Yet Rachel's successes with the classics hastened romanticism's demise.

The next great French actress continued the

Marguerite in Dumas *fils's La dame aux camélias* (*The Lady of the Camellias*). She continued to tour even after her leg was amputated in 1914. In *The Art of the Theatre*, Bernhardt designates a Schopenhauerian "will" as the most important aspect of an actor's skill. She quotes advice given to her by a Madelaine Brohan on what to do with her original genius:

> . . .there is nothing you can do; you cannot help being original; you have a dreadful head of hair that is intractable and naturally curly: your figure is excessively slender; in your throat you possess a natural harp; all this renders you a being apart, which constitutes a crime in vulgar eyes. So much for your physical, now for your moral qualities. You cannot conceal your thoughts or stoop to anything. You will have nothing to do with either hypocrisy or compromise, which is a crime in the eyes of society. Under these circumstances, how can you expect not to arouse jealousy, not to wound people's susceptibilities, and not to make them spiteful? If you despair because of these attacks, you are lost. But if you wish to remain yourself, my dear, prepare to mount on a little pedestal compounded of calumnies, injustices, flatteries, and lies, with the truths as make weight. When you are on the pedestal, stand firm and cement it by your talents, your work and your kindness. Be determined. All the spiteful people who have unwittingly provided the first materials for the edifice will kick it then, in hopes of destroying it. But if you are determined, they will be powerless."[7]

Playwrights carefully supervised the actors' work in increasingly complex settings. Pixérécourt, Dumas *père*, and Hugo worked as stage directors interested in stage composition and picturization. They worked against the neo-classical habit of lining actors across the edge of the stage. New directors insisted that actors occasionally sit on and use the furniture.

The *Comédie Française* refused to accept the new techniques. Since Napoleon had restricted the number of theatres and assigned a type of drama to each, the *Comédie Française* cherished its monopoly on regular spoken drama. Minor theatres sprouted with *mélodrame* to circumvent the monopoly. With the fall of Napoleon minor theatres prospered even more. They ran without subsidy; managers hired actors and chose plays to cover expenses. The repertoire system lasted until the midcentury's love of the long run ended the age-old practice of hiring actors for a season. Hugo's *Hernani*, for example, ran over 100 nights.

***Scenic Innovation*** After Napoleon the number of theatres tripled by midcentury. Minor unsubsidized theatres such as the *Vaudeville* and the *Gymnase* tended to be more experimental because they depended upon luring an audience. In addition, the new long run allowed scenery to become more elaborate.

While romanticism's texts moved toward idealism, the scenery moved toward realism. Spectacle and "local color" pleased audiences. But special machinery was needed to advance the melodramatic plots. Louis Jacques Mandé Daguerre (1787–1851) thus developed the *panorama* and *diorama*. The panorama was used for essentially undramatic theatrical spectacles. A circular painting inside of which sat an audience, the panorama was seen through one of two seventy-one by forty-five foot proscenium picture frames as the audience rotated every fifteen minutes toward one of the openings. The diorama put the panoramic painting on large spools for flat, sequential viewing on a theatre's proscenium arch stage. Characters on treadmills in front of the diorama created the illusion of movement. In 1839 Daguerre's experimentation led him to invent the most influential form of photography, the daguerreotype. Photography would lead to the origin and eventually the demise of the realistic theatre.

Opera usually led the development of French theatre technology. In 1822 gas lighting was installed. A water system for fountains and waterfalls entered the theatre the same year Ciceri opened the first independent scenic shops in Paris. In the shops Ciceri designed over 400 plays, including *Hernani*. The *Comédie Française* installed gas in 1843. The year before, a revival of *Le Cid* had brought historical accuracy to the *Comédie*'s neo-classical repertoire.

With the introduction of urban melodrama the box setting appeared for interior locations.

***New Dramatic Theory***    The audience at the opening of Hugo's *Hernani* typified the enthusiasm, passion, and diversity of the French theatre-going public. French audiences loved to battle over the theatre. Declarations, opinions, manifestoes, and prefaces always announced spirited debates.

Napoleon had favored classical drama. But Stendhal urged the French to model their dramas on Shakespeare rather than on Racine. Each Parisian theatre, major or minor, had a paid *claque* (hired applauders) to lead the audience in the correct response. Hugo insisted that the house *claque* not be used for *Hernani*; he wanted the audience to find inspiration naturally from characters like Juliet, Ophelia, Iago, Tartuffe, Basile, Polonius, Harpagon, Bartolo, Falstaff, Figaro, and, in the middle ages, Apuleius's *The Golden Ass*, the *Roman de la Rose*, court jesters, Cervantes, and Rabelais.

Hugo's Preface to *Cromwell* originated the romantic challenge; it laid out the ideals of the new romantic audience. "We are constructing no system here," Hugo wrote, "God protect us from systems." He advocated "the fruitful union of the grotesque and the sublime types," typical of genius. Shakespeare seemed to unite the best of Corneille, Molière, and Beaumarchais.

Hugo also attacked the neo-classical ideal: "A plot confined within twenty-four hours is as absurd as one confined within a peristyle." And lest his love for Shakespeare be misconstrued, he hastened to add, "There are neither rules nor models; or, rather, there are no other rules than the general laws of nature, which soar above the whole field of art, and the special rules which result from the conditions appropriate to the subject of each composition." Genius "divines rather than learns. . . .Let the poet beware especially of copying anything whatsoever; . . .we must draw our inspiration from the original source."

Attacking the growing realism around him, Hugo warned that "art cannot produce the thing itself." He predicted a theorist who would come to believe "there is no reason why he should not go on to demand that the sun should be substituted for the footlights, *real* trees and *real* houses for those deceitful wings." Finally, Hugo declared, "Nature and art are two things—were it not so, one or the other would not exist."

Hugo insisted on verse for the stage to lift the theatre away from "a vice that kills it—the commonplace." Although some verse may be stiff, ostentatious, and "pomposo," he urged playwrights to write better verse rather than abandon it for prose. Blame the versifiers, he argued, not verse: "Verse is the optical form of thought" for the dramatic theatre, the "concentrating mirror." Verse helps both actor and audience by engraving thoughts more deeply in the mind; it prevents actors from improvising. It also lasts longer in the auditors' memories. For Hugo "mediocrity is at its ease in prose." Nevertheless, prose became the language of democracy, industry, and, in the next age, dramatic diction.

In *The Law of the Drama*, another critic, Ferdinand Brunctière, combined philosopher Ar-

*The audience gathers outside the Théâtre Déjazet in Paris in 1878.*    (Lilly Library)

thur Schopenhauer's idea of will with romantic mystery: "Drama is a representation of the will of man in conflict with the mysterious powers or natural forces which limit and belittle us; it is one of us thrown living upon the stage;

against one of his fellows; against himself, if need be; against the ambitions, the prejudices, the folly, the malevolence of those around him." Conflict, like prose, came to be central ingredients in the realistic theatre.

# AMERICA

***Expansion and Warfare*** The democratic revolution rebounded to America from Europe with the election of Thomas Jefferson as president of the United States in 1800. The political revolution moved west as log-cabin settlers elected Andrew Jackson president. The German aesthetic revolution entered New England through the doors of Unitarian churches. Utopian communities rejected the growing industrial revolution. The Civil War forced the democratic revolution on larger numbers of people but brought America further from national unity.

Jefferson championed a strong central government and purchased the Louisiana Territory from Napoleon in 1803. In 1819 Florida was acquired and in the 1840s, California and Texas. The East divided North against South; consequently, America's political heroes—Jackson and Lincoln—and stage heroes came from the West.

Lincoln upheld Jefferson's and Jackson's beliefs that property rights were secondary to other rights. Lincoln came to side with the abolitionists when westward expansion aggravated the slavery issue. The Compromise of 1850 let some new states retain slaves while other states entered the union free from slavery. The South countered growing abolitionism by pointing to the northern practice of wage slavery in mills and factories. To Lincoln, wage slavery at least held out the possibility that the exploited would someday do the exploiting.

Lincoln's election in 1860 represented a victory for forces upholding union over the rights of states. The War between the States, called by southerners The War of Northern Aggression, challenged the growing power of the central government. The South fought for its right

to end the social contract; the North fought to end slavery; President Lincoln fought to preserve the union. During the war some theatres closed while others housed the military. Actors enlisted or toured with patriotic readings. In theatres that remained open, plays functioned as newsreels: *Bull Run* (1861), *The Capture of Fort Donelson* (1862), *How to Avoid Drafting* (1862), and *The Unionist Daughter* (1864).

The Civil War weakened the power of individual states and accentuated the tensions between regions of the country. A national dramatic theatre grew more remote. America's national character, however diffuse before the war, was torn asunder. The theatre could do little more than present foreign visions or parade native costumes and dialects before happy audiences.

***The National Character*** Before the war Europeans sent visitors to America to see how the experiment in democratic society was progressing. Harriet Martineau reported to England in 1837 after Alexis de Tocqueville reported to France in 1835. De Tocqueville came to Jackson's America looking for answers to Europe's problems. In America he saw the development of reform movements for public education and universal suffrage. But de Tocqueville found Americans unsuited for the collective experience of theatre: "Each man is narrowly shut up in himself, and from that basis makes the pretension to judge the world. This American way of relying on themselves alone to control their judgement leads to other mental habits."[8] He found fewer ignorant and fewer learned people than anywhere he had ever been.

All Europeans were interested in the American Negro, the theatrical symbol of oppression and natural goodness. De Tocqueville reported that in the North

> the negro is free, but he cannot share the rights, pleasure, labors, griefs, or even the tomb of him whose equal he has been declared; there is nowhere where he can meet him, neither in life nor in death.
>
> In the South, where slavery still exists, less trouble is taken to keep the Negro apart: they sometimes share the labors and the pleasures of the white man; people are prepared to mix with them to some extent; legislation is more harsh against them, but customs are more tolerant and gentle.[9]

Harriet Martineau agreed with many of de Tocqueville's observations. She found a respect for intelligence: "Men rank according to their supposed intellect." Americans "reverence intellect more than wealth and fashion. . . .The vainest fops and the most solid capitalists readily succumb before men and women who are distinguished for nothing but their minds." But Martineau objected to the treatment of women in America.

In America women were treated worse than in most parts of Europe. Martineau found American men lying to the women: "While women's intellect is confined, her morals crushed, her health ruined, her weaknesses encouraged, and her strength punished, she is told that her lot is cast in the paradise of women: and there is no country in the world where there is so much boasting of the chivalrous treatment she enjoys." Hearing the reviews of foreigners, many Americans redoubled their efforts to reform society.

***Reforms*** In 1840 American delegates to the International Anti-Slavery Congress were denied seats because they were female. Back home the delegates organized the Seneca Falls Convention of 1848 to launch the American Women's Suffrage movement.

Horace Mann (1796–1859) led efforts to establish a free elementary education system that even the affluent would want their children to attend. But educational reform was limited to northern states until after the Civil War. Compulsory education had not yet arrived; children were put to farm chores or factory work as soon as they were able. And coeducation, too, was a radical concept. A Lyceum circuit of speakers evolved to bring education to adults. Reformers, poets, actors, writers, politicians, scientists, and crackpots toured 3000 locations—the most famous of which was New York's Cooper Union—to speak on a variety of topics.

Utopian communities also put education at the center of their affairs. The socialist ideas of Europe found homes in rural America. Brook Farm, New Harmony, Oneida Community, Amana Community, Nashoba, Modern Times, the Mormons, the Shakers, the Rappites, and the Millerites returned to nature to create model communities. Abolitionists worked to make the entire nation a utopia.

The South, meanwhile, justified slavery with the belief that Negroes were by nature and God's design a vicious, inferior race not capable of prospering in freedom. Southerners used Greek history and the Bible to legitimize the practice of slavery. They also argued that slavery was vital to the nation's economic prosperity. On the other hand, abolitionists worked to eliminate all slavery by printing journals and newpapers. William Lloyd Garrison, the editor of *The Liberator*, and Theodore Parker, a Unitarian minister, were the most hated men in America for their abolitionist activities. But slave rebellions increased, and the executed terrorist John Brown was eulogized across the North.

After the war reformers concentrated on other evils, especially wage slavery and working conditions in northern urban factories and mills. The industrial revolution had placed factories in the North but found raw materials in the South and West. All parts of the nation thus needed one another. Like their plantation counterparts, factory managers exploited immigrant workers with poor wages and working conditions. After the war, waves of immigrants forced America to move by urban realities rather than by rural utopian visions.

*Immigration*   Immigration to America increased as ships once tied up with the Napoleonic wars were freed to take Europeans to utopia. In the 1820s, 150,000 immigrants arrived; in the 1830s, 600,000; in the 1840s, 1.8 million. In time the nation housed more immigrant than native-born Americans. Small theatres catered to ethnic tastes. Aristocrats and wealthy bourgeois formed associations and organizations to trumpet the length of their Americanization; the immigrants were to be second-class citizens. The upper classes accused Europe of dumping its poor and criminal classes in America.

The immigrants came in waves—Irish, German, Norwegian, Italian, Polish, Baltic, Balkan, Levantine. Europeans had revived medieval laws against Jews. Consequently, by 1840, 15,000 Jews had found safety in America. Playwright Mordecai Noah staked many newcomers to lives as peddlers. By the end of the Civil War a quarter of a million mostly German Jews had injected America with their passion for learning.

Immigrants, political machines, new capitalist wealth, and alcoholism brought increased violence to the changing nation. The simplicity and idealism of romanticism loomed as very appealing in an age of growing pragmatism.

Change brought violence, both inside and outside the theatres. In the North abolitionist meetings were broken up by mobs. Reform leaders were run through the streets to lynchings. Arsonists terrorized immigrant ghettos. Abolitionist, feminist, and ethnic presses were destroyed. School students often chased their teachers out of the classrooms. Utopians were tarred and feathered. Shaker homes were ransacked, and their leaders beaten up. Mormons were driven from town to town, and their leaders lynched. Masons were attacked. The Anti-Masonic Party also spread anti-Catholicism. Catholics were denounced as secret agents of the Vatican working to turn America into a medieval Spain. Catholic schools were firebombed, and many states denied Catholics the right to vote. The Ku Klux Klan was born. Fear and loathing appeared as distinctive traits of the emerging American character. New immigrants were physically attacked in the streets. In the theatres the immigrants, the utopians, the Catholics, the Jews, and the reformers were ridiculed. "Local color" thus came to the American stage.

But Americans kept moving. Writer Washington Irving (1783–1859) noted in *The Legened of Sleepy Hollow* that ghosts "have scarcely time to turn themselves in their graves, before their surviving friends have travelled away from the neighborhood." Mobility and immigration worked against the development of a national dramatic theatre. Ambition seemed the only common trait. De Tocqueville noted that "Every American is eaten up with a longing to rise, but hardly any of them seem to entertain very great hopes or to aim very high. All are constantly bent on gaining property, reputation, and power, but few conceive such things on a grand scale." Philadelphia centered America's social set, New York America's financial axis, and Boston America's intellectual community.

*Transcendentalism*   The French Enlightenment had infiltrated America through the South. The German romantic movement passed through northern immigration. Unitarianism did for New England what Jeffersonianism did for the South and West: disseminate the ideals of democratic liberalism. Whereas Jeffersonian liberalism found political expression, Unitarian liberalism took a philosophical and artistic bent. Unitarianism had broken with Calvinism by emphasizing moral action over supernatural awe as the primary sphere of religion. Unitarianism proclaimed individual intuition superior in all ways to ecclesiastical authority. Following the spirit of German romanticism, Unitarianism espoused an attitude rather than a creed whose hallmarks were an open mind and free inquiry. Unitarian minister William Ellery Channing declared, "Let the full heart pour itself forth!" and romanticism entered America.

From the Unitarians emerged the Transcendentalists, people who found truth and inspiration not in the revelation of the Christian

Bible but in "intuitive perception," "intuitive reason," and "consciousness." Essayist Ralph Waldo Emerson (1803–1882) and other lapsed Unitarians interpreted German romantic philosophy as an affirmation of life, as a reinforcement of the utopias sprouting up in America. But by 1850 the impending war and the problems of industrialization diminished the Transcendentalists' hopes. The philosophy turned to social activism and reform.

The mysticism of Emerson gave way to the common sense of Theodore Parker. Looking back on his earlier thoughts and hopes Emerson concluded, "'Tis all mere nightmare; false instincts; wasted lives." But romantic despair, touching Americans only fleetingly, did not crush permanently, as in Europe. As a result, the American theatre remained ever-blithe. Transcendentalists became leaders of abolitionist and women's suffrage movements. But literature remained the Transcendentalists' greatest contribution to American romanticism.

Harriet Martineau said that "If the American nation be judged by its literature, it may be pronounced to have no mind at all." De Tocqueville found the most common books in America to be those of European authors, religious treatises, and political pamphlets. He observed that Americans pay "less interest to literature than any other civilized country." Before the Transcendentalists, American readers read English authors; they waited for European critics to judge their own writers before reading them.

*New Themes* James Fenimore Cooper (1789–1851), who was expelled from Yale, explored the tensions between dualities—freedom and law, natural goodness and social order, the individual and society, and religious intuition and theology—in novels featuring frontier hero Natty Bumpo. Cooper, in fact, established the American hero with his *Leatherstocking Tales* between 1823 and 1841. Like the character in almost all romantic literature, Natty travels into the wilderness and displays natural courage, toughness, enterprise, modesty, loyalty, and morality. In urban society

Natty is uncomfortable. Cooper's native American Indians are drawn as vicious moral inferiors. Other Indians, however, became stage heroes.

The West's dark forest, Indian fights, riverboat men, wandering families looking for homes, outlaws, and adventurers provided fertile ground for romantic theatrical visions. James Kirk Paulding penned *Westward Ho!* and *The Lion of the West*. Robert Montgomery Bird wrote *Nick of the Woods*. Later, Ned Buntline wrote *The Scouts of the Plains* for Wild Bill Cody. As late as 1882, *The Buffalo Bill Show* began another national tour. The new nation's literature thus developed a mythology of heroes, real, imagined, and both—Rip van Winkle, Peter Stuyvesant, Natty Bumpo, Nimrod Wildfire, The Noble Savage, Evangeline, Pocahontas, Hiawatha, Paul Revere, and Davy Crockett. By midcentury families were reading the works not only of England's Sir Walter Scott but of America's Cooper and Henry Wadsworth Longfellow.

Like English romantics, Edgar Allan Poe (1809–1849), the son of an actor and actress, declared imagination to be the "soul" of poetry. Poe was the first American writer interested only in beauty. He, like England's Walter Pater and Oscar Wilde, was irked by attempts to make art or literature do anything practical. Influenced by the German Schlegels and England's Coleridge, Poe always felt isolated from society.

Romanticism found its greatest champions in New England. Ralph Waldo Emerson served as unofficial head of the American Transcendentalists, who circled about him as French romantics circled around Victor Hugo. Like their German counterparts, the Transcendentalists based their work partly on Asian literature. Emerson read Sanskrit texts and wrote "Brahma" under the influence of the *Bhagavad-Gita*: "If the red slayer thinks he slays,/ or if the slain think he is slain,/ they know not well the subtle ways/ I keep, and pass, and turn again." Nature and the Orient increased the Transcendentalists' reliance on intuition and experience.

The Transcendentalists were the heirs of the

German romantics. Unlike the French or English, the Transcendentalists thus shared the German seriousness, humorlessness, and pedantic approach to life and art. American theatre seemed too frivolous for them to write for it. Nature was their antidote to despair and disillusionment. Intuition and the experience of nature could connect them with the fundamental common truth of all religious experience, what Emerson called the Over-Soul.

Like the Germans and Asians, Emerson called music "sensuous poetry." Like the romantic hero, Emerson urged "whoso would be a man must be a nonconformist." Emerson reaffirmed Hegel's belief that God did not exist until He came to consciousness of Himself in someone's mind. "Emerson" became a European synonym for newness in literature, for freedom, and for genius. Even German philosopher Friedrich Nietzsche admired Emerson for his mental solidarity. Emerson's hired hand, Henry David Thoreau (1817–1862), who shared his friend's views, translated such Greek poetry and plays as *Seven against Thebes* and *Prometheus Bound*.

Emerson attracted writers other than Thoreau. One young poet, Walt Whitman (1819–1892), traveled to Concord to present a copy of his poems to Emerson. Emerson found Whitman to be the poet for whom he had been looking. In his Preface to *Leaves of Grass* (1855) Whitman advocates the democratic poet: "He is a seer...the others are as good as he, only he sees it and they do not." Whitman's romantic spirit produced what critics consider the first "realistic" American poetry, even though the poet says "one's self I sing, a simple separate person."

Harriet Beecher Stowe (1811–1896) felt a need to "sing" about slavery. The wife of a Bowdoin College professor, Stowe became the friend of Lord Byron's widow after the publication of *Uncle Tom's Cabin* (1852). The most famous episode of Stowe's novel reeks of romantic theatricalism: Eliza escapes with her infant Harry into the frozen wilderness. Like good romantics, they flee the corrupt world of slavery. When her husband follows, they escape to Canada and Africa.

The first edition of *Uncle Tom's Cabin* sold out in two days; 10,000 copies sold in the first week, 300,000 in just the first year in America. To meet the demand, eight power presses and three paper mills ran around the clock. During the first year 1.5 million copies sold in the British Empire. The book was translated into twenty-two languages, and countless stage versions played throughout America. Melodramatic realism rather than transcendental idealism created this dramatic work, which made the Fugitive Slave Law unenforceable.

Another woman writer captured an aspect of American romanticism in both her life and her work. Emily Dickinson (1830–1886) withdrew to a room in her parents' Amherst, Massachusetts, home to write 1,775 poems without fear of societal influence. Dickinson yearned for supernatural love, "perfect... paralyzing Bliss." Her work features the great romantic ideas of love, death, and the truth of poetry. Her life became the subject of dramatic treatment in the twentieth century.

Dickinson's passion for the unattainable found a fictional counterpart in the work of Herman Melville. Born in New York, Melville (1819–1891) later taught school in Pittsfield, Massachusetts; he also worked as a cabin boy, whaler, and south sea adventurer. On board a warship, he read the classics of Elizabethan drama. In 1851 he wrote the novel *Moby Dick*. In the novel Ishmael, a schoolteacher, leaves the life of the mind for a romantic adventure in the wilderness of the sea. As a whaler, he meets Ahab, a Faustian character who is obsessed with dominating a great white whale, a symbol of untamed nature. Ahab seeks dominion over nature rather than romantic oneness with nature. He declares, "Talk not to me of blasphemy, man; I'd strike the sun if it insulted me." Ahab dies in pursuit of the whale. Melville died an ailing New York customs officer. Many of Melville's works were adapted to the stage.

Like Melville's, Mark Twain's career overlapped the beginning of realism with the end of romanticism. The son of a land speculator, Mark Twain—born Samuel L. Clemens (1835–1910)—began his romantic quest at an early age. At one time Clemens even worked as a Western drama critic. The success of his *Innocents Abroad* (1869) tranformed Twain from a bohemian romantic to a gentleman of the Gilded Age. Yet he continued to escape to the simpler past of his boyhood days in Hannibal, Missouri. The despair and desolation Twain experienced made him both a participant in and a critic of the realistic era.

Twain's *Huckleberry Finn* (1885) is America's most widely translated book. Huck, the romantic hero, takes a trip down the river, escapes from civilization, and seeks the freedom of nature with another fugitive, Jim, a runaway slave. Along the escape route the boy and the native see the corruptions of bourgeois morality. At the end, the slave is freed, but Huck, faced again with civilization, declares the eternal romantic words, "I reckon I got to light out for the territory ahead of the rest, because Aunt Sally she's going to adopt me and sivilize me, and I can't stand it. I been there before."[10] The book was banned for its language, characters, and ridicule of religion. Naturally, the stage tried to make a play of it.

As a gentleman Twain participated in amateur theatricals and helped his neighbor, William Gillette, get started as an actor. Twain loved minstrel shows and disliked melodramas. He recognized the inferiority of American playwrighting to other American literatures. He liked romantic fantasy and escape; he even took children to see Maude Adams in the play *Peter Pan*. German poetic, metaphysical dramas such as Adolf Wilbrandt's *The Master of Palmyra* especially suited Twain's taste because they "gave me the sense of the passage of a dimly connected procession of dream-pictures." Twain believed in an important American theatre: "It would make better citizens, honest citizens. One of the best gifts a millionaire could make would be a theatre here and a theatre there. It would make . . . a real Republic, and bring about an educational level."

***New Audiences*** American romantic drama generally represented the worst of European practices. But that suited American audiences

just fine. "The Americans have little dramatic taste: and the spirit of puritanism still rises up in such fierce opposition to the stage, as to forbid the hope that this grand means of intellectual exercise will ever be made the instrument of moral good to society there that it might be made," Harriet Martineau anticipated Mark Twain. She continued her observation by saying that "there is not the remotest comprehension of what the drama is. If a reader of Shakespeare occurs, here and there, it usually turns out that he considers the plays as collections of passages, descriptive, didactic, etc."

Americans were not temperamentally suited to appreciate the pessimism of much romantic drama. De Tocqueville saw that Americans did not like to lose control of their emotions. Americans would rather drink indoors than dance outdoors. They were, he concluded, "the most serious minded people on earth" but "are nonetheless often carried away; far beyond the bounds of common sense, by some sudden passion or hasty opinion. They will in all seriousness do strangely absurd things." Americans lived the romantic dramas enjoyed only on stage in Europe. They "want profit as well as delight."

Educated Americans like Twain could not influence American tastes. De Tocqueville concurred: "It has always been the theater that the learned and the educated have had the greatest difficulty in making their tastes prevail over that of the people and preventing themselves from being carried away by them. The pit often lays down the law for the boxes." Even less than their counterparts in England did American writers attempt to write for the stage.

American audiences only wanted sympathetic characters like themselves speaking native dialects, wearing native clothing, and succeeding. That satisfied them. Probability mattered little to men and women whose own lives were improbable. The audience de Tocqueville found did not attend "for the pleasures of the mind, but for lively emotions of the heart." Playwrights who failed to please an American audience were in trouble; playwrights even failed when successful. De Tocqueville noted that "a democratic public often treats its authors much as kings usually behave toward their courtiers; it enriches and despises them."

American audiences divided along class lines. In New York, sophisticated audiences attended the Park Theatre. The "people" went to the Bowery Theatre. Whitman described the Bowery crowd as "alert, welldress'd, full-blooded young and middle aged men, the best of average American born mechanics." Often they could be seen "bursting forth in one of those long kept-up tempests of handclapping peculiar to the Bowery—no dainty kid-glove business, but electric force and *muscle* from perhaps two thousand fullsinew'd men."

Average Americans demanded average Americans plays. The percentage of American plays in repertoire thus increased during the century. Melodrama drew the biggest audiences. New plays, like new countries, were thought best. At the Bowery, as at many other theatres, casually dressed men who smelled of whiskey freely spit tobacco juice, while whores worked the upper gallery. Theatres were built in the tough parts of town along with saloons, billiard parlors, gambling houses, and brothels.

An evening's bill offered something for everyone. A one-act licentious or "breeches" forepiece usually preceded a five-act drama interspersed with novelty acts. At the end, an afterpiece of "breeches" or buffoonery closed the affair. The audience freely interrupted the action with applause, cheers, jeers, and boos, as if at a spectator sport. The audience wanted to socialize, and it complained if the auditorium was too dark.

The box, pit, and gallery arrangement let Americans gather with people of their own sort. In the gallery, the whores watched with Negroes, apprentices, and the servants of people seated in the boxes. The gallery frequently housed rowdies throwing things at the actors, the orchestra, and the middle class seated in the pit. The merchants preferred the pit despite the missiles thrown from the gallery and the candle wax dripping from the chandeliers. In the North, women were banned from the pit. Ladies, fashionable theatre patrons, and the rich sat in boxes.

***Theatre Missionaries***   The western territories opening up for settlers also provided virgin territory for theatrical entrepreneurs. Touring troupes brought theatre to the American West as itinerant companies played in small-town concert halls, town halls, and opera houses located sometimes on the upper floors of office buildings.

Noah M. Ludlow, the Albany, New York, theatre manager who presented the premiere of *Rip van Winkle*, was one of the early pioneers in "showboating." In 1817 Ludlow used a river flatboat to tour productions to the towns along the rivers between Nashville, New Orleans, and St. Louis. Likewise, James Caldwell managed a chain of theatres along the Mississippi River that led to his great American Theatre in New Orleans. The territory controlled by Ludlow and Caldwell also found Solomon Franklin Smith managing a rival company. In 1831 the Chapman family built the first major "showboat." The Chapmans actually pioneered showboat variety entertainment that ranged from minstrel shows to Shakespeare.

A trip to the theatre put one amid the cracking of peanuts, tobacco spit, crying babies, mothers nursing infants, tapping feet, and singing. Occasionally an audience member, carried away by the on-stage action, jumped to the stage to save the persecuted innocent or assault the villain. William Macready wrote of playing Hamlet on tour in America:

> Acted Hamlet to a rather rickety audience, but I tried my utmost, and engaged the attention of at least half the audience. In the scene after the play with Rosencrantz and Guildenstern, an occurrence took place that, for disgusting brutality, indecent outrage, and malevolent barbarism, must be without parallel in the theatre of any civilized community.... A ruffian from the left side gallery threw into the middle of the stage the half of the raw carcase of a sheep.[11]

Twain, too, attacked the American theatre goer's taste:

> You are trying to make yourself believe that life is a comedy, that its sole business is fun, that there is nothing serious in it. You are ignoring the skeleton in your closet.... You are neglecting a valuable side of your life; presently it will be atrophied. You are eating too much mental sugar; you will bring on Bright's disease of the intellect. You need a tonic; you need it very much.[12]

College dramatic societies began to separate themselves from literary societies to produce serious drama. In 1795 Harvard's Hasty Pudding Society organized; in 1866 Brown University's Thalian Dramatic Society appeared. Other college associations were founded as well: St. Johns Dramatic Association (1871), Williams College Dramatic Association (1872), and Cornell Amateur Dramatic Association (1875). Classroom productions of Latin and Greek plays revived earlier European Renaissance pedagogical tools. In 1890 Plautus's *Twin Menaechmi* was staged at the University of Michigan, produced by classroom actors who had studied the drama. Harvard produced Sophocles's *Oedipus the King* in 1881.

The lateness of the educated Americans' acceptance of the theatre reflected the entrenched belief that the theatre was unrighteous. Moral and cultured Americans avoided the theatre. Even by midcentury Americans read only Edgar Allan Poe, novelist Nathaniel Hawthorne (1804–1864), and Ralph Waldo Emerson. Publishers had to give away copies of Whitman's *Leaves of Grass*. European authors still dominated American literary tastes. In addition, all arts surpassed America's theatre. But social observer Harriet Martineau did not despair: "The faith that America is to have an artist of some order is universal; and such a faith is a sufficient guarantee of the event."

***Home-Grown Stars*** The first American theatre artists of any note were actors, and ro-

manticism in the American theatre could best be seen in their acting. In the *Brooklyn Eagle* of 1846 critic Walt Whitman characterized American acting as "loud mouthed ranting" and "tearing everything to shivers." He continued, "If they have to enact passion, they do so by all kinds of unnatural and violent jerks, swings, screwing of the nerves of the face, rolling of the eyes, and so on."

Foreign stars came to profit from America's growing audience. Native actors needed to develop novelties, mostly passion, to compete. American acting had come to be known for very physical and passionate portrayals. As stock companies closed, actors hired for individual productions worked hard to get noticed. As their European counterparts, American actors created the long run. By the 1860s an anonymous critic defined a star as "an advertisement in tights, who grows rich and corrupts public taste." Actors were obviously still considered immoral, and families panicked when sons or daughters took to the stage. American actors' reputations for brawling, insolvency, drunkenness, and divorce were especially aggravated by the career of Edwin Forrest.

Brooding and selfish, Edwin Forrest (1806–1872) reigned as America's first great tragic actor. His large body and voice, plus his torrential energy and passion, made him the idol of American workers, who especially loved him in roles symbolizing masculine rebellion, such as Metamora or Spartacus. Forrest actually turned several stage fights into real fights.

As a boy, Forrest read Shakespeare. He joined a traveling troupe at age 16. In 1829 Forrest began a seven-year stay at the fashionable Park Theatre. In 1836 he embarked on a European tour. But the English preferred their own William Macready's intellectual and subdued acting to the passion of Forrest. Back home, Americans seethed at the slight England gave their hero. Thus, when Macready came to America to play in New York in 1849, Forrest's fans rioted outside his theatre at Astor Place. Twenty-two people even died.

When playing Othello, Forrest discovered his wife in the off-stage arms of his Iago. The

*Edwin Forrest as Richard III.* (Lilly Library)

not permitted on the "white" stages of America. A small Negro company, the African Company, led by James Brown and James Hewlett, had produced Shakespeare's *Richard III* and *Othello* and Brown's *King Shotaway*, the first known play by a black person to receive a professional production, in New York, but harassment by whites forced the company to disband. Negroes werre not allowed on the stage, in fact, until after the Civil War and then only in minstrel shows invented by white performers. The minstrel show had been created by Thomas Dartmouth Rice (1818–1860), who blackened his face and made people laugh as an "Ethiopian delineator," a shuffling, simple, carefree slave named "Jim Crow." The first all-Negro minstrel company, "Georgia Minstrels," was assembled by George Hicks in 1865.

Ira Aldridge would have nothing to do with such a country. In England he thrilled audiences as Othello, Shylock, Lear, Aaron, and as melodramatic runaway slaves and rebel

*Ira Aldridge as Othello.* (Lilly Library)

ensuing divorce suit became a national scandal. Forrest lost the case but continued to make curtain speeches about his wife, "the whore." As his voice gave out Forrest cut back on his stage appearances to give public readings.

The greatest American actor of the romantic age could not even play in his native country. Ira Aldridge (1807–1867), who was born in New York, became a British citizen at age 17 so that he could act, because Negroes were leaders. He even played the title character, *Oroonoko* in the play by Aphra Behn. Aldridge made five European tours, played Lear in St. Petersburg, received Prussia's highest medal, and was knighted in Saxony.

Meanwhile, in America, Edwin Forrest's female counterpart was a tall, masculine, husky-voiced descendant of original Pilgrims, Charlotte Cushman (1816–1876). Cushman was dubbed by the *Sunday Sun* as the greatest theatrical genius since Edmund Kean. William Macready made her Lady Macbeth after seeing her perform. She played Romeo to her sister's Juliet but had her greatest triumph as Meg Merrilies in an adaptation of Scott's *Guy Mannering*. In Shakespeare's *Henry VIII* Cushman played both Queen Catherine and later Cardinal Wolsey; critic Walt Whitman commented particularly on her passionate face. In America, Cushman lived with Rosalie Sully, a painter, and, in England, with poet Eliza Cook. Late in her career she played Hamlet and lived with her costar Matilda Hays.

*Charlotte Cushman as Romeo.*   (Lilly Library)

Third in a family of actors, Joe Jefferson III (1829–1905) began in blackface with Thomas Rice's minstrels. In 1858 he played in Tom Taylor's *Our American Cousin*; in 1865 he began his greatest portrayal—Boucicault's *Rip van Winkle*—which he played for forty years.

Another family dynasty centered around the acting of Junius Brutus Booth (1796–1852). English born and Eton educated, Booth lived a troubled life. At 13, for example, he was convicted of seducing his neighbor's maid. He sailed with the navy, practiced law, and sculpted before latching onto a European touring company. Booth played Shakespeare's Richard III to rival Kean in some critics' eyes. Later he played Iago in Shakespeare's *Othello* to Kean as Othello. Booth even tried playing Shylock in Hebrew.

In 1821 Booth deserted his wife and fled to America with Mary Anne Holmes. In America, Booth's life and performances of Richard III created a sensation. He also tried to play Racine in French in New Orleans. In time Booth grew so superstitious that his sanity weakened. Violent on stage and drunk off stage, Booth discouraged his sons, John Wilkes and Edwin (named after Edwin Forrest), from going on the stage. Critic Walt Whitman said the elder Booth "illustrated Plato's rule that to the forming of an artist of the very highest rank a dash of insanity (or what the world calls insanity) is indispensable." Before he died on a tour of the West Coast, Booth had created an American taste for tragedy and Shakespeare.

One of Booth's sons—John Wilkes—killed President Lincoln; the other, Edwin (1833–1893), established the idea of Hamlet as a melancholy, overly thoughtful prince. Edwin Booth himself might have been accused of melancholy and overthoughtfulness. Beginning with (what else?) Richard III in 1839, Edwin Booth brought new grace and spontaneity of expression to American acting: he modulated passion. But in 1863 Booth's wife died, and the next year he was forced to retire from the stage for over a year after his brother assassinated the President. When he returned Booth set a record for 100 performances of Hamlet and

Joe Jefferson as Rip Van Winkle. (Lilly Library)

Barrett could have used the help of America's impresario P. T. Barnum (1810–1891), the prototype of American commercial theatre entrepreneurs. "The Prince of Humbugs" paraded freaks, ventriloquists, curiosities, deformed animals, exotic animals, variety acts, mermaids, and fantasy creatures past the gaping American public. Barnum made millions by creating entertainment and money out of anything. He was, in fact, the romantic American demigod, shaping nature and profiting on nature's chance occurrences. In 1835, for instance, Barnum bought a supposedly 161-year-old slave, Joice Heth, and exhibited her for a fee. Her autopsy, of course, showed she was only about 80 years old. Then in 1856 Barnum negotiated for a twenty-one inch tall 5-year-old boy, whom he billed as General Tom Thumb. He made a fortune on this exhibit as well. Barnum's management of opera singer Jenny Lind demonstrated how to make an interna-

Edwin Booth as Hamlet. (Lilly Library)

won great applause for his *Richelieu*. In 1868 he opened his own theatre with a *Romeo and Juliet* decorated in historically accurate and picturesque Italianate scenery. As an actor Booth boasted that he observed nature; "I am an interpreter, I reveal the soul of masterpieces."

Working in the shadow of the Booths, Laurence Barrett (1838–1891), the son of Irish immigrants, tried to compensate for a poor voice with hard work. He was also criticized for having a weak body and even a lack of basic talent. His mannered and mechanical style of performance characterized his career's highlight: Cassius to Booth's Brutus in Shakespeare's *Julius Caesar*.

tional star out of nothing but effective public relations. Who needed drama when America had such entertainment wizards?

*Places for Spectacle*    New York and Philadelphia housed the dominant theatres in America at the beginning of the nineteenth century. In 1807 New York's Park Theatre seated over 2300 patrons, but in 1820 and 1848 fire destroyed the building. Each time the building reopened larger than it had been before. Spectacle and local color drew audiences to four rows of boxes and a gallery that faced the forty-five by seventy foot stage in the new 1821 Park. The new building also had a shallower apron than the old one and no proscenium boxes. Seats cost seventy-five, fifty, and thirty-seven cents, depending upon the location.

In 1812, the Walnut Street Theatre opened in Philadelphia. Then in 1816 Philadelphia's Chestnut Street Theatre became the first theatre in the world to use gas lighting for illumination. When Boston built the Tremont Street Theatre in 1827 New York had already become the nation's theatrical center: in 1826 the Bowery, the nation's largest theatre, proclaimed New York's leadership. The gas-lit 75 by 170 foot Bowery Theatre was the first New York theatre to compete directly with the 80 by 160 foot Park Theatre. But new management in 1830 redirected the Bowery's mission. The "Bowery Slaughter House" went after the masses with melodramatic spectacle. For one thing, the Bowery's 4000 seats cost much less than those at the Park. In addition, as the population increased, new theatres opened to gain a piece of the action. Wallack's Theatre opened in 1852; it expanded in 1861 and again in 1882.

In 1869 a 184 by 100 foot theatre opened on the corner of New York's Sixth Avenue and Twenty-Third Street. Booth's Theatre, designed and managed by Edwin Booth, held

*The exterior of Booth's Theatre in 1869.*    (Lilly Library)

1750 seats in the pit alone. Three galleries—the balcony, the gallery, and the amphitheater—overlooked a fifty-five foot deep by seventy-six foot high stage house. A steam-driven fan cooled the auditorium. Hydraulic rams flew and dropped scenery through cuts in the stage floor. The orchestra pit was submerged to improve sight lines. Thirty dressing rooms and a scene shop served the theatre's commitment to expensive spectacle. Renovations in 1876 extended the stage over the orchestra pit. But in 1883 financial troubles transformed the Booth into a dry goods store.

Spectacle and sensation climaxed in America in 1862, when Adah Isaacs Menken rode bareback in a flesh-colored body stocking (to appear naked) in Juliusz Slowacki's *Mazeppa* at the Bowery. Dioramas, too, brought more technological illusions of reality to the stage by creating the effects of trips down the Hudson, climbs over the Rockies, voyages down the Mississippi, and battles.

Mark Twain complained about the American theatre's preoccupation with scenery:

> It is only within the last dozen years that men have learned to do miracles on the stage in the way of grand and enchanting scenic effects; and it is at such a time as this that we have reduced our scenery mainly to different breeds of parlors and varying aspects of furniture and rugs.[13]

The Realistic age made Twain's complaint a principle of dramatic art.

***Sentiment and Melodrama*** The best authors of America's romantic literature kept away from the stage. A few penned closet dra-

*Backstage at Booth's Theatre in 1870.* (*Appleton's Journal*, Vol. III, May 28, 1870, p. 1.)

mas—for example, poet Henry Wadsworth Longfellow (1807–1882) wrote *The Spanish Student* (1843), feminist Julia Ward Howe (1819–1910) wrote *The World's Own* (1855), and poet Edgar Allan Poe wrote *Politian* (1835). Others found their fiction adapted to the stage by other writers—Nathaniel Hawthorne's novel *The Scarlet Letter* in 1857 and 1858 and Poe's short story *The Gold Bug* in 1843.

For the most part, however, playwrighting for the American stage was left to lesser talents. James Nelson Barker (1784–1858), for instance, made history by writing the first American Indian into a drama and by writing the first American play performed in England. The honored play was *The Indian Princess or Pocohantas* (1808). Then, actor Edwin Forrest made much out of John Augustus Stone's (1801–1834) play *Metamora* (1829). But not enough. Dissatisfied with his career, Stone committed suicide. Another of Forrest's finds, Robert Montgomery Bird (1806–1854), wrote for Forrest's strengths with *The Gladiator* (1831) and *The Broker of Bogota* (1834). Bird, however, gave up the stage at age 30 to write such romantic fiction as *Nick of the Woods*. Meanwhile, in Canada, Charles Heavysege (1816–1876) wrote the verse drama *Saul* (1857).

George Henry Boker (1823–1890) tried his hand at poetic drama. His *Francesca da Rimini* (1855) remains the best American poetic tragedy of the Romantic age. John Brougham (1810–1880) and others profited from burlesquing Americans' attempts to write serious drama. Brougham travestied Barker's play with his own *Po-co-hon-tas*.

Women authors were represented by Anna Cora Mowatt (1819–1870), who was famous for her watered-down nineteenth-century social comedy, *Fashion* (1845). The play satirizes New Yorkers aping the French; Mowatt's Mrs. Tiffany is an American Mrs. Malaprop. Poe reviewed the play and said, "Compared with the generality of modern dramas, it is a good play—compared with most American dramas it is a *very* good one—estimated by the natural principles of dramatic art, it is altogether unworthy of notice."

Negroes could not even get this much attention for their plays. Black playwrights had to settle for readings in public halls. Nevertheless, plays were written: escaped slave William Wells Brown's *Experience* (1856) and *The Escape* (1858); John S. La Due's *Under the Yoke* (1876), starring J. A. Arneux, the leading black actor; and Louise A. Smith's children's play, *The Little Mountain Fairies* (1887). Emma G. Hatcher's *Lazette* (1888) toured the nation, while William Edgar Easton wrote *Dessalines* (1893), a drama of the Haitian revolution.

These authors worked to counteract the messages of Jim Crow and the minstrel shows, which instilled the idea that blacks were naturally comic. Seeing "them dressed-up niggers" imitating the whites' manners, "their betters," was a riot. Sentimental and comic songs loaded with references to watermelon, chicken, stealing, and "yaller gals" just could not be topped as entertainment.

Minstrel Dan Emmett wrote "Dixie" for his 1859 show. White audiences across the nation found great comfort in seeing Dixie's white "Mister Interlocutor" patronize and oversee the child-like frolicking of his "Mr. Bones" and "Mr. Sambo," fools trying to ape the whites' ways and words. The minstrel show did for blacks what medieval drama did for Jews: it confirmed people's fears and prejudices, thereby locking a minority out of full cultural participation.

***The Musical*** The good feelings of the minstrel show met the narcotic panaceas of the traveling medicine show to produce, in the hands of American entrepreneurs, the American musical, America's chief contribution to the Romantic age. Some historians credit America with inventing the dramatic form, though it actually extends back to the Greek playwright Aristophanes, French *mélodrame* and *vaudeville*, and English ballad opera.

In 1866 the New York Academy of Music burned down, leaving a Parisian ballet troupe homeless. P.T. Barnum added the troupe to his production of the play *The Black Crook* by Charles M. Barras. The addition saved the

*Scenes from minstrel shows were depicted on the covers of sheet music.* (Lilly Library)

show and created a year's run for the six-hour entertainment. *The Black Crook*, in fact, grossed over a million dollars and won a review from Charles Dickens: "preposterous." Dickens continued, "The people who act in it have not the slightest idea of what it is about, and never had."

The burlesque-extravaganza *Evangeline* (1874) first used the term "musical comedy." Sheet music from the show *A Trip to Chinatown* (1893) by Charles A. Hoyt was the first such music sold. "The Bowery," "Reuben, Reuben," and "After the Ball" were played across America on the upright pianos invented by John Isaac Hawkins in 1800. Continuing to demonstrate to black audiences that black Americans could improve upon any white entertainment, black musicians turned out *A Trip to Coontown* (1898) and *Clorindy* (1898).

Between 1855 and 1900 seventy-two musicals and eighty-three operettas played in New York. The operetta oozed into the twentieth century with the works of Victor Herbert (1859–1924), Sigmund Romberg (1887–1951), and Rudolf Friml (1879–1972).

*Local Color*  Subject matter mattered most in a text. Local color and topicality were especially popular. From the beginning of the nineteenth century playwrights wrote about current events: the inauguration of President Jefferson, the purchase of Louisiana, the border disputes involving both Maine and Oregon, the War of 1812, the Barbary pirates, the Mexican War, the Civil War, the Mormons, Westward expansion, temperance, and slavery. Historical figures likewise proved popular: William Penn, Hernando De Soto, and General Putnam, for example. Native characters like Mose the Bowery B'hoy, the Yankee, the Negro, the Indian, the Backwoodsman, and various ethnic immigrants let Americans celebrate themselves.

Harriet Beecher Stowe's *Uncle Tom's Cabin* found stage form in 1852, the same year her novel was published. The work set a vogue for plays about moral problems. Stowe, however, objected to any stage version: "If the barrier which now keeps young people of religious families from theatrical entertainments is broken down by the introduction of respectable and moral plays, they will then be open to all the temptations of those which are not such." Her father called the theatre "The Centre of the Valley of Pollution."

Moral problem plays dealt with emancipation: *Star of Emancipation* (1841), *Ossawatomie Brown* (1850), and *Neighbor Jackwood* (1857) are examples. Temperance was the topic of *Ten Nights in a Bar Room* (1858). Crime in the city and virtue in the country were explored in *Shore Acres* (1882), *The Old Homestead* (1887), and *The County Fair* (1889). Urban problems began to be discussed with Dion Boucicault's *The Poor of New York* (1857).

Melodrama took on more realistic details near the turn of the century with such writers as Augustin Daly (1838–1899), David Belasco (1859–1931), William Gillette (1855–1937), and Augustus Thomas (1857–1934). Daly tied a persecuted innocent to a railroad track in *Under the Gaslight* (1867). David Belasco, named "The Bishop of Broadway" because he wore a clerical costume, offered *The Girl I Left Behind Me* (1883), *The Heart of Maryland* (1895), *Madame Butterfly* (1900), and *The Girl of the Golden West* (1905). Gillette presented *Held by the Enemy* (1886), *Secret Service* (1895), and *Sherlock Holmes* (1899). Thomas pictured *Alabama* (1891), *In Mizzoura* (1893), *Arizona* (1899), *Colorado* (1901), and *Rio Grande* (1916). America thus moved into the age of Realism.

# RUSSIA

*The End of Isolation*  The Romantic age brought the influence of Western culture to Russia. Although Orthodox Christianity had always dominated Russia, even at the time of the Mongol conquests in the thirteenth century, the fall of Constantinople in 1492 actually brought the center of Orthodox Christianity to Moscow. Because the Church was immune from change, Russian princes depended on its stability.

Russian princes also oversaw the increase of agricultural production through deforestation. Surplus crops brought about trade and the growth of cities. By the fifteenth century, Moscow presided as the chief Russian trading center. Moscow's Ivan III (1462–1505) expelled the Mongols, dominated the other principalities, and named himself tsar. Political unification was complete. Such political and religious stability in an urban setting let the theatre develop.

As princes had in the East and the West, Russia's tsars turned to the dramatic arts to glorify their reigns. As elsewhere, Russian leaders imported the arts and artists they admired. Early Renaissance explorers seeking furs and forest products had brought some Western culture to Russia. Russians welcomed the Westerners for their technology but guarded their Orthodox traditions from foreign influence.

In 1613 the Romanov family took charge of Russian absolutism. Like the French Bourbons, the Russian Romanovs had but a small middle class between them and the peasants. The tenuous position of the ruling aristocrats intensified the suspicion of foreigners. Visitors were even isolated in special sections of cities lest their radical ideas topple either the government or the religious hierarchy.

*"Frenchification"* In 1698 Peter the Great (reigned 1689–1725) returned from a tour of Europe undaunted by what he had seen. Indeed, he wished to remake Russia in the French mold. He prohibited traditional Russian costumes, and he adopted the Western calendar. He also moved his capital to St. Petersburg, his Russian Versailles. To further Westernize his nation, Peter moved the theatre from his palace to a new state theatre, built in 1702 in Moscow. In 1709 the theatre moved to St. Petersburg. Under Peter Russia also began to amass a great military force to compete with the armies of the West.

An industrial revolution was needed to complete Peter's cultural revolution. Conse-

quently, Peter elevated the status of landed nobles and encouraged the growth of middle-class manufacturing and commerce. He also educated Russians in Western mathematics and science to build the economy. As a result, an elite corps of educated administrators and military officers formed around him. In addition, the power and influence of the Russian church declined. The theatre could, therefore, grow.

When the wife of Peter II became Tsarina Catherine II, or Catherine the Great (reigned 1762–1796), she continued Peter the Great's love for the culture of Enlightened France. In 1756 F. G. Volkov opened the first professional theatre in St. Petersburg. In 1757 Catherine established an Academy and began an exchange of letters with French writer Voltaire. Catherine even tried her hand at playwriting eleven comic scenes. She also wrote an imitation of Shakespeare's *The Merry Wives of Windsor*. During Catherine's reign urban population, manufacturing, and exporting increased. By 1750 middle-class capitalism had started to form within medieval feudalism. In addition, some nobles imported French and German tutors for their children, whereas other nobles were sent away to study. Scholars, too, accepted invitations to Russia.

*Enter Romanticism* Under Alexander I (reigned 1801–1825), the son of the mad Pavel I (reigned 1796–1801), the classical versus the romantic struggle began in Russian aesthetics. Capitalism increased the demand for agricultural products for export. With more produce going to export, however, Russian peasants had even less to consume. Russia, moreover, helped defeat Napoleon, the embodiment of the democratic spirit that had caused Russia's serfs to rise up at the end of the eighteenth century. Conservative paranoia grew among the Russian aristocracy. Liberal poet Aleksandr Pushkin (1799–1837) was expelled in 1820. And Nicholas I (reigned 1825–1855) established a secret police force. (He also spent a lot of time at the Imperial Theatre enjoying lavish historical plays and performances by foreign stars.) Finally, when further economic progress proved impossible without resolving the problem of increasing numbers of serfs, the serfs were freed.

When Alexander II (reigned 1855–1881) freed the 22.5 million serfs in 1861, he established *zemstovs* (regional assemblies) to diffuse potentially revolutionary situations. Urban population increased as the number of workers in industry tripled between 1820 and 1860. But the industrial revolution in Russia was slowed by poor transportation systems. Peasants rented small land allotments and capitalism developed quickly. As the bourgeois demanded more participation in the government, feudal monarchy became a bourgeois monarchy like that in England. Workers demanding justice organized unions. Peasants looked for economic relief. Discontent was growing, and Alexander II was assassinated.

Alexander III (reigned 1881–1894) rejected reform proposals. Marxist circles formed in Russia to discuss Karl Marx's *Das Kapital* (1867; published in Russia in 1872), just as literary circles had formed around Victor Hugo in France and Ralph Waldo Emerson in America. Revolutionist Vladimir I. Lenin (1870–1924) joined a circle in St. Petersburg. The Marxist political party developed. Alexander III, distrusting anyone smarter or more cultured than himself, revived the persecution of the Jews. In 1890 he force-marched all Jews to the Western provinces. Many kept going.

Meanwhile, strikes increased among the workers. The literacy rate tripled as serfs sought education as a way to prosperity and property. The number of university students, in fact, increased eightfold in the nineteenth century. Nicholas II (reigned 1894–1917), realizing the need to move with the times, attempted to modernize industry; he also built railroad systems. But disillusionment with World War I, political corruption, bankruptcy, famine, shortages, and the ever-present demand for democratic liberalism proved too much for the monarchy.

In 1905 almost 3 million workers struck, including those aboard the battleship Potemkin and among the military at Sevastopol. When urged to convene a new legislative body, Tsar Nicholas II responded with executions and jailings. By April, 1906, 14,000 had been executed and 75,000 waited in prison. Six hundred unions were dissolved. One thousand newspapers were closed. Political and economic turmoil once again frustrated theatrical development.

***Revolution*** In March of 1917 St. Petersburg workers revolted against another food shortage. When the army sided with the workers, the revolt spread. Workers' councils, known as *soviets*, formed to organize the areas in revolt. Tsar Nicholas II abdicated for his brother Michael. But the workers demanded immediate reform. Even a provisional government led by Alexander Kerensky could not deal with the problems.

Kerensky's government divided power between the bourgeoisie and the soviets. Lenin later wrote: "Dual power could not last for long: It contained irreconcilable contradictions that had to be resolved through the establishment of a dictatorship—a dictatorship either of the soviets or of the Provisional Government." England, America, and France had resolved their revolutionary crises in favor of the bourgeoisie; later they reformed their governments to allow more participation by the workers. Russia took the opposite route: the workers took control, and only late in the twentieth century did reform allow minimal bourgeois activity.

In 1917 workers thought the bourgeois were suppressing their rights, delaying reform, urging caution, and ignoring the need to change the civil service and the judiciary. Titles had not yet been abolished, as they had been during the French Revolution. Nobles and clergy retained their wealth and privilege. The provisional government dispatched forces to suppress peasant uprisings. And the theatre allied itself with the power brokers.

In April Lenin returned to Russia from exile in Switzerland where the Austrians had sent him at the outbreak of World War I. Elected leader of the Bolshevik Party, Lenin mobilized the Red Guard. The soviets sided with the Bolsheviks. In October a congress of soviets transferred governmental power to itself. The Tsar's

Winter Palace was stormed and the provisional government arrested. The Congress of Soviets elected Lenin chairman. All land, minerals, forests, and bodies of water were nationalized. The government instituted free education and free medical services and an eight-hour work day. Ranks and titles were abolished. Freedom of conscience was proclaimed. Women were guaranteed the rights of men. The church was formally separated from the government and the schools.

***Revolutionary Romanticism***   The romantic utopia envisioned by Karl Marx in the British Museum had become the dictatorship of the Russian proletariat. Whatever disparity existed between the romantic ideal and the realistic fact would become apparent in time.

Russian theatrical romanticism arose as an antibourgeois posture. Young Russians considered the bourgeois to be banal, prosaic, soulless, and egotistical bedmates of the oppressive ruling elite. Russian romantics despaired at unnatural individuals, the irrationality of fate, and the monotony of everyday life. The disparity between the real and the ideal created passion, which was accentuated by the problems with the serfs. The defeat of Napoleon had destroyed the hope for a democratic revolution; the victory of the Bolsheviks revived the Russian hope for it.

Romanticism issued forth in music and poetry. Fedor Tiutchev (1803–1873) wrote lyric poetry expressing the doom of individuals in conflict with nature. Nature imagery abounded along with a belief in the universal consciousness of all things. Sergei Rachmaninoff (1873–1943) set Tiutchev's poems to music.

Sixteen operas by Nikolai A. Rimsky-Korsakov (1844–1908)—the most famous of which was *The Golden Cockerl*, (1906)—found their subjects in Russian history and legend. Russian romantic music achieved almost perfect expression in the work of Petr Ilich Tchaikowsky (1840–1893), the son of a mine inspector. His opera *Voyevoda* (*Dream on the Volga*, 1868) was not as successful as his *Eugeny Onegin* (*Eugene Onegin*, 1879). But Tchaikowsky did find enthusiastic theatre audiences for his bal-

lets *Swan Lake* (1895), *The Sleeping Beauty* (1890), and *The Nutcracker* (1892).

***Imitative Dramas***   As in Germany, native Russian folk comedy held the stage despite reformers' efforts to supplant it with French neoclassicism. Alexander Petrovich Sumarokov (1718–1777) was the first Russian to write in the neo-classical style for the stage. His *Khorev* (1749) was produced in 1750 at court after premiering at a military academy. In 1756 Sumarokov, called "the Russian Racine," was appointed head of the Russian theatre in St. Petersburg.

Shakespeare and Byron came to influence the work of Ivan Andreevich Krylov (1768–1844). Krylov was Russia's greatest satirist; he wrote such works as *Urok dochkam* (*A Lesson to Daughters*, 1807) and *Modnaya Lavka* (*The Fashion Shop*, 1806).

Romanticism produced the first great Russian authors. Alexander Sergeivich Pushkin (1799–1837), regarded by the tsarist government as a dangerous revolutionary, wrote little plays in French when he was 8 years old. Considered Russia's Dante, Goethe, and Shakespeare, Pushkin used Russian myths and history in his works. He mixed prose and poetry in *Boris Godunov* (1825), an imitation of Shakespeare's style that was not produced until 1870. Before he died in a duel defending his wife's honor, Pushkin also wrote a few one-act tragedies.

Influenced by the German and English romantics, Mikhail Yurevich Lermontov (1814–1841) read England's Lord Byron intensely. He subsequently wrote *Ispantsy* (*The Spaniards*, 1830) and an Othello drama entitled *Maskarad* (*Masquerade*, 1835). He was called "Russia's Byron."

Alexander Sergeivich Griboedov (1795–1829), wrote the masterpiece of Russian comedy, *Gore ot umar* (*Woe from Wit*, 1822). In the play the misanthrope Chatski returns from Europe a hero but confronts a hometown bourgeois morality antipathetic to his liberal ideas. Griboedov was murdered in Teheran while working for the government.

After the Tsar saw Nikolai Vasilievich Gogol's (1809–1852) *Revizor* (*The Inspector General*, 1836), a satire on bureaucracy and an attack on serfdom, Gogol tried to flee to the United States but only got as far as Germany. He moved to Rome and lived there for twelve years. In 1847 Gogol wrote another play, *Zhenitba* (*Marriage*). His novel *Dead Souls*, written when he was on the verge of an emotional breakdown, led him on a pilgrimage to the Holy Land in 1848. But Gogol eventually went mad and lost his will to live.

Count Alexei Konstantinovich Tolstoi (1828–1910) moved Russia away from the domestic subjects Gogol tackled. Tolstoi's trilogy of history plays about Ivan the Terrible—*Tsar Feodor* (1860), *Smert Ioanna Groznogo* (*The Death of Ivan the Terrible*, 1866), and *Tsar Boris* (1870)—were romanticism's last major explorations of the past.

With Gogol, Russian playwriting moved toward realism. Gogol had said "only a great, deep rare genius can catch what surrounds us daily." Realistic genius limited itself to what could be perceived by the five senses. Playwrights began to organize scenes according to cause and effect logic. Subplots disappeared. And contemporary characters and familiar situations replaced Russian history and mythology.

***Struggling Players*** Russian actors inherited both the French classification of lines of business and the demarcation of particular theatres for particular genres of drama. Peter the Great had imported actors from the West to train Russian serf performers. In 1756 Sumarokov directed the St. Petersburg theatre, where he worked to raise the level of performance. Nobles owned serf actors and often traded them, as they had in medieval Europe.

Various actors became especially well known. Fyodor Volkov (1729–1763), actor, teacher, director, and translator, was considered the founder of the Russian theatre. Volkov excelled in the heroic acting of French neoclassical characters. Ivan A. Dmitrieviskii (1734–1821) was the first Russian actor to tour abroad (1765–1768). His acting of classical Russian drama helped improve the status of the actor and establish a Russian style of acting. Best as Alceste in Molière's *Le misanthrope*, Dmitrieviskii also produced Beaumarchais's *Eugène* and translated sentimental *drame*.

The son of a serf actor, Pavel Mochalov (1800–1848) began his career playing *Horace* by Corneille and *Tancrede* by Voltaire. But he gave up the classical repertoire for the passion and depth of feeling in romanticism. Acting by inspiration and impulse, he played Alexander Dumas's *Kean*, August Kotzebue's *The Stranger*, *Hamlet*, the Moor in Schiller's *The Robbers*, Ferdinand in Schiller's *Love and Intrigue*, Othello, Lear, and Richard III. Mochalov also acted in stage adaptations of works by Aleksandr Pushkin, and he played Chatski in Griboedov's *Woe from Wit*. His unexpected transitions of emotion established emotional spontaneity as a desirable quality in performance and won the praise of playwrights Nikolai Gogol, Mikhail Lermontov, Ivan Turgenev, and Alexandr Ostrofsky. Actor Constantin Stanislavsky called Mochalov "Russia's Kean," one of the geniuses of the world theatre.

By moving romantic acting toward realism, Mikhail Shchepkin (1788–1863) developed a larger following than Mochalov. The son of a serf butler, Shchepkin won freedom in 1821 and joined the Moscow Imperial Theatre. His best roles were in comedy, especially as Fumusov in Griboedev's *Woe from Wit*, the Mayor in Gogol's *The Government Inspector*, Podkoleosin in Gogol's *The Marriage*, and Polonius in *Hamlet*. In 1823 he joined the Maly Theatre and made it "The House of Shchepkin." He looked for objective rules for acting, eschewed acting based on momentary inspiration, and worked for a science of acting. Constantin Stanislavsky said Shchepkin laid the basis for an artistic dramatic theatre.

With the Russian Revolution political unification of greater Europe was complete. Throughout the West countries developed national pride and distinctive national characters as the industrial revolution both produced prosperity and demanded ever more raw materials and markets. Technology and science seemed ready to deliver the utopias dreamed about by the romantics.

Realists, meanwhile, insisted that attention be focused on the facts of the present world, and they turned the theatre's attention to the current problems of urban societies. Science and technology provided theatre artists with a methodology for making the theatre a laboratory of science. They believed this laboratory of the theatre helped reform society and bring about the progress promised by science. The scientific theatre of fact and accurate observation envisioned itself contributing to the reformation of the world's problems. Realists sought a better theatre and a better world through science. Progress would be their most important product.

# NOTES

[1] William Hazlitt, "On the Comic Writers of the Last Century," in *European Theories of the Drama*, ed. Barret Clark (New York: Crown, 1969), p. 427.

[2] Friedrich Nietzsche, *The Birth of Tragedy and the Case against Wagner*, Walter Kaufman, trans. (New York: Vintage Books, 1967), p. 73.

[3] Ibid., p. 74.

[4] Charles Dickens, *The Life and Adventures of Nicholas Nickleby* (London: Chapman & Hall, Ltd. nd.), pp. 374, 375.

[5] Sarah Bernhardt, *The Art of the Theatre* (New York: Benjamin Blom, 1924), p. 98.

[6] Ibid., p. 137.

[7] Ibid., pp. 94–95.

[8] Alexis de Tocqueville, *Democracy in America*, J.P. Mayer and Max Lerner, eds. (New York: Harper & Row, 1966), p. 316.

[9] Ibid.

[10] Mark Twain, *The Adventures of Huckleberry Finn* (New York: New American Library, 1959), p. 283.

[11] *Macready's Reminiscences and Selections from His Diaries and Letters*, Sir Frederick Pollock, ed. (New York: Macmillan, 1875), p. 613.

[12] Mark Twain, "About Play-Acting," in *The Man Who Corrupted Hadleyburg and Other Essays and Stories* (New York: Harper & Brothers, 1901), p. 213.

[13] Ibid., p. 215.

# 8

# THE REALISTIC THEATRE

*Now, what I want is Facts. Teach these boys and girls nothing but Facts. Facts alone are wanted in life. Plant nothing else, and root out everything else. You can only form the minds of reasoning animals upon Facts: nothing else will ever be of any service to them.*

Mr. Gradgrind in *Hard Times*\*

## OVERVIEW

The speed of transportation and communication increased during the Industrial Revolution. With goods and orders traveled ideas. Movements and countermovements developed and spread more rapidly than ever before. Even before romanticism had run its course, theatrical realism arose. And in time the seeds of the Modern theatrical era hit fertile soil. Although attempts to separate the movements distort the dynamic interplay of the concurrent lines of thought, they may help clarify the lines' theoretical bases. Mr. Gradgrind, for example, epitomized the realistic theatrical position.

***Age of Science***   The scientific method, the harbinger of economic prosperity, was applied to most aspects of life. In 1859 the word "tech-

nology" appeared to refer to the practical arts. The same year Charles Darwin (1809–1882) published an abstract of a longer work, *On the Origin of Species by Means of Natural Selection, or the Preservation of Favored Races in the Struggle for Life*. Darwin was hailed as the "Newton of Biology," and anthropocentric consciousness collapsed with Darwin as anthropocentric space had fallen with Copernicus.

After scientific expeditions around the world, Darwin concluded that the same factors that check population growth also keep down the number of animals and plants. When faced with accident, disease, war, and famine, favorable species survive and unfavorable ones perish. New species develop from the process of "natural selection," a "struggle for existence" for "the survival of the fittest." In his conclusion Darwin noted that one could infer from analogy the probability that all organic beings had descended from a common pri-

\* Charles Dickens; *Hard Times* (New York: W. W. Norton, 1966), p. 1.

mordial form, "into which life was first breathed." The realistic theatre would demonstrate Darwin's theory.

Nonetheless, Darwin's work created quite a stir. Churches attacked Darwin for challenging the biblical story of creation. Christians ridiculed Darwin for claiming that humans were descendants of monkeys and for proposing that turnips might grow into people. Leading university libraries banned his book, but noted scientists attacked and defended Darwin's evidence and conclusions. Capitalists considered that Darwin justified an economic system that weeded out the "unfit" by means of poverty, hunger, and disease. To them, utopian romantics and social reformers seemed hindrances to the forces of natural selection working to improve the human species.

Darwin's ideas envisioned humans as unfinished products descending from other life forms through evolutionary processes. Scientists, humanitarians, racists, and naturalists preferred to think of humans as ascending—progressing toward greater abilities. Evolution came to mean upward progress. The age produced an avalanche of technological "advances" proving human progression. To avoid being left behind to die out, even theatre workers hurried to adapt the scientific method to their profession.

Systematic laboratory research conducted by trained staffs of engineers and scientists replaced the serendipitous individual romantic genius puttering around in home-made labs. Educational systems copied the factory method to produce mass-educated citizens trained as scientifically aware workers for nations' struggle to survive as the "fittest."

Science changed the world. In 1839 vulcanized rubber, electroplating, and the electric clock appeared. A new device for dramatic exposition, the telegraph, sent messages between Washington and Baltimore in 1844; the same year wood pulp paper debuted. By 1845 power looms threatened weavers with extinction. New clocks measured the speed of light in 1849. The following year scientists perfected the gas burner. New technological breakthroughs rapidly changed the quality of Western life: Goe-

bel's light bulb (1854), the transatlantic cable (1857), the storage battery (1859), bicycles (1867), color photography (1873), the telephone (1876), the phonograph (1877), the microphone and the repeater rifle (1878), large steel furnaces and canned foods (1880), the recoil machine gun (1882), the six-cylinder motor car engine (1885), celluloid film (1887), the cloth zipper (1891), x-rays, the motion picture camera, and the wireless radio (1895), radioactivity (1896), the electron (1897), the zeppelin airship (1898), oil drilling in Persia (1901), the aeroplane (1903), telegraphic transmission of photographs (1904), and Einstein's Special Theory of Relativity (1905). When Halley's Comet passed over in 1910, it marked the end of one age and the beginning of another.

But Albert Einstein (1879–1955) in particular located the limits of Newtonian science, and announced the end of the realistic dream. Meanwhile, Newtonian science discovered what was thought to be indestructible matter—molecules, atoms, and subatomic particles. The tiny pieces contained inestimable sources of energy. Humanity stood on the threshold of dominion over the universe. The objective understanding of the facts of nature, the utilization of dispassionate reason, had put humanity in a position to dream not just of new products but of new matter. Science promised to make people equal to God as creator. Science became the new religion and scientists the new gods. Science also worked wonders for the theatre. The theatre, too, made dispassion the medium and the message.

Science affected industry as well. Mass production resulted from the standardization of the industrial process. The amount of goods produced and available increased. Communication and transportation networks further facilitated industry's needs: railroads led to new markets, new audiences, and new sources of raw materials. Steamships carried new materials to mills, manufactured goods to market, and theatre companies to remote sites. The modern postal system developed to help industry carry out business.

But at the same time, local artisans in both

industrialized and nonindustrialized lands were driven out of business. Individual artisans could not compete with inexpensive, mass-produced, imported goods. Unemployment grew. The jobless gravitated to cities looking for work. The lucky ones found work on assembly lines as dispensable gears in the industrial machine. As the workers' frustrations grew along with the complexity of the machinery, industries grew susceptible to work stoppages and strikes. As a result, communities formed local police forces and drew up anti-union legislation.

***The Science of Society*** The development of unions and factory turmoil were only two of the urban problems prompting reform movements. August Comte (1798–1857) believed science should apply itself to society as well as to biology, chemistry, and physics. Comte was credited with developing the modern social sciences. He founded "positivism" with his *Positive Philosophy* (1830–1842) and *Positive Polity* (1851–1854). Positivism insisted on the scientific investigation of society to discover the true basis for moral action. Comte claimed science, rather than religion, as the best basis for morality. The theatre followed his lead.

Comte ranked the sciences hierarchically. The results of mathematical science led to astronomy, astronomy to physics, physics to chemistry, chemistry to biology, and biology to the most complex science, sociology. Comte defined civilization as "the increasing power of man over nature." The basic sociological unit in Comte's civilization was the family: "The family is the basis of the state." Not since the Chinese philosopher Confucius had the family been so elevated and venerated. For Comte, as the family went, so went the nation. The family symbolized the dominant bourgeois ethic of respectability and morality. Family dramas proliferated.

The realistic, scientific family of sociology relied on the dominance of the male: "Sociology will prove that the equality of the sexes, of which so much is said, is incompatible with all social existence." Comte found woman "unfit" for "the requisite continuousness and intensity of mental labor, either from the intrinsic weakness of her reason or from her lively moral and physical sensibility, which are hostile to scientific abstraction and concentration." Women are, he found, "superior to men in a spontaneous expansion of sympathy and sociability as they are inferior to men in understanding and reason." Sexual chauvinism became the domestic counterpart to both political nationalism and international economic imperialism.

The realistic bourgeois dramatic theatre, created by men, reinforced Comte's values. Women were portrayed with their biologically unique ability to place social good above personal feelings. Popular playwrights drew women who proved Comte's belief that woman "merits always our loving veneration, as the purest and simplest impersonation of humanity." Comte insisted that man rule the family, business, and the state despite "his inferiority in goodness. Success in all great undertakings depends more upon energy and talent than upon goodwill."

Comte urged scientists to observe the facts of society. He found observation more important to human progress than imagination; discovery furthered social evolution more than invention. Comte attacked the romantic idea of genius: "The isolated power of genius is greatly less than that with which it has been credited." Comte thought that individuals' achievements were always based on the work of predecessors. In fact, Comte named environment and heredity as the primary factors in human evolution: "Placed in a given system of exterior circumstances a definite organism must always act in a necessarily determinate manner."

Despite Comte's insistence that dramatic art be banned from the positivist utopia, the dramatic theatre tried to envision the reality observed by the sociologists. Comte believed the theatre too irrational, too immoral, and too dependent upon imagination. Realists working in the theatre agreed and vowed to apply the principle of factual observation to the creation of dramatic art.

*A New Bourgeois Aesthetic*   Both industry and the bourgeoisie controlling the popular theatre liked to see male values prevail on stage. Conservative capitalism, they were sure, would survive the liberalism of the working classes, women, and ethnic minorities struggling for power under the banner of either social justice or socialism. Artists consciously and unconsciously took sides in the struggle. Playwrights wrote either to show the virtues of male family life or to demonstrate the hypocrisy of bourgeois capitalism. Socialism, the child of utopian romanticism, gradually embraced the scientific and realistic view of economics, art, and politics. Everyone defined people sociologically, in life and in art.

Romantic theatre artists had fled the present. Realistic theatre artists took responsibility for the present. Romantic artists valued emotion. Realistic artists considered emotion harmful to the ability to observe, analyze, and conclude objectively, dispassionately, and scientifically. Realistic theatre wished to study the human character, and realistic art became the case study. Ideology was suspect to scientific artists who considered heredity and environment to be determinants of human destiny regardless of individual conviction. Scientific determinism led many playwrights to deny free will to the characters they drew. Artistic composition eschewed selectivity as distortion. Realists believed that all subjects should be open to investigation. As a result, realistic theatre artists portrayed what had been ignored: the poor, the oppressed, the sick, and the sexual.

Bourgeois realism raised the family institution to new heights of importance and value in capitalist society. The first Christmas card was sent in 1846 and a chorus of new Christmas carols praised the ideal Christian bourgeois family of Joseph, Mary, and the infant Jesus. Music remained a powerful and popular Protestant merchant art. On the other hand, socialist realism exposed the hypocrisy and immorality of the image. While one group of realists expressed bourgeois optimism, another championed proletarian pessimism. Norwegian playwright Henrik Ibsen's bourgeois family, for example, crumbles in *A Doll's House* Christmas celebration. Capitalists encouraged workers to think positively by increasing productivity to "get ahead." But socialists urged the workers to forsake membership in the middle class for action designed to subvert the ruling class's grip on power.

Bourgeois realists raised the theatrical picture of familial domestic love to oppose the romantics' vision of passionate and wild love. Socialist realists used the theatre to depict class solidarity and social humanism as individuals' greatest allies. One side excused men and punished women for violations of bourgeois morality; the other side punished men and excused women. On stage the family was drawn as either the source of all goodness or the root of all evil. Women came to represent the family as the family represented the state. The realistic theatre presented differing objective pictures of the "truth" about women, the family, and the nation.

*The Science of Race*   While dramatic visions competed for survival on realist stages, athletic competition revived among nations. The Olympic Games returned in 1896, for example, as a way for nations to demonstrate their athletes' "fitness." However, from 1908 to the Modern age, the Games were used to promote various nations' prides, biases, and antagonisms. Racial bias, in fact, found an easy outlet in sport. In 1910, when Jack Johnson became the first black heavyweight boxing champion of the world, racial violence erupted in fifty cities. Even clergy asked that films of the fight be suppressed, because Johnson's triumph violated the scientific truth of white racial superiority revealed by Count Arthur de Gobineau (1816–1882).

Gobineau, who authored two plays, applied both Darwin's evolutionary theory and Comte's hierarchial view to race. He also extended the social evolution theory of Herbert Spencer (1820–1903), which saw history marching toward a better world in the future. Spencer had applied the idea of evolution to every aspect of life, thereby making evolution and progress synonymous. Scientists worked to hasten the evolution Spencer described. Gobineau worried that racial mixing might pollute the natural biological forces working toward the progress of the species. His *Essay on the Inequality of Human Races* (1854) claimed race as the key factor in the formation and decline of societies. Naturally, his hierarchy of races placed his white race on top, the "yellow" race in the middle, and black people on the bottom.

Like Comte, Gobineau championed the nuclear family. He also extended family values to race: white people valued family life more than other races. The white race and the bourgeois family were the last line of defense for human security and stability. Other races were more "rootless." Gobineau worried that urbanization might bring about intermarriage among the races and the consequent pollution of superior strains. His nationalism went hand in hand with racism: "Lack of patriotism together with frivolity in matters of national interest are vices that deeply strain the character of a people." Gobineau linked racism, patriotism, and sexual chauvinism; as the white, male-dominated family went, so went the nation; as the nation went, so went the white race; as the white race went, so went civilization.

As a result of Gobineau and Comte, the Renaissance's great chain of being found sociological verification when white male industrialists replaced kings as God's chosen measure of all things. The earth seemed humanity's to dominate; whites could, and should, dominate individuals of other races. Males could, and should, dominate women and children. Science, moreover, was the handmaiden of white male dominance. In 1899 American sociologist Thorstein Veblen (1857–1929) satirically described *The Theory of the Leisure Class* atop white Western civilization. Industrial titans created awe and inspired power over lesser men and women through "conspicuous leisure," "conspicuous consumption," and "conspicuous waste." The more of each one had, the greater one's prestige. The invention of photography further enhanced the conspicuousness of the leisured class and domestic social climbing.

*Imperialism*   Such social climbing had its counterpart in foreign policy. Western imperialism even found humanitarian justification. According to the so-called "White man's burden," the whites brought European culture and dramatic theatre—the pinnacle of social, moral, aesthetic, and religious evolution—to the barbarian primitives of the world. Europeans, and later Americans and Russians, built miniature versions of their own economic systems and dramatic theatres all around the globe. Back home, nationalism grew as citizens heard reports of their country's efforts at humanitarian and missionary colonization. So successful was colonization in creating an admiration for Western nationalism that eventually native populations demanded their own nations, just like the conqueror's homelands.

Imperialism spread both nationalism and democratic revolution throughout the world as well as throughout the theatre. Beginning in 1913 The William Ponty School at Dakar trained African theatre artists who would, during the next decades, spread Western dramatic technique throughout most parts of French-speaking Africa. Meanwhile, theatre programs in colleges and universities in British African colonies introduced Western theatrical technique into English-speaking territories.

The nonindustrialized world was explored, divided, and conquered for both raw materials and markets for manufactured goods. As Western powers competed for colonies, tension increased the number of international crises. England's early industrialization gave the British an edge in colonization: Singapore (1819), Burma (1824), Aden (1839), Hong Kong (1842), Natal (1843), the Punjab (1845), India (1858), Beijing (1860), the Suez Canal (1875), Transvaal (1877), Afghanistan (1878), New Guinea, Nigeria, Bechuanaland, and South Africa (1885), Zanzibar (1890), Sierra

Leone and East Africa (1896), the Orange Free State and Northern Nigeria (1900), and Jerusalem (1917). France followed: Cochin-China (1862), Mexico City and Cambodia (1863), Indochina (1885), the Ivory Coast (1893), Madagascar (1896), and Morocco (1912). Germany moved into the competition: Togoland, Cameroon, and Southwest Africa (1884), East Africa (1885), and Heligoland (1890). In 1885 Belgium took the Congo. Italy won Ethiopia in 1899 and Tripoli, Libya, in 1911. In 1908 Austria picked up Bosnia Herzegovina.

Latecomers America and Russia continued to spar into the Modern age for "spheres of interest." In fact, realism and science found their most enthusiastic and enduring advocates in the two nations. America and Russia continued to operate from realistic premises. World Wars I and II removed all but the United States and the Soviet Union from international competition. Science and technology remained key weapons in the two nations' competition to emerge "the fittest."

Imperialism directed attention away from domestic problems. The tensions and ills of industrialization found some relief in social programs. Sociology, the science of society, tried to isolate all the variables so that problems could be solved. The variables were thought to be finite in number. In time, prosperity would trickle down to the workers. But hope merely intensified the workers' demands for equity and justice.

Worker agitation spread throughout the West as industrialization and colonization increased the overall standard of living. Universal military conscription took some disgruntled men off to foreign lands to protect civilization from nonwhite races. The ideal of the citizen-soldier revived. The popular press headlined slogans about national honor, patriotic pride, and individual acts of selfless honor overseas. New chivalric codes developed for the military. Parades gave workers a chance to vent their emotions. Nationalistic sentiment became very popular. And the theatre jumped on the bandwagon. As a result, international incidents or crises, quickly re-layed by the media, mobilized intense mass reactions to real or imagined slurs on national honor or pride. The themes of French neo-classical drama became national foreign policies. World War I, the result of such a reaction, began the decline of the Realistic age.

*Asian Influence* But before then, Japan influenced the realistic theatre as China had teased the social theatre and India had inspired the romantic theatre. Japan opened its doors to Western gunboats and altered the world of Western art. In France, for example, realistic and naturalistic writers collected the Japanese prints that decorated the kabuki theatres. The French authors, the Goncourt brothers, collected prints of Japanese actors and geishas; in the brothers' novels Japanese actors became Western acrobats and courtesans. Emile Zola (1840–1902), the founder of naturalism, collected Japanese prints of exotic subjects and admired Japanese artists' unique angle of vision. French painter Henri de Toulouse-Lautrec (1864–1901) collected and sketched Japanese prints. In America, artist James McNeill Whistler (1834–1903) collected Japanese prints, porcelain, and curios. Russian movie maker and stage director Sergei Eisenstein (1898–1948) wrote *The Cinematograph Principle and the Ideograph* and took "cut," "disintegrate," "slow motion," and "super close-up" techniques from kabuki stage practice. Even American impresario P. T. Barnum displayed Japanese coins.

Realists used subject matter that shocked the public. In addition, realistic painters and scene designers reacted to the invention of photography by rediscovering painting. Japan's influence also helped reconcile three-dimensional illusion with the flat surface of canvas. Impressionists, for instance, found freshness in the color, unorthodox composition, and everyday subject matter of Japanese prints. Impressionism bloomed as a climactic stage of realistic painting. Impressionists, believing truth to reside in sense impressions, painted only what they saw around them; they invented nothing. They captured the prismatic quality of natural light in compositions of snapshot casualness. At age 16, Toulouse-Lautrec declared of his painting: "I have tried to make it true and not idealized." Painting whores, lesbians, dancers, and actresses as victims of society, Lautrec moved art away from traditional subject matter. American painter Thomas Eakins (1844–1916) practiced a scientific realism that eventually led him to the new art of photography.

*Photography* In 1839 Louis Jacques Mandé Daguerre (1787–1851), a painter and scene designer, invented photography, which altered human perception and consciousness in a way unsurpassed since the introduction of the printed book. Romanticism found its truest expression in opera. Realism found its natural form in photography, and, later, in its extension, motion pictures.

Photography recorded, objectively, everything in front of the lens. Photography did not select; it provided the ultimate in realistic observable detail. Photography enabled individuals to freeze and own experience, because like science, photography broke nature into manageable bits for framing. Photography also increased people's sense of power and faith in science. In addition, photographic equipment could go anywhere and record anything. Because anyone could create an illusion of reality, the goal of visual art for over 100 years, photography in effect democratized artistic creation. Photography also reinforced individuals' reliance on the senses as the most effective way to perceive the truth of nature. The camera did not imagine or invent. The truth of bourgeois happiness—captured at weddings, births, parties, and holidays—could be exhibited for all to see. Photography made the world seem smaller by bringing the exotic, the foreign, and the distant into every home.

In *Fathers and Sons* Russian novelist Ivan Turgenev (1818–1883) wrote, "A picture shows me at a glance what it takes dozens of pages of a book to expound." Because photography captured reality more effectively than words, photography made words less impor-

tant. Individuals could possess the thing itself instead of merely printed symbols describing the thing. Alphabet symbols needed imagination to recreate the image; the photograph was the image itself—no imagination was necessary. Photography consequently diminished the human capacity to remember and imagine.

Photography increased individuals' dependence on the present as well. It froze time, thereby making the recorded experience an artifact of the past. Captured on film, experience aged more than when kept only in the living, imaginative memory of the present. Consequently, photography made the past more distant and more alien; in a photograph bygone experiences yellowed and cracked with time.

Photography achieved the visual goal of romantic and realistic theatre workers: complete accuracy in the creation of observable phenomena. Photography directed attention toward gesture and movement, and away from the spoken word. Photography kindled a new interest in movement, mime, dance, and nonverbal communication. Psychologists Sigmund Freud (1856–1939) and Carl Jung (1875–1961) eventually described the subconscious as a communicator that uses dream images rather than words. Theatre artists and poets were freed from the depiction of external reality; photography could do it better. As media theorist Marshall McLuhan wrote, "Art moved from outer matching to inner making."[1] Modern theatre artists forsook the creation of products to explore the process of creation itself.

*Motion Pictures* But Daguerre was not content with a still picture. He, and many others, wanted to create the illusion of motion. Inventions came in a flurry: the thaumatrope, phenakistoscope, and stroboscope (1825), the magic lantern (1853), the phonautagraph (1857), the zoetrope (1860), the kinematoscope (1894), and the Lumière brothers' motion picture camera in 1895. In 1896 a kinetoscope opened on Broadway in New York City. But such movies lost popularity—until one came along with a story line. In 1903 *The*

*Great Train Robbery* took from the theatres an audience trained to want spectacle without imaginative effort. As a result, theatrical touring shows ended and resident companies closed; the movies won the audience.

The theatre audience had been trained for almost 100 years to value accuracy in visual detail, local color in setting and costume, and historicity in the representation of the past. As a result, the theatre's audience went where the realistic ideal was best achieved. The realistic theatre actually sired a rival that forced the modern dramatic theatre to rediscover its historical nature.

***Scientific Art***   While the movies presented real, visual detail, the realistic novel provided enough facts to make it the second most important realistic art. Most movies upheld bourgeois family values; many novels, however, attacked the bourgeoisie. Novelists showed individuals struggling in a propertied society, businesspeople exploiting the poor, morality being corrupted, and materialism destroying human relationships. Realistic literature addressed intellectuals rather than the popular audience of England's Sir Walter Scott and Charles Dickens. By confronting contemporary moral problems, realistic novels laid the foundation for the realistic theatre.

The coldly rational, antiromantic Hippolyte Adolphe Taine (1828–1893) insisted on the use of the scientific method in both literary criticism and creation. Literature "resembles that admirable apparatus of extraordinary sensibility, by which physicians disentangle and measure the most recondite and delicate changes of a body." Therefore, the realistic critic must scientifically analyze literature to arrive at the truth about a particular time and people.

The realistic theatre valued the thought of a scientific thesis more than dramatic character or plot. Consequently, realistic playwrights marshaled facts to prove a thesis rather than organize action in a plot. Bourgeois realism ended happily; romantic realism ended unhappily. Both occurred in the drawing room. Some playwrights sent in a *raisonneur*, a character who expressed the playwright's thesis. The realistic stage was both a scientific laboratory and a platform for persuasion.

Realistic playwrights did not speak of unities, genre, or form. Their dramas rejected plot considerations as artificial. Instead, they concentrated on an inner, psychological action of characters shaped by biological determinism and social environment. The demonstration of scientific ideas required the language of science: prose. Richard Wagner's success with music-drama and poetry led English critic William Archer to write in *The Old Drama and the New* (1923), that "the two elements of the old drama, imitation and lyrical passion, have at last consumated their divorce. For lyrical passion we go to opera and music drama, for interpretation through imitation we go to the modern realistic play." Poetry was confined to the expression of emotion, a quality harmful to a scientific theatre of objective fact. Poetry was not real or natural or truthful; poetry was merely another contrivance, like soliloquies and asides, to be discarded.

***Ibsen and Strindberg***   Two Scandinavian playwrights, Henrik Ibsen and August Strindberg, though arch enemies, demonstrated both the transition from the romantic to the realistic theatre, and the shift from the realistic to the fledging modern theatre. The realistic dramas of Ibsen and Strindberg were located in the rooms of bourgeois family homes, the symbol of familial, national, and racial stability, progress, and virtue. These playwrights used the family image to motivate audiences. Their plays demonstrated the effects of heredity and environment on characters' behavior. The prose diction of everyday life both hid and revealed the psychological needs and desires of the characters. Spectacle was limited to what could happen in a contemporary domestic situation to a contemporary bourgeois family.

In 1814 Norway gained independence from Denmark. The ensuing patriotism and nationalism let Henrik Ibsen (1828–1906), the son of a bankrupt bourgeois merchant, rise to fame as the new nation's chronicler. After fathering a child out of wedlock, Ibsen went to work at the Bergen National Theatre as dramaturg and playwright. In 1855 Ibsen began to write a long line of historical dramas with *Lady Inger of Ostrat*, in which a mother's ambitions both destroy her son and lead one daughter into the arms of her dead sister's seducer.

In 1858 Ibsen wrote *The Vikings of Helgeland* but could not get the play produced. In the drama, a Viking wife's love for her best friend's husband leads her to torment her husband and sister, kill her lover, and finally commit suicide. Ibsen then worked as a stage director, married, fathered another child, but went bankrupt. He was forced to borrow money to support his family. In 1864, however, his first stage success, *The Pretenders*, enabled him to secure a government grant and move to Europe, where he lived for over twenty-five years. In this drama, a self-righteous man competes with a shy idealist for the throne of Norway.

In Rome Ibsen wrote *Brand* (1866), a verse play revealing his debt to the philosophy of Soren Kierkegaard (1813–1855). The idealistic Brand lives by an "all or nothing" creed. The next year *Peer Gynt*, another verse epic, presented Brand's opposite in the person of an expedient antihero. In 1873 Ibsen wrote what he considered—though no one else agreed—his greatest play, *The Emperor and the Galilean*. Ibsen consequently abandoned verse and history; he said, "Prose is for ideas, verse for visions."

In 1877 *The Pillars of Society* presented Ibsen's ideas in a new form. Ibsen took the "well-made play" popularized by bourgeois French realists and made it organic to character and situation. Melodrama's fixed characters gave way to evolving personalities. Ibsen focused on the struggle between an individual and bourgeois values in plays reintroducing the unity of place. In *The Pillars of Society* the unearthing of the leading citizens' sordid pasts ruin many reputations.

With *A Doll's House* (1879) Ibsen began his gallery of great independent women, heretofore the symbols of happy bourgeois family life. Nora, the heroine, discovering that her husband is not the man she hoped, leaves him to educate herself in the ways of the world. Parallel to the action, Mrs. Linde abandons her independent life for the man she loves. One family is thus broken as another begins. Money propels the action in both plots. When Ibsen explained how, and after whom, Nora was named, someone suggested the information irrelevant to his dramatic art. Ibsen answered with the realist's credo: "But facts are still facts."

Ibsen's facts were not popular. His notes for *Ghosts* (1881) said, "The play is to be like a picture of life." But no one wanted to see the picture Ibsen snapped. *Ghosts*, in fact, had to premiere in Chicago after being turned down by every other major theatre in other cities. Ibsen countered, "People demand reality, no more and no less. That art should elevate is not a popular conception." His play *The Wild Duck* (1884) applied Charles Darwin's account of how wild ducks degenerate in captivity to individuals caught in bourgeois society. More importantly, *The Wild Duck* raised a major theme of modern drama: Illusions may be more important to happiness than the truth. (Interestingly, the hero of *The Wild Duck*, whose family and life are based on illusion, is a photographer.) In *The Wild Duck* an unsuccessful husband is visited by his idealistic friend who insists on forcing the family to confront the truth about its relationships. As a result the family is destroyed, and the daughter is killed.

Ibsen admired the Russian realistic novelists but not the French Emile Zola: "Zola descends into the sewer to bathe in it; I, to cleanse it." Ibsen elaborated on his dramatic method, similar to the technique of the realistic novelists:

> Before I write one word, I must know the character through and through, I must penetrate into the last wrinkle of his soul. I always proceed from the individual; the stage setting, the dramatic ensemble, all of that comes naturally and causes me no worry, as soon as I am certain of the individual in every aspect of his humanity. But I have to have his exterior in mind also, down to the last button, how he stands and walks, how he bears himself, what his voice sounds like. Then I do not let him go until his fate is fulfilled.[2]

*When We Dead Awaken* (1899), Ibsen's last play, reveals a mystical and symbolical side, which began to emerge in *The Master Builder* (1892). In the latter play an aging builder falls in love with a young girl who seeks to inspire his dormant creativity. The master builder dies trying. In *When We Dead Awaken* an aged sculptor, unhappily married to a young woman, encounters the woman who was his greatest inspiration. Together they head off to certain death in a mountain storm.

Ibsen's mystical symbolism both anticipated the modern theatre and found fuller expression in the late plays of Ibsen's most famous critic, Swedish playwright August Strindberg. Ibsen kept a portrait of Strindberg hanging over his desk. He called the picture "Insanity Emergent" and told visitors it helped him write: "He is my mortal enemy, and shall be there and watch while I write." Ibsen died after he was paralyzed by a stroke.

Strindberg (1849–1912) disliked Ibsen's *A Doll's House* but praised the fact that "marriage was revealed as being a far from divine institution, people stopped regarding it as an automatic provider of absolute bliss, and divorce between incompatible parties came at last to be accepted as conceivably justifiable." But Strindberg called Ibsen "an ignorant women's writer." He hated Ibsen's *Hedda Gabler* (1890) because he was sure the wild womanizer Eilert Loevborg was modeled on himself. He likewise thought Ibsen mocked him as a source for Hjalmar Ekdal in *The Wild Duck*: "His shit will rebound on him."

Throughout his life a great deal, in fact, rebounded on August Strindberg. The son of a bankrupt bourgeois merchant and his maid, Strindberg blurred his life with his work in a romantic manner. He loved the theatre because there he could witness his troubled life on stage. He abandoned early historical and fanciful plays to travel to Europe where he wrote most of his sixty-two plays.

Strindberg wished to reveal the warfare between the sexes in marriage. With *The Father* (1887), a tale of a tortured family, Strindberg joined the new realistic writers. In this play, a husband is slowly driven insane by his wife. To cap her victory, the wife challenges her husband's role in fathering their daughter. The husband, though a captain, cannot control his

*August Strindberg's 1910 production of his play* Comrades. (Courtesy Drottningholms Teatermuseum)

household; though a scholar, he cannot even know the parentage of his child. Strindberg distanced himself from the French naturalists who "hold that art merely consists of drawing a piece of nature in a natural way; it is not the great naturalism which seeks out the points where the great battles are fought, which loves to see what you do not see everyday, which delights in the struggle between natural forces. . . ''. Strindberg wrote the "great naturalism."

Yet, like other, realistic writers, Strindberg discounted plot: "Life does not move as regularly as a constructed drama." In *Miss Julie* (1888) Strindberg condensed the struggle into one act to "let people's brains work irregularly, as they do in actual life." In the self-styled "naturalistic tragedy," an aristocratic young woman seduces her valet, only to find herself under his power. When the valet forces her to steal from her father, she commits suicide. Strindberg's next plays furthered his belief that "the psychological process is what chiefly interests the newer generation."

Strindberg gave up the stage to explore the occult and alchemy, but a spiritual and mental breakdown confined him to a sanatorium. After six years he resumed writing for the stage, but with new interests. He wrote history plays and "chamber plays" but found greatest satisfaction in writing such subjective plays as *Easter* (1901), *The Dance of Death* (1901), *To Damascus I, II, III* (1898 and 1904), *A Dream Play* (1902), and *The Ghost Sonata* (1907). These plays began the modern theatre as Strindberg imitated "the disconnected but seemingly logical form of the dream."

***Luigi Pirandello*** Realism took another twist before giving way to the modern theatre. Luigi Pirandello (1867–1936) initiated a new direction for the modern theatre by penning realistic plays that questioned the very fact of reality.

He created plays in which the "given circumstances," to use Russian director Constantin Stanislavsky's term, are hidden thoughout the play. The truth of the dramatic situation, like the truth of life, can never be known. Moreover, his dramatic characters

*August Strindberg's 1909 production of* The Dance of Death *at the Intimate Theatre.* (Courtesy Drottningholms Teatermuseum)

usually need to hide some truth to protect other characters from unnecessary pain. Often a *raisonneur* (voice of reason) denies the existence of hidden secrets, thereby leading both the characters and the audience away from the answers they are seeking. Pirandello saw existence as a confused layering of masks and faces—some internal, others external, some self-made, others demanded by society. Where could one find reality, truth, or even identity? Because layers of illusion and numerous masks are stripped away to no avail, the truth remains just beyond the next layer or mask.

In *Cosi e'se vi pare* (*Right You Are*, 1916) a remarried widower must keep his new wife away from his ex-mother-in-law who, he explains, continues to believe that her daughter is still alive. On the other hand, the mother-in-law claims the second wife is really her daughter humoring her son-in-law's strange tastes. Who is telling the truth? A *raisonneur* keeps the question from resolution while seeming to pursue an answer. *Sei personaggi in cerca d'autore* (*Six Characters in Search of an Author*, 1921) interrupt the rehearsals of a play by Pirandello. Abandoned by their author, they search for meaning in their lives. *Enrico IV* (*Henry IV*, 1922) was a wealthy man who fell from his horse during a pageant and awoke believing himself to be the medieval king Henry IV. When he comes to his senses, the businessman decides to keep his fictional identity rather than return to the real world he despises. The action of *Questa sera si recita a soggetto* (*Tonight We Improvise*, 1930) examines Diderot's paradox of the actor: real emotion and the illusion of emotion.

Pirandello himself was a partner in an arranged marriage. His wife suffered a mental breakdown and lived as a paranoid sadist who almost drove their daughter to suicide. Pirandello was eventually forced to commit his wife to an asylum. Although his dramatic form remained realistic, his ideas started a main current of the modern theatre.

*A New Acting Style*   The growing accuracy in scenic decor and acting found theatrical justification in the realistic theatre. Henrik Ibsen insisted, ''No declamation! No theatricalities! No grand mannerisms! Express every mood in a manner that will seem credible and natural. Never think of this or that actress whom you may have seen. Observe the life that is going on around you, and present a real and living human being.''

The greatest practitioners of such a realistic school of acting came from Italy. The Italian revolutionary and actor Gustavo Modena

A 1936 production of Luigi Pirandello's Six Characters in Search of an Author. (Vandamm Photo Theatre Collection, New York Public Library)

(1803–1861), for example, inspired the realistic Italian actors who followed him. Modena had his own company by 1843. Under 20 years of age, the actors in his company were trained to be truthful and spontaneous in the playing of romantic and "well-made" dramas. Unlike some later theorists, Modena was interested in having actors work on ideas rather than talk about them. By the age of 19, Tomasso Salvini (1829–1915), born into an acting family, became a world-famous actor of tragedy by playing Shakespeare's Othello and Hamlet. Although he retired in 1890, he reigned as the idol of the Russian actor Constantin Stanislavsky. Adelaide Ristori (1822–1906) acted with Modena in Paris. Born into an acting family, she was playing leading roles by the age of 15. A rival of Rachel, Ristori played Racine's Phèdre, Shakespeare's Lady Macbeth, and Schiller's Mary Stuart with great passion. She toured the world as Juliet before retiring in 1885. Ernesto Rossi (1829–1896) was Modena's favorite student. Famous for his Macbeth, Othello, Lear, and Hamlet, Rossi was the first actor to play Shakespeare in South America.

Italy's Eleanore Duse (1859–1924) ruled the international stage as a realistic star. Her acting without extravagance in realistic plays especially confirmed her as a genius of realism. She toured the world after her first hit, Emile Zola's *Thérèse Raquin*. Duse fell in love with Italy's romantic poet, Gabriele D'Annunzio (1863–1938). She played Henrik Ibsen's great heroines in *Hedda Gabler*, *A Doll's House*, and *The Lady from the Sea* following her 1897 performance of Dumas *fils*'s *La Dame aux caméllias*, about which English playwright George Bernard Shaw said that "I should say without qualification that it is the best modern acting I have ever seen."

Realism had critics from the beginning. Some thought the movement antithetical to the conventional nature of the dramatic theatre. Others blamed realism for a failure of the imagination. Realists could only present what

*Eleanora Duse on the set of a 1906 production of Henrik Ibsen's* Rosmersholm. (Nationaltheatret, Oslo)

they could observe rather than what they envisioned as possible. Critics complained that the realists had violated the Aristotelian order of drama by elevating character and thought over plot. Realism made tragedy and comedy impossible; determinism removed the individual's responsibility for heroic or laughable action. Realists could only be drawn as pitiable tragicomediens, innocent victims of biological and sociological circumstance.

# FRANCE

In 1880 France celebrated the fiftieth anniversary of Victor Hugo's *Hernani*; five years later a grand state funeral bid adieu to Hugo. The Franco-Prussian War had dealt Hugo's liberalism a severe blow. The Commune of Paris, the city's municipal body, believed that the national government had sold out to the Prussians. Consequently, Parisians resisted, disarmed the national guard, took hostages, and demanded decentralization of power. The conservative Republic destroyed the Commune, killing 17,000 Parisians. Because Hugo's pleas for understanding and mercy were ignored, he fled to exile. Throughout the world the word "communist" came to symbolize liberal rebellion against monarchy and conservative intransigence.

**Naturalistic Dramas**  Realism, the dominant mode of the twentieth century, had its birth, like many artistic movements, in France. In 1856 a liberal review called *Réalisme* appeared and popularized the term "realism" throughout world cultural centers. Naturalism consciously defined itself as something quite different from the so-called realistic works of Alexandre Dumas *fils* (1824–1895). Dumas *fils*'s success in the theatre had brought realism to the stage for the first time. The illegitimate son of Dumas *père*, Dumas *fils* rejected his father's romanticism for the prose styling of the writer of "well-made plays," Eugène Scribe (1791–1861).

Unlike his father, Dumas *fils* also insisted that dramatic diction could be grammatically incorrect. In a Preface Dumas *fils* urged playwrights to put the characters of the novelist Honoré de Balzac in the plays of Scribe. In 1852 Dumas *fils* attacked romantic bohemianism with *Le Demi-monde*. In the play a prostitute who has gained access to polite society is exposed and expelled. With *Le Fils naturel* (*The Illegitimate Son*, 1858) Dumas *fils* created a play with a "social thesis" for a useful theatre. Jacques, an illegitimate son, overcomes his birth by the strength of his upright character.

**The Triumph of Dramatic Structure**  The son of a silk merchant, Eugène Scribe had invented the *pièce bien faite* (well-made play) for a bourgeois theatre of fun:

> You go to the theatre, not for instruction or correction, but for relaxation and amusement. Now what amuses you most is not truth, but fiction. To represent what is before your eyes every day is not the way to please you; but what does not come to you in your usual life, the extraordinary, the romantic, that is what charms you, that is what one is eager to offer you; . . .The theatre is then very rarely the expression of society; . . .it is very often the inverse expression.[3]

Scribe developed a formula to accomplish the "inverse expression." In the formulation plot is the most important element. Unlike the romantic playwrights, Scribe placed the drama's point of attack close to the *dénouement*. His goal was always to keep his audience's attention, and he displayed true genius in maintaining suspense. Each theatrical effect is prepared carefully and is spaced for greatest impact on an audience. Initial scenes introduce various plot entanglements designed to interest an audience in their outcome. Sensational discoveries, revelations, reversals, and confrontations build the action to a *scene à faire* (obligatory scene), which contains a major discovery and leads to a speedy resolution.

The most successful playwright of his day,

Eugène Scribe wrote such drawing-room melodramas as the favorite of actresses Rachel and Sarah Bernhardt, *Adrienne Lecouvreur* (1849). Bourgeois plays for bourgeois audiences upheld the morality of the white, patriarchal bourgeois family. The husband always knows best and triumphs over his wife's lover. The wife always wins back her husband. Parents always succeed with their children. Age always convinces youth to follow its advice. Men lead women. The working class thanks the middle class for providing stability and prosperity. Eugène Labiche (1815–1888) was Scribe's comic counterpart. The well-made formula and bourgeois morality endured in the work of other dramatists. Victorien Sardou (1831–1908) refined the pattern to something easier to imitate. His early play pleased audiences but won jeers from the critics. Sardou's plays feature short and clear expositions, numerous misunderstandings, secreta, lost objects, and overheard conversations that lead to major climactic confrontations. Quick unwindings of the plots follow last-minute discoveries or reversals. Another disciple of Scribe's, George

Feydeau (1862–1921), was the comic counterpart to Sardou.

Alexander Dumas *fils* kept the well-worn form but altered the content. His subject matter more clearly reflected contemporary problems. Whereas Scribe had sacrificed the study of a problem to the pyrotechnics of plot, "realistic" dramatists like Dumas *fils* made a social problem their drama's point of attack or thesis. The realists thought that their predecessors had used too much imagination or invention in plot construction:

> . . .invention does not exist for us. We have nothing to invent; we have only to see, to remember, to feel, to coordinate, and to reestablish, under a special form, that which all spectators must immediately remember long felt or seen without having up to that time been able to take notice of it.[4]

Consequently, Alexander Dumas *fils's* plays feature "real-life" problems, simulate everyday conversation, and present interior rooms resembling those of contemporary society.

*The original 1907 production of Georges Feydeau's* A Flea in her Ear. *(Le Thé-âtre, 1907)*

All the while Dumas *fils* and the realists maintained that a difference existed between truth in the novel and truth on stage:

> The book speaks in low tones, in a corner, with a door and windows closed, to one single person; it emanates from the alcove and from the confessional. On the other hand, the theatre speaks to twelve or fifteen hundred persons in a group and emanates from the public platform and the public square. The painting of truth in public therefore has its limits.[5]

Dumas thought that the drama was suited for different subjects:

> The artist, the true artist, has a higher and more difficult mission than that of reproducing that which exists; he has to discover and to reveal to us what we do not see in all that we observe about us everyday.[6]

In time some disagreed.

**Emile Zola** Chief among the dissenters was novelist Emile Zola (1840–1902), who grew up in proverty and dropped out of school to work. Zola's writings observed the causes and effects of, among other things, prostitution, alcoholism, debased aristocracy, class struggle, and warfare. He began writing with a hypothesis or thesis. He then tested his hypothesis by placing the evidence in dramatic form.

Zola's novel and play *Thérèse Raquin* (1867) expressed his fatalistic philosophy, passion for detail, understanding of environmental influences, and interest in the animal nature of humans. In the play, *Thérèse Raquin* drowns her husband for her lover, but guilty consciences lead the lovers to a double suicide. Though set in the bourgeois world, the play was hissed off the stage for presenting impolite subjects.

In his Preface to *Thérèse Raquin* Zola rejected the realists' ''science of the theatre'' as a ''heap of clever tricks.'' He proposed ''life'' rather than ''thesis,'' and ''living'' rather than ''arguments.'' Zola was impatiently waiting for France's playwrights ''to put a man of flesh

and bones on the stage, taken from reality, scientifically analyzed, without one lie.''

> I am waiting for them to rid us of fictitious characters, of conventional symbols of virtue and vice, which possess no value as human data. I am waiting for the surroundings to determine the characters, and for characters to act according to the logic of facts, combined with the logic of their own temperament. I am waiting until there is no more juggling of any kind, no more strokes of a magical wand, changing in one minute persons and things. I am waiting for the time to come when they will no longer spoil the effects of just observation by romantic incidents, the result being to destroy even the good parts of a play. I am waiting for them to abandon the cut and dried rules, the worked-out formulas, the tears and cheap laughs. I am waiting until a dramatic work free from declamations, big words, and grand sentiments has the high morality of truth, teaches the terrible lesson that belongs to all sincere inquiry.[7]

Plot was the enemy:

> When we have gotten rid of the child's play of a plot, the infantile game of tying up complicated threads in order to have the pleasure of untying them again; when a play shall be nothing more than a real and logical story—we shall then enter into perfect analysis; we shall analyze necessarily the double influence of character over facts, of facts over characters.[8]

Zola advocated a ''naturalism'' that would subordinate plot to character and character to the influence of heredity and environment.

**Drama as Case Study** Zola's drama sought to eliminate the ''thesis'' from a play and to apply strictly the scientific principle of observation. Wishing to avoid an author's prejudice resulting in blatantly good or bad characters, Zola created plays in believable environments and presented all classes of society on stage. By applying the principles of ''natural science'' to the drama, the naturalistic playwright functioned as a scientific doctor of society. Presenting case studies to reveal the ills of society, the playwright sought an appropriate diagnosis and remedy.

Zola's plays were to be *lambeaux d'existence* (fragments of existence). "Naturalism" meant "simply a formula, the analytical and experimental method namely."[9] One formula replaced another formula:

> Science is, then, to speak truly, but explained poetry; the savant is a poet who replaces imaginary theories by the exact study of men and things.[10]

Nature was conceived as human beings' reacting in circumstances that determine evolution. Truth became the knowledge of the laws governing change in human behavior. Even though Zola's plays failed to accomplish his goals, he nonetheless remained the head of the French "naturalists."

Playwright Jean Jullien (1854–1919) invented the phrase *une tranche de vie* (a slice of life) to describe the naturalists' goal. The naturalists were "natural" relative to the plays that preceded them. Later realistic playwrights made their work seem quite "well-made." Despite claims to the contrary, naturalist playwrights constructed a clear cause-to-effect ordering of scenes developing suspense, surprise, crisis, and climax. Conventional stage diction disappeared; language grew out of character and situation. Brilliant language vanished to make room for the "commonplace" feared by romantic playwright Victor Hugo. Gradually slang and inarticulateness brought naturalism and realism to their logical ends.

In 1865 Hugo's supporters tried to boo realism from the *Comédie Française* stage. But the theatre of Zola would not be denied. Henri Becque (1837–1899) was credited with writing the first great naturalist drama, *Les corbeaux* (*The Vultures*, 1882). In the drama a deceased industrialist's family is destroyed by his greedy partner. Becque wrote other plays but disillusionment forced him to become a stockbroker. Bankruptcy later encouraged his return to playwrighting.

**Delsartism** Henrik Ibsen thought that "French actors are more suited than many others to act my plays. People have not fully appreciated that a passionate writer needs to be acted with passion, and not otherwise." Scientific analysis, in constrast, came to acting in France with the work of François Delsarte (1811–1871).

Orginally a voice student at the Conservatorie, Delsarte lost his voice due to poor and conflicting instruction. He vowed to eliminate such possibilities by systematizing the instruction of voice. Delsarte developed the first objective analysis and mathematical formulation of the laws of speech and movement. He never published anything, however, because like the work of all good teachers, his work continued to evolve.

From 1839 to the time of his death, Delsarte taught "Applied Aesthetics," a system based on his observation that the effects of emotion on the body result in characteristic gestures and speech. Delsarte also based his system on the belief that emotion caused movement, which, if truthfully and freely expressed, led the body to positions expressive of the felt emotion. False or feigned emotion led to artificial poses. Delsarte taught actors William Macready and Rachel and found great popularity for his technique in America. (His student, Steele Mackaye, founded the American Academy of Dramatic Art.) Delsarte defined grace scientifically—as efficiency of movement. But Delsarte insisted that scientific truth differed from artistic truth; the former must be proved but the latter can only be revealed: "Art is not an imitation of nature. It elevates in idealizing her." As a result Delsarte espoused what might be called scientific romanticism.

Delsarte also believed in genius: "Many artists do not possess an atom of genius. Many geniuses are poor artists. . . . The great artist must first be a genius and then through training become the artist." Geniuses know "If you cannot conquer your defect, make it beloved." Delsarte anticipated later realistic insistence on psychological motivation: "Nothing is more deplorable than a gesture without a motive, without meaning.'' His ''Trinity'' of the universe was applied to aesthetics: ''the unity of three things, each of which is essential to the other, each co-existing in time, co-penetrating in space, and cooperative in motion.'' His description was echoed early in the twentieth century by quantum physicists describing the essential processes of the universe.

Physicists who ushered in the Modern age also proved Delsarte's belief that motion has but three tendencies—remaining centered and static, going out from the center, and going in toward the center. Delsarte described the ways emotion and movement combine these three tendencies in various parts of the body. In addition, Delsarte associated certain areas of the body with particular spheres of motion, as did the Indian dramaturg Bharata's *Natya Sastra*. In the Modern age, in fact, dance and nonverbal theatre found great inspiration in both Delsarte and India's theoretical *Natya Sastra*. Delsarte was the first acting teacher to develop relaxation exercises to make the body more sensitive to inner impulses.

Delsarte, ignoring the realism of his day, bridged the romantic with the modern. He thought naturalism nothing but ''atheism disguised under the precious title of a new science and which they pretend, to-day, constitutes the basis of aesthetics.'' Even though Delsarte objected to realism as ''cold reasoning condemned to a profound sterility,'' he gave his own art the precision of mathematics.

Like the realists, Delsarte objected to simple inspiration as the basis of performance: ''Trusting to the inspiration of the moment, is like trusting to a shipwreck for your first swimming lesson.'' Genevive Stebbins, Delsarte's American enthusiast, claimed ''What Comte has done for exact science and Spencer for culture, Delsarte has done for action, for expression.'' But realists, especially in America, misinterpreted Delsarte's system as they did the technique of the Russian acting teacher Constantin Stanislavski.

Benoit Constant Coquelin (1841–1909), the son of a baker, kept the skepticism of Delsarte but moved his own acting style toward the realistic ideal. Coquelin debuted at the *Comédie Française* in 1860 and played Figaro the following year. He wrote *Art and the Actor* (1880) to revive the debate over Denis Diderot's *Paradox of the Actor*.

With their scientific approach to art, realists had been attacking Diderot with great ferocity. Coquelin replied, ''The actor needs not to be actually moved. It is as unnecessary as it is for a pianist to be in the depths of despair to play the Funeral March of Chopin or of Beethoven aright.'' He defined the theatrical illusion as a joint creation of the actor and the audience; the actor suggests a part so that the audience may imagine the whole. For Coquelin, actual reality on the stage denied the audience its essential role in the creative process of illusion making. As a result, the total effect of the dramatic theatre was weakened: ''We must not destroy all truth in the theatre by too frequent use of conventions; but neither must we destroy the theatrical illusion by too great fidelity to fact.''

***The Theatre Libre***   André Antoine (1858–1943) was accused of ''too great fidelity to fact.'' A gas company employee so fascinated with the theatre that he moonlighted as a member of the *Comédie Française claque*, Antoine discovered Emile Zola's theories and decided to do something about them. With his followers and friends—clerks, architects, dressmakers, bookbinders, and postal employees—he rented a room in a pool hall behind a wine store to rehearse new naturalistic plays. Antoine, the oldest of four children, borrowed his mother's furniture and carted it across Paris to his makeshift theatre. In 1887 he and his group produced two evenings of plays that established the realistic technique of production.

Antoine's actors intentionally used sloppy diction and turned their backs to the audience. This acting style, rejected by most actors, found a perfect match in plays rejected by most companies. Subscriptions were sold to Antoine's private *Théâtre Libre* (1887–1895). Only seven or eight bills of plays were offered a year due to the rocky finances of the group. In 1888 the group produced Leo Tolstoy's *The Power of Darkness* (1887), a play banned from the Rus-

Constant-Benoît Coquelin in Edmund Rostand's Cyrano de Bergerac.   (Le Théâtre, 1898)

sian stage, and toured Brussels. The *Théâtre Libre* also produced August Strindberg's *Miss Julie* (1893), German playwright Gerhart Hauptmann's *The Weavers* (1892), and Henrik Ibsen's *Ghosts* (1888). Jean Jullien, working as the theatre's dramaturg and playwright, insisted that actors never display an awareness of the audience. In 1889 Jullien, editing the periodical "Art et Critique," coined the terms "fourth wall" and "slice of life." Strindberg said the plays of the *Théâtre Libre* "appear in all their pleasing naiveté and completeness, without embellishments and puerile abbreviations." Andre Antoine also reconceived his theatre's playing space.

Later Antoine organized a new theatre, *Théâtre Antoine* (1896–1906), which capitalized on his fame. In 1906 Antoine moved his energies to the Odeon Theatre.

***Reality on Stage***  The realists' conception of stage space revived some ideas of Denis Di-
derot. But the realists moved Diderot's "fourth wall" from the rear of the auditorium to along the footlights, thereby making the audience a group of voyeurs. Thus, environment dominated character action in the realistic theatre, and stage settings influenced and determined the action as never before. The exactness of minute detail created a scenic ideal that insisted that stage environment actively participate in shaping the characters' actions.

Everything on stage duplicated exactly what existed in reality. Designers plotted four-sided rooms and then selected the wall to remove along the footlights. The furniture along the invisible fourth wall remained in place. Some designers showed only two sides of a room in order to crush the characters in a deterministic corner space. For the play *Butchers*, Antoine hung real quarters of beef on stage. And for the play *Old Heidelberg*, he purchased a student dormitory room and moved it to the stage.

Emile Zola insisted that the footlights be removed to eliminate the unnatural illumination of place and characters. Motivational lighting entered the stage picture. Antoine created new settings and built new flats for each play. Scene design rose to unprecedented importance in the dramatic theatre as environment rose in importance in discussions of human behavior.

Alexander Dumas *fils* had objected to Zola's insistence that the truth of life replace the conventional truth of the stage. He maintained that, to work effectively, the group psychology of a theatre audience demanded a different truth. He seems to have been correct. French audiences were baffled and unhappy when they could not clearly see and hear the on-stage action. Antoine tried to hush the traditionally rowdy, smoking, joking, and yelling audience. But the audience got even more restless when they saw actors' ignoring them. Yet, in time, the realist ideal prevailed. In the twentieth century most audiences both hoped the actors would ignore them and preferred a hushed auditorium. The realists thus created an audience appropriate for the art of the film. By 1890 leadership in realism and naturalism had nonetheless shifted away from France.

# GERMANY

*Nationalism*   Prussia's victory over France resulted in the unification of Germany in 1871. General Otto von Bismarck (1815–1898) wielded power even though the King of Prussia became the German Caesar, the *Kaiser*. Germany became a federation of states, like the United States and the Soviet Union. But the German federal government was not answerable to the parliament.

As German industry prospered the number of angry socialists grew. Workers became social democrats as Chancellor Bismarck defended the rights of the wealthy bourgeoisie. Conservative aristocrats, using Anti-Semitism to lure the rising middle class away from the workers' plight, claimed that social democrats were manipulated by atheists and Jews. Racial theorist Count Gobineau was hailed in Germany. Charles Darwin was used to move the nation to the right, and national Darwinism climaxed in the twentieth century. Meanwhile, socialists found theatrical realism a powerful weapon in the battle for the hearts and minds of middle-class intellectuals.

The wealthy bourgeois were the targets for German realistic playwrights as princes had been for German romantic playwrights. Munich especially seemed to attract realist rebels attacking German materialism and economic values.

German nationalism grew with Chancellor Bismarck's plan to isolate France by forging alliances. Germany failed to strike a bargain with Russia or England but signed a mutual defense pact with Austria. An insecure politician rather than a leader, the Kaiser increased German international competition and urged university professors to oppose "modern art."

*New Plays*   Friedrich Hebbel's (1813–1863) *Maria Magdelena* (1844) paved the way for Ibsen and German realists by making character the most important aspect of the drama. Hebbel's insistence that German drama deal with the inner psychology of character rather than external plot devices fell on the eager ears of Gerhart Hauptmann (1862–1946).

The son of a hotelkeeper, Hauptmann studied art before writing *Vor Sonnenaufgang (Before Sunrise*, 1889). The play's production in Berlin was violently opposed. In the drama an idealistic young socialist, investigating workers' conditions, discovers exploitation by his old college roommate, now the workers' boss. After turning down his friend's bribe, the investigator leaves when he discovers that his fiancee's family is plagued by alcoholism and inbreeding. Alone, the fiancee commits suicide. In 1892, Hauptmann wrote a first-class tragedy about *Die Weber* ( *The Weavers*), the class heroes of the play. The action shows that horrible working conditions cause the proletariat to rise up and destroy the home of their capitalist boss. The play inspired a series of prints by painter Kathe Kollwitz (1867–1945).

Hebbel had described the German ideal for realistic diction in his journal. Poor dramatic diction ''is the counterpart of 'how beautifully put!' in conversation. Chintz, chintz, and more chintz! It may glitter but it gives no heat!'' Gerhart Hauptmann followed Hebbel's advise but, like Hebbel, abandoned realism later in his career.

*The Duke of Saxe-Meiningen* The court theatre company of the Duke of Saxe-Meiningen advanced practices of realism in production, even though the repertoire consisted mostly of romantic plays. In 1866 George II (1826–1914), the Duke, took control of the duchy. A sophisticated world traveler, the Duke wanted to improve the court's theatre.

He replaced Karl Grabowski, his stage director between 1870 and 1873, with Ludwig Chronegk (1837–1891), who was the director for the next eighteen years. The Duke of Saxe-Meiningen had the ideas, Chronegk the theatre know-how. Ellen Franz (1839–1923), the Duke's third wife, chose the plays and worked as the troupe's vocal coach.

The dictatorial methods of the director, backed by the political power of the Duke, made directing a chief ingredient in this realistic theatre. Every element of the production, including interpretation, came under the director's unifying hand. The director shone as the new theatrical star. Planning every detail, the director eliminated both accident and inspiration by recording every detail in a promptbook. In addition, the Meiningen company displayed a new respect for stage tech-

*A sketch by the Duke of Saxe-Meinigen for an 1867 production of Shakespeare's* Julius Caesar. *(Deutsches Theatermuseum)*

nicians and backstage personnel. Ensemble playing and detailed crowd scenes highlighted the company's work.

The Duke of Saxe-Meiningen pioneered in the use of realistic sound and lighting effects. Chronegk's scenes were lit by a variety of motivated light sources. Actors wore their costumes and used the production properties early in rehearsal to ensure ease of movement. The ensemble's stage compositions mirrored the asymmetry of Japanese prints. Historical accuracy in costume and scenery extended to authentic materials, properties, and furniture.

In 1876, the Meiningen company staged Ibsen's *The Pretenders*. Also, their tours of Europe influenced the production work of Antoine and Strindberg.

**The Freie Bühne**  Albert Basserman (1867–1952), the great German actor of the late nineteenth and early twentieth centuries, trained with the Meiningen company. Otto Brahm (1856–1912), who had been a newspaper critic of Henrik Ibsen's plays, cast Basserman in the plays of Ibsen, Leo Tolstoy, and Gerhart Hauptmann for his theatre, the *Freie Bühne*. Brahm had opened this German independent theatre in 1889, two years after Antoine had opened the *Théâtre Libre*, on which the *Freie Bühne* was modeled.

But unlike Antoine's *Théâtre Libre*, the *Freie Bühne* closed after its second season. Nevertheless, the company premiered Hauptmann's socialist *Before Sunrise* (1889) and Ibsen's *Ghosts* (1889).

Later the *Freie Volksbühne* presented Sunday afternoon performances like those at the *Freie Bühne*. Socialists Bruno Wille, Julius Tuk, and Wilhelm Bolsche managed the theatre and gave Ibsen the premiere of his *Pillars of Society* in 1890. But police barred women from the theatre by claiming the performances were political meetings.

Bruno Wille founded the *Neue Freie Volksbühne* in 1892 after being ousted from the *Freie Volksbühne* for apparently softening his advocacy of socialism. In 1894 Brahm managed the *Deutsches Theatre* as realism grew in acceptability. Nevertheless, a well-known German actress, about to play Ibsen's *A Doll's House*, announced "I would never leave *my* children." She wanted to change the ending. Ibsen decided to write an alternative ending for her rather than leave the job to a hack writer of her choosing. As a result, the German Nora could not bring herself to leave the German Torvald.

# ENGLAND

**Victoria and After**  Queen Victoria reigned between 1837 and 1901 after succeeding her uncle. Her reign was a time of change in England. Puritanism and conservatism revived, especially in matters of sexuality. Prosperity improved the living conditions of the working class and dampened the zeal of the socialists. Utilitarians championed Scottish economist Adam Smith's (1723–1790) industrialism, free from governmental interference. The wealthy middle-class theatre audience was a quieter lot than the once-frequent prostitutes, gamblers, and people about town. In sum, Queen Victoria presided over a change in the nation's popular tastes and fashions.

Parliamentary acts and social activism held off the threats of the socialists. The Reform Act of 1867, for example, enfranchised the working class, exclusive of farmers and miners. The 1870 Education Act ensured a primary education for all English citizens. The Reform Act of 1884 enfranchised farmers and miners. "Social settlements" brought some cultural decency to London slums while the tale of Dick Whittington kept alive the rags-to-riches dream among the workers and the unemployed. By 1905 Britain's population was awed by submarines, motor taxis, motor buses, and a subway. Realism likewise arrived in literature.

William Makepeace Thackeray (1811–1863) published the serialized novel *Vanity Fair*, a review of life's cruelties and ironies, in installments between 1847 and 1848. Later, the stage enjoyed his unprincipled and cunning heroine Becky Sharp. Poetry took a realistic turn with the pen of Matthew Arnold (1822–1888), a poet and critic of literature, religion, society, politics, and education. Arnold's poetry describes the decay of sensitivity within a materialistic society, the alienation of individuals in an acquisitive world, and the age's loss of faith in traditional religion. In "Dover Beach" Arnold saw that the world

> Hath really neither joy, nor love, nor light,
> Nor certitude, nor peace, nor help for pain;
> And we are here as on a darkling plain
> Swept with confused alarms of struggle and
> flight,
> Where ignorant armies clash by night.[11]

The naturalist novel grew dark with the writings of the Polish-born orphan Joseph Conrad (1857–1924), whose books echoed the naturalists' refrain in a seaside setting. Conrad said he wrote "a meticulous precision of statement" to "bring out the true horror behind the appalling face of things." Some of the novelist's works were adapted to the stage.

Although the son of a wealthy lawyer and businessman, John Galsworthy (1867–1933) shared Conrad's gloom a bit. His education at Harrow and Oxford, plus his world travels, led him to write a series of socially conscious novels, *The Forsythe Saga* (1906–1922), about a bourgeois industrialist family. Later Galsworthy turned his attention to the stage.

***Problem Plays*** At the time they were written, the plays of John Galsworthy, rooted in the social problems of the moment, created great interest in both social ills and realistic drama. Nonetheless, they did not survive the passage of time. *The Silver Box* (1906) reveals different justice for rich and poor. *Strife* (1909) examines the struggles between workers and management. *Justice* (1910) indicts the penal system. *The Fugitive* (1913) is a woman unable to find happiness or love in any relationship.

*The Mob* (1914) looks at the dangers of rampant patriotism. *The Skin Game* (1920) pits gentleman against self-made man. *Loyalties* (1922) exposes aristocratic anti-Semitism.

Social problems also edged into the dramas of Henry Arthur Jones (1851–1929). His one-act play, *It's Only Round the Corner* (1878), was followed by an adaptation of Ibsen's *A Doll's House* called *Breaking a Butterfly* (1884). The two titles summarize the difference between Ibsen's and Jones' realism: Jones's Nora repents for her rebellion.

Arthur Wing Pinero (1855–1934), a playwright whose name is usually uttered in the same breath as Jones, contributed realistic farces like *The Magistrate* (1885) and *Dandy Dick* (1886) before portraying the "fallen woman," *The Second Mrs. Tanqueray* (1893) for Mrs. Patrick Campbell to play. In *The Magistrate* a husband is shocked to discover the true ages of his wife and stepson. A respectable widower, trying to make a "woman with a past" into *The Second Mrs. Tanqueray*, finds polite society avoiding Paula. Jealous of her stepdaughter, Paula invites her old friends to her new home. When she discovers that her stepdaughter's fiancé is her old lover, Paula concludes that one is always trapped by one's past. *Trelawney of the "Wells"* (1898) was Pinero's last successful play. In the drama a retired actress, bored with respectable society, makes a comeback.

***George Bernard Shaw*** When asked by the new Independent Theatre to provide a play, critic George Bernard Shaw (1856–1950) sent his own *Widowers' Houses* (1892), "An Original Didactic Realistic Play," and began a career in playwrighting. In the play the bourgeoisie battle the aristocracy for control of the slums; when faced with economic realities, social conscience crumbles.

Shaw's realistic "comedies of ideas" blasted romanticism by unmasking the romantic hero's false integrity. Shaw also blasted sentimentality and the refusal to face facts. An Irish socialist philosopher and anti-imperialist, Shaw dramatized the most outrageous ideas of his time, pricking conservative balloons and destroying liberal idols along the way. He described his method as "to take the utmost trouble to find the right thing to say, and then say it with the utmost levity."

Shaw, unlike lesser realistic playwrights of ideas, did not illustrate the truth of any one idea. Instead, he choreographed a dance of ideas, circling thesis around antithesis, accommodating one to the other's variations. Whenever one idea took the lead, the dominance was only partial and temporary. Besides examing the prostitution business, for example, *Mrs. Warren's Profession* (1896) confronts the relationship between environmental determinism and individual free will: "The people who get on in this world are the people who get up and look for the circumstances they want, and if they can't find them, make them."[12] In the play prostitution is shown as the result of economic need rather than lust. Women decide to merchandise themselves rather than go through traditional, acceptable economic channels. Businessmen without a conscience "are more dangerous in modern society than poor women without chastity."

Shaw admired Ibsen's view of morality as something up for discussion and debate rather than for blind obedience. In *The Quintessence of Ibsenism* (1891) Shaw noted his admiration for Ibsen's dramaturgical technique: "It was held that the stranger the situation, the better the play. Ibsen saw that, on the contrary, the more familiar the situation, the more interesting the play." As Shaw's characters dance around looking for a viable morality, his plays lose the fixed character types of melodrama. In a Shaw play there is no clear hero or villain, and the persecuted are rarely innocent.

In plays as varied as *Arms and the Man* (1894) and *Back to Methuselah* (1919–1920), Shaw's technique rearranged facts into a parable of conflicting, dialectical ideas. In the former Shaw destroys the romantic notions of war and love. In *Back to Methuselah* he illustrates his theory of creative evolution leading to human longevity. Shaw presented pragmatism as the chief dramatic, social, political, and metaphysical tool. *Candida* (1893) decides to remain with her husband rather than run off with a young poet because her husband needs her more; being a

*Noel Coward, Gertrude Lawrence, and Laurence Olivier in the original production of Coward's* Private Lives. (Courtesy Mander and Mitchenson Theatre Collection)

*George Bernard Shaw (right) directing his play* Androcles and the Lion *(1913).* (Victoria and Albert Museum, London)

wife is like being a mother. In *Caesar and Cleopatra* (1899) Shaw debunks the Shakespearean and historical Caesar by presenting him as a bald, middle-aged, common-sense man, one of Shaw's "supermen" whose power comes from the use of reason. *Man and Superman* (1901) uses the comic battle of the sexes, perfected by Congreve, to reveal the woman as superman. Likewise, Shaw shows the force of creative evolution as superior to the power of human revolution. The hero's dream in the middle of the play reveals Don Juan in Hell. But Shaw's Hell is the home of "the seven deadly virtues." And his Don Juan wants to escape women because he fears losing his power to marriage: "The confusion of marriage with morality has done more to destroy the conscience of the human race than any other single error."[13] *Major Barbara* (1905) shows a munitions–making Greek professor as the superman, philanthropy perpetuating the social ills it seeks to eliminate, and charitable organizations fawning at the knees of munitions makers. "A Fantasia in the Russian Manner on English Themes," the *Heartbreak House* (1914) of Captain Shotover works as a metaphor for the English ship of state.

The plots of Shaw's plays seek a reconciliation of ideals with reality. Shaw believed that drama must "take this unmeaning, haphazard show of life, that means nothing to you, and arrange it in an intelligible order, and arrange it in such a way as to make you think very much more deeply about it than you ever dreamed of thinking about actual incidents that come to your knowledge." No surprise then that Shaw gave his Nobel Prize money for better translations of August Strindberg's plays.

Shaw contributed to the art of stage direction as well as dramaturgy. He realized the importance of psychology in working with actors: "It discourages and maddens an actor to be told merely that you are dissatisfied." Actors are irritable so "do not tell an actor too much all at once." Shaw knew that the ensemble necessary for realism depended on nonstars: "The fact and judgement of directors in their very delicate relations with players are sometimes strained to the utmost."

**The Irish Renaissance**   In 1899 the Irish Literary Theatre, patronized by Miss Horniman, daughter of a wealthy merchant, led by poets William Butler Yeats (1865–1939) and

Lady Gregory (1852–1932)—who wrote thirty plays about Irish life—moved to the Abbey Theatre where Yeats's protégé, John Millington Synge (1871–1909), became the Irish Ibsen. Synge realistically portrayed people's relationships with nature in such plays as *Riders to the Sea* (1904) and *The Playboy of the Western World* (1907). The former is a one-act tragedy that explores the grief of a peasant family confronting a sudden death. The latter is the story of how the ne'er-do-well Christy Mahon wins and loses his position as town hero.

The last of thirteen children of a Dublin slum family, Sean O'Casey (1889–1964) read Shakespeare and Dion Boucicault's melodramas before writing realistic tragicomedies. O'Casey's plays reflected his socialism, anticlericalism, and support of the Irish Citizen Army. *The Shadow of a Gunman* (1923), for example, compares a loud-mouthed revolutionary with a quiet man of action. *Juno and the Paycock* (1924) examines the effects of money on a poor family held together by the mother while the father and his best friend go off on drinking bouts. The audience rioted at *The Plough and the Stars'* (1926) portrayal of Irish patriots as immoral personally and high minded politically.

**The Legacy of Realistic Drama**   Realism survived in the plays of later British playwrights. Noel Coward (1899–1973) drew realistic comedies of manners that revealed the shallowness of leisured life. In *Private Lives* (1930) a divorced couple accidentally meet and elope from their current spouses. In *Blithe Spirit* (1941) two couples and a medium accidentally conjure the novelist's first wife, now deceased.

John Osborne (1929–     ), the original "angry young man," revived naturalism with such social protest plays as *Look Back in Anger* (1956). Jimmy Porter, the play's misanthropic working-class hero, looks back on his life in anger and strikes out at his wife and the class she represents. David Storey (1933–     ) extended realism to collective action and silence. *The Contractor* (1970) presents the erection and dismantling of a wedding tent. *Home* (1970) presents two old men reminiscing on the terrace of a mental hospital. Amateur rugby players are dissected in *The Changing Room* (1973).

*The original production of John Osborne's* Look Back in Anger *(1956).*   (Photo by Houston Rogers)

Realism travelled with the British Empire. In Lebanon, Sa' id Tagi al-Din (1904–1960) wrote an angry critique of the social structure, *al-Manbudh* (*The Outcast*, 1953). In Egypt, Mahmud Taymur (1894–1973) penned bitter social satires. In Australia, the Little Theatre movement encouraged Leon Brodsky to found the Australian Theatre Society (1904) in Melbourne, and Doris Fitton the Independent Theatre (1930) in Sydney. Australian Alexander Buzo (1944–      ) wrote a naturalistic black comedy, *Norm and Ahmed* (1967). David Williamson's (1942–      ) *The Club* gave a hyper-realistic picture of a Melbourne rugby club.

In South Africa, Athol Fugard (1932–      ) chronicled the tragedy of apartheid with *The Blood Knot* (1961), a story of two brothers; *Boesman and Lena* (1969), the tale of a black couple forced to move; *Sizwe Bansi Is Dead* (1974); and *Master Harold . . . and the Boys* (1982), a drama of a white teenager coming to grips with black servants.

In Canada, realism prospered at the University of Toronto's Hart House Theatre (1919) under the direction of Roy Mitchell. Elsewhere, the novelist Robertson Davies (1913–      ) wrote a satiric comedy of manners about an old Casanova, *General Confession* (1972), which also revealed the playwright's interest in Jungian psychology. Marcel Dube (1930–      ) wrote about the class struggle of poor French Canadians with *Au retour des oies blanches* (*At the Return of the White Geese*, 1966). John Coulter (1888–      ) focused attention on an Irish rebellion in western Canada in an epic trilogy. John Herbert (1926–      ) explored the Canadian penal system with *Fortune and Men's Eyes* (1965). Michel Tremblay (1942–      ) put the Quebecois dialect of Montreal on stage in *Les belles-soeurs* (*The Sisters-in-Law*, 1968). In Newfoundland, Michael Cook's (1933–      ) *The Head, Guts, and Soundbone Dance* (1972) combined liberal politics with regional folk tales.

***Actors and Managers*** England's star, Henry Irving (1838–1905), decided to debate France's actor Coquelin over Denis Diderot's old paradox of the actor. William Archer (1856–1924), a critic and editor of Ibsen, moderated the 1888 debate commissioned by Longman's Magazine. The magazine published the results of Archer's scientific investigation into the validity of Denis Diderot's paradox. Later, Archer published the articles as *Masks or Faces? A Study in the Psychology of Acting*. Archer concluded that great actors habitually yield to the "sympathetic contageion" of the emotions of the characters they are playing. He used Charles Darwin's *Expression of the Emotions* to prove "sympathetic contageion" in other species' play: "When two dogs fight together in play (this is, when they imagine and act the emotion of anger) their hair at once bristles up, just as in actual warfare."

When her husband and children deserted her, Mrs. Patrick Campbell (1865–1940) turned to acting. In 1893 her performance of Paula in Pinero's *The Second Mrs. Tanqueray* dazzled London. She subsequently played Rita in Ibsen's *Little Eyolf*. In addition, Shaw wrote his *Pygmalion* for Campbell to perform. Not particularly scientific in her acting, Campbell nevertheless dominated English realistic acting.

To systematize the study of acting in England, Herbert Beerbohm Tree (1853–1917) founded the Royal Academy of Dramatic Art in 1904. Tree also brought realistic detail to the production of Shakespeare. He produced *A Midsummer Night's Dream* with real rabbits, *The Tempest* with a boat in real water, and *Richard II* with a real horse.

Squire Bancroft (1841–1926) and his wife, actress Marie Wilton (1839–1921), brought realistic settings to their Prince of Wales Theatre. In new comfortable seats, the Prince of Wales's audience enjoyed the Bancrofts' realistic scenery detailing contemporary drawing rooms.

Henry Irving employed the German Meiningen company's use of extras to create realistic historical environments on his stage. Irving concentrated on creating the actual outer reality of scene and character. For example, he electrically wired the swords for a duel in Goethe's *Faust* so that flashes of electricity ap-

*Mrs. Patrick Campbell in Arthur Wing Pinero's* The Second Mrs. Tanqueray
*(1893).* (Culver Pictures)

peared whenever the swords met. He even visited Nurenberg before selecting the scenery. As a result of his attention to spectacle, however, the language in the productions lost importance and value.

The English audience loved realism. A member of an audience once wrote to Henry Irving to offer her own baby as a replacement for the doll in *Henry III* so that the audience would not laugh when Irving kissed it. George Bernard Shaw observed that theatrical technique consisted of nothing more than "the art of making the audience believe that real things are happening to real people."

The premiere critic was William Archer, whose *Playmaking* (1928) scientifically prescribed the technique for writing a realistic play. Archer insisted that verse drama had been dead for a century. Soliloquies and asides were likewise outdated. For Archer, "style, in prose drama, is the sifting of common speech."

## RUSSIA

Following the abolition of serfdom the literacy rate in Russia rose to 21 percent by 1897. The number of university students increased eightfold by the end of the nineteenth century. Despite socialism's birth in romanticism, realism became the Soviet theatrical style. The form suited the Soviets' desire for the artistic penetration of true social reality. Realism, in fact, found its greatest addicts in Russia and America.

The novel and the drama became the chief art forms of socialist realism, which was founded by playwright Maxim Gorky (1868–1936). Typical characters in typical situations let audiences study the relationship between personality and social reality. Socialist realist artists made, according to socialist leader Friedrich Engels (1820–1895), "poetic judgments" of the lives they presented. However, when the judgments failed to find organic expression and appeared imposed, the work fell into the category of didacticism.

Socialist realism and the Soviet Union rejected the modernist trends that appeared at the end of the Realistic era. Soviets objected to the arbitrary nature of the modern artists' subjective visions. Modern art and theatre also failed to remain accessible to the mass of people. Socialist realism extended realism to its logical end: Realism is what most of the people can understand easily.

*New Plays* Early literary realism was expressed by the son of an alcoholic physician who was murdered by his serfs: Fedor Mikhailovich Dostoyevsky (1821–1881). Dostoyevsky loved Friedrich Schiller and the romantics, but his six great novels are landmarks of Russian realism. Director Vladimir Nemirovich-Danchenko (1858–1943) staged adaptations of Dostoyevsky's novels.

At age 19 Ivan Sergeyevich Turgenev (1818–1883), the son of a cavalry officer and a tyrannical mother, published poems and short stories attacking serfdom. Turgenev, who lived with opera singer Pauline Viardot-Garcia for forty years, became the first Russian to win a European reputation with such works as *Ottzy i deti* (*Fathers and Sons*, 1862) and the great comedy, *Mesyats v derevne* (*A Month in the Country*, 1850). In this comedy a landowner's wife falls in love with her son's tutor, only to find her 17-year-old maid as her rival for the boy's affections.

Alexander Ostrovsky (1823–1886) dominated Russian theatre and drama to the time of his death. In 1859 the photographic exactness of representation in his masterpiece, *The Storm*, laid the basis for Maxim Gorky and Anton Chekhov. In the play a neglected wife begins a love affair. But when her lover jilts her, she commits suicide rather than face her angry husband. *The Storm's* Katerina became a favorite role among Russian actresses.

A spiritual conversion inspired Leo Nikolaevich Tolstoy (1828–1910) to write for the stage. The son of a noble family—but raised by his aunts—Tolstoy worked to educate and emancipate the serfs. The drama *Vlast' t'my* (*The Power of Darkness*, 1886), which explored moral emptiness, established Tolstoy's reputation. In the play, a peasant has an affair with his boss's wife. The peasant's mother con-

vinces the boss's wife to murder her husband. The lovers marry but the peasant seduces the stepdaughter. The peasant's mother then convinces him to crush his stepdaughter's infant. But guilt makes the peasant confess. Emile Zola, Shaw, Antoine, and Brahm loved the play. Tolstoy eventually died of pneumonia while waiting for a train.

When Maxim Gorky (1868–1936), a poor orphan, was thrown out of his grandparents' home when he was 8 years old, he became a vagabond. Eventually he chose a name meaning "bitter." In fourteen plays Gorky depicted the lowest states of human life so realistically that audiences feared to sit in the front rows. Nonetheless, Gorky's novels and plays, such as *Na dne* (*The Lower Depths*, 1902), led to his appointment as chief of the state propaganda bureau in 1918. In this play, society's outcasts live in *The Lower Depths*, a cave owned by a receiver of stolen goods. The pilgrim Luka arrives and hands out illusions to keep everyone going. He especially urges the outcasts to try the gospel of kindness. When they pursue the new goal, however, they find discord, violence, murder, and suicide as Luka slips away. They conclude that the truth, however unpleasant, is preferable to illusions.

An ardent supporter of the Bolsheviks, Gorky was elected first President of the Soviet Writers Union (1932), from which position he helped form the official literary method, socialist realism.

Another abandoned child was Anton Chekhov (1860–1904), whose tyrannical father deserted him to avoid creditors. Chekhov struggled to become a doctor. He also authored over 700 realistic stories. He began playwriting with short farces. Chekhov's plays depict the boredom, impotence, and disappointment of the leisured class. His plots are made of the small actions of failed and lonely characters confronting helplessness and hopelessness.

The 1896 production of *Chayika* (*The Seagull*), was a failure. The play paints the portrait of a quartet: an aging actress; her son, an aspiring avant-garde playwright; an aging but wealthy novelist; and a budding young actress. Though it ends with the son's suicide, the play

*The Moscow Popular Art Theatre's 1902 production of Maxim Gorky's* The Lower Depths. *(Moscow Art Theatre)*

mingles laughter and pathos in a unique manner. Through the subtle use of everyday objects as symbols, Chekhov creates a poetic mood even though the language is prosaic and the technique is naturalistic.

Two years later the new Moscow Popular Art Theatre staged Chekhov's play *Dyadya Vanya* (*Uncle Vanya*) a rewrite of his play *The Wood Demon*, and revived *The Seagull*. In *Uncle Vanya* a widowed professor lives in retirement with his daughter, his brother-in-law Uncle Vanya, and his new young bride. The pro-

*The Moscow Popular Art Theatre's 1899 production of Anton Chekhov's* Uncle Vanya. *(Bakhrishin Theatre Museum, Moscow)*

fessor's doctor loves the daughter, the daughter loves the uncle, and the uncle loves the wife. The success of the plays established both the theatre company and the playwright at the top of the Russian theatre. The work of the Moscow Popular Art Theatre on Chekhov's plays also established the Russian realistic production technique.

In 1901 the Moscow Popular Art Theatre produced *Tri sestry* (*The Three Sisters*) and in 1904 *Vishnyovyi sad* (*The Cherry Orchard*). *The Three Sisters*—Olga, Masha, and Irina—live in a small town but dream of life in the big city. The play chronicles the deterioration of the dream. Aristocrats who frittered away time and money must confront the loss of both their ancestral home and *The Cherry Orchard* to a former slave.

*The Moscow Popular Art Theatre* In 1880 the Imperial Theatres monopolized Russian drama, underpaid playwrights, and cast foreign stars in the leading roles. The next year Alexander Ostrovsky appealed to the tsar for an inexpensive peoples' theatre without stars. When Ostrovsky was named director of Moscow theatres in 1882 the monopoly indeed

ended. Private theatres flourished. Ostrovsky opened the Russian Academy of Dramatic Art but died before his plans could be enacted completely. In 1885 the German Meiningen company toured Russia and brought a new vision to Russian theatre workers.

In 1897 Nemirovich-Danchenko, a drama teacher, theatre critic, and playwright (who had graduated in physics and mathematics from Moscow University), urged the Maly Theatre, the house of Ostrovsky, to move toward more realistic production techniques. When his hope for success with the Maly evaporated, Nemirovich-Danchenko met with Constantin Sergeyevich (Alekseev) Stanislavski (1863-1938), the founder of the amateur Society of Art and Literature (1888), to discuss the prospects for an independent art theatre in Russia. The stage director of the Moscow Philharmonic Society, Nemirovich-Danchenko decided to form a theatre with Stanislavski, a merchant's son whose stage name was taken from a retired Polish actor named "Stanislavski," to search for "truth" through new realistic production techniques and ensemble acting.

The new company consisted of students

The Moscow Popular Art Theatre's 1904 production of Anton Chechov's The Cherry Orchard.

from Nemirovich-Danchenko's class at the School of Music and Drama of the Moscow Philharmonic Society and amateur players from Stanislavski's Society of Art and Literature. That summer the company began rehearsals in the country and returned to Moscow in the fall as the Moscow Popular Art Theatre. Nemirovich-Danchenko selected the repertoire and codirected many of the plays with Stanislavski. Their first play was Tolstoy's *Tsar Fyodor*. The company researched the play in libraries and traveled to towns to absorb the atmosphere of the play. Shakespeare's *The Merchant of Venice*, Goldoni's *The Mistress of the Inn*, Merezhkovsky's new play *There Will Be Joy*, Sophocles's *Antigone*, Ibsen's *Hedda Gabler*, and Chekhov's *The Seagull* rounded out the first season.

As directors, Stanislavski and Nemirovich-Danchenko imitated the Meiningen style and method. With Chekhov, the two directors developed an interest in deep character analysis. Chekhov enjoyed a close association with the company and wrote for the particular actors. He also married Nemirovich-Danchenko's prize student, Olga Knipper. The directors insisted on analyzing not just the play's text but also the *subtext*, the deep buried life of meaning. Without verse to play, actors looked for vocal and psychological excitement by discovering implications in the subtext's inarticulated desires and unspoken needs. For Gorky's *The Lower Depths* (1902), for example, actors visited the hiding places of thieves and outcasts. Peasants were brought to the theatre as consultants for the 1906 production of Tolstoy's *The Power of Darkness*. Even Rome was researched, for the 1903 *Julius Caesar*.

The company developed a subtle acting style keyed to psychological truth and an ensemble sensitivity to mood, tone, and environment. Ibsen's plays were popular: *When We Dead Awaken* (1900), *Pillars of Society* (1903), *Brand* (1906), and *Rosmersholm* (1908). Stanislavski also acted with the company—as Doctor Stockman in Ibsen's *An Enemy of the People*, Satin in Gorky's *The Lower Depths*, Astrov in Chekhov's *Uncle Vanya*, Vershinin in Chekhov's *The Three Sisters*, Famusov in Griboedev's *Woe from Wit*, Argan in Molière's *The Imaginary Invalid*, and Gayev in Chekhov's *The Cherry Orchard*. Around 1906 Stanislavski began to work for a

*Members of the Moscow Popular Theatre listening to Anton Chekhov reading his play* The Seagull *(1896).* (Society for Cultural Relations with the U.S.S.R.)

Tsar Fyodor, *the first production of the Moscow Popular Art Theatre.*

technique whereby actors themselves could create a mood for creativity. Rehearsals became experiments in finding that technique.

*The Stanislavski System* Stanislavski investigated the nature of the subconscious creative process so that actors found inner justification for their actions. The actors' belief in a psychological need let the audience believe in the truthfulness of the actors' behavior. Belief in the reality of the illusion was enhanced by the "magic if": an actor asked what he would do if he were the character in a particular situation. The analysis of the situation gave rise to the concept of "given circumstances." A psycho-technique gradually developed for consciously tapping unconscious creativity.

Analysis led Stanislavski's actors to integrate themselves with their characters. Acting was subordinated to the text, the springboard for creative imagining about character. Imagining about a character drew upon the actor's own personal experiences, recollections, and associated emotions. Action became the key

tool for creating a sense of truth anew in each performance.

Stanislavski's great discovery was the importance of physical actions in mustering the inner psychological life of a role. His "method of physical actions" let an actor improvise actions toward the character's goal within the given circumstances of the play. Only after an actor understood the role physically would Stanislavski allow him or her to add the words of the text. A through-line of physical action gave the actor's performance clarity and unity. Obstacles to character goals activated emotion in the actor. Emotion arose either from pursuing an objective or by sensing images that recalled past events in the actor's own life. During his career Stanislavski moved away from this emotional recall technique and toward a psycho-technique based completely on physical actions. Throughout his life Stanislavski believed his system to be incomplete, ever-changing, and constantly adapting to new times, new plays, and new actors.

In 1912 Stanislavski established the First Studio of the Moscow Popular Art Theatre, with Leopold Sulerzhitskii, to test his techniques. In 1919 Nemirovich-Danchenko, who invented the concept of an inner character monologue playing silently inside the actor's head, founded the Moscow Popular Art Theatre Musical Theatre as an adjunct to the main school. When confronted with nonrealistic texts the directors established studios and found directors eager to investigate methods for acting in nonrealistic dramas. In 1920 the theatre's extensive educational mission changed the name to the Moscow Art Academic Theatre. Finally in 1932 the theatre was renamed the M. Gorky Moscow Art Academic Theatre.

In America in 1924, Stanislavski prepared an American edition of the first draft of *My Life in Art* to satisfy an American, Elizabeth Reynolds Hapgood, who had been pestering him. In 1926 a rewritten Russian edition appeared. In 1929 Stanislavski began a new book, which he continued to write throughout his life. Again Hapgood published sections of the work sporadically in American editions. Characters in Stanislavski's book have fictitious yet symbolic names: Tortsov derives from the Russian *tvortsov* for creator and Shustov from the Russian *chuvstov* for emotion. Stanislavski's work and writing influenced world theatre practice, but nowhere more than in America.

# AMERICA

***Rags and Riches*** America's economy boomed after the Civil War. This so-called "Gilded Age" saw the completion of coast to coast settlement. Domestic prosperity fueled America's Manifest Destiny. Profits increased as industry boomed. The first oil well was drilled in 1859, and eleven years later John D. Rockefeller (1839–1937) founded the Standard Oil Company. In 1904 Ida M. Tarbell investigated *The History of Standard Oil Company* and directed America's attention to the harmfulness of monopolies to the general welfare.

In 1893 Henry Ford's (1863–1947) first car rolled down the street. Ten years later Ford founded the Ford Motor Company. In 1909 Ford competed against the new General Motors Corporation (1908) by introducing assembly-line production. In 1904 New York City opened its subway, and in 1912 F. W. Woolworth (1852–1919) opened a variety store chain. The twentieth century had arrived.

Money was made almost everywhere by just about anyone with luck. Gold was discovered in Wyoming in 1867. The first skyscraper appeared in Chicago in 1883. In 1901 J. P. Morgan (1837–1913) organized the United States Steel Corporation. In 1914 the Federal Trade Commission was formed to investigate the fairness of the struggle among businesses for

"the almighty dollar," as writer Washington Irving described the national pastime in 1854.

The Gilded Age was also the Age of the "self-made man": John Jacob Astor (1763–1848) rose with New York real estate; Daniel Drew, with steamboats and railroads; Cornelius Vanderbilt (1794–1877), with shipping and railroads; John Wanamaker and Marshall Fields, with department stores, and Andrew Carnegie (1835–1919), with textile mills.

In 1867 Horatio Alger Junior (1834–1899), a Harvard-educated minister, published his first novel, *Ragged Dick, or Street Life in New York*. Two hundred million copies of the original rags-to-riches novel encouraged Americans to rely on luck, circumstance, and deference to their "betters" as the road to riches. By 1890 1 percent of the population owned as much as the other 99 percent combined.

As ready-made goods replaced hand-made and custom-made products, America became a world power. Success through science and technology encouraged America to flex its muscle in the Spanish-American War (1898). America thus found itself with Puerto Rico, Guam, the Philippines, and Cuba.

***Social Problems*** While America got itself into problems overseas, Americans organized to tackle domestic problems. In the South the Ku Klux Klan decided to protect the nation from immigrants and Negroes. The Society for the Prevention of Cruelty to Children began to address the serious urban problems of 1874. The American Federation of Labor organized in 1886. In 1906 the Pure Food and Drug Act responded to collective concerns about industrial processing and marketing practices. Margaret Sanger (1883–1966) opened the first birth-control center in 1918. The National Association for the Advancement of Colored People grew out of continued lynchings and W. E. B. Du Bois's (1868–1963) insistence on the self-advancement of black Americans.

*Up From Slavery* (1901), Booker T. Washington's (1856–1919) autobiography, made him the most influential man in America next to President Theodore Roosevelt. Hundreds of thousands of copies were sold all over the world. As a result, some white Americans' esteem for blacks rose, along with shame for actions of the past. After the Civil War Union troops and Northern "carpetbaggers" had run the South and had worked to secure the blacks' emancipation. Black colleges and universities were built. But the withdrawal of the troops in the 1870s had let states rewrite their constitutions to disenfranchise Negroes. "Jim Crow" laws, for example, limited black freedom and rights. And sharecropping established wage slavery in the South.

In 1903 W. E. B. Du Bois's *The Souls of Black Folk* raised black pride and consciousness, as Washington's book had tried to raise white respect. The book went through thirty editions. Du Bois kindled a new interest in black nationalism by reestablishing the bonds between American blacks and Africa. Du Bois urged blacks to gather in cities both to increase their solidarity and to struggle for civil rights.

American cities, meanwhile, gave sociologists nightmares. Electricity, for instance, cast a harsh light on the grime in America's cities. In 1880 New York City's streets were lit with electric light; the first neon sign appeared in 1905. When Spencerites John Fiske of Harvard and William Graham Sumner of Yale founded American sociology, they saw capitalism working to better the race and society. They also considered interfering with the marketplace process on anyone's behalf to be a crime against nature. Consequently, "social Darwinism" let the tensions of the cities fester. In *A Traveler from Altruria* (1894) writer William Dean Howells (1837–1920) observed that the "American ideal is not to change the conditions for all, but for each to rise above the rest if he can."

Black immigrants came to northern cities from the South. European immigrants came to American cities for the 160 free acres promised in the Homestead Act of 1862. French Canadians moved to New England textile and shoe-manufacturing cities. Chinese arrived in California until the Act of 1882 banned free Chinese immigration to stop the "Yellow Peril." Irish Protestants and Catholics battled away in Irish ghettos. In Pennsylvania such groups as the Mollie Maguires, a secret miners' protection association, fought against ethnic discrimination in the coal mines. New Jewish immigrants arriving between 1881 and 1914 fueled growing Anti-Semitism. Earlier German Jews had assimilated. But in America the almost 1.5 million Jews from Russia and Poland who had fled the tsar maintained the closed society that had proved to be their only defense in Europe. Americans saw them as being unwilling to assimilate into the American "melting pot." Young Russian Jews, meanwhile, found the arts and theatre to be their only escape from stultifying family traditions. And all ethnic groups went to the theatre to learn English. In the theatre, however, they saw themselves ridiculed as Kikes, Micks, Wops, and Niggers.

In 1892 President Harrison announced that "American workmen are subjected to peril of life and limb as great as a soldier in time of war." At first labor organized to protect jobs secretly. Terence Powderly led the Knights of Labor, and Eugene V. (for Victor Hugo) Debs (1855–1926) led the American Railway Union. Immigrant workers from class-conscious Europe brought America a socialist interpretation of the labor situation. Bosses labeled the unionists "communists" in reference to the

Paris Commune of 1870. Anarchists' bombs put everyone on edge. In addition, rail strikes in 1877 brought America to the brink of all-out civil revolution.

America promised to be a socialist paradise by the year 2000, according to Edward Bellamy's (1850–1898) *Looking Backward* (1888), which sold as well as Stowe's *Uncle Tom's Cabin*. But city officials and industrial philanthropists encouraged the workers' taste for spectator sports. Baseball and football purged the irrational impulses first released by the Greek Cult of Dionysus. After World War I ice hockey and basketball filled out a year-round schedule of watching and rooting. Secure in stadiums, and later isolated in home living rooms in front of television sets, America's exploited workers vented their angers and hopes between a few drinks of alcohol, and returned to work purged and passive.

But Henry Adams (1838–1918), the leisured grandson of an American president, looked back on his life in this Gilded Age as a failure. In *The Education of Henry Adams* (1918), Adams found religion and science incapable of answering life's essential questions. Adams believed himself unfit to live in the technological age.

*A Ragtime Rhythm* As the technological age teetered a new rhythm gradually found an outlet and an audience. Late in the nineteenth century revivalist camp meetings and banjo playing in black communities produced musical syncopation and off-beat stress. The Fiske University Singers toured the nation popularizing syncopated black gospel music, America's original contribution to world music. By 1890 pianists had made their instrument imitate the banjo's sound; in St. Louis the efforts produced a "ragtime" music. Turkey trots and cakewalks swept the nation into its first classless and colorless dance craze. Delighted black and white dancers started America moving. The music of Tom Turpin and Scott Joplin attracted the attention of both New York music publishers and theatrical impresarios.

The improvisational quality of the new music made it "hot." When sung solo, however,

as a melancholy lament, the "cool" music, flattening various "true" notes, was called the "blues." The ragtime piano and the blues vocalist combined around 1915 as small instrumental ensembles in New Orleans played "jazz." In 1915 Ferdinand Morton's "Jelly Roll Blues" arrangement was published. Two years later Victor Records produced the first so-called "jass" recordings—performed, of course, by white musicians. The same scenario plagued jazz's descendants: rhythm and blues and rock and roll. Black artists made the music, but white musicians and publishers made the money.

Nevertheless, the rhythm and sound of the Modern age was born at the end of the realistic era. America, and in time the world, started to communicate nonverbally through dance. The dance renaissance in the American theatre derived from both the newfound thrill of erotic social dancing and the method of physical expression taught by François Delsarte's American disciple, Steele Mackaye (1842–1894). In the Modern age dance theatre would catch a new vision of the truth of the human condition.

*A New Literature* Meanwhile, American realists found the novel to be an appropriate vehicle for the communication of the realistic truth of the human condition. Self-educated novelist, editor, and critic William Dean Howells (1837–1920) wrote about European realism and urged Americans to read Emile Zola. Howells also wrote such plays as *The Sleeping Car* (1883) and *The Elevator* (1885). His friend Henry James (1843–1916) lived in England, wrote twelve plays, and adapted a few of his novels to the stage. James's *Berkeley Square*, for example, was an adaptation of one of Howells's tales. But James's *Daisy Miller*, originally penned as a play with a happy ending, became a novel. Later James dramatized his novel *The American* but gave it, too, a happy ending.

Theodore Dreiser (1871–1945), the son of poor, religious immigrant parents, took pen against the materialism corroding American society. In 1900 *Sister Carrie* bothered the censor as did *The Financier* (1912), *The Titan* (1914),

*The Genius* (1915), and *An American Tragedy* (1925). Dreiser also wrote such plays as *Plays of the Natural and Supernatural* (1916) and *The Hand of the Potter* (1918).

***Toward O'Neill*** As in the Romantic age, in the Realistic age America's best authors either did not write for the stage or did not understand the dramatic theatre's peculiar demands. Realism was left to lesser talents working in the theatre. For example, James A. Herne (1839–1901), an actor from *Uncle Tom's Cabin, East Lynne*, and *Oliver Twist*, turned his attention toward writing for the stage. Influenced by Charles Dickens, Herne wrote "Art for Truth's Sake" using Leo Tolstoy and William Dean Howells as examples of the new realistic art. He wrote *Margaret Flemming* (1890) for his wife, actress Katherine Corcorun, and successfully premiered this realistic drama of adultery in Lynn, Massachusetts. The next year, however, Herne discovered that New York was not Lynn, Massachusetts. In the play, a bourgeois husband is revealed to be the father of an illegitimate child. His wife adopts the child but goes blind. The husband must live with guilt but without reconciliation. The play failed.

Considered by some historians to be the first serious American drama, *The Great Divide* (1906) by William Vaughn Moody (1869–1910), the son of a steamboat pilot, presented the problems of a New England woman married to a western frontiersman. In the play the woman abandons society to live in the West with the man who saved her from a rapist in the Arizona desert. The tension between the refinement of eastern wealth and the roughness of western poverty are resolved when the man's mine brings him riches. Moody followed up with *The Faith Healer* (1908), a drama about a midwestern farmer, an advocate of Charles Darwin and Herbert Spencer, in competition with a faith healer for the soul of the farmer's lame wife.

***Eugene O'Neill*** Realism dominated the twentieth-century American stage. Eugene O'Neill (1888–1953), a student of Harvard's George Pierce Baker, emerged as America's

A scene from a 1906 production of William Vaughn Moody's The Great Divide. (*The Theatre Magazine*, 1906)

first world-class playwright. Like Ibsen and Strindberg, O'Neill tried romanticism, realism, and nonrealism. But O'Neill's most popular plays came from the realistic mold.

The son of romantic actor James O'Neill (1847–1920), young O'Neill went to sea like the novelist Herman Melville. Later, when he enrolled in Harvard's pioneering playwriting workshop taught by George Pierce Baker, he penned one-act realistic dramas about life at sea. In the summer he worked with the Provincetown Players on Cape Cod and learned about the particular requirements of the dramatic theatre. Inspired by the independent theatres of Europe, the Provincetown Players moved to New York City's Greenwich Village in the fall.

Working with a producing theatre company, O'Neill blossomed as America's first, and some would say only, great playwright. *Beyond the Horizon* (1921), a naturalistic study of father and sons torn between the land and the sea, won the Pulitzer Prize. In 1924 *Desire under the Elms* continued the naturalistic portraiture of the father and son relationship. To get pregnant, the young wife of an old New England farmer seduces his son. But she murders the baby when the son confesses. In the play O'Neill mixed elements from Sophocles's *Oedipus the King*, Euripides's *Medea*, and Racine's *Phèdre*. A realistic comedy of family life, *Ah,* *Wilderness* (1933), was followed in 1956 by a serious autobiographical drama, *Long Day's Journey into Night*. Pretensions and illusions are ripped apart during an evening with the Tyrone family. By dawn the family members stare at the horrible truths of their lives.

O'Neill claimed "Strindberg was the precurser of all modernity in our present theatre." Like Strindberg, O'Neill tried his hand at nonrealism in midcareer: He announced, "I am interested in the relation between man and God." Returning to realism at the end of his career, O'Neill continued to use a prose style that did little more than highlight the need for compelling stage diction. Nonetheless, O'Neill's success and international acclaim sealed America's destiny with realism, just as Anton Chekhov's success had locked Russia into socialist realism.

**Black Playwrights** Black playwriting increased with the new respect generated by Booker T. Washington and W. E. B. Du Bois. *The Cannibal King* (1901), a comedy by Paul Dunbar and James Weldon Johnson, never got off the ground, but Celia Parker Wooley's dramatization of *The Wife of his Youth* (1907) by Charles W. Chestnutt was produced by an amateur group in Chicago. Angela Grimke, the daughter of an NAACP Vice-President, staged *Rachel* (1916), a drama of urban white

*The Provincetown Players' Wharf Theatre in 1916.* (Brown Brothers)

The 1946 production of Eugene O'Neill's The Iceman Cometh. (Vandamm Photo Theatre Collection, New York Public Library)

racism in Washington, D.C. In 1925 Du Bois instituted the Krigwa Playwriting Contest. In time the Krigwa Players produced plays in the basement of a Harlem library. The same year arrived the first black play to open on Broadway—*Appearances* by Garland Anderson. Life in a Harlem apartment was dramatized in *Harlem* (1929) by William Jourdan Rapp and Wallace Thurman.

Realism continued as a popular style for black playwrights. Langston Hughes's (1902–1967) 1935 tragedy of the old south, *Mulatto*, was produced at the Harlem Suitcase Theatre. *Big White Fog* (1938) by Theodore Ward suggested that black people's only hope lay with socialism. Paul Green and Richard Wright's dramatization of *Native Son* opened in 1941. *Raisin in the Sun* (1959) by Lorraine Hansberry (1930–1965) presented the hopes and conflicts of a South Side Chicago family who refuse to sacrifice integrity to a greedy racist society. The play illustrates the words of the poet Langston Hughes: "What happens to a dream deferred? Does it dry up? Like a raisin in the sun?"[14] In 1966 Alice Childress's *Wedding Band* continued the social realistic tradition by examining interracial dating in 1918 South Carolina. Imanu Baraka (nee LeRoi Jones) (1934– ) founded the Black Arts Repertory Theater

School of Harlem and wrote *Dutchman* (1964), about the murder of a black man by a white woman; *The Toilet* (1965), about black students beating up a white student in a school lavatory; and *Slave Ship* (1969), about the forced movement of Africans to America.

But black theatre artists still suffered from the double-bind described by W. E. B. Du Bois in 1897:

> The innate love of harmony and beauty that set the ruder souls of people a-dancing, a-singing, and a-laughing raised but confusion and doubt in the soul of the black artist; for the beauty revealed to him was the soul beauty of a race which his larger audience despised, and he could not articulate the message of another people.[15]

*Realism's Legacy*   Paul Green (1894–1981) brought his North Carolina experiences to the stage with plays like *In Abraham's Bosom* (1926) and *The House of Connolly* (1931). *In Abraham's Bosom* the mulatto hero, determined to help blacks through education, encounters indifference from blacks and hostility from whites. In an American Chekhovian drama, the *House of Connolly* can survive only if the son marries "white trash." New blood, however alien, is the only hope for revitalizing the land.

*Sidney Poitier, Claudia McNeil, Ruby Dee, and Diana Sands in the 1959 production of Lorraine Hansberry's* A Raisin in the Sun. *(Photo by Friedman-Abeles)*

Another Southerner, Lillian Hellman (1905–1984), stuck to realism when not scandalizing America with trips to the Soviet Union. Hellman's plays skirted scandalous subjects, too. In *The Children's Hour* (1934), for example, a student hints at a possible lesbian relationship between her teachers. And Regina, the matron of *The Little Foxes* (1938), murders her husband to gain control of the family business.

Meanwhile, in the North, Clifford Odets (1906–1963) wrote about the poor of New York with plays such as *Awake and Sing* (1935). In the drama the Berger family is racked by the Great Depression until the grandfather's suicide gives his grandson a chance to help both himself and his fellow workers.

Two of America's leading playwrights at midcentury toyed with nonrealistic elements in essentially realistic plays. Tennessee Williams (1911–1983) recorded the struggle between violence and sensitivity. In his lyrically realistic plays, the forces of beauty and sensitivity are crushed by the aggression and vi-

olence of modern society. For example, *The Glass Menagerie* (1945) is a "memory" of a young man forced to desert his mother and sister to pursue his own career dream. In *A Streetcar Named Desire* (1947) the sensitive Blanche battles the brutal Stanley for control of her sister.

Arthur Miller (1916– ) combined Odets's social responsibility with personal *angst*. In *Death of a Salesman* (1949), for example, Willie Loman's family is torn apart by his desire to pursue the American dream rather than face reality. The Salem witch trials became *The Crucible* (1953) in which a man's conscience and character are tested. In *A View from the Bridge* (1955) a dock worker dies trying to save his family honor. *After the Fall* (1964), like *Death of a Salesman*, uses nonrealistic techniques to relate a realistically drawn lawyer's search for both the source of his guilt and the nature of his responsiblity. Grown children explore *The Price* (1968) of guilt and responsibility in their family's relationships.

Realism blossomed in American drama.

*The Living Theatre's 1959 production of Jack Gelber's The Connection.*
(Courtesy The Living Theatre)

Jack Gelber (1932–    ) convinced audiences they were seeing real drug addicts in *The Connection* (1959). Edward Albee (1928–    ) shocked audiences with his analysis of the games couples play in *Who's Afraid of Virginia Woolf?* (1962). At an all-night party, two college faculty couples play psychological games designed to hide and expose the truths of each other's relationships. By morning all illusions are shattered. Ed Bullins (1935–    ) continued to make the black experience a part of the mainstream American theatre; he worked on a twenty-play cycle of the black experience in America.

Some modern American playwrights shifted style from realistic to nonrealistic. Ronald Ribman (1932–    ) mixed realistic dialogue and Pirandellian circumstances in plays such as *Harry, Noon, and Night* (1965), *Buck* (1983), and *Sweet Table at the Richelieu* (1987). David Mamet (1947–    ) captured the inarticulateness of the contemporary world in short cinematic scenes with plays such as *American Buffalo* (1977) and *Glengarry Glen Ross* (1983). In *American Buffalo* three punks plan a robbery and

dream of becoming businessmen. *Glengarry Glen Ross* then exposes the humor and horror of American businessmen.

Like Ribman, Sam Shepard (1943–    ) kept the circumstances of his dramas vague. In realistic pictures of the contemporary American West, such as *Curse of the Starving Class* (1976) and *Buried Child* (1978), Shepard shows the American family as both confused and in search of new meaning. Marsha Norman (1947–    ) drew studies of mothers and daughters with *Getting Out* (1979) and *'Night, Mother* (1983), while Beth Henley (1952–    ) spun Gothic tales of sisters in *Crimes of the Heart* (1980) and *The Wake of Jamie Foster* (1982).

Even the American musical tried realism. The new black-rooted music entered the theatre with Marion Cook's *Clorindy* (1898). In 1903 Scott Joplin wrote the first ragtime opera, *A Guest of Honor*. The opera *Porgy and Bess* (1935) led to a realistic musical about an antihero, *Pal Joey* (1940); *Regina* (1949) was based on Hellman's *The Little Foxes; Raisin* (1973) was based on Hansberry's play, *Raisin in the Sun;* and *Working* (1982) was based on Studs Terkel's oral history of American workers. *A Chorus Line* (1975) attempted to realistically portray a dancer's life in the theatre.

**The Syndicate**   Realism had to fight a theatrical monopoly for a place on the American stage. All 5000 theatres for "legitimate" drama were controlled first by the Theatrical Syndicate and then by the Syndicate and the Shubert brothers. The Syndicate gave the most profitable shows the best theatres. Indeed, until the Shuberts broke the monopoly in 1905, the American theatre was run completely by a few businesspeople.

Charles Frohman believed he ran a theatrical "department store." He and his brother Daniel, Sam Nixon, Alf Hayman, J. F. Zimmerman, Marc Klaw, and Abe Erlanger merged their controlling theatres to bring order to a chaotic booking system. Run by Erlanger, the group was known as the "Syndicate" or the "Trust." Together the theatre owners controlled all first-class playhouses and took a high percentage of all profits received by the plays in their theatres.

In 1900 the Shubert brothers tried to make a deal for 25 percent of the Syndicate. David Belasco, who had been forced to pay 50 percent of his profits to the Syndicate, sued the Trust in 1902 by charging antitrust violations. In 1904 Belasco joined with the Shuberts to run a rival chain of theatres using second-rate playhouses. The Shuberts had challenged the Syndicate by both signing actors to contracts and purchasing more theatres. Sarah Bernhardt's 1906 tour and the popular productions of David Belasco finally helped break the monopoly of the Trust.

With the monopoly broken independent theatres modeled their repertoires on European companies. Minnie Maddern Fiske (1865–1932), the daughter of a New Orleans theatre manager, married a second husband, playwright and critic Harrison Grey Fiske. Mrs. Fiske used both her popularity as an ingenue and her success in Ibsen's *A Doll's House* to open and manage, with her husband, the Manhattan Theatre (1903). The theatre brought the plays of Pinero, Shaw, Ibsen, and Wilde to American audiences. As an actress Mrs. Fiske anticipated some of the theories of Constantin Stanislavski. She advised, "Go where you can find something fresh to bring back to the stage."

**Independent Theatres**   By 1901 romantic realism had made New York, with its forty-one playhouses, the world's theatre capital. And by 1915 independent theatres were opening all around the country. Beginning in 1915, the Provincetown Playhouse played on New York's Macdougal Street under the direction of George Cram "Jig" Cook. The Washington Square Players performed at the Bank Box Theatre on Fifty-Seventh Street. In 1915 Anita Bush founded the Harlem Lafayette Players to produce black versions of current Broadway successes. Emily Hapgood's Negro Players presented plays such as *The Rider of Dreams* (1917) by Ridgely Torrence. In Chicago, Raymond O'Neill founded the Ethiopian Art Theatre. Chicago also had the Hull House Players. Mrs. Lyman Gale ran Boston's Toy Theatre. Maurice Browne and Ellen Van Volkenburg operated the Chicago Little Theatre. Winthrop Ames managed a Little Theatre after his New Theatre closed. The Neighborhood Playhouse started in 1915 at New York's Henry Street Settlement House. And in Fargo, North Dakota, Alfred G. Arnold brought the new drama to the Little Country Theatre.

The "little theatre" movement, America's version of the European independent theatre, found a home in America's colleges and universities. With the demise of resident companies, America's colleges became the primary training and testing grounds for new theatre practices. In time, the university theatres in America would become the largest subsidized theatres in history. But the growth came slowly. In 1900 Columbia University named Brander Matthews the first professor of dramatic literature. Harvard's George Pierce Baker began a playwriting class at Radcliffe College in 1904. The next year the course was offered at Harvard as "English 47: The Forms of the Drama." In 1913 Baker established the "47A Workshop" for students to stage plays extracurricularly. In time Baker's students included Edward Sheldon, Sidney Howard, Steele Mackaye's son Percy, Eugene O'Neill, and Thomas Wolfe. One of Baker's students, Frederick Koch, moved to the University of North Dakota in 1905 to teach theatre. Before Koch moved from North Dakota to the University of North Carolina to teach a student named Paul Green, he found an able student named Maxwell Anderson, who later wrote poetic dramas. In 1914 The Carnegie Institute of Technology formed the first department of dramatic arts, offered a degree in theatre, and named Thomas Wood Stevens chair.

Acting was taught as early as 1906 at the University of Wisconsin. In general, the western states' land-grant universities introduced theatre courses more easily than did the puritanical private colleges of the east. Baylor University in Texas taught technical production in 1901. In 1925 Hallie Flanagan Davis came to direct Vassar College's Experimental Theatre. Also in 1925 Yale University lured Professor Baker away from Harvard with promises of a graduate school of drama, great financial support, and a new theatre. Baker directed the Yale Drama School until his death in 1935.

After studying at the Royal Academy of Dramatic Art, Eva Le Gallienne (1899–    ) moved to New York and delighted audiences with performances in the plays of Ibsen and Hauptmann. She also founded the Civic Repertory Theatre (1926–1933) and made Chekhov acceptable to American audiences. Before closing in the economic depression, the "Civic Rep" produced Chekhov's *The Three Sisters, The Seagull,* and *The Cherry Orchard* and Ibsen's *The Master Builder.* A few years before Le Gallienne opened the Civic Rep, Lawrence Langer and the founders of the Washington Square Players decided to create the Theatre Guild to produce important new plays.

***The Group Theatre***    In time, a few workers at the Theatre Guild met to discuss the possibility of creating a theatre group devoted to the "truth" sought by Stanislavski in Russia. In 1931, three people became directors of the new Group Theatre: Cheryl Crawford (1902–1986), Lee Strasberg (1901–1982), and Harold Clurman (1901–1980) collected theatre people dedicated to working on Stanislavski's ideas in an American context. Between 1931 and 1941 the company produced twenty-three plays under the inspiration and unifying spirit of Harold Clurman. One member said that if a history of the Group Theatre were written, it would be called "The Group Theatre: The Man and His Works."

In 1931 twenty-eight actors retreated to Brookfield, Connecticut, as the Moscow Popular Art Theatre had retreated to the countryside, to rehearse Paul Green's *The House of Connolly.* Mordecai Gorelick, the designer for the Group Theatre's production of Sidney Kingsley's *Men in White,* suggested that the Group Theatre's motto was "What shall it profit a man if he gain the whole world and lose his own soul?" While Americans pursued The Almighty Dollar and millions stood in bread lines, the Group Theatre's Chekhov, Clifford Odets, proclaimed in *Awake and Sing,* "Life is not printed on dollar bills."[16]

Lee Strasberg taught the actors his understanding of the Stanislavski method, relying on the Russian's early experiments with "inner truth" and emotion recall. Strasberg created "The Method" of acting, which dominated twentieth-century American performance. But in 1934, Stella Adler, the premiere actress in the company, and Harold Clurman, returned from five weeks of discussion and work with Stanislavski. Their new understanding of the Russian technique showed the Group Theatre's prior work to have been misguided. "Given circumstances" and "the method of physical action" were the keys, Adler announced, to Stanislavski's work. Debates erupted about "The Method." Strasberg and his followers ignored Adler's report. Tensions mounted. Financial worries and a lack of new plays intensified the company's anxieties.

Finally, in 1937, actors petitioned the directors for reorganization, better wages, and more opportunities to act. Crawford and Strasberg resigned. Robert Lewis formed a Group Studio in 1938. Clurman tried to preserve his dream as the company began work on *The Three Sisters* in 1939. In 1940, however, the Group Theatre presented its last play. Debt and disarray ended America's important theatre company.

The techniques and philosophy of the Group Theatre continued in the work of the members who went off to interpret Stanislavski in their own light. Sanford Meisner, for example, worked at the Neighborhood Playhouse. Elia Kazan and Strasberg created The Actors' Studio. Clurman, Lewis, and Kazan took the Group Theatre's social realistic approach to careers as stage directors. Adler, Lewis, and Clurman opened their own acting studios. The Group Theatre, through its theatrical grandchildren, thus maintained the tradition of American social realism and psychological truth in acting.

*Life on Stage* Realism in scene design came from the hand of David Belasco (1854–1931), the author of many romantic melodramas. In *Theatre through the Stage Door* (1919), Belasco wrote, "He who goes direct to nature for the effects he introduces on stage can never be wrong, because nature itself is never wrong." Belasco began his career in San Francisco at the Baldwin Theatre. In 1881 his *The Curse of Cain* created a realistic gypsy camp with a donkey, horses, hens, roosters, ducks, and a pig. Belasco pioneered the use of projected scenery as well. For *Hearts of Oak* (1879) his design included real water, beans, potatoes, a cat, and a baby. In New York, Belasco's first hit, *The Girl I Left Behind Me* (1893), featured a realistic Indian raid and a cavalry charge.

Belasco managed the Madison Square Theatre, the best equipped playhouse in America, built by Steele Mackaye. Mackaye's theatre, seating around 1000, was smaller than most. The Madison Square had its orchestra located over the proscenium arch and boasted New York's only marquee. In the proscenium, Belasco used a "luxuriator" to correct shadows cast by the footlights. A two-story elevator stage, as wide as the proscenium opening, shifted complete settings. The Madison Square's lighting system came from the hand of Thomas Edison himself. Belasco replaced footlights with front-of-the-house lighting. He said "Lights are to drama what music is to the lyrics of a song."

But after working for Daniel Frohman at the Lyceum, Belasco launched a career as an independent producer with *The Heart of Maryland* (1895). The production had real lilacs growing before an old Colonial mansion built on stage. For *The First Born*, Belasco spewed the odor of incense from the stage to create the illusion of San Francisco's Chinatown. He converted the Stuyvesant Theatre to the Belasco Theatre in 1906. The next year he moved an actual boarding house room into the theatre for Eugene Walter's *The Easiest Way*.

Belasco worked for detailed reality on stage. For *Madame Butterfly* (1900) he timed a Japanese

*Blanche Bates in David Belasco's* The Darling of the Gods. *(Lilly Library, Indiana University, Bloomington, Indiana)*

*The Madison Square Theatre in 1879.* (*The Scientific American,* April 5, 1884.)

sunrise to recreate the fourteen-minute effect on stage. *The Girl of the Golden West* (1905) had a realistic snowstorm outside a log cabin. Belasco was even known to stop people in the street to buy their clothing if it was appropriate for the play he was directing. *DuBarry* (1902)

featured materials ordered from France and items actually owned by the real DuBarry. *The Darling of the Gods* used real Japanese properties. A Child's Restaurant was built on stage for *The Governor's Lady;* real food and drink were served. For *Tiger Rose* (1917) a real log cabin was built over a pine needle floor; a realistic rainstorm beat on the action. Belasco ordered real French law books for Brieux's *The Advocate* (1925).

American theatre critics resisted the European realism. William Winter thought Ibsen's plays "flaccid, insipid, tainted, obfuscated and nauseous." He thought Shaw was a "man of very little importance." As critic for the *New York Tribune,* Winter defended America's morals, praised stars, and attacked realism. On the 1894 production of Ibsen's *Ghosts,* Winter commented: "Drama falls very low when it can do no more for the service of the community than to suggest contemporaneous indigestion is attributable to prehistoric circumstances or antediluvian buns." Heredity and Ibsen have "nothing more important to communicate than the fact that if a girl is quick-tempered her great-grandmother ate too many pickles."

Other critics, like George Jean Nathan and even Alexander Woollcott, were kinder and more receptive to European realism. But before realism could become the style of an American theatrical renaissance, two world wars knocked the theatre and the world spinning.

## THE GREAT WAR: AN END TO REALISM

In 1914 Archduke Ferdinand, the heir to the Austrian throne, was assassinated by supporters of democratic revolution in Serbia. In time, almost the entire world was involved in warfare. Military forces stalemated in trench warfare. Machine-gun assaults and artillery bombardment replaced old-fashioned infantry assaults. "The Great War" was the first scientific and technological war, the first modern war using nationalistic sentiments to mobilize

drafted troops. Submarines, airplanes, air raids, machine guns, heavy cannon, balloons, bombs, trucks, tanks, and poison gas debuted on the battlefield. The scientific instruments of death—along with trenches of lice, flu, fever, starvation, freezing cold, dirt, and human excrement—made The Great War unlike any other before it.

For the first time entire populations, civilian and military, became involved in the war effort. Soldiers in the field depended upon workers in home industries. Industries retooled to build armaments, prepare canned foods, and supply materials. Railroads and steamships linked home supplies with the front lines of battle. And, for the first time, radio and photography brought the horrors of war home for all to see and hear in stark reality.

All believed that science, despite the atrocities endured, would make The Great War the "war to end all wars." After the war reasonable people would create a peaceful order in which war could never again be an option. Finally, in 1918, President Wilson of the United States broadcast by radio to Europe his Fourteen Points to accomplish a peaceable world. But the United States, a newcomer on the international stage, did not have enough clout.

Wilson's points were rejected by all. Instead, the victors dictated a severe peace and created new European states out of the losers' land. Western powers feared Bolshevism as they had once feared Napoleon. The victors' actions were designed more to frustrate the revolutionary sentiments in Russia than to build a stable world order. Wilson had advocated self-determination as the way to decrease the need for war. His League of Nations was formed to resolve international tensions peacefully through negotiation. The United States Senate, however, refused to participate and thereby doomed the League.

*The Seeds of Modernism*   The Great War had created a wasteland, unlocked unimagined scientific barbarism, and reignited Romantic despair. Science's faith in the evolutionary progress of humanity had resulted in the deaths of over 10 million soldiers and over 25 million noncombatants. Millions suffered from poverty, starvation, homelessness, and unemployment as a result of the war. Domestic industries, faced with mass human need, continued to produce munitions. The unprecedented violence and barbarism of the war, and the callousness of the victors to the suffering of the participants after the war, seemed to lower the world's acceptable level of human morality.

Soldiers returned home to find not only parades of welcome but also capitalists grown rich from the war effort. Power seemed to rest with the unscrupulous. After receiving the nation's thanks soldiers were left to search for jobs. The tempo of industry, agriculture, and daily life had accelerated in the war effort. Consequently, soldiers felt alienated in their own land. Inflation spurred workers to demand wage increases. Home construction, stopped during the war, did not resume. Shortages produced overcrowding, congestion, and landlord profiteering. As a result, socialism and "communism" found more and more converts.

The romantic theatre had offered escape; the realistic theatre's faith in science and observable reality now seemed misguided. The theatre found a new vision in the late works of realistic playwrights. The modern theatre rejected science and realism to fly off in a thousand different directions as the old faith in objectivity, science, and progress was shattered.

The war trauma sent people searching for meaning in communism and fascism, secularity and religiosity, decadence and puritanism, escape and social awareness. The Modern age and the modern theatre were characterized, therefore, by extremes, eclecticism, and diffusion. A second World War doubled the doses of disillusionment and despair. As men and women looked for a new explanation of the human condition, the dramatic theatre looked for a vision of a new reality.

# NOTES

[1] Marshall McLuhan, *Understanding Media* (New York: McGraw-Hill, 1964), p. 194.

[2] Michael Meyer, *Ibsen* (New York: Doubleday, 1971), p. 560.

[3] Eugène Scribe, quoted in Donald Stuart, *The Development of the Drama* (New York: Dover Publications, 1960), pp. 516–517.

[4] H. Stanley Schwarz, *Alexander Dumas fils, Dramatist* (New York: Benjamin Blom, 1977), pp. 13–14.

[5] Ibid., p. 15.

[6] Ibid., p. 16.

[7] Emile Zola, ''To the Young People of France,'' in *The Experimental Novel and Other Essays*, Belle M. Sherman, trans. (New York: Haskell House, 1964), pp. 142–143.

[8] Ibid., pp. 150–151.

[9] Ibid., p. 94.

[10] Ibid., p. 89.

[11] *The Poems of Matthew Arnold, 1840–1866* (London: Oxford University Press, 1930), p. 402.

[12] George Bernard Shaw, *Plays* (New York: New American Library, 1960), p. 82.

[13] George Bernard Shaw, *Man and Superman* (London: Penguin Books, 1967), p. 156.

[14] Langston Hughes, *The Langston Hughes Reader* (New York: George Braziller, 1958), p. 123.

[15] W. E. B. Du Bois, *A Reader*, Meyer Weinberg, ed. (New York: Harper & Row, 1970), p. 21.

[16] Clifford Odets, *Six Plays* (New York: The Modern Library, 1939), p. 97.

# 9
# THE MODERN THEATRE

*Should you then, in time, discover all there is to be discovered, your progress must then become a progress away from the bulk of humanity. The gulf might even grow so wide that the sound of your cheering at some new achievement would be echoed by a universal howl of horror.*

Bertolt Brecht.*

*Teach him again to dance wrong side out as in the frenzy of dance halls and this wrong side out will be his real place.*

Antonin Artaud**

*Roll over, Beethoven!*

Chuck Berry[†]

## OVERVIEW

While realism enjoyed great popularity, scientists announced discoveries that ushered in the Modern age and theatre. In 1900, for example, physicist Max Planck (1858–1947) formulated the Quantum Theory in physics, for which he won the Nobel Prize in 1918. Physicist Albert Einstein (1879–1955) published his Special Theory of Relativity in 1905 and his General Theory of Relativity in 1915. As the twentieth century progressed, physicists announced more principles to complete a new picture of the universe. In 1930 A. S. Eddington tried to unite the General Theory of Relativity with Quantum Theory. In 1932 physicist Werner Heisenberg (1901–1976), the originator of the Uncertainty Principle, received the Nobel Prize for his Matrix Theory of quantum mechanics. Modern science progressively reduced Newtonian physics to a minor subset of a new universal order. In 1986 physicists discovered a new physical force, "hypercharge," which counteracts the force of gravity. A new vision was forming.

***The Modern Cosmology*** The new conclusions of science astounded and redirected the wonderings of the modern theatre world just as other cosmologies had affected past civilizations. Modern scientists discovered that the universe was not as it appeared to common-sense observation. Reality was redefined as the creation of subjective and personal reactions. Each person perceived, influenced, and created what was called "reality." Reality necessarily was different for each person and species. One could neither observe nor describe an objective reality. Whenever an attempt was made at objectivity, reality responded by changing. Things in the world were so interrelated that the point at which one thing, process, and idea ended and another began could not be located. Science discovered the non-existence of objectivity, the guiding light of theatrical realism since the Renaissance.

Scientists concluded that physical reality was not what the senses suggested. The world was made neither of matter nor of substances, but rather of "tendencies," things made of equal parts idea and matter. All living and nonliving things shared the same fundamental "tendencies." Tendencies resembled what the Greek philosopher Aristotle once called "potentia," a middle ground between the idea tional sphere and the actual world. Tendencies possessed characteristics of both ideas and actualities but were, in fact, neither.

*The End of Reason*    Scientists discovered that tendencies could not be understood by rational thought. Indeed, the essential nature of the universe blurred with each rational attempt to explain and understand it. Rational thought itself, the basis of Western civilization and dramatic theatre, the major cultural divergence from Eastern thought, was, scientists concluded, the major obstacle to understanding the nature of the universe, to getting at the "truth"—Westerners' quest since the classical Greeks.

Rational thought was an obstacle because it differentiated and analyzed. Differentiation and analysis negated the possibility of understanding a universe operating on opposite principles. The existence of tendencies as the basic stuff of the universe belied science's previous conclusions based on differentiation and analysis. All things of the universe lived in a mutually interacting, organic, and conscious process.

*The Age of Transformation*    The organic process of interrelated tendencies and patterns did not unfold in time, as Western Newtonian common sense once believed. Time and space, in the modern world, were not uniform and absolute. Instead, the universe existed already complete, in what Albert Einstein called a "space-time continuum." The modern universe was a four-dimensional continuum. Time was but one dimension moving matter toward increasing entropy and disorder. Facts, matter, and neutral observers did not exist in the modern universe; they would not exist in the modern theatre. Only a space-time continuum and motion existed. And the space-time continuum and motion were, in effect, the same thing.

The modern universe, the modern world, and, consequently, the modern theatre, were defined as processes of change and transformation. Reality, on stage and in life, was a continuous forming, creating, breaking, and destroying process. Things existed not as things, but as various states and stages in the process of change and transformation. The categories of the old Renaissance chain of being were no longer separate identities; they were but temporary manifestations of motion in the space-time continuum. In fact, the chain of being itself was redefined as horizontal rather than vertical; no person or object had dominion. All were but tendencies changing into other manifestations.

Everything and everybody was a temporary stage in the great universal flux. The modern universe was so abstract, scientists said, that one could not even picture it in the imagination. Physicists Einstein and Planck had demonstrated the limits of reason, rationality, and common sense as effective tools for yielding the "truth" about the nature of humanity. Modern playwrights aped them.

*More Scientific Advances*    But the scientists of realism continued to make new, progressive "achievements" by sticking to their observable "facts." The nature of scientific "advances" brought hope to some and despair to others. The breakthroughs of Planck and Einstein led other physicists to unleash the power of atomic energy. At midcentury outer space received satellites from the United States and the Soviet Union. By 1962 the United States boasted 200 atomic reactors to the Soviet Union's thirty-nine. The two nations raced each other in space and on Earth. In 1968 the United States landed a spacecraft on the moon; the next year men followed. In 1974 the Soviet Union probed Mars. The same year India became the sixth nation to enter the nuclear arms race on Earth. In 1984 the arms race moved to outer space.

Newtonian scientists turned to dominate inner space as well. In 1976 scientists at the Massachusetts Institute of Technology constructed the first synthetic gene, and researchers began to dream of the scientific management of species' evolution through genetic engineering. Evolution would be controlled by people rather than be left to Charles Darwin's natural selection. In 1977 British scientists determined, for the first time, the complete genetic structure of a living organism. In time scientists discovered *methanogens*, a new form of life distinct from bacteria, plants, and animals. But it, too, could be killed by the United States' neutron bomb, which was designed to leave only property intact. In 1978 an English baby girl was born after being conceived outside a womb. As the century neared a close, machinery and animal parts replaced defective human organs.

*Psychology*   Throughout the century modern theatre artists turned away from the advances of realistic science. They urged instead a world order based on a peaceful acquiescence with the order revealed by quantum physicists. Doctors investigating mental disturbances came upon another unobservable reality, one that created great anxiety for many patients. Psychologists Sigmund Freud (1856–1939) and Carl Jung (1875–1961) challenged reason's dominance in human behavior by claiming that consciousness was merely a superficial aspect of human reality.

The pioneers of psychology found that irrational actions were caused by unconscious desires. Strindberg's notes for his modern drama *A Dream Play* (1902) echoed what scientists saw happening in their patients' minds: "The characters are split, double and multiply, they evaporate, crystallize, scatter, and converge. But a single consciousness holds sway over them all, that of the dreamer." Freud and Jung attributed the "sway" to unconsciously repressed or transferred motivations. In 1904 Freud published *The Psychopathology of Everyday Life* to supplement his *The Interpretation of Dreams* (1900). Jung issued *The Psychology of the Unconscious* in 1917. Psychologists found human minds and personalities behaving like subatomic particles. The modern theatre dramatized the new reality of both physics and psychology.

*Dreams and Symbols*   Every human dream was considered an inner drama based on a conflict with the outer world. Conversely, playwrights made their dramas inner dreams based on conflicts with the outer world. Dreams were written by the id, the ego, and the superego. The id was one of three mental levels that sought the satisfaction of primitive, instinctive, impulsive, and amoral desires. The ego was the conscious level of mental activity that tried to keep control of the id. The superego, a subconscious level like the id, censored the id with learned morality and a sense of guilt. Only one-ninth of human mental activity was considered conscious by the psychologists. Consequently, dreams visualized the necessary conflicts between conscious and unconscious minds. To skirt the censorious ego and superego, the id created dreams in symbols. Thus, by interpreting the symbolism, dreamers could discover the nature of their psychological troubles.

Some modern playwrights freed their ids with plays of dark, inaccessible symbols that represented feelings, instincts, and impulses. The plays represented the dramatists' dreams and the stage the playwright's minds. The audience was to interpret the dramatic symbols, resolve the mysteries, and alleviate the troubles. The playwrights' dreams mirrored human existence. Symbols would unlock the mysteries of the world and free humanity from pain and suffering. A well-written dream-drama could have the power to tap the universal mythic dreams among the spectators. When psychologists proposed that sex and death were the two great urges and fears lurking in the unconscious, playwrights made sex and death the two major themes of the modern theatre.

Dreamers and psychologists' patients used the technique of "free association" to unlock psychological desires and gain serenity of mind. Playwrights used the technique to structure the actions and images of the modern theatre. The interpretation of dreams required activity by both patient and psychologist. An appreciation of the modern theatre required active participation on the part of the audience. Intuition and pragmatism became values for patients, therapists, artists, and audiences in the Modern age. Both intuition and pragmatism thus found champions among modern philosophers.

*A New Philosophy* C. S. Pierce (1839–1914) founded the philosophy of pragmatism, which won acclaim as interpreted by American William James (1842–1910), the brother of novelist Henry. Pragmatism took science's idea that the value and truth of a proposition exist only if it works. But William James broke with the realists' belief in an objective reality by claiming truth to be simply the opinion upon which a particular community agrees.

James founded "radical empiricism," the claim that experience was the basic material of all things. He moved from philosophy to "psychology," the science of the unconscious; observable reality was not, he concluded, the whole picture. He immediately objected to the realists' faith in determinism. In *The Will to Believe* (1897) James insisted upon individual will as an important ingredient in human action: "If this life be not a real fight, in which something is eternally gained for the universe by success, it is no better than a game of private theatricals. . . . Be not afraid of life. Believe that life *is* worth living, and your belief will help create the fact." James's belief became more difficult as the twentieth century wore on.

Philosopher Henri Bergson (1859–1941) shared James's faith in life with his theory of "vitalism," a philosophy based on intuiting the existence of a "life-force." Life based on intuitive intelligence was, for Bergson, the highest form of life. Bergson saw a life-force moving through history and leading humanity on. Bergson thought that all matter was made of the life-force, just as physicists thought "tendencies" were the basic stuff of things.

Bergson looked at technology and machinery and laughed. Laughter, he said, was the result of seeing intuitive and pragmatic individuals behaving as nonintuitive and nonpragmatic machines. Yet, as the century advanced, machine-like behavior became more admired and imitated by compartmentalized specialists. But Bergson insisted that "any arrangement of acts and events is comic which gives us, in a single combination, the illusion of life and the distinct impression of a mechanical arrangement. . . .We laugh every time a person gives us the impression of being a thing." Bergson made intuition and non-machine-like behavior respectable again. He laughed when people behaved like objective, dispassionate, and impersonal machines. But his view, like the modern view as a whole, remained outside the current of realism shaping society.

*Technological Civilization* Realism formed a society that made modern theatre artists outsiders. The Industrial Revolution, the engine of realism, transformed society to a scientific civilization. Historian William Irwin Thompson illustrated the change: the communication and transportation revolutions created an information explosion. An electronic revolution eventually threatened printed books with extinction. Information had been accumulating exponentially since the Renaissance; an individual had not been able to know everything since the Medieval age. Rarely in the Modern era could individuals attain enough information to free themselves from dependence on specialists.

The basic functions of society divaricated. Culture fragmented. Specialists worked for,

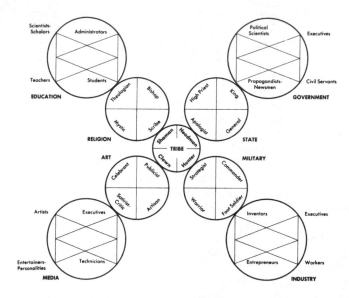

*William Irwin Thompson's diagram of the evolution of industrial civilization.* (William I. Thompson, *At the Edge of History,* p. 125. Copyright © by William Irwin Thompson. Reprinted by permission of Harper & Row, Publishers, Inc.)

and spoke to, one another rather than for and to society at large. Critic Jacques Barzun noted that:

> By this delegation of culture the importance of art and the humanities is shifted to a new ground. These good things are no longer valuable for their direct effect on the head and the heart; they become valuable as professions, as means of livelihood, as badges of honor, as goods, to be marketed, as components of the culture industry.[1]

Realism, familiar and available, became the most profitable and marketable theatrical art in modern society. Modernism remained for the shaman and clowns furthest from the center of modern society.

Thompson's model encapsulated the operation of modern scientific civilization. Democratic revolutions produced a modern society ruled by elected or appointed executives rather than by kings. World War I initiated the modern symbiotic relationship between industrial and military interests. Old polarities remained, however: Universities housed both protesters to military and industrial activities and researchers working for industrial and military interests. Educational administrators, media executives, industrial magnates,

and governmental officials became interchangeable. Scholars and scientists doubled as political scientists, inventors, and creative artists. Media personalities and entertainers shifted to work as journalists, teachers, industrial entrepreneurs, and politicians. Students, civil servants, workers, and technicians lived in the lower depths of the modern scientific civilization.

Mass production created the art industy of "media." Media criticized and investigated both government and industry to turn a profit. Government and industry, in turn, purchased media to manipulate public opinion. Democratic revolutions had made "the people" the primary patron of the arts. Consequently, mass media glorified and flattered the tastes and achievements of its patrons, the common people. Just as kings' tastes had ruled the art of the past, the majority taste of "the people" ruled in the Modern age. Money and power resided not with executives, but with the people, and the white people at that; the artists catered to the powerful. Like their antecedent patrons, the people used the media to celebrate themselves and their values; the media, in turn, used the celebrations to make money.

***New Artistic Visions*** Modern theatre artists, rebelling against the realist vision locked into the scientific society, lived necessarily outside the favor of the majority of the people. The modern reality envisioned by dramatic artists thus did not find a receptive audience. Science and realism had brought the people to power but had diminished the people's ability and need to imagine anything else. Specialization further eroded the people's need to wonder or imagine; experts did that for them. When modern artists' theatrical visions were found incomprehensible, specialists were called upon to explain what the artists had imagined. The modern vision found "truth" outside common sense, reason, and observable facts.

Modern theatrical art, unlike realistic art, demanded something more from the audience. Gordon Craig (1872–1966), a founder of the modern theatre, insisted that the "sense of being beyond reality" permeated all great art. For Craig, "drama which is not trivial, takes us *beyond* reality. . . ."[2] The modern theatre, seeking to distinguish itself from realism, created the term "poetic drama," thereby continuing to separate poetry from drama by implying a need to synthesize two distinct modes.

The modern prophet Antonin Artaud (1896–1948) foresaw the end of realism: "An art based entirely on a power of illusion which it is incapable of obtaining has no choice but to disappear."[3] Even the gentlemanly stage director Michel Saint-Denis (1897–1971) acknowledged the end of realism: "To reveal life the theatre cannot use the means of life. It has got to use the means of theatre. The Chinese say, 'It is not doors that are interesting, but what happens behind them: so why have doors?'"[4]

*Non-Western Influences* Modern artists found reinforcement for their views in non-Western cultures. So-called "primitive" natives had created cultures delighting in the modern values of spontaneity and instinct. Anthropologists unearthed non-Western art, mythology, and religion in support of the modern notion of the universe. Modern artists tried to imitate the natives' methods of artistic composition. Artist Pablo Picasso (1881–1973) collected non-Western sculpture and masks before reconceiving the Western picture. Like "primitive" works, modern paintings were not window frames to the observable realistic world, but surfaces for the arrangement of complex forms. African and Eastern aesthetic principles found a home in the West.

Most Western theatre artists, however, came to their conclusions without the direct influence of Oriental art. Indeed, Western science had come to Eastern conclusions; modern men and women arrived at an Eastern perspective unaided. Western artists and scientists abandoned the long-held belief in a finite world comprised of permanent matter. Modernists considered process rather than matter to be the essence of nature. Finally, the West came to see the rendering of visible reality in art, literature, and theatre not as a help in individuals' search for the "truth," but rather as a lie and a hindrance. In the Modern age, Eastern and Western theatre artists and scientists arrived at common metaphysical and aesthetic grounds.

Western theatre workers studied Eastern theatre practices as never before. In the 1920s Mei-Lan Feng (1894–1961), a Beijing opera performer, toured the West and opened the eyes of Russians Eugene Vakhtangov (1883–1922), Vsevolod Meyerhold (1874–1940), Sergei Eisenstein (1878–1948), the German Bertolt Brecht (1898–1956), the French Paul Claudel (1868–1955), and countless other leaders of the modern theatre. Critic Antonin Artaud saw a Balinese dance troupe. French director Jacques Copeau (1879–1949) began to train his students at the *Vieux Columbier* in noh techniques. French actor Jean-Louis Barrault (1910–    ) read about Zen archery. The history of the modern theatre traced the acquisition of Eastern theatre practices.

Modern artists revived the historical connection between shamanism and clowning. In the modern global village created by science, the poet and player regained old functions. The oral reading of poetry revived with the Welsh poet Dylan Thomas (1912–1953). American poets like Alan Ginsberg (1926–    ) and Gary Snyder (1930–    ) studied Zen. Folk singers sang rhapsodic epics of contemporary heroes. Some of the sagas became movies and plays. Artist Jackson Pollock's (1912–1956) theory of composition resembled that of Zen ink painting. Performers reacted against reasoned and logical composition by making chance an artistic principle.

***New Aesthetic Theory*** Modern theatrical art revolutionized aesthetic theory. In 1909 painter Vasily Kandinsky (1866–1944) had announced, *Alles ist erlaubt* (everything is permitted): everything, that is, except the "accurate" representation of external appearances. Kandinsky had maintained that "the form is the outer expression of the inner content."

Theatre artists valued spontaneity, instinct, and automatic expression. Swiss artist Paul Klee (1879–1940) insisted that "creation must of necessity be accompanied by distortion of the natural form; only in that way can nature be reborn and the symbols of art revitalized." Abstraction and subjectivity in dramatic art paralleled the quantum physicists' discovery that space represented the essence of nature more faithfully than solids. Consequently, space became more important than solid matter in modern art, theatre, scene design, and architecture. White space on pages and "white noise"—silence—in performances appeared in modern literature, music, and theatre.

In time, wave systems replaced matter in the physicists' picture of the universe; matter became energy. Modern theatre artists responded by invalidating the concept of substance in their work. Solidity was portrayed as an illusion in visual art, music, poetry, dramatic character, and stage setting. Science and modern art envisioned a universe so abstract that men and women could not even picture it in their imaginations. Only motion and equilibrium came close to capturing the essential characteristics of the modern universe.

Modern artists started over again with basic questions: What is a novel? What is music? What is painting? What is theatre? What is performance? What is the relationship between theatre and ritual? What is the relationship between theatre and dance, theatre and music, theatre and art? Science's vision was so profound and the World Wars' demonstration of technology so overwhelming that modern artists decided to reconsider every old answer.

Modernists wondered whether art, music, painting, and performance were products or processes. They considered each art's existence in time and space. Because the universe and humanity had been defined as processes, the modern arts became processes. Modernists asked how the process of each art differed one from another. They concluded that if nature was a dynamic continuum, then one art could never be differentiated precisely from another, or even from life itself.

Modern artists demonstrated and explored the unconfined universe. Composer John Cage (1912–    ) summarized the work: "The highest purpose is to have no purpose at all. This puts one in accord with nature in her manner of operation."[5] Cage claimed that the purpose of the theatre was simply to increase people's awareness of life. Each person had to create meaning for theatrical art, just as each person had to find meaning for life. Each person, each spectator, had to decide for him- or herself what to see, do, or hear, and in what order. Because no one could dictate meaning in life, artists did not wish to dictate meaning to the audience.

The modern universe was a meaningless process in which each person had to find or create his or her own order. The modern theatre, like all modern arts, mirrored the age's search. All of the various modern "isms" shared, however, a common faith in the theatrical process's ability to communicate the search. Critic Albert Bermel noted that "Theatricalism is rightly considered *the* dramatic mode of the century, theater turning in on itself, pondering its nature as a form of life and a form of art, usually by setting up a dialogue of a sort between the outer and the inner play."[6] The proliferation of electronic media in the Modern age gave the theatre a practical need to reexamine its nature.

*New Media*   In 1927, the year of the first talking movie, 280 plays, the largest number ever, opened in New York. By 1933, however, half of New York's theatres were dark. By 1947 more than one-third of the plays in New York were revivals. By 1950 only 2 percent of Americans admitted that they went to the theatre and of that, only 1 percent was under 25 years of age.

Radio, motion pictures, television, and the realistic theatre had created the context for the modern theatre. Actors and writers moved to more lucrative and popular media. But movies suffered with the advent of television. Nevertheless, in 1939, 80 percent of the people said they would rather listen to the radio than see a movie. The same year the National Broadcasting Corporation began regular television transmissions. The next year many movie studios reported record losses. Radio listening dropped, and music replaced radio drama. Radio and movie actors and writers went to television for more regular employment and a larger audience. In 1949 the first cable television broadcast went on the air; the next year the first pay television collected its fee. Movie studios set up television divisions in 1951. Cinerama and 3-D movies tried to coax customers back to movie houses. By 1954 television's gross revenue had surpassed radio's. The introduction of color broadcasting the same year plunged movie attendance to its all time low since talking pictures.

In 1962 an orbiting satellite relayed instantaneous video communication around the world. Movie studios made movies for television. Theatre did little more than decentralize to various regions of the country and introduce subscription tickets to ensure an economic base of operation.

In 1975 Sony introduced the video cassette recorder-player. After video cassette movies went on sale in 1979, movie and television companies made films for video cassette sale. Theatrical companies filmed their plays for broadcast or sale as well.

Television gave the world a glut of realistic drama and performance: it burned the realistic form on to the retinas of the people. And television, like radio earlier, brought spectator sports to greater numbers. Italian dictator Benito Mussolini (1883–1945) had created a Department of Physical Education. German dictator Adolph Hitler (1889–1945) had decreed: "There should be no day in which a boy should not have at least one hour's physical training, both in the morning and afternoon." His Reich Federal Sports Association's theoretician Kurt Munch wrote that "athletics and sports are the preparatory school of political driving power in the service of the state." Men, who once constituted a majority of the theatre's audience, now preferred to watch sporting events. Thus, women made up most of the movie and theatre audiences. Consequently, artists wrote and performed for their tastes. As a result, many modern theatre workers looked to the sporting arena for inspiration in rethinking the roots of the theatrical experience.

The realistic theatre created the audience for movies, television, and spectator sports. Technology had worked to capture a true illusion of reality in the realistic theatre; realistic playwrights strove to put real-life people on the stage. Science guided both attempts. Movies were the logical result of the realists' efforts: a machine created movies, and a machine showed movies. Technology made the realistic theatre obsolete. The modern theatre was left to rediscover the nature of the theatrical event.

***The Theatre Responds***   Most theatre workers reacted to movies and television by trying to compete. But as theatres closed or converted to movie houses, the victory was clear. At first movies aped the realistic theatre's techniques: a single fixed camera filmed continuous, chronological action. In time cinematic techniques developed. The modern theatre borrowed many of the later movies' techniques: the position of the movie camera (and spectator) moved; the film editor freely manipulated time and space; action proceeded faster or slower than normal. Movie scenes cut away, dissolved, wiped off, or faded away. Panning and tracking techniques developed.

The modern theatre imitated the movies consciously and unconsciously. Plays were written and staged to incorporate the movies' dream-like fluidity. The modern theatre replaced the assumed objectivity of realism with the movies' subjective point of view. Directors of the surrealist, futurist, expressionist, and constructivist art movements all worked in both the movies and the modern theatre.

The movies forced the theatre to reconsider many assumptions. If a director was the dominant creative artist in the movies, then the director's vision should prevail over the playwright's in the theatre. If the theatre required a more active participation by the spectator than did the movies, efforts were made to determine the nature of that participation. Realism left little for the movie or stage audience to imagine. Modern artists wondered what the theatre could show and how it could show it.

A movie was a finished product to be reviewed; the modern theatre defined itself as an event created anew with each performance. To see a modern play was to participate in the process of creation. The difference between process and product suggested different concepts and portrayals of time and space. Realistic theatre action had always been continuous and sequential in time. The movies sped, retarded, froze, and even reversed time; the movies repeated or omitted time. Movie time was more subjective than realistic stage time. The movies presented action differently than the theatre had. Movies flexed space and action; presented simultaneous times, spaces, and actions; leapt about among past, present, and future; dissolved objects; and even transformed people. The modern theatre wanted to do the same. But the movies were just colored lights on a wall; the theatre had to work with living people.

Confronted with the movies, the theatre rediscovered its essence. Movies-as-products aged with time, but theatre-as-process was reborn at each performance and remained as fresh as the players and the audience. The movies were trapped in time; the modern theatre existed beyond time.

The modern theatre's discoveries became a theatrical image for modern individuals rediscovering themselves and their world. Modern individuals became actors playing roles in the universe, their stage. Modern actors, like modern individuals, had to discover what it meant to act. The modern theatre self-consciously used and exploited the theatre as a metaphor for the human condition. Polish director Jerzy Grotowski (1933–    ) concluded that "The theatre must recognize its own limitations. If it cannot be richer than the cinema, then let it be poor. If it cannot be as lavish as television, let it be ascetic. If it cannot be a technical attraction, let it renounce all outward technique. Thus we are left with a 'holy actor in a poor theatre.'"[7] The modern theatre's history consisted of various conclusions about what the theatre should be *vis à vis* realism on stage or film.

*A New Consciousness*   While the modern media forced the theatre to confront itself, the media also reoriented modern humanity's way of perceiving nature. The telegraph, telephone, radio, and television united the world and increased people's sensitivity to time and space. Messages arrived as soon as they were sent. People saw and heard immediately events and people in the remotest corners of the earth and outer space. Minicameras and microphones probed the innermost places of the human body.

Electronics replaced the visual dominance of reading with multisensory experiences. Reading's interest in the past fell to the media's interest in present "news." Books told what had happened; the media showed what was happening now. The linear sequentiality of the printed word gave way to the simultaneous multifocus of electronic media.

Modern men and women unconsciously developed new sensitivities, fluencies, and appreciations for auditory, tactile, kinetic, and gustatory sensations. The media replaced the desire to understand events with the desire to experience events. Modern people relied more frequently on intuitive feelings rather than on intellectual analyses. The phrase "I feel" began to replace "I think" in everyday discourse. Process and motion invaded modern consciousness as people reported what others "went" rather than what people "said." The media changed *how* modern people experienced the world far more than *what* they thought or experienced.

Rather than encourage uniformity of thought and experience, television and radio increased the modern urge for uniqueness and diversity. Through media the modern world saw the diversity of nature; heterogeneity got the go-ahead signal. Television and radio encouraged in-depth involvement with experience. According to media theorist Marshall McLuhan (1911–1980), the electronic media disseminated "symbolist and mythic structures" that required immediate audience translation. The multifocal medium of television required the viewer to select and recreate images. Vague or ill-defined images let the viewer engage and share in the process of creation. Unlike movies, television was the modern medium that required the most active viewer participation in a multisensory experience.

Television viewing required the audience to integrate fragmented and differentiated sensory experiences. All of the viewer's senses were needed to interpret the medium's discontinuous, simultaneous, and illogical images. The process of television viewing paralleled the process of watching a modern theatre performance. Television was a fluid collage, a dynamic mosaic, requiring viewer interpretation. Like the theatre, television presented men and women with an iconographic experience. With the rise of television, theatre workers adapted television techniques to the dramatic art.

While the electronic media reoriented modern consciousness, modern heads of the "global village" sought to manipulate the messages. Mass consumption brought mass advertising. Psychological research yielded information used to manipulate human behavior for the benefit of politicians and industrialists. In 1922 John B. Watson, the founder of modern behavioral psychology, left the John Hopkins University to become a Vice-President in the J. Walter Thompson advertising agency. Mass psychology was employed to manipulate the people's unconscious demands. Economic and political systems, based on the operation of reason, were driven by mass media messages that sought to break down individual habits, create a desire for newness, and link the marketplace with utopian ideals of freedom, well-being, and the fulfillment of private fantasies. Media artists and scholarly psychologists united to make people feel more emotional about things than about other people. The work of advertisers seemed to incarnate the irrational world depicted in the novels of Czech Franz Kafka (1883–1924). But Kafka was upstaged by the irrational terror brought by the century's two great world wars.

***The Rise of Geopolitics***   World War I had a devastating and profound effect on the world. Disillusioned Germans, Italians, and Spaniards turned to fascism. Dictator Benito Mussolini (1883–1945) rose to power by capitalizing on Italy's discontent with the war's settlement. A beerhall war veteran who liked to argue politics, Adolf Hitler (1889–1945) blamed Germany's defeat on internal problems, Jews, and socialists. Modeling his career on Mussolini's, Hitler came to power with the National Socialists during the 1929 depression. The depression of worldwide magnitude produced massive unemployment, bankruptcy, and disillusionment with capitalism and democracy. As a result, socialism and fascism found numerous adherents throughout the world. In the East, new-found nationalism became Western-styled imperialism.

Nations rearmed to bring themselves out of depression. Hitler blamed German Jews for betraying German nationalism to the forces of international socialism, and the Jews again became the scapegoats for human frustrations. Eventually Germany inaugurated the "Final Solution," the extermination of Jews, homosexuals, and political opponents by gas and cremation. Millions of Jews were sent to concentration camps. And biological experiments made these concentration camp inmates guinea pigs for odd surgical procedures and sterilization. New depths of human depravity and barbarity were discovered.

Western nations did not stop the shipment of Jews, Poles, and liberals to concentration camps. Many Germans who tried to escape were denied entrance to some Western countries and were themselves forced to return to imprisonment and death. In all 6 million Jews and 9 million gypsies and Slavs died in the "Final Solution." But Hitler wooed the world's Christian religious leaders who still officially blamed the Jews for the death of Jesus. In 1933 he signed a concordat with Pope Pius XI (1922–1939). Either fearful of the wrath of the rearmed German state or subconsciously turning their eyes, most clergy muffled their proclamations of Christian morality. War failed to stop Hitler's extermination of racial and political undesirables.

War weary nations, however, wanted peace. World War I had disillusioned most people with war as a tool for resolving international differences. Faced with German and Italian aggression, the world conceded for peace, and the worldwide peace movement was very strong. Nevertheless, Germany invaded Czechoslovakia, Poland, Norway, Denmark, the Netherlands, France and Russia. Air raids terrorized Britain. Meanwhile, the United States sent supplies to England and Russia but insisted on isolation and neutrality lest World War I be repeated. Not until Japanese imperialism clashed with American interests in the Pacific did the United States join the war. Within German-occupied Europe, socialist and communist resistance fighters struggled beside capitalists to defeat the fascists. The allies invaded. Massive bombings of German cities produced "firestorms"; by mixing incendiary and high-explosive bombs, the United States destroyed 75 percent of Hamburg and Dresden and killed numerous allied flyers. The Germans retaliated by attacking London with missiles that killed 6000 people and destroyed 750,000 buildings. Finally, a resolution to the war was inevitable.

But the allies had to win the war in the Pacific. The United States retook lost islands and announced the existence of an atomic bomb capable of destroying an entire city. Despite the objections of the Supreme Allied Com-

mander and many physicists who created the weapon, the United States dropped atomic bombs on Hiroshima and Nagasaki. Japan surrendered, and the world sighed at the end of World War II.

Peace in Europe left Germany divided into occupational zones and the Soviet Union dominant in Central Europe. The allied victors gasped at the horrors they found in liberated concentration camps. As the Nazis were tried, the world learned that the Nazis were not animal barbarians but, more shocking, cultured, educated, and sophisticated men and women who just happened to have committed "crimes against humanity."

The wartime alliance between the United States and the Soviet Union collapsed as the two nations entered a "cold war." Fearful of each other, both nations worked secretly and overtly to undermine the rival. Each anxious nation forged alliances with other nations. The world once again committed itself to mutual defense treaties; pressure mounted for every nation to choose sides.

***The Age of Despair*** World War II accelerated human disillusionment and despair. The Russians, who had condemned fascism so vehemently, were themselves discovered to have eliminated thousands of political opponents in forced labor camps. The Americans, who had persecuted the Nazis so vigorously at the Nuremberg trials, were themselves seen making the mass extermination of life a legitimate tool of war by dropping atomic bombs. The war had brought radar, jet planes, firestorms, missiles, and nuclear weaponry to the world.

The entire world was thus transformed into a global concentration camp awaiting mass nuclear extermination. Over 15 million deaths and almost 27 million casualties resulted from the war; almost half were Russian. Modern warfare had eliminated military fronts and the differentiation of civilian from military targets. The entire world became a target and every person an imminent casualty. Mass murder moved from the category of human aberation to legitimate foreign policy. The aim of mod-

*Vaudevillian Bert Lahr in an American production of Samuel Beckett's* Waiting for Godot. *(The New York Public Library Theatre Collection. Photo by Ben Mancuso)*

ern war became, not the destruction of military targets, but the elimination of whole peoples and civilizations. Modern warfare became capable of destroying not only people but also the philosopher Bergson's life-force itself.

Modern theatre artists, poets, and philosophers created within this reality. Poet and playwright Samuel Beckett (1906-    ) drew dramatic characters who could only wait; there was "nothing to be done." Efforts at disarmament could not erase the knowledge of mass destruction acquired during the war. Humanity hoped that it could somehow refrain from using the knowledge it had acquired. Modern men and women scrambled to find some basis for hope, faith, and belief. Alcoholism, drug addiction, political action, religious devotion, and violent outbursts of terrorism all increased and attested to the vigor of the search.

***The Debasement of Language***   The surfeit of information and the excessive rhetoric of the wars led people to distrust language's ability to convey meaning or truth. Language seemed a distortion of the human experience. The study of semantics and linguistics blossomed to work on the problem. Philosopher Ludwig Wittgenstein (1889-1951), the son of an engineer, fueled the development of semantics. His *Tractatus Logico-Philosophicus* (1921) proved that there was very little that could be said. Wittgenstein concluded that "whereof one cannot speak, thereof one must be silent." He asserted that the belief in cause and effect relationships was nothing but a "superstition" and that the "so-called laws of nature" were all merely an "illusion."

The modern theatre, like all modern art, attempted to articulate the inarticulateness of modern existence. The theatre tried to provide a dramatic presentation of an experience beyond the power of words to communicate. Rumanian playwright Eugène Ionesco (1912-    ) explained that "when words are worn out, the mind is worn out." Silence appeared more frequently on the modern stage, especially during climactic moments of heightened awareness. Modern playwrights wrote "pauses" or "silence" into their scripts. Pantomimic action played a prominent role in the modern theatre.

***The Revival of Dance***   Movement returned to rival language for supremacy in the modern theatre. England's critic Gordon Craig (1872-1966) insisted that movement be considered a primary part of the dramatic theatre. He wanted the respect for pantomine, dance, and masks that had existed in the classical theatres of the East and West. His lover, Isadora Duncan (1877-1927), was the first modern dancer.

A native of San Francisco, Isadora Duncan lived most of her life in Europe. Duncan studied dance with, among others, a ballerina from *The Black Crook.* The dance movement called "Delsartism" in America, however misapplied, broke down the nation's inhibitions about the body and provided the theoretical and practical basis for the modern dance theatre. Isadora was the first international star of the new freedom in movement and dress. Although unwelcome in America as a "Red Menace," Duncan acquired scores of international fans and disciples. She hated classical ballet for the hollowness she found in its passion and formalism. Duncan owned and studied a book on Delsartism; she applied the principles to her desire to copy the ancient Greek sculptural studies of nature. Duncan wished to bring "the soul back to the mystical sources."

Modern dance had romantic roots as well. Duncan called herself and her disciples "the spiritual offspring of Walt Whitman." She marked her favorite passage in her favorite book, *Thus Spake Zarathustra* by German philosopher Friedrich Nietzsche: "Only in dance do I know how to tell the parable of the highest things." Duncan established schools in Germany, France, and Russia. Modern dance, however, was born in America.

Another student of Delsartism, Ruth St. Denis (1878–1968), was a ballerina from *The Black Crook*. Finding her inspiration in the East, after seeing Japanese dancer Sad Yacco at the 1900 Paris Exposition, St. Denis investigated Egypt's god Isis and India's goddess Indra. In 1906 St. Denis danced her East Indian ballet, *Radha*, and studied yoga in Europe. In later years she added the dances *Yoga*, *Incense*, *The Cobras*, and *Nautch*.

In 1914 another student of Delsartism, Ted Shawn (1891–1972), joined St. Denis to form the "Denishawn" organization of performing groups and schools, which, by 1931, had spread acceptance of modern dance. Doris Humphrey (1895–1958), Martha Graham (1894– ), and Charles Weidman (1900–1975) studied with Denishawn. In the 1930s Shawn led an all-male troupe and St. Denis an all-female troupe. The Denishawn Jacob's Pillow Dance Festival and school opened in 1933. Modern dance evolved from Denishawn. Martha Graham, Doris Humphrey, and Charles Weidman formed their own companies and toured extensively.

Nietzsche's announcement of the death of God found confirmation in the reality of the modern world. Christianity's historic suppression of the dance, which had caused the rhythmic impulse to flow into Renaissance me-

*Modern dance pioneer Ruth St. Denis.* (Lilly Library, Indiana University, Bloomington, Indiana)

tered language, thus faded as people began to dance once again. Modern dance theatre captured the reality described by modern physicists, investigated by modern psychologists, and painted by modern artists.

***Art and Music*** The old rules of perspective and coloration, and the Renaissance's desire to capture three-dimensionality on a flat surface, disappeared. Paul Gauguin (1848–1903) painted his dreams and memories in visual metaphors and symbols. Vincent van Gogh (1853–1890) painted what he felt. Edvard Munch (1863–1944) expressed on canvas his dark introspection, obsessions, and fatalism.

In 1915 painter Henri Matisse (1869–1954) and his friends created so much excitement with their paintings that modern art was said to have begun at that moment. Modern artists wanted to express freely what they felt, rather than represent, in accordance with the rules, what others saw. Free, expressive color was their first daring experiment. In time, painting, like the other modern arts, became interested in process; as always, modern artists kept abreast of modern science.

In the late 1950s and early 1960s artists presented "Happenings." Influenced by the aesthetic theories of John Cage (1912– ), painters and musicians like Allan Kaprow (1927– ) staged simultaneous, diverse actions scattered about and among an audience. The work gave formal theory to the activities of earlier futurist and dadaist artists. Space became the medium for art; by being in the performance space the audience became part of the art. Happenings were a process in which an audience participated simply by being there and by experiencing the events occurring around them. Happenings were three-dimensional action collages involving all media. The assembled audience experienced a sequence of arbitrary and chance perceptions; meaning was created rather than received by the audience. When the process ended nothing remained of the Happening. Art imitated life so faithfully that the artificial and illusory distinction between art and life disappeared.

Modern music followed suit by rejecting the "internal logic" of past composition. Modern musical principles arose from the process of composition itself. Composer Arnold Schoenberg (1874–1951) perfected twelve-tone composition; many of his "motifs" were more apparent on the printed sheet than in performance.

Such electronic media as tape recorders, synthesizers, electronic instruments, and computers revolutionized the possibilities of sound production. John Cage, rejecting the mathematical complexity of serial composition, advocated chance as a technique for both composition and performance. Cage used the ancient Chinese *I Ching* to decide matters and explored the visual and spatial dimensions of music. Robert Wilson (1944– ), an architect and opera creator, joined with composer

Phillip Glass (1937– ) to develop operatic architectures without libretti or traditional time restrictions. In their works, singers, dancers, actors, and instrumentalists climbed over and around architectural playing spaces of tableaux, pausing only occasionally to pose. Taped and live music combined to produce novel effects.

*Literature* Charles Baudelaire (1821–1867) was considered the first modern poet. In addition, his theory of correspondences started the symbolist movement. Baudelaire, who defined the modern poet as a shaman communing with and becoming God in the process of artistic creation, used the ancient ninth-century Caballa as an inspiration. Stéphane Mallarmé (1842–1898), another symbolist poet, envisioned a ceremonial theatre of gestures, images, and ritualized poetry, dance, and mime.

Symbolists and imagists imitated Eastern poetic and artistic styles. Paul Fort (1872–1962) and other French symbolists favored the Japanese poetic form known as *haiku*. Irish poet William Butler Yeats (1865–1939), finding lyric and dramatic inspiration in the East, translated noh plays and penned originals. German writer Hermann Hesse (1877–1962) combined Christian mysticism with Buddhist philosophy in symbolist novels. Ezra Pound (1885–1972) displayed the influence of haiku in his *Pisan Cantos*. In the "Essay on the Chinese Written Character" (1920), Pound used Chinese characters in poems as magical pictures. Pound also translated noh plays and classical Greek dramas.

Modern poets tried again to write for the theatre. The modern rejection of logical prose language seemed an invitation to a new type of stage language. But like romantic poets, most modern poets knew more about poetry than about the theatre.

T. S. Eliot (1888–1965) wrote poetic dramas. The 1170 assassination of Thomas à Becket, the archbishop of Canterbury who opposed English King Henry II, inspired Eliot's *Murder in the Cathedral* (1935), in which he examined the making of a martyr who wrestles with the possibility of doing the right deed for the wrong reason. *The Cocktail Party* (1940) takes inspiration from Euripides's *Alcestis*. With the drama Eliot seeks to combine elements of the medieval morality play with traditional drawing-room comedy. Based on the Orestes legend, *The Family Reunion* (1939) presents a misanthropic murderer pursued by invisible Furies while relatives, attending his mother's birthday party, act as chorus. None of these plays achieved the stature of Eliot's monumental poems, "The Waste Land" (1922) and "Ash Wednesday" (1930).

Other poets attempted to write for the stage, as well. Christopher Fry (1907–    ) penned *The Lady's Not for Burning* (1949), a play that showed a clever romantic existential hero's attempts to save a medieval girl from burning as a witch. Maxwell Anderson (1888–1959) extolled democracy and freedom in heroic blank verse in *Elizabeth the Queen* (1930). In the play the hero is destroyed by petty power-seeking bureaucrats. *Winterset* (1935) was Anderson's drama of an American ethnic Hamlet in New York's tenements, seeking vengeance for his father's death. Federico Garcia Lorca (1898–1936) penned earthy, theatrical poetic dramas about individuals' search for meaning in a wasteland of worthless codes and traditions. Before his murder by fascists, Lorca wrote a trilogy: *Bodas de sangre* (*Blood Wedding*, 1933), *Yerma* (1934) and *La casa de Bernarda Alba* (*The House of Bernarda Alba*, 1935).

In Martinique, surrealist visionary poet, Aimé Césaire (1913–    ) wrote *Et les chiens se taisaient* (*And the Dogs Keep Quiet*, 1956), a lyrical mixture of Greek tragedy and surrealistic form. His major work for the stage was a trilogy exploring the black struggle for independence from white suppression. *Le tragédie du roi Christophe* (*The Tragedy of King Christophe*, 1963) begins the saga in Haiti. The second play, *A Season in the Congo* (1966) reveals the global scope of racism. The final play, *Une tempête* (*A Tempest*, 1986) reinterprets Shakespeare's play to call attention to the black struggle.

In Nigeria, Kola Ogunmola (1923–1972) mixed song, dance, and native elements in lyric folk plays. Hubert Ogunde (1916–    ) found inspiration in the Western music hall as he combined African folk elements, transvestism, and jazz in plays of social and political protest. Wole Soyinka (1934–    ), an important adaptor of the plays of Euripides, also wrote powerful dramas of the conflict between the African past and the demands of modern industrial society. Critics compared his play *A Dance of the Forests* (1960), a mysterious celebration of tribal animism, with Ibsen's great verse epic, *Peer Gynt*.

e. e. cummings (1894–1962) offered the play *him* (1927), a combination of expressionist, surrealist, and cubist techniques exploring the process of writing plays, the nature of creativity, the relativity of existence, and the modern search for meaning. Robinson Jeffers (1887–1962) wrote *Medea* (1947), *The Cretan Women* (1959), and a version of *Hippolytus* (1928). Richard Eberhart (1904–    ) imagined *Visionary Farms* (1952). Wallace Stevens (1879–1955) explored the effect of nature on objects and objects on nature with *Three Travellers Watch a Sunset* (1916). With Christopher Isherwood (1904–1986), W. H. Auden (1907–1973) wrote *The Ascent of F6* (1936), a mixture of farce, tragedy, symbolism, and realism in verse and popular slang depicting rival attempts to climb a sacred mountain. Alone, Auden authored plays portraying the moral and spiritual disintegration of Western civilization, translated plays by Bertolt Brecht, adapted some plays by John Webster and Ernst Toller, and wrote opera libretti. Archibald MacLeish (1892–1982) put Job in modern dress with *J.B.* (1958) and concluded that humanity might "get by" if we blew "on the coal of the heart."

**Novelists**  French novelist André Gide (1869–1951) suggested a return to the conventions of the classical theatre. He produced new translations of Shakespeare, an *Oedipus* (1930), and a stage adaptation of Kafka's novel *The Trial* (1947). Before dying of tuberculosis, Franz Kafka (1883–1924) had written *The Trial* (1925) and *The Castle* (1926), "testimonials of my solitude," which chillingly depicted modern humanity's situation. Kafka's hero was a victim trapped and entangled in an unknowable and uncontrollable system. In Kafka's world individuals, without God or love, eventually agree to their own destruction by falling for the lure of technology. Thomas Mann (1875-1955) wrote of Western bourgeois decay and depravity in *Death in Venice* (1913) and *The Magic Mountain* (1924). Ralph Ellison's (1914-    ) *The Invisible Man* (1952) chronicled a young black man's disillusionment. Marcel Proust (1871-1922) detailed the inescapability of time's destruction of all things in the seven-part *Remembrance of Things Past* (1913-1927).

Subjectivity reigned as the modern writer's perspective. James Joyce (1882-1941) used psychology's ''stream of consciousness'' as a narrative technique in his epics of modern alienated men, *Ulysses* (1922) and *Finnegan's Wake* (1939). His only play, *Exiles* (1918), infused a realistic problem play with stunning symbolism. Gertrude Stein (1874-1946), a student of William James, moved to France and made her home a literary salon. A friend of Picasso and Matisse, Stein hosted the ''lost generation'' of American writers. Her opera libretto, *Four Saints in Three Acts* (1934), and her play, *Yes Is for a Very Young Man* (1944), extended the cubist use of language to the theatre. *Yes Is for a Very Young Man* shows the German occupation of France dividing a family.

Modernism became worldwide. William Faulkner (1897-1962) wrote novels and stories of rural America with an inner psychological flow of memories, dreams, and recollections. Russian author Vladimir Nabokov (1899-1977) played with words, reality, and identity with *Ada* (1969) and *Pnin* (1957). Gabriel Garcia Marquez (1928-    ) made *One Hundred Years of Solitude* (1967), his magical story of a Columbian family's epic struggle for existence, a metaphor for the Modern age. Czechoslovakian Milan Kundera (1929-    ) reinvigorated the novel with *The Book of Laughter and Forgetting* (1980) and *The Unbearable Lightness of Being* (1984); his play, *Jacques and his Master* (1985), saluted his hero, Denis Diderot.

A major current in modern literature sought to accomplish the romantic dream of integrating individuals in nature. Poets like W. H. Auden, Wallace Stevens, Theodore Roethke (1908-1963), Robert Bly (1926-    ), Denise Levertov (1923-    ), and Gary Snyder (1930-    ) mirrored the physicists' image of a single consciousness permeating the universe. Bly explained:

The poet does not insist on presenting all the events of his life, and doesn't refuse to present them either. He brings in enough to make his poem his, but is sparing, so that space opens behind the details, just as there is space between stars in a constellation, so that through space the reader may see the outer world, may see the mountain night.[8]

This description could apply equally well to modern theatre workers. Modern theatre people selected from their subjective experiences and arranged the pieces in the four dimensions of the space-time continuum. Space framed the stage action; the action framed the stage space. Each depended on the other for existence.

***The Critics Respond***   Since the subject of modern art and theatre was the process of creating art and theatre, modern criticism occupied itself with criticizing that very process. Modern critics like Roland Barthes (1915-1980), Michel Foucault (1926-1984), Jacques Derrida (1930-    ), and Jacques Lacan (1901-1981) focused attention on how art and theatre are conceived, perceived, and received. They extended the critical perspective to consider all things—history, the weather, wine—as ''texts'' worthy of serious and detailed critical analysis. Since earlier critics had sought to understand art works and plays by providing coherent interpretations which revealed a clear and stable meaning, modern critics outside the theatre took the name ''postmodern'' to announce their different goals.

Post-modern criticism in literature and the visual arts joined modern theatre criticism in revealing art's equivocations and contradictions. Critics found modern theatre and postmodern art self-deconstructing; the art both made assertions and undercut its assertions at the same time. "Deconstruction" delighted in locating points at which art and theatre violated the very rules and conventions they seem to have established.

The philosophy of Edmund Husserl (1859–1938) and Martin Heidegger (1889–1976) known as *phenomenology* invaded criticism, as theatrical meaning and artistic unity came to reside neither in the work of art nor on the stage, but rather in the audience of a particular historical moment. Deconstructionism went so far as to deny the possibility of separating or differentiating the reader from the poem, the viewer from the painting, or the audience from the performance. Spectators and critics could separate themselves from art no more than physicists could separate themselves from laboratory experiments.

The modern theatre also challenged the dominance of "the word" in art. English theatre critic Gordon Craig blasted the "literary" theatre and advocated a "perishable" theatre of process like the *commedia dell'arte*. The prophet Antonin Artaud (1896–1948) marshaled his own considerable gift with language to redefine the role of diction in the modern theatre:

> THE DUTY
> of the writer, of the poet
> is not to shut himself up like a coward in a
>     text, a book, a magazine from which he
>     never comes out
> but on the contrary to go
> into the world
>         to jolt,
>         to attack
>         the mind of the public,
>         otherwise
>         what use is he?
> And why was he born?[9]

The electonic media brought the glut of language under close scrutiny. Language in the modern theatre needed a unique dimension to set it apart from all the words blaring at people.

***The Cold War***  Language blurred people's awareness of the political and economic realities existing at the end of the twentieth century. Competition between the two superpowers led Western and Eastern corporations to move factories close to raw materials, thereby cutting transportation and labor costs. In some cases Christian wealth and power rode roughshod over regional religious beliefs. But as the "underdeveloped" nations holding the raw materials and inexpensive labor prospered, their demands for political, economic, and social justice increased. Prosperity thus increased political instability. Imperialist nations had to choose between removing the industries or risking local takeover. Unemployed workers, both in the industrialized and nonindustrialized nations, demanded jobs to replace the ones lost. Governments responded with incentives to lure industrial investment. As a result, capitalist nations inched toward socialism and socialist nations crept toward capitalism. Economic realities reduced actual political differences. Multinational corporations, the Modern age's primary economic and political forces, cut across national and ideological boundaries. In aesthetic endeavors multinational corporate subsidies to the arts provided not only tax advantages but also favorable public images.

While the educational opportunities necessary for economic advancement increased throughout the modern world, the traditional educational and religious values disappeared. Polish playwright Stanislaw Ignacy Witkiewicz (1885–1939) suggested in 1920 that dramatic art seek to restore some of the feelings lost with the demise of religion:

> It is possible, even if only for a short period, for a form of theatre to arise in which contemporary man, independent of dead myths and beliefs, could experience the metaphysical feelings which ancient man expressed through those myths and beliefs?[10]

Process ruled modern religion and education. Students and congregants concentrated on methodology. Students and teachers, believers and priests, devoted more time to technique than knowledge. Tests of faith and wisdom judged familiarity with procedures and processes.

As the twentieth century closed, modern individuals faced new social challenges. The world's natural resources—oil, fertile soil, forests, fisheries, and grazing land—were fast being depleted. The standard of living in both industrialized and nonindustrialized nations was falling. Governmental deficits increased and spread throughout the world. The threat of famine spread to more regions. Worldwide unemployment rose. The population continued to increase at an annual rate of 2 percent. Military exports to nonindustrialized nations exceeded food exports. Nuclear weaponry multiplied and spread. The opportunity for species' annihilation increased. This was the context for the dramatic theatre at the beginning of the twenty-first century.

## THEATRE MOVEMENTS AND MANIFESTOES

The modern theatre began at the close of the nineteenth century. One movement after another announced a new approach to the theatrical event. Ideas about art and theatre constituted important players in the modern theatre. In fact, some argued that the modern theatre rarely gave the plethora of ideas successful concrete representation.

*Symbolism* One of the first challenges to realism brought poet Charles Baudelaire's theory of correspondences to the theatre. "Symbolism" found truth in the subconscious imagination of fantasy. Baudelaire and the symbolists, who denied that bourgeois civilization had progressed spiritually, found the world an ugly and evil place. In the theatre, symbolists employed color, line, and mass to express abstractly their emotional reactions to the world. The symbolists were the last romantics and the first modernists.

In 1886 Jean Moreas issued a Symbolist Manifesto. Symbolists announced their intention to use symbols, as in dreams, to objectify subjective experience. They did not wish to present a subjective view of objective reality. (Expressionists would do that later.) Symbolists replaced external facts with internal feelings, instincts, moods, and opinions. Idealism and spiritualism combined with antirealism to form the symbolist theatre.

Symbolists used language for its suggestive rather than denotative abilities. Symbolist language tried to recapture the magic of shamanistic poetical incantation. Words were thus valued for sound and rhythm rather than for sense or meaning. But the process of naming things also interested the symbolists. Language on stage created an atmosphere of inner reality rather than the logic of psychological discourse. Silences and voids both framed the symbolists' sounds and heightened the atmospherics. Symbolist truth echoed Eastern tranquility rather than Western passion.

In 1890 symbolist poet Paul Fort (1872–1960) opened the *Théâtre Mixte*, which shortly became the *Théâtre d'Art*. Fort's symbolist theatre presented the dark, mysterious, evil, and violent sides of nature housed in nightmares, dreams, fantasies, insanity, perversion, and debauchery. Fort used symbolist words to create the stage decor. Simple settings with few details, resembling Japanese prints, framed the words and the void to evoke the audience's imagination of dark mystery. Maurice Maeterlinck had the first production of his plays at Fort's theatre.

Aurelien-François-Marie Lugne-Poe (1869–1940) also produced symbolist works. Addicted to the works and spirit of American romantic poet Edgar Allen Poe, Lugne-Poe wore black and presented dark, moody productions at his *Théâtre de l'Oeuvre* (founded in 1892). Lugne-Poe produced the modern plays of August Strindberg, Chinese and Sanskrit dramas, and French playwright Alfred Jarry's (1873–1907) *Ubu Roi* (*King Ubu*, 1896), a comic-grotesque Polish *Macbeth*, before closing his theatre in 1899. In the United States and England the "little" and "independent" the-

*A 1910 production of Maurice Maeterlinck's* The Blue Bird. (Culver Pictures)

atres produced symbolist plays along with re-alistic fare.

***Futurism*** In Italy, poet Filippo Tommaso Marinetti (1876–1944) presided over an ide-ological theatre known as "futurism." His *Fu-turist Manifesto* (1905) debuted in Paris, the city of manifestoes. Futurism found inspiration in the speed, energy, and noise of the modern city. The past held all evil for the futurists; they ad-mired newness of any kind. New materials for art and theatre design—glass, sheet metal, wire, electricity, iron, cardboard, leather, and mirrors—were used in new ways. Futurist scenographer Enrico Prampolini (1894–1960) borrowed ideas from Gordon Craig. Futurist sets revealed no painted scenery. Instead, neu-tral architecture created a mechanical mobile of moving scenic panels and units. Moving il-lumination lit the stage. In time Prampolini hoped to devise a set that would both illumi-nate itself and act as a character in the dramatic action.

Industrial machinery became the model for futurist stage scenery, costume, acting, and dramaturgy. The theatrical event was to pre-sent a complex, efficient assemblage of pieces working together. Actors imitated the sound and movement qualities of machines. Futur-ists took old plays apart and reassembled the pieces more efficiently. Machine-like shapes and actions filled the stages. And because ma-chines employed simultaneous actions, the fu-turist theatre presented the simultaneity of events in time.

Machines, moreover, did not speak words, so movement and sound increased in impor-tance in futurist theatre. War, the epitome of machine movement, sound, energy, power, and speed, was glorified. Futurist dancers moved to the sounds of shrapnel and machine gun fire. Futurists advocated urban warfare, burning libraries, and flooding museums; the past had to be erased to make room for the future. Futurists, denying the past's separa-tion of the arts, mixed arts to create picture-poems and kinetic sculptures. Futurist per-formers confronted audiences in their own and others' theatres. They moved audiences around. Performers played among audiences.

Found objects, expecially mass-produced objects, were hailed as great works of futurist art. The dynamic sounds of life were consid-ered music known as *bruitsme*. In *The Art of Noise* (1913) futurists declared all sound, including both everyday sounds and sounds made from found objects, useful material for music. They developed new musical notation and instru-ments. The brevity, multiple focus, and en-ergy of music halls and variety theatres were declared superior to anything the bourgeois theatre could offer. The futurist essay "The Variety Theatre" (1913) was published by Gordon Craig in his *The Mask* of 1914. Other futurists wrote short, energetic, "synthetic" dramas called *sintesi*, each of which was less than a minute long. Futurist playwrights condensed traditional dramas into *sintesi*.

The futurists first employed many of the characteristic principles and techniques of the modern theatre. Futurist drama, for example, eschewed plot, character, thought, psychological motivation, dramatic exposition, climax, and resolution. Instead, futurists presented *The Theatre of Surprise* (1921), as the manifesto labeled it. The logic of realism disappeared, as futurism destroyed the separation of audience from performance space. The fourth wall of realism crashed down with a vengeance, as well. Futurist theatre also moved all media into the performance event. In France, artist Marcel Duchamp (1887–1968), and, in America, artist Joseph Stella (1877–1946), continued to work in the visual arts under the influence of futurist notions, but the movement as a whole ended in 1916. The energy of World War I destroyed even the futurists.

While the futurists attacked Italian audiences, a group of French artists exhibited their work in the Paris Exhibition of 1911 and won the label "cubists." Unlike the futurists, the cubists worked infrequently in the theatre. And unlike the futurists, the cubists thought subject matter unimportant. But the few cubist excursions into the theatre, and the impressive nature of their achievement, influenced other movements more interested in the theatre.

Cubists concentrated on the process of creation. Because they depicted nature as geometrical shapes, objects transformed in cubist paintings and dance-theatre presentations. A newspaper, for example, could become a violin. And real objects were used unnaturally in cubist collages. Found objects were arranged in novel ways, as well. Everyday material became material for sculpture and stage decoration. The cubists thus contributed to the modern questioning of the boundaries between art and life.

***Dada and Surrealism***    After World War I a group of artists in a Zurich cabaret created a movement called "dada" that investigated similar issues. Roumanian poet Tristan Tzara (1886–1963) led group discussions on the death of art and literature in the world of bourgeois greed and materialism. Futurist Marcel Duchamp briefly joined the dadaists and explained their technique: They "took an ordinary article of life, placed it so that its useful significance disappeared under the new title and point of view—created a new thought for that object."

Dada made chance a central player in the modern theatre. Chance, in fact, gave dada its name: it was the first name Tzara and his friends found in the dictionary. A dada performance might include simultaneous box beating, poetry reading, grunting, and duck waddling. Tzara said logic and reason were "the dance of those impotent to create."

In 1923 poet André Breton (1896–1966) broke with dada. He thought it silly—more interested in notoriety than in art. Breton founded "surrealism," a movement taking a name coined by French poet and playwright Guillaume Apollinaire (1880–1918) in 1917. A former medical student, Breton visited psychologist Sigmund Freud and found that the theory of dreams and the unconscious held exciting possibilities for art. Breton wanted art and theatre to explore the psychic world, to fuse the dream and everyday worlds into a "surreality." In 1924 Breton issued the *First Surrealist Manifesto* advocating, like Constantin Stanislavski in Russia, a conscious technique for tapping unconscious creativity.

Surrealism claimed to have descended from romanticism. Like romanticism, surrealism attacked hypocrisy in families, nations, and religions. Surrealists aimed at, in Breton's words, "the total recovery of our psychic force by a means which is nothing other than the dizzying descent into ourselves, the systematic illumination of hidden places and the progressive darkening of other places, the perpetual excursion into the midst of forbidden territory." Surrealist art and theatre questioned the line between reality and unreality, reason and nonsense, deliberation and instinct, knowledge and ignorance, foolishness and utilitarianism. Breton looked for the "point of the mind at which life and death, the real and the imagined, past and future, the communicable and the incommunicable, high and low, cease to be perceived as contradictions."[11]

"Automatism" became a favorite surrealist technique. Artists and writers wrote or painted automatically, without reflection or hesitation, whatever passed their minds. They followed their instincts without censorship or selection. Chance, accident, spontaneity, and free-flowing action and emotion characterized the surrealist technique. *Frottage*, a visual art resulting from the taking of rubbings from everyday objects, became another popular surrealist art.

In 1930 Breton issued the Surrealists' *Second Manifesto*, but the movement broke apart. The rise of fascism and World War II demonstrated that surrealism had made little impact on the world's apparent desire to destroy itself.

***Expressionism*** The term "expressionism" was first used in Germany in 1911 by a group of like-minded artists and theatre workers to describe the spontaneous expression of feeling in art. The next year artist Vassily Kandinsky (1866–1944) published *Concerning the Spriritual in Art*, and critic Rudolf Steiner (1861–1925) explained that art was the best way to understand the spiritual. Like other modern movements, expressionism sought to bring to the stage a dimension of life missing in realism. In 1912 the production of Reinhold Sorge's (1892–1916) *Der Bettler* (*The Beggar*) marked the arrival of expressionism on stage.

Plays became "dream pictures" and "visionary abstracts of reality." Expressionist theatre expressed an "ego" rather than an idea. As with symbolism, the expressionist stage presented a world seen through the eyes of one character in the drama. The expressionist stage was, in addition, often a black void in which flashes of light illuminated fleeting scenes. But expressionism found the world to be distorted rather than symbolical. Exaggerated lines, masses, colors, and sounds revealed a character's "distorted" view of the world. Reality was presented as something that ex-

isted only through the unique perceptions of individuals. Expressionist theatre accused audiences, condemned society, damned God, and rejected the Western civilization that had produced World War I.

Leopold Jessner (1878–1945), director of the Berlin State Theatre from 1919 to 1925, developed mobile platforms and stairs to capture expressionistic fragments of subjective environment. In general, such innovations, as well as projections and cycloramas, played important roles in the expressionist theatre. Max Reinhardt (1873–1943), the director of the *Grosses Schauspielhaus*, also advanced the expressionist movement by touring productions of August Strindberg's late plays and a cycle of dramas by German playwright Frank Wedekind (1864–1918). Reinhardt's development of the revolving stage and innovative use of spotlights futher contributed to the expressionists' ability to create the inside of a mind on stage. With the rise of fascism expressionists moved to safe quarters outside Europe.

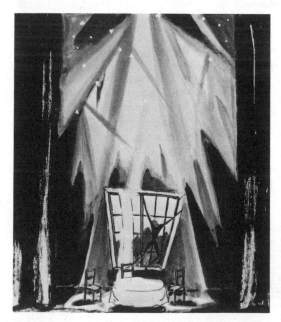

*An expressionist design for a 1919 production of Walter Hasenclaver's* The Son. *(Deutsches Theatermuseum, München)*

*Constructivism*   In Russia playwright Anatoly Lunacharsky (1875–1932), the first head of Soviet education and art, encouraged non-realistic artists like Marc Chagall (1887–1985) and Vassily Kandinsky. "Constructivism" developed as a way to put utilitarianism in abstract form. Constructivists did not believe in "art for art's sake"; art had to have a practical function in the revolutionary order. Like the futurists, constructivists admired the formal efficiency of machines, manufacturing, photography, and technology.

The scientific time-management studies of American Frederick Winslow Taylor (1856–1915) were greatly admired. Constructivist theatre workers experimented with time and motion to make scenery, sculpture, and actors as efficient as machines. Such directors as Vsevelod Meyerhold (1874–1940) and Alexander Tairov (1885–1950) worked to make the form of a stage production fit the function of the play. Theatrical form had to express the thought of the playwright. Often the constructivist stage was an abstract metaphor of the playwright's idea. But when powerful realists questioned the usefulness of constructivism to the masses, constructivist artists left Russia. Finally, in 1932, constructivism was suppressed in an all-out effort to eliminate modernism.

Evolving from a school in Weimar, the *Bauhaus* school of art, architecture, and handicrafts gave constructivism a German outlook. Like cubism, the *Bauhaus*'s direct influence on the theatre was small. Most of the *Bauhaus*'s theatrical efforts, in fact, featured dance. Nevertheless, *Bauhaus* ideas were in the air for the modern theatre to breathe. From the first *Bau-*

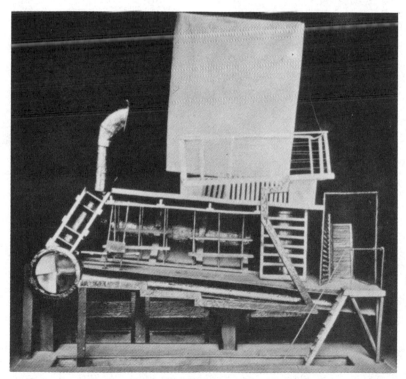

*Alexander Tairov's constructivist setting for Eugene O'Neill's* The Hairy Ape. (Margot Berthold, Weltgeschichte des Theaters, Alfred Kroner Verlag, Stuttgart)

*haus* director, Walter Gropius (1883–1969), to Mies van der Rohe (1886–1969), the last director, the school fused art with technology to produce a social revolution.

Like constructivism, *Bauhaus* form derived from function. French architect Le Corbusier (1887–1965) defined a house as a "machine for living." Everything in art and craft was conceived as a machine. With the advent of World War II *Bauhaus* artists joined the growing number of exiled European artists living in New York.

**Epic Theatre**   While director of Berlin's *Volksbühne*, Erwin Piscator (1893–1966) explored the relationship between the epic and the dramatic modes first contrasted by Aristotle. With an assistant named Bertolt Brecht (1898–1956), Piscator invented "epic theatre." Piscator's theatre narrated, with frank theatrical presentations of raw data, a story of many episodes and characters. Films, photos, charts, and an array of stage technologies let Piscator stage newspaper accounts, short stories, and novels. The epic theatre later evolved into America's story theatre, the dramatization by openly presentational means of fairy tales, folk myths, short stories, and novels.

Piscator and Brecht produced an ideological theatre. They thought the perilous times denied anyone the right to neutrality. Their epic staging resulted in such expressionistic dramas as Ernst Toller's (1893–1939) *Hoppla, wir leben!* (*Hurrah, We Live*, 1927), Alexei Tolstoy's *Rasputin* (1925), and Jaroslav Hasek's (1883–1923) landmark, *The Good Soldier Schweik* (1927).

Brecht produced a table contrasting the "dramatic" with the "epic" theatres:

| DRAMATIC THEATRE | EPIC THEATRE |
|---|---|
| plot | narrative |
| implicates the spectator in a stage situation | turns the spectator into an observer, but |
| wears down his capacity for action | arouses his capacity for action |
| provides him with sensations | forces him to make decisions |
| experience | picture of the world |
| the spectator is involved in something | he is made to face something |
| suggestion | argument |
| instinctive feelings are preserved | brought to the point of recognition |
| the spectator is in the thick of it, shares the experience | the spectator stands outside, studies |
| the human being is taken for granted | the human being is the object of the inquiry |
| he is unalterable | he is alterable and able to alter |
| eyes on the finish | eyes on the course |
| one scene makes another | each scene for itself |
| growth | montage |
| linear development | jumps |
| man as a fixed point | man as a process |
| thought determines being | social being determines thought |
| feeling | reason[12] |

Piscator, meanwhile, introduced film and projection both to narrate his story and to act in the plot. Moving platforms carried the epic action. When fascists accused Brecht and Piscator of being Bolshevik Jews the two German Lutherans went to America.

In the United States, Piscator formed a Dramatic Workshop at the New School for Social Research and Brecht, before wrangling with the House Committee on Un-American Activities, wrote his best plays. The East German government invited Brecht back to Germany after the war to establish the Berliner Ensemble, where his great plays were finally produced. After the war Piscator rocked the West with a production of Rolf Hochhuth's *The Deputy*, an examination of the Pope's activities during World War II.

Americans applied Piscator's epic techniques in Living Newspapers presented by the Federal Theatre Project of the Works Progress Administration. Plays like *Triple-A Plowed Un-*

*Erwin Piscator's 1927 epic production of Ernst Toller's* Hurrah, We Live! *(Margot Berthold, Weltgeschichte des Theaters, Alfred Kroner Verlag, Stuttgart)*

*der, Ethiopia, One-Third of a Nation,* and *Spirochete* let Americans understand the tumultuous events of the Great Depression. Created by playwright Elmer Rice (1892–1967), the Living Newspaper Unit pioneered group-created theatre events. Each Newspaper was written by an editorial staff.

Piscator's epic theatre, along with the Living Newspapers, created a theatrical newsreel. Projections, direct quotations, montages of short scenes, typed characters, shadowgraphs, and shadow plays responded to the comments and editorials of a Loudspeaker and answered the questions of a character named the Common Man.

Other artists modified the epic theatre's techniques. In *The Cradle Will Rock* (1938), for example, Marc Blitstein (1905–1964) attacked capitalism. American playwright Thornton Wilder (1897–1975) applied epic technique to middle-class America. Wilder's plays celebrate the human survival instinct in an existential world. *Our Town* (1938)—Grover's Corners, New Hampshire—for example, houses common people experiencing life's heartaches and joys while affirming the dignity of humanity. A stage manager narrates the action and addresses the audience directly. Pantomime and presentational scenic elements on a bare stage induce imaginative participation by the audience. The history of Excelsior, New Jersey, from primitive society to 1942, shows humanity getting on by *The Skin of Our Teeth* (1943). Wilder's epic play mixes drawing-room comedy with expressionistic techniques. Actors talk about the play while presenting the characters.

Playwright Paul Green (1894–1981) and German composer Kurt Weill (1900–1950) revolutionized American musicals and opera with the epic antiwar drama *Johnny Johnson* (1936). Johnny, a small-town innocent, gets caught up in love and World War I fever but ends up a disillusioned beggar selling war toys on a street corner. Expressionist scenes, such as one presenting the League of Nations in an asylum, present an honest man destroyed by an insane world.

In Australia, the poet Dorothy Hewett (1923–    ) explored epic technique with both *The Chapel Perilous* (1971) and her rock opera, *Catspaw* (1974). Louis Nowra (1950–    )

likewise experimented with Piscator's ideas with *Inner Voices* (1977). In Canada, James Reaney (1926–    ) went directly to the epic theatre's Asian sources to create *Colours in the Dark* (1967), a forty-two scene transformational drama told from within the mind of an ailing child. George Rya (1932–    ) depicted the place of the American Indian in contemporary society using epic technique in *The Ecstasy of Rita Joe* (1967).

The epic theatre continued realism's so-called objectivity but replaced realism's scientific determinism with a political and ideological bias. The epic theatre abolished illusionism by mixing epic, dramatic, and lyric modes in a total theatre event. Coordinating the massive undertaking accelerated the modern director's rise to power.

***A Director's Theatre***   The modern theatre's eclecticism demanded a director to decide the style of each production. Directors controlled the shape of the modern theatre both from their writing desks and in their rehearsal halls. One of the first great formulators of the modern vision was Gordon Craig.

In 1905 Craig's *The Art of the Theatre* announced that the dramatic art was comprised of "action which is the very spirit of acting; words, which are the body of the play; line and colour, which are the very heart of the scene; rhythm, which is the very essence of dance."[13] Craig stunned many by insisting that no one part of the theatrical art should dominate, though he did concede that action was the most valuable component. Indeed, he restored plot action to the structural dominance over character first described by Aristotle.

Craig favored a theatre ruled by a strong stage director who would ensure unity in the production. Craig's chief enthusiast was director Max Reinhardt (1873–1943), a former bank clerk and actor for Otto Brahm. Reinhardt suited the style, form, and methodology of his productions to the particular style and form of the plays he directed. Reinhardt's eclecticism borrowed from both Eastern and Western historical styles and periods. Teams of assistants followed the meticulous plans Reinhardt outlined in his *Regiebuch* (promptbook) for each production. Reinhardt stated that "there is no one style of theatre which is more artistic than the others. All the old forms are equally valuable if illuminated by the genius of a director." The subsequent history of the theatre validated Reinhardt's claim.

*Gordon Craig's design for a setting utilizing mobile screens.   (Stage Yearbook, 1914)*

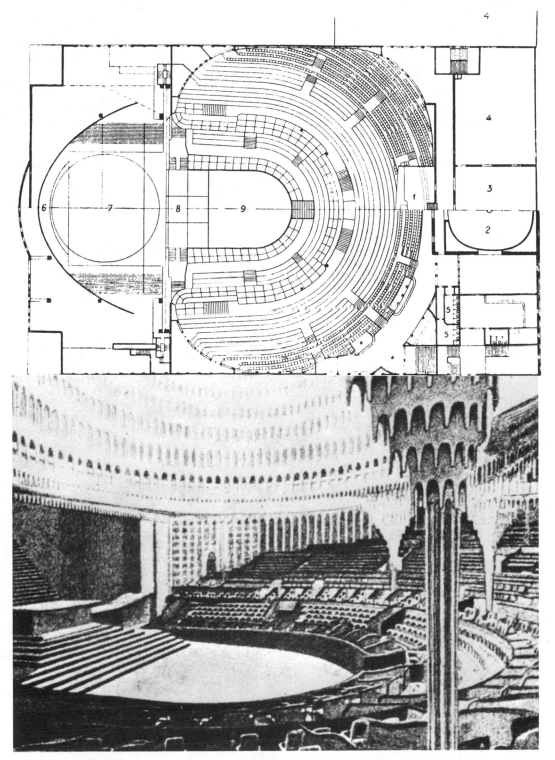

*A floorplan and interior of Max Reinhardt's Grosses Schauspielhaus in 1919.*
(Barkhin, *Teatra Architectura,* Moscow)

Directors' names often topped the titles of the plays. Among these directors was Yevgeny Vakhtangov (1883–1922), who departed from Constantin Stanislavski's realism as head of the Moscow Popular Art Theatre's First Studio. His constructivist ideas created a "fantastic realism." Another, Alexander Tairov (1885–1950), founded Moscow's Kamerny Theatre to create a "synthetic theatre," which combined the rhythms and techniques of the music hall, circus, sporting arena, opera, and ballet.

In France, Gaston Baty (1885–1952) wrote *Sire la Mot*, which attacked the supremacy of the text and advocated a total theatre event. By playing with mime, dance, Japanese techniques, and the *commedia dell'arte*, Charles Dullin (1885–1949) explored the possibilities of spectacle as a replacement for language. Jean-Louis Barrault (1910–    ), his student, directed the premieres of many plays by Bertolt Brecht and Eugène Ionesco.

In England, Peter Brook (1925–    ) directed opera, Shakespeare, and the premieres of plays by Swiss playwright Friedrich Durrenmatt (1921–    ), author of *The Visit* (1956), and German playwright Peter Weiss (1916–1982). To find common theatrical techniques and vocabularies that cut across cultural boundaries, Brook investigated Antonin Artaud's Theatre of Cruelty before founding the *Centre International de Créations Théâtricales*. Peter Hall (1930–    ) directed Great Britain's National Theatre and presented new interpretations of Shakespeare and the premieres of modern authors, including Harold Pinter (1930–    ). Charles Marowitz (1934–    ), codirector of Brook's Theatre of Cruelty Workshop, founded the Open Space Theatre and continued the investigation and application of Artaudian ideas.

Jerzy Grotowski (1933–    ) stripped the dramatic theatre to the bone in his Polish Laboratory Theatre. Eliminating all nonessentials, his "Poor Theatre" left only the actor with the audience. Grotowski rearranged texts and actor-audience proximities for each production. His actors, who lived as communal ascetics, appeared as shamen to reveal the depths of their psyches in sacrificial performances. Texts, confronted and disassembled, created a unique experience for both actor and audience. Grotowski's company found inspiration in theatres as diverse as Constantin Stanislavski's Moscow Popular Art Theatre, the Indian kathakali, and the Japanese noh.

*Peter Brook's Persian* Orghast Part II.    (Nicolas Tikhomiroff)

*Peter Brook's 1984 production of Verdi's* Carmen.    (Martha Swope)

*Jerzy Grotowski's* Akropolis.    (Teatr-Laboratorium)

In time, Grotowski drifted to an interest in psychodrama and personal, therapeutic theatrical activities. In 1976 Grotowski disbanded his company. In America, his Theatre of Sources extended his interest in private psychological and physical confrontations. Grotowski's prominence brought other central European directors, such as Andrei Serban (1943–    ) and Livui Ciulei (1923–    ), to Western attention. Their reinterpretation of Western classics confirmed Craig's belief in a balanced use of the full spectrum of theatre arts in performance.

In America, the central Europeans witnessed the work of other directors. Joseph Papp (1921–    ) founded the New York Shakespeare Festival to produce new interpretations of Shakespeare and the plays of such modern authors as Sam Shepard (1943–    ). In 1946 Julian Beck (1925–1985) started the Living Theatre and presented the plays of such modernists as Gertrude Stein, T. S. Eliot, Alfred Jarry, August Strindberg, and Bertolt Brecht. In time, the company's political and social convictions led to group-created pieces that confronted the audience with political challenges and social ultimata.

Other directors were visible as well. One member of the Living Theatre, Joseph Chaiken (1935–    ) began the Open Theatre in 1964 to develop collective theatre works through theatre games invented by Viola Spolin. Richard Schechner (1934–    ), a university professor and coproducer of the Free Southern Theatre, founded the Performance Group in 1968 to develop a collective company within an environmental theatre. Schechner tested some of Grotowski's ideas in an American context. In 1970 Peter Schumann (1934–    ) moved his Bread and Puppet Theatre commune to rural New England, where giant puppet shamen and live performers created contemporary rituals and dramatized modern myths with music and dance. Each performance ended with actors' sharing bread with the audience. Robert Wilson (1944–    ) and his Byrd Hoffman School of Byrds revived Walter Pater's aestheticism in abstract mod-

*The Living Theatre's* Frankenstein *in 1969.* (Gianfranco Mantegua)

*The Open Theatre's production of* The Serpent. (Karl Bissinger)

ern dress. Architecture, dance, pantomime, and music combined to form human mobiles and collages that challenged the audience's sensitivity to time and space.

Modern directors drew inspiration from Gordon Craig and other early superstar di-

rectors. One of the most influential modern directors was Jacques Copeau (1879–1949), who founded the *Théâtre du Vieux Colombier* in 1913 to simplify the theatrical event by getting rid of technology. Copeau worked mostly with classical texts as "an antidote to bad taste and

*The Bread and Puppet Theater's Domestic Resurrection Circus.* (Photo by Ron Levin)

aesthetic fad.'' He eliminated the footlights and the proscenium arch. In his acting school and dramatic productions *le treteau nu* (bare stage) let the text alone stimulate the imaginations of both actors and audience. Copeau spent two years in New York during World War I. He returned to France and withdrew his company to the countryside, where it explored mask work and noh technique to discover the essence of acting.

Copeau set the standard for later modern directors' ability to transform a text into theatrical poetry. But in 1929 Copeau retired, leaving his company to Michel Saint-Denis (1897–1971), who created the *Compagnie des Quinze* and reopened the *Vieux Colombier* in 1931. With instruction in mime, acrobatics, musical instrumentation, singing, and improvisation, Saint-Denis continued Copeau's attention to acting. In 1934 Saint-Denis's company disbanded, but he continued the Copeau tradition in the acting schools he opened in London, Montreal, and New York. Copeau's assistant, Louis Jouvet (1887–1951), also continued his mentor's work with revolutionary reinterpretations of the classics.

***Bertolt Brecht*** Like Copeau, Bertolt Brecht (1898–1956), Erwin Piscator's disciple and a modern superstar director, respected the dramatic text. In fact, Brecht wrote and rewrote the plays he directed. He worked to create a theatrical experience that placed the audience in a skeptical point of view toward what happened on the stage. Because Brecht believed a bit more skepticism would have prevented the horrors of the Modern age, his theatre tried to develop the habit of skepticism in the modern audience. Brecht wanted neither actor nor audience to lose themselves, to escape, or to forget that the events on stage were not real. He wanted actors and audiences to confront, consciously and rationally, both themselves and the stage, so that they might learn what needed to be done in society.

The means of Brecht's theatre visibly reminded the audience of the artificial nature of both the stage picture and, by analogy, the events of everyday life. The stage's illusion of reality was just as changeable and unrealistic as people's illusion of everyday reality. Emotional sympathy or empathy with characters and situations interfered with the actors' and audience's ability to remain skeptical. Brecht wanted his audience to ask whether situations and people, both on stage and in life, deserved sympathy or empathy.

The classical Chinese theatre inspired Brecht to envision the modern epic theatre. In the article ''Alienation Effects in Chinese Acting'' (1936), Brecht first mentioned the *Verfremdungseffekt* (the alienation effect) in acting. After watching the great Beijing actor Mei-lan Feng, Brecht concluded that Chinese actors kept the audience at a distance by, paradoxically, playing directly to the audience. Direct playing to the audience kept both actors and audience self-conscious; they could thus not

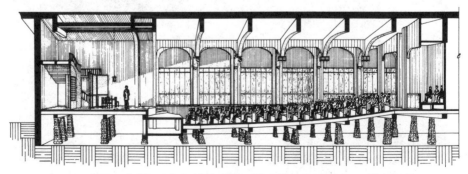

*Jacques Copeau's Theatre du Vieux Colombier, France.* (Izenour, *Theatre Design,* p. 196. By permission of McGraw Hill Book Company.)

Caspar Neher's setting for the 1926 production of Bertolt Brecht's first play, Baal.

lose themselves in the characters. For his theatre Brecht wanted to distill the objectivity of science from the hypnotism of realism. Brecht favored the science of human relationships over the science of biological determinism.

In both directing and writing Brecht underlined the man-made "historical conditions" that alter human relationships. Historical circumstances were more important to him than the psychological circumstances of any individual character. A Marxist, Brecht envisioned a theatre that showed the social effects of dialectical materialism. Change would be displayed as basic to life; men and women would see that they could change life and the world. Brecht observed, "If art reflects life it does so with special mirrors."[14]

Brecht's stage direction emphasized the episodic nature of a plot by providing spaces and silences for reflection and judgment between the scenes. He directed each scene as a little self-contained play; each scene's title summarized the scene's *gestus* (point). Brecht deliberately avoided the motivation of songs or dances; he wanted abrupt shifts to keep the audience from making an emotional investment in the action.

When working with composers such as Kurt Weill and Paul Dessau, Brecht insisted that music neither support nor accompany the lyrics. Music, like each element of the epic theatre, was to comment on and react to the lyrics. As Brecht's music refrained from creating atmosphere, his settings did not represent place. Brecht created a Marxist *Gesamtkunstwerk* (master art work) in which each individual art maintained its independence. Brecht's epic theatre gathered the arts, employing each according to the moment's need, and using each according to the art's ability to clarify the moment. Brecht observed that "Every art contributes to the greatest art of all, the art of living."[15]

***Vsevelod Meyerhold***   In the Soviet Union, Vsevelod Meyerhold (1874–1940) worked to celebrate the Russian Revolution with a revolutionary approach to the theatrical event. The son of a rich merchant, Meyerhold gave up law school to study with Nemirovich-Danchenko at the Moscow Philharmonic School. Later he joined the Moscow Popular Art Theatre. A great actor, Meyerhold nevertheless had difficulty with Stanislavski's approach to

*A 1980 production in New York of Bertolt Brecht's* Mother Courage and her Children. (Martha Swope)

acting. Meyerhold had read Gordon Craig and the symbolists. He wondered why actors should ignore the audience, the center of the dramatic theatre. Meyerhold suggested the audience "accept instead a theatre that speaks to you directly, that doesn't try to move you to believe in a palpable falsehood." In 1905 Stanislavski gave Meyerhold the leadership of the Moscow Popular Art Theatre's new First Studio and launched him on a career that explored alternatives to realistic performance.

Meyerhold, who worked throughout Russia under the name "Dr. Dappertuto," began by working on a play by Maurice Maeterlinck. In 1906 he staged *The Life of Man* by Leonid Andreyev (1871–1919). The production featured a grey cyclorama, one lighting instrument, and mask-like make-up. In Minsk, Meyerhold developed an interest in circus and music-hall techniques. He concluded that mime was superior to language in the theatre.

To train actors Meyerhold reintroduced gymnastics and *commedia dell'arte* improvisation. He also explored ways to break down the barrier between stage and auditorium. He once placed actors in the aisles and urged audience participation. For his 1910 *Don Juan* by Molière, Meyerhold took out the proscenium and front curtain, hung chandeliers over the stage and auditorium, costumed the stage hands to move scenery and properties, and left the house lights on during the action.

Constructivism appealed to Meyerhold as an exciting alternative to bourgeois realism. He revised his theatre by permanently removing the front curtain and cyclorama to expose the back wall and lighting instruments. He also used scaffolding to create a stage machine for acting. "Biomechanics" was Meyerhold's acting version of constructivism; the physical movement of the actors—who wore overalls—would stir the emotions of the audience. Throughout his career Meyerhold worked to develop an alternative to psychologically based acting. His 1926 version of Nikolai Gogol's *The Government Inspector* capped his career and prompted an investigation of experimentation in Soviet arts.

*Vsevolod Meyerhold's production of Dumas's* Lady of the Camellias. *(University of Bristol Theatre Collection)*

From 1928 to 1953 Soviet dictator Joseph Stalin (1879–1953) denounced modernism as an enemy of socialist realism; in 1938 Meyerhold was condemned as an enemy of the state. Yet just before he died, Stanislavski supposedly said, "Take care of Meyerhold; he is my sole heir in the theatre—here or anywhere else."[16] Still, three days after Meyerhold defended experimentation at the All-Union Convention of Theatre Directors in 1939, he was

*Vsevolod Meyerhold's production of Molière's* Don Juan. *(University of Bristol Theatre Collection)*

*Vsevolod Meyerhold's production of Gogol's* The Government Inspector. (University of Bristol Theatre Collection)

deported to a concentration camp and never seen again. His wife's mutilated body was discovered not long after.

*Antonin Artaud*   Though his practical experience in the theatre was minimal, no one shaped the direction of the modern theatre, or personally understood the cruelty of the Modern age, more than Antonin Artaud (1896–1948). Essays Artaud wrote between 1931 and 1937, collected as *The Theatre and Its Double*, inspired, challenged, confounded, and infuriated generations of theatre workers. Artaud attacked Western theatre for having a psychological and intellectual bias; he preferred the Eastern religious and metaphysical theatre. Artaud urged Western theatre to return to the ceremonial roots of magic, myth, ritual, and dance. In Artaud's theatre modern individuals could submerge their personal troubles for group purgation in the collective miseries of humanity.

A visit to a Balinese dance troupe at the 1931 Paris Exposition started Artaud's impassioned writing about the theatre. He witnessed a dancer enter a trance, become possessed by dance, and thereby acquire a mysterious power over the audience. With the surrealists, Artaud had edited an issue of *La révolution surréaliste*, and praised the Asian interest in the inner theatrical life as superior to Western dramatic materialism and logic. In 1927 Artaud had founded the *Théâtre Alfred Jarry* with playwright Roger Vitrac (1899–1952). The search for a magical theatre even took Artaud to live among, and smoke peyote with, the Tarahumara Indians. This search, however, finally put Artaud in an asylum, between 1937 and 1946.

Artaud's theatre was to be a sensory experience where people and the forces of the universe met and communed. Like Brecht, Artaud was moved by the enormity of the problems facing modern humanity. Like Brecht, too, Artaud believed the theatre could help humanity. But Artaud's prescription could not have been more different than Brecht's. Artaud's theatre would exorcise the emotional, psychological, and moral demons plaguing modern people. If Brecht's theatre were a classroom, Artaud's would be a hospital operating room.

Artaud's medical theatre would heal the sick with whatever means were necessary. For severe cases like modern humanity, healing would have the cruelty of a plague. Artaud maintained that "in the theatre everything is permissible except barrenness and banality." He cried, "Retheatricalize the theatre. . . . We must wait and seize the images that arise in us, naked, natural, excessive, and follow these images to the very end."[17]

Artaud's theatre would be different at each performance. Each performance, in fact, had to be different and seemingly unrepeatable. Artaud wanted metaphysics in action, incantational language, danger, puppets, dance, music, magic, exorcism, sensory hieroglyphics, masks, and distorted objects. A director must invent the performance without a text and, with the spectators at the center of the action, directly confront and commune with them. The purpose was "to drain abcesses collectively."[18] Artaud would attack the audience's central nervous system and go directly at the collective subconscious. His Theatre of Cruelty would be aesthetic shock therapy involving moral cruelty—first cleansing, then transfiguring, and finally exalting humanity. Artaud's theatre would be cruel to be kind.

*New Acting Theory*  Modern directors and theoreticians placed the actors at the center of the modern theatre. But chief among the modern theatre's problems was the creation of an acting style to replace the psychological, detailed impersonation of realism.

Gordon Craig raised actors' ire with his use of the term *Uber-marionette* to describe his vision of the modern actor. He used the image to challenge actors to return to the masked performance conventions of the Eastern and Western classical theatres. Craig disliked the Stanislavski goal of making actors seem "natural" by repeating everyday psychological behavior. Craig wanted actors who seemed "supernatural." In any event he thought great actors were "born" rather than educated. And Craig tossed off the troublesome "paradox" of Denis Diderot by espousing Jamesian pragmatism: Actors should "feel" as much or as little as they need.

The development of electronic media increased the pressure on actors to seem "natural" by withdrawing their bodies and voices to a scale appropriate to the microphone and camera lens. In time, the ability to play convincingly on a stage declined. Theatres installed microphones and reduced size so that audiences could see and hear the electronically conditioned actors' performances.

The great directors offered advice to modern actors. Brecht worked with actors to develop a style that discouraged audience identification. He urged actors, rather, to identify and stress the dissimilarities between themselves and the characters. Brecht asked his actors to analyze not the characters but what took place in a scene. Brecht pointed out the differences between a play's circumstances and those of the actors' world. He even suggested that, rather than *become* a character, an actor *present* a character for evaluation by the audience. Brecht thus suggested that actors quote the characters in third-person voices. Brecht hoped to break the realistic "illusion of the first time." He encouraged actors to acknowledge frankly the changes in the manner of playing prose, poetry, and song. In rehearsals Brecht also asked actors to swap roles to gain wider social perspectives on their characters.

The wide variety of ideas about acting made modern actors leery about claiming their position at the center of the theatrical event. With each director came new ideas about the appropriate style for the play and period. Most actors did, in fact, become the puppets Gordon Craig had envisioned. The high unemployment rate among actors forced them to make their modern dominance only theoretical. Directors interpreted plays and characters, and designers selected the costumes and properties. The actors were left with little more to do than show up and be heard. After all, the electronic media rewarded actors who did just that before a lens and microphone. Great acting came to mean the ability to just live in public without change. In an incredible age, believability in acting was the ultimate goal. Modern actors faced a perplexing situation.

In America Viola Spolin devised improvisational games to free actors "to relate and act, involving [themselves] in the moving changing world. . . .'' In keeping with the modern conception of humanity and the universe, Spolin's actors worked from intuition, seeking an organic involvement with the environment. Actors were encouraged to strive for spontaneity—to trust their immediate responses. Spontaneity was the key to truth in acting: ''Through spontaneity we are re-formed into ourselves. It creates an explosion that for the moment frees us from handed-down frames of reference, memory choked with old facts and information and undigested theories and techniques of other people's findings.''[19] Acting could not follow objective criteria; subjectivity guided the modern actor's work.

Like matter in the universe, Spolin's actors developed techniques of transformation. ''Transforming, whether it be of character, object, or idea, seems to be essentially what must take place within every scene improvisation. It is the excitement and energy of every scene—it's life process.''[20] Spolin's exercises could have been modern physicists' descriptions of quantum mechanics or modern psychologists' analyses of contemporary behavior: Character Agility, Difficulty with Small Objects, Exchanging Where, Exploration of Larger Environment, Gibberish, Give and Take, Feeling Self with Self, Hidden Problem, How Old Am I?, Inability to Move, Object Moving Players, Ruminating, Seeing the World, Shadowing, Silent Scream, Space Substance (Transformation of Objects), Television Exercise, Trapped, Wandering Speech, What Am I Listening To? What Time Is It? Who Started the Motion? As always, actors played the envisioned world order.

In the West, mainstream theatres continued to feature white actors. Despite the fact that the white race constitutes a global minority, nonwhite faces on the Western stage were a rarity. At the same time, nonwhite theatre companies suffered from a weak economic base, dependent for the most part on grants from white corporations and foundations. Nonwhite theatre artists continued to be excluded from full participation in the modern theatre.

***Reconceived Stage Space*** Space was reconstituted not only by physicists but also by modern scenographers. In part, modern scene design compensated visually for the lack of spiritual resonance in realistic prose texts. Stage space took over the metaphor construction once carried out by poetic language, and mass, line, and color created the rhythm once carried by verse. In fact, realistic productions often employed modern scenic designers to provide the missing mythic, rhythmic, spiritual, and poetic dimensions.

Modern scene design, first of all, abandoned the quest to reproduce on stage the accumulated details of observable reality. Gordon Craig and Adolph Appia (1862–1928), a shy Swiss, pioneered the modern reassessment of stage space. In the pamphlet ''Staging Wagnerian Drama'' (1891) and in *Die Musik und Die Inscenierung* (1899), Appia presented an abstract rendition of Richard Wagner's vision of a synthesis of scenery with actor. Light was Appia's harmonizing medium. His stage housed elements that created a sensory atmosphere rather than an observable appearance. Suggestive and evocative scenery let the audience complete the vision in its imagination.

In Appia and Craig's designs, three-dimensional masses, illuminated to accentuate height, width, and depth, made the three-dimensional actor appear at home on the stage. Geometric shapes, ramps, and staircases replaced painted perspective wings, drops, and flats. Like Craig, Appia considered dynamic movement the key to stage design. In time, modern designers worked to make every element on stage mobile.

Stage space thus came alive in the modern theatre. Moreover, the changing nature of the universe found representation in the fluidity of modern stage space. Realistic painted details had presented false, static illusions. Modern designers painted with light instead, thereby defining, revealing, and constantly changing the visible atmosphere of the on-stage mood. Light became the visual equivalent of music; it was as important to modern theatre designers as to modern physicists. Physicist Albert Einstein, too, had discovered that space was a

*Adolph Appia's 1895 design for Wagner's* Parsifal.

player. And, just as physicists abandoned observation for imagination, modern designers forsook observable reality for the products of the imagination.

The stage space became the manifestation of what a play conjured in the designer's unconscious imagination. Modern scenery represented the inner consciousness of a designer rather than the exterior historical reality of a particular fixed time and place. The place and time of modern scene design resided in the imagination of a designer's inner reality. Modern stage design thus presented a subjective vision of the inner nature of particular times and places.

In America, the ideas of Appia and Craig were labeled the "new stagecraft" to distinguish them from the realistic objectives of scene design. Robert Edmund Jones (1887–1954), Donald Oenslager (1902–1975), Norman Bel Geddes (1883–1958), Boris Aronson (1900–1980), Howard Bay (1912–1986), and Jo Mielziner (1901–1976) brought America prominence in the representation of modern stage pictures, even in the design of realistic texts.

The epic theatre presented a different conception of stage space. Mordecai Gorelik (1899–     ), a designer who moved between epic and new stagecraft techniques, called the epic space "the inductive setting." Like the new stagecraft, the epic design was nonillusionistic. But unlike new stagecraft, the epic design sought neither beauty nor psychological effect. The inductive setting was, above all, utilitarian. As in the *Bauhaus*, form followed function.

Epic design echoed Vsevelod Meyerhold's insistence that beauty be utilitarian: "We must realize that the beauty of Ford's car is a direct outcome of its efficiency and reliability."[21] The epic setting neither imitated nor symbolized; it presented what was necessary for the action in a scene. Bertolt Brecht explained:

> It's more important nowadays for the set to tell the spectator he's in a theatre than to tell him he's in, say, Aulis. The theatre must acquire *qua* theatre the same fascinating reality as a sporting arena during a boxing match. The best thing is to show the machinery, the ropes and the flies. If the set represents a town it must look like a town that has been built to last precisely two hours . . . there mustn't be any faking.[22]

Epic light was just stage light, not an imitation of some other kind of natural or artificial light.

During the Modern era theatre spaces shrank, both to facilitate the actors' diminished ability to fill large spaces convincingly and to accommodate the reduced number of people who wanted and could afford attendance. As a result, stage settings of necessity

*Robert Edmund Jones's 1921 design for Sakespeare's* Macbeth. (*Theatre Arts Magazine,* 1924)

*Jo Mielziner's design for Arthur Miller's* Death of a Salesman. (By permission of the estate of Jo Mielziner.)

were simplified. Plays were staged in churches, public halls, public works, hotel lobbies, airplane hangers, parking lots, boxing arenas, swimming pools—any place, in fact, either appropriate to the plays or inexpensive to use. In addition, with increasing production costs brought on by unionization, designs relied more and more on costume, light, and suggestive set pieces. At the same time, alternative actor-audience relationships were sought to replace box, pit, and gallery proscenium theatres. Thrust stages, arena stages, and "environmental theatres" also appeared.

***Environmental Theatre*** Environmental theatre created new actor and audience performance spaces for each production. As in Happenings, environmental theatres used all of the available space for actors and audience alike. Like Happenings, environmental theatres gave actors and audience a multiple focus on events. Richard Schechner, an environmental theorist and practitioner, explained:

Environmental theater encourages give-and-

take throughout a globally organized space in which the areas occupied by the audience are a kind of island or continent in the midst of the audience. The audience does not sit in regularly arranged rows; there is one whole space rather than two opposing spaces. The environmental use of space is fundamentally collaborative; the action flows in many directions sustained only by the cooperation of performers and spectators.[23]

The arrangement of the environmental performance space grew out of the rehearsals; action, text, and space evolved through group collaboration. Schechner listed the principles:

1. For each production the whole space is designed.
2. The design takes into account space-senses and space-fields.
3. Every part of the environment is functional.
4. The environment evolves along with the play it embodies.
5. The performer is included in all phases of planning and building.[24]

The environmental theatre, along with col-

*The Performance Group's* Dionysus in 69.   (Max Waldman)

lective creation, reflected a desire for society to move in the direction of collective and creative solutions to world problems. Schechner, like Brecht before him, drew a table to contrast the "new" theatre with the "traditional" theatre:

| TRADITIONAL | NEW |
|---|---|
| plot | images/events |
| action | activity |
| resolution | open-ended |
| roles | tasks |
| themes/thesis | no pre-set meaning |
| stage distinct from house | one area for all |
| script | scenario or free form |
| flow | compartments |
| single focus | multifocus |
| audience watches | audience participates, sometimes does not exist |
| product | process.[25] |

Josef Svoboda (1920–    ), the Czechoslovakian National Theatre designer from 1948, worked in traditional theatre spaces but pioneered in the design and use of technology in scene design. Svoboda's Polycran system of simultaneous projections allowed multimedia to advance in the modern theatre. In addition, his *Laterna Magika* integrated actors with still and moving pictures.

**Texts and No Texts**   "ALL WRITING IS GARBAGE. People who come out of nowhere to try to put into words any part of what goes on in their minds are pigs."[26] Antonin Artaud, obviously, could be counted on to state the modern position succinctly. Nevertheless, poets and playwrights continued to shape words into a modern idiom, even though design, direction, and acting all combined to reduce the status of the text in the modern theatre.

In 1909 August Strindberg called realism "useless." He began to draw upon his soul, his subconscious, to write characters who changed and transformed. The action of his plays was perceived through the eyes of one character, such as Indra's daughter in *A Dream Play* and The Unknown in *To Damascus* (1898, 1904). These plays present an expressionistic dream trilogy.

*A Dream Play* (1902) is one of the most influential modern dramas in both form and content. Strindberg attempted to place on stage an action not observable in everyday life—the dream-life of the imagination. The theatre, historically the place of dream visions, would reveal its inner workings, the very process of imagination.

Influenced by his studies of Eastern philosophy and religion, Strindberg evisioned human life as frustrated by *maya*—material perceptions that prevent mortals from glimpsing the oneness of all things. To penetrate the *maya*, Strindberg employed Eastern and Western symbols to suggest a reality beyond those presented by realistic dramatists.

In the play the Indian god Indra, the god who asked Brahma to create the Hindu theatre, allows his daughter Agnes to descend to earth to learn why humans are so unhappy. Agnes enters the *maya* of human existence at the Castle. The Castle holds men and women anesthetized by material things. When Agnes becomes a human to understand humanity, the "dream" begins; in Hinduism human existence is only a dream, an illusion.

The men and women of Agnes's dream—glazier, father, officer, lawyer, dean, billposter, naval officer, mother, doorkeeper, dancer—are but momentary physical manifestations of Jung's *anima* and *animus*, complementary female and male energies, presented by Strindberg as natural enemies. Consequently, the characters' identities, like the locations, transform into one another. The *anima* and *animus* created the Castle, a symbol both of human achievement and enslavement. Agnes journeys from human misery to human misery, only to end up back at the Castle with her Poet. Separation from her home has resulted in her initiation into humanity; she is ready to return to heaven.

To penetrate the *maya*, to glimpse the truth of human existence, to attain enlightenment, to free Agnes for her heavenly home, the men and women of the Castle must sacrifice their most prized possessions. Their sacrifices release Agnes in a conflagration that allows the flaming Castle to blossom into a lotus flower of enlightenment, like the *hana* of the noh actor. Agnes's journey and sacrifice should enable a modern audience to leave the theatre with a fuller understanding of the nature of human existence than is found in the realistic theatre of *maya*.

German playwright Benjamin Franklin Wedekind (1864-1918) wrote episodic plays in which similar characters wrestle with life instincts. *Der Erdgeist (Earth Spirit*, 1895), written in expressionistic verse, reveals Lulu, the symbol of sexual ecstasy, as actually the destructive force in the universe. In the second part of the Lulu saga, *Die Büchse der Pandora (Pandora's Box*, 1904), the heroine becomes the victim of Jack the Ripper. The plays resulted in charges of obscenity against the playwright. The works of Wedekind and Strindberg, and the symbolism of Belgian playwright Maurice Maeterlinck (1862-1949), began altering the writing styles of modern playwrights.

Inspired by American essayist Ralph Waldo Emerson, and the late works of Henrik Ibsen, Maeterlinck wrote to create an atmosphere of death, mystery, and unreality within a symbolic stage mysticism. Maeterlinck preferred language that left a mysterious effect on an audience. In his plays silence fell the moment a truth was revealed, when the mystery cracked. Dramas such as *Pelleas et Melisande* (1892) and *L'oiseau bleu (The Blue Bird*, 1905) were more to be experienced than understood. Melisande, one of the fated lovers, is married to a man she does not love. Her husband kills her lover, Pelleas. Melisande flees, gives birth, and dies of a broken heart. In the other play children follow an old fairy in search of *The Blue Bird* of happiness. Despite a cat's plots to stop them, the children learn that the dead continue to live in our memories and that happiness is at home.

Expressionism had more practitioners than did symbolism. Ernst Toller (1893-1939) wrote *Masse Mensch (Man and the Masses*, 1921) with scenes seen through the eyes of both the "masses" and a character named Sonia. In the drama, Sonia, the leader of a workers' strike, battles her government-employed husband. Bankers dance to the music of coins. The masses overrule Sonia's pleas for nonviolence. But the revolution is suppressed, and Sonia is jailed. She refuses the efforts of both the masses and her husband to free her; her guilt causes her to choose execution instead. Toller later wrote Piscator's success, *Hoppla, wir leben!* (*Hurrah, We Live*, 1927), the story of the suicide of a political idealist. Toller divided the stage in half and employed loudspeakers and newsreels.

In expressionist plays only individualized characters are given personal names. Actors, in fact, play moral problems rather than characters. Numerous scenes house only a few bits of furniture and properties; expressionist action is usually unlocalized. At most, a property is used to indicate the location.

Georg Kaiser (1878-1945) wrote over sixty expressionist plays including the trilogy *Die Koralle (The Coral*, 1917), *Gas I* (1918), and *Gas II* (1920). In the Gas trilogy an idealistic son and daughter rebel against their billionaire industrialist father. As they succeed him, generations of industrialists try, but fail, to aid the workers. The billionaire's descendants conclude that a global holocaust is the only solution to the human dilemma. *Von Morgens bis Mitternachts (From Morn to Midnight*, 1916) remained Kaiser's most popular play.

Meanwhile, in Poland, Stanislaw Ignacy Witkiewicz (1885-1939) wrote both expressionist and surrealist plays. One, *Wariat i zakonnica (The Madman and the Nun*, 1925), presents science and religion as inmates of an asylum who find freedom only through violence and sex. His play *Szewcy (The Shoemakers*, 1934) depicts the end of Western civilization.

In America, Eugene O'Neill gave expressionism a whirl. In *The Emperor Jones* (1920) the West Indian emperor Brutus Jones flees into the jungle for freedom in the natural, premodern world. In *The Hairy Ape* (1922) Yank seeks a place in modern society but is rejected even by the apes in the zoo. In *The Great God Brown* (1926) the masks of the artist Dion Anthony (Dionysus and St. Anthony) vie with successful American William Brown for the hand of Margaret, Faust's heroine. And in *Lazarus Laughed* (1927) Lazarus announces that death is only laughter and joy.

Elmer Rice (1892–1967) produced America's most popular expressionist work, *The Adding Machine* (1923). The hero of this play, Mister Zero, a fired clerk, goes mad and murders his boss. In heaven Mr. Zero finds reemployment with his beloved adding machine. George S. Kaufman (1889–1961) and Marc Connelly (1890–1981) adapted expressionism to comedy with *Beggar on Horseback* (1924). John Howard Lawson (1894–1977) applied expressionism to *Roger Bloomer* (1923), the dream of a young man following the suicide of his girlfriend. Lawson's *Processional* (1923) exposes the American class struggle, racism, and chauvinism as miners battle the mine owners' police.

The founder of surrealism, Guillaume Apollinaire (1880–1918), though severely wounded in World War I, gave the surrealist movement both *Les mamelles de Tirésias* (*The Breasts of Tiresias*, 1903) and a name. Set in 1917 Zanzibar, Apollinaire's play examines feminism and overpopulation with such characters as a dancing kiosk, a megaphone, and a single-person "people of Zanzibar." In the surrealistic masterpiece breasts fly off like balloons, and beards and mustaches grow full size in an instant.

Between nervous breakdowns, the homosexual, opium-addicted son of a lawyer, Jean Cocteau (1889–1963), led the surrealistic salon world. With *Parade* (1917) Cocteau revolutionized ballet by making dance a metaphor for everyday experience. *Parade* boasted choreography by Serge Diaghilev, music by Eric Satie, and scenery by Pablo Picasso. Cocteau also wrote *Les mariés de la Tour Eiffel* (*The Marriage*

*The original production of Guillaume Apollinaire's* The Breasts of Tiresias *(1917).*

*on the Eiffel Tower*, 1921), a play narrated by two phonographs and consummated when the photographer's camera envelops everyone. In Cocteau's *Orphée* (*Orpheus*, 1925) a horse that taps out poetry has come between Orpheus and Euridyce, who dies from poisoned envelope glue while plotting the death of the horse, her rival. Orpheus goes to the afterworld to fetch Euridyce, but is beheaded. The police interrogate the decapitated head as the lovers are united in death. *La machine infernale* (*The Infernal Machine*, 1934), which combines the stories of Hamlet and Oedipus, recasts the gods as a gigantic machine causing pain for humankind.

Much of the surrealist vision had been anticipated by Alfred Jarry (1873–1907) in *Ubu Roi* (*King Ubu*, 1896). Jarry hated realism, especially realism's reliance on words. He wanted a theatre of gestures, masks, and signs. Jarry lived an eccentric life as the "Father Ubu" of his play. As at the premiere of Hugo's *Hernani*, cheers and jeers filled the theatre after *Ubu Roi*'s opening line, "Shit!" The ambitious bourgeois Ubu goes on to steal the Polish throne from King Wenceslas. He is pursued to France, however, and defeated.

Bertolt Brecht (1898–1956) wrote plays tailor-made for the epic theatre: *Die Dreigroschenoper* (*The Threepenny Opera*, 1928), an updated, anticapitalistic version of John Gay's *The Beggar's Opera*; *Leben des Galilei* (*Galileo*, 1938), an examination of the underside of heroism in which the coward Galileo announces "Unhappy the land that needs a hero!"; *Mutter Courage and ihre Kinder* (*Mother Courage and her Children*, 1937), a chronicle of both the Thirty Years' War and a mother who must choose between war profiteering and the welfare of her children; *Der aufhaltsame Aufsteig des Arturo Ui* (*The Resistible Rise of Arturo Ui*, 1941), the story of a Chicago gangster whose life reveals traces of Hitler, Richard III, and Faust; *Der gute Mensch von Sezuan* (*The Good Woman of Setzuan*, 1938–1939), the Chinese-influenced parable of mutual exploitation; and *Der Kaukasische Kreiderkreis* (*The Caucasian Chalk Circle*, 1944–1945), a reworking of the classical Chinese play to illustrate the socialist credo: "From each according to his ability, to each according to his need." Brecht's plays reveal both a romantic anarchy and a belief in the dialectical contradiction of all things.

Brecht's epic theatre inspired documentary dramatists. Peter Weiss (1916–1982) wrote *The Persecution and Assassination of Jean-Paul Marat as Performed by the Inmates of the Asylum of Charenton under the Direction of the Marquis de Sade* (1964), the Marquis de Sade's drama-debate on the history and nature of revolution staged in an 1808 French mental institution; *Die Ermittlung*

*Pablo Picasso's design for Jean Cocteau's* Parade *(1917).* (Editions Cercle d'Art, Paris)

*Jean Cocteau's* The Wedding on the Eiffel Tower.

(*The Investigation*, 1965), an account of the trials of the Auschwitz concentration camp officials at the end of World War II; *Gesang vom lusitanischen Popanz* (*The Song of the Lusitanian Bogey*, 1969), a documentation of the Portuguese imperialists' exploitation of Angola and Mozambique; and *Trotzki im Exil* (*Trotsky in Exile*, 1970), a procommunist but anti-Soviet account of the Russian revolutionary Leon Trotsky.

Other playwrights tried to write docudrama. Eric Bentley (1916–    ), Brecht's English translator, for example, offered *Are You Now or Have You Ever Been?* (1972), an exposé of the American government's attempts to identify communists and dampen free speech in the arts. Heinar Kipphardt (1922–1982) wrote *In der Sache J. Robert Oppenheimer* (*In the Matter of J. Robert Oppenheimer*, 1964), the security trial of an American physicist who hesitated to contribute to the development of the hydrogen bomb. After *Der Stellvertreter* (*The Deputy*, 1963), Rolf Hochhuth (1931–    ) produced *Die Soldaten* (*Soldiers*, 1967), a verse drama about British Prime Minister Winston Churchill's involvement in clandestine political and military activities during World War II. In England, Joan Littlewood (1914–    ) created a music-hall documentary entitled *Oh, What a Lovely War!* (1963), counterpointing the horrors of World War I with nostalgic songs of the era. In America, Donald Freed considered the Rosenberg spy trial with *Inquest* (1970), and the Reverend Daniel Berrigan reported *The Trial of the Catonsville Nine* (1971), who destroyed draft records during the Vietnam War.

With the onset of World War II artists and writers fled to America. In time New York replaced Paris as the West's cultural capital. In New York, Europe's various modern visions and movements married and gave birth to new, unnamed breeds of art and dramatic theatre. Abstract expressionism, for instance, was one of the first names applied to paintings about painting's process or action: The art of painting became the subject of paintings. Pictures revealed the artists' emotions as they struggled to paint. Surrealism, fed on images of American consumerism, produced pop art. *Bauhaus* notions revived with minimalism's desire to reduce art to its essentials. Neorealism painted reality with a focus sharper than color photography. Conceptual art eliminated the art product entirely; when the process of creation was over nothing remained but the initial concept. Postmodernism rejected even that.

In the dramatic arts, however, labels did not

*Erwin Piscator's 1964 production of Peter Weiss's* Marat/Sade.

fly as freely. Critic Martin Esslin summarized the theatrical situation as the "theatre of the absurd." French existential philosophy dominated the immediate postwar drama. In fact, the leading philosophers of existentialism, Jean-Paul Sartre (1905–1980) and Albert Camus (1913–1960), wrote plays. Sartre wrote *Les mouches* (*The Flies*, 1943), in which the legendary Orestes becomes an existential hero faced with creating meaning for his life by social engagement. In *No Exit* (1944), a one-act "philosophical melodrama," a pacifist journalist, a lesbian postal worker, and a society lady find Hell to be a room without exit in a sleazy hotel: "Hell—is other people."[27]

Samuel Beckett (1906–    ), a friend of James Joyce and a French resistance fighter during the war, solidified France's position as the center of modern dramatic writing. Beckett's characters have no pasts and live alone with no prospects of a future. Two vagabonds are *Waiting for Godot* (1953): "Nothing happens, nobody comes, nobody goes, it's awful," one concludes. *Endgame* (1957) finds an aged and blind master, his servant, and trash-can–inhabiting parents searching for ways to pass the time, apparently after the destruction of human civilization. A bourgeois matron enjoys *Happy Days* (1961) as she goes optimistically about her daily trivia while sinking into a mound of earth. In *Not I* (1971) an aged couple shares a free flow of reminiscences, despairs, and disappointments. Beckett's characters in *Catastrophe* (1984), *Ohio Impromptu* (1984), and *What There* (1984) also exist in incomprehensible situations.

*Erwin Piscator's 1965 production of Peter Weiss's* The Investigation.

Like Beckett, Eugène Ionesco (1912–    ) went beyond social reality to the fundamental alienation of individuals and society. Ionesco believed that humanity suffered from a lack of metaphysics; it was "flattened" out. But unlike Beckett, Ionesco drew characters so alienated that they did not even know it. Consequently, Ionesco's plays were funny and tragic at the same time. Ionesco believed the world needed a metaphysical solution rather than a political or social one. In the foreword to his 1959 *Plays*, Ionesco described an Eastern transcendental experience of enlightenment. He said that during the experience he "felt so completely free, so relaxed, that I had the impression I could do anything I wished with the language and the people of a world that no longer seemed to me anything but a baseless and ridiculous sham."[28]

Ionesco's plays present the modern world from his enlightened perspective. In *La can-tatrice shuave* (*The Bald Soprano*, 1949) an English bourgeois couple's trivial discussion is interrupted by the visit of another couple. When the maid's boyfriend, a fire fighter, joins the discussion, the conversation degenerates into abstract sounds. *La leçon* (*The Lesson*, 1951), another "tragedy of language," presents a young geography doctoral student and her professor. The professor insists on teaching the student mathematics, but she suffers from a toothache. He stabs her, and the maid helps him dispose of the body and prepare for the next student-victim. In a circular tower, surrounded by water, an elderly couple arrange *Les chaises* (*The Chairs*, 1952). They welcome an invisible audience that has come to hear a speech explaining the meaning of life. When the speaker arrives the couple jumps out of the window. The silent orator writes a cryptic message on the blackboard, smiles, and leaves.

*Amédée* (1954) presents a bourgeois play-

*Joan Littlewood's* Oh, What a Lovely War! *(1963).* (Photo courtesy *The Report*)

wright and his wife boarded up in their house. While they argue, mushrooms and a gigantic corpse grow in the home. The wife believes the corpse to be her lover; the husband thinks the corpse is the neighbor's baby. With the help of an American soldier and a prostitute, they struggle to dispose of the corpse, which threatens to drive them out of the house. The corpse lifts the playwright into the sky so that he can fly away from everyone. An average bourgeois citizen of a model city confronts *Tueur sans gages* (*The Killer*, 1959) that is ravaging the population. In *Rhinocéros* (1959) the average citizen searches for meaning, love, and identity in a world in which people transform into identical

rhinoceri. A dying king, the hero of *Le roi se meurt* (*Exit the King*, 1962), searches for reasons to despise life. Finally, Ionesco retells Shakespeare's tragedy with his *Macbett* (1972).

Other playwrights continued the French existentialist vision and technique. Jean Genet (1910–1986), for example, focused on society's outcasts. *Les bonnes* (*The Maids*, 1947) are lesbian sisters who alternately play the roles of madam and maid. *Haute surveillance* (*Death-watch*, 1949) presents the fantasies of three prisoners struggling for dominion within the prison society. Real and imaginary sexual fantasies are played on *Le balcon* (*The Balcony*, 1956) of a brothel, which mirrors society's fascination

*Charles Dullin's 1943 production of Jean-Paul Sartre's* The Flies.

with power and domination. In *Les nègres* (*The Blacks*, 1959) masks confuse both the audience-performer relationship and the master-slave relationship.

England's Harold Pinter (1930–    ) put Maeterlinck's mystery and menace in Beckett's language. In *The Birthday Party* (1958) a former concert pianist, hiding in a seaside boarding house, is discovered, interrogated, straitjacketed, and led away. A brother brings an old man home to be *The Caretaker* (1960). But when the old man tries to pit brother against brother, he is thrown out. *The Homecoming* (1965) of a university professor and his new wife ends as the wife decides to remain with her father and brothers-in-law in a life of prostitution. A couple entertains the wife's old roommate as recollections of *Old Times* (1971) become struggles for control. In *No Man's Land* (1975) two old writers transform their relationship. *Betrayal* (1978) moves backward in time to reveal a husband's real role in the affair between his wife and his best friend.

In Spain, Fernando Arrabal (1932–    )

presented *La cimetière des voitures* (*Automobile Graveyard*, 1958), a mystery play in which a jazz musician-pimp plays the role of Jesus among wrecked cars that serve as the mansions. *L'Architecte et l'Empereur d'Assyrie* (*The Architect and the Emperor of Assyria*, 1967) explores the dynamics of both the master-slave relationship and the relationship of primitivism to Western civilization. In . . .*Et ils passèrent des menottes aux fleurs* (. . .*And They Put Handcuffs on the Flowers*, 1970) prisoners dream of freedom and violence.

In Germany, Peter Handke (1942–    ) confronted audiences with both Wittgenstein's limits of what could be said and a personal statement of what to expect in the modern theatre. Characters who are actors confront and ''offend'' the bourgeois audience, the source of the problems of the modern world. Handke's actor-characters refuse to perform, impersonate, or do anything expected of them. In *Kaspar* (1968) Handke shows the civilization and cultivation of a wild man, whose acquisition of Western values, language skills, and behavior lead to breakdown. Similar interests charac-

*The original production of Samuel Beckett's* Waiting for Godot *(1953).* (Photo by Pic)

*Sameul Beckett's* Ohio Impromptu *(1984).* (Martha Swope)

*Jean-Louis Barrault directed and acted in the original production of Eugene Io-nesco's* Rhinoceros *(1960).* (Photo by Pic)

*A production in Washington, D.C. of Dario Fo's* Accidental Death of an Anarchist *in 1984.* (Martha Swope)

terize Handke's *Der Ritt über den Bodensee* (*The Ride across Lake Constance*, 1971), *Die Unvernünftigen sterben aus* (*The Foolish Ones Die Out*, 1974), and *Wanschloses Unglück* (*A Sorrow beyond Dreams*, 1977). In *The Ride across Lake Constance* two famous actors create an evening party that features the legend of a horseman's ignorance of his ride across an ice-covered lake.

Surrealist Charles Ludlam (1943–1987) burlesqued all dramatic literature in plays like *The Conquest of the Universe* (1967), *Bluebeard* (1970) *Camille* (1973), *Stage Blood* (1974), *Der Ring Gott Farblonjett* (1977), *Reverse Psychology* (1980), *Le Bourgeois Avant-Grade* (1983), *The Mystery of Irma Vep* (1984), *Salammbo* (1985), and *The Artificial Jungle* (1986) with his Ridiculous Theatrical Company. Richard Foreman (1937–    ) explored the process of theatrical processing with plays like *Rhoda in Potatoland* (1975) and *Pandering to the Masses* (1975). In Italy, Dario Fo (1926–    ) and Franca Rame created a theatre of anarchist vaudevilles with Fo's *Non Si Paga! Non Si Paga!* (*We Won't Pay! We Won't Pay!* 1975) and *Morte accidentale di un anarchico* (*Accidental Death of an Anarchist*, 1979).

Following World War II an interest in collective creation developed. The Living Theatre (founded in 1946) made *Paradise Now* (1968), a political shock therapy featuring direct confrontation and harassment of the audience. The play worked to create the conditions for a social revolution leading to an anarchist paradise. *Mysteries and Smaller Pieces* (1966) had continued the group's interest in Asian rituals and left-wing politics. The Open Theatre (founded in 1963) presented *The Serpent* (1969), a ritualistic examination of the issues of the Book of Genesis, the nature of evil, and the source of responsibility. Transformation was again the group's principal performance technique with *The Mutation Show*, a collective meditation of death.

The Polish Laboratory Theatre (founded in 1959) constructed *Akropolis*, a reinterpretation of a nineteenth-century Romantic play into the Auschwitz concentration camp. *The Constant Prince*, based on a Calderón play, examined the nature of martyrdom. *Apocalypsis cum Figuris*

featured actors who awoke to portray assorted Biblical characters. The Performance Group (founded in 1968) offered *Dionysus in 69*, an environmental and collective production based on Euripides's *The Bacchae*. Peter Brook's company assembled *US*, a collectively created anti-Vietnam War play, and *The Ik*, a performance piece seeking a theatrical vocabulary that cut across cultural lines. Marrowitz's Open Space Theatre (founded in 1963) contributed *Artaud at Rodez*.

Following World War II, the decentralization of the professional theatre, begun earlier in the century, accelerated. Starting in 1920, France's Théatre Nationale Populaire had presented plays at reduced rates until 1951, when Jean Vilar took a new company on tour. After the war, the French government encouraged theatre in the provinces by establishing "drama centers" in large cities. Louis Durreux at Colmar, Jean Daste at St. Etienne, Maurice Sarrazin at Toulouse, Hubert Gignoux at Rennes, Gaston Baty at Aix, and Roger Planchon at Lyon moved the theatre to the people. Regional centers were also founded at Strasbourg, Villeurbanne, Tourcoing, Bourges, and Nice. Annual festivals at Avignon, Strasbourg, Bordeaux, and Toulouse likewise enhanced the professional theatre scene.

In 1948 Britain's Parliament authorized local governments to subsidize resident professional theatre companies. Building upon the work of Barry Jackson in Birmingham and Annie Horniman in Manchester, dynamic professional theatres appeared in Bristol, Glasgow, Coventry, and Nottingham. In Germany the Volksbühnen revived the professional theatres of Dusseldorf, Weimar, Dresden, Munich, and Hamburg.

Americans created professional regional theatres outside the sphere of New York's Broadway. Raymond O'Neill opened the Cleveland Playhouse, and Bagley Wright the Seattle Repertory Theatre, while others did the same in other cities: Nina Vance in Dallas, Zelda Finchandler in Washington, Jules Irving and Herbert Blau in San Francisco, Ty-

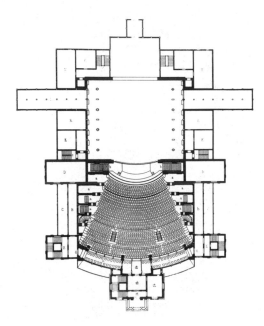

*Richard Wagner's Festspielhaus in Beyreuth, Germany, designed in the Romantic period, is still today a popular type of theatre construction.* (Lilly Library)

rone Guthrie in Minneapolis, Adrian Hall in Providence, Gordon Davidson in Los Angeles, and Robert Brustein in Boston.

At the end of the twentieth century modern dramaturgical wheat and chaff awaited history's sifting. Playwrights seemed to be writing plays using the process detailed by the artist Mark Rothko to describe modern painting:

> Neither the action nor the actors can be anticipated, or described in advance. They begin as an unknown adventure in an unknown space. It is at the moment of completion that in a flash of recognition, they all seem to have the quantity and function which was intended. Ideas and plans that existed in the mind at the start were simply the doorway through which one left the world in which they occur.[29]

In England, Caryl Churchill (1938– ) penned *Cloud Nine* (1980), a music hall–styled exploration of political and sexual imperialism; *Top Girls* (1982), an examination of self-made women, past and present; and *Fen* (1983), a portrait of women land workers facing multinational corporate interests. David Hare (1947– ) presented *Slag* (1969), a play about militant feminists in a girls' school; *Fanshen* (1975), a study of the effects of the Chinese communist revolution on a remote village; *Plenty* (1978), a look at a French resistance fighter's life after the war; and *A Map of the World* (1984).

America's Ronald Ribman (1932– ) wrote *Buck* (1983), a modern morality play set in a cable television station, and *Sweet Table at the Richelieu* (1987). Sam Shepard (1943– ) wrote *Operation Sidewinder* (1970), the collision of snakes, Indians, and the United States Air Force in the American desert; *Tooth of Crime* (1972), a mythical showdown between old and young rock and rollers; *Angel City* (1976), the story of a young man torn between integrity and Hollywood success; *Suicide in B Flat* (1976), the story of two detectives' investigating the murder of a jazz musician; and *A Lie of the Mind* (1985), a love story within two feuding families, each of whom falsely accepts and attributes responsibility.

Nonrealism became international both in form and content. Yusuf Idris of Egypt (1927– ) wrote a symbolist allegory, *al-Farafir* (*The*

*David Hare's* A Map of the World *(1985) at the New York Public Theatre.* (Martha Swope)

*Farfoors*, 1964) to show the human tendency to exploit one another. In Mexico, Carlos Fuentes y Fuentes (1929–   ) mixed realism with nonrealistic techniques to examine Mexican history in *Todos los gatos son pardos* (*In the Dark All Cats Are Dark*, 1971). Roberto Athayde (1949–   ) revealed the relationship between education and totalitarianism in *Apa-*

*recen a Margarida* (*Miss Margarida's Way*, 1977). In Canada, George F. Walker (1947–   ) used popular characters and icons to expose contemporary mythology with plays like *Ramona and the White Slavers* (1976), a metaphor for the modern family.

*Looking for an Audience*   The modern the-

*Andrei Serban's production of Ronald Ribman's* Sweet Table at the Richelieu *(1987).* (American Repertory Theatre; photo by Richard Feldman)

atre asked much of the audience—so much, in fact, that many preferred to stay away. Groomed by realism to passive, silent anonymity, the modern audience resented the attention it received in modern works. It also associated the theatre with realism. In an age when experts wondered for them, many people either could not, would not, or did not know they should participate in the imaginative creation of a theatrical event. The wide range of demands placed on the modern audience was dizzying.

For example, the epic theatre placed the audience in a classroom atmosphere, and insisted that it learn the truth necessary to change the world. Modern audiences sighed when their fun in empathizing and relating with dramatic characters was denied them. Troubled men and women preferred a fix of bourgeois sentimentality to the epic demand for "suspicious inquiry."

But Antonin Artaud had hope for the modern audience. He blamed the theatre for the audience's reaction:

> I believe that the public will always accept something that conflicts with its opinions and goes against its habits as long as it understands the intention with which it's been done. And I believe that those so-called new masterpieces which the public receives with volleys of hisses because they conflict with its attitudes must have been badly acted and produced; otherwise they would have succeeded.[30]

Many modern theatrical adventures did suffer from poor artistry. When that was not the case, audiences did not understand the theatre's intention. Even when the intention was understood, however, the modern theatre was often associated with a special social class. Indeed, the rising costs of theatre and movie production stratified the public by wealth. Television was available to all regardless of income, and movies entertained the moderate-income people. The theatre catered to the wealthy. Ticket prices, even with corporate and governmental subsidy, locked out many of the very people depicted in the modern vision. As a result, the

modern theatre began to feed those who could afford attendance. It often wrapped its harrowing vision in bourgeois values and chic pseudo-modernism. Vsevelod Meyerhold's condemnation grew more accurate with time:

> The stage has become estranged from its communal religious origins; it has alienated the spectator by its objectivity. The stage is no longer *infectious*, it no longer has the power of *transformation*.[31]

Meyerhold demanded that a "theatrical performance should be a joyous event which rouses the public emotions; . . . only via the sports arena can we approach the theatrical arena. . . . Unless the theatre shouts as lustily as the streets, it won't attract an audience for love nor money."[32]

As late as 1985 critic David Denby revealed the modern audience as still interested in seeing observable reality on stage:

> The theatre seems caught in a gigantic double bind. The closer it comes to realistic representation, the more it betrays how inadequate it is next to the cinema; the further away from representation it moves, the more it loses contact with what interests us in the world and becomes preoccupied with the means of its own existence.[33]

Modern theoreticians believed Denby's "double bind" could be overcome by eliminating the conventions established by Russian realist Constantin Stanislavski and the Moscow Popular Art Theatre. The problem was to find conventions to take their place. Meyerhold thought the fourth wall had to disappear; actors needed to directly welcome the audience into the theatre and communicate with them directly. Viola Spolin said, "The actor must no more forget his audience than his lines, his props, or his fellow actors." The modern player was to see the audience "as a group with whom he is sharing an experience."[34] An alienated, lonely, and confused public would appreciate some shared conversation about important matters:

> When our theater training can enable the future playwrights, directors, and actors to think through the role of the audience as individuals and as a part of the process called theater, each one with a right to a thoughtful and personal experience, is it not possible that a whole new form of theater presentation will emerge?[35]

Others believed the popularity of the musical comedy derived more from the form than from the content. Consequently, experiments sought to present nonmusical characters directly to the audience.

The modern theatre, relatively young, continued to search for the means to communicate a new reality directly to an audience without offending, confusing, or frightening. The modern audience presented a great challenge to the theatre. The modern vision defied common sense, reason, logic, and tradition. While audiences decreased, the urgency of the vision increased.

Ezra Pound, a poet who, like Antonin Artaud, lived in a dimension outside of modern society, warned:

> A nation which neglects the perceptions of its artists declines. After a while it ceases to act, and merely survives.
>
> There is probably no use in telling this to people who can't see it without being told.
>
> Artists and poets undoubtedly get excited and "overexcited" about things long before the general public.
>
> Before deciding whether a man is a fool or a good artist, it would be well to ask, not only "is he excited unduly," but: "does he see something we don't?"
>
> Is his curious behavior due to his feeling an oncoming earthquake, or smelling a forest fire which we do not yet feel or smell?
>
> Barometers, wind-gauges, cannot be used as engines.[36]

# NOTES

[1] Jacques Barzun, "Scholarship versus Culture," *The Atlantic*, 254, no. 5 (November 1984), p. 97.

[2] J. Michael Walton, ed., *Craig on Theatre* (London: Methuen, 1983), p. 21.

[3] Antonin Artaud, *Selected Writings*, Susan Sontag, ed. (New York: Farrar, Straus and Giroux, 1976), p. 155.

[4] Michel Saint-Denis, *Theatre: The Rediscovery of Style* (New York: Theatre Arts Books, 1960), p. 55. This excerpt is used by permission of the publisher. Copyright © 1960 by Michel Saint-Denis.

[5] John Cage, *Silence* (Middletown, Conn.: Wesleyan University Press, 1973), p. 155.

[6] Albert Bermel, *Farce: A History from Aristophanes to Woody Allen* (New York: Simon & Schuster, 1982), p. 339.

[7] Jerzy Grotowski, *Towards a Poor Theatre* (New York: Simon & Schuster, 1969), p. 41. Copyright © 1968 by Jerzy Grotowski and Odin Teatrets, Forlag, Denmark.

[8] Robert Bly, *News of the Universe* (San Francisco: Sierra Club Books, 1980), p. 127.

[9] Artaud, *Selected Writings*, p. 582.

[10] Stanislaw Ignacy Witkiewicz, "The Analogy with Painting," Daniel C. and Eleanor S. Gerould, trans., in *Avant Garde Drama. A Casebook*, Bernard F. Dukore and Daniel C. Gerould, eds. (New York: Thomas Y. Crowell, 1976), p. 490.

[11] André Breton, "Second Manifesto of Surrealism," in *Manifestoes of Surrealism* (Ann Arbor: The University of Michigan Press, 1969), p. 123.

[12] John Willett, ed., *Brecht on Theatre* (London: Methuen, 1964), p. 37.

[13] Walton, *Craig on Theatre*, p. 52.

[14] Willett, *Brecht on Theatre*, p. 204.

[15] Ibid., p. 277.

[16] Edward Braun, ed., *Meyerhold on Theatre* (London: Methuen, 1969), p. 251.

[17] Artaud, *Selected Writings*, p. 55.

[18] Ibid., p. 245.

[19] Viola Spolin, *Improvisation for the Theater* (Evanston, Ill.: Northwestern University Press, 1963), p. 4.

[20] Ibid., p. 272.

[21] Braun, *Meyerhold on Theatre*, p. 270.

[22] Willett, *Brecht on Theatre*, p. 233.

[23] Richard Schechner, *Environmental Theatre* (New York: Hawthorn Books, 1973), p. 39.

[24] Ibid., p. 39.

[25] Richard Schechner, *Public Domain* (Indianapolis: Bobbs-Merrill, 1969), p. 146. Copyright © 1969 by Richard Schechner. Used by permission of the publishers, Bobbs-Merrill Company, Inc.

[26] Artaud, *Selected Writings*, p. 85.

[27] Jean-Paul Sartre, *No Exit and Three Other Plays* (New York: Random House, 1955), p. 47.

[28] Eugène Ionesco, *Plays*, vol. 1, Donald Watson, trans. (London: John Calder, 1959), p. vii.

[29] Herschel B. Chipp, *Theories of Modern Art* (Berkeley: University of California Press, 1968), p. 548.

[30] Artaud, *Selected Writings*, p. 297.

[31] Braun, *Meyerhold on Theatre*, p. 60.

[32] Ibid., p. 174, 200, 263.

[33] David Denby, ''Stranger in a Strange Land,'' *The Atlantic*, 255, no. 1 (January 1985), p. 50.

[34] Spolin, *Improvisation for the Theatre*, p. 12.

[35] Ibid. p. 13.

[36] Ezra Pound, *ABC of Reading* (New York: New Directions Books, 1960), pp. 82–83. Copyright 1934 by Ezra Pound. Reprinted by permission of New Directions Publishing Corporation.

# TIME LINE

<table>
<tr><td>**The Theatre**</td><td></td><td>**The World**</td></tr>
<tr><td>1500 B.C.</td><td></td><td></td></tr>
<tr><td></td><td>1375 B.C.</td><td>Head of Akhenaten</td></tr>
<tr><td></td><td>1257</td><td>Temple of Ramses II</td></tr>
<tr><td></td><td>1250</td><td>The Exodus</td></tr>
<tr><td></td><td>1200</td><td>*The Epic of Gilgamesh*</td></tr>
<tr><td></td><td>1193</td><td>Destruction of Troy</td></tr>
<tr><td></td><td>1027</td><td>Zhow Dynasty begins</td></tr>
<tr><td></td><td>900-</td><td>Homer's *The Iliad*</td></tr>
<tr><td></td><td>800</td><td>Homer's *The Odyssey*</td></tr>
<tr><td></td><td>776</td><td>First Olympic Games</td></tr>
<tr><td></td><td>753</td><td>Founding of Rome</td></tr>
<tr><td></td><td>720</td><td>Lamassu</td></tr>
<tr><td></td><td>660</td><td>Founding of Byzantium</td></tr>
<tr><td></td><td>630</td><td>Zoroaster born</td></tr>
<tr><td></td><td>605</td><td>Pisistratus born</td></tr>
<tr><td></td><td>604</td><td>Lao Ze born</td></tr>
<tr><td></td><td>594</td><td>Solon archon of Athens</td></tr>
<tr><td></td><td>581</td><td>Pythagoras born</td></tr>
<tr><td></td><td>570</td><td>Kouros from Tenea</td></tr>
<tr><td></td><td>563</td><td>Buddha born</td></tr>
<tr><td></td><td>560</td><td>Pisistratus archon of Athens</td></tr>
</table>

| The Theatre | | The World | |
|---|---|---|---|
| 365 | First Roman theatrical performance | | |
| | | 356 | Alexander the Great born |
| 350 | Theatre at Epidarus | 350 | *Mahabharata* |
| | | 347 | Plato dies |
| 342 | Menander born | | |
| 335 | Aristotle's *Poetics* | | |
| | | 323 | Alexander the Great dies |
| | | 322 | Aristotle dies |
| | | 321 | Maurya Dynasty begins |
| 316 | Menander's *The Grouch* | | |
| | | 303 | Yayoi period begins |
| 291 | Menander dies | | |
| 284 | Livius Andronicus born | | |
| | | 274 | King Ashoka begins rule |
| 264 | First gladiator contests | 264 | First Punic War begins |
| | | 256 | Zhow Dynasty ends |
| 254 | Plautus born | | |
| | | 241 | First Punic War ends |
| 240 | Livius Andronicus's plays performed | | |
| | | 232 | King Ashoka ends rule |
| | | 218 | Second Punic War begins |
| | | 214 | Great Wall started |
| | | 206 | Han Dynasty begins |
| 205 | Plautus's *Miles Gloriosus* | | |
| 204 | Livius Andronicus dies | | |
| | | 201 | Second Punic War ends |
| 200 | Bharata's *Natya Sastra* | | |
| 191 | Plautus's *Pseudolus* | | |
| | | 190 | Victory of Samothrace |
| 185 | Terence born | | |
| 184 | Plautus dies | 184 | Maurya Dynasty ends |
| 161 | Terence's *Phormio* | | |
| 159 | Terence dies | | |
| | | 150 | Venus de Milo |
| | | 149 | Third Punic War begins |
| | | 146 | Third Punic War ends |
| 75 | Theatre at Pompeii built | | |
| | | 73 | Spartacus slave revolt |
| | | 70 | Virgil born |
| 65 | Horace born | | |
| | | 60 | First Triumvirate |
| 55 | First permanent Roman theatre built | | |
| | | 45 | Julius Caesar dictator |
| | | 44 | Julius Caesar assassinated |
| | | 43 | Ovid born |
| | | 37 | Antony marries Cleopatra Herod begins reign |

| The Theatre | | The World | |
|---|---|---|---|
| | | 30 | Suicide of Antony and Cleopatra |
| 19 | Horace's *Ars Poetica* | 19 | Virgil dies |
| 15 | Vitruvius's *De Architectura* | | |
| 8 | Horace dies | | |
| 4 | Seneca born | | |
| | | 1 A.D. | Jesus born |
| | | 5 | Ovid's *Metamorphoses* |
| | | | Herod ends reign |
| | | 18 | Ovid dies |
| | | 30 | Jesus dies |
| | | 32 | Saul converts |
| | | 54 | Emperor Nero |
| | | 64 | Fire destroys Rome |
| 65 A.D. | Seneca commits suicide | 65 | *Gospel of Mark* |
| | | 68 | Nero dies |
| 80 | Colosseum built | | |
| | | 121 | Marcus Aurelius born |
| | | 124 | Pantheon built |
| | | 135 | Diaspora of Jews |
| 160 | Tertullian born | | |
| | | 161 | Emperor Marcus Aurelius |
| | | 180 | Marcus Aurelius dies |
| | | 181 | Column of Marcus Aurelius |
| | | 220 | Han Dynasty ends |
| 240 | Tertullian dies | | |
| 300 | Sudraka's *The Little Clay Cart* | 300 | Yayoi period ends |
| 304 | St. Genesius dies | | |
| | | 306 | Emperor Constantine begins reign |
| | | 312 | Constantine converts |
| | | 320 | Gupta Dynasty begins |
| | | 325 | Council of Nicea |
| | | 337 | Constantine ends reign |
| | | 350 | Council of Nicea ends |
| 373 | Kalidasa born | | |
| | | 396 | Augustine becomes Bishop of Hippo |
| 400 | Kalidasa's *Sakuntala* | | |
| | | 413 | Augustine's *City of God* |
| 415 | Kalidasa dies | | |
| | | 432 | Patrick in Ireland |
| | | 476 | Fall of Rome |
| | | 532 | Hagia Sophia |
| | | 535 | Gupta Dynasty ends |
| | | 552 | Buddhism introduced to Japan |
| 568 | Lombards stop Roman spectacles | | |
| | | 570 | Mohammed born |
| | | 600 | Chinese book printing |
| | | 618 | Dang Dynasty begins |

| The Theatre | | The World |
|---|---|---|
| | 622 | The Hegira |
| | 632 | Mohammed dies |
| | 638 | Moslems take Jerusalem |
| | 698 | Lindisfarne Gospels |
| | 701 | Li Po born |
| | 715 | Great Mosque, Damascus |
| | 732 | Moors defeated at Tours |
| | 742 | Charlemagne born |
| | 762 | Li Po dies |
| | 792 | Palatine Chapel |
| | 794 | Heinan period begins |
| | 800 | *Book of Kells* |
| | 814 | Charlemagne dies |
| | 907 | Dang Dynasty ends |
| 925 | *Quem quaeritis trope* | |
| 935 | Hroswitha born | |
| | 960 | Sung Dynasty begins |
| | 961 | Cordoba mosque |
| 965 | Ethelwold's *Regularis Concordia* | |
| | 980 | Cologne Cathedral |
| 1000 | Hroswitha dies | 1000 | *Beowulf* |
| | 1002 | Leif Ericson explores North America |
| | 1018 | Moslems invade India |
| | 1027 | Omar Khayyam born |
| | 1040 | Macbeth kills Duncan |
| | 1054 | Christian Church splits East and West |
| | 1066 | Battle of Hastings |
| | 1096 | First Crusade |
| | 1100 | *The Song of Roland* Angor Wat |
| | 1123 | Omar Khayyam dies |
| | 1128 | Durham Castle |
| | 1129 | Heinan period ends |
| | 1140 | St. Denis Abbey Church |
| 1150 | *The Play of Adam* | |
| | 1160 | Leonin of Paris |
| | 1184 | Kamakura period begins |
| | 1191 | *Niebelungenlied* |
| 1200 | Bodel's *St. Nicholas Play* | |
| | 1203 | *Parzival* |
| | 1209 | Cambridge University founded |
| | 1210 | Chartes Cathedral |
| | 1212 | Children's Crusade |
| | 1215 | Magna Carta |
| | 1220 | Amiens Cathedral |

| The Theatre | | | The World | |
|---|---|---|---|---|
| | | 1225 | Thomas Aquinas born | |
| | | 1233 | Inquisition established | |
| | | 1256 | Gunpowder invented | |
| | | 1260 | Kublai Khan born | |
| 1261 | Rutebeuf's *Miracle of St. Théophile* | | | |
| | | 1264 | Feast of Corpus Christi first ordered | |
| | | 1265 | Dante born | |
| | | 1266 | Giotto born | |
| | | 1271 | Marco Polo visits Kublai Khan | |
| | | 1274 | Thomas Aquinas dies | |
| 1276 | de la Halle's *The Play of the Greenwood* | | | |
| | | 1277 | Roger Bacon imprisoned | |
| | | 1279 | Sung Dynasty ends | |
| | | | Yuan Dynasty begins | |
| | | | Ciambue's "Virgin and Child" | |
| 1283 | de la Halle's *The Play of Robin and Marion* | | | |
| | | 1294 | Kublai Khan dies | |
| | | 1304 | Scrovegni creates chapel frescoes | |
| | | 1307 | Dante's *The Divine Comedy* | |
| 1315 | Mussato's *Eccerinis* | | | |
| | | 1321 | Dante dies | |
| | | 1324 | Polyphony banned | |
| | | 1325 | Aztec Tenochtitlan | |
| | | 1335 | Kamakura period ends | |
| | | 1336 | Ashikaga Dynasty begins | |
| | | | Giotto dies | |
| | | 1337 | 100 Years' War begins | |
| | | 1347 | Black Death begins | |
| | | 1348 | *The Decameron* begun | |
| | | | Black Death ends | |
| 1350 | *The Chalk Circle* | | | |
| | *Lute Song* | | | |
| | | 1354 | Alhambra | |
| | | 1362 | Langland's *Piers Plowman* | |
| 1363 | Zeami Motokiyo born | | | |
| | | 1364 | de Machaut, "Mass for Four Voices" | |
| | | 1368 | Ming Dynasty begins | |
| | | | Yuan Dynasty ends | |
| 1375 | *Second Shepherd's Play* | | | |
| | | 1377 | Filippo Brunelleschi born | |
| | | 1382 | Wyclif expelled from Oxford | |
| | | 1387 | *The Canterbury Tales* begun | |
| 1390 | *Paulus* | | | |
| | | 1392 | Ashikaga family rules | |

| The Theatre | | The World | |
|---|---|---|---|
| 1398 | Confrerie de la Passion produces plays | | |
| | | 1399 | Richard II deposed |
| 1400 | *Pride of Life* | | |
| | | 1401 | Masaccio born |
| | | 1411 | Hus excommunicated |
| | | 1412 | Brunelleschi, *Rules of Perspective* |
| | | 1415 | Henry V at Agincourt |
| | | | Hus executed |
| | | 1424 | Ghiberti designs doors of Florence Baptistry |
| 1425 | *The Castle of Perseverance* | | |
| | | 1428 | Masaccio dies |
| | | 1431 | Joan of Arc executed |
| | | 1432 | Van Eyck, Ghent altarpiece |
| | | 1434 | Cosimo di Medici rules Florence |
| | | 1438 | Inca Empire in Peru |
| | | 1440 | Platonic Academy |
| 1444 | Zeami dies | | |
| | | 1446 | Filippo Brunelleschi dies |
| | | 1451 | Christopher Columbus born |
| | | 1452 | Leonardo da Vinci born |
| | | 1453 | Turks take Constantinople |
| | | | 100 Years' War ends |
| 1454 | Angelo Poliziano born | 1454 | Movable type press invented |
| 1465 | Fernando de Rojas born | | |
| | | 1466 | Erasmus born |
| 1469 | Juan del Encina born | 1469 | Ferdinand marries Isabella |
| | | | Niccolo Machiavelli born |
| | | | Platonic academy established |
| 1470 | *Pierre Pathelin* | | |
| | *Mankind* | | |
| 1471 | Poliziano's *Orfeo* | | |
| | | 1472 | Leon Battista Alberti dies |
| | | 1473 | Sistine Chapel built |
| 1474 | Lodovico Aristo born | 1474 | Michelangelo Buonarroti born |
| | | | Reign of Isabella begins |
| 1475 | Sebastiano Serlio born | | |
| 1478 | Gian Giorgio Trissino born | 1478 | Spanish Inquisition begins |
| | | 1482 | Portuguese settle Gold Coast |
| | | 1483 | Richard III's rule begins |
| | | | Martin Luther born |
| | | | Raphael born |
| | | 1484 | Botticelli, "Birth of Venus" |
| | | 1485 | Richard III killed |
| | | | Henry VII's rule begins |

| | The Theatre | | The World |
|---|---|---|---|
| 1486 | Vitruvius's *De Architectura* printed | | |
| | | 1491 | St. Ignatius Loyola born |
| | | 1492 | Columbus in West Indies |
| | | | Leonardo draws flying machine |
| 1494 | Hans Sachs born | | |
| | Angelo Poliziano dies | | |
| | | 1495 | Michelangelo's "The Last Supper" |
| 1497 | Medwall's *Fulgens and Lucrece* | | |
| | John Heywood born | | |
| | | 1498 | Michelangelo's "Pieta" |
| 1499 | de Rojas's *The Comedy of Calisto and Melibea* | | |
| 1500 | *Everyman* | 1500 | Machu Picchu |
| | *Nature* | | |
| | | 1501 | Michelangelo's "David" |
| 1502 | Angelo "Ruzzante" Beolco born | | |
| | | 1503 | De Vinci's "Mona Lisa" |
| 1504 | Giambattista Giraldi Cinthio born | 1504 | Reign of Isabella ends |
| 1508 | Aristo's *The Casket* | | Michelangelo begins Sistine Chapel ceiling |
| | | 1509 | Henry VII dies |
| | | | Henry VIII's rule begins |
| | | | John Calvin born |
| 1510 | Lope de Rueda born | 1510 | Raphael's "Alba Madonna" |
| 1513 | *La Calandria* | 1513 | Machiavelli's *The Prince* |
| 1515 | Trissino's *Sofonisba* | 1515 | Bosch's "Triptych" |
| | | | Desprez's "Pange lingua" |
| | | | Francis I begins reign |
| 1516 | *Magnificence* | 1516 | Aristo's *Orlando Furioso* |
| | | | More's *Utopia* |
| | | 1517 | Luther's 95 Theses |
| | | 1519 | Leonardo da Vinci dies |
| 1520 | Machiavelli's *The Mandrake* | 1520 | Raphael dies |
| | | 1522 | Magellan circumnavigates the globe |
| 1523 | Etienne Jodelle born | | |
| | | 1524 | Pierre de Ronsard born |
| | | 1526 | Mongol Empire begins |
| | | | Durer's "Four Apostles" |
| | | 1527 | Niccolo Machiavelli dies |
| | | 1528 | Castiglione's *The Book of the Courtier* |
| 1529 | Juan del Encina dies | | |
| 1530 | James Burbage born | | |
| 1532 | Thomas Norton born | 1532 | Rabelais's *Pantagruel* |
| 1533 | Heywood's *Johan Johan* | 1533 | Pizarro conquers Peru |
| | Lodovico Aristo dies | | Ivan the Terrible born |
| | | | Michel de Montaigne born |
| | | | Queen Elizabeth born |
| 1534 | *Ralph Roister Doister* | | Henry VIII heads English Church |
| | | | Society of Jesus founded |

| | The Theatre | | | The World |
|---|---|---|---|---|
| 1536 | Thomas Sackville born | | 1536 | Tyndale executed<br>Michelangelo's "Last Judgment"<br>Erasmus dies |
| 1537 | Thomas Preston born | | | |
| 1538 | Battista Guarini born<br>Bales *Kynge Johan* | | 1538 | Titian's "Venus of Urbino" |
| 1541 | Cinthio's *Orbecche*<br>Fernando de Rojas dies | | | |
| 1542 | Angelo Beolco dies | | | |
| 1544 | Torquato Tasso born | | | |
| 1545 | *The 4 P's*<br>Serlio's *De Architecttura* | | 1545 | Council of Trent begins |
| | | | 1546 | Martin Luther dies |
| | | | 1547 | Ivan the Terrible becomes first tsar<br>Cervantes born<br>Henry VIII dies<br>Francis I dies<br>Henry II of France begins reign |
| 1548 | France bans religious plays<br>*Hotel de Bourgogne* built | | | |
| 1550 | Sachs's *The Wandering Scholar from<br>Paradise*<br>Gian Giorgio Trissino dies | | | |
| 1552 | Jodelle's *Cleopatra Captive*<br>Jodelle's *Eugene* | | | |
| 1554 | Sebastiano Serlio dies<br>Cinthio's *Discourse on Comedy and<br>Tragedy*<br>Sir Philip Sidney born | | 1554 | Palestrina's "Book of Masses" |
| | | | 1556 | Cranmer executed<br>St. Ignatius Loyola dies |
| 1557 | Thomas Kyd born | | | |
| | | | 1558 | Elizabeth I begins reign |
| | | | 1559 | Henry II of France dies |
| 1561 | Scaliger's *Poetics*<br>Preston's *Cambises*<br>Sackville and Norton's *Gorboduc* | | | |
| 1562 | Lope de Vega Carpio born | | | |
| | | | 1563 | Council of Trent ends<br>Index of Prohibited Books |
| 1564 | William Shakespeare born<br>Christopher Marlowe born | | 1564 | French Psalter<br>Galileo Galilei born<br>Michelangelo Buonarroti dies<br>John Calvin dies |
| 1565 | Lope de Rueda dies<br>*La Confanaria* presented | | 1565 | Breugel's "Harvesters" |
| 1566 | Edward Alleyn born | | | |
| 1567 | Richard Burbage born<br>Claudio Monteverdi born | | | |
| | | | 1568 | Ashikaga Dynasty ends |
| 1569 | Tirso de Molina born | | | |

| The Theatre | | The World |
|---|---|---|
| 1572 | Ben Jonson born | |
| 1573 | Inigo Jones born | |
| | Tasso's *Aminta* | |
| | Giambattista Giraldi Cinthio dies | |
| | Etienne Jodelle dies | |
| | | 1574 | Henry III begins reign |
| 1575 | John Webster born | |
| | Alexandre Hardy born | |
| 1576 | Hans Sachs dies | |
| | Wakefield cycle suppressed | |
| | "The Theatre" opens | |
| | Blackfriars opens | |
| | John Marston born | |
| 1579 | Gosson's "The School of Abuse" | |
| | *Corral de la Cruz* built in Madrid | |
| | John Fletcher born | |
| 1580 | John Heywood dies | 1580 | Montaigne's *Essays* |
| 1583 | *Corral del Principe* built in Madrid | |
| | Sidney's "The Defense of Poesy" | |
| 1584 | Francis Beaumont born | 1584 | Ivan the Terrible dies |
| | Thomas Norton dies | |
| 1585 | *Teatro Olympico* opens | 1585 | Pierre de Ronsard dies |
| 1586 | Sir Philip Sidney dies | |
| | | 1587 | Monteverdi's madrigals |
| 1588 | Marlowe's *Doctor Faustus* | 1588 | Spanish Armada defeated |
| | *Teatro di Sabionetta* opens | |
| | | 1589 | Henry III dies |
| | | | Henry IV of France begins reign |
| 1590 | Guarini's *The Faithful Shepherd* | 1590 | Spenser's *The Faerie Queen* |
| | | | Microscope invented |
| 1592 | Kyd's *The Spanish Tragedy* | 1592 | Michel de Montaigne dies |
| | Valeran Le Comte born | |
| 1593 | Christopher Marlowe dies | |
| 1594 | Rinuccini and Peri's *Dafne* | |
| 1595 | Shakespeare's *A Midsummer Night's Dream* | |
| | Shakespeare's *Romeo and Juliet* | |
| | Torquato Tasso dies | |
| | Thomas Kyd dies | |
| 1597 | James Burbage dies | 1597 | El Greco's "Resurrection" |
| 1598 | Thomas Preston dies | |
| 1599 | Shakespeare's *Henry V* | 1599 | Oliver Cromwell born |
| | Shakespeare's *Julius Ceasar* | |
| | The Globe erected | |
| 1600 | Calderon born | 1600 | Giordano Bruno executed |
| | Peri's *Euridice* | |
| 1601 | Shakespeare's *Hamlet* | |
| | Shakespeare's *Twelfth Night* | |
| | | 1602 | East India Company |
| 1603 | Okuni dances | 1603 | Elizabeth I dies |
| | Lope de Vega's *Madrid Steel* | | James I begins reign |

| | The Theatre | | The World |
|---|---|---|---|
| 1604 | Jean Mairet born | | |
| 1605 | Shakespeare's *King Lear* | | |
| 1606 | Jonson's *Volpone* | 1606 | Cervantes' *Don Quixote* |
| | Pierre Corneille born | | |
| | Shakespeare's *Macbeth* | | |
| | Marston's *Tragedy of Sophonisba* | | |
| | William Davenant born | | |
| 1607 | Monteverdi's *Orfeo* | 1607 | The Virginia Colony |
| 1608 | Giacomo Torelli born | 1608 | Telescope invented |
| | Monteverdi's *Arianna* | | |
| | Thomas Sackville dies | | |
| 1610 | Jonson's *The Alchemist* | 1610 | Henry IV of France assasinated |
| | | | Louis XIII begins reign |
| | | | Galileo sees Jupiter's satellites |
| 1611 | Shakespeare's *The Tempest* | 1611 | *King James Bible* |
| 1612 | Battista Guarini dies | | |
| 1613 | The Globe burns | 1613 | François de La Rochefoucauld born |
| | Valleran de Comte dies | | |
| 1614 | Webster's *The Dutchess of Malfi* | | |
| | Lope's *The Sheep Well* | | |
| | | 1615 | Inigo Jones named England's architect |
| 1616 | William Shakespeare dies | 1616 | Cervantes dies |
| | Ben Jonson first poet laureate | | Galileo ordered to cease research |
| | Francis Beaumont dies | | |
| 1618 | *Teatro Farnese* built | 1618 | Thirty Years' War begins |
| 1619 | Richard Burbage dies | 1619 | Negro slaves arrive in Virginia |
| | | 1620 | Massachusetts Bay Colony |
| | | | Submarine invented |
| 1622 | Molière born | | |
| | Middleton and Rowley's *The Changeling* | | |
| 1623 | Shakespeare's First Folio | | |
| | | 1624 | Bernini's "Baldacchio" |
| 1625 | John Fletcher dies | 1625 | James I dies |
| | | | Charles I begins reign |
| 1626 | Edward Alleyn dies | | |
| | | 1628 | Taj Mahal |
| 1629 | Ford's *'Tis Pity She's a Whore* | 1629 | Poussin, "Arcadian Sheperds" |
| 1630 | Mairet's *Silvanie* | | |
| | Cornelle's *Mélite* | | |
| 1631 | John Dryden born | 1631 | Michael Wigglesworth born |
| 1632 | Alexandre Hardy dies | 1632 | John Locke born |
| | Jean Baptiste Lully born | | |
| 1634 | *Théâtre du Marais* built | 1634 | Wallenstein dies |
| | Mariet's *Sophonisba* | | |
| | George Etherege born | | |
| | John Marston dies | | |
| | John Webster dies | | |
| 1635 | Lope de Vega dies | 1635 | Rubens's "Landscape with Rainbow" |

| The Theatre | | The World | |
|---|---|---|---|
| 1636 | Calderon's *Life Is a Dream*<br>Corneille's *Le Cid* | 1636 | Harvard College founded |
| 1637 | Ben Jonson dies<br>Venetian public opera house | | |
| 1639 | Jean Racine born | | |
| 1640 | Coliseo built in Madrid<br>Corneille's *Horace*<br>William Wycherley born | 1640 | English Civil War begins<br>Sir Isaac Newton born<br>Giotto dies<br>Rembrandt's "Night Watch" |
| 1642 | Monteverdi's *L'Incoronazione di Poppea* | 1642 | Galileo Galilei dies |
| 1643 | Claudio Monteverdi dies | 1643 | Louis XIII dies<br>Louis XIV begins reign |
| | | 1644 | Ming Dynasty ends<br>Jing Dynasty begins |
| 1645 | Calderon's *The Great Theatre of the World* | | |
| | | 1646 | English Civil War ends |
| 1648 | Tirso de Molina dies | 1648 | Thirty Years' War ends<br>Society of Friends founded<br>English Commonwealth |
| | | 1649 | Charles I dies |
| | | 1651 | Hobbes's *Leviathan* |
| | | 1652 | Inigo Jones dies |
| 1653 | Chikamatsu Monzaemon born | | |
| 1656 | Davenant's *The Seige of Rhodes*<br>Jeremy Collier born | 1656 | Velasquez's "Las Meninas" |
| | | 1658 | Oliver Cromwell dies |
| | | 1660 | English Commonwealth ends<br>Restoration of Charles II |
| 1662 | Molière's *L'Ecole des femmes* | 1662 | Wigglesworth's *The Day of Doom* |
| 1663 | Drury Lane theatre opens | | |
| 1664 | Molière's *Tartuffe* | | |
| | | 1665 | Newton's Laws of Gravitation<br>LaRochefoucauld's *Maxims*<br>Vermeer's "The Artist's Studio" |
| 1666 | Molière's *Le Misanthrope* | | |
| 1667 | Racine's *Andromaque* | 1667 | Milton's *Paradise Lost* |
| 1668 | Molière's *L'Avare*<br>William Davenant dies | | |
| 1669 | Racine's *Britannicus* | | |
| 1670 | Racine's *Bérénice*<br>Molière's *Le Bourgeois Gentilhomme*<br>William Congreve born | | |
| 1671 | Colley Cibber born | | |
| 1672 | Richard Steele born<br>Joseph Addison born | | |
| 1673 | Molière dies<br>*Théâtre du Marais* closes | | |
| 1674 | Lully's *Alceste* | | |

| | The Theatre | | The World |
|---|---|---|---|
| 1675 | Wycherley's *The Country Wife* | | |
| 1676 | Etherege's *The Man of Mode* | | |
| 1677 | Dryden's *All for Love* | | |
| | Racine's *Phèdre* | | |
| 1678 | Giacomo Torelli dies | 1678 | Bunyan's *The Pilgrim's Progress* |
| 1679 | *Comédie Française* founded | | |
| | | 1680 | François de La Rochefoucauld dies |
| 1681 | Calderon dies | | |
| | | 1682 | Peter the Great named tsar |
| | | 1683 | Edward Young born |
| 1684 | Pierre Corneille dies | | |
| 1685 | John Gay born | 1685 | Charles II dies |
| | | | James II begins reign |
| | | | Handel born |
| 1686 | Jean Mariet dies | | |
| 1687 | Jean Baptiste Lully dies | 1687 | Newton's *Philosophiae Naturalis Principia Mathematica* |
| 1688 | Pierre Carlet de Chamblain Marivaux born | 1688 | "The Glorious Revolution" |
| | | | Genroku period begins |
| | | | James II flees to France |
| 1689 | Purcell's *Dido and Aeneas* | 1689 | Samuel Richardson born |
| | | | Peter the Great begins reign |
| 1691 | George Etherege dies | | |
| 1692 | Adrienne Lecouvreur born | 1692 | The College of William and Mary founded |
| | | | Salem witch trials |
| 1693 | George Lillo born | | |
| 1694 | Voltaire born | | |
| 1696 | Cibber's *Love's Last Shift* | | |
| 1698 | Collier's *Short View of the Immorality and Profaneness of the English Stage* | | |
| 1699 | Jean Racine dies | | |
| | Charles Macklin born | | |
| 1700 | John Dryden dies | | |
| | Congreve's *The Way of the World* | | |
| 1703 | Scena per angolo | 1703 | Genroku period ends |
| | | 1704 | John Locke dies |
| | | 1705 | Michael Wigglesworth dies |
| 1707 | Carlo Goldoni born | 1707 | Henry Fielding born |
| 1709 | LeSage's *Turcaret* | 1709 | Steele's *The Tatler* |
| | | 1710 | Georg Wilhelm Friedrich Hegel born |
| 1711 | Handel's *Rinaldo* | 1711 | Addison and Steele's *The Spectator* |
| 1712 | Pear Garden Conservatory | 1712 | Jean-Jacques Rousseau born |
| 1713 | Addison's *Cato* | | |
| | Denis Diderot born | | |
| | | 1714 | George I begins reign |
| 1715 | William Wycherley dies | 1715 | Louis XIV dies |
| | | | Louis XV begins reign |
| 1717 | David Garrick born | 1717 | Handel's "Water Music" |
| | | | Matteau's "Fête champêtre" |

| The Theatre | | The World | |
|---|---|---|---|
| 1719 | Joseph Addison dies | 1719 | Defoe's *Robinson Crusoe* |
| 1720 | Carlo Gozzi born | | |
| | Haymarket Theatre opens | | |
| | | 1721 | Walpole first Prime Minister |
| | | | Bach's "The Brandenburg |
| | | | Concerto" |
| 1722 | Steele's *The Conscious Lovers* | | |
| | | 1724 | Immanual Kant born |
| | | | Bach's "Mass in B Minor" |
| 1725 | Chikamatsu Monzaemon dies | 1725 | Peter the Great dies |
| 1726 | Jeremy Collier dies | 1726 | Swift's *Gulliver's Travels* |
| | | | Voltaire flees to England |
| | | 1727 | Sir Isaac Newton dies |
| | | | George I dies |
| | | | George II begins reign |
| 1728 | Gay's *The Beggar's Opera* | | |
| 1729 | Henri-Louis Lekain born | | |
| | Gotthold Lessing born | | |
| | Fyodor Volkov born | | |
| | William Congreve dies | | |
| | Richard Steele dies | | |
| 1730 | Adrienne Lecouvreur dies | | |
| | Oliver Goldsmith born | | |
| 1731 | Lillo's *The London Merchant* | | |
| 1732 | Covent Garden Opera House opens | 1732 | "Poor Richard's Almanac" |
| | Beaumarchais born | | |
| | John Gay dies | | |
| | Voltaire's *Zaire* | | |
| 1733 | Pergolesi's *La Serva Padrone* | | |
| 1737 | Licensing Act | 1737 | Herculaneum excavated |
| | Marivaux's *Les fausses confidences* | | |
| 1739 | George Lillo dies | 1739 | Methodism |
| | | 1740 | Richardson's *Pamela* |
| 1741 | David Garrick's London debut | 1741 | Handel's "The Messiah" |
| | | 1743 | Hogarth's "Marriage à la Mode" |
| 1746 | Goldoni's *The Servant of Two Masters* | | |
| 1747 | Alain René Le Sage dies | | |
| 1748 | Izumo's *Chushingura* | 1748 | Pompeii excavated |
| 1749 | Johann Wolfgang von Goethe born | | |
| | | 1750 | Voltaire's *Candide* |
| | | | Peking Forbidden City |
| 1751 | Richard Brinsley Sheridan born | | |
| 1752 | Hallams sail for America | | |
| 1753 | Goldoni's *The Mistress of the Inn* | | |
| | | 1754 | Henry Fielding dies |
| 1755 | Lessing's *Miss Sara Sampson* | 1755 | Dr. Johnson's *Dictionary* |
| | Sarah Siddons born | | |
| 1756 | George Frederick Cooke born | | |
| | Wolfgang Amadeus Mozart born | | |

| **The Theatre** | | **The World** | |
|---|---|---|---|
| 1757 | Diderot's *Le Fils naturel*<br>John Philip Kemble born<br>Royall Tyler born<br>Colley Cibber dies | 1757 | England rules India<br>Young's *Conjectures on Original Composition* |
| 1759 | Friedrich Schiller born<br>Spectators banished from French stage | 1759 | Handel dies |
| | | 1760 | George II dies |
| 1761 | Gozzi's *The Love for Three Oranges* | 1761 | Mongol Empire ends<br>Samuel Richardson dies |
| 1762 | Gozzi's *King Stag* and *Turandot*<br>Gluck's *Orpheus and Euridice* | 1762 | Catherine the Great begins reign<br>Rousseau's *The Social Contract* |
| 1763 | Fyodor Volkov dies<br>Talma born<br>Pierre Carlet de Chamblain de Marivaux dies | | Edward Young dies |
| | | 1764 | Voltaire's *Philosophical Dictionary* |
| 1765 | Autos sacramentales banned | | |
| 1766 | Southwark Theatre opens<br>William Dunlap born | | |
| 1767 | Lessing's *Minna von Barnhelm*<br>John Street Theatre opens<br>August Wilhelm Schlegel born<br>Godfrey's *The Prince of Parthia* | | |
| | | 1768 | Royal Academy, Joshua Reynolds President |
| 1769 | Diderot's *La Paradoxe sur le comédien* | 1769 | Napoleon Bonaparte born |
| 1770 | Beethoven born<br>Goethe's *Faust Part I* | 1770 | Boston Massacre<br>Gainsborough's "The Blue Boy" |
| 1772 | Lessing's *Emilia Galotti* | 1772 | Friedrich Schlegel born<br>Samuel Taylor Coleridge born<br>Slavery abolished in England |
| 1773 | Goldsmith's *She Stoops to Conquer*<br>Ludwig Tieck born<br>Goethe's *Goetz von Berlichingen*<br>Guilbert de Pixérécourt born | 1773 | Boston Tea Party<br>J. B. P. Du Sable founds Chicago |
| 1774 | Oliver Goldsmith dies | 1774 | Louis XV dies<br>Louis XVI begins reign<br>Goethe's *Sorrows of Young Werther*<br>First Continental Congress |
| 1775 | Sheridan's *The Rivals*<br>Beaumarchais's *Le Barbier de Séville*<br>Sarah Siddon's London debut | 1775 | Steam engine invented |
| | | 1776 | Smith's *Wealth of Nations*<br>Declaration of Independence<br>Gibbon's *Decline and Fall of the Roman Empire* |
| 1777 | Sheridan's *The School for Scandal*<br>Heinrich von Kleist born | | |

| | The Theatre | | The World |
|---|---|---|---|
| 1778 | Voltaire dies<br>Henry-Louis Lekain dies | 1778 | Rousseau dies |
| 1779 | Sheridan's *The Critic*<br>Lessing's *Nathan the Wise*<br>David Garrick dies | | |
| 1781 | Gotthold Lessing dies<br>Schiller's *Die Räuber* | 1781 | Kant's *Critique of Pure Reason* |
| | | 1783 | Stendhal born |
| 1784 | Beaumarchais's *Le Mariage de Figaro*<br>James Sheridan Knowles born<br>Denis Diderot dies | 1784 | The Treaty of Paris |
| 1785 | Argand lamp | | |
| 1786 | Mozart's *The Marriage of Figaro* | | |
| 1787 | Tyler's *The Contrast*<br>Edmund Kean born<br>Mozart's *Don Giovanni*<br>Louis Jacques Mandé Daguerre<br>  born<br>Goethe's *Iphegnia in Tauris* | 1787 | Steamboat invented |
| 1788 | Lord Byron born<br>Mikhail Shchepkin born | 1788 | Arthur Schopenhauer born<br>"Auld Lang Syne" |
| 1789 | William Macready born<br>Kotzebue's *The Stranger*<br>Talma debuts | 1789 | French Revolution<br>Blake's *Songs of Innocence*<br>George Washington becomes<br>  President |
| 1790 | Mozart's *Cosi fan Tutte* | | |
| 1791 | Eugène Scribe born<br>Goethe at Weimer Theatre<br>Mozart's *The Magic Flute*<br>Mozart dies | 1791 | Paine's *The Rights of Man*<br>U.S. Bill of Rights |
| 1792 | Gioacchino Rossini born<br>Percy Bysshe Shelley born | 1792 | *A Vindication for the Rights of Women* |
| 1793 | William Charles Macready born<br>Carlo Goldoni dies | 1793 | Louis XVI decapitated<br>Reign of Terror begins<br>Marat killed<br>David's "Dead Marat" |
| 1794 | Chestnut Street Theatre opens | | |
| | | 1796 | Catherine the Great dies |
| 1797 | Charles Macklin dies<br>Pixérécourt's *Victor* | 1797 | Coleridge's *Kubla Khan* |
| 1798 | Park Theatre opens | 1798 | Auguste Comte born |
| 1799 | Schiller's *Wallensteins Tod*<br>Beaumarchais dies | | |
| 1800 | Frédérick Lemaître born<br>Schiller's *Maria Stuart* | 1800 | Electric battery invented<br>Jefferson becomes President |
| 1801 | John Augustus Stone born | | |
| 1802 | Victor Hugo born<br>Alexandre Dumas père born | | |
| 1803 | Edward Bulwer-Lytton born<br>Gustavo Modena born<br>Douglas William Jerrold born | 1803 | Louisiana Purchase<br>Beethoven's "Heroic Symphony"<br>Ralph Waldo Emerson born |

| | The Theatre | | The World |
|---|---|---|---|
| 1804 | Samuel Phelps born | 1804 | Emperor Napoleon Bonaparte<br>Steam locomotive invented<br>Immanuel Kant dies<br>Haiti independence |
| 1805 | Friedrich Schiller dies<br>Beethoven's *Fidelio* | 1805 | Turner's "Shipwreck" |
| 1806 | Edwin Forrest born<br>Carlo Gozzi dies | | |
| 1807 | Ira Aldridge born | 1807 | England stops slave trade |
| 1808 | Goethe's *Faust, Part I* | | |
| 1809 | Fanny Kemble born<br>Nikolai Gogol born | 1809 | Felix Mendelssohn born<br>Charles Darwin born |
| 1810 | Kleist's *Prinz Friedrich von Homburg* | 1810 | P. T. Barnum born |
| 1811 | Heinrich von Kleist dies<br>François Delsarte born | 1811 | Harriet Beecher Stowe born |
| 1812 | George Frederick Cooke dies | 1812 | Grimm, *Fairy Tales*<br>Charles Dickens born |
| 1813 | Richard Wagner born<br>Giuseppe Verdi born<br>Friedrich Hebbel born<br>Georg Büchner born | 1813 | Austen's *Pride and Prejudice*<br>Madame de Staël's *On Germany* |
| 1814 | Kean debuts | 1814 | Goya, "The Third of May 1808"<br>Constable, "Vale of Dedham" |
| 1815 | Eugène Labiche born<br>William Wells Brown born | 1815 | Battle of Waterloo<br>Congress of Vienna<br>Otto von Bismarck born |
| 1816 | Rossini's *The Barber of Seville*<br>Charlotte Cushman born<br>Gas lighting introduced at Chestnut<br>  Street Theatre<br>Richard Brinsley Sheridan dies<br>Limelight invented | 1816 | Arthur de Gobineau born |
| 1817 | Byron's *Manfred* | 1817 | Frederick Douglass born |
| 1818 | Ivan Sergeyevich Turgenev born | 1818 | Shelley's *Frankenstein*<br>Schopenhauer's *The World as Will and<br>  Idea*<br>Karl Marx born |
| 1819 | Shelley's *The Cenci*<br>Anna Cora Mowatt born | 1819 | Walt Whitman born<br>Herman Melville born |
| 1820 | Shelley's *Prometheus Unbound*<br>Knowles's *Virginius* | 1820 | Keats, "Ode to a "Nightingale"<br>Friedrich Engels born |
| 1821 | Charles Beaudelaire born<br>Rachel born<br>Byron's *Cain*<br>The African Company<br>von Weber's *Der Freischutz* | 1821 | Napoleon Bonaparte dies<br>Costa Rica independence<br>Mexico independence<br>Fedor Mikhailovich Dostoyevsky<br>  born |
| 1822 | Dion Boucicault born<br>Griboyedov's *Woe from Wit*<br>Percy Bysshe Shelley dies | | |
| 1823 | John Philip Kemble dies<br>Brown's *King Shotaway*<br>Stendhal's *Racine and Shakespeare* | | |

| The Theatre | | The World | |
|---|---|---|---|
| 1824 | Alexander Ostrovsky born<br>Ira Aldridge leaves America<br>Charles Fechter born<br>Alexandre Dumas fils born<br>Lord Byron dies | 1824 | Beethoven's "The Ninth<br>Symphony" |
| 1826 | Talma dies<br>Royall Tyler dies<br>Duke of Saxe-Meiningen born<br>Edwin Forrest debuts<br>Bowery Theatre opens | 1826 | Cooper's *The Last of the Mohicans* |
| 1827 | Hugo's *Cromwell* | 1827 | Beethoven dies |
| 1828 | Henrik Ibsen born<br>Leo Nikolaevich Tolstoy born | | |
| 1829 | Tomasso Salvini born<br>Stone's *Metamora*<br>Jerrold's *Black-Eyed Susan* | 1829 | Friedrich Schlegel dies<br>Chopin debuts |
| 1830 | Hugo's *Hernani* | 1830 | Delacroix's "Liberty Guiding the<br>People"<br>Berlioz's "Symphonie Fantastique" |
| 1831 | Sarah Siddons dies<br>Goethe's *Faust, Part II*<br>Victorien Sardou born | 1831 | Darwin sails on H.M.S. Beagle<br>Georg Wilhelm Friedrich Hegel dies |
| 1832 | Johann Wolfgang von Goethe dies<br>Dunlap's *History of the American<br>Theatre*<br>Hugo's *The King Takes his Pleasure* | | |
| 1833 | Edmund Kean dies<br>Edwin Booth born | | |
| 1834 | John Augustus Stone dies | 1834 | Samuel Taylor Coleridge dies<br>Hugo's *The Hunchback of Notre Dame*<br>Schumann's "Carnival" |
| 1835 | Büchner's *Danton's Death* | 1835 | Mark Twain born |
| 1836 | Büchner's *Leonce and Lena*<br>Gogol's *The Inspector General*<br>Büchner's *Woyzeck* | 1836 | The Alamo |
| 1837 | Georg Büchner dies<br>Henri Becque born | 1837 | Queen Victoria begins reign<br>Telegraph invented |
| 1838 | Henry Irving born<br>Hugo's *Ruy Blas*<br>F. Calderon's *The Tourney* | 1838 | Dickens's *Oliver Twist* |
| 1839 | Bulwer-Lytton's *Richelieu*<br>William Dunlap dies<br>James Herne born | 1839 | Poe's *Fall of the House of Usher*<br>Photography (Daguerreotype)<br>invented<br>Walter Pater born |
| 1840 | Emile Zola born | | |
| 1841 | Benoit Constant Coquelin born<br>Boucicault's *London Assurance* | 1841 | Emerson's *Essays* |
| | | 1842 | Hong Kong granted to England<br>Turner's "Snow Storm"<br>Stendhal dies |
| 1843 | Gas installed at *Comédie Française*<br>"Virginia Minstrels" | | |

|  | The Theatre |  | The World |
|---|---|---|---|
| 1844 | Guilbert de Pixérécourt dies | 1844 | Friedrich Nietzsche born |
|  | Hebbel's *Maria Magdelena* |  |  |
|  | Dumas père's *Les trois mousquetaires* |  |  |
| 1845 | Wagner's *Tannhäuser* |  |  |
|  | Mowat's *Fashion* |  |  |
|  | Sarah Bernhardt born |  |  |
|  | Ellen Terry born |  |  |
|  | August Wilhelm Schlegel dies |  |  |
|  | Dumas père's *Le Comte de Monte Cristo* |  |  |
|  |  | 1846 | Segregation in S. Africa |
|  |  | 1847 | Felix Mendelssohn dies |
|  |  | 1848 | Republic of Liberia |
|  |  |  | Marx's *The Communist Manifesto* |
|  |  |  | European Revolutions |
|  |  |  | California Gold Rush |
|  |  |  | Seneca Falls Women's Convention |
|  |  |  | Italian unification |
| 1849 | Scribe's *Adrienne Lecouvreur* | 1849 | Mendelssohn's "Elijah" |
|  | Astor Place Riots |  |  |
|  | August Strindberg born |  |  |
|  | Edwin Booth debuts |  |  |
| 1850 | Turgenev's *A Month in the Country* | 1850 | Hawthorne's *The Scarlet Letter* |
|  |  |  | Edward Bellamy born |
| 1851 | Labiche's *Le Chapeau de paille d'Italie* | 1851 | Melville's *Moby Dick* |
|  | Louis Jacques Daguerre dies |  |  |
| 1852 | Dumas fils's *La dame aux camélias* | 1852 | Stowe's *Uncle Tom's Cabin* |
|  | Boucicault's *The Corsican Brothers* |  |  |
|  | Nikolai Gogol dies |  |  |
|  | Dumas fils's *Le Demi-Monde* |  |  |
| 1853 | Verdi's *La Traviata* |  |  |
|  | Ludwig Tieck dies |  |  |
| 1854 | David Belasco born | 1854 | Thoreau's *Walden* |
|  | Oscar Wilde born |  | Light bulb invented |
|  | Jean Jullien born |  | Gobineau's *Essay on the Inequality of Human Races* |
|  |  |  | Liszt's "Faust Symphony" |
|  |  |  | Lincoln University founded |
|  |  | 1855 | Whitman's *Leaves of Grass* |
| 1856 | Otto Brahm born | 1856 | Flaubert's *Madame Bovary* |
|  | George Bernard Shaw born |  | Sigmund Freud born |
|  | *Realisme* appears |  | Booker T. Washington born |
|  | Oscar Wilde born |  |  |
|  | Brown's *Experience* |  |  |
| 1857 | Douglas William Jerrold dies | 1857 | Auguste Comte dies |
|  | Heavysege's *Saul* |  |  |
| 1858 | Rachel dies |  |  |
|  | André Antoine born |  |  |
|  | Dumas fils's *Le fils naturel* |  |  |
|  | Vladimir Nemirovich-Danchenko born |  |  |
|  | Brown's *The Escape* |  |  |

| The Theatre | | The World | |
|---|---|---|---|
| 1859 | Gounod's *Faust*<br>Eleonora Duse born<br>Boucicault's *The Octaroon*<br>Ostrovsky's *The Storm* | 1859 | Darwin's *On the Origin of Species*<br>Mill's *On Liberty* |
| 1860 | Anton Chekhov born | 1860 | Arthur Schopenhauer dies |
| 1861 | Eugène Scribe dies<br>Gustavo Modena dies | 1861 | U.S. Civil War begins<br>Dickens's *Great Expectations*<br>Russian serfs freed<br>Machine gun invented |
| 1862 | Adolph Appia born<br>Georges Feydeau born<br>Maurice Maeterlinck born<br>Gerhart Hauptmann born<br>Sarah Bernhardt debuts<br>James Sheridan Knowles dies | 1862 | Hugo's *Les Misérables*<br>Bismarck Prime Minister |
| 1863 | Mikhail Shchepkin dies<br>Constantin Stanislavski born<br>Friedrich Hebbel dies | | |
| 1864 | Benjamin Franklin Wedekind born | 1864 | Tolstoy's *War and Peace*<br>U.S. purchases Alaska |
| 1865 | Wagner's *Tristan und Isolde* | 1865 | Lewis Carroll's *Alice in Wonderland*<br>U.S. Civil War ends<br>Slavery abolished in the U.S. |
| 1866 | Henry Irving debuts<br>Ibsen's *Brand*<br>*The Black Crook* | 1866 | Dostoyevsky's *Crime and Punishment*<br>Trans-Atlantic cable laid |
| 1867 | Charles Beaudelaire dies<br>Ibsen's *Peer Gynt*<br>Luigi Pirandello born<br>Zola's *Thérèse Raquin*<br>Ira Aldridge dies<br>Albert Basserman born<br>John Galsworthy born | 1867 | Marx's *Das Kapital*<br>Manet's ''Execution of the Emperor Maximillian''<br>Alger's *Ragged Dick*<br>Howard University |
| 1868 | Maxim Gorky born<br>Gioacchino Rossini dies | 1868 | Renior's ''The Skaters''<br>Meiji Period begins<br>W. E. B. Du Bois born |
| 1869 | William Vaughn Moody born<br>Booth's theatre opens in New York | 1869 | Suez Canal opens<br>Brahms's ''A German Requiem'' |
| 1870 | Alexandre Dumas père dies<br>Anna Cora Mowat dies | 1870 | Franco-Prussian War<br>Charles Dickens dies<br>Vladimir I. Lenin born |
| 1871 | Verdi's *Aida*<br>Lewis's *The Bells*<br>François Delsarte dies<br>John Synge born | 1871 | Kaisar Wilhelm I<br>''L'Internationale''<br>Barnum's ''Greatest Show on Earth''<br>Paris Commune<br>Marcel Proust born<br>James Weldon Johnson born |
| 1872 | Gordon Craig born<br>Edwin Forrest dies<br>Eleanora Duse debuts<br>Nietzsche's *The Birth of Tragedy from the Spirit of Music* | 1872 | Whistler's ''Mother''<br>Monet's ''Impression of Sunrise'' |

| | The Theatre | | The World |
|---|---|---|---|
| 1873 | William Charles Macready dies<br>Alfred Jarry born<br>Max Reinhardt born<br>Edward Bulwer-Lytton dies<br>Ibsen's *The Emperor and the Galilean* | 1873 | Pater's *The History of the Renaissance* |
| 1874 | Vsevelod Meyerhold born<br>Paris Opera House<br>Gertrude Stein born | 1874 | Degas's "Ballet Rehearsal"<br>Bruckner's "Romantic Symphony"<br>Mussorgsky's "Pictures at an<br>    Exhibition" |
| 1875 | Bizet's *Carmen* | 1875 | Schliemann, *Troy and Its Remains*<br>Carl Jung born<br>Thomas Mann born |
| 1876 | Charlotte Cushman dies<br>Frédérick Lemaître dies<br>Wagner's *The Ring of the Nibelung*<br>Bayreuth *Festspielhaus* opens<br>LaDuc's *Under the Yoke* | 1876 | Telephone invented |
| 1877 | Isadora Duncan born<br>Ibsen's *The Pillars of Society* | 1877 | Phonograph invented |
| 1878 | Samuel Phelps dies<br>Georg Kaiser born | 1878 | Dvorak's "Slavonic Dances" |
| 1879 | Jacques Copeau born<br>Ibsen's *A Doll's House*<br>Gilbert and Sullivan's *The Pirates of<br>    Penzance*<br>Madison Square Theatre<br>Alla Nazimova born<br>Charles Fechter dies | 1879 | Albert Einstein born |
| | | 1880 | Dostoyevsky's *The Brothers Karamazov*<br>*Uncle Remus*<br>Rodin's "The Thinker" |
| 1881 | Gilbert and Sullivan's *Patience*<br>Ibsen's *Ghosts*<br>Fedor Mikhailovich Dostoyevsky<br>    dies | 1881 | Pablo Picasso born<br>Tuskegee Institute<br>Renior's "The Boating Party" |
| 1882 | John Barrymore born<br>Becque's *The Vultures*<br>Sybil Thorndike born | 1882 | Tchaikovsky's "1812 Overture"<br>Ralph Waldo Emerson dies<br>Charles Darwin dies<br>Franck's "The Accursed<br>    Huntsman"<br>Arthur de Gobineau dies<br>James Joyce born |
| 1883 | Buffalo Bill's Wild West Show<br>The Metropolitan Opera House<br>Richard Wagner dies<br>Ivan Sergeyevich Turgenev dies | 1883 | Franz Kafka born<br>Karl Marx dies<br>Seurat's "Bathers"<br>Munch's "The Scream" |
| 1884 | Ibsen's *The Wild Duck*<br>Shaw joins Fabian Society<br>William Wells Brown dies | 1884 | Grieg's "Holberg Suite" |
| 1885 | Victor Hugo dies<br>Stanislaw Ignacy Witkiewicz born<br>Henry Irving knighted<br>Gilbert and Sullivan's *The Mikado* | 1885 | Twain's *Huckleberry Finn* |

| The Theatre | | The World |
|---|---|---|
| 1886 | Alexander Ostrovsky dies<br>Tolstoy's *The Power of Darkness* | |
| 1887 | *Théâtre Libre* founded<br>Strindberg's *The Father*<br>Verdi's *Otello*<br>Lynn Fontanne born<br>Smith's *The Little Mountain Fairies* | |
| 1888 | Edith Evans born<br>Strindberg's *Miss Julie*<br>Eugene O'Neill born<br>T. S. Eliot born<br>Eugène Labiche dies<br>Maxwell Anderson born | 1888 | Kaisar Wilhelm II<br>Rimsky-Korsakov's *Scheherazade*<br>Jack the Ripper<br>Bellamy's *Looking Backward*<br>Van Gogh's "Night Cafe" |
| 1889 | Hatcher's *Lazette*<br>Hauptmann's *Before Sunrise*<br>*Freie Bühne* opens<br>Noel Coward born<br>Sean O'Casey born<br>Jean Cocteau born | 1889 | Ludwig Wittgenstein born |
| 1890 | Herne's *Margaret Flemming*<br>*Théâtre d'Art* opens<br>Dion Boucicault dies<br>Ibsen's *Hedda Gabler* | 1890 | Frazer's *The Golden Bough*<br>Cézanne's "The Card Players" |
| 1891 | The Independent Theatre<br>Wedekind's *Spring's Awakening* | 1891 | Herman Melville dies<br>P. T. Barnum dies |
| 1892 | *Théâtre de l'Oeuvre* founded<br>Shaw's *Widower's Houses*<br>Reinhold Sorge born<br>Alfred Lunt born<br>Maeterlinck's *Pelleas et Melisande*<br>Hauptmann's *The Weavers*<br>Archibald MacLeish born<br>Fanny Kemble dies | 1892 | Tchaikovsky's "The Nutcracker"<br>Walt Whitman dies<br>Gaughin's "Spirit of the Dead<br>Watching" |
| 1893 | Edwin Booth dies<br>Pinero's *The Second Mrs. Tanqueray*<br>Hoyt's *A Trip to Chinatown*<br>Shaw's *Candida*<br>Erwin Piscator born<br>Ernst Toller born<br>Katherine Cornell born<br>Easton's *Dess alines* | |
| 1894 | Mei Lan Feng born<br>Shaw's *Arms and the Man*<br>Paul Green born<br>e. e. Cummings born | 1894 | Debussy's "Prelude to 'Afternoon of<br>a Faun'"<br>Walter Pater dies |
| 1895 | Wilde's *The Importance of Being Ernest*<br>Alexandre Dumas fils dies<br>Gillette's *Secret Service* | 1895 | Yeats's *Poems*<br>Tchaikovsky's "Swan Lake"<br>X-rays invented<br>Strauss's "Thus Spake Zarathustra"<br>Frederick Douglass dies |
| 1896 | Chekhov's *The Seagull*<br>Shaw's *Mrs. Warren's Profession*<br>Antonin Artaud born<br>Jarry's *Ubu Roi* | 1896 | Olympic Games revived<br>Harriet Beecher Stowe dies |

|  | The Theatre |  | The World |
|---|---|---|---|
| 1897 | Rostand's *Cyrano de Bergerac*<br>Michel Saint-Denis born<br>Thornton Wilder born | 1897 | Debussy's "Nocturne" |
| 1898 | Paul Robeson born<br>Moscow Popular Art Theatre<br>  founded<br>Lilian Baylis at the Old Vic<br>Morris Carnovsky born<br>Bertolt Brecht born<br>Federico Garcia Lorca born<br>Cole and Johnson's *A Trip to*<br>  *Coontown*<br>Cook's *Clorindy* | 1898 | Otto von Bismarck dies<br>Edward Bellamy dies |
| 1899 | Henri Becque dies<br>Noel Coward born<br>Shaw's *Caesar and Cleopatra* | 1899 | Veblen's *The Theory of the Leisure Class* |
| 1900 | Oscar Wilde dies<br>Puccini's *Tosca*<br>Tyrone Guthrie born<br>Gertrude Lawrence born<br>Helen Hayes born | 1900 | Friedrich Nietzsche dies<br>Freud's *The Interpretation of Dreams*<br>Quantum Theory formulated |
| 1901 | Giuseppi Verdi dies<br>Chekhov's *The Three Sisters*<br>Harold Clurman born<br>Strindberg's *The Dance of Death*<br>Lee Strasberg born<br>Shaw's *Man and Superman*<br>James Herne dies | 1901 | Queen Victoria dies<br>Washington's *Up From Slavery*<br>Commonwealth of Australia<br>  proclaimed |
| 1902 | Ralph Richardson born<br>Cheryl Crawford born<br>Cook's *In Dahomey*<br>Emile Zola dies<br>Gorky's *The Lower Depths*<br>Strindberg's *A Dream Play*<br>Williams and Walker's *Sons of Ham* | 1902 | James's *The Varieties of Religious*<br>  *Experience*<br>Langston Hughes born |
| 1903 | Madelaine Renaud born<br>Apollinaire's *The Breasts of Tiresias* | 1903 | First opera recording<br>Airplane invented<br>*The Great Train Robbery* movie opens<br>Du Bois's *The Souls of Black Folk* |
| 1904 | John Gielgud born<br>Australian Theatre Society<br>Abbey Theatre<br>Chekhov's *The Cherry Orchard*<br>Barrie's *Peter Pan*<br>Synge's *Riders to the Sea*<br>Anton Chekhov dies<br>Janécek's *Jenufa*<br>Christopher Isherwood born | 1904 | Cohan's "I'm a Yankee Doodle<br>  Dandy" |
| 1905 | Craig's *The Art of the Theatre*<br>Henry Irving dies<br>Shaw's *Major Barbara*<br>Maeterlinck's *The Blue Bird*<br>Marinetti's *Futurist Manifesto*<br>Strauss's *Salome* | 1905 | Einstein's *Special Theory of Relativity* |

| The Theatre | | The World |
|---|---|---|
| **1905** | Lehar's *The Merry Widow*<br>Theatrical Syndicate broken<br>Jean-Paul Sartre born<br>Lillian Hellman born | |
| **1906** | Moody's *The Great Divide*<br>Henrik Ibsen dies<br>Clifford Odets born<br>Samuel Beckett born | **1906** Matisse's "The Joy of Life" |
| **1907** | Laurence Olivier born<br>Peggy Ashcroft born<br>Strindberg's *The Ghost Sonata*<br>Synge's *The Playboy of the Western World*<br>Alfred Jarry dies<br>*Ziegfeld Follies*<br>W. H. Auden born | **1907** Picasso's "Demoiselles d'Avignon"<br>Frank Lloyd Wright's Robie house<br>Dominion of New Zealand proclaimed |
| **1908** | Victorien Sardou dies | |
| **1909** | Benoit Constant Coquelin dies<br>Elia Kazan born<br>Galsworthy's *Strife*<br>Jessica Tandy born<br>John Synge dies | **1909** Assembly-line automobile production introduced<br>Mahler's "Ninth Symphony"<br>Stravinsky's "The Fire Bird"<br>Schoenberg's "Anticipation"<br>Rachmaninoff's "Isle of the Dead" |
| **1910** | Jean-Louis Barrault born<br>Jean Genet born<br>Leo Nikolaevich Tolstoy dies<br>William Vaughn Moody dies | **1910** Mark Twain dies<br>N.A.A.C.P. founded |
| **1911** | Tennessee Williams born | **1911** Braque's "The Portuguese"<br>Webern's "Five Pieces for Orchestra" |
| **1912** | August Strindberg dies<br>Otto Brahm dies<br>Actors' Equity Association<br>Eugène Ionesco born<br>Sorge's *The Beggar* | **1912** Meiji period ends<br>*Titanic* sinks<br>Chinese Republic<br>Schoenberg's "Pierrot lunaire"<br>Jing Dynasty ends |
| **1913** | *Théâtre du Vieux Colombier* founded<br>Albert Camus born<br>Vivien Leigh born<br>William Ponty School opens<br>Aime Cesaire born | **1913** Husserl's *Phenomenology*<br>Armory show<br>Mann's *Death in Venice*<br>Proust's *Remembrance of Things Past*<br>Stravinsky's "The Rite of Spring"<br>Kandinsky's "Composition VII" |
| **1914** | Duke of Saxe-Meiningen dies<br>Joan Littlewood born<br>Shaw's *Heartbreak House*<br>Alec Guinness born<br>Denishawn founded | **1914** Panama Canal opens<br>World War I begins<br>Louis Armstrong band<br>Ralph Ellison born |
| **1915** | Tomasso Salvini dies<br>Neighborhood Playhouse opens<br>Provincetown Playhouse opens<br>Joplin's *Treemonisha* | **1915** "The Birth of a Nation"<br>Morton's "Jelly Roll Blues"<br>Einstein's *General Theory of Relativity* |
| **1916** | Eric Bentley born<br>Arthur Miller born<br>Peter Weiss born<br>Reinhold Sorge dies | |

| | The Theatre | | The World |
|---|---|---|---|
| 1916 | Irene Worth born | | |
| | Pirandello's *Right You Are* | | |
| | Kaiser's *From Morn to Midnight* | | |
| | Grimke's *Rachel* | | |
| 1917 | Cocteau's *Parade* | 1917 | Russian Revolution |
| | Ossie Davis born | | Jung's *The Psychology of the Unconscious* |
| | Torrence's *The Rider of Dreams* | | Duchamp's "The Fountain" |
| | Kaiser's *The Coral* | | Tommasini's "The Good-Humoured Ladies" |
| 1918 | Benjamin Franklin Wedekind dies | 1918 | World War I ends |
| | Brecht's *Baal* | | Spengler's *Decline of the West* |
| | Allan Schneider born | | *The Education of Henry Adams* |
| | Kaiser's *Gas I* | | Stravinsky's "Ragtime for Eleven Instruments" |
| 1919 | The Theatre Guild | 1919 | League of Nations |
| | Hart House Theatre | | The Bauhaus |
| | Uta Hagen born | | Booker T. Washington dies |
| | Shaw's *Back to Methuselah* | | |
| | Jean Jullien dies | | |
| 1920 | *Théâtre National Populaire* | 1920 | Lewis's *Main Street* |
| | Joseph Svoboda born | | "Cabinet of Dr. Caligari" |
| | Kaiser's *Gas II* | | Television invented |
| | O'Neill's *The Emperor Jones* | | Satie's "Socrates" |
| 1921 | Pirandello's *Six Characters in Search of an Author* | 1921 | Lawrence's *Women in Love* |
| | Toller's *Man and the Masses* | | Wittgenstein's *Tractatus Logico-Philosophicus* |
| | Georges Feydeau dies | | |
| | Friedrich Duerrenmatt born | | |
| | Joseph Papp born | | |
| | Cocteau's *The Marriage on the Eiffel Tower* | | |
| | O'Neill's *Beyond the Horizon* | | |
| 1922 | Pirandello's *Henry IV* | 1922 | Union of Soviet Socialist Republics |
| | O'Neill's *The Hairy Ape* | | Eliot's "The Waste Land" |
| | Paul Scofield born | | Hesse's *Siddhartha* |
| | Heinar Kipphardt born | | Joyce's *Ulysses* |
| | | | Marcel Proust dies |
| 1923 | Sarah Bernhardt dies | 1923 | Secretary General Stalin |
| | Shaw's *St. Joan* | | Fascist Italy |
| | Luvui Ciulei born | | Buber's *I and Thou* |
| | Donald Sinden born | | Gershwin's "Rhapsody in Blue" |
| | Rice's *The Adding Machine* | | Bessie Smith's "Down Hearted Blues" |
| | John Galsworthy dies | | |
| | O'Casey's *The Shadow of a Gunman* | | |
| 1924 | Eleanora Duse dies | 1924 | Lenin dies |
| | O'Neill's *Desire under the Elms* | | Franz Kafka dies |
| | Stanislavski's *My Life in Art* | | Forster's *A Passage to India* |
| | Marlon Brando born | | |
| | O'Casey's *Juno and the Paycock* | | |
| | *First Surrealist Manifesto* issued | | |
| | Geraldine Page born | | |
| 1925 | Berg's *Wozzeck* | 1925 | Kafka's *The Trial* |
| | Yale Drama School | | "Battleship Potempkin" |
| | Peter Brook born | | "The Gold Rush" |
| | Julian Beck born | | Malcolm X born |

| The Theatre | | The World |
|---|---|---|
| **1925** | Witkiewicz's *The Madman and the Nun*<br>Richard Burton born<br>Julie Harris born | |
| **1926** | Dario Fo born<br>Green's *In Abraham's Bosom*<br>Civic Repertory Theatre founded<br>Colleen Dewhurst born<br>O'Casey's *The Plough and the Stars* | **1926** Twelve-tone composition perfected<br>Bartok's "Mikrokosmos" |
| **1927** | Isadora Duncan dies<br>Hacek's *The Good Soldier Schweik*<br>Toller's *Hurrah, We Live!*<br>cummings's *him*<br>Hammerstein and Kern's *Showboat*<br>George C. Scott born<br>Robert Brustein born | **1927** "The Jazz Singer" |
| **1928** | Adolph Appia dies<br>Brecht's *The Threepenny Opera*<br>Edward Albee born<br>Leslie's *Blackbirds of 1928*<br>Kern's *Showboat*<br>Ellen Terry dies | **1928** Penicillin discovered<br>Ravel's "Bolero"<br>Gabriel Garcia Marquez born |
| **1929** | Joan Plowright born<br>John Osborne born<br>Christopher Plummer born | **1929** First Mickey Mouse cartoon<br>Milan Kundera born<br>Martin Luther King Jr. born |
| **1930** | Coward's *Private Lives*<br>Pirandello's *Tonight We Improvise*<br>DuBois's *Star of Ethiopia*<br>Peter Hall born<br>Harold Pinter born<br>Douglas Turner Ward born<br>Lorraine Hansberry born | |
| **1931** | David Belasco dies<br>James Earl Jones born<br>Green's *The House of Connelly*<br>Group Theatre founded<br>Rip Torn born<br>Ann Bancroft born<br>Rolf Hochhuth born | **1931** Dali's "The Persistence of<br>Memory"<br>Dominion of Canada proclaimed |
| **1932** | Jack Gelber born<br>Athol Fugard born<br>Fernando Arrabal born<br>Ronald Ribman born | |
| **1933** | Lorca's *Blood Wedding*<br>Jerzy Grotowski born<br>David Storey born<br>O'Neill's *Ah, Wilderness*<br>Schönberg's *Moses and Aaron*<br>Peter O'Toole born | **1933** Franklin Roosevelt becomes<br>President<br>Reichstag fire |
| **1934** | Cocteau's *The Infernal Machine*<br>Wole Soyinka born<br>Alan Bates born<br>Lorca's *Yerma*<br>Jonathan Miller born<br>Maggie Smith born<br>Stein's *Four Saints in Three Acts* | **1934** Hitler leads Germany<br>Magritte's "Le viol"<br>Hindemith's "Matthias the Painter" |

| | The Theatre | | The World |
|---|---|---|---|
| 1934 | LeRoi Jones born | | |
| | Peter Schumann born | | |
| | Hellman's *The Children's Hour* | | |
| | Charles Marowitz born | | |
| | Richard Schechner born | | |
| 1935 | Gershwin's *Porgy and Bess* | 1935 | Radar invented |
| | Odets's *Awake and Sing* | | Berg's "Violin Concerto" |
| | Ed Bullins born | | |
| | Edward Bond born | | |
| | Hughes' *Mulatto* | | |
| | Eliot's *Murder in the Cathedral* | | |
| | Anderson's *Winterset* | | |
| | Joseph Chaiken born | | |
| | Federal Theatre Project | | |
| | Lorca's *The House of Bernarda Alba* | | |
| 1936 | Isherwood and Auden's *The Ascent of F-6* | 1936 | Spanish Civil War begins |
| | | | Chaplin's "Modern Times" |
| | Fascists murder Federico Garcia Lorca | | |
| | Green's *Johnny Johnson* | | |
| | Albert Finney born | | |
| | Glenda Jackson born | | |
| | Luigi Prandello dies | | |
| | Maxim Gorky dies | | |
| 1937 | Blitzstein's *The Cradle Will Rock* | 1937 | Xerox invented |
| | Dustin Hoffman born | | |
| | Vanessa Redgrave born | | |
| | Richard Foreman born | | |
| | Lee Breur born | | |
| | Joanne Akalaitis born | | |
| | Tyrone Guthrie leads Old Vic | | |
| 1938 | Constantin Stanislavski dies | 1938 | Huinziga's *Homo Ludens* |
| | Artaud's *The Theatre and Its Double* | | James Weldon Johnson dies |
| | Wilder's *Our Town* | | |
| | Ward's *Big White Fog* | | |
| | Derek Jacobi born | | |
| | Peter Stein born | | |
| | Nicoll Williamson born | | |
| | Brecht's *Galileo* | | |
| | Caryl Churchill born | | |
| | Hellman's *The Little Foxes* | | |
| | Brecht's *The Good Woman of Setzuan* | | |
| | Brecht's *Mother Courage and her Children* | | |
| 1939 | Ernst Toller dies | 1939 | Spanish Civil War ends |
| | Liv Ullmann born | | World War II begins |
| | Stanislaw Ignacy Witkiewicz dies | | "Gone with the Wind" |
| | | | "The Wizard of Oz" |
| | | | Sigmund Freud dies |
| 1940 | Root's *Cabin in the Sky* | 1940 | Adler's *How to Read a Book* |
| | Al Pacino born | | Wilson's *To the Finland Station* |
| | Rodgers and Hart's *Pal Joey* | | |
| | Eliot's *The Cocktail Party* | | |
| | Trevor Nunn born | | |
| | Vsevelod Meyerhold dies | | |

| The Theatre | | The World | |
|---|---|---|---|
| **1941** | Coward's *Blithe Spirit*<br>Green and Wright's *Native Son*<br>Stacy Keach born | **1941** | "Citizen Kane"<br>James Joyce dies |
| **1942** | John Barrymore dies<br>Robert Wilson born<br>Peter Handke born<br>Wilder's *The Skin of Our Teeth* | **1942** | Battle of Stalingrad |
| **1943** | Vladimir Nemirovich-Danchenko dies<br>André Antoine dies<br>Rogers and Hammerstein's *Oklahoma*<br>Wilder's *The Skin of Our Teeth*<br>Robeson's *Othello*<br>Max Reinhardt dies<br>Andrei Serban born<br>Elizabeth LeCompte born<br>Sam Shepard born<br>Charles Ludlam born<br>Robert DeNiro born<br>Meredith Monk born<br>Sartre's *The Flies* | **1943** | Transistor invented<br>Camus's *The Myth of Sisyphus* |
| **1944** | Sartre's *No Exit*<br>Robert Wilson born<br>Brecht's *The Caucasian Chalk Circle* | **1944** | Normandy invasion<br>Copland's "Appalachian Spring" |
| **1945** | Williams's *The Glass Menagerie*<br>Georg Kaiser dies<br>Britten's *Peter Grimes*<br>Alla Nazimova dies | **1945** | Franklin Roosevelt dies<br>Atomic bombing of Japan<br>World War II ends<br>United Nations<br>Orwell's *Animal Farm*<br>Van der Rohe's Farnsworth house |
| **1946** | O'Neill's *The Iceman Cometh*<br>Gerhart Hauptmann dies<br>Living Theatre founded<br>Fritz Weaver born<br>Franz Xavier Kroetz born<br>Gertrude Stein dies | **1946** | Electronic computer invented |
| **1947** | Williams's *A Streetcar Named Desire*<br>Genet's *The Maids*<br>Poulenc's *The Breasts of Tiresias*<br>David Mamet born<br>David Hare born<br>Marsha Norman born<br>Kevin Kline born<br>Rainer Werner Fassbinder born<br>International Theatre Institute<br>Actors' Studio<br>Alley Theatre | **1947** | India's independence<br>Sessions's "Montezuma" |
| **1948** | Porter's *Kiss Me, Kate*<br>Sinead Cusack born<br>Antonin Artaud dies | **1948** | Ghandi assassinated<br>State of Israel founded |
| **1949** | Jacques Copeau dies<br>Miller's *Death of a Salesman*<br>Genet's *Deathwatch*<br>Arena Stage<br>Maurice Maeterlinck dies | **1949** | Chinese Communist Revolution<br>Cable television inaugurated<br>Orwell's *1984* |

| The Theatre | | The World |
|---|---|---|
| **1949** | The Berliner Ensemble<br>Eliot's *The Cocktail Paty*<br>Fry's *The Lady's Not for Burning*<br>Ionesco's *The Bald Soprano*<br>Meryl Streep born | |
| **1950** | George Bernard Shaw dies | **1950** "Un-American activities"<br>investigated<br>"Rashomon"<br>Pollock's "Autumn Rhythm"<br>DeKooning's "Excavation" |
| **1951** | Kate Nelligan born<br>Ionesco's *The Lesson* | **1951** Ludwig Wittgenstein dies<br>Libya independence |
| **1952** | Ionesco's *The Chairs*<br>Gertrude Lawrence dies<br>Beth Henley born<br>Albert Basserman dies | **1952** Ellison's *The Invisible Man* |
| **1953** | Miller's *The Crucible*<br>Eugene O'Neill dies<br>Beckett's *Waiting for Godot*<br>Stratford Shakespeare Festival<br>John Malkovich born<br>al-Din's *The Outcast* | **1953** Stalin dies<br>Skinner, *Science and Human Behavior*<br>DNA structure determined |
| **1954** | New York Shakespeare Festival<br>Ionesco's *Amedée* | **1954** Golding's *Lord of the Flies*<br>U.S. segregation declared<br>unconstitutional<br>Tolkien's *Lord of the Rings*<br>"La Strada"<br>Boulez's "*Le Marteau sans maître*" |
| **1955** | Miller's *A View from the Bridge* | **1955** Albert Einstein dies<br>Thomas Mann dies<br>Marian Anderson debuts at the Met. |
| **1956** | Osborne's *Look Back in Anger*<br>Lerner and Loewe's *My Fair Lady*<br>O'Neill's *Long Day's Journey into Night*<br>Cesaire's *And the Dogs Kept Quiet*<br>Bertolt Brecht dies<br>Genet's *The Balcony*<br>Duerrenmatt's *The Visit* | **1956** "The Seventh Seal"<br>"Heartbreak Hotel"<br>Rothko's "Green on Blue"<br>Sudan independence<br>Tunisia independence |
| **1957** | Bernstein's *West Side Story*<br>Beckett's *Endgame* | **1957** Space satellite launched<br>"Great Balls of Fire"<br>"Lucille"<br>Ghana independence |
| **1958** | MacLeish's *J. B.*<br>Pinter's *The Birthday Party*<br>Arrabal's *Automobile Graveyard* | **1958** Johns's "Three Flags"<br>"Johnny B. Goode" |
| **1959** | Hansberry's *Raisin in the Sun*<br>Ionesco's *The Killer*<br>Ionesco's *Rhinoceros*<br>Polish Laboratory Theatre founded<br>Gelber's *The Connection*<br>Genet's *The Blacks*<br>San Francisco Mime Troupe<br>Maxwell Anderson dies | **1959** "Hiroshima mon amour"<br>"La Dolce Vita"<br>Cuban Revolution |

| The Theatre | | The World | |
|---|---|---|---|
| **1960** | Lerner and Loewe's *Camelot* | **1960** | Updike's *Rabbit, Run* |
| | Bart's *Oliver* | | "Let's Do the Twist" |
| | Albert Camus dies | | Malagasy Republic independence |
| | Pinter's *The Caretaker* | | Somali independence |
| | Soyinka's *A Dance of the Forests* | | Central African Republic independence |
| | | | Nigeria independence |
| | | | Cameroon independence |
| | | | Chad independence |
| | | | Congo independence |
| | | | Niger independence |
| | | | Senegal independence |
| **1961** | Mei Lan Feng dies | **1961** | Man in space |
| | Beckett's *Happy Days* | | Bay of Pigs invasion |
| | Bricusse and Newley's *Stop the World—I Want to Get Off* | | Cage's "Silence" |
| | | | Heinlein's *Stranger in a Strange Land* |
| | Royal Shakespeare Company | | *New English Bible* |
| | Owens's *Futz* | | Heller's *Catch-22* |
| | Bread and Puppet Theatre founded | | Carl Jung dies |
| | Fugard's *The Blood Knot* | | The Beatles |
| | | | Tanzania independence |
| **1962** | Ionesco's *Exit the King* | **1962** | Feldman's "Last Pieces" |
| | Albee's *Who's Afraid of Virginia Woolf?* | | Cuban missile crisis |
| | La Mama E.T.C. | | Britten's "War Requiem" |
| | Brook at the Royal Shakespeare Company | | "Blowin' in the Wind" |
| | | | Uganda independence |
| | Duerrenmatt's *The Physicists* | | Jamaica independence |
| | e. e. cummings dies | | Rwanda independence |
| **1963** | Littlewood's *Oh, What a Lovely War!* | **1963** | Nuclear Test Ban Treaty |
| | Simon's *Barefoot in the Park* | | President Kennedy assassinated |
| | Open Theatre founded | | Kenya independence |
| | Clifford Odets dies | | Arendt's *Eichmann in Jerusalem* |
| | Hochhuth's *The Deputy* | | "Dr. Strangelove" |
| | The Guthrie Theatre | | W. E. B. Du Bois dies |
| | Cesaire's *The Tragedy of King Christophe* | | |
| | Olivier heads National Theatre | | |
| | Jean Cocteau dies | | |
| **1964** | Jones's *Dutchman* | **1964** | "I Want to Hold Your Hand" |
| | Weiss's *Marat/Sade* | | Warhol's "Disaster 22" |
| | Idris's *The Farfoors* | | Malawi independence |
| | Bock's *Fiddler on the Roof* | | Zambia independence |
| | Herman's *Hello, Dolly* | | |
| | Miller's *After the Fall* | | |
| | Kipphardt's *In the Matter of J. Robert Oppenheimer* | | |
| | Sean O'Casey dies | | |
| **1965** | Weiss's *The Investigation* | **1965** | Winston Churchill dies |
| | Simon's *The Odd Couple* | | Foucault's *Madness and Civilization* |
| | Herbert's *Fortune and Men's Eyes* | | Lichtenstein's "Big Painting #6" |
| | Leigh's *Man of La Mancha* | | Venturi's Chestnut Hill house |
| | Ribman's *Harry, Noon, and Night* | | Malcolm X assassinated |

| | The Theatre | | The World |
|---|---|---|---|
| 1965 | T. S. Eliot dies | | |
| | Pinter's *The Homecoming* | | |
| | Lorraine Hansberry dies | | |
| 1966 | Gordon Craig dies | 1966 | Chinese Cultural Revolution |
| | Kander and Ebb's *Cabaret* | | Frye's *Anatomy of Criticism* |
| | Handke's *Offending the Audience* | | Mao's *Quotations from Chairman Mao* |
| | Erwin Piscator dies | | Botswana independence |
| | Cesaire's *A Season in the Congo* | | |
| | Barber's *Antony and Cleopatra* | | |
| | Dube's *At the Return of the Wild Geese* | | |
| 1967 | Ragni and Rado's *Hair* | 1967 | Six Day War |
| | Vivien Leigh dies | | Marquez's *One Hundred Years of Solitude* |
| | Buzo's *Norm and Ahmed* | | First heart transplant |
| | Reaney's *Colours in the Dark* | | "Sergeant Pepper" |
| | Rya's *The Ecstasy of Rita Joe* | | Langston Hughes dies |
| 1968 | Handke's *Kaspar* | 1968 | Tet Offensive in Vietnam |
| | Performance Group founded | | Martin Luther King, Jr. assassinated |
| | Miller's *The Price* | | "2001: Space Odyssey" |
| | Tremblay's *The Sisters-in-law* | | LeWitt's "Untitled Cube (6)" |
| | Negro Ensemble Company founded | | Swaziland independence |
| 1969 | Fugard's *Boesman and Lena* | 1969 | Men land on the moon |
| | Van Itallie's *The Serpent* | | "Z" |
| | Jones's *Slave Ship* | | Messiaen's "The Transfiguration" |
| | Fo's *Mistero Buffo* | | |
| | Mabou Mines | | |
| | Hare's *Slag* | | |
| 1970 | Brook's *A Midsummer Night's Dream* | | |
| | Guare's *The House of Blue Leaves* | | |
| | Storey's *The Contractor* | | |
| | Gordone's *No Place to Be Somebody* | | |
| | Bread and Puppet Theater moves to New England | | |
| 1971 | Weber and Rice's *Jesus Christ Superstar* | 1971 | McLuhan's *Understanding Media* |
| | Tyrone Guthrie dies | | Stravinsky dies |
| | Schwartz's *Godspell* | | "A Clockwork Orange" |
| | Hewett's *The Chapel Perilous* | | The Republic of Zaire |
| | Fuentes's *In the Dark all Cats Are Dark* | | |
| | Michel Saint-Denis dies | | |
| | Pinter's *Old Times* | | |
| | Handke's *Ride across Lake Constance* | | |
| 1972 | Shepard's *The Tooth of Crime* | 1972 | Ezra Pound dies |
| | Ionesco's *Macbett* | | "The Discreet Charm of the Bourgeoisie" |
| | Davies's *General Casanova* | | Republic of Sri Lanka |
| 1973 | Sondheim's *A Little Night Music* | 1973 | Cease-fire in Vietnam |
| | Peter Hall at the National Theatre | | Pynchon's *Gravity's Rainbow* |
| | Wilson's *The Life and Times of Joseph Stalin* | | President Nixon resigns |
| | | | "The Godfather" |

| The Theatre | | The World | |
|---|---|---|---|
| 1973 | W. H. Auden dies<br>Noel Coward dies | 1973 | Pablo Picasso dies |
| 1974 | Hewett's *Catspaw*<br>Katharine Cornell dies<br>Fugard's *Sizwe Bansi Is Dead* | 1974 | Solzhenitsyn's *The Gulag Archepelago* |
| 1975 | Fo and Rame's *We Won't Pay! We Won't Pay!*<br>Hamlisch's *A Chorus Line*<br>Thornton Wilder dies<br>Wooster group founded | 1975 | Snyder's *Turtle Island*<br>Videocassette recorders marketed<br>Crumb's "Makrokomos II" |
| 1976 | Edith Evans dies<br>Paul Robeson dies<br>Walker's *Ramona and the White Slaves*<br>Fassbinder dies<br>Wilson's *Einstein on the Beach*<br>Shange's *For Colored Girls Who Have Considered Suicide/When the Rainbow is Enuf*<br>Shepard's *Curse of the Starving Class*<br>Sybil Thorndike dies | 1976 | Synthetic gene technology<br>Mozambique independence |
| 1977 | Fornes's *Fefu and Her Friends*<br>Mamet's *American Buffalo*<br>Athayde's *Miss Margarida's Way*<br>Alfred Lunt dies<br>Nowra's *Inner Voices* | 1977 | "Star Wars"<br>Djibouti independence |
| 1978 | Shepard's *Buried Child*<br>Hare's *Plenty*<br>Pinter's *Betrayal*<br>Kroetze's *Mensh Meier* | 1978 | First test-tube baby |
| 1979 | Sondheim's *Sweeney Todd*<br>Fo and Rame's *Accidental Death of an Anarchist* | 1979 | Iranian Revolution<br>Three-Mile Island nuclear accident<br>AIDS diagnosed |
| 1980 | Churchill's *Cloud Nine*<br>Henley's *Crimes of the Heart*<br>Harold Clurman dies<br>Jean-Paul Sartre dies<br>American Repertory Theatre | 1980 | Reagan elected President<br>John Lennon assassinated<br>Kundera's *The Book of Laughter and Forgetting*<br>Zimbabwe independence<br>Nicaraguan revolution |
| 1981 | Paul Green dies | | |
| 1982 | Peter Weiss dies<br>Lee Strasberg dies<br>Churchill's *Top Girls*<br>Fuller's *A Soldier's Play*<br>Fugard's *Master Harold...and the Boys*<br>Archibald MacLeish dies<br>Heinar Kipphardt dies | | |
| 1983 | Ralph Richardson dies<br>Lynne Fontanne dies<br>Mamet's *Glengarry Glen Ross*<br>Tennessee Williams dies<br>Ribman's *Buck* | | |

|  | The Theatre |  | The World |
|---|---|---|---|
|  | Norman's *'Night, Mother* |  |  |
|  | Strehler's Théâtre de l'Europe |  |  |
| **1984** | Hare's *A Map of the World* | **1984** | Johnson's AT&T Building |
|  | Lillian Hellman dies |  | Glass's "Aknaten" |
|  | Alan Schneider dies |  | Kundera's *The Unbearable Lightness of Being* |
|  | Richard Burton dies |  |  |
|  | Breur's *Gospel at Colonus* |  | U.S. Strategic Defense Initiative proposed |
| **1985** | Shepard's *A Lie of the Mind* |  |  |
|  | Julian Beck dies | **1985** | Mikhail Gorbachev becomes General Secretary of USSR |
|  | Kundera's *Jacques and his Master* |  |  |
|  | Brook's *Mahabharata* |  |  |
| **1986** | Jean Genet dies |  |  |
|  | Christopher Isherwood dies | **1986** | USSR nuclear accident at Chernobyl |
|  | Cheryl Crawford dies |  |  |
| **1987** | Ribman's *Sweet Table at the Richelieu* |  |  |
|  | Wilson's *Fences* |  |  |
|  | Charles Ludlam dies |  |  |
|  | Geraldine Page dies |  |  |
|  | Foreman's *Film Is Evil, Radio Is Good* |  |  |

# BIBLIOGRAPHY

## GENERAL WORKS

ADAMS, HAZARD, ed. *Critical Theory Since Plato*. New York: Harcourt Brace Jovanovich, Inc., 1971.

ARNOTT, PETER. *The Theatre in Its Time*. Boston: Little, Brown, 1981.

AUERBACH, ERICH. *Mimesis. The Reproduction of Reality in Western Literature*. Princeton: Princeton University Press, 1953.

BECKERMAN, BERNARD. *Dynamics of Drama*. New York: Drama Book Specialist Publishers, 1979.

BELCHER, FANNIN. ''*The Place of the Negro in the Evolution of the American Theatre, 1767 to 1940*.'' Ph.D. Thesis, Yale University, 1945.

BENTLEY, ERIC. *The Life of the Drama*. New York: Atheneum, 1964.

BENTLEY, ERIC. *What Is Theatre?* London: Dobson, 1956.

BERMEL, ALBERT. *Farce*. New York: Simon & Schuster, 1982.

BROCKETT, OSCAR G. *History of the Theatre*. Boston: Allyn and Bacon, 1982.

CAMPBELL, JOSEPH. *The Masks of God*. New York: Penguin Books, 1962.

CASSIRER, ERNST. *An Essay on Man*. New Haven: Yale University Press, 1944.

CLARK, BARRETT H., ed. *European Theories of the Drama*. New York: Crown, 1965.

COLE, DAVID. *The Theatrical Event*. Middletown: Wesleyan University Press, 1975.

COLE, TOBY, and CHINOY, HELEN K., eds. *Actors on Acting*. New York: Crown, 1980.

DORNER, ALEXANDER. *The Way beyond Art*. New York: Wittenborn, Schultz, Inc., 1947.

DUERR, EDWIN. *The Length and Depth of Acting*. New York: Holt, Rinehart, and Winston, 1962.

DUKORE, BERNARD F., ed. *Dramatic Theory and Criticism*. New York: Holt, Rinehart, and Winston, 1974.

GASCOIGNE, BAMBER. *World Theatre*. Boston: Little, Brown, 1968.

GASSNER, JOHN. *Masters of the Drama*. New York: Dover, 1954.

GASSNER, JOHN, and ALLEN, RALPH, eds. *Theatre and Drama in the Making*. Boston: Houghton Mifflin, 1964.

GREBANIER, BERNARD. *Then Came Each Actor*. New York: McKay, 1975.

HAUSER, ARNOLD. *The Social History of Art*. New York: Vintage, 1951.

HEFFNER, HUBERT C. *The Nature of Drama*. Boston: Houghton Mifflin, 1959.

HILL, ERROL. *Shakespeare in Sable*. Amherst: The University of Massachusetts Press, 1984.

HILL, ERROL. *The Theatre of Black Americans*, 2 Volumes. Englewood Cliffs, N.J.: Prentice-Hall, 1980.

HOCHMAN, STANLEY, ed. *McGraw-Hill Encyclopedia of World Drama*. New York: McGraw-Hill, 1984.

HONOUR, HUGH, and FLEMING, JOHN. *The Visual Arts*. Englewood Cliffs, N.J.: Prentice-Hall, 1982.

JUNG, C. G *Memories, Dreams, Reflections*. New York: Pantheon Books, 1961.

KIRBY, E. T., ed. *Total Theatre*. New York: Dutton, 1969.

LEACROFT, RICHARD. *The Development of the English Playhouse*. Ithaca: Cornell University Press, 1973.

MCLUHAN, MARSHALL. *The Gutenberg Galaxy*. Toronto: University of Toronto Press, 1962.

MCLUHAN, MARSHALL. *Understanding Media*. New York: McGraw-Hill, 1964.

MCNEILL, WILLIAM. *The Rise of the West*. Chicago: University of Chicago Press, 1963.

NAGLER, ALOIS M. *Sources of Theatrical History*. New York: Dover, 1952.

NICOLL, ALLARDYCE. *The Development of the Theatre*. New York: Harcourt Brace and World, 1966.

NICOLL, ALLARDYCE. *World Drama*. New York: Harcourt Brace, 1976.

POULET, GEORGES. *Studies in Human Time*. Baltimore: Johns Hopkins Press, 1956.

ROBERTS, VERA MOWRY. *On Stage*. New York: Harper & Row, 1962.

SOUTHERN, RICHARD. *The Seven Ages of the Theatre*. New York: Hill and Wang, 1961.

STUART, DONALD C. *The Development of Dramatic Art*. New York: Dover, 1928.

THOMPSON, WILLIAM IRWIN. *At the Edge of History: Speculations on the Transformation of Culture*. New York: Harper & Row, 1972.

THOMPSON, WILLIAM IRWIN. *The Time Falling Bodies Take to Light: Mythology, Sexuality, and the Origin of Culture*. New York: St Martin's Press, 1981.

USHER, A. P. *The History of Mechanical Inventions*. Boston: Beacon Press, 1959.

# CHAPTER 1: WHAT IS THEATRE?

BREASTED, JAMES HENRY. *Ancient Records of Egypt*. Chicago: University of Chicago Press, 1906.

BROWN, IVOR. *The First Player*. New York: William Morrow, 1928.

CASSIRER, ERNST. *Symbol, Myth and Culture*. New Haven: Yale University Press, 1955.

CASSIRER, ERNST. *The Philosophy of Symbolic Forms*. New Haven: Yale University Press, 1955.

CHARLES, LUCILLE HOERR. "The Clown's Function," *Journal of American Folklore*, 58 (1945), 25–34.

CRUMRINE, N. ROSS. "Ritual Drama and Culture Changes," *Comparative Studies in Society and History*, 12 (1970), 361–372.

DEWEY, JOHN. *Experience and Nature*. New York: Macmillan, 1958.

ELIADE, MIRCEA. *Myths, Rites, Symbols: A Mircea Eliade Reader*. New York: Harper and Row, 1976.

ELIADE, MIRCEA. *Patterns of Comparative Religion*. New York: Sheed and Ward, 1958.

FRAZER, JAMES G. *The Golden Bough*. New York: Macmillan, 1922.

GASTER, THEODOR. *Thespis*. New York: Schuman, 1950.

GOFFMAN, ERVING. *Frame Analysis*. New York: Harper & Row, 1974.

GROSSE, E. *The Beginnings of Art*. New York: D. Appleton and Co., 1898.

HARRISON, JANE. *Themis: A Study of the Social Origins of Greek Religion*. Cambridge: The University Press, 1912.

HUIZINGA, JOHANN. *Homo Ludens: A Study of the Play Element in Culture*. Boston: Beacon Press, 1955.

HUNNINGHER, BENJAMIN. *The Origin of the Theatre*. New York: Hill and Wang, 1961.

KIRBY, E. T. *Ur-Drama: The Origins of Theatre*. New York: New York University Press, 1975.

LANGER, SUZANNE. *Feeling and Form*. New York: Scribner, 1953.

LANGER, SUZANNE. *Problems of Art*. New York: Scribner, 1957.

LEVI-STRAUSS, CLAUDE. *The Savage Mind*. Chicago: University of Chicago Press, 1966.

LEVI-STRAUSS, CLAUDE. *The Way of the Masks*. Seattle: The University of Washington Press, 1979.

MACGOWAN, KENNETH, and ROSSE, HERMANN. *Masks and Demons*. New York: Harcourt, Brace and Co., 1923.

MARITAIN, JACQUES. *Distinguish to Unite, or The Degrees of Knowledge*. New York: Scribner, 1959.

NASH, JUNE. "The Passion Play in Maya Indian Communities," *Comparative Studies in Society and History*, 10 (1968), 318–326.

RIDGEWAY, WILLIAM. *The Dramas and Dramatic Dances of Non-European Races*. New York: B. Blom, 1964.

SCHUON, FRITHJOF. "The Degrees of Art," *Studies in Comparative Religion*, 10 (1976), 194–207.

SPENCE, LEWIS. *Myth and Ritual in Dance, Game, and Rhyme*. London: Watts, 1947.

TURNER, VICTOR. *From Ritual to Theatre*. New York: Performing Arts Journal Publications, 1982.

WELSFORD, ENID. *The Fool, His Social and Literary History*. Gloucester: P. Smith, 1966.

WILLEFORD, WILLIAM. *The Fool and his Scepter*. Evanston: Northwestern University Press, 1969.

## CHAPTER 2: THE CLASSICAL THEATRE

ALLEN, JAMES T. *Greek Acting in the Fifth Century*. Berkeley: University of California Press, 1916.

ALLEN, JAMES T. *Stage Antiquities of the Greeks and Romans and their Influence*. New York: Longmans, Green, 1927.

ALLEN, JAMES T. *The Greek Theatre of the Fifth Century before Christ*. Berkeley: University of California Press, 1920.

ARNOTT, PETER D. *Greek Scenic Conventions in the Fifth Century, B.C.* London: Clarendon Press, 1962.

ARNOTT, PETER D. *The Ancient Greek and Roman Theatre*. New York: Random House, 1971.

BAILEY, CYRIL, ed. *The Legacy of Rome*. Oxford: Clarendon Press, 1923.

BEARE, WILLIAM. *The Roman Stage*. London: Methuen, 1963.

BIEBER, MARGARETE. *The History of the Greek and Roman Theatre*. Princeton: Princeton University Press, 1961.

BRANDT, PAUL. *Sexual Life in Ancient Greece*. New York: Barnes and Noble, 1952.

BREASTED, JAMES HENRY. *The Conquest of Civilization*. New York: Harper, 1926.

BULTMAN, RUDOLF. *Primitive Christianity in its Contemporary Setting*. New York: Meredian Books, 1956.

BUTLER, JAMES H. *The Theatre and Drama of Greece and Rome*. San Francisco: Chandler Publishing, 1972.

CARY, M., and HAARHOFF, T. T. *Life and Thought in the Greek and Roman World*. New York: Crowell, 1942.

CORNFORD, FRANCIS M. *The Origin of Attic Comedy*. London: Cambridge University Press, 1914.

DODDS, ERIC. *The Greeks and the Irrational*. Berkeley: University of California Press, 1951.

DOVER, K. J. *Greek Homosexuality*. Cambridge: Harvard University Press, 1978.

DUCKWORTH, GEORGE E. *The Nature of Roman Comedy*. Princeton: Princeton University Press, 1952.

ELSE, GERALD F. *The Origin and Early Form of Greek Tragedy*. Cambridge: Harvard University Press, 1965.

FLICKINGER, ROY C. *The Greek Theatre and its Drama*. Chicago: The University of Chicago Press, 1936.

FRIEDLANDER, LUDWIG. *Roman Life and Manners under the Early Empire*. New York: E. P. Dutton, 1910.

GOODENOUGH, ERWIN R. *The Church in the Roman Empire*. New York: H. Holt and Co., 1931.

GUIGNEBERT, CHARLES. *Jesus*. New York: University Books, 1956.

HAMILTON, EDITH. *The Greek Way*. New York: W. W. Norton and Co., 1952.

HAMILTON, EDITH. *The Roman Way*. New York: W. W. Norton and Co., 1932.

HANSON, J. A. *Roman Theatre-Temples*. Princeton: Princeton University Press, 1959.

HARRISON, JANE ELLEN. *Ancient Art and Ritual*. New York: H. Holt, 1913.

HARSH, PHILIP W. A. *A Handbook of Classical Drama*. Stanford: Stanford University Press, 1944.

KITTO, H. D. F. *Greek Tragedy*. New York: Barnes and Noble, 1950.

KITTO, II. D. F. *The Greeks*. Baltimore: Penguin Books, 1957.

KLAUSNER, JOSEPH. *The Messianic Idea in Israel*. New York: Macmillan, 1955.

LAWLER, LILLIAN B. *The Dance of the Ancient Greek Theatre*. Iowa City: University of Iowa Press, 1964.

LINDSAY, JACK. *The Origins of Astrology*. London: F. Muller, 1971.

NICOLL, ALLARDYCE. *Masks, Mimes, and Miracles*. New York: Cooper Square Publishing, 1931.

PERRIN, NORMAN. *The New Testament: An Introduction*. New York: Harcourt Brace Jovanovich, 1974.

PICKARD-CAMBRIDGE, A. W. *Dithyramb, Tragedy, and Comedy*. London: Clarendon Press, 1962.

PICKARD-CAMBRIDGE, A. W. *The Dramatic Festivals of Athens*. London: Clarendon Press, 1968.

PICKARD-CAMBRIDGE, A. W. *The Theatre of Dionysus in Athens*. London: Clarendon Press, 1946.

SAUNDERS, CATHERINE. *Costume in Roman Comedy*. New York: Columbia University Press, 1909.

TAPLIN, OLIVER. *Greek Tragedy in Action*. Berkeley: University of California Press, 1978.

TAPLIN, OLIVER. *The Stagecraft of Aeschylus*. London: Clarendon Press, 1977.

THOMSON, GEORGE. *Aeschylus and Athens*. New York: Haskell House, 1972.

WALTON, J. MICHAEL. *The Greek Sense of Theatre*. London: Methuen, 1985.

WALTON, J. MICHAEL. *Greek Theatre Practice*. Westport, Conn.: Greenwood Press, 1980.

WEBSTER, T. B. L. *Greek Theatre Production*. London: Methuen, 1970.

## CHAPTER 3:   THE CLASSICAL ASIAN THEATRE

AMBROSE, KAY. *Classical Dances and Costumes of India*. London: A. and C. Black, 1951.

ANAND, MULK RAJ. *The Indian Theatre*. London: D. Dobson, 1950.

ARAKI, J. T. *The Ballad-Drama of Medieval Japan*. Berkeley: University of California Press, 1964.

ARLINGTON, L. C. *The Chinese Drama*. New York: B. Blom, 1966.

ARNOTT, PETER. *The Theatres of Japan*. New York: St. Martins, 1969.

BENEGAL, SOM. *A Panorama of Theatre in India*. Bombay: Popular Prakashan, 1968.

BHARATA. *Natya Sastra*, M. Ghosh, trans. Calcutta: Manisha Granthalaya, 1961.

BOWERS, FAUBION. *Dance in India*. New York: AMS Press, 1957.

BOWERS, FAUBION. *Japanese Theatre*. New York: Hermitage House, 1952.

BOWERS, FAUBION. *Theatre in the East*. New York: T. Nelson, 1956.

BRANDON, JAMES R. *Guide to Theatre in Asia*. Honolulu: University Press of Hawaii, 1976.

BRANDON, JAMES R. *Theatre in Southeast Asia*. Cambridge: Harvard University Press, 1967.

BUSS, KATE. *Studies in the Chinese Drama*. New York: J. Cape and H. Smith, 1930.

CHANG, PECHIN. *Chinese Opera and Painted Face*. Taipei: Mei Ya Pub., 1978.

CHEN, JACK. *The Chinese Theatre*. New York: Roy, 1951.

CRAVEN, ROY C. *A Concise History of Indian Art*. New York: Praeger, 1976.

CRUMP, J. I. *Chinese Theatre in the Days of Kublai Khan*. Tucson: University of Arizona Press, 1980.

DAS GUPTA, HEMENDRA NATH. *Indian Stage*. Calcutta: Metropolitan Printing and Publishing House, 1944.

DOLBY, WILLIAM. *A History of Chinese Drama*. New York: Barnes and Noble, 1976.

ERNST, EARLE. *The Kabuki Theatre.* New York: Oxford University Press, 1956.

FENOLLOSA, ERNEST F., and POUND, EZRA. *Noh, or Accompaniment.* New York: A. A. Knopf, 1917.

GARGI, BALWANT. *Theatre in India.* New York: Theatre Arts Books, 1962.

GHOSH, M. M. *History of Hindu Drama.* Calcutta, 1957.

GUNJI, MASAKATSU. *Kabuki.* New York: Kadansha International, 1969.

HACHIMONJIYAS, JISHO. *The Actor's Analects.* New York: Columbia University Press, 1969.

HALSON, ELIZABETH. *Peking Opera, A Short Guide.* London: Oxford University Press, 1966.

HAMAMURA, YONEZO. *Kabuki.* Tokyo: Kenkyusha, 1956.

HORROWITZ, E. P. *The Indian Theatre.* New York: B. Blom, 1967.

HUNG, JOSEPHINE HUANG. *Ming Drama.* Taipei: Heritage Press, 1966.

IMMOOS, THOMAS, and MAYER, FRED. *Japanese Theatre.* New York: Rizzoli, 1977.

JOHNSTON, REGINALD F. *The Chinese Drama.* Shanghai: Kelly and Walsh, Ltd., 1921.

JONES, CLIFFORD R., and TRUE, BETTY. *Kathakali.* New York: American Society for Eastern Arts, 1970.

KALE, PRAMOD. *The Theatric Universe.* Bombay: Popular Prakashan, 1974.

KAWATAKE, SHIGETOSHI. *Development of the Japanese Theatre Art.* Tokyo: Kokusai Bunka Shinkokai, 1935.

KEITH, ARTHUR B. *The Sanskrit Drama.* Oxford: Clarendon Press, 1924.

KINCAID, ZOE. *Kabuki.* New York: B. Blom, 1965.

KOMPARU, KUNIO. *The Noh Theater.* New York: Weatherhill, 1983.

KONOW, STEN. *The Indian Drama.* Calcutta: General Printers and Publishers, 1969.

LEITER, SAMUEL L. *The Art of Kabuki.* Berkeley: University of California Press, 1979.

LIU, WU-CHI. *An Introduction to Chinese Literature.* Bloomington: Indiana University Press, 1966.

LOMBARD, FRANK ALANSON. *An Outline History of the Japanese Drama.* London: G. Allen & Unwin, Ltd., 1928.

MACKERRAS, COLIN. *Chinese Theater.* Honolulu: University of Hawaii Press, 1983.

MACKERRAS, COLIN. *The Chinese Theatre in Modern Times.* Amherst: University of Massachusetts Press, 1975.

MACKERRAS, COLIN. *The Performing Arts in Contemporary China.* Oxford: Clarendon Press, 1981.

MACKERRAS, COLIN. *The Rise of the Peking Opera 1770–1870.* Oxford: Clarendon Press, 1972.

MANKAD, D. P. *The Ancient Indian Theatre.* Anand: Charotar Book Stall, 1960.

McKINNON, RICHARD N. "Zeami on the Art of Training," *Harvard Journal of Asiatic Studies,* 16 (1953), 200–223.

NAKAMURA, YASUO. *Noh, The Classical Theatre.* New York: Weatherhill, 1971.

NOGAMI, TOYOICHIRO. *The Noh and Greek Tragedy.* Sendai: Sendai International Cultural Society, 1940.

NOGAMI, TOYOICHIRO. *Zeami and his Theories on Noh.* Tokyo: Hinoki Shoten, 1955.

O'NEILL, P. G. *Early No Drama.* London: Lund Humphries, 1958.

POUND, EZRA, and FENELLOSA, ERNEST. *The Classic Noh Theatre of Japan.* Westport, Conn.: Greenwood Press, 1977.

PRONKO, LEONARD C. *Guide to Japanese Drama.* Boston: G. K. Hall, 1973.

PRONKO, LEONARD C. *Theater East and West.* Berkeley: University of California Press, 1967.

RANGACHARYA, ADYA. *Indian Theatre.* New Delhi: India Book House, 1971.

RAZ, JACOB. *Audience and Actors.* Leiden: E. J. Brill, 1983.

SCHUYLER, M. A. *A Bibliography of the Sanskrit Drama with an Introductory Sketch of the Dramatic Literature of India.* New York: Columbia University Press, 1906.

SCOTT, A. C. *An Introduction to the Chinese Theatre.* Singapore: D. Moore, 1958.

SCOTT, A. C. *The Classical Theatre of China.* New York: Macmillan, 1957.

SCOTT, A. C. *The Kabuki Theatre of Japan.* London: Allen and Unwin, 1955.

SCOTT, A. C. *Theatre in Asia.* New York: Macmillan, 1973.

SHEKHAR, INDU. *Sanskrit Drama.* Leiden: E. J. Brill, 1960.

SHIH, CHUNG WEN. *The Golden Age of Chinese Drama.* Princeton: Princeton University Press, 1976.

SUZUKI, D. T. *Zen and Japanese Culture*. Princeton: Princeton University Press, 1970.

SUZUKI, D. T. *Zen Buddhism*. New York: Doubleday, 1956.

TOITA, YASUJI. *Kabuki*. New York: Weatherhill, 1970.

UEDA, MAKOTO. *Zeami, Bashō, Yeats, Pound: A Study in Japanese and English Poetics*. The Hague: Mouton, 1965.

VARADPANDE, M. L. *Traditions of Indian Theatre*. New Delhi: Abhinav Publications, 1979.

VATSYAYAN, KAPILA. *Classical Indian Dance in Literature and the Arts*. New Delhi: Sangeet Natak Akademi, 1968.

WALEY, ARTHUR. *The Nine Songs: A Study of Shamanism in Ancient China*. London: Allen and Unwin, 1955.

WALEY, ARTHUR. *The No Plays of Japan*. New York: Grove Press, Inc., 1957.

WALEY, ARTHUR. *Three Ways of Thought in Ancient China*. New York: Allen and Unwin, 1939.

WALEY, ARTHUR. *The Way and its Power*. Boston: Houghton Mifflin, 1942.

WATTS, ALAN. *This Is It*. New York: Pantheon Books, 1973.

WELLS, H. W. *Classical Drama of India*. Westport, Conn.: Greenwood Press, 1975.

YAJNIK, R. K. *The Indian Theatre*. New York: Haskell House, 1970.

ZEAMI. *On the Art of the No Drama*. Princeton: Princeton University Press, 1984.

ZUCKER, ADOLPH E. *Chinese Theatre*. Boston: Little, Brown, 1925.

ZUNG, CELIA. *Secrets of the Chinese Drama*. New York: B. Blom, 1964.

## CHAPTER 4: THE MEDIEVAL THEATRE

ANDERSON, M. D. *Drama and Imagery in English Medieval Churches*. Cambridge: Cambridge University Press, 1963.

ANGLO, SYDNEY. *Spectacle, Pageantry and Early Tudor Policy*. London: The Clarendon Press, 1969.

AXTON, RICHARD. *European Drama of the Early Middle Ages*. Pittsburgh: University of Pittsburgh Press, 1975.

BEVINGTON, DAVID. *From Mankind to Marlowe*. Cambridge: Harvard University Press, 1962.

BRADBROOK, MURIEL C. *The Rise of the Common Player*. Cambridge: Harvard University Press, 1962.

BRODY, ALAN. *The English Mummers and their Plays*. London: Routledge Kegan Paul, 1971.

CARGILL, OSCAR. *Drama and Liturgy*. New York: Columbia University Press, 1930.

CHAMBERS, E. K. *The Medieval Stage*. London: Oxford University Press, 1903.

CHAYTOR, HENRY J. *From Script to Print*. Cambridge: Cambridge University Press, 1945.

COLLINS, FLETCHER. *The Production of Medieval Church Music-Drama*. Charlottesville: The University of Virginia Press, 1971.

CRAIG, HARDIN. *English Religious Drama of the Middle Ages*. London: Oxford University Press, 1960.

CRAIK, THOMAS W. *The Tudor Interlude*. Leicester: University Press, 1958.

CRAIK, THOMAS W., ed. *The Revels History of Drama in English*. New York: Barnes and Noble, 1980.

DAVIDSON, CLIFFORD. *Drama and Art*. Kalamazoo: Western Michigan University, 1977.

DEWULF, MAURICE. *Philosophy and Civilization in the Middle Ages*. Princeton: Princeton University Press, 1922.

DONOVAN, R. B. *Liturgical Drama in Medieval Spain*. Toronto: University of Toronto Press, 1958.

DUBY, GEORGES. *The Chivalrous Society*. Los Angeles: University of California Press, 1977.

DUCHESNE, LOUIS. *Christian Worship: Its Origin and Evolution*. New York: Macmillan, 1923.

EVANS, MARSHALL B. *The Passion Play of Lucerne*. New York: Modern Language Association of America, 1943.

FARNHAM, WILLARD. *The Medieval Heritage of Elizabethan Tragedy*. Berkeley: University of California, 1936.

FRANK, GRACE. *The Medieval French Drama*. Oxford: Clarendon Press, 1954.

GARDINER, HAROLD C. *Mysteries' End. Yale Studies in English*, Vol. 103. New Haven: Yale University Press, 1946.

HARDISON, O. B. *Christian Rite and Christian Drama in the Middle Ages*. Baltimore: Johns Hopkins University Press, 1965.

HENSHAW, MILLETT. "The Attitude of the Church toward the Stage to the End of the Middle Ages," *Medievalia et Humanestica*, 7 (1952), 4–17.

HUIZINGA, J. *The Waning of the Middle Ages*. New York: Doubleday, 1949.

KINGHORN, ALEXANDER M. *Medieval Drama*. London: Evans Brothers, 1968.

KOLVE, V. A. *The Play Called Corpus Christi*. Stanford: Stanford University Press, 1966.

MEHL, DIETER. *The Elizabethan Dumb Show*. London: Methuen, 1982.

NAGLER, A. M. *The Medieval Religious Stage*. New Haven: Yale University Press, 1976.

NELSON, ALAN H. *The Medieval Pageants and Plays*. Chicago: University of Chicago Press, 1974.

PHILLIPS, WILLIAM J. *Carols: Their Origin, Music, and Connection with Mystery Plays*. London: G. Routledge & Son, 1921.

POLIAKOV, LEON. *The History of Anti-Semitism*. New York: Schocken Books, 1974.

POTTER, ROBERT A. *The English Morality Play*. London: Routledge, Kegan Paul, 1975.

PROSSER, ELEANOR. *Drama and Religion in the English Miracle Plays*. Stanford: Stanford University Press, 1961.

RUDWIN, MAXIMILLIAN J. *The Origin of the German Carnival Comedy*. New York: G. E. Steckert and Co., 1920.

SALTER, F. M. *Medieval Drama in Chester*. Toronto: University of Toronto Press, 1955.

SHERGOLD, N. D. *A History of the Spanish Stage from Medieval Times until the End of the 17th Century*. Oxford: Clarendon Press, 1967.

SHOEMAKER, WILLIAM H. *The Multiple Stage in Spain during the Fifteenth and Sixteenth Centuries*. Westport, Conn.: Greenwood Press, 1973.

SOUTHERN, RICHARD. *The Medieval Theatre in the Round*. London: Faber and Faber, 1957.

STICCA, SANDRO. *The Latin Passion Play*. Albany: State University of New York Press, 1970.

STICCA, SANDRO, ed. *The Medieval Drama*. Albany: State University of New York Press, 1972.

STRATMAN, CARL J. *Bibliography of Medieval Drama*. New York: F. Ungar, 1972.

STUART, D. C. *Stage Decoration in France in the Middle Ages*. New York: Columbia University Press, 1910.

SWAIN, BARBARA. *Fools and Folly during the Middle Ages and Renaissance*. New York: Columbia University Press, 1932.

TRACHTENBERG, JOSHUA. *The Devil and the Jews*. New Haven: Yale University Press, 1943.

TUNISON, JOSEPH S. *Dramatic Traditions of the Dark Ages*. Chicago: University of Chicago Press, 1907.

TYDEMAN, WILLIAM. *The Theatre of the Middle Ages*. New York: Cambridge University Press, 1979.

WHITE, LYNN. *Medieval Technology and Social Change*. Oxford: Clarendon Press, 1962.

WICKHAM, GLYNNE. *Early English Stages, 1300–1660*. New York: Columbia University Press, 1959–1972.

WICKHAM, GLYNNE. *The Medieval Theatre*. London: Weidenfeld and Nicolson, 1974.

WILLIAMS, ARNOLD. *The Drama of Medieval England*. East Lansing: Michigan State University, 1961.

WOOLF, ROSEMARY. *The English Mystery Plays*. Berkeley: University of California Press, 1972.

WRIGHT, EDITH A. *The Dissemination of the Liturgical Drama in France*. Bryn Mawr: Bryn Mawr Press, 1936.

YOUNG, KARL. *The Drama of the Medieval Church*. Oxford: Clarendon Press, 1933.

## CHAPTER 5: THE RENAISSANCE THEATRE

ADAMS, JOHN C. *The Globe Playhouse*. New York: Barnes and Noble, 1961.

ADAMS, JOSEPH Q. *Shakespearean Playhouses*. Gloucester: P. Smith, 1917.

ARNOTT, PETER. *An Introduction to the French Theatre*. Totowa, N.J.: Rowman and Littlefield, 1977.

BALDWIN, T. W. *The Organization and Personnel of the Shakespearean Company*. New York: Russell and Russell, 1961.

BARROLL, J. L., ed. *The Revels History of Drama in English*. New York: Barnes and Noble, 1975.

BECKERMAN, BERNARD. *Shakespeare at the Globe, 1599–1609*. New York: Macmillan, 1962.

BENTLEY, GERALD E. *The Jacobean and Caroline Stage*. Oxford: Oxford University Press, 1941–1956.

BENTLEY, GERALD E. *The Profession of Dramatist in Shakespeare's Time, 1590–1642*. Princeton: Princeton University Press, 1971.

BJURSTROM, PER. *Giacomo Torelli and Baroque Stage Design*. Stockholm: National Museum, 1961.

BRADBROOK, MURIEL C. *Elizabethan Stage Conditions*. Cambridge: Cambridge University Press, 1932.

BRADBROOK, MURIEL C. *Themes and Conventions of Elizabethan Tragedy*. Cambridge: Cambridge University Press, 1960.

CAMDEN, CHARLES CARROLL. *The Elizabethan Woman*. Mamaroneck, N.Y.: P. P. Appel, 1975.

CAMPBELL, LILY BESS. *Scenes and Machines on the English Stage during the Renaissance*. Cambridge: Cambridge University Press, 1923.

CHAMBERS, E. K. *The Elizabethan Stage*. Oxford: Clarendon Press, 1923.

COHEN, WALTER. *Drama of a Nation*. Ithaca: Cornell University Press, 1985.

DEBANKE, CECILE. *Shakespearean Stage Production*. New York: McGraw-Hill, 1953.

DUCHARTE, PIERRE L. *The Italian Comedy*. New York: Dover, 1966.

ELLIS-FERMOR, UNA. *The Jacobean Drama*. New York: Vintage, 1964.

GALLOWAY, DAVID, ed. *Elizabethan Theatre*. Hamden, Conn.: Shoestring Press, 1973.

GILDERSLEEVE, VIRGINIA. *Government Regulation of the Elizabethan Drama*. New York: Columbia University Press, 1908.

GURR, ANDREW. *The Shakespearean Stage, 1574–1642*. Cambridge: Cambridge University Press, 1970.

HARBAGE, ALFRED. *Shakespeare's Audience*. New York: Columbia University Press, 1958.

HARBAGE, ALFRED. *Shakespeare and the Rival Tradition*. New York: Macmillan, 1952.

HATHAWAY, MICHAEL. *Elizabethan Popular Theatre*. Boston: Routledge and Kegan Paul, 1982.

HAWKINS, FREDERICK. *Annals of the French Stage from its Origins to the Death of Racine*. New York: Greenwood House, 1969.

HEINEMANN, MARGO. *Puritanism and Theatre*. Cambridge: Cambridge University Press, 1982.

HERRICK, MARVIN. *Italian Comedy in the Renaissance*. Urbana: University of Illinois Press, 1960.

HERRICK, MARVIN. *Italian Tragedy in the Renaissance*. Urbana: University of Illinois Press, 1965.

HERRICK, MARVIN. *Tragicomedy: Its Origin and Development in Italy, France, and England*. Urbana: University of Illinois Press, 1955.

HEWITT, BERNARD, ed. *The Renaissance Stage*. Coral Gables: University of Miami Press, 1958.

HODGES, C. W. *The Globe Restored*. New York: Norton, 1973.

HODGES, C. W. *Shakespeare and the Players*. New York: Coward-McCann, 1948.

HODGES, C. W. *Shakespeare's Second Globe*. London: Oxford University Press, 1973.

HOTSON, LESLIE. *Shakespeare's Wooden O*. New York: Macmillan, 1960.

JOSEPH, BERTRAM. *Acting Shakespeare*. New York: Theatre Arts Books, 1969.

JOSEPH, BERTRAM. *Elizabethan Acting*. London: Oxford University Press, 1962.

KENNARD, JOSEPH S. *The Italian Theatre*. New York: William Edwin Runge, 1932.

KERNODLE, GEORGE. *From Art to Theatre*. Chicago: University of Chicago Press, 1943.

KING, T. J. *Shakespearean Staging, 1599–1642*. Cambridge: Harvard University Press, 1971.

LAWRENCE, WILLIAM. *Those Nut-Cracking Elizabethans*. London: Argonaut Press, 1935.

LAWRENCE, W. J. *The Elizabethan Playhouse and Other Studies*. New York: Russell and Russell, 1963.

LAWRENCE, W. J. *The Physical Conditions of the English Public Playhouse*. New York: Cooper Square Publishers, 1968.

LAWRENCE, W. J. *Pre-Restoration Stage Studies*. New York: B. Blom, 1967.

LEA, KATHLEEN M. *Italian Popular Comedy*. Oxford: Clarendon Press, 1934.

LEES-MILNE, JAMES. *The Age of Inigo Jones*. London: Batsford, 1953.

LINTHICUM, MARIE C. *Costume in the Drama of Shakespeare and his Contemporaries*. New York: Hacker Art Books, 1972.

LOUGH, JOHN. *Paris Theatre Audiences in the Seventeenth and Eighteenth Centuries*. London: Oxford University Press, 1957.

MULLIN, DANIEL C. *The Development of the Play-house*. Berkeley: University of California Press, 1970.

NAGLER, A. M. *Shakespeare's Stage*. New Haven: Yale University Press, 1958.

NAGLER, A. M. *Theatre Festivals of the Medici, 1539–1637*. New Haven: Yale University Press, 1968.

NEWTON, STELLA. *Renaissance Theatre Costume*. New York: Theatre Arts Books, 1975.

NICOLL, ALLARDYCE. *Stuart Masques and the Renaissance Stage*. New York: B. Blom, 1963.

OREGLIA, G. *The Commedia dell'Arte*. New York: Hill and Wang, 1968.

ORGEL, STEPHEN. *The Illusion of Power*. Berkeley: University of California Press, 1975.

ORGEL, STEPHEN, and STRONG, ROY. *The Theatre of the Stuart Court*. Berkeley University of California Press, 1973.

PHILLIPS, HENRY. *The Theatre and Its Critics in Seventeenth-Century France*. New York: Oxford University Press, 1950.

RENNERT, HUGO A. *The Life of Lope de Vega*. Philadelphia: Campion and Co., 1904.

RENNERT, HUGO A. *The Spanish Stage in the Time of Lope de Vega*. New York: Hispanic Society of America, 1909.

REYNOLDS, GEORGE F. *The Staging of Elizabethan Plays at the Red Bull Theatre, 1605–1625*. New York: Modern Language Association of America, 1940.

SCHOENBAUM, S. *Shakespeare: The Globe and the World*. New York: Oxford University Press, 1979.

SCHWARTZ, ISIDORE A. *The Commedia dell'Arte and its Influence on French Comedy in the Seventeenth Century*. Paris: H. Samule, 1933.

SMITH, IRWIN. *Shakespeare's Blackfriars Playhouse*. New York: New York University Press, 1964.

SMITH, IRWIN. *Shakespeare's First Playhouse*. Dublin: Liffey Press, 1981.

SMITH, WINIFRED. *The Commedia dell'Arte*. New York: New Era Printing Company, 1912.

SOUTHERN, RICHARD. *The Staging of Plays before Shakespeare*. New York: Theatre Arts Books, 1973.

SPRAGUE, A. C. *Shakespearean Players and Performances*. Cambridge: Harvard University Press, 1953.

SPRINGARN, JOEL E. *A History of Literary Criticism in the Renaissance*. New York: Columbia University Press, 1908.

STRONG, ROY. *Splendor at Court*. Boston: Houghton Mifflin, 1973.

STYAN, J. L. *Shakespeare's Stagecraft*. Cambridge: Cambridge University Press, 1967.

THOMPSON, ELBERT. *The Controversy between the Puritans and the Stage*. New York: Russell and Russell, 1966.

WEINBERG, BERNARD. *A History of Literary Criticism in the Italian Renaissance*. Chicago: University of Chicago Press, 1961.

WELSFORD, ENID. *The Court Masque*. New York: Russell and Russell, 1927.

WHITE, JOHN. *The Birth and Rebirth of Pictorial Space*. New York: Thomas Yoseloff, 1958.

WILEY, WILLIAM. *The Early Public Theatre in France*. Cambridge: Harvard University Press, 1920.

WILSON, EDWARD M. *The Golden Age: Drama 1492–1700*. London: Benn, 1971.

WILSON, MARGARET. *Spanish Drama of the Golden Age*. New York: Pergamon Press, 1969.

YATES, FRANCIS. *The Theatre of the World*. Chicago: The University of Chicago Press, 1969.

## CHAPTER 6: THE SOCIAL THEATRE

BERNBAUM, ERNEST. *The Drama of Sensibility*. Boston: Ginn, 1915.

BOOTH, MICHAEL, ed. *The Revels History of Drama in English*. London: Methuen, 1975.

BRUFORD, WALTER H. *Germany in the Eighteenth Century*. Cambridge: Cambridge University Press, 1935.

BURNIM, KALMIN. *David Garrick, Director*. Pittsburgh: University of Pittsburgh Press, 1961.

CARLSON, MARVIN. *Goethe and the Weimar Theatre*. Ithaca: Cornell University Press, 1978.

CIBBER, COLLEY. *An Apology for the Life of Colley Cibber*. Ann Arbor: The University of Michigan Press, 1968.

DIDEROT, DENIS. *Writings on Theatre*. Cambridge: Cambridge University Press, 1936.

GAY, PETER. *The Enlightenment*. New York: Norton, 1966.

*Goethe on the Theatre*, trans. John Oxenford. New York: Dramatic Museum of Columbia University, 1919.

GOSSIP, C. J. *An Introduction to French Classical Tragedy*. Totowa, N.J.: Barnes and Noble, 1981.

GREEN, FREDERICK C. *Minuet: Critical Survey of French and English Literary Ideas in the Eighteenth Century*. St. Clair, Mich.: Scholarly, 1935.

GREGOR, JOSEPH. *The Russian Theatre*. Philadelphia: J. B. Lippincott, 1930.

HEITNER, R. R. *German Tragedy in the Age of Enlightenment, 1724-1768*. Berkeley: University of California Press, 1963.

HOTSON, LESLIE. *The Commonwealth and Restoration Stage*. Cambridge: Harvard University Press, 1928.

JOURDAIN, ELEANOR F. *Dramatic Theory and Practice in France, 1690-1808*. London: Methuen, 1924.

LANCASTER, H. C. *A History of French Dramatic Literature in the Seventeenth Century*. Baltimore: Johns Hopkins University Press, 1929-1942.

LANCASTER, H. C. *French Tragedy in the Reign of Louis XVI and the Early Years of the French Revolution, 1774-1792*. Baltimore: Johns Hopkins University Press, 1953.

LANCASTER, H. C. *French Tragedy in the Time of Louis XV and Voltaire, 1715-1774*. Baltimore: Johns Hopkins University Press, 1950.

LANCASTER, H. C. *Sunset: A History of Parisian Drama in the Last Years of Louis XIV, 1701-1715*. Baltimore: Johns Hopkins University Press, 1945.

LAWRENSON, T. E. *The French Stage in the Seventeenth Century*. Manchester: Manchester University Press, 1957.

LOFTIS, JOHN, ed. *The Revels History of Drama in English*. New York: Barnes and Noble, 1976.

*The London Stage, 1660-1880*. Carbondale: Southern Illinois University Press, 1960-1968.

LYNCH, JAMES J. *Box, Pit, and Gallery*. Berkeley: University of California Press, 1953.

MARTINEAU, HARRIET. *Society in America*. New York: Anchor Books, 1962.

MAYOR, A. H. *The Bibiena Family*. New York: H. Bittner & Co., 1945.

MELCHER, EDITH. *Stage Realism in France between Diderot and Antoine*. Bryn Mawr: Bryn Mawr College Press, 1928.

MILHOUS, JUDITH. *Thomas Betterton and the Management of Lincoln's Inn Fields 1695-1708*. Car-

bondale: Southern Illinois University Press, 1979.

NICOLL, ALLARDYCE. *History of English Drama, 1660-1900*. Cambridge: Cambridge University Press, 1955-1959.

ODELL, GEORGE C. D. *Shakespeare from Betterton to Irving*. New York: C. Scribner, 1920.

PALMER, JOHN L. *The Comedy of Manners*. New York: Russell and Russell, 1962.

PASCAL, ROY. *The German Sturm und Drang*. Manchester: Manchester University Press, 1953.

PEDICORD, HARRY W. *The Theatrical Public in the Time of Garrick*. Carbondale: Southern Illinois University Press, 1954.

POWELL, JOCELYN. *Restoration Theatre Production*. Boston: Routledge and Kegan Paul, 1984.

PRICE, CECIL. *Theatre in the Age of Garrick*. Totowa, N.J.: Rowman and Littlefield, 1973.

PRUDHOE, JOHN. *The Theatre of Goethe and Schiller*. Oxford: Blackwell, 1973.

RANKIN, HUGH F. *The Theatre in Colonial America*. Chapel Hill: University of North Carolina Press, 1965.

ROOT-BERNSTEIN, MICHÈLE. *Boulevard Theater and Revolution in Eighteenth-Century Paris*. Ann Arbor: UMI Research Press, 1984.

SCHOLZ, JANOS. *Baroque and Romantic Stage Design*. New York: H. Bittner, 1950.

SEILHAMER, GEORGE O. *History of the American Theatre*. Philadelphia: Globe Printing House, 1888-1891.

SLONIM, MARC. *Russian Theatre from the Empire to the Soviets*. Cleveland: World Publishing, 1961.

SOUTHERN, RICHARD. *Changeable Scenery*. London: Faber and Faber, 1952.

SOUTHERN, RICHARD. *The Georgian Playhouse*. London: Pleides Books, 1948.

SPENCER, HAZLETON. *Shakespeare Improved*. New York: F. Ungar, 1963.

SUMMERS, MONTAGUE. *The Playhouse of Pepys*. London: Kegan, Paul, 1935.

SUMMERS, MONTAGUE. *The Restoration Theatre*. New York: Macmillan, 1934.

TURNELL, MARTIN. *The Classical Moment*. New York: New Directions, 1948.

VARNEKE, B. V. *History of the Russian Theatre*. New York: Macmillan, 1951.

WILCOX, JOHN. *The Relation of Molière to Restoration Comedy*. New York: B. Blom, 1964.

WILDEBLOOD, JOAN, and BRINSON, PETER. *The Polite World*. New York: Oxford University Press, 1965.

WILLIAMS, SIMON. *German Actors of the Eighteenth and Nineteenth Centuries*. Westport, Conn.: Greenwood Press, 1985.

WILLOUGHBY, LEONARD A. *The Classical Age of German Literature, 1749–1832*. London: Oxford University Press, 1926.

WRIGHT, RICHARDSON. *Revels in Jamaica, 1682–1838*. New York: Dodd, Mead, 1937.

# CHAPTER 7:  THE ROMANTIC THEATRE

ABRAMS, M. H. *The Mirror and the Lamp*. New York: Oxford University Press, 1953.

APPLETON, WILLIAM W. *Madame Vestris and the London Stage*. New York: Columbia University Press, 1974.

ARVIN, NEIL E. *Eugène Scribe and the French Theatre, 1815–60*. Cambridge: Harvard University Press, 1924.

CARLSON, MARVIN. *The French Stage in the Nineteenth Century*. Metuchen: The Scarecrow Press, 1972.

CARLSON, MARVIN. *The German Stage in the Nineteenth Century*. Metuchen: The Scarecrow Press, 1972.

CARLSON, MARVIN. *The Theatre of the French Revolution*. Ithaca: Cornell University Press, 1966.

CARSON, WILLIAM G. B. *The Theatre on the Frontier*. Chicago: University of Chicago Press, 1932.

CHRISTY, A. K. *The Orient in American Transcendentalism*. New York: Octagon Books, 1972.

CLEMENT, NEMOURS H. *Romanticism in France*. New York: Modern Language Association, 1939.

DISHER, MAURICE. *Blood and Thunder*. London: F. Muller, 1949.

DONOHUE, JOSEPH W. *Theatre in the Age of Kean*. Totowa, N.J.: Rowman and Littlefield, 1975.

DONOHUE, JOSEPH W., ed. *The Theatre Manager in England and America*. Princeton: Princeton University Press, 1971.

GRIMSTED, DAVID. *Melodrama Unveiled*. Chicago: University of Chicago Press, 1968.

HEWITT, BERNARD. *Theatre USA, 1668–1957*. New York: McGraw-Hill, 1957.

HODGE, FRANCIS. *Yankee Theatre*. Austin: University of Texas Press, 1964.

JOHNSON, EDGAR and ELEANOR, eds. *A Dickens Theatrical Reader*. London: Victor Gollancz, Ltd., 1964.

LACEY, ALEXANDER. *Pixérécourt and the French Romantic Drama*. Toronto: University of Toronto Press, 1928.

MATTHEWS, BRANDER. *The Theatres of Paris*. New York: Scribner, 1880.

MATTHEWS, BRANDER, ed. *Papers on Acting*. New York: Hill and Wang, 1958.

MOODY, RICHARD. *America Takes the Stage*. Bloomington: Indiana University Press, 1955.

QUINN, ARTHUR H. *A History of the American Drama*. New York: F. S. Crofts, 1943.

ROBERTSON, PRISCILLA. *The Revolutions of 1848: A Social History*. Princeton: Princeton University Press, 1952.

ROWELL, GEORGE. *The Victorian Theatre, 1792–1914*. Cambridge: Cambridge University Press, 1979.

SHATTUCK, CHARLES H. *Shakespeare on the American Stage*. Washington: Folger Books, 1976.

STEIN, JACK M. *Richard Wagner and the Synthesis of the Arts*. Detroit: Wayne University Press, 1960.

VARDAC, A. N. *Stage to Screen*. Cambridge: Harvard University Press, 1949.

*Wagner on Music and Drama*, selected and arranged by Albert Goldman and Evert Sprinchorn; H. Ashton Ellis, trans. New York: E. P. Dutton Co., 1964.

WALZEL, OSKAR F. *German Romanticism*. New York: G. P. Puttnam and Sons, 1932.

WATSON, ERNEST B. *Sheridan to Robertson*. Cambridge: Harvard University Press, 1926.

WILLOUGHBY, LEONARD A. *The Romantic Movement in Germany*. London: Oxford University Press, 1930.

WILLSON, A. LESLIE. *A Mythical Image: The Ideal of India in German Romanticism*. Durham: Duke University Press, 1964.

WILSON, GARFF B. *A History of American Acting*. Bloomington: Indiana University Press, 1966.

WILSON, GARFF B. *Three Hundred Years of American Theatre*. Englewood Cliffs, N.J.: Prentice-Hall, Inc., 1973.

ZORN, JOHN W., ed. *The Essential Delsarte*. Metuchen, N.J.: Scarecrow Press, 1968.

## CHAPTER 8: THE REALISTIC THEATRE

ANDRESKI, STANISLAV, ed. *The Essential Comte*. New York: Barnes and Noble, 1947.

ANTOINE, ANDRÉ. *Memories of the Theatre Libre*. Coral Gables: University of Miami Press, 1964.

ARCHER, WILLIAM. *The Old Drama and the New*. New York: Dodd and Mead, 1929.

ARCHER, WILLIAM, and DIDEROT, DENIS, *Masks or Faces? and The Paradox of Acting*. New York: Hill and Wang, 1957.

BELASCO, DAVID. *Theatre Through its Stage Door*. New York: Harper's, 1919.

BENTLEY, ERIC. *The Playwright as Thinker*. New York: Harcourt, Brace, and World, 1946.

BIDDISS, MICHAEL. *The Social and Political Thought of Count Gobineau*. London: Weybright and Talley, 1970.

CARTER, LAWSON A. *Zola and the Theatre*. New Haven: Yale University Press, 1963.

CLAUS, HORST. *The Theatre Director Otto Brahm*. Ann Arbor: UMI Research Press, 1981.

CLURMAN, HAROLD. *The Fervent Years*. New York: Harcourt Brace Jovanovich, 1975.

COLE, TOBY, ed. *Playwrights on Playwriting*. New York: Hill and Wang, 1961.

DEHART, STEVEN. *The Meininger Theater*. Ann Arbor: UMI Research Press, 1981.

GLASSTONE, VICTOR. *Victorian and Edwardian Theatres*. Cambridge: Harvard University Press, 1975.

GRUBE, MAX. *The Story of the Meininger*. Coral Gables: University of Miami Press, 1963.

HOPKINS, ALBERT A. *Magic*. New York: Arno Press, 1977.

HUGHES, HENRY STUART. *Consciousness and Society: The Reorientation of European Social Thought, 1890–1930*. New York: Knopf, 1958.

HUNT, HUGH, ed. *The Revels History of Drama in English*. New York: Barnes and Noble, 1979.

JOSEPHSON, MATTHEW. *Zola and his Time*. New York: Garden City Publishing, 1928.

LAMM, MARTIN. *Strindberg*. New York: B. Blom, 1971.

MATTHEWS, BRANDER. *French Dramatists of the Nineteenth Century*. New York: Scribner, 1914.

MESERVE, WALTER J. *An Outline History of American Drama*. Totowa, N.J.: Littlefield Adams and Co., 1965.

MEYER, MICHAEL. *Ibsen*. New York: Doubleday and Company, 1971.

ROPP, THEODORE J. *War in the Modern World*. Durham: Duke University Press, 1962.

ROWELL, GEORGE. *Theatre in the Age of Irving*. Totowa, N.J.: Rowman and Littlefield, 1981.

SANDERSON, MICHAEL. *From Irving to Olivier*. New York: St. Martins, 1984.

SCHAEFFER, LOUIS. *O'Neill: Son and Playwright*. Boston: Little, Brown, 1968.

SCHAEFFER, LOUIS. *O'Neill: Son and Artist*. Boston: Little, Brown, 1973.

SHAWN, TED. *Every Little Movement*. New York: Dance Horizons, 1963.

SMITH, HUGH A. *Main Currents in Modern French Drama*. New York: Holt, 1925.

SONDEL, BESS SELTZER. *Zola's Naturalistic Theory with Particular Reference to the Drama*. Chicago: University of Chicago Press, 1939.

STANISLAVSKI, KONSTANTIN. *An Actor Prepares*. New York: Theatre Arts Books, 1936.

STANISLAVSKI, KONSTANTIN. *My Life in Art*. Moscow: Foreign Languages Publishing Co., n.d.

TAINE, HIPPOLYTE. *A History of English Literature*. London: Chatto and Winders, 1880.

TAYLOR, FRANK A. *The Theatre of Alexandre Dumas fils*. Oxford: Clarendon Press, 1937.

TAYLOR, JOHN R. *The Rise and Fall of the Well-Made Play*. London: Methuen, 1967.

WEINBERG, BERNARD. *French Realism*. London: Oxford University Press, 1937.

WEST, E. J., ed. *Shaw on Theatre*. New York: Hill and Wang, 1958.

# CHAPTER 9: THE MODERN THEATRE

APPIA, ADOLPHE. *The Work of Living Art and Man Is the Measure of All Things*. Coral Gables: University of Miami Press, 1960.

ARONSON, ARNOLD. *The History and Theory of Environmental Scenography*. Ann Arbor: UMI Research Press, 1981.

ARTAUD, ANTONIN. *Selected Writings*. New York: Farrar, Straus, Giroux, 1976.

BENTLEY, ERIC. *In Search of Theatre*. New York: Alfred A. Knopf, 1953.

BERMEL, ALBERT. *Artaud's Theatre of Cruelty*. New York: Taplinger, 1977.

BERMEL, ALBERT. *Contradictory Characters*. New York: Dutton, 1973.

BLY, ROBERT, ed. *News of the Universe*. San Francisco: Sierra Club Books, 1980.

BRAUN, EDWARD. *The Director in the Modern Theatre*. New York: Holmes and Meier, 1982.

BRAUN, EDWARD. *Meyerhold on Theatre*. New York: Hill and Wang, 1969.

BRAUN, EDWARD. *The Theatre of Meyerhold*. London: Eyre Methuen, 1979.

BRECHT, BERTOLT. *Brecht on Theatre*. London: Methuen, 1964.

BRETON, ANDRÉ. *Manifestoes of Surrealism*. Ann Arbor: University of Michigan Press, 1969.

BROCKETT, OSCAR G. *Perspectives on Contemporary Theatre*. Baton Rouge: Louisiana State University Press, 1971.

BROCKETT, OSCAR G., and FINDLAY, ROBERT R. *Century of Innovation*. Englewood Cliffs, N.J.: Prentice-Hall, Inc., 1973.

BROOK, PETER. *The Empty Space*. New York: Atheneum, 1968.

BRUSTEIN, ROBERT. *The Theatre of Revolt*. New York: Little, Brown, 1964.

BURIAN, JARKA. *The Scenography of Joseph Svoboda*. Middletown: Wesleyan University Press, 1971.

CAGE, JOHN. *Silence*. Middletown: Wesleyan University Press, 1973.

CHAMPAGNE, LEONORA. *French Theatre Experiment Since 1968*. Ann Arbor: UMI Research Press, 1984.

CHIPP, H. B. *Theories of Modern Art*. Berkeley: University of California Press, 1968.

CORRIGAN, ROBERT, ed. *Theatre in the Twentieth Century*. New York: Books for Libraries, 1963.

CRAIG, EDWARD. *Gordon Craig*. New York: Alfred A. Knopf, 1968.

CRAIG, EDWARD GORDON. *On the Art of the Theatre*. Chicago: Browne's Bookstore, 1911.

CROYDEN, MARGARET. *Lunatics, Lovers, and Poets*. New York: McGraw-Hill, 1974.

DAVY, KATE. *Richard Forman and the Ontological-Hysteric Theatre*. Ann Arbor: UMI Research Press, 1981.

DUKORE, BERNARD F., and GEROULD, DANIEL C., eds. *Avant Garde Drama*. New York: Crowell, 1967.

GORELIK, MORDECAI. *New Theatres for Old*. New York: Dutton, 1940.

GREENE, NAOMI. *Antonin Artaud*. New York: Simon & Schuster, 1970.

GROPIUS, WALTER, ed. *The Theatre of the Bauhaus*. Middletown: Wesleyan University Press, 1961.

GROTOWSKI, JERZY. *Towards a Poor Theatre*. New York: Simon & Schuster, 1968.

KIRBY, MICHAEL. *The Art of Time*. New York: Dutton, 1969.

KIRBY, MICHAEL. *Futurist Performance*. New York: Dutton, 1971.

KIRBY, MICHAEL. *Happenings*. New York: Dutton, 1966.

KIRBY, MICHAEL, ed. *The New Theatre*. New York: New York University Press, 1974.

KOSTELANETZ, RICHARD. *The Theatre of Mixed Means*. New York: Pitman, 1968.

LEY-PISCATOR, MARIA. *The Piscator Experiment*. New York: Heinemann, 1967.

PASOLLI, ROBERT A. *A Book on the Open Theatre*. Indianapolis: Bobbs-Merrill, 1970.

ROOSE-EVANS, JAMES. *Experimental Theatre*. London: Studio Vista, 1973.

SAINT-DENIS, MICHEL. *The Rediscovery of Style*. New York: Theatre Arts Books, 1960.

SANDROW, HANMA. *Surrealism*. New York: Harper, 1972.

SCHECHNER, RICHARD. *Environmental Theatre*. New York: Hawthorn, 1973.

SCHECHNER, RICHARD. *Public Domain*. Indianapolis: Bobbs Merrill, 1969.

SCHEVILL, JAMES. *Breakout!* Chicago: Swallow Press, 1972.

SELDEN, RAMAN. *A Reader's Guide to Contemporary Literary Theory*. Lexington: The University of Kentucky Press, 1985.

SHATTUCK, ROGER. *The Banquet Years*. New York: Vintage, 1961.

SPOLIN, VIOLA. *Improvisation for the Theatre*. Evanston: Northwestern University Press, 1963.

TEMKINE, RAYMOND. *Grotowski*. New York: Avon, 1972.

VOLKER, KLAUS. *Brecht Chronicle*. New York: Seabury, 1975.

WADDINGTON, C. H. *Behind Appearances*. Edinburgh: Edinburgh University Press, 1969.

WALTON, J. MICHAEL, ed. *Craig on Theatre*. London: Methuen, 1983.

WILLETT, JOHN. *Expressionism*. New York: McGraw-Hill, 1970.

WILLETT, JOHN. *The Theatre of Bertolt Brecht*. New York: New Directions, 1959.

WILSON, EDMUND. *Axel's Castle*. New York: Scribners, 1931.

WITT, HUBERT, ed. *Brecht as They Knew Him*. New York: International Publishers, 1974.

# INDEX

**457**

**459**

**460**

461

**466**